RAPHAEL MAHLER was born in Nowy
Sącz, western Galicia, i
educated at the local
gyr sium, and then
He received h doctorate in
phy from the Uni-
turned

HASIDISM *and the* JEWISH ENLIGHTENMENT

Translated from the Yiddish by
EUGENE ORENSTEIN

Translated from the Hebrew by
AARON KLEIN *and*
JENNY MACHLOWITZ KLEIN

The Jewish Publication Society of America
Philadelphia • New York • Jerusalem 5745/1985

HASIDISM *and the* JEWISH ENLIGHTENMENT

Their Confrontation in Galicia and Poland in the First Half of the Nineteenth Century

RAPHAEL MAHLER

 First edition
Manufactured in the United States of America

Library of Congress Cataloging in Publication Data
Mahler, Raphael, 1899–1977
Hasidism and the Jewish Enlightenment.
Translation of: ha-Ḥasidut veha-Haśkalah.
Pt. 1 originally in Yiddish; pt. 2 originally in Hebrew.
Bibliography: p. 339
Includes index.
1. Hasidism—Galicia (Poland and Ukraine)—History—19th century. 2. Hasidism—Poland—History—19th century. 3. Haskalah—Galicia (Poland and Ukraine)—History—19th century. 4. Haskalah—Poland—History—19th century. I. Title.
BM98.M2513 1985 296.8′33 83-23890
ISBN 0-8276-0233-2

Translator's Note

The following excerpts of this book have previously appeared as articles in English translation:

"The Austrian Government and the Hasidim During the Period of Reaction," *Jewish Social Studies* (1938), pp. 195–240. (This article comprises fragments of chapters 1 and 2 of the book.)

"The Social and Political Aspects of the Haskalah in Galicia," *YIVO Annual*, vol. 1 (New York, 1946), pp. 64–85. (Originally published as part of chapter 2 of the author's *Der Kamf tsvishn Haskole un Khsides in Galitsye.*)

"Censorship of Hasidic, Kabbalistic and Yiddish Literature in Galicia During the Period of Reaction," *Journal of Jewish Bibliography* 1:2 (January 1939): 35–39, 1:3 (April 1939): 71–82 (this article consists of a part of chapter 4).

"The Hebrew Almanacs of Joseph Perl," *Journal of Jewish Bibliography* 3:1–2 (January–April 1942): 22–31, 3:3 (July 1942): 75–83.

Design: ADRIANNE ONDERDONK DUDDEN

Contents

I GALICIA

The Suppression of Galician Jewry / The Social Character of Hasidism / Beliefs and Values of Hasidism / Hasidism and Germanization / Jew, Gentile, and the Messianic Age / Charity in Hasidic Life / Hasidic Solidarity / Social Alliances and the Roles of the Rebbes / The Emergence of the Hasidic Reign

The Economic Base / The Program of the Haskalah: Pride and Practicality / Language: The Question of Yiddish; the Dominance of German; the Emergence of Hebrew / The Vein of Rationalism in the Haskalah / Anachronism and Paradox in Haskalah Internationalism / Messianic Redemption and Return to Zion in Haskalah Thought / Unequivocal Loyalty of the Haskalah to the Absolutist Monarchy / The Poor, the Masses, and the Jewish Bourgeoisie / The Contrast and Conflict between Hasidism and the Haskalah

From Hostile Suspicion to Guarded Accommodation / The Development of an Official Policy toward Hasidism / The Perl Memorandum / The Concurrent Maskil-Inspired Persecutions

Prefatory Note

RAPHAEL MAHLER
(1899–1977)

Born in Nowy Sącz (Tsandz), western Galicia, under Hapsburg rule, Raphael Mahler studied in the local yeshivah and completed the course of study of the gymnasium before attending the University of Vienna, earning his doctorate in history in 1922. He returned to the newly restored sovereign state of Poland and served as a teacher of general and Jewish history in Jewish secondary schools.

During his fifteen years in Poland, Mahler concentrated on researching the history of Polish Jewry. He was a leading member of the Seminar for Jewish History, which was founded in 1923 by his intimate friend and colleague, the martyred historian of the Warsaw Ghetto, Emanuel Ringelblum. This seminar was first established under the patronage of the Jewish Academic Home in Warsaw, the club of Jewish university students, and was later affiliated with the historical section of the YIVO Institute in Vilna. Mahler was an editor of the publications of this seminar, *Der yunger historiker* ("The Young Historian," 1926, 1928) and *Bleter far geshikhte* ("Historical Leaves," 1934, 1938).

Raphael Mahler combined public activity with his academic work, as did many of his contemporaries and fellow community members. He was a member of the Left Po'alei Zion Party in Poland and later in Israel became a leading member of *Mapam*, the left-wing Labor-Zionist party.

In 1937 Mahler emigrated to the United States and became a staff member of the YIVO Institute for Jewish Research in New York. In 1950 he settled in the state of Israel. From 1951 to 1958 he lectured on the economic history of the Jews at the Tel Aviv School of Law and Economics and in 1959 was appointed professor of Eastern European Jewish history at the University of Tel Aviv. Shortly before his death Raphael Mahler was honored with the Israel Prize, the Jewish state's most prestigious award, for his contribution to the field of Jewish studies.

Influenced by the historian Ignacy Schiper, Mahler stressed social and economic problems. He championed a theoretical and methodological approach to the study of Jewish history in accordance with historical materialism. Mahler viewed his work as a corrective to the dominant trends in modern Jewish historiography, particularly to the orientation of Simon Dubnow. In the preface to the English translation of his major work, Mahler explained his approach to Jewish history.

> Notwithstanding the good intentions of the adherents of the school described by its originator, S. Dubnow, as "sociological-realistic," it must be said that they were unable to grasp the exuberant and colourful reality of Jewish life, its past and its present alike: they overlooked the principal factor in the development of the people—namely, its social dynamics. Social antagonisms, class struggle and social opposition within the community have never been accorded their appropriate place in the history of the Jews of any period, and they have been almost completely omitted from the portrayal of the events of modern times for fear of overstepping political bounds and, sometimes, precisely because of obvious political intentions. Phenomena and institutions concerning the ruling classes among the Jewish people were presented as general, national matters, and the Jewish policy of the ruling nations with regard to each and every class of the people under their rule was not properly analysed. Thus, instead of a national history of the Jews, we have been presented by the dominant school in Jewish historiography with a history that is largely nationalistic.
>
> Nor was justice done to the economic aspect of life, the basis of the national and social development of the Jewish people, as of all other people in the world. The economic structure of the people, its economic activities and the functions it fulfilled in the economic life of the countries of its dispersion in each particular period, were given only sporadic mention rather than exhaustive treatment. Because of this disregard of economic problems, no explanation was given for the causal nexus with those aspects of the people's life which occupy pride of place in the portrayal of modern history—the legal and political status. There was no clarification either of the fundamentals of the spiritual trends which shaped the structure of Jewish culture in modern times. Their social roots were not laid bare, and no attempt was made to establish how those trends reflected the interests, aspirations and ideals of the social classes which originated them.[1]

---

[1]Raphael Mahler, *A History of Modern Jewry: 1780–1815* (London: Vallentine, Mitchell, 1971), pp. xi–xii.

In a reassessment of his own approach, fostered by the Holocaust, Mahler also stressed the importance of the attitude of the Jewish people in the Diaspora—and that of its various classes in particular—toward the historical desire for the Return to Zion and the Restoration in Zion.

Based on an abundance of archival sources, *Hasidism and the Jewish Enlightenment* is a prime example of Raphael Mahler's analysis of movements that shaped the spiritual and cultural life of modern Jewry. Whether the central thesis of the book is accepted or rejected, in total or in part, the work remains a challenging study in modern Jewish social and intellectual history.

EUGENE ORENSTEIN

Introduction

Hasidism and the Haskalah, two movements that clashed for the first time in the social and cultural life of the Jewish people at the threshold of the nineteenth century, were crucial factors in shaping Jewish culture in the modern period. Deepening our knowledge and understanding of these two trends is therefore not merely of academic interest; it will very likely clarify the nature of the traditional sources from which the renewed culture of the Jewish people draws its ideological nourishment to this day.

An objective historical evaluation of these two trends can be achieved only by investigating their contrasting social foundations. Only by exposing these bases can criteria be established to determine whether a movement's tendency is toward progress or reaction. These social criteria are also a necessary condition for a sociological classification of Hasidism and the Haskalah in comparison with other sociocultural currents—secular and religious—in Jewish history or in world history.

The climax of the bitter war between the two rival trends took place in the first half of the nineteenth century, during the period of reaction which dominated Europe after Napoleon's defeat. This was a period of transition in the history of Hasidism when its flowering came to an end and its social and ideological decline began. Insofar as

Hasidism lost its original character of a social opposition movement and compromised with the Mitnaggedim, its previous adversaries, it was emptied of its pre-Humanist, antinomian, and individualist world view.

This process varied in tempo according to the geographical regions of eastern Europe. The Ukraine, though the cradle of the movement, also preceded the other regions in the negative development of Hasidism, namely the cult of the zaddik, the arrogant rule of the dynasties, and the loss of even a trace of a desire for religious renewal and social reform. In Galician Hasidism, the popular nature of the movement was still preserved to a great extent at the beginning of this period in the field of social morality. In central Poland, where Hasidism was late in coming, the movement was still strong enough to curb the decline to vulgarity. As opposed to the tawdry Hasidism of petty miracle workers, there emerged a movement of renewal which brought with it an abundance of fresh ideas that were astonishingly profound and incisive. Even these, however, were but the afterglow, the historical twilight of the movement.

All characteristic differences in the various regions of eastern Europe at the stage of its decline notwithstanding, Hasidism, in general, was still remarkable with regard to its innate character as a national movement. This is no wonder, considering that the national oppression of the Jewish population in Poland under the Saxon kings in the days of the Ba'al Shem Tov was not eased under the tyrannical regime of the Austrian and Russian rulers; it only changed form. Persecution at the hands of the landowners and churchmen was replaced by harsh governmental decrees, insufferable special taxes, military service, and severe residential and occupational restrictions. It was thus only natural that the concept of redemption was, as before, the pivot on which the Hasidic doctrine revolved. A keen national sense, though veiled by inflexible conservatism, was also the root of the vigorous opposition of the Hasidic masses to all attempts of "official" enlightenment, which were, in fact, directed toward the assimilation of the Jews. Official documents reveal yet another aspect of the absolute national solidarity of the Hasidim, namely, their organized action to passively resist governmental decrees, in particular the special levies that disgracefully impoverished the masses.

Archival documents also cast a new light on the movement of the Jewish Enlightenment, the Haskalah. The historians of the Haskalah, relying in their research primarily on the literature of the movement itself, described it merely as a cultural-literary current. From other official sources, it is possible to learn more about the nature of the Haskalah and its sociopolitical tendencies. These tendencies were indeed expressed in the literature itself, although some scholars have been unaware of their significance. It can be shown that the Haskalah movement, in its political view and Weltanschauung, adhered to the ruling absolutism, even if it was the reactionary absolutism that inherited the place of an enlightened absolutism.

Nevertheless, this characteristic of the Haskalah does not conceal its ideas of renewal, its program for the revival of the people by reforming its economic foundations, linking the people closer to European culture, and raising the standards of its education. Despite all its limitations, the function of the Haskalah in the history of the Jewish people was determined by its progressive aim, namely, to battle against medievalism in the social and cultural life of the Jews. This was the source of its creativity. The progressiveness of the Haskalah is measured by the degree of progressiveness of the bourgeoisie, the class that carried on the struggle against social and political feudalism, which was developing in Jewish society just as it was elsewhere in the world.

The very rise of the Haskalah served as evidence that Hasidism had become outmoded. Rather than a progressive force, it became a stumbling block on the road of development. The contribution of Hasidism to modern Jewish culture is rooted not as much in the period following the Napoleonic wars, despite the fact that the remnants of its vital powers could still be seen at that time in central Poland, but in its period of florescence, when it launched a rebellion against the decrepit rule and outmoded world view of what it considered a fossilized orthodoxy.

A certain idealization of Hasidism prevalent today makes no distinction between the periods of rise and fall in its development and, at the same time, belittles the role of the Haskalah in the development of modern Judaism and underestimates it to the degree of deliberate omission. It was thus possible that the bicentennial of the death of the Baʿal Shem Tov in 1960 was observed in the state of Israel with elaborate publicity, yet the public was unaware that the same year marked the centennial of the death of Isaac Ber Levinsohn, the father of the Russian Haskalah. This want of knowledge of the Haskalah as opposed to Hasidism is certainly a disquieting sign of a turning away from the values of rationalism in our cultural heritage in preference to those of irrationalism and mysticism.

We should not defend this demeaning distinction on the ground that it allegedly issues from a persistent aim at arousing our national consciousness. This has mistakenly led to the claim that Hasidism was a movement of redemption and, thus, a typical national movement, whereas the Haskalah, in general, did not see the need to emphasize the national element of Judaism and, to a certain extent, was even misled into a tendency to actual assimilation. This argument is based on a complete misunderstanding of the special character of the cultural trends in the history of the Jewish people as an exterritorial nation.

The conditions of the Jews in the Diaspora induced the popular currents to exalt the concept of redemption, whereas in the rationalistic currents, whose standard bearers were the upper strata of the people, this idea was not emphasized, often because of the desire to draw nearer to the ruling nation. In this respect, the opposition between Hasidism and the Haskalah is of the same nature as the rivalry between the zealots on the one hand and the rationalists on the other in the controversy that flared up in Spain and Provence after the death of Maimonides, or between the Kabbalists and the men of the Renaissance in Italian Jewry, or between the guardians of traditional Jewish belief in their struggle against philosophy in Dutch Judaism. Cultural progress in the history of the Jewish people in the Diaspora—since it is a history of Diaspora—did not always parallel the historic desire of the people for redemption in Zion.

The paths to progress in the development of the Jews have not been straight. Yet, the power of progress is great throughout Jewish history, and only progress can guide a people on the main road to liberation, the road to autoemancipation and the return to Zion. It was not by coincidence that Hasidism, the last and most powerful of all the religious movements of Jewish redemption, reached at its final stage the impasse of passivity and weakness; in contrast, the Haskalah, inasmuch as it struck root among the people, deepened its hold by becoming more realistic until it gave birth to a new movement, the "Lovers of Zion," which paved the way for the revival of the nation in its homeland.

The first part of this book, which discusses Galician Hasidism and the Haskalah, was published in Yiddish in 1942 by the YIVO in New York. In the Hebrew edition (*Sifriyat Po'alim,* 1961), on which this translation is based, the number of documents in the appendix was doubled and a sixth chapter was added dealing with Joseph Perl's almanacs, which first appeared in English in the *Journal of Jewish Bibliography* (1942, nos. 1–3) and then in Yiddish in the bimonthly *Getseltn* (1946–47, nos. 10–13). This edition contains a number of changes in the formulation of the Haskalah's national stand, and of the problem of the social foundations of Hasidism, aspects of which became clearer to me following further research into the history of the movement. Therefore, the portrait of Hasidism in Galicia presented here is, I believe, richer and more detailed.

In the second part of the book, a description of the Hasidic system and Haskalah literature in Congress Poland is given. The scope is much broader here than in Part I because whereas the creative powers of Galician Hasidism weakened, the Hasidic doctrine in Poland, especially in that period, excelled in the originality of its ideas. As far as the Haskalah in Poland is concerned, I chose to elaborate on its writers and literature since, due to its sparsity, it did not succeed in entering the written history of modern Hebrew literature as did the Haskalah in Galicia.

Sincere thanks go to Dr. Michael Wonsowicz, director of the Central State Archives in Warsaw, who courteously allowed me to use its documents during my stay in Warsaw in the summer of 1957. He was also of great assistance during my work in the State Archives in Lemberg (Lwów) in the summer of 1937, when he served there as chief archivist.

Last, I remember with deep reverence my beloved friend, the renowned martyred historian Dr. Emanuel Ringelblum, hero of the Warsaw Ghetto and creator of its archives. He, in faithful friendship, copied for me the documents of the Public Education Archives (AOP) in Warsaw concerning Hasidism and sent them to me in New York just before the outbreak of World War II, during which the entire collection was destroyed by the Nazis.

RAPHAEL MAHLER
Summer 1961

I

GALICIA

1

The Sociopolitical Foundations of Hasidism in Galicia in the First Half of the Nineteenth Century

The Suppression of Galician Jewry

The period between 1815 and 1848, when the struggle between Haskalah and Hasidism in Galicia reached its most heated phase, was the most difficult in the history of the Jews in this province of the Austrian monarchy. The policy of brutal suppression of Galician Jewry, initiated in the era of so-called enlightened absolutism, was carried out in a more overt and shameless fashion by the Austrian government under the powerful Metternich. Not only did all previous restrictions of Jewish rights remain in effect but also new and highly oppressive edicts were issued.

As early as 1784–85, during the reign of Emperor Joseph II, Jews in the villages were forbidden to engage in trade, operate taverns or lease mills, and collect tolls; and the Edict of Toleration of 1789 banished Jews from the villages unless they were engaged in handicrafts or agriculture. Although this harsh edict was difficult to enforce, it did make life miserable for the village Jews, who lived in constant fear of being caught by the police. A Jew who was apprehended for selling liquor or for not having a special permit to reside in the village would, under this law, be returned under guard to his place of birth.[1] Jews were not allowed to reside in such towns as

Żywiec, Kęty, Biała, Wadowice, Andrychów, Ciężkowice, Zakliczyn, Pilzno, Jasło, Bochnia, Wieliczka, and Mikołajów. Modern ghettos were introduced in the larger cities such as Lemberg (Lwów), Nowy Sącz, Tarnów, and Sambor, and even in the smaller ones, like Gródek Jagielloński and Jaryczów. Only individuals with an academic education or the vast fortune of thirty thousand gulden were permitted to settle outside these Jewish quarters. A Jew needed a special passport to travel from one city to another. Jews who came to Galicia had to pay the high poll tax which formerly they had paid in medieval Germany. Even for Jews involved in handicrafts there were difficulties because the Christian guilds did not admit Jews as members. Jews were forbidden to purchase either property in the cities or agricultural land from Christians, except for several hundred Jewish colonists whose number decreased from year to year due to harassment by Austrian officials.

The heaviest burden on the impoverished Jewish population in Galicia were the taxes specific to Jews which dated back to the time of Empress Maria Theresa and Emperor Joseph II. These were increased many times and new ones were frequently levied. For example, the special tax on *sheḥita* (ritually slaughtered meat), introduced in 1784, was so greatly increased in 1789, 1810, and 1816 that it came to three times the original levy and resulted in an increase in the price of kosher meat to twice that of nonkosher meat. Michael Stöger, a Christian scholar writing at that time, noted that "beef was either never or very seldom eaten by the poorer classes." The ignominious exploitation of the Jewish population by the pious Catholic Austrian monarchy was thus described by the well-known Viennese writer and Jewish communal leader Joseph von Wertheimer in his book, *Die Juden in Oesterreich* (On the condition of the Jews in Austria), which, due to censorship, was published in Leipzig:

> Now this is not Shylock who, according to Shakespeare's slander, wanted to deprive a Christian of a pound of flesh but these are hundreds of thousands of Jews who are being deprived of substantial pounds of flesh on the ground of decrees of a Christian state.[2]

Still more invidious was the introduction in 1797 of the candle tax, which was trebled in the course of two decades. Every married Jewish woman was required to pay the candle tax of ten kreutzers on two candles to the tax lessee before the Sabbath began, whether or not she had any money to buy candles! The homes of those who could not pay promptly were raided by the tax collector on Friday night, and he was empowered to confiscate the household goods, including even the bedding. According to the reliable testimony of Wertheimer, one would often meet impoverished people on the street on Fridays begging for a few kreutzers in order to pay the candle tax.

In addition to these two imposts, the Galician Jews were burdened with a special marriage tax, a heavy residence tax, and an annual tax on *battei keneset* (houses of worship) and *minyanim* (private religious assemblies). Jews suspected of avoiding payment of any of these taxes, especially the candle tax, were required to take an oath of purgation every year, sometimes twice a year, wearing a *talit* (prayer shawl) and *kittel* (white ritual robe), in the presence of the rabbi and the district commissioner. The Austrian government also assumed the role of guardian of Jewish piety in order to increase its financial exploitation of the Jews. Thus, the eating of nonkosher meat was punishable by fine or imprisonment, and any Jewish woman who did not light Sabbath candles was subject to arrest, forced labor, and even whipping.

The institution of the *kehillah,* the autonomous administration of the Jewish community, was deeply demoralized by its being in effect handed over arbitrarily to the lessees of the candle tax. The *kehillah* became a private domain of the Jewish plutocracy. In the smaller Jewish communities, only those who regularly paid the tax on three to four candles a week were enfranchised and in the larger communities the tax was on seven candles a week. And, to be a candidate for *parnas* (trustee of the *kehillah*) or for rabbi, one had to furnish certification of regularly paid taxes on four to seven candles in the smaller communities and on eight to ten candles in the larger communities. Moreover, the candle tax lessee often issued false tax receipts for those men, including himself, whom he wanted appointed trustees. Thus, for example, in Lemberg in 1817, the candle tax lessees held four out of the five trusteeships in the *kehillah*.

In an 1818 report of the imperial chancellery, the government cynically acknowledged its financial exploitation of the Jewish masses: "The higher taxation [of the Jewish population] was maintained because a reduction of this taxation would be possible only if [the tax burden] were transferred to the rest of the population and this would create an unfavorable impression."[3]

Parallel with this economic exploitation of Galician Jews was the Austrian government's concerted attempt to germanize its Jews by attempting to eradicate their national distinctiveness, by, among other measures, destroying the Yiddish language. Having failed to germanize the Polish and Ukrainian population, this policy was rigorously applied to the Jews, first out of sheer frustration and malice, and second in the hopes that the Jews, scattered as they were throughout the land, would serve as disseminators of the German language among the Gentiles. The closing of the German-Jewish schools is an example of an even stronger attempt to germanize the Galician Jews by legislative means. In 1806, the year the German-Jewish schools were closed, a court decree was issued requiring all officials of the larger Jewish communities to have a command of German. In 1810 the scope of this decree was broadened to require that every Jewish voter in *kehillah* elections prove his literacy in German. In 1814 an edict was issued declaring Hebrew and Yiddish documents inadmissable as evidence in the courts and invalid in government bureaus. The decree that every Jewish couple, prior to their marriage, be examined in German on the *Bnei Ẓion* catechism (published by the notorious school inspector Herz Homberg in 1812), was especially oppressive. The extent of the government's intention to germanize Galician Jewry is indicated in the imperial decree of January 22, 1820, which stated that, after a specified time, all synagogue services must be conducted in German or at least in the official local language.

Thus, the Jewish population of Galicia was under the double yoke of extreme poverty and governmental exploitation. According to official estimates, at least one-third of the Jewish population consisted of *luftmentshn* (persons without a definite occupation), who subsisted on odd jobs or who had no trade and often no means of subsistence at all.[4] However, even those directly engaged in trade, approximately one-third, were primarily petty tradesmen and shopkeepers.[5] About one-fifth were engaged in crafts and small industry, of which one-half were employed in the garment industry as tailors, furriers, hatters, and shoemakers; the others were for the most part butchers, bakers, weavers, blacksmiths, goldsmiths, and watchmakers.[6] The mass of Galician Jewry lived in small towns, which at that time were still mostly the private property of the Polish nobility, as were several larger cities such as Tarnopol and Brody. Approximately one-fifth of the Jewish population lived in villages as innkeepers, tradesmen, and brokers,[7] despite all the legal restrictions, and were therefore subject to the whims of the Polish landowners and the malevolence of Austrian officials.

The extraordinary impoverishment of the Jewish population in Galicia is clearly illustrated by the fact that the government was initially forced to exempt 4,000 Jewish families from the candle tax and to reduce the tax by half for 11,000 families.[8] Since the entire Jewish population consisted of about 45,000 families (about 225,000 to 250,000 people),[9] it appears that one-third of the Jews were in such an extreme state of poverty that even the ruthless, reactionary administration had to make allowances .

The grave economic and political situation also accounts for the fact that the number of Jews in Galicia increased very little during the first half of the nineteenth century, while the gentile population approximately doubled during the same period. In 1773 the gentile population of Galicia numbered just above 2 million. Galician Jewry numbered 224,981 in 1773, and about 246,000 in 1827. Since the natural rate of increase of the Jews was certainly no less than that of the Gentiles, owing to the tradition of early marriages, it is probable that many more Galician Jews than Gentiles migrated to the neighboring provinces of Poland, the Ukraine, and Hungary.[10]

Thus, to seek solace from their grievous needs and sufferings and to express their yearning for redemption, the enslaved Jewish multitude in the small towns and villages of Galicia turned to the Hasidic movement. The nature of Hasidism in Galicia in this era of reaction (1815–48) is reflected in the Hasidic literature of the time, in official government documents, and in some of the utterances of the enemies of Hasidism, the Maskilim.

The Social Character of Hasidism

The answer to the question of which strata the adherents of Hasidism were recruited from can be found in the official acts. In the gubernatorial ordinance of July 29, 1823, regarding Hasidism, the Hasidic rebbes are described as those who exert influence on the "plebeian class" of Jews.[11] The district commissioner of Brody, in a report in 1827 to the gubernium, explains the class status of the adherents of Hasidism in the following words:

> One recognizes such a Jew very easily. He goes about with a bare throat, with rolled up sleeves and usually is very dirtily and shabbily dressed. . . . The commonest Jews belong to this sect. They attach themselves to no profession, are usually common tavernkeepers, swindlers and soothsayers [*Sagerer*], for they have the firm conviction that God will provide for and help them even in the face of complete indolence.[12]

In an 1838 memorandum, the Lemberg police commissioner wrote to the gubernium:

> The Hasidic leaders have discarded the outmoded and sometimes burdensome ceremonies of the Hebrew worship. The rabble hastily seized this opportunity. There are very few merchants among the Hasidim. For the most part they are idlers, drunkards and hypocritical, lazy fanatics.[13]

Although these characterizations are charged with hatred and contempt, they do state explicitly that the Galician Hasidim were a "common rabble" of tavernkeepers,[14] small shopkeepers, brokers, petty tradesmen (officially termed *Betrüger,* or swindlers), and poor, unemployed people. A similar characterization of the Hasidim is found in the casual comments in the letters of the Maskilim.

In his letter "le-Yadid Mitḥassed" of 1815, Solomon Judah Rapoport wrote that the Hasidim were lenient in interpreting the commandments "and therefore everyone of the poor people follows them."[15] A Maskil in the town of Jarosław, Ungar, described the Hasidim who came to welcome the zaddik Hersh of Żydaczów when he arrived in 1822 as a "crowd of ragged beggars."[16]

The Hasidic leader Moses of Sambor (brother of Hersh of Żydaczów) presented a similar picture of a reception for a zaddik. According to this account, "devotees hoping to catch a spark from his holy fire run to receive him. . . . As his star begins to rise the poor hasten to greet him; then the youths—like arrows from the hand of the mighty—flash by. Finally, as the noonday sun appears overhead, the princes of our generation and the leaders of the nation come to pay homage."[17]

In "Katit la-Ma'or," a series of letters in *Kerem Ḥemed* concerning the Rabbi Meir Ba'al ha-Nes boxes (alms boxes for the benefit of the poor in Ereẓ Yisrael that were distributed by Hasidim), Joseph Perl stated that R. Meir Ba'al ha-Nes "has no significance nor reputation at all among the great men but has been exalted by the poor people who do not understand how to differentiate between right and left." He described this as a new "custom that the ignorant and the poor are very fond of."[18] In Perl's *Megalleh Temirin* (Revealer of secrets), the Hasid Reb Zaynvl of Verkhevke complains in a letter to Reb Zelig of Letitshiv that, because of the favors the Maskil "Mordecai, may his name be erased," prevailed upon the landowner to concede, "only the few poor men in our little *bet ha-midrash* [house of study] still adhere to the truth with us."[19] In *Boḥen Ẓaddik* (The tester of the righteous), a review of his own *Megalleh Temirin*, Perl tells of his astonishment in meeting a very wealthy man in "Bitsuk" who was an adherent of "our company" and he immediately infers that this rich man probably sought esteem and honor in the eyes of the Hasidim "just to gain respect within the clique."[20]

In a letter of consolation written in 1827 by Nachman Krochmal,[21] the distinguished philosopher and leader of the Galician Haskalah, to Abraham Goldberg, a young Maskil of Mosty Wielkie, whose books had been burned by the Hasidim, Krochmal wrote that Hasidism is found only in eastern Europe:

In our province, too, they have been successful only in small towns such as the celebrated Mosty and environs, where they have made progress and taken root among the villagers dwelling on the Hungarian frontier, in the Wallachian hideouts of robbers,[22] and in the desolate Ukrainian steppes, all of them new communities recently established by refugees and exiles from the adjacent countries. The opposite is true of the old communities renowned for their learning, wisdom and large population, such as Cracow, Lemberg, Lublin, Brody, Tarnopol, Vilna, Brest, and the like. And in our areas the Maskilim leave them alone due to their insignificance and misery.

Even more characteristically, Krochmal encouraged his young friend to continue his secular studies, for "enlightenment will elevate you, will remove you from the wretched poor people and place you among the rich. The recognition and prestige bestowed upon the followers of knowledge, the genuinely enlightened, by the leaders of our people, as well as by kings and rulers, is a well-known fact." He pokes fun at the poor Hasidic rebbe who "is forced to flatter women, children and villagers . . . in order to alleviate his poverty and to satisfy his own hunger as well as that of his partisans and admiring followers. . . . The leprosy of poverty shines forth from his forehead," Krochmal writes. He wanders and begs "like those wretched gypsy families." Krochmal's letter speaks volumes not only about the social structure of the Hasidim but also about the relationship between the Haskalah, plutocracy, and ruling absolutism.

The works of the Maskilim from Poland and Volhynia also reflect their contempt for the "wretchedly poor" Hasidim. In *Teyator fun Khsidim,* a play written by Ephraim Fischl Fischelsohn of Zamość,[23] the "paupers" motif appears in the opening as well as the finale. In the beginning, one of the characters, the Hasid reb Shmuel Yerukhem of Bełz, says,

By all means, do tell, why you don't like the Hasidim.
What do you know! Though they're wretchedly poor
Really naked and bare
Without a shirt on their backs
And indeed terrible paupers
Still they flock to the rebbes.

Concerning the dispute between the Maskil and the Hasid, the yeshivah students conclude that Leybele the Maskil "is a fine fellow":

And our Hasidim, those paupers,
Are indeed vagabonds and fools. . . .

The hero of Isaac Ber Levinsohn's anti-Hasidic satire *Emek Refa'im* (Valley of ghosts)[24] relates that, when already "famous among the masses as a wonder worker," he decided to become a rebbe. He avoided settling down in the big cities, where enlightened merchants, men of keen intellect, and the very wealthy lived, in favor of a very small town where "people who, because of extreme poverty, are constantly occupied eking out a living." He did become widely known outside his own town in all the surrounding towns and villages, but he began his "rounds" in the villages. In his will, he advises his son how to find favor with "the rabble and the poor." In the satire *Divrei Ẓaddikim* (Words of the righteous), also by Levinsohn,[25] the two protagonists, the Hasidim Reb Henekh Soyfer and Reb Hirsh Itsik, are also portrayed as indigents who lack the money to travel to their rebbe and sometimes receive alms even from Maskilim. In a letter written in 1840 by Levinsohn to Daniel Hartenstein of Radziwiłłów[26] he complains about his poverty, requests material assistance, and asks rhetorically: To whom shall I turn? Perhaps to the holy people in the land or to their gang? Or to the poor people who do not know their way about and for want of wisdom seek protection under the wings of Hasidism?

From the very beginning of Hasidism, its character was set by the middle class, which occupied the lower level of the social hierarchy vis-à-vis the Talmudists, and the merchant class, with which the Hasidim were connected. This middle class consisted of liquor franchise holders in the villages and small towns, the more prosperous innkeepers, and the brokers at the courts of the nobility. In the Polish provinces adjacent to Galicia the communal strong men and tax lessees took over. As will be shown, prior to the social transformation of Hasidism, prosperous elements from the feudal sphere joined its ranks and were a component of the movement's social structure. What all these social elements had in common was their dependence on the feudal economy within both the local community and the province at large—a feudalism weakening with the slow but steady growth of capitalism and with the increasing strength of the absolutist regime.

Thus, the wretched living conditions of the Jewish petty bourgeoisie, its concerns and hopes, dreams and ideals, are all reflected in Hasidic philosophy and practices.

Beliefs and Values of Hasidim

Hasidic doctrine is usually expressed through the exegesis of Torah passages, although comprehension of the text is not its aim. On the contrary, the Torah is merely a point of departure for homilies on conduct, consolation, assurances of imminent redemption, and the like. For example, the Exodus from Egypt provides ample material for sermons on the contemporary Exile and the promise of Redemption and the Koraḥ story for tirades against heretics and Mitnaggedim who find no need for a rebbe. Moreover, the use of kabbalistic interpretation of the Torah (Abraham, for example, represents mercy; Isaac, judgment) always made it possible to link the Hasidic doctrine in the sermons preached at the rebbe's Sabbath table to the weekly Torah portion.[27]

The basic idea in all Hasidic doctrine of this period in Galicia is the primacy of the kabbalistic notion of *midat ha-ḥesed* (divine grace) as personified in the *sefirah Ḥesed*.[28] All the calamities of the *galut klali* (the exile of the Jewish people), as well as of the *galut prati* (the exile of the individual Jew), derive from the dominance of *midat ha-din* (stern judgment) over *midat ha-ḥesed*. This is manifested by the lack of unity in God's name; that is to say, of the four Hebrew letters which compose the tetragrammaton, the first two—the *yod* and the *he*, representing the Holy One, blessed be He—and the second two—the *vav* and the *he*, representing the *Shekhinah* (Divine Presence)—are separated. Every Jew is in a position—through fervent prayer, good deeds, and inner love of God—to restore this kabbalistic unity of God and thereby to secure the rule of *midat ha-ḥesed*. Devotion in prayer is not merely an emotion but, in a tradition that derives from the teachings of the Ba'al Shem Tov, is also the intention to unify the higher spheres. In this vein, Rebbe Hersh of Żydaczów explained the dictum of *Pirkei Avot* (Ethics of the Fathers) that "all your deeds should be done in the name of Heaven," instead of simply "for Heaven," as an exhortation to intend each act and word "for uniting God's names."[29] Furthermore, he claimed, the zaddik reaches the stage whereby his mere breathing achieves this unification: He exhales with the name *Elohim* (attribute of judgment) and inhales with *yod he vav he* (attribute of mercy).[30]

Thus, every Jew is responsible in his conduct not only for himself but also for the entire Jewish people. As piety, love of God, and good deeds increase, so does the abundance of God's grace that streams down upon the entire Jewish people and on each individual Jew. "However, faith is primary, for if a man believes with perfect faith that the Lord delivers the abundance of his livelihood to him every day, and truly believes in his heart in God, then this evil spirit is subjugated and is unable to rob him of that abundance."[31]

Undoubtedly, zaddikism also plays an important role in the Hasidic conception of the category of *midat ha-ḥesed*. Several Hasidic books of that period, as in the earlier works (such as the *No'am Elimelekh)*, constantly repeat the warning that, without the mediation of the zaddik or at least without his guidance, God's abundance cannot be attained.[32] In this respect, the conception of *midat ha-ḥesed* in Hasidism is similar to that of the dogma of God's grace in Catholicism, in which salvation cannot be imagined without the mediation of the Church, the "mediatrix of divine grace." The Hasidic teaching of divine grace and complete faith in God primarily reflects the pitiful, uncertain, and haphazard existence of the Jewish village tavernkeeper, small shopkeeper, or broker of the time who did not know in the evening if he would earn a piece of bread for himself and his family the following day.[33]

In Volhynia and Congress Poland, where because of various legal restrictions there were fewer tavernkeepers than in Galicia, smugglers (peklmakhers) held a significant position among the Hasidim. Rebbes are portrayed cooperating with smugglers by Levinsohn in *Emek Refa'im,* in the anonymous *Di Genarte Velt* (The deceived world), and by Fischelsohn in his *Teyator fun Khsidim.* Abraham Ber Gottlober tells in his memoirs of knowing "such persons who call themselves Hasidim" who come over the border to Galicia to the son of Rebbe Israel of Ruzhin and whose visits are "merely coverups" for smuggling contraband on their way back home.[34]

It is not surprising that the most solid economic element among the Jewish petty bourgeoisie, the artisan, is least represented in the Hasidic stories.[35] Gottlober described the Hasidim of his youth as "particularly hating the crafts and making fun of artisans living from manual labor." Generalizing about the vocational spectrum of the Hasidim, he said, "Hardly anyone in those circles takes up a trade," but he stressed this applied to declared Hasidim and not to those who just believed in rebbes and presented them gifts, among the latter of which there were some "unlettered" artisans.[36] We may guess that these artisans were from small towns. In larger communities, they either inclined toward the Mitnaggedim or removed themselves from the controversy altogther, as the ignorant of ancient days essentially kept their distance from the Sadducee-Pharisee struggle. In *Teyator fun Khsidim,* Reb Shmuel the Hasid conjoins (in the course of rhyme), of all things, "tailor's apprentices, nothing but servants" ("Shnayderyungen, same meshorsim") with "such great heretics" ("Azoyne groyse apikorsim").[37]

"Children, life and daily bread" is the earthly undertone in all the consolatory teachings of the Hasidic leaders. In *Teyator fun Khsidim* the Maskil, Reb Leybele, mocks the Hasidim:

You argue that a Hasid cries day and night,
Why shouldn't he, isn't he right?

How can he be happy when he thinks about his brood
And about his creditors?
What's surprising about that?[38]

The Hasidic collections of stories very often tell of people, for the most part penniless lessees and tenant innkeepers, whose deep faith remained despite their woes. Even in the second half of the nineteenth century, the folksinger Velvl of Zbaraż depicted the Hasid as a pauper whose faith never fails him for a moment.[39]

If, according to the Hasidic teachings, all the woes of the Jewish people and of each individual Jew are caused by the domination of the power of *midat ha-din*, this domination reveals itself first of all in the oppression of the Jews by the gentile nations. Almost all the Hasidic books of this period are replete with complaints about the oppressive burden of exile placed upon the Jewish people by the gentile nations. This contrasts significantly with the position of the Maskilim of that time, who not only did not mention the oppression of the Jews, but also preached loyalty, devotion, and gratitude to the "gracious" government.

"The holy sparks spread among the Gentiles and nourish them; they have grown up strong and are successful in their wickedness and make ever more difficult our burden of bondage and of exile," complained Naphtali of Ropczyce.[40] "On Passover today—as opposed to the Temple era—we eat bitter herbs before matzoh," explained Mendel of Rymanów a generation earlier in Napoleonic times. "Matzoh symbolizes redemption; bitter herbs, exile. In dispersion we first acknowledge the bitter, then the fervent hope for deliverance and restoration of our glory."[41]

Hersh of Żydaczów bade Jews to divide their time between studying the Kabbalah and earning a living. He justified this on the ground that "especially in our generation, with its burden of taxes and tolls and under the yoke of exile in our generation, which is the period preceding the coming of the Messiah,[42] the people of the country are becoming ever more impoverished."[43] He specifically mentioned the taxes as a tribulation of the cruel Exile; legend in fact represents him as the defender of the Jewish people against the special Jewish taxes. It is told that in keeping with an old Purim custom, Hersh's brother Kopl once disguised himself as a prince of the realm. Intoxicated and accompanied by a retinue, Kopl went to his brother Hersh, who honored him as a king and implored him to revoke the burdensome candle and kosher meat taxes. The Purim king agreed to this and even signed his name to one such edict. However, when Kopl refused his brother's request to rescind the onerous decree of military service, Hersh held it against him for some time.[44] In contrast, Rebbe Hersh, through intercession on high, was able to nullify the decree banishing Jewish tavernkeepers from the villages. He accomplished this, it was explained, because the taverns provided not only food but also prayer shawls and phylacteries for Jewish travelers.[45]

Hasidism and Germanization

In view of the Hasidim's vigilance with regard to matters of religion, the attempts of the Austrian government to germanize the Jews were considered as repressive as the taxes. Thus, the rebbes stubbornly defended the Yiddish language and the old modes of dress and customs. Mendel of Rymanów saw in the decrees concerning "new clothing" and "new languages" the work of the *kelipah gedolah,* "the shell" (i.e., the evil spirit) that precipitated the gentile nations' gaining power over the people of Israel. He cited the talmudic statement that the Jews were redeemed from slavery in Egypt because they did not change their names, their language, or their dress.[46] In this regard, Ẓevi Elimelekh of Dynów, a student of Hersh of Żydaczów, spoke of the edict declaring Hebrew and Yiddish documents invalid in the government bureaus and courts and the edict requiring a Jewish bride and groom to pass an examination in German as a precondition for legal marriage:

> And now, because of our many sins, an unsparing, evil decree has been issued declaring that our holy tongue has become an invalid coin, God forbid. Who would have believed this about the language that has from time immemorial been regarded even among the wise men of the Gentiles as the best and most magnificent language; the language in which the world was created and that was given as a gift through divine revelation to His chosen people. Now fortune has changed through this evil decree that prohibits any document in matters of business and any bill of sale in our holy tongue. . . . The decree that a marriage cannot be performed until the couple is versed in the foreign writing and tongue.

Consequently, he demands that the Yiddish language be maintained with devotion and that it not be supplanted by German.

> Therefore, my beloved brothers and friends, guard the lock on your mouth and speak to one another only in the language that was instituted by our ancestors in the Diaspora, with its admixture of the holy tongue, so that the language of Judaism should be visible as a distinct [language] from the languages of the Gentiles. Keep your children as much as possible from foreign tongues and God will bring his nation to speedy deliverance in our day as He did for our forefathers in Egypt.

The same author pours out his wrath and mockery upon "the wicked who are proud of the foreign language and consider it a disgrace to mix even a word of our holy tongue into their speech."[47]

It was not only their attachment to the Yiddish language and tradition that strengthened the Hasidim in their struggle against the attempts at germanization. The Hasidim viewed the germanizing policy as but another element in the Austrian system of oppression and fiscal exploitation of the Jews. "These were obviously our enemies," Ẓevi Elimelekh said of the proponents of German, namely, the Maskilim, "through denunciations, robberies and the burden of taxes."[48] The fact that Herz Homberg, the brutal germanizer of Galician Jewry, was one of the initiators of the institution of the candle tax was probably still fresh in the memory of the Hasidim.[49] The moderate Maskilim also offered the government their unqualified support. It is therefore not surprising that the Hasidim held them responsible for the anti-Jewish decrees.

The Hasidim vigorously opposed not only the study of German, but also all secular studies. Although the fear of cultural assimilation played a large part in the Hasidim's struggle against enlightenment, the principal factor was their kabbalistic Weltanschauung. According to Hersh of Żydaczów and Ẓevi Elimelekh of Dynów, every secular area of inquiry is opposed to God, as it originates in *ḥokhmah ḥiẓonit* (external science) which comes from the *sitra aḥra* (other side), and is thus essentially empty and false.

Like many of the Christian sects during the Middle Ages and the Reformation, Hasidism attacked science not only because it was hostile to enthusiastic, inwardly directed religion but also because it was closely allied to the new socioeconomic order of capitalism, which was undermining the old relationships of production and the medieval ways of life connected with them. For the occupations of the Hasidic masses were rooted in the old, essentially feudal relations of production between lord and serfs, with the small-town Jew and village Jew serving as middlemen between city and countryside, as well as between the landowner and his peasants.

Science was regarded by the Hasidim to be such a great threat to faith that even medicine was rejected by some of the rebbes. When the terrible cholera epidemic of 1831 broke out, Hersh of Żydaczów deemed it necessary to write a letter enjoining his Hasidim in Munkacs against being treated by a physician. He justified this prohibition by claiming that the true healer is the zaddik, who is the link (*kav ha-emẓa'i*) between the Jews and the Almighty, the "healer of the sick among his people, Israel." His remedy for cholera was to "recite all of Psalms every week, pledge to charity after completing each of the five books of the Psalms, recite the *ketoret* [the biblical portions concerning burning of incense in the Tabernacle] before 'May it be Thy will,' and examine the mezuzahs to insure that they are ritually fit."[50]

Rebbe Nachman of Bratslav preceded Rebbe Hersh in the absolute prohibition against physicians.[51] Rebbe Simon of Jarosław, also known as Simon of Dobromil, repeated Nachman's extreme antirationalist saying over and over, "The ultimate in wisdom is not to be wise at all."[52]

In contrast to the religious and rationalistic Christian sects which opposed superstitions as adamantly as they did secular science, the Hasidic movement was permeated by superstitions of all kinds. The Hasidim believed as much in magical remedies, amulets, exorcisms, demonic possession (dybbuks), ghosts, devils, and teasing, mischievous genies as they did in the almost unlimited heavenly power of the zaddik. Thus, the distance between the religious rationalism of most of the medieval Christian sects and the superstitious mysticism of Hasidism was in a sense as great as the socioeconomic difference between those sectarians, workers, and artisans who were directly involved in the processing of raw materials and the Jewish shopkeeper and declassé elements who, for hundreds of years, were cut off from any direct contact with the production process.

Jew, Gentile, and the Messianic Age

The views of the Hasidim about their native land and the land of Israel, Jews and Gentiles, and the Messiah and Redemption were a direct outgrowth and development of the Weltanschauung of the Kabbalah. The Jewish people were not simply the chosen, but were the only people of God; "Israel and the Torah and the Holy One, blessed be He, are one." According to the Midrash, the whole world was created only for the sake of the Jews. The Jews are dispersed in order to gather together the holy sparks that are scattered over the earth. Consequently, their feelings of social involvement did not reach beyond their own people.

The positive expression of this attitude was the principle of the unconditional solidarity of the Jews and the idea of *ahavat yisrael* (love of the Jewish people). *Ahavat yisrael*, the leitmotif of the teachings of Levi Isaac of Berdichev, as well as of the legends about him, is just as characteristic a motif in the stories and legends of the prominent Hasidic rebbes in the first half of the nineteenth century.[53] However, a negative attitude toward Gentiles, which took the form of contempt, was also an unavoidable consequence of this position. As Mendel of Rymanów put it, "A Gentile does not have a heart, although he has an organ that resembles the heart."[54] Simon of Jarosław asserted that the Gentiles will be held responsible not for their evil decrees—these were actually divinely inspired and had been prophesied in order to "cleanse [the Jews] of their sins"—but for their "vengefulness and revelry in the distress of the Jews."[55] The symbol for the Gentile in the Hasid's consciousness was the brutal landowner or the enslaved and boorish peasant.

In practice, however, the folk character of Hasidism caused the Hasid to relate to the peasants with a certain sympathy. This can be inferred both from the Jewish and Ukrainian legends about the Ba'al Shem Tov and from the stories about Meyer of Przemyślany and other rebbes of his time. The fact that peasants would sometimes come to a rebbe for help is also related by Levinsohn in his *Emek Refa'im.*[56] In fact, the peasants were often exploited in their daily economic relations with the Jewish tradesmen and brokers, especially with the tavernkeepers, though the exploiters were themselves impoverished. But this resulted from the general phenomenon of exploitation of the village by the landowner and the city which had prevailed for hundreds of years prior to the inception of Hasidism. Only the Maskilim, who saw Hasidism as the cause of all the miserable and deceitful aspects of Jewish life, held this movement responsible even for the evils which were often an unavoidable product of the economic activities of most small-town and village Jews. In *Teyator fun Khsidim*, Leybele the Maskil admonishes the Hasidim,

> The Gentile works bitter and hard.
> For all his pain, the Jew
> Comes by and steals his gain.[57]

As to the fate of the gentile nations in the Messianic Age, Hasidic books highlight two biblical positions—one positive, one negative. Even those that speak of revenge and judgment against the gentile nations[58] paint the prophetic picture of the Messianic Age, when all nations will be converted to Judaism and will devote themselves to the Torah.[59]

Just as all the nations exist, according to the Hasidim, only by virtue of the Jewish people, so the earth endures thanks only to the land of Israel because "Ereẓ Yisrael is the essence of the world and all vitality stems from it."[60] The life of the Jews in the Diaspora is considered to be a merely temporary phenomenon. Mendel of Rymanów surprisingly regards the laws permitting Jews to purchase houses as a ruse intended to bind them more closely to the lands of the exile and subsequently to assimilate them. By way of contrast, he points to the Jews of Egypt, who lived in tents because they did not want to become permanent inhabitants in their diaspora.[61] It was not only Mendel of Rymanów, who, active in Napoleonic times when messianic expectations were heightened by the world upheaval, spoke of the Messianic Age and imminent Redemption, but also the rebbes of the later generation, such as Mendel of Kosów, Simon of Dobromil, Naphtali of Ropczyce, Hersh of Żydaczów and his student Ẓevi Elimelekh of Dynów.[62] "The time of redemption has already arrived," writes one rebbe, "and all the predestined dates have passed and the matter depends only on great repentance."[63] The faith of the ordinary Hasidim in the imminent advent of the Messiah and the Redemption was as firm as their rebbes'. "Even though he tarries, I await him daily" was the cardinal principle of faith set forth by Maimonides and observed quite literally by the Hasidim. It is told of Rebbe Sholem Rokeakh of Bełz that, when greeted with "Next year in Jerusalem" while drawing water to bake matzoh before Passover, he replied, "Why should it be next year? We hope and pray that the water we have just drawn will be used tomorrow to bake matzoh in Jerusalem."[64]

With unwavering faith in the ancient religious tradition rooted in prophetic vision, the expositors of Hasidic doctrine taught the concept of a total redemption—both national and spiritual. Rebbe Moses of Sambor, brother of Hersh of Żydaczów, stressed a triple goal: "We seek the Kingdom of Heaven, the Kingdom of David and the rebuilding of the Temple."[65]

While these Hasidic teachings reflect the social distress and political oppression of the Jewish masses and their yearning for Redemption, the Hasidic movement did not propose any social or political programs. The healthy social instinct of self-help and self-defense did, however, thrust the Hasidic masses closer together and strengthened mutual assistance and unified resistance to the oppressive measures of the government. The spontaneity of these actions in the total absence of any social or political goals reveals even more clearly the tragic contradiction between the potential of the masses and their feeling of powerlessness. This powerlessness found expression first and foremost in greater piety and in mysticism.

Charity in Hasidic Life

Though Hasidism was a petty bourgeois movement, it never regarded wealth as a direct product of social exploitation. The Kabbalah theory of *midat ha-ḥesed* determined from the very outset that the Hasid should be resigned to the existing class differences in Jewish society. In this teaching, the rich man was the one who received a greater portion of *midat ha-ḥesed*.[66] The poor man's recourse was to increase the influx of *midat ha-ḥesed* both for himself and for all the Jews through his conduct, prayer, learning, and good deeds. The poverty of the Jewish masses was attributed to national oppression, "the bondage of the exile" caused by the sins of the Jewish people. When the Jews were worthy and the Messianic Age arrived, the disproportionately large share previously held by the gentile nations would be held by the people of Israel.

In practice, the desire to reconcile the class differences and the drive for social reform could find expression only in charity, the one possible form of self-help under the prevailing conditions. Hasidic works of that time contain numerous injunctions concerning the importance of charity. Mendel of Kosów reiterates the teachings of the Talmud[67] and the works of ethical literature[68] which oblige the prosperous Jew to regard his money as a loan from God and not as an unconditional possession. Naphtali of Ropczyce interprets the prayer of grace after meals, "Lord our God, O make us not dependent on the gifts and loans of men but rather on Thy full, open and generous hand . . . ," as saying that one should not be dependent upon those who regard the giving of charity as a gift to the poor or as a loan to God, but upon those who understand that they have received money from God's hand as a trust which was intended to be distributed to the poor.[69]

Of the three things on which the world is based—Torah, divine service, and the practice of kindliness—Meyer of Przemyślany believed the most important one to be the practice of kindliness (*gemilut ḥasadim*). In support, he cites Ps. 89:3—*olam ḥesed yivneh* (usually translated as "forever is mercy built")—understanding *olam* as "world" instead of "forever," thus "the world is built on kindness."[70] It is on account of the poor who do not receive enough charity, says Simon of Dobromil, that misfortune is brought upon the entire Jewish people, thus causing, as it were, "dissension in Heaven."[71] The matter of charity is thus closely related to the foundations of the system of the kabbalistic-Hasidic Weltanschauung—*midat ha-ḥesed* is directly dependent upon earthly grace. If kindliness is not practiced on earth, *midat ha-din* will dominate the world.[72] Even biblical verses having no relation at all to charity were ingeniously interpreted as alluding to it.[73] Furthermore, to encourage charitableness, there was no hesitation about altering a simple interpretation of a talmudic injunction. For example, the reform of the Academy of Usha: "One who is extravagant [in alms-giving] should not squander more than one-fifth of his holdings"[74] was reinterpreted by R. Uri of Strelisk as follows: "The person for whom giving charity is the same as being robbed, should not donate more than one-fifth of his holdings; he may give more, however, if he is one who is inspired by the act of giving." This interpretation is based on the similarity between the Hebrew roots for booty (*bzh*) and squander (*bzbz*).[75]

The Hasidic legends, even more than the rabbinic legislation, reflect the role that charity played in the Hasidic movement. There are folk tales about the alms-giving and charitableness not only of the earlier generation of leaders of the Galician Hasidim, such as Moses Leyb of Sasów[76] and Mendel of Rymanów, but also of the later zaddikim, Hersh of Żydaczów, his nephew Yitskhok Ayzik of Żydaczów, and Naphtali of Ropczyce,[77] and even stories of zaddikim giving everything to the poor, for example Meyer of Przemyślany.[78] For the Hasidim, the zaddik was regarded as a kind of philanthropic administrator, receiving fees for his advice and returning them to the neediest, in the form of both cash and room and board for the steady followers at his court. In *Emek Refa'im*, even Levinsohn acknowledged that the zaddik contributed money to the poor people of his town, though he was quick to point out that those alms amounted to only a small fraction of the sum he collected during his trips to the surrounding small towns and that his true motive was to become known as a philanthropist.[79] Austrian officials of that time also attested to the fact that charity was one of the chief characteristics of Hasidism. In the 1827 report of the district chief of Stryj to the provincial presidency, we read, "They have assumed the name Hasidim, or more pious Jews, because they turn their attention to the alleviation of the misery and to the support of their unfortunate coreligionists."[80]

Hasidic Solidarity

Like charity and benevolence, unconditional solidarity was a distinctive feature of the Hasidim during that period. In a letter to his Hasidim in Drohobycz and Brody, Hersh of Żydaczów addressed them as "comrades" and emphasized repeatedly that the basis of Hasidism is love for one another and unity among them. In this letter, he added that "all poverty stems from disunity of hearts," and that it is "critical" to "join with one's fellow in love, for that is the goal of Hasidism and its source."[81] In the same vein, Uri of Strelisk preached that it is "essential to Israel that all be bound in a single unity."[82] And Moses of Sambor preached that the Jews would be able to draw compassion from heaven only when love, brotherhood, and friendship reigned among them.[83]

Solidarity was also listed in the official reports of the Austrian civil servants as one of the characteristic traits of the Hasidic movement. The commissioner of Brody wrote in his report for the year 1827: "The Hasidim are bound to each other with heart and soul."[84] The same was recorded by the district chief of Przemyśl in his report of that same year[85] and by the Lemberg chief of police in a report from 1838, in which he also pointed out the strict discipline and conspiratorial methods of the Hasidim.[86] In 1837 Levinsohn wrote to the Warsaw censor, Jacob Tugendhold, in connection with his plan to organize an association of Maskilim under the name "Zion," asking, "How much longer will we tolerate the Hasidic sect, which is united by such a strong bond and whose members help one another?"[87]

Indeed, the Hasidim responded to the oppressive policies of the Austrian government by emphasizing solidarity among themselves and the rest of the Jewish community, and by offering a form of organized passive resistance.

Thus, the village Jews could violate the governmental prohibition of the sale of liquor in the villages through the cooperation of the landowners from whom they had rented the taverns. According to an estimate of the imperial chancellery, in 1836 Jewish tavernkeepers were to be found in at least three-quarters of the Galician villages.[88] The Jewish masses likewise evaded the excessive wedding taxes and the law concerning the German language examination of all prospective bridal couples on Homberg's catechism, *Bnei Ẓion*, by dispensing with the civil regulations and merely undergoing the religious wedding ceremony. From the official statistics for the year 1826, it is apparent that the actual number of marriages among the Jews of Galicia was 1,122, while only 137 legal marriages were recorded.[89] Jews generally shunned the official government courts, resorting instead to the *bet din* (rabbinical court). Similarly, they circumvented the governmental requirement of a special permit for *minyanim* and the payment of the high tax by meeting secretly in the small *shtiblekh* (Hasidic houses of prayer). When the government outlawed the publication of Hasidic and kabbalistic works, the Hasidim established secret presses and printed false dates and places of publication. In spite of the decree of 1800 that forbade the importation of Hebrew and Yiddish books from abroad, the Jews smuggled books from Russia. Despite the prohibition on transferring money abroad without a special permit, the Hasidim succeeded in making regular collections on behalf of Jewry in Palestine and in secretly forwarding the sums there.[90] Many denunciations of the Hasidim by the Maskilim include, among their other sins, the offense of collecting money for Ereẓ Yisrael.[91]

To evade military service, which, under the circumstances, was considered tantamount to forced conversion, the Jews either furnished incorrect birth dates or, if possible, simply neglected altogether to register their sons. Perl, who nevertheless undoubtedly knew the true reason for this "negligence," expressed astonishment in his denunciation to the government in 1838 over the fact that the Jews "place obstacles in the way of regular registration." The Jewish masses also banded together to protect Jews from foreign lands, primarily emigrants from Russia. In the same denunciation, Perl complained that every time the police in Tarnopol arrested Russian Jews, the Jews of Tarnopol would go en masse to the prison and claim that those captured were truly native-born inhabitants. Perl further related that the officials became so confused that they were finally forced to release the imprisoned Jews.

The Hasidim and the masses offered their strongest and most organized resistance to the candle and kosher meat taxes, and they fought the lessees of those taxes by any means at their disposal. In one of the oldest denunciations against the Hasidim found on record, namely that against the local Hasidic rebbe Jacob Groynem of Tomaszów in 1824 by Ḥayyim Herbst of Mosty Wielkie in the district of Żółkiew, it is alleged that this rebbe lured Jews not only into "fanaticism" but also "to illegal acts that are detrimental to the imperial treasury," and that he cursed the tax lessees and put them under bans.[92] Perl justified his denunciation of 1838, in which he proposed that the government put the houses of study (*battei midrash*) under its control, with the argument that "all bans against the Jewish taxes and against the tax lessees are planned there." In a later denunciation of the same year, Perl mentioned boycotts organized by the rebbes against those tax lessees who opposed them. In such cases, "anonymous bans are proclaimed against the consumption of meat." Perl also related that the Hasidim avoided the payment of the kosher meat tax by having their *shoḥatim* operate secretly in the villages where there was no control, since ritual slaughter was legal only in the cities. In the 1841 denunciation of the Hasidim of Buczacz by Joseph Tepper, a Tarnopol Maskil, the offenses of the rabbi–rebbe–Halakhist Abraham David Kru, who had died the previous year, include the charge that "he used to excommunicate every tax lessee."[93] In the 1827 report of the district chief of Stryj, it is said of the Hasidim that "even the fact alone that the kosher meat [tax] lessee of the whole district has not yet been exposed to any attack can serve as evidence that the adherents of this sect have not yet slipped into the Stryj district."[94] This bureaucrat was obviously ignorant of what transpired in his domain if he concluded Hasidim were not present there. However, the struggle of the Hasidim against the tax lessees was so widely known that any region where a tax lessee had peace of mind was thought to be without Hasidim. In Lemberg the candle tax lessees were so hated that in 1808 they submitted a request to the government for permission to reside outside the Jewish quarter because of the attacks against them.[95]

Furthermore, the power of bans, particularly against the consumption of meat, was great. Even those not sympathetic to such restrictions would submit to the pressure of unified mass actions and refrain with the rest of the Jewish population from eating meat, and eat dairy dishes even on the Sabbath and holidays. When such a ban was proclaimed in a town, the district chief would send the district rabbi there to effect its repeal. Travel expenses for the rabbi came from the district chief, who later collected them from the rebellious *kehillah*. However, such "punitive expeditions" had little effect. In Lemberg, the government also attempted to counteract the bans against tax lessees by calling assemblies of the most prominent Galician rabbis. From the end of the eighteenth century there were six such rabbinical assemblies, to which several of the nineteen district rabbis and other prominent rabbis of smaller towns were invited. The last of these assemblies was convened in 1830. These assemblies issued bans against all those who "defrauded" the government by avoiding payment of the candle and kosher meat taxes. Such a ban was then printed and posted on a special black tablet in all the synagogues. Every rabbi was obliged to proclaim this ban orally in the synagogue four times a year. However, these solemn bans seldom deterred anyone. In 1830, at the very same time that a rabbinical assembly in Lemberg was issuing such a ban, leaflets were distributed there forbidding the consumption of meat under penalty of a Hasidic ban. Since the solidarity of the people was stronger than the official ban of the rabbis, the meat tax lessee was, in such instances, forced to reduce the tax.[96]

Thus, Hasidism was a significant factor in uniting the Jewish masses in Galicia to resist the oppression and fiscal exploitation of Austrian absolutism. "The nonpartisan observer who merely glances at Galician Jewry," said Perl in his anti-Hasidic denunciation of 1838, "is immediately faced with the great problem of explaining its complete disregard of almost all the state laws issued in its behalf."[97]

Social Alliances and the Roles of the Rebbes

Just as the Hasidim succeeded in gathering under their banner the greater part of Galician Jewry by their solidarity and their clandestine struggle against the oppressive decrees of the Austrian government, so Hasidism eventually became a conservative force that carried with it the Jewish middle class because of its defense of religion and tradition against the attacks of the Haskalah. Non-Hasidic orthodoxy discerned in the Haskalah a much greater danger to the Jewish religion and to its own hegemony in Jewish life than in Hasidism, and, therefore, its struggles against Hasidism gradually gave way to the struggle against the modernization of Jewish life.

At the beginning of the nineteenth century, the borderline between the Hasidic petty bourgeoisie and the non-Hasidic Orthodox middle class in Galicia was still discernible. Mendel of Kosów, the author of *Ahavat Shalom*, enumerated in his treatise four "classes" ("kitot") among the Jews, characterizing them as follows: (1) the completely wicked; (2) the ignorant people; (3) the scholars; and (4) the Hasidim.[98] It is not difficult to infer that his "completely wicked" are the Maskilim, while the class of "ignorant people" denotes chiefly the artisans, that petty bourgeois element that was always furthest from the Hasidic movement. If the social base of the Hasidim was the petty bourgeois tradesmen, tavernkeepers, and the *lumpenproletariat*, then the class of "scholars"—i.e., Orthodox opponents (*Mitnaggedim*) of Hasidism—found its primary social support in the "respectable burghers" who constituted the Jewish middle class. I. B. Levinsohn's *Emek Refa'im* leaves no doubt that the "wealthy, the prosperous, and the merchants" were, as a rule, Mitnaggedim, adherents of the "scholars" and the "sagacious."[99] The following of the Mitnaggedim was initially much weaker than that of the Hasidim since the Jewish middle class was much smaller than the Jewish petty bourgeoisie. As early as 1837, Perl submitted a report to the Austrian government[100] in which he divided the Galician Jews, according to their religious views, into almost the same four classes as the "kitot" that Mendel of Kosów had enumerated several decades earlier. His division was: (1) "the common mass, the ignorant multitude"; (2) the Orthodox, or strictly rabbinic class; (3) fanatics, or the so-called Hasidim; (4) "the very small number of Maskilim." Perl explained that the "common mass," having no doctrine of its own on religious questions, fell under the influence of whichever group it came in close contact with. The fact that this was written at the end of the 1830s, when Perl was submitting one memorandum after another to the Austrian government, indicates that, in his view, Hasidism had already captivated the Jewish people to such an extent that there was almost nothing left to save. In his report, Perl still thought of the Orthodox class as distinct from the Hasidim. Ẓevi Elimelekh of Dynów also complained that the scholars (*ba'alei torah*) did not live in harmony with the reverent (*ba'alei yir'ah*)—the Hasidim.[101]

Thus, the oppressive measures taken by the Austrian government, together with the necessity of consolidating all conservative religious forces in the face of the Haskalah, resulted in the virtual triumph of Hasidism in Galicia by the middle of the nineteenth century. In his *Neuere Geschichte der Israeliten*, which appeared in 1847, Jost relates that according to information he received from Galicia, only about one-seventh of its Jews did not belong to the Hasidic movement.[102] The gradual process of domination of Jewish religious and communal life by the Hasidim was described by Joseph Perl in his books as well as in his memoranda to the government. The zaddikim attained such a position of power that opposing rabbis were forced out of the community (as in the case of the Rabbi of Kolne in Perl's *Megalleh Temirin*). Through their unity, the Hasidim succeeded in placing their adherents in the positions of *shoḥatim*, thereby wielding considerable power, as, for example, they would pronounce meat from the ritual slaughter of other *shoḥatim* nonkosher. They used similar means to extend their influence into neighboring areas. In *Emek Refa'im*, Levinsohn related that whenever the rebbe arrived in a town, he would summon the *shoḥet* to present his knife for inspection. If the latter did not appear, his *sheḥita* would be declared invalid.[103] This tradition stems from the early days of the movement, when *shoḥatim* were barred from showing their knives "to any but a distinguished rabbi, and then only with the knowledge of the *parnas* of that month" as in Brody in 1772.[104]

These *shoḥatim* became "the janissaries" of the Hasidic rebbes, as Perl calls them in his memorandum of 1838, and they succeeded in breaking the resistance of even the most ardent of the anti-Hasidic rabbis. The *mohalim* (ritual circumcisers), too, Perl reported, were almost all adherents of the Hasidim and used all sorts of strategems against their opponents. Levinsohn indicated that even the administration of the donations for Ereẓ Yisrael passed into the hands of the rebbes and that rabbis and highborn intending to travel to Ereẓ Yisrael had to have recourse to them.[105]

In addition to the *shoḥatim* and *mohalim*, other members of the clergy, "minor scholars" who from the beginning added a bit of intellectualism[106] to Hasidism and aided its spread, were the *maggidim* (preachers), and, especially, the cantors and the less formal prayer leaders. Gottlober, in fact, considered the prayer leaders the main factor in the movement's success. Their influence grew out of a system of mutual promotion with the rebbes: the latter drew the cantors to their side in order to promote the "Sefardic" liturgy, which in turn raised the status of the prayer leaders and drew them to the movement. Under this system, cantors whose service was both pleasant and inspiring would often become rebbes themselves.[107]

The gradual amalgamation of rabbinic orthodoxy and the Hasidic movement could not have been imagined, however, had Hasidism not gradually lost its initial character of being opposed to the social order. This amalgamation, which began in the Ukraine at the end of the eighteenth century, first appeared in Galicia and Poland in the early nineteenth century and gained momentum over the years.

The same anti-Hasidic satires that depict the Hasidim as a mass of wretchedly poor people also tell of wealthy men who come to the rebbe for advice. In *Teyator fun Khsidim*, Leybele the Maskil mocks the Hasidic rebbes:

Both rich and poor flock to them
And they're taken for a ride.[108]

In *Emek Refa'im*, Levinsohn tells how the rebbe conducts his table. He personally serves the rich guests large portions, while the poor Hasidim bring their own repast from home.[109] In this satire, Levinsohn paints a portrait of such "wealthy men" as intimates of the rebbe. The rebbe advises his son, for example, not to retain the ways of the preachers of morals, not to admonish his people for their deviousness or "the rich and powerful" for robbing the poor.

To the contrary, always latch onto the strong. Honor the wealthy; show favor to the officials. Express concern for the welfare of officials like: *ratmanes* [city council members], *gemines* [town council members], communal heads, *otkuptshikes*,[110] *odavtshikes*,[111] *faktoyrim*,[112] *baley-takses*,[113] *tsekhmaysters* [guildmasters], *kvartirne komisarn*[114] and the like. Keep close to smugglers and advise them how to prosper. Do not forget the *faktoyrim* [115] either. From these you will strengthen your throne and grow rich.[116]

In short, the above are "rich men without money" who "live on businesses without substance," "on an appointment, illicit taxes, etc.," according to Levinsohn's succinct description in the well-known satire *Di Hefker-velt* (The chaotic world).[117]

The famous rebbes who restricted their attention to the poor were the exception. Uri of Strelisk—called the "Seraph" for his fervor in prayer—claimed the indigent style of life of his followers was in imitation of their rebbe. Nevertheless, this did not prevent the rebbe from accepting aid in time of need from a wealthy enthusiast. At the other extreme were the cohorts of Uri's contemporary, Rebbe Hersh of Żydaczów, the majority of whom were considered "well off."[118]

The first elements of the middle class that petty bourgeois Hasidism attracted were originally involved in insubstantial trades like those of the poor brokers and smugglers, only in a higher social stratum. Both strata gave Hasidism its popular, democratic flavor.

As the middle class prospered and its merchant-scholars drew closer to Hasidism, the power, respectability, and often also the wealth of the rebbe grew, as was the case for the Rebbe of Ruzhin and his dynasty in Galicia and Bukovina. Later in the nineteenth century the social ascent increased, precipitating a more opulent style of living for the rebbes. Perl admitted in the sermon he delivered in the Tarnopol synagogue in 1838 that the rebbes of the generation of Levi Isaac of Berdichev still "excelled in their prayer, charity and ransoming of prisoners—at that time they used to do this."[119] Dr. Nathan Horowitz, Nachman Krochmal's son-in-law, said of Perl that when he was a Hasid the rebbes were still honest, sincere people, free of sin and leading an ascetic life. He contrasted them to the rebbes of his generation (1846), who were swindlers, lacking conviction and intending to cheat "the rich and poor rabble" of its money. They undertook to heal barren women and sick people and to exorcise dybbuks, while living in palaces that glittered with gold and silver, their tables well laden.[120] This description of the rebbes' comfort and wealth, however, really reflects the conduct of the Ukrainian zaddikim and of the Sadagura dynasty that also settled in eastern Galicia. According to such witnesses as Joseph Ḥayyim Halberstam, Solomon Rubin, and other Hasidic sources, the generation of the rebbes Naphtali of Ropczyce, Meyer of Przemyślany, and Hersh of Żydaczów generally maintained a simple or even ascetic life, although rebbes who exploited their position in order to amass wealth and live in luxury had already begun to appear in Galicia, e.g., Hersh "the Attendant," Rebbe of Rymanów.

The struggle between the old and the new conception of the social role of the rebbes, which began in the early nineteenth century, is succinctly reflected in the following Hasidic tradition.

An old Hasid of Lublin mocked Rebbe Meyer of Przemyślany for living in hardship and want. He recited a teaching of his rebbe, Jacob Isaac of Lublin, based on the talmudic *aggadah (Ta'anit* 24b*)*: "Every day a Heavenly Voice is heard declaring, the whole world draws its sustenance *bishvil* (because of) Ḥanina my son, and Ḥanina my son satisfies himself with a *ḳab* of carobs from one Sabbath eve to another."[121] Jacob Isaac of Lublin interpreted this *aggadah* as a rhetorical question: How can the whole world draw its sustenance because of Ḥanina my son if he satisfies himself with a *ḳab* of carobs from one Sabbath eve to another? If the zaddik who draws abundance to the earth acts so frugally, he further explained, the whole world will obviously live in want. Meyer of Przemyślany, in an antielitist Hasidic spirit, argued that the meaning of this *aggadah* is to be understood as a conditional sentence. By dividing *bishvil* into "bi" and "shvil" ("in the path" in Hebrew), *bishvil* can be rendered "according to the conduct of." Thus, only when the zaddik is satisfied with little, like Ḥanina, can the world be worthy of drawing sustenance because of his merit.[122]

The Emergence of the Hasidic Reign

The struggle of the Rebbe of Tsandz (Nowy Sącz), Joseph Ḥayyim Halberstam, against the intemperance of the Sadagura dynasty that broke out in 1868 in connection with the "Reb Berenyu affair" was the last belated attempt to retain in zaddikism the remnants of its former folk character.

As a result of this social transformation the rebbes, as a matter of course, also lost their militancy in the clandestine struggle against Austrian government oppression. Characteristic is the fact elucidated both in the reports of the Austrian officials and in Perl's memoranda. Instead of imposing bans upon the kosher meat and candle tax lessees, the Hasidic leaders were now satisfied to obtain tax exemptions for themselves and their adherents and also the confirmation of their own appointees as *shoḥatim*. This is corroborated in Hasidic literature. In a pre-1815 letter to the tax lessees of Żurawno, Hersh of Żydaczów adjured them not to eat the meat of an opposing *shoḥet*.[123] As early as the beginning of the nineteenth century, a prominent Hasidic leader in Cracow, Berl Luxenburg, was a candle tax lessee.[124] Thus, the struggle between Hasidism and anti-Hasidic orthodoxy continually lost every vestige of ideological content, and in its last phase it was no more than a struggle for power in the Jewish community.

Along with the social transformation, Hasidic doctrine also underwent a substantial change. In many Hasidic works of the period there is not only the call to charity but also a reiterated emphasis upon peace and harmony which ought to unite both the learned and the masses (according to the author of *Toledot Ya'akov Yosef*), as well as the poor and rich.[125] There was also a change in the position on the study of the Talmud and Jewish religious scholarship. Whereas originally piety was given priority over the study of the Talmud in attaining a higher spiritual plane, now the intensive study of the Talmud and its commentaries was proclaimed as an indispensible religious duty, and those who were lax in this regard were admonished.[126]

Not only had the Rebbe of Żydaczów already established a good personal relationship with the leading rabbis of his time, such as Jacob Ornstein, rabbi of Lemberg, author of *Yeshu'ot Ya'akov*, but he also promoted mutual respect between Talmudists and Kabbalists in general.[127] His contemporary, Uri of Strelisk, advocated the approach of "the Jew" (*ha-Yehudi*) of Przysucha: "Study of Torah and prayer go hand in hand." He explained, "Study leads to depth of prayer which in turn brings to greater depth of Torah study."[128]

As early as the 1830s, this new movement in Hasidism,[129] the so-called *Ḥadushim* (the new), was widespread in the land and in the course of a short time became the officially accepted tendency (as indicated by the Rebbe of Tsandz, Ḥayyim Halberstam, author of *Divrei Ḥayyim*). The process of amalgamation with rabbinism had progressed to such an extent that most Hasidic leaders also occupied the rabbinic posts in their *kehillot*. The titles "rabbi" (rav) and "rebbe" had not yet become identical only because there still were rabbis who were not Hasidic leaders.[130] Yet Hasidism in Galicia, as in Congress Poland and the Ukraine, was, by the beginning of the nineteenth century, transformed from a popular religious movement into the reigning faith of the majority of Polish Jewry.

2

The Sociopolitical Foundations of the Haskalah in Galicia

The Economic Base

The development of capitalism proceeded at a very slow pace in the first half of the ninteenth century in feudal-agrarian Galicia. The growth of industry was hampered there by the very low purchasing power of the peasants, who remained serfs until the Revolution of 1848 and were even poorer than their brethren in the rest of Poland because their landholdings were so fragmented. The Austrian government had already deliberately suppressed the development of industry in Galicia in order to retain that province as a market for the products of German-Austrian and Bohemian industry.

Trade, however, developed considerably, particularly in eastern Galicia, along the Russian border, and was concentrated in three cities: Lemberg, Tarnopol, and the free city of Brody.[1]

Brody, the largest city after Lemberg, because of its geographical location and mainly because of its privileges as a "free city," developed during the first half of the nineteenth century into one of the most important centers of both European and world trade. Raw materials were exported through Brody from Russia to Austria, Germany, Italy, and other European countries. And through this city Russia imported manufactures, fancy goods, and provisions from Austria, Prussia, Saxony, and southern Germany.[2] The Jews of Brody, who in 1820 composed approximately 88 percent of the population (16,292 out of a total of 18,471 persons) and represented the largest Jewish community in Galicia, dominated the world trade of the city and controlled all its local trade. Although the few gentile merchants in Brody were the richest in the city and operated with the largest capital,[3] the concentration of capital among Jewish merchants was also pronounced. In 1840 fifty-six Jewish merchants of the city together accounted for one-half million (521,000) florins, almost eight times as much as the more than five hundred registered Jewish merchants and traders who operated altogether with barely 69,000 florins.[4]

These three commercial cities were virtually the exclusive centers of the Haskalah movement in Galicia.[5] The newly risen class of wealthy merchants provided the spokesmen as well as the patrons of the Galician Haskalah. When the second part of Samson Bloch's Hebrew geography *Shevilei Olam* (Paths of the world) was published in 1828, of the 360 subscribers 86 percent lived in these three cities, and of these, 48 percent lived in Brody itself. Even for Isaac Ber Levinsohn's *Te'udah be-Yisrael* (Testimony in Israel), which was published the same year with the help of subscribers from Volhynia, Podolia, Lithuania, and Galicia, Brody accounted for more subscribers than any other city in all these provinces.

It is no wonder then that the Austrian administration identified Maskilim in general with the Jews of Brody. For example, with regard to the inquiry of the Supreme Imperial Police and Censorship Office in 1806, about the response of the Austrian Jews to the call of a Sanhedrin in Paris, the governor of Galicia replied that in Galicia the Jews were divided into Orthodox, Hasidim, and Karaites; "one finds enlightened Jews only in Brody."[6]

The Maskilim themselves were well aware of the close relationship between the rise of wholesale trade in these Galician border cities and the Haskalah. Samson Bloch wrote in 1828 in the dedication of his book to Solomon Judah Rapoport:

> Since God has taken pity on us and brought us under the rule of our lord, the Emperor, may his majesty be exalted . . . trade with foreign lands has begun to flourish in our parts and instead of a life of poverty, a life of enjoyment has arrived . . . and since then the few brave ones have attempted to cast off the disgrace of ignorance and the shame of idleness and of poverty and they teach their children the vernacular and other languages and disciplines that men live by.[7]

Nachman Krochmal, in a letter to Isaac Erter, described Brody as a city "where wisdom and wealth, Torah and understanding, commerce and faith are united."[8] In his *Moreh Nevukhei ha-Zeman* (Guide to the perplexed of the time), Krochmal enumerated among those who scoffed at the *aggadot* of the Talmud, and even at the Talmud itself, the Jews who were versed in the sciences and who did not have sufficient religious education, "and with them a great multitude of scoffers who travel about around the world on account of commerce."[9]

Abraham Ber Gottlober tells in his memoirs of the immense importance that the merchants of Brody and other Galician cities had in the dissemination of the Haskalah in Russia:

> The Jews who lived in the large Galician cities were the first to be enlightened by the light of the wisdom of the RaMbeMaN[10] and his students. On account of their commercial affairs they would travel to various Russian cities and bring with them at the same time the spices of their enlightenment and knowledge. . . . In this regard Brody especially excelled, being a city of scholars and Maskilim who used to do business mostly with Russia. Everywhere that a merchant of Brody would come, he would excite the youth with his fine speaking—their eyes opened . . . and they would take up education. . . .[11]

The Haskalah literature itself acknowledged the support extended to Maskilic writers by wealthy patrons. Meyer Letteris noted the patrons who supported Isaac Erter while he was in Brody:

> And at the head of his reverers and admirers who used to support him when it was necessary were the dear Kallir sons and especially the wealthy Maskilim, our teacher and master Meyer and his brother, our teacher and master, Moses Kallir; the beloved Herzenstein brothers and the Nathansohn family; the wealthy man, our teacher and master R. M. Nirenstein and his sons with their precious spirit and the manager of his commercial firm, the enlightened and understanding R. Mordecai Auspitz, of blessed memory; and the wealthy Trachtenberg brothers who now reside in Odessa; and the sage, the magnificent, our teacher and master Leybush Landau . . . and our teacher, master I. A. Finkelstein and Jacob Samuel Byk (Bick), the beloved sage and deft writer, and his son-in-law . . . the august rich man, our teacher and master Isaac Oser Rothenberg and many more honorable people. . . .[12]

These same Nathansohns and Kallirs, and also the Bernstein family, were mentioned by Joseph Perl in his memorandum to the government in 1838 as the most prominent families of Brody which assisted the district rabbi, Michael Kristianpoller, in his struggle against the "fanatic rabbi," Solomon Kluger.[13]

Not only Krochmal and Erter but also all the other distinguished Maskilim had friendly relations with the wealthy families in Brody, Lemberg, and Tarnopol. Solomon Judah Rapoport, writing to Bloch in 1822, asked that he send regards in his name to their mutual friends and "in particular to Jacob Landau and his sagacious, wise, and wealthy son, and to the wealthy and distinguished honorable prince

Joshua Nathansohn, his son and grandchildren, and to our friend, the wise, sagacious, august, wealthy man Alexander Ziskind Kallir."[14] Bloch noted that he settled in Brody on the advice of Krochmal because of its "*kohanim,* wise and wealthy men . . . admirers of sages, who rejoice in their honor, support their right hand. . . ."[15]

The same patronal families in Brody appear in the city's commercial history. Among the six largest Jewish commercial firms in Brody in 1840 are M. Nathansohn with 40,000 florins in capital, and Yidl Nathansohn and Nirenstein with 30,000 florins each.[16]

Tarnopol played a lesser role in Galician commerce than Brody, but the nature of its trade was the same. Perl used to travel to Hungary for his father to buy wine and to Vienna to sell wax, honey, tallow, and other agricultural products.[17] Like Jacob Samuel Byk of Brody and Judah Leyb Mieses of Lemberg, Joseph Perl and Samuel Leyb Goldenberg of Tarnopol belonged to that social category of Maskilim who combined in their person the roles of both patron and artist.

The wealthy merchant, the social foundation of the Haskalah movement, was held up in the Haskalah literature as a model for Jews. The only positive figure in Perl's anti-Hasidic satire *Megalleh Temirin* was that of the wealthy enlightened merchant and supplier Mordecai Gold.[18] The hero and social ideal of the anonymous comedy *Di Genarte Velt* is "a prominent merchant in Russia." Similarly, in the comedy *Teyator fun Khsidim*, written by Ephraim Fischelson, a Russian-Polish Jew brought up in Lemberg, the hero is Leybele the philosopher, an exporter in Cracow. In his anti-Hasidic satire *Emek Refa'im*, Levinsohn contrasted the obscurant Hasidim with "the merchant Maskilim from the big city who travel about the world and are worldly wise."[19]

The bookkeepers and clerks of these wealthy merchants also came to be associated with the Haskalah. Among patrons of Isaac Erter in Brody, Mordecai Auspitz, the manager of Nirenstein's commercial house, also figured prominently. Before he became an independent merchant,[20] Nachman Krochmal's father was employed by the commercial house of Fayvl Tsipris, one of the largest firms in Brody. The spokesman of the Maskilim in *Di Genarte Velt* was "an Austrian bookkeeper" employed by a wealthy merchant.

Lessees of the special Jewish taxes were also found among the Maskilim. The father of Solomon Judah Rapoport was employed as an assessor in the revenue office in Lemberg. Rapoport himself was employed for many years as a secretary of the association of the lessees of the taxes on kosher meat and Sabbath candles in Lemberg and was also a partner in the business.[21] Later he held this post in Brody, before he became the Rabbi of Tarnopol. Perl's father and brother-in-law were lessees of the tax on kosher meat in Tarnopol,[22] and the well-known Maskil and teacher of Isaac Erter, Joseph Tarler, who later converted and became the Hebrew censor in Lemberg, made a fortune in this profession. There were also lessees for the monopolies of the landowners among the Maskilim. In addition to leasing the kosher meat tax, Perl's father also held the lease to the mills in Tarnopol,[23] and Krochmal held the only liquor sale franchise in the district of Żółkiew.[24]

In the Austrian monarchy, which was based on class privileges, clerical intolerance, and national suppression, Jews were, as a rule, not permitted in government positions. Some exceptions, however, were made, particularly in those positions and honorary offices that were connected with business, banking, and the free professions. In Lemberg and in Brody, Jews were assessors in the local "mercantile and exchange courts." Jews were also appointed to posts in revenue offices and as licensed brokers, managers of state banks, interpreters, censors, and teachers in conservatories. In Brody, Brzożów, and Nowy Sącz, Jews held the position of city physician ("Physicus").[25] Among these real and titular officials, there were a number of patrons and followers of the Haskalah movement. Disregarding his own declaration to list all subscribers "without any title at all" with the exception of rabbis, Bloch mentions, among the subscribers to the second volume of his *Shevilei Olam*, the following officials with their full titles: R. Mordecai Berish Margolis, "Royal and Imperial Mining Agent, Exchange Court Assessor and Branch Manager of the Austrian Savings Bank" (eight copies!) and R. Note Sokal, "Royal and Imperial Assessor of the Galician Mercantile and Exchange Court," both of Lemberg.

In the ranks of the Maskilim must also be included the Jewish professional intelligentsia, consisting largely of teachers, employed in the almost one hundred German-Jewish schools and, upon their closing in 1806, in the Tarnopol and Brody schools,[26] and in private homes.[27] Jewish physicians composed a fairly prominent group in Galicia, as can be seen from the number of doctors in the list of subscribers to Bloch's geography (1828): from Brody, Moses Mahl, Leyb Neustein (surgeon), and Heller (oculist);[28] from Tarnopol, Frankenfeld and Nathan Horowitz; from Lemberg, Aaron Gussman, Jacob Rapoport, and his son-in-law Kossowitz. A number of physicians of this sort felt called upon to spread science among their people by giving lectures to Maskilim.[29] Some of them, like Isaac Erter and Moritz Rappaport of Lemberg, became well known in the field of letters. Court versifiers and other writers who were maintained or aided by wealthy Jewish patrons were included among the professional intelligentsia. Their number must have been considerable, for Joseph Perl in his *Boḥen Ẓaddik* satirized the Maskilic poets "that raise to the skies the wealthy merchants of Brody."[30] Aryeh Leyb Kinderfreund, the author of *Shirim Shonim* (Various poems), was typical of such court poets. Meyer Letteris wrote a great number of panegyrics in honor of wealthy philanthropists. The well-known Maskil of Brody, Dov Ber Ginzburg, Perl's teacher, lived on an allowance given by the benefactor Alexander Kallir before he became secretary of the Jewish community of that city. Samson Bloch, who published his works with the aid of "noble-minded" and "wealthy men," justified himself to Perl in a letter from 1832 as a poor man to a rich one, saying, "There still are sages and wise men prominent among us, of whom the nobles of other nations boast, and they do favors for their people in the courts of kings."[31]

On the whole, the number of the poor among the Maskilic intelligentsia in Galicia, as in Poland and Russia,[32] was quite large; Maskilic writers particularly, with the exception of a handful such as Perl, Byk, and Mieses, had to struggle to earn a living.[33] But just as the humanist scholars and poets had represented the interests and strivings of their protectors, the princes and patricians, so the Maskilim in their writings expressed the interests and the outlook of the rising class of the wealthy Jewish merchants, who were their material protectors and their social ideal. The extent to which the Maskilim had identified with their wealthy benefactors can be seen from an analysis of the program of the Haskalah in economics, politics, and culture.

The Program of the Haskalah: Pride and Practicality

"Education for Jews," the main watchword of the Galician Haskalah, as it was of the earlier German and the later Russian Haskalah, was by no means an abstract postulate but a result of the circumstances and the demands of life of the main standard bearers of the concept—the wealthy merchant class. Whereas the small tradesman could get along in his commercial activities on a smattering of Polish and Ukrainian, the merchant with business in Leipzig, Berlin, and Vienna or with the local authorities had to resort to the German language. The practical necessity of studying languages, geography, and other fields in connection with the demands of business was explicitly stressed by the spokesmen of the Haskalah themselves. Erter, in his *Ha-Ẓofeh le-Bet Yisrael* (The watchman of the house of Israel), asked the ghost,

> And why did your parents fail to teach you about the nature of the earth and its various lands, so that you might know the merits and the needs of each

land? Why did they not teach you the languages of the nations with whom the merchant corresponds?[34]

Berish Goldenberg praised the achievements of Perl's German school in his monograph *Ohel Yosef*: "His students are the ornament of the merchants of the land, they have a fine quality of composition in modern languages and show their forte in a nice style."[35] Letteris told that his father Gershon was popular among the highest Austrian officials because of his intellect and character as well as the correctness of his German when speaking "with princes and lords of the land."[36] The good relations of the Maskilim with the administrative authorities were also noted by Krochmal. He consoled Bloch, who lamented his having returned from Germany, "the paradise," to Poland, "the hell of ignorance," with the observation that "there still sparkle among us men of wisdom and understanding of whom even the noble-minded of the nations boast and they obtain favors for their people in the courts of kings."[37]

Education played another and no less important role in the Haskalah, namely, as a factor in the Jewish plutocracy's gaining social equality with their gentile counterparts. Among practically all Galician Maskilim, education was regarded as a means of proving to the nations that the Jews were also a people of learning and culture and that not all Jews were to be identified with the fanatical, ignorant, and superstitious Hasidim. In Erter's satire, this "sin" of the Maskilim is classified with the "sin of donning the garb of the people in whose midst the Jews live."[38] In the dialogue between wisdom and Hasidism in the same satire, wisdom (education) boasts that "she rolls away the shame of the people of Israel before the Gentiles."[39] Perl formulated the aim of the Haskalah almost in the same words in his description of the groupings of Jews in the city of Tarnopol: "The second class consists of people whose great aspiration is that Israel shall not be a disgrace and a mockery in the eyes of the nations, that, therefore, various languages and sciences should be studied. . . ."[40] In his popular Hebrew almanac *Ẓir Ne'eman* (Faithful messenger), for the year 5576 (1816), Perl concluded a description of the distinctive branches of science with the following invocation:

> God who bestows wisdom to the wise, open our hearts and enlighten our eyes so that we may become intelligent and understanding and cast off from ourselves the disgrace before the nations and not be ashamed when they have the occasion to speak to us in public.

In a letter to a friend concerning the study of languages and sciences, Solomon Judah Rapoport also cited the argument that "every Jew who cannot speak their language or read their books is an object of disgrace among nations and of disapproval among peoples."[41] In the anonymous *Di Genarte Velt*, the merchant states: "Throughout the world the greatest people edify the public and encourage them to study languages, sciences, and handicrafts, [and] to support themselves honestly, so that they will not have to be humiliated before all the nations."[42]

The goals for studying the modern languages German and Russian were specifically set forth by the father of the Russian Haskalah, Isaac Ber Levinsohn: (1) conducting business; (2) dealing with government officials; and (3) enhancing the dignity of the Jewish people. And Dr. Max Lilienthal asked rhetorically, "Will they [the Gentiles] still do us ill when the farmer can speak Russian, the craftsman studies writing and arithmetic, the merchant knows [modern] languages and even rabbis will be able to stand before kings and speak a correct language to their community?"[43] In the *Hefker-Velt*, Levinsohn portrayed the messenger of the *kehillah* who speaks to a lord in such a "mutilated language" that it is "a shame and a disgrace." Abraham Ber Gottlober, who typified the Maskil in Russia, was angry with the Jews who wore long caftans "that trail behind like a woman's gown" and who, when they had occasion to speak to a "prince and judge," did so in a "stammering tongue." He appealed to the Jews to dress like their gentile neighbors and to send their children to the modern schools "so that your disgrace will be cast off."[44]

Given this aim of the Maskilim, namely, education as a means of "becoming like all the nations," it is not surprising that a knowledge of western European languages, primarily German, was considered essential. This attitude toward languages is clear from the works of Erter, Perl, and from *Di Genarte Velt* (which advocated the study of languages and then sciences), and it found expression in all the works of the Galician Maskilim. In David Caro's *Tekhunat ha-Rabbanim* (The qualities of the rabbis), published by Mieses, one of the first duties demanded of a modern rabbi was that "he should be proficient in modern scholarship and sciences and especially in the language of the people of the land."[45] In this regard, the wording of the lifting of the ban against the Maskilim by the Rabbi of Lemberg, Jacob Ornstein, in 1816 is significant: "The conclusion is that a Jew may and should study the languages of the peoples under whose rule, and in the shade of whose grace, he finds shelter."[46] In his introduction to a new edition of Menasseh ben Israel's *Teshu'at Yisrael* (Israel's salvation),[47] Bloch stated that "deliverance came to Israel only at the hands of rabbis and scholars conversant with the languages of the nations." As one of the main signs of the modern age that followed the dark Middle Ages, he cited the fact that the wise men of the gentile nations had shown the Jews the path to the sciences and modern languages.

The fact that the Maskilim were the spokesmen of the interests and the outlook of the business plutocracy among the Jews did not deter certain Maskilim from castigating those rich men who regarded wealth as the only possession and placed it above learning. Both Erter in his *Ha-Ẓofeh* and Perl in his *Boḥen Ẓaddik* ridiculed the wealthy illiterates who look upon learning as superfluous,[48] and "who cannot even speak the language of the country and think of themselves as highly accomplished because they have taken two or three trips to large cities in Germany. . . ."[49]

Language: The Question of Yiddish; the Dominance of German; the Emergence of Hebrew

The study of German meant much more to the Galician Maskilim than simply a means for achieving economic and social goals. German was also part of the Galician Haskalah's program for the daily life and the cultural and linguistic future of the entire Jewish population. No Maskil (with the exception of the interesting figure of Byk, who was therefore indeed sharply attacked by his fellow Maskilim) looked upon Yiddish as anything more than a mutilated jargon that must be swept away in favor of the "pure" German language. This is how the author of *Tekhunat ha-Rabbanim* wrote about Yiddish:

> Many of the rabbis in our time do not understand the language of the land at all. . . . Their language is no more than a bastard tongue that can point to neither a father nor a mother, but is an admixture of the languages of the peoples among which our ancestors were cast away, a torn, ragged, and corrupt language. . . .[50]

Bloch called Yiddish "the corrupt language that is spoken by our masses."[51] Elsewhere he cited with approval the teacher of the Mishnah, Rabbi Judah the Prince, for his objection to the use of the Syrian language in the land of Israel. "Either use the holy tongue or Greek!" For the Aramaic (Syrian) language was, Bloch wrote, "a stammering tongue without understanding and was mutilated like the German language that is spoken by the sons of our people in many lands."[52] Rapoport, in a letter written in 1822 to his friend M. O.,[53] drew the same parallel to Yiddish as did Bloch: "Why use the Judeo-German language in the land of Poland? Either use the holy tongue or Polish."[54]

Yiddish was used by Mendel Lefin, Joseph Perl, and later Isaac Ber Levinsohn as a necessary evil without which the broad masses could not be approached with the slogans of enlightenment. Even Mieses stated in his *Kinat ha-Emet* (The zeal for truth) that "popular works should be written in the vernacular in order to combat superstitions and fanaticism."[55] However, it was hoped that with the reopening of German schools for Jewish children (to which end requests were continually submitted to the government) and with the dissemination of the enlightenment literature, the Jewish population of Galicia would in time become sufficiently educated that it could speak German.

German was the language of instruction in the school that Perl founded and directed in Tarnopol, and Perl regularly preached sermons in German in the synagogue of the city. The only time he delivered a sermon in Yiddish was in 1838, in connection with the feud against the newly appointed rabbi, Solomon Judah Rapoport. In the introduction to this sermon, Perl justified his not speaking in a "refined language," that is, German, but in the "crude language," explaining that Yiddish was the language of the initiators of the feud and that the feud was a threat.[56] Apart from Hebrew, the Maskilim would often correspond with each other in German (for the most part written with Hebrew characters,[57] but not in Yiddish), and they would also write to their closest family members in German.[58]

Just as the spokesmen for the Haskalah unanimously advocated the widespread adoption of the language of the country by the Jews living in it, so, too, the Haskalah was united in its love and devotion to the Hebrew language. Indeed, the revival of Hebrew literature in modern times can be traced to the fact that the literary works of the Maskilim were all written in Hebrew. This position of the Hebrew language within the Haskalah movement and its program was determined by the Haskalah's stand on religion and tradition, as well as on the historical and cultural unity of the Jewish people.

The Vein of Rationalism in the Haskalah

The Haskalah, which to some extent is correctly designated as Jewish rationalism, was very far from western European rationalism in its attitude toward religion. Even Mieses, the most radical rationalist of all the Galician Maskilim of his time, published *Tekhunat ha-Rabbanim*, in which Caro railed against those who believed "that Voltaire and Mirabeau represent the last word in wisdom and progress and scoff at God and his Torah, without comprehending what is the truth."[59] But within the camp of the radical Maskilim there were those—and Mieses fell within this camp as well—who, though their attitude toward the Talmud was one of respect, obliquely but unmistakably rejected the absolute authority of the Talmud as the source of Jewish law. The majority of the Maskilim, however, not only did not tamper with the holiness of the Talmud but also sanctified the very essence of the rabbinic tradition. Most of them did not go beyond expressing opposition to Hasidism, to its faith in zaddikim and to the superstitions that were widespread among the people.

The Maskilim relied upon "the Grand Eagle" Maimonides as a facade for their program of rationalistically purifying the Jewish religion; they did not in fact go much beyond him on their road to deism. Their moderate rationalism fit well into the nineteenth-century cultural and political framework of reactionary absolutism in which remnants of enlightened absolutist ideology could still be discerned. It did not formally repudiate the principle of religious tolerance and "love of humanity," and it affirmed opposition to superstition, mysticism, and "fanaticism." In essence, however, it strengthened clericalism and attempted very energetically to suppress the intellectual currents of deism, materialism, and atheism. In connection with the rabbinical assembly in Frankfurt-am-Main in 1845, Rapoport wrote that he was convinced that were the Reform rabbis to insist upon imposing on the Orthodox their abbreviated form of prayer and their procedure in the matter of divorce, "a complaint with the authorities would bring desirable results, for we have nowadays gracious rulers who have eyes to see who is religious and follows the true path and who is an enemy of religion and corrupts the people."[60]

There is no doubt that among the Maskilim the authority of the biblical precepts was considerably weakened by a rationalistic explanation of their origin, as in the case of the rationalist followers of Maimonides in Spain. Nevertheless, the leading Galician Maskilim complied with the traditional observance in all its details, if only so as not to alienate the Orthodox masses.[61] Others, such as Krochmal, undoubtedly, adhered to Orthodox observance out of honest conviction. Krochmal, in a well-known letter of 1814 to Wolf Schiff defending his contacts with the Karaites, professed his piety:

> Thank God, it is well-known to all who come in the gates of my city that I have not cast off, God forbid, the yoke of the precepts and of the words of our sages of blessed memory and that I observe all the minutiae of the law and pursue regularly a course in the Scriptures, the Mishnah and the Gemara. . . .[62]

Later, in a letter of 1839 to Samuel Leyb Goldenberg, Krochmal claimed such religious observance to be critical to the Judaism of his day. "Faith and service of the heart are insufficient," he wrote, "till they are realized through action. That is fundamental to our Torah in every age and place."[63]

Concerning Krochmal's correspondent, in a letter to Isaac Samuel Reggio from 1831, S. J. Rapoport stressed that although Goldenberg was a wealthy merchant and it was difficult for him to observe all the commandments, he never violated any of the stricter ones such as those relating to the desecration of the Sabbath and forbidden foods, or even many of the less rigorous ones.[64]

Joseph Perl instituted the study of the Talmud in his school in Tarnopol and he saw to it that his students said the morning, afternoon, and evening prayers in the temple adjacent to the school. He dismissed a teacher because of a report that smoke had been seen coming out of the chimney of his house on the Sabbath, and also the sexton of the temple because he scoffed at the oid custom of spreading hay on the floor of the synagogue after *Kol Nidrei*.[65] In his Hebrew almanac he preached about fear of God at every opportunity, and in his sermons he would always contrast true piety with what he called the hypocrisy of the Hasidim.

Indeed, one of the highly characteristic features of the Haskalah's stance on the commandments was its polemic against Hasidism. Like the Mitnaggedim, the Maskilim castigated the Hasidim for their degradation of the talmudic scholar. Gottlober, for one, in "Masa Ẓafon," rebuked the Hasidim for this:

> Upon God's word their heels tread;
> The Torah's honor did they malign
> And shame the outspoken man of truth.[66]

The sins that the Maskilim reproached the Hasidim for were essentially the same "transgressions" that the first Mitnaggedim could not forgive during the controversies in their time. Thus, for example, Joseph Perl closed his denunciation to the government in 1838 concerning the *battei midrash* and *mikva'ot* (ritual baths) with the admonition that the Hasidim so lose themselves in conversation in the *mikveh* that they miss "the time for prayer that is fixed according to the law," that is, the time for the recitation of the *Shema*.[67] In *Teyator fun Khsidim*, the hero of the play, Leybele the philosopher, chides the Hasidim:

> You know! If the Hasidim would not show the way,
> Who would dare our Talmud to disobey?

And in the note, the author explained what the sin was against the Talmud and why the Hasidim were transgressors: Hamnuna said that

Jerusalem was destroyed only because the reading of the *Shema* morning and evening was neglected.[68] The *melamed* (a teacher in the *ḥeder*), the personification of the Hasid in *Di Genarte Velt*, was also ridiculed for being late to prayer because of his dawdling in the *mikveh*.[69] A great part of this comedy consists of debates between the Maskil clerk and the *melamed*, whom he shows that the Hasidim do not adhere to the law of the Talmud and the *Shulkḥan Arukh*, the code of Jewish Law. The author derides the rebbes for believing that it is permissible to read the Book of Esther without the proper musical accents used in the cantillation of the text and for permitting themselves similar "sins."[70]

Even if the Maskilim voiced these complaints for the sake of propaganda among the Mitnaggedim, the fact that they made use of such arguments demonstrates that in the domain of religious practice, they did not significantly depart from the anti-Hasidic Orthodox. They saw themselves essentially as heirs to the Mitnaggedic tradition by way of the Maimonidean method of inquiry. Even their work of spreading enlightenment among the masses was seen by Maskilim as restoration rather than innovation. In the introduction to his *Bet Yehudah*, Levinsohn bears witness to his own efforts: "You know, O God, my intent in this work is to uplift the lot of Israel in both Torah and wisdom and to enhance our holy Torah and the pure sayings of our talmudic sages, whose words stand forever and whose tradition stems truly from the living God."

The continuation of the Mitnaggedic tradition by the Maskilim was expressed most strongly in the war on Hasidism. After the Mitnaggedic Orthodox dropped the "struggle" with the "sect," the Maskilim took up the banner with enthusiasm. The Hasidim, who had been the rebels in the earlier fight, became the conservative opposition to the rising Maskilim in the first half of the nineteenth century. The latter viewed Hasidism as such a national disgrace that its various ideological factions united for the battle. There was hardly a Haskalah writer who did not see his duty to inveigh against the movement in satiric prose, poetry, and comedies.

Although the Maskilim were unanimous in their bitterness against their opponents, there were important gradations in attitude within their own camp. Whereas the moderate Maskilim limited their criticism of Hasidism, the radicals bore down against all religious fanaticism and agitated against the steadily increasing burden of precepts and prohibitions, against traditional religious education, and against all the obsolete religious customs that barred the way of progress. Thus, non-Hasidic rabbis fell under attack along with the rebbes.

Reforms of religious belief and practice were urged. Mieses and his followers, such as Abraham Goldberg, went so far as partially to reject talmudic authority and to rely more on a purely ethical or deistic interpretation of the Torah and the Prophets.

Anachronism and Paradox in Haskalah Internationalism

A characteristic aspect of eastern European Jewish culture was its backwardness regarding general European cultural developments. This lay at the root of the paradoxical attitude of the Maskilim toward nationalism in general and its Jewish application in particular. The Haskalah was spreading among eastern European Jewry in the early nineteenth century when the notion of nationalism prevailed in European literature, philosophy, and social sciences. The intelligentsia were captivated by it, especially in oppressed nations where it stirred hearts to struggle for national liberation. While this was happening, the Maskilim were still basking in the cosmopolitanism of the Age of Enlightenment, with its eighteenth-century notions of world citizenship and its dedication to rationalism. Cosmopolitanism also served the Maskilim as a theoretical basis for their cardinal watchword—cultural and social rapprochement with the dominant culture. Love of man without distinction of race, nation, or creed was a favorite motif and a popular literary theme with all the Maskilim. Yet along with their internationalism went the belief in the Jews as a religious and national unit.

The Maskilim followed ancient tradition in maintaining the indivisibility of Jewish religion and nationhood. Although they focused upon the religious aspect of that unity, they never forgot its national aspect. In Levinsohn's *Bet Yehudah*, the terms "religion of Yeshurun," "Israelite nation," and "our holy nation" are used interchangeably. Perl referred to the Jews as a nation not only in his correspondence but also in his memoranda to the government. Even Mieses, the most extreme Galician Maskil in his rationalist leaning toward linguistic assimilation, spoke of "our people" and "God's people."[71]

The attitude of the majority of the leading Galician Maskilim toward the concept of the Jews as a nation was closest to the attitude later assumed by Graetz, who, incidentally, was strongly under the influence of the works of Krochmal and Rapoport. According to that view, the Jews are indeed a race (*Volksstam*), forming part of the surrounding nations linguistically and culturally, but at the same time they represent an international entity, united by religion, history, and cultural heritage.[72] The principal difference between this attitude of the Maskilim and the later attitude of Graetz is one of emphasis. The Maskilim primarily struggled against the cultural isolation of the Jews; therefore, in their propaganda they underscored the task of Jewish adaptability to the surrounding languages and cultures. Graetz's attitude, by contrast, was the result of a reaction against the extreme assimilation of the German Reform rabbis, and, therefore, his historical work could provide inspiration for the later, consciously nationalistic movement among the Jews. The Maskilim, despite their stress on adapting to surrounding cultures, did not look upon Hebrew as mere heritage, but as a language of a living culture. When they modernized Hebrew literature, it was with absolute faith in its future.

In the Haskalah scheme, Hebrew also fulfilled a practical role: that of a propaganda medium for reaching the wider circles that had received their training at the yeshivah and in the *bet midrash* and for whom Hebrew was the language of learning. Thus, even the most extreme assimilationists of *Wissenschaft des Judentums* like Jost and Geiger hailed the growth of Hebrew literature. Paradoxically—and perhaps unknowingly—Hebrew was also used to reinforce the sense of elitism among Maskilim, in much the same way wealthy humanist patricians and their court of intellectuals used Latin. The Maskilim in effect raised themselves above the masses by reading and composing poems and articles in the biblical idiom.[73]

Nevertheless, neither of these uses of Hebrew overshadowed its main importance for the Maskilim, as a language of the Jewish people and its religion which united their generation with all past generations. Letteris, in his introduction to *Ha-Ẓefirah*, a literary magazine published in 1824, stated that the purpose of the publication was to "awaken in the young a love for the old tongue, more precious than pearls." He gave two reasons: "in it was written the Law and the Prophets, which bind us unto our God with bonds of love and faith"; and in it were also included "the precious thoughts that elicited admiration from the wise men of the nations." Nachman Krochmal advised his son Abraham to master Hebrew and German no less than Talmud and mathematics.[74] In the introduction to *She'erit Yehudah*, the Hebrew adaptation of Racine's *Esther*, Solomon Judah Rapoport exalted the value of the Hebrew language, "through which one is reminded of the origins and becomes acquainted with the ancient times and all of the precious things that once were and the soul yearns for God and for the people that he created for himself."

Along with the historical bond, the Maskilim also stressed the geographical bond of Hebrew as a means of communication among the Jews of all countries. In the article "Toledot he-Ḥaluẓ" in *Ha-Ẓofeh le-Bet Yisrael*, Erter asserted that "for my people the holy tongue is their pasigraphy. All Children of Israel, wherever they be scattered on the face of the earth, understand it. They need no other pasigraphy, for this one has been passed on to them by their forefathers. How could they then abandon it?"

Levinsohn viewed the knowledge of Hebrew "in the Diaspora as a great imperative," in that "it forms a bond of religion and national survival, and provides the global axis along which all Jews dispersed among peoples and tongues are linked. Only this binds their hearts to serve God; without it where else would the people of Yeshurun and Torah find a haven today?"[75] The virtue of Hebrew as unifier of world Jewry was noted even in the Hebrew periodical *Ẓiyyon,* edited by Jost, in an article by the well-known Rumanian Maskil, J. M. Barasch, entitled "*Kol Medabber Meyekar Leshon Ever.*"[76]

Yet for all Levinsohn's identification of religion with nationhood, he made quite clear in *Te'udah be-Yisrael* that nationhood is a function of language:

> Just as one would not call a person wise without the trappings of wisdom nor a hero one who had not the trappings of strength so is one unworthy of the title Jew if he has not the proper qualifications. How does one define a person or a people if not by language. . . ? Ought not one be ashamed to call himself Jew while ignorant of the Hebrew tongue?[77]

If in a general sense Hebrew had to share equal status with the vernacular of the country, this was not so within Jewish culture itself, where it was given great prominence. Rapoport reiterated on several occasions that the best in foreign literature ought to be included within Jewish culture through Hebrew translation:

> . . . From the treasures of the nations
> I'll choose to offer at her feet. . . .
> If there be wisdom in their tongues,
> I shall pour it into a vessel
> to give my people fresh fruits
> for its ancient tongue. . . .[78]

Similarly, in "Toledot he-Ḥaluẓ" Erter urged the establishment of Hebrew schools to supplement vocational and secondary schools. According to his program, Hebrew would be used not only for Torah and other religious study but also for the study of ethics (as Naphtali Herz Wessely advocated), Jewish history, and ancient writings. Conversely, the more radical rationalist, Mieses, was extreme in his tendencies toward linguistic assimilation, and he reduced the role of Hebrew in his curriculum to a minimum. In an article in the anthology *Ha-Ẓefirah* of 1824, he drafted a program for Jewish schools in which the only Jewish subjects mentioned were a German translation of the Bible "and a little history of the children of Israel." Mieses believed that every Jew should be introduced to the Torah in a vernacular translation.[79] In regard to the language of prayer, he contended that not only ought women to pray in German but also all Jews should pray "in the language of the land" because the majority do not understand the meaning of the Hebrew prayers at all. He even offered a prayer to God that the rabbis will decide to follow the example of the German Reform rabbis in this respect:

> The Jews there did very well in the German lands by altering the prayers to their own language, so they would be understood. If only the rest of the Jews would be so wise as to realize the great advantage to this from the standpoint of ethics. May God inspire the rabbis, whose responsibility is our well-being, to follow the enlightened of those places.[80]

Messianic Redemption and Return to Zion in Haskalah Thought

On the matter of belief in messianic Redemption and the Return to Zion, absolute political loyalty to the regime did not mend the rift between the conservative and extreme rationalist wings of the Haskalah. The moderates, whether openly or more subtly, tended to take a negative view toward belief in messianic Redemption as a religious absolute. Perl, in an 1837 statement to the Austrian government on the attitude of the Galician Jews toward Siegfried Justus's (Karl Gustav Seyfart's) plan to establish a Jewish state in Palestine, explained at length why the "few enlightened," the fourth class of Galician Jewry after the ignorant, the Orthodox, and the Hasidim, were against it:

> . . . the truly educated Jews who represent the fourth class by no means picture the Messiah as a real individual personality but see in him only a symbol of the idea of redemption and universal peace which awaits its realization; when Israel, free of all oppression, will be accepted into the family of nations and will enjoy equal rights with all the other free nations. This opinion, as paradoxical as it may seem to the strictly rabbinite Jew, is, however, substantiated in the Talmud (Sanhedrin 97), where it is written: the present time differs from the days of the Messiah only in that then the subjugation of the Jews by the kingdoms will cease. The Messianic era is, therefore, to the clearly thinking Israelite, nothing else than a time of love, respite, peace and joy as the prophet Isaiah (11:6; 65:25) so aptly describes it. . . .[81]

It is superfluous to dwell upon the fact that Perl gave the cited opinion of the Talmud a false interpretation. The passage speaks of servitude to foreign powers in the sense of the political domination of the Jews by foreign nations, and Maimonides even rendered a legal decision according to it.[82] Perl interpreted it in the spirit of the age of emancipation as a condition in which the Jews do not yet have full equality of civil rights. Nor did Perl hesitate, like the Reform assimilationists, to interpret prophetic statements on restoration of the Kingdom of Israel other than figuratively.

Just as Perl chose from the entire discussion of the millennium in the Talmud the opinion of Samuel, which he interpreted as it suited him, so in *Teyator fun Khsidim* Fischelsohn, who was raised in Galicia, cited a talmudic passage according to which it appears that the Messiah will never come. Leybele the philosopher presents this argument to Reb Shmuel Yerukhem, the Hasid from Bełz:

> How dare that nobody brand everyone as an apostate and sinner;
> The Talmud tells us that one of the sages
> Launched into a thorough exposition.
> Rabbi Hillel, one of the Tannaim, believed
> That the Messiah had come to the Jews
> In the days of Hezekaiah[83]
> The other sages heard this and let it pass.
> What does that indicate?
> . . . The Tannaim said: "May God forgive him" [for saying so].
> But it seems that Rabbi Hillel could not accept the thought
> That the advent of the Messiah is an essential article of faith. . . .[84]

Ephraim Fischelsohn's complete argumentation was taken from *Sefer ha-Ikkarim* (Book of principles) by Joseph Albo.[85] It is clear that the author identified himself with R. Hillel's standpoint, as can be seen later in his play where he mocked the great faith of the Hasidim that personal conquest of the evil inclination and protracted mourning over Jerusalem would bring the Messiah.[86]

Just as Fischelsohn quoted Joseph Albo—albeit in order to deny the faith in the Messiah—so the author of *Tekhunat ha-Rabbanim* relied upon a quotation from Maimonides' commentary on the Mishnah to persuade the Jews to break with the religious traditions that link the Jewish people with Ereẓ Yisrael. He opposed the recitation of the special prayer for rain (*Tefillat Geshem*) on the festival of Shemini Aẓeret with the following argument: "Due to the fact that of old we were in a land of the East, where we were forced to pray for rain in the winter because it does not rain there during that season, must we, too, the inhabitants of Europe, pray [for rain] during the time of our winter, when it is, in any case, the rainy season?"[87]

The same tendency to disparage the traditions of Ereẓ Yisrael in Jewish life is found in the works of Gottlober, a typical representative of the Haskalah in Russia. In his memoirs, he ridiculed the *ḥeder*, both because the pupils were taught all the tractates of the Talmud with commentaries that were incomprehensible to them and because "the laws of the Temple and its sacred objects are taught as if the Temple existed now and the priests have to perform the divine service and the Jews have returned to their land and every difficult question has to be decided by a Jewish judge."[88]

Gottlober went even further than his teacher Joseph Perl with respect to interpreting the prophecies concerning the Redemption as referring to the process of emancipation. While both saw their time as a golden age in contrast to the dark times of the Middle Ages, Perl emphasized that the emancipation of the Jews had yet "to be brought to blessed perfection."[89] Gottlober, however, sang a hymn to the redemption that was announced by the prophets and that had already arrived. In his poem "Shir Higgayon" he used as a motto the verse from Isaiah, "To appoint unto them that mourn in Zion, to give unto them beauty for ashes" (Isa. 61:3). In the first part of the poem, entitled "The Pained Voice of My People Weeps," the Jewish people bemoans the sufferings that were inflicted upon it during the Middle Ages. In the second part, "A Voice from On High Announces Consolation," he calls upon the people to end its mourning because the Jews are "saved in the shadow of kings and princes" and religion has united with wisdom:

> But now
> Behold, you have taken refuge
> From traps and ensnarements
> In the shadow of kings and princes. . . .
> For religion and faith
> Have forged a bond
> With wisdom and understanding. . . .
> If you shall seek wisdom,
> Then you shall secure your crown.
> Forget your mourning,
> Blossom forth like a lily,
> And I shall call you Ruḥamah. . . .[90]

It is no wonder that such opinions were expressed by only a few Maskilim. Even the extreme rationalists in the movement tended for political reasons to exercise constraint in treating fundamental articles of faith.

Unlike the rationalists, including some of the more moderate, the outspoken conservatives were unanimous in upholding traditional beliefs concerning the national future. Samson Bloch polemicized in a letter to his friend Isaac Blumenthal that Maimonides "emphasized three times in chapter 3 of his *Guide for the Perplexed* that belief in the Messiah's coming is one of the cardinal articles of faith."[91]

Nevertheless, even Krochmal's conservatism did not prevent him from expressing an opinion—however tactfully it was couched—about the Messiah's coming. In a letter to Samuel Goldenberg he wrote:

> There is yet another important matter that requires consideration . . . , namely, that which is considered in one or in several generations as a fundamental principle may revert in other generations to the stage of a proper faith, which is subject to the degree of knowledge of the believers and to their interpretation. And everyone will agree that when Israel is finally redeemed as expected, we shall no longer have to consider the advent of the Messiah as a fundamental principle, just as even today the attributes and the characteristics of the Messiah are not a matter of principle and on this point every believer has his own opinion and conception. . . .[92]

Thus even though Krochmal allows for various conceptions of the person of the Messiah, the notion itself of "eternal redemption of the Jews by the redeemer" is not in doubt. The steadfastness of conservative Maskilim concerning messianic deliverance is further evidenced by the fact that a group of Haskalah writers in Congress Poland expressed its anticipation of the Return to Zion and rebuilding of Jerusalem.[93]

Conservative Haskalah leaders in Galicia and the Pale of Settlement felt compelled to challenge the argument that the belief in the Return to Zion is irreconcilable with loyalty to the ruling regime. In Rapoport's *She'erit Yehudah*, Queen Esther defends the Jews against the contention that because of hopes of Zion they are not attached to their new homeland:

> It seems to you that because we yearn for another land,
> We do not cherish loyalty to the peoples of your land,
> Indeed, it is true, [Jews] hope for and eagerly await the return to Zion
> But they also seek and desire the welfare of your kingdom. . . .[94]

Twenty years later, in 1845, Rapoport attacked the German Reform rabbis who would rid the Jewish religion of those national elements. He argued that "the Jews are considered by the nations to be loyal subjects who love their present homeland, though they cherish the hope of [return to] the Holy Land, the land of their ancestors."[95]

Levinsohn found it necessary to reiterate the well-known talmudic prohibition against war or revolution in the name of the Return to Zion.[96] "The Jewish people," he wrote, "rejects any natural means (in order not to violate its oath) to return to its ancient status. Deliverance is to come neither by sword nor by crime and rebellion, but by quietly waiting for restoration from God on High."

Levinsohn strongly cleaved to tradition, asserting, contrary to the naturalist-realist outlook of Maimonides, that through the Messiah, God will perform "wonders and miracles as in the exodus from Egypt." He also viewed the advent of the Messiah as a cardinal article of faith. He explained Joseph Albo's omitting it from his list of "principles" as necessary "because his debating opponents built the foundations of their argument on the issue of the Messiah."[97]

The fact that certain Haskalah writers did not mention Zion and Redemption does not mean they despaired of the goal or were apathetic toward it. For example, the Lithuanian Maskil I. M. Dick never said a word about Zion and Jerusalem in his moralistic folktales, but in his pamphlet *Ha-Oreiaḥ*, in which he described Moses Montefiore's visit to Lithuania in 1846, he noted that "many Jews whose hearts were touched by the love of the people for their land, shed tears of sorrow and joy over 'Jerusalem' engraved on his coach."[98]

By its very program, Ereẓ Yisrael and Return to Zion could not occupy a prominent place within the Haskalah movement or its literature. As opposed to the religious movements, especially the mystical ones, the Haskalah was seen as realistic, intent on improving the national condition in many areas—political, economic, social, and cultural. To most Maskilim who held to their people's ideals, Ereẓ Yisrael expressed a longing for the past and hope for the future, but it was not relevant to the present. On the contrary, as though foreseeing the sequence of modern Jewish social currents, some of the Maskilim had a clear notion about the fulfillment of the Haskalah program as a historic precondition to a Return to Zion and redemption of the Land. A clear expression of this concept is found in "Masa Ẓafon" by Abraham Goldberg of Rawa, one of the Haskalah pioneers in Galicia. This work, which was written in 1846, appeared in a special edition together with the author's *Ma'aseh Rokeaḥ*, in 1848, the year of the revolution. The occasion that prompted Goldberg to write the propagandistic poem was the founding of governmental schools for Jews in Russia. It is precisely in this paean both to "the benevolence" of Czar Nicholas the "king of mercy" and to the Haskalah program itself that Goldberg chose to declare fulfillment of that program as a precondition of the Return to Zion. The Jews must prepare themselves in the Diaspora, he wrote, in the following ways: reject Ḥasidism; discard superstition, especially belief in zaddikism, as that is nothing less than idol worship; increase enlightenment and scientific knowledge; learn to speak "a correct language" of the land fluently; recognize all mankind as brothers; engage in more productive trades and professions; conduct business honestly and without usury; and take up farming like the majority of the population. Also needed, for the program to be fully implemented, were simplicity of dress and abstinence from luxury. Only when the nation was completely reformed would it be delivered to its land:

> Then shall the Daughter of my People take pleasure in the land
> of her birthright
> And tend its soil, its nectars to suck.
> In regal splendor shall she appear
> And she will rejoice in God's anointed. . . .
> Lo, then shall Zion be made steadfast, Jerusalem firm;
> And her mourners shall delight sevenfold. . . .

Thus, the transformation of Haskalah into the Lovers of Zion movement in the following generation was not so radical as it might seem. For the opinions of people like the author of "Masa Ẓafon" had a decisive influence in shaping the Haskalah's attitude toward the idea of the return.

Concern for both religion and the Hebrew language compelled the Maskilim to wage a two-front war. The brunt of the struggle was directed primarily against the fanaticism and ignorance of the "super-righteous" Hasidim. But the moderate Maskilim also reproached, albeit with less intensity, the "pseudowise," who in their enlightenment went so far as to reject religion. In "Sha'ar ha-Aggadah," Nachman Krochmal differed from those extreme Maskilim—professional intellectuals, readers of European literature and the "merchant-chiefs"—who scoffed at the *aggadot,* then at the Talmud and finally at the authors of the Talmud. At the same time, he attacked "all obscurantist experts" who "confuse homiletic explication with the simple meaning of a text and even interpret obscure legends . . . as God's sharing his secrets with the reverent."[99]

In *Boḥen Ẓaddik*, Perl depicted Tarnopol Maskilim as persons who strive to "learn languages and disciplines, in a faithful and God-fearing manner without discarding our ancient traditions."[100] The position of conservative Galician Maskilim was shared by the Russian Isaac Ber Levinsohn, who denounced "enlightened" possessors of scant, superficial knowledge who profaned the Torah's commandment and became apostates.[101]

Even more than religious zeal, Haskalah writings defended the importance of Hebrew against those "cognoscenti" who scoffed at it.

In the introduction to *She'erit Yehudah* and in his letter to his friend M. O.,[102] Rapoport opposed those who proclaimed Hebrew an outmoded tool because it had been "rooted out of every tongue," or had "lost all meaning." Jacob Eichenbaum, in his introduction to *Kol Zimrah*, a collection of his poetry, lashed out against the abandonment of Hebrew by both observant and "enlightened" alike who "heap calumny upon the Hebrew tongue, because it has departed from the land of the living and is dying out together with its speakers."

In the same vein, Abraham Mendel Mohr in his preface to Toviah Feder's "Kol Meḥaẓeẓim," rebuked two extreme "factions" equally: Hasidim, on the one hand, who "oppose the study of the Bible and the Hebrew language in loud voices"; "and the other extreme, those pursuing foreign tongues, and are not with God . . . and are ignorant of his word."

Regarding their second theater of war, the Maskilim saw fit to use the rod of satire to chastise empty-headed pseudointellectuals who were lured by the glamor of European culture or the life of the wealthy. In *Boḥen Ẓaddik*, Perl held up for derision the people of Brody ("Abdari") who drew their enlightenment from "catalogues, theaters, novels, lexicons, and encyclopedias," or studied French or Italian, "but lack decent characters."

The Maskil writer most critical of the "cognoscenti" was Isaac Erter, who castigated them for their egotism and for turning their backs upon the needs of their people. "They are not enlightened," he said, "because the love of their people cannot illuminate the darkness of their hearts. . . ."[103] With this reproach Erter expressed the deepest feelings of all who took up the banner of the Haskalah to wage the difficult struggle to "uplift Israel's glory from the dust piles."

Unequivocal Loyalty of the Haskalah to the Absolutist Monarchy

One issue uniting all the Maskilim—be they conservative, moderate, or radical—was loyalty to the absolutist monarchy, which was seen as the means whereby Jews could become integrated into the civil life of the country. Moreover, there was no doubt in their minds that the regime was in utter accord with their program of opposing religious fanaticism, raising the level of culture through government schools, and improving their depressed economic situation through engaging in agriculture and crafts.

The greatest factor in promoting loyalty to the regime was the social base of the Maskilim. Haskalah spokesmen belonged to that class of Jews that did not suffer national oppression, but prospered as a result of the general economic expansion in Austria and Russia. An important segment of this class even benefited directly from government franchises: the tax lessees and their employees from Galicia and Congress Poland. As merchants they, like members of the Russian merchant guilds, were even exempt from the draft.

The Maskilim considered the propagation of loyalty to the monarch, the state, and its officials as cardinal a task as propaganda for education. The periodical *Bikkurei ha-Ittim* abounds in eulogies for the Emperor Françis I and his dignitaries. "The gracious will of His Majesty and his adjutants is well known," the editor of this periodical, Judah Jeiteles, wrote in 1829. "Their aim and wish are that we improve our ways through a good and normal education of our children. In this way you will win the goodwill of the government."[104] In 1822 Rapoport wrote a dirge upon the death of the Galician governor Franz von Hauer. Joseph Perl devoted a considerable part of the Hebrew almanac which he edited (1813–15) to expounding loyalty to and love of the gracious kings and princes. His memoranda are full of flattery of the very government that taxed the Jews unmercifully. The book *Tekhunat ha-Rabbanim* is permeated with the same spirit of servility in relation to the Emperor and the government: "The individual will must be subjugated to the will of the monarchy which cares for the general welfare . . . , and if a war breaks out we must arise as one man and all together say to the king: we are your servants!"[105] Letteris included in his handbook *Mikhtevei Benei Kedem* the following letter of condolence to a father whose son fell on the battlefield: "A reason for consolation that will comfort you before all others: Your brave son died as a defender of the fatherland, for his king, for his fellow citizens, on the field of honor."[106] The seriousness and sincerity of Letteris's profession of loyalty to the emperor is seen in a letter he wrote to a friend after the death of Emperor Francis I in 1835 in which he compared the late monarch to an angel of God![107]

Using a passage in Proverbs (21:1), Abraham Goldberg, in "Masa Ẓafon," emphasized the importance of carrying out the ruler's decrees, as though such a transgression would be against God himself:

> The heart of the reigning king
> is as streams of water in the hand of God, who bends it at will.
> Therefore, keep ye the king's decrees;
> Not his laws does he fashion, but those of God on high.

The fact that under the rule of those "gracious rulers" the Jews were still restricted in their rights and exploited by means of special taxes did not dampen the loyalty of the Maskilim. They were so pleased at the few concessions granted to the Jews in the field of civil rights under the rule of absolutism that they looked upon this period as a golden age in Jewish history. Like the reactionary government, they, too, maintained that Jews must first of all "reform," become more "ethical" and more educated, so as to deserve full equality with the rest of the citizenry. Mieses expressed this conviction in his *Kinat ha-Emet* where he contrasted with his own time the evil decrees of former kings,[108] and it can be seen even more clearly in *Tekhunat ha-Rabbanim* where he urged that "we mend our ways as much as possible and draw near to them [our neighbors] by every means of approach so as to pass our days on earth in peace. . . ."[109] Rapoport, in a letter to S. D. Luzzatto, waxed enthusiastic over ". . . our times when practically all the rulers of Europe are moved to change our state for the better; some of them accord us all citizenship rights and others signify their willingness to grant them in the course of time."[110]

Perl, however, in his memorandum to the government, admitted that the Jews had not yet attained equal rights, but justified the government on the grounds that the juridical restrictions were intended to benefit the Jews.

Eliezer Kirschbaum of Sieniawa, Galicia, also attributed the shameful condition of the Jews to their low ethical standards and lack of culture. As in the time of the Exodus from Egypt, "So, too, today there is no respite from slave labor forced upon us, till we return from evil. Let us mend our ways and from our folly we shall go free."[111]

Just as the difference between Maskilim and Mitnaggedim was not great in matters of religious practice, so, too, the Mitnaggedim's loyalty to the absolute monarchy did not lag far behind the Maskilim's. After the death of the Galician governor, Letteris was commissioned to write an elegy in German and Hebrew under the name of the Rabbi of Lemberg, Jacob Ornstein.[112] In 1838, Letteris translated into Hebrew a poem by Baron von Sedlitz in honor of the Emperor, the receipts from which were designated for the victims of the flood in the city of Pest; the *Ḥatam Sofer* wrote an approbation for it (in rhyme).[113] In contrast to the Hasidim, the Mitnaggedic rabbis regarded loyalty to the government as a religious duty and viewed the government as a source of support in the struggle against heresy. In 1833 the *Ḥatam Sofer* complained to the imperial chancellery in Vienna about Viennese Jews who kept their offices open on the Sabbath, thereby corrupting other Jews. But, unlike the Mitnaggedim, the Maskilim did have a crystallized political Weltanschauung according to which the absolute monarchy was the ideal sociopolitical order.

There is a historical irony in the fact that precisely in the Kingdom of Poland, the land which most oppressed the Jews, Maskilim raised allegiance to the monarchy to the level of a fundamental axiom in their theological-sociological system. One such writer, Moshe Tannebaum, author of *Mataei Moshe*,[114] was the antirevolutionary spokesman for all Maskilim.

The issue was not simply a theoretical one. Underground liberation movements were being formed thoughout reactionary western and central Europe that were undermining the institutions of absolutism, feudalism, and clericalism. The "Young Europe" movement staged open attacks in 1830 that succeeded in setting up constitutional regimes in France and Belgium, and effected tangible political reform in a few German and Italian principalities. Yet, in that era of revolutionary ferment, the hand of the Maskilic clock still pointed to absolute monarchy. According to Jacob Eichenbaum, it was even to the credit of the Holy Alliance that its members plugged "the breach" after Napoleon's collapse. In his "Elegy" composed at the death of Czar Alexander I, Eichenbaum sings the praises of the departed Russian monarch:

> Out of the West once came
> a foe, mighty in arms, with
> a host numberless like the stars.
> Who crushed them and brought them here to their grave?
> Who entered a sacred covenant with the rulers of the world
> to create peace and truth and stop the breach?
> Alexander is his name; he is the one.[115]

In Russia, while the echo of the Decembrist rebellion was still reverberating, Levinsohn, in *Te'udah be-Yisrael*, praised the Jewish people for never having supported a revolt against a government. He went so far as to claim it their duty, like that of the biblical Mordecai, to inform the regime of any underground activity.[116]

Galician Maskilim, like those of the Pale of Settlement, unequivocally condemned all revolutions and revolutionary movements. In Perl's declaration to the Austrian government concerning the movement launched by Siegfried Justus for the restoration of a Jewish state in Ereẓ Yisrael, Perl stated:

> This Siegfried Justus with all his projects belongs to [the] Young Germany [movement] which upholds, as is well known, all extravagant ideas and sanctions all plans—no matter how utopian, if only thereby what exists is destroyed—to overthrow the social order and to disseminate revolutionary ideas.

The same aversion for revolution was expressed by Gottlober in his poem "A Flower on the Grave of the Year 5608 [1848]," in which he said goodbye to that year when

The earth was nearly overturned
And only weeping and sighing were our share. . . .

He took leave of the year that

Drew forth all the weapons of anger from the inferno
And all the evils and plagues from hell . . .
Incited city against city and state against state
And against his masters the slave arose. . . .[117]

For Maskilim, the French Revolution served as a telling illustration of the destructiveness of any upheaval. David Luria, a well-known Maskil and communal activist from Minsk, claimed the only function of such activity was

to turn one man against his brother, to obliterate all order and national authority, and to do away with domestic tranquility, as evidenced in the previous generation. A great and dignified nation saw nothing but destruction for thirty years and still has not found its mooring. Why? Because it rose up against the regime.[118]

Jacob Samuel Byk, though the most democratic (at least in his attitude toward Yiddish) among the Galician Maskilim, in his letter of 1827 to Samson Bloch cited the French Revolution as an example of the consequences of the spirit of controversy and of the insistence upon a definite political stand without tolerance of opposition:

The French curse the memory of Voltaire and Rousseau, for they were accustomed (in order to gain a hearing among the people) to cry havoc against their oppressors, who existed only in their imagination. For their contemporaries became excessively critical about every imperfection and became accustomed to the use of shouting and through them the people of France became infuriated like a feverish patient and a revolution broke out in their land and thousands and tens of thousands perished in Europe and the blood of children, young men and old, indiscriminately, flowed like water.[119]

Rapoport displayed a far keener historical insight into the causes of the revolution than Byk, but essentially he too viewed it as a misfortune that could have been avoided through enlightenment. In his correspondence with S. D. Luzzatto in 1831, Rapoport cited a letter he had written to Byk in which he was replying to Byk's hypothesis that the French Revolution was the result of the enlightenment and irreligion, and in which he had stated that "the origin of the French Revolution of 1789 is known to every historian, that is, only the misery of the people and the indulgence of the aristocracy led to all their difficulties and the rebels did not cry we are hungry for knowledge, but for bread." Rapoport concluded that "wisdom musters no armies and kills no opponents, but convinces with sensible words; only stupidity operates with hatred and sword and spear, the last arguments of force."[120]

Thus, in sociopolitical questions, the horizon of the Maskilim did not extend beyond the reforms of eighteenth-century rationalist and enlightened absolutism. Samson Bloch, contrasting on several occasions the "paradise" of enlightened western Europe with the squalor of eastern Europe,[121] criticized the latter because there the nobility rule over their subjects with an unlimited power,[122] but he found no fault with the institution of feudalism itself.

The Poor, the Masses, and the Jewish Bourgeoisie

As unqualified adherents of political absolutism, which, even in its most reactionary phase in the nineteenth century, they viewed as a continuation of enlightened absolutism, the Maskilim also staunchly defended the absolutist motto: "All for the people, nothing by the people." In the eyes of the Maskilim, the people were an ignorant mob that had to be trained and enlightened so as to come to their senses. Both Rapoport and Krochmal quoted verbatim Frederick the Great, who characterized the populace as a "many-mouthed and eyeless beast."[123] "The populace," said Bloch, "regardless of nation and class is ever accustomed to its way of folly."[124] Gottlober also called the Jewish masses who had no respect for his works "the uneducated multitude."[125] The changed attitude toward the Jews on the part of the gentile nations in modern times in comparison with the Middle Ages was regarded by Bloch as a result not only of the policy of enlightened rulers but also of the fact that "their wise men preach good and correct ideas in their books for their masses, that they should do good for our people and join with us." In his autobiography, Meyer Letteris wondered why the "genteel and prominent people," the "distinguished people" of his home town Żółkiew, used to pray in the old house of study, whereas "the poor people and the obscurant mass" would pray in the new synagogue.[126] The author of *Tekhunat ha-Rabbanim* was incensed at "the arrogance that has grown among the Jews to the extent that even people of the poor classes have the audacity to speak openly against the wise, the God-fearing and the perfect."[127] Nachman Krochmal's contempt for the "wretchedly poor" and veneration of the "wealthy of our people" and "rich men" in connection with the social characterization of Hasidism has already been discussed. The same conceit and contempt for the "rabble" is displayed in *Teyator fun Khsidim*. Leybele the philosopher concludes his conversation with the Hasidim:

> From now on please keep away from me
> For you yourselves realize that we are not equals.

Leybele's servant calls him away from the debate with the Hasidim with the following words:

> Should you suffer harm at the hands of such lousy people?
> They're not in your class! Let them do something befitting their kind.[128]

The disdain of the Maskilim for the "populace" and the poor was in accord with their views on social questions. *Enrichissez-vous*!, the motto of emerging capitalism, was also the motto of the Maskilim, the pioneers of the capitalist ideology in Jewish life. Like the rising capitalist class, the Maskilim maintained that wealth is a natural reward for economic initiative, energy, and education; while poverty is the result of indolence, inertia, and illiteracy. Bloch spoke in the same breath of "the shame of ignorance and the disgrace of idleness and poverty" and characterized the members of the "lowest" class as "those devoid of everything, wealth, wisdom, and honor."[129] Perl, in two articles in his Hebrew almanac, dwelled upon the problem of the origin of poverty in the world and came to this conclusion: There are cripples, invalids, and aged persons whose poverty is a matter of fate; the majority of the poor, however, consists of people notorious for their indolence and negligence, or of such as have squandered their fortunes on luxuries, in gambling, etc.[130] In the same vein, Krochmal observed:

> All that is called the fortune or misfortune of a man is not something that comes upon him from without, but from his inner nature and the man who is God-fearing, who has learned a profession or trade and strenuously opposes, from his youth, the inclination that is evil, may be assured of succeeding on his way in this world, if he desires no luxuries.[131]

The social philosophy of the Maskilim is also revealed in their interpretation of the motto of productivization of the Jewish masses, which was one of the foundations of their program. In their conception, the Maskilim remained true to the interests of the class which they represented and to the interests of the government that they faithfully served. Neither Perl in *Boḥen Ẓaddik* nor Mieses in *Tekhunat ha-Rabbanim* decried commerce as an unproductive occupation. On the contrary, the rich merchant is the only positive type in Perl's

Megalleh Temirin, and is presented as the ideal of *Di Genarte Velt* and of the *Teyator fun Khsidim*. The mass of Jewish small shopkeepers, tavernkeepers, and brokers who languished in poverty and misery[132] were urged to become artisans and farmers. This would affect the prestige of the wealthy Jews and their esteem in the eyes of the government,[133] for the decrease in the number of Jewish shopkeepers, tavernkeepers, and brokers would lead to the equalization in the social hierarchy of the rich Jewish merchant with the German merchant, so that the former would no longer be identified in the "public mind" with the poor, ragged Jewish petty tradesmen.[134] In the idiom of the Maskilim this was "Honest trade but no swindle and robbery."[135] In *Di Genarte Velt*, the Maskil defines productivization as thorough vocational training both in "business," which is "the greatest and most honorable occupation," and in various handicrafts. He chastises "our merchants" for deception and dishonest competition.[136] The productivization of the masses was also directly in the interests of the rising Jewish capitalist class, for the impoverished nonproductive elements constituted a deterrent to the expansion of the internal market.

Since the government did nothing to help the Jewish masses in their transition to productive occupations but only reiterated its charges that the Jews refused to reform morally and persisted in their old callings, the Maskilim refrained from mentioning the government's responsibility for the horrible plight of large segments of the Jewish population, and continually reproached these Jews for their alleged recalcitrance. Just as the Maskilim maintained that the Jews must first "enlighten" themselves and only then would they be deserving of the "favor of royalty," so in the matter of productivization did they also reverse the order. This inverted logic was due not to the naïveté of the Maskilim but to their political outlook, which did not permit them to level any criticism at the government, and to their social philosophy that, as in the Latin proverb, "every man forges his own fate."

The same concern with increasing the buying power and raising the social prestige of the Jewish bourgeoisie prompted the Maskilim to wage war on idleness, luxuries, and waste, to combat the rule of the communities by despots who were seen as a cancerous growth on economic life, and to oppose excessive philanthropy.

In a 1789 French brochure about the reform of the Jews in Poland, Mendel Lefin had already demanded that workhouses be instituted for lazy paupers.[137] In 1857, Samuel Deutsch, the Reform rabbi of Sambor, in his project for the reform of Galician Jewry proposed to the government such measures as the opening of poor-houses, the compulsory modernization of Jewish dress, and the establishment of modern schools for Jewish children.[138] The author of *Tekhunat ha-Rabbanim* demanded a concentration of all philanthropic activities in the hands of the *kehillah* and compulsory labor for the healthy but lazy beggars, who could become "servants" or "hewers of wood and drawers of water."[139]

In its opposition to idleness and philanthropy, the Haskalah adopted the same capitalist attitudes which appeared among Gentiles as early as the period of Humanism. The Humanists had denounced the large number of monasteries as nests of idleness that were detrimental to society. The Haskalah adopted the slogans for its struggle against idleness and philanthropy from the mercantilistic economy which prevailed in the period of enlightened absolutism, and added the specific motive of the Jewish bourgeoisie, namely, of raising its prestige among the Gentiles. In his article "Toil of One's Hands" in his almanac for 1814, Perl reproached those Jews who lived on charity for "exposing their shame before the eyes of the peoples of the land."

As a corollary of the program of productivization, the Galician Maskilim also decried luxury and waste. Perl devoted considerable space to this problem in his almanac for the years 1813–15 and also in his satire *Boḥen Ẓaddik*.[140] In *Di Genarte Velt*, the Maskil reproaches the merchants who "live like lords" and demands of the artisans, in addition to vocational training, modesty and thrift.[141] In *Boḥen Ẓaddik*, Perl also inveighed against those who depended for their livelihood on their posts in the *kehillah*, and who often enriched themselves at its expense.[142] In *Di Genarte Velt*, the Maskil speaks in the same breath of the insubstantial existences of *melamedim*, emissaries for institutions of charity and learning, agents, brokers, dealers in old clothes, and about powerful men and trustees and wardens of *kehillah* institutions who make a living from communal affairs.[143] A similar struggle against the parasitism of influential men of the *kehillah* in the Russian Haskalah was initiated by Levinsohn in *Di Hefker-velt* and *Emek Refa'im*, where he spoke of a hypocritical crowd of communal functionaries who made a living through "various appointments."

The powerful cliques and their intimates, whose communal roosts were their source of livelihood, exploited their positions to tax the poor and powerless. Thus, just as among pre–French Revolution rationalists a radical faction arose that not only opposed the aristocratic-clerical regime but also espoused the poverty issue, so too among Haskalah writers, a half century later, there were those who championed the social issue. However, the fact that these two rationalist manifestations shared a point in common does not obliterate their sharp differences.

Among western European rationalists, a number of thinkers, like Meslier, Morelly, and Mably, extended their social criticism to cover the entire notion of a capitalist regime. They saw the solution to social ills only in the abolition of private property and the establishment of a society with social equality and collective property. The Maskilim, on the other hand, never considered such egalitarianism as a solution to societal ills. In their biting satires and other chastisements, they exposed only those phenomena that had been acknowledged as evils by capitalist society itself, like accumulation of wealth by extortion and other forms of oppression or feudal exploitation of the masses by means of violence. Class society itself, like political absolutism, they found quite natural and acceptable.

All this notwithstanding, there were many Maskilim—men of conviction, compassion, charity, and ethics—who went beyond their sociopolitical horizons and took up the claims of the poor against their oppressors.

Levinsohn was one of the most outspoken of these Maskilim. His satires, *Di Hefker-velt* and *Toledot Peloni Almoni ha-Kezavi*, cried out with the utmost sympathy for the poor who were oppressed by communal functionaries, and against the practice of drafting the children of the poor as ransom for those of the rich. Even in his satires on Hasidim, Levinsohn included some sharp social criticism.

Among Galician Maskilim, Erter, in his collection of satires *Ha-Zofeh le-Bet Yisrael*, censured in very harsh terms those who grew rich by exploiting the poor, and who regarded the unfortunate with disdain or indifference. It is no accident, considering the social thinking of the Maskilim, that the social types who became objects of satire grew out of a degenerate communal leadership and a Hasidism which in its decline became a national nuisance.

In addition to doctors who amassed wealth from their patients' ills, flattered the rich, and turned their backs on the poor, Erter, in *Gilgul ha-Nefesh*, satirized the following as oppressors of the people: zaddikim, the rebbes, burial society officials, rabbis, and meat and candle tax lessees. The rebbe and "wonder worker," an incarnation of a fox, confesses: "Fools be my flock; I warm myself from their wool. . . . A mansion have I built for myself, a king's palace." The well-born rabbi, a confederate of the rich and an incarnation of "an inflated turkey," acknowledges only two values: pedigree and money. This privileged cleric is symbolic of the entire rabbinic class. In "Toledot he-Ḥaluẓ" Erter placed all blame for cultural decline—especially neglect of Hebrew—upon the "benefactors of the people," the rabbis who "spend their days with generations long gone," and "walk with the dead, pay no heed to the living, except the rich in order to join them in marriage."

Erter's critique of social wrongs reached its pinnacle in his depiction of the meat or candle tax lessee as the incarnation of the shark, who "swallows his brother and members of his nation."

This criticism is interesting in that it was never directed against the Austrian government—an attitude similar to that of Levinsohn toward the Russian regime. The government that decreed the meat and candle taxes was never blamed. Erter contended that the rulers would have preferred to lighten the Jews' burden, but the Jewish tax lessees themselves lobbied for its retention. When a tax lessee heard "it was the King's intention to relieve the land of this duty," he died of a heart attack.

Hirsh Reitman of Galicia, in his poem "Der Kitl," lashed out against the tax lessees for their oppression of the poor. This work was not published until 1863, but it circulated in the Haskalah circles of Brody years beforehand.[144] Reitman, who started as a teacher in Perl's school, later became principal of the communal school in Brody.

Gottlober of Volhynia was an outstanding social satirist in the mold of his revered mentor, Levinsohn, although he was also influenced by Erter's work. His satires, all composed in Yiddish in the first half of the nineteenth century, are unequalled in Haskalah literature for the way in which he uses humor to criticize the ancien régime of the Jewish community. He revealed the paradox of creating communal posts to benefit the populace and filling the positions with extortionists and liars. Like his predecessors, Gottlober aimed his arrows primarily at the community leaders such as the rebbe, whom he characterized as a "shearer of the flock," and the wealthy and patricians whose pride was based upon their relationship to a rabbinical family.

The usurer was seen as a social parasite who both sucked from the poor and burdened the rich. He was a precapitalist vestige impeding the development of modern capitalism—a common concern in Haskalah writings. In "Masa Ẓafon," Abraham Goldberg termed the exacting of interest a "felony," and the usurer was said to "ensnare in his net poor and affluent alike."[145]

Benjamin Mandelstamm, an admirer of Erter and the most radical Lithuanian Maskil of the day, also lashed out against usurers, describing them as an "abomination" who had "three quarters of the Jewish population of Vilna" in their debt.[146] Thus, in the realm of social protest, there were in the first half of the nineteenth century indications of the direction the movement would take during the peak period of J. L. Gordon, *Yehalel* (Judah Leyb Levin), M. L. Lilienblum, and the young Mendele Mokher Sefarim.

The Contrast and Conflict between Hasidism and the Haskalah

In all fields and in every respect, the Haskalah was the opposite of Hasidism, an antithesis that reflected the conflicting interests and philosophies of two classes of the Jewish people, who were separated by a deep social abyss: Hasidism—the impoverished, suffering, retarded petty bourgeois and *lumpenproletarian* masses—and Maskilim—the rising Jewish bourgeoisie and the intelligentsia associated with it. In addition to this interclass dichotomy, there existed an internal one: between the feudal-based "aristocrats" and the emerging bourgeois merchants—and, outside Galicia, manufacturers. The merchants stood for onrushing capitalism within the Jewish economy.

Hasidism viewed the Diaspora as the main calamity of the Jewish people, its only remedy being messianic Redemption and the Return to Zion. For the Maskilim, the problem of the Diaspora did not exist. Their solution to the abnormal situation of the Jewish masses was education and linguistic assimilation. The Hasidim, who were fanatically attached to the Jewish tradition and to the Yiddish language, zealously resisted even the least cultural influence from the outside; while the main object of the Maskilim was to merge with the dominant nationality in language, dress, and external bearing. To the Hasidim, Galicia was a foreign land, the Austrian government, an unbearable ruler; while the Maskilim vied with one another in their expression of loyalty toward the Austrian "fatherland," toward the "gracious monarch" and his rule. The Hasidim shunned secular learning as the greatest danger for Jewry; the Maskilim made education the central pillar of their program. The Hasidim elevated emotion to the highest category of religious values, and the Hasidic world of discourse and action was permeated with a belief in miracles and in the preternatural order of the universe; the Maskilim subscribed to a rationalistically purified religion that remained halfway on the road to deism. The Hasidim combatted as an evil decree every attempt to advance economic life; the Maskilim regarded the old, unproductive Jewish occupations as a curse. The Hasidim regarded social suffering as a result of the oppression of the Diaspora and the mystic play of the forces of divine abundance, and philanthropy was seen as the greatest social commandment; the Maskilim viewed poverty as a deserved penalty for economic inertia and opposed philanthropy as encouraging idleness.

In view of this complete antithesis, it is understandable why the Haskalah waged a life-and-death struggle against Hasidism. (With Mitnaggedim the Maskilim sensed an affinity, and they tried unsuccessfully to draw them to their camp.) The Maskilim rightly saw in Hasidism the greatest obstacle to the realization of their program in Jewish life. Just as in relation to all other aspects of the Haskalah program—the problems of language, education, and productivization—the subject of the social and political prestige of the rising Jewish middle class figured significantly in their struggle against Hasidism. Solomon Judah Rapoport, in a letter of 1815, decried the Hasidim for "having made us a disgrace among our neighbors."[147] Similarly, Perl complained to Gottlober upon the occasion of the latter's visit in 1828 that "these Hasidim . . . bring us harm in every land and because of them we have become a disgrace among the neighbors."[148] The leading spokesmen of the Haskalah in Russia also could not forgive the Hasidim for this. In addition, they explicitly mentioned the damage that the Hasidim did to the cause of equal rights for the Jews. In 1837 Levinsohn wrote to Jacob Tugendhold, the Vilna censor, suggesting a plan for a Maskilic organization for the purpose of promoting solidarity and of working in behalf of the community at large,

> in order to find favor and understanding in the eyes of God and men, and particularly in the eyes of the mighty Emperor, may his majesty be exalted, and in the eyes of his rulers and of the entire people in whose midst we live: for they truly seek the welfare of our people and desire our success; but the foolish Hasidim, through their evil and distorted deeds, have caused the hatred without reason of the land. . . . And certainly the government would also bestow upon us grace and truth and would join with us in love if not for these stupid Hasidim who isolate us with their great folly. . . .[149]

As late as 1869, Gottlober asked rhetorically in the introduction to his *Toledot ha-Kabbalah ve-ha-Ḥasidut* (History of the Kabbalah and Hasidism), "How then can a man who loves his people look on . . . as the whole people, on account of one sect of obscurants, is put to shame and is a mockery in the eyes of the people that rules the land and it cannot ascend the rungs of citizens to inherit political honor like all the other inhabitants of the land, regardless of creed. . . ?[150]

The Maskilim's boundless hatred of the Hasidim, for which Byk reproached them because they preached tolerance and love of one's fellow men toward everyone except the Hasidim[151] can be seen more clearly as sociopolitically motivated when one considers that these very same Maskilim undoubtedly took into account several attributes of Hasidism and evaluated them correctly. In his letter to a friend about Hasidism, "Ner Miẓvah," Rapoport allowed that the conscious swindlers were a minority among the zaddikim and were even scorned by some of the Hasidim. He also mentioned that the impoverished masses followed the Hasidim because they were lenient in interpreting the commandments. However, Rapoport contended that the majority of the zaddikim, while not deliberate swindlers, acted out of ambition and other egoistic motives.[152] On the other hand, Krochmal, in a letter to his son, wrote that the haughtiness and egocentrism of the rabbinic scholars was the chief complaint that the Hasidim lodged against the Mitnaggedim.[153] Gottlober regarded the tyranny of the rabbis as the main cause of the rise of Hasidism and he conceded that unintentionally, the Hasidim had undermined orthodoxy in general and prepared the way for the Haskalah.[154]

Like every cultural and political movement, the Maskilim advanced their program not in the name of the class whose interests they represented but in the name of the entire people. The Maskilim were firmly convinced that their program would solve the cultural, economic, and political problems of the broadest sectors of the Jewish masses. Insofar as it was within the scope of their limited possibilities, the Maskilim indeed endeavored to transpose Jewish life in accordance with their views. Perl not only founded and conducted a German school for Jewish children and flooded the government with memoranda on the establishment of such schools in other cities, but also introduced handicrafts into the curriculum of his school, apprenticed Jewish boys to Christian masters, and organized a "Society for the Promotion of Useful Trades among the Jews in Galicia." Other Maskilim were wholeheartedly devoted to the colonization of Jews on the land. Isaac Erter, Ẓevi Natkes, and Leyb Pastor in Lemberg gave free instruction to young people desiring knowledge, and Mieses even founded a society for the support of Jewish high school and medical students.[155] The Hebrew almanac, a great part of which was devoted to popular presentations of the natural sciences, is a further indication that the Maskilim not only advocated education but also dedicated their best efforts, abilities, and experience to the dissemination of knowledge among the Jews.

In light of the analysis of the social foundations of the Haskalah, it becomes even clearer that the Haskalah was relatively progressive in all of its slogans (even if not in its formulation and according to its social intentions), while in the same period Hasidism was already a reactionary trend. The Maskilim pioneered the way for capitalism in Jewish life, while Hasidism clung to the precapitalist feudal forms of life.

The principles of secular education, of the abolition of the spiritual segregation between Jew and Gentile, of participation in the political and cultural life of the country were progressive, provided they were dissociated from the Maskilic propaganda of linguistic assimilation and loyalty to the prevailing reactionary order. The rationalism of the Haskalah, the tireless struggle against superstition and the belief in miracles were progressive if divorced from the Maskilic insensibility to the national ideas of the Kabbalah and Hasidism. Similarly, the propaganda for the productivization of Jewish life and the opposition to philanthropy were progressive, although their program was restricted by the class interests of the rising Jewish bourgeoisie.

3

The Policy of the Austrian Government toward Hasidism

From Hostile Suspicion to Guarded Accommodation

The policy of the Austrian government toward the Hasidic movement during the first half of the nineteenth century was determined, on the one hand, by the nature and evolution of this religious movement, and, on the other, by the general national, religious, and cultural policies of reactionary absolutism.

Generally, the government was suspicious of Hasidism. As a religious mass movement, Hasidism ran counter to the policy of absolutism which tried to control every aspect of social life, including so important a domain as religion. As late as 1838, the Lemberg police director stressed in his memorandum to the provincial presidency that the Hasidic sect "seems to possess not only a religious but also a political tendency." The cult of the zaddikim and the unconditional obedience to them are described in all official reports as dangerous to the state. The basic attitude of Hasidism toward the state as the foreign yoke of Gentiles seems to have remained unclear to the Austrian officials, but they must have realized, as is evident from all official correspondence, that Hasidism did not "demand reverence and obedience to the laws and the authorities."

Likewise, religious mysticism, the basic feature of Hasidism, ran counter to the interests of absolutism. The Austrian government feared every religious movement characterized by fanatic, visionary, and apocalyptic tendencies, although it did not regard them as direct a threat as the revolutionary tendencies of students and demagogues. All such religious movements were suspected of being secret political opposition groups.[1] In this, the religious policy of reactionary absolutism was a continuation of the cultural policy of enlightened absolutism. It is true that, contrary to the absolutism of the Age of Enlightenment, the successively even more reactionary brand of Austrian absolutism in the nineteenth century combatted the earlier modern deism and philosophic rationalism; yet it still advanced religious rationalism as the only position in accord with the aims of the government.[2]

It was the explicitly national trait of Hasidism, rather than its popular religious character and mystical basis, that prompted the Austrian government to oppose this movement so rigorously from the outset. The attachment of the Hasidim to Yiddish and to the Jewish national and religious tradition was the greatest obstacle to the success of the government's policy of germanizing Galician Jewry. Their stubborn resistance to forced assimilation was euphemistically described in official reports as "antagonism to all education." However, the harsh policy toward Hasidism stemmed more from the fact that the government had abandoned all attempts to germanize the Galician Jews by means of education. While the government had created a system of approximately one hundred German schools for Jewish children in Galicia, it was not deemed necessary to persecute the Hasidim in order to intensify germanization.[3] The reactionary monarch Francis I abolished the German-Jewish schools in Galicia in 1806 as a concession to the Catholic Church, with which he had concluded a concordat the previous year restoring the administration of the schools to the clergy. But the decisive consideration was the fact that reactionary absolutism became apprehensive about the revolutionary influence of education on Galician Jewry.[4] Educated Jewish masses could easily fall under the influence of revolutionary propaganda and enter the struggle against both clericalism[5] and absolutism.[6] With the discontinuation of the German schools, the government had to place all its hopes for the germanization (still termed "enlightenment" in the official jargon) of the Galician Jews on coercion to use the German language in Jewish communal and religious life and on repressive police measures against Hasidism.

The first steps of the Austrian government, taken in 1814, against Hasidism demonstrated its complete ignorance concerning the nature of this "sect." The president of the Supreme Imperial Police and Censorship Office designated the Hasidim as "freemasons," although he correctly indicated their tendency toward mysticism as one of their characteristic traits. In 1816, Count Joseph Sedlnitzky, the new president of the court police commission, accused the Hasidim of strange imaginary offenses, but he already regarded them as enemies of "education," and hence asked the Galician governor's office not only to keep a close watch on the "sect" but also "if possible to suppress it altogether." Not only the central government in Vienna but also even the Galician administration had been unaware at first of how widespread the Hasidic movement was in Galicia. As late as 1829, the Galician governor reported to Sedlnitzky that "the number of Hasidim is constantly diminishing," whereas the opposite was true. The harsh policy toward Hasidism, exaggeratedly described as a great danger to the state, culminated in the governor's decree of October 31, 1823, which threatened severe measures against Hasidic activity.

This severity, however, began to ease in 1824 when the provincial presidency explained that the government's principle was one of "toleration and neutrality toward the various religious practices of the Jews," and that repressive measures should be applied only with respect to the Hasidic leaders. This principle of toleration was reiterated in a decree of the provincial presidency in 1831. When the Lemberg police director attempted to renew the previous austere policy against Hasidism in 1838 and suggested to the provincial presidency that it nullify the principle of toleration of this movement, which was "dangerous to the state," the provincial presidency categorically rejected this proposal, replying that "although the Hasidim are superstitious, there is no notable difference between them and 'blatant' (*krassen*) Judaism," and that the abrogation of toleration appeared altogether impractical.

The Galician provincial presidency was essentially correct. In view of the growing amalgamation of Mitnaggedic orthodoxy with Hasidism, there was no "notable difference" between Hasidism and "blatant Judaism." As Hasidism lost its original character of political and social aggressiveness, it became rooted more deeply in the Jewish petty bourgeoisie and middle class, and the government was forced to recognize that it would be "altogether impractical" and unfeasible to suppress such a mass movement through violent police repression. Moreover, the change in the government's policy toward Hasidism was due more to a revision of its previous position than to these tactical motives. The more the government became acquainted with the true nature of Hasidism, the more it realized that the Hasidic ideology possessed certain essential features which might be sympathetic to an absolutist regime. In its report of 1827, the district office of Stryj emphasized that the Hasidim, in their striving for greater piety, were "less prejudicial to the state in the civic moral sense" than "the talmudic Jews who for the most part limit themselves to ceremonial religiosity." Hasidic conservatism and the dogged Hasidic hostility toward every attempt to modernize Jewish life matched the aims of absolutism, which strove with all its might to stem social, political, and cultural progress. The romantic *Schwärmerei* of the Hasidim proved to be even less of a political threat than romanticism in general, which was the dominant spiritual current in Europe at that time. Hasidism combined the yearning for a better and more beautiful world order with a turning away from the actual problems of life and, like every other form of mysticism, transferred the notion of redemption from the real world to the sphere of heavenliness and metaphysics.

The government probably took all these factors into consideration when it turned down the suggestions of the Maskilim to suppress the Hasidic movement. For the same reasons, the government also rejected the Maskilic projects for educating the Jews, as well as their earlier requests for the reestablishment of the government German schools for Jewish children. It continued to pay lip service to the concept in all its official reports, but nothing whatsoever was done to raise the cultural level of Galician Jewry. In fact, the low level of general education among the Jews was exploited in official declarations as justification for their civil inequality and economic need.[7]

Although the government had softened its attitude toward Hasidism, it continued to press vigorously for the germanization of Galician Jewry. This reflected general official inconsistency and indecisiveness in relation to the Hasidic movement in this phase, since the Hasidic movement still was under governmental pressure from time to time. The Hasidic rebbes were still kept under surveillance and persecuted by the police; kabbalistic and Hasidic books remained outlawed; and Hasidic congregations were raided sometimes because they lacked government permits. They were not shut down, however, the denunciations of the Maskilim notwithstanding.

The difference in attitude toward Hasidism between the local and provincial authorities must also be considered. The local officials—the district chiefs and commissioners who were themselves raised in the atmosphere of enlightened absolutism—adopted the government's phraseology concerning its feigned intentions to disseminate education among the Jews, and they viewed with great favor all the projects proposed by the Maskilim. In their accompanying letters to the governor they supported all the Maskilic denunciations against the Hasidim,[8] and on their own initiative or under the influence of the Maskilim they submitted projects for the complete suppression of the Hasidic movement in Tarnopol, Brody, and Lemberg. The "ultimate" goals of the government's religious and cultural policies remained unknown to these junior officials. Its inconsistent policy, the attitude of the local authorities, as well as the continuous denunciations by the Maskilim all greatly contributed to the continuation of sporadic persecutions of the Hasidim to the end of the period of the first reaction and, to a certain extent, into the period of the second reaction.

The Development of an Official Policy toward Hasidism

Through a study of official documents, the development of the Austrian government's policy toward the Hasidic movement in Galicia can be traced.

There are no official documents related to Hasidism in Galicia for the period from 1788, when the government issued a favorable verdict about Hasidism in response to an inquiry from the district office of Rzeszów,[9] until 1814. Some information is reported by the Mitnagged Israel Loebl, the author of *Sefer Vikkuaḥ*. Loebl stated[10] that in the beginning of 1799 he had an audience in Vienna with Emperor Francis II, to whom he personally gave his two works about Hasidism. The Emperor promised that he would carefully investigate the matter. Loebl's report concluded that "both in that part of the former Poland that belongs to the Emperor of Russia and in the Austrian part, this sect has been forbidden under a strict penalty to assemble publicly."

Loebl's report about the persecution of Hasidim in Austria is for the most part highly exaggerated and self-congratulatory. Even concerning Russia, the Mitnaggedic preacher credited himself with instigating the investigation of the Hasidim of Karlin in connection with the second arrest of Shneur Zalman of Lyozna in 1800, which actually took place because of the denunciation by Rabbi Avigdor of Pinsk. In Austria, Loebl's audience with the emperor probably resulted only in an investigation, and nothing is mentioned about a prohibition of Hasidic meeting places in the later documents where the previous decrees concerning the Hasidim are cited. In a decree of the court chancellery of 1810 about *minyanim,* the previous tax on religious assemblies was replaced by an annual stamp tax in the amount of twenty gulden to be paid on application for a special permit to conduct a *minyan.* Participating in a *minyan* or holding one in one's home without a permit from the district office was regarded as participation in a secret society and punishable according to the laws of "serious violations of police regulations."[11]

In 1813–14 the administrative authorities became interested in the Hasidic movement in relation to the spread of Hasidism in the district of Zloczów. Since the city of Brody, the center of the Galician

Haskalah, belonged to the district of Zloczów, it is easy to understand that the initiative in drawing the government's attention to the Hasidic movement came from the Maskilim as it did in almost all the later cases. It seems that the district office of Zloczów questioned the Galician provincial authorities about this matter, and from there a report was forwarded to the supreme imperial police headquarters in Vienna. A decree was issued by the court chancellery on February 14, 1814, citing the verdict of 1788, which declared that "Hasidim or pious Jews cannot be persecuted because the law of toleration of the Mosaic religion also applies to them." This decree was transmitted on April 1, 1814, through the Galician provincial presidency to the district office of Zloczów as a directive.[12]

This episode was the last expression of tolerance by the government toward Hasidism in the Age of Enlightenment. A half year later, the government, in complete disregard of the Edict of Toleration of Joseph II (1789), began to look closely into the activities of the Hasidim, and the period of their persecution began.

On July 28, 1814, the president of the Supreme Imperial Police and Censorship Office, Baron Franz von Haager, advised the governor of Galicia, Baron Peter von Goess, in connection with the censorship of *Sefer Ḥasidim* (Book of the Pious), that he should pay particular attention "to the ever-spreading Jewish sect of Hasidim in Poland, i.e. a freemasonry society." Baron von Haager described this sect as fond of everything that is "mystical, obscure, and absurd."[13] The designation of the Hasidim as freemasons probably stemmed from the fact that the Hasidim were also regarded as a secret society based on mysticism.[14] Baron von Goess, who was in Vienna at the time, transmitted the orders of the imperial police to the provincial administration of Galicia. He addressed himself to Brody Police Director Kandrany, who could be particularly helpful in investigating this matter because he both was in Brody and knew Hebrew. At the end of August 1814, the provincial presidency issued a circular to all the district offices, the censorship office (Book Inspection Board) of Lemberg, and the Lemberg police directorate, as well as to Kandrany, summoning them to give exact information concerning the Hasidic sect. On the basis of the reports received, Baron Franz von Hauer, the successor to von Goess as governor of Galicia, issued a decree in July 1816 against the Hasidim and ordered the district offices to investigate the Hasidic rebbes.[15] The measures against the Hasidim were particularly intensified after the ban against the leaders of the Maskilim—S. J. Rapoport, Ẓevi Natkes, Isaac Erter, Judah Pastor, and their adherents—was pronounced in the Lemberg synagogue in the autumn of 1815.[16] During this period, Hasidim attacked the German-Jewish

Realschule in Brody which was about to open. The guilty Hasidim were punished by order of the governor.[17]

The vice-president of the imperial police office, Count Sedlnitzky, in a note of September 20, 1816, sanctioned both the punishment of the originators of the bans against the Maskilim in the Lemberg synagogue[18] and Governor von Hauer's decree concerning strict police surveillance of the Hasidic movement. In doing so, he characterized the Hasidim as hypocrites who were not at all as pious as they pretended to be, judging by the way they indulged their passions on certain holidays. Moreoever, they had opposed all the attempts made by the state administration to improve education for the Jews. Accordingly, he instructed the governor to scrutinize this sect carefully in order to punish it for all its misdeeds and to suppress it as far as possible.[19]

Needless to say, if Sedlnitzky correctly designated the Hasidim as enemies of education, his accusation of hypocrisy and debauchery rested mainly upon information given him by the Jewish censors of Vienna and Lemberg, who envied the "sect" its ecstatic, joyful dances on the holidays.

In a report of December 15, 1816, Governor von Hauer informed Count Sedlnitzky that the "efficacy" of the Hasidic sect had been diminished for a time owing to the appropriate measures taken by the Galician provincial authorities, "although it has not been completely extirpated." All the district chiefs were instructed to combat all attempts at a revitalization of the sect. At the same time, however, the governor turned over to Count Sedlnitzky the manuscript of Joseph Perl's treatise, "Über das Wesen der Sekte Chassidim aus ihren eigenem Werken gezogen" (Concerning the Nature of the Sect of Hasidim on the Basis of Quotations from their own Books),[20] which Perl had submitted to him with a request for permission to have it printed. In his petition to the governor, Perl had also asked that he be permitted to dedicate the book to him. The governor remarked to Sedlnitzky that he could not consent "since it is in his interest as provincial chief to maintain the goodwill of all classes and sects of the population, so that he cannot, by accepting the dedication of this pamphlet, place himself in opposition to one sect even though it may run counter to the aims of the state through its fanatical principles."[21]

The caution which the highest Galician authorities exercised toward Hasidism, even in the period of severest repression, is characteristic and was to lead to a thoroughgoing modification of the official policy.

Sedlnitzky's reply to Governor von Hauer, dated February 11, 1817, dealt first with the question of allowing Perl's work to be printed. Based on the opinions of both the Hebrew and the theological censors, he forbade the publication of this work, citing the censors' argument that the book might evoke indignation against the Jews among the enlightened Gentiles. He added that "The uncultivated Jews, however, who understand neither the writings nor the language [German], would not desist from adhering to this sect." Moreover, Sedlnitzky reported that both censors had described the Hasidic movement as being so dangerous politically as to warrant an investigation by the governor to verify their information. He considered it most important to investigate carefully the Hasidic and kabbalistic works mentioned in Perl's pamphlet. Finally, Sedlnitzky recommended that the rabbis and zaddikim belonging to this sect be sought out and placed under police surveillance. "In general, one is to proceed so as to stamp out this evil at its roots."[22]

The Galician governor fully carried out the order of the imperial police office concerning the confiscation of forbidden Hasidic and kabbalistic books.[23] In the same year, 1817, he also submitted a report to Sedlnitzky in which he referred to the fact that on July 26, 1816, he had issued pertinent ordinances with respect to the investigation and surveillance of the Hasidic rebbes. He also found it necessary to remark that he was convinced effective action against this sect could be taken only by the government, exerting its influence on the "spiritual education" of the Jews. Therefore, the governor regretted that, after closing the German-Jewish schools, the government had done nothing in this area, despite the fact that in 1812 the Galician provincial presidency had strongly emphasized the necessity for systematic education of the Jews. It even had submitted the necessary proposals in connection with the projected new Jewry ordinance, which had been presented to the central government at that time. However, the governor concluded that to date, no high-level decision concerning the Jewry ordinance had been made.[24]

The Austrian government did not take seriously the advice of the governor of Galicia and also categorically rejected Perl's proposals to reopen the German schools for Jewish children, proposals supported by the provincial authorities.

The Perl Memorandum

The proposals were contained in a memorandum addressed by Perl at the end of 1819 to the provincial presidency, in which he argued for reestablishment of German-Jewish state schools. The court chancellery in Vienna, to which Perl's memorandum had been referred by the Galician administration, did not respond until April 29, 1820. Their note referred to an imperial decree issued just after the arrival of Perl's memorandum, on January 22, 1820, which contained many new decisions concerning the forced germanization of the Jews,[25] and orders "to consider that, except for the subject of religion, the Jewish youth ought to receive its instruction in Christian schools." Therefore, the court chancellery asked the Galician provincial presidency if, in the light of this imperial decree, it was still of the opinion that Perl's project should be considered.[26]

In reply to the notice of the court chancellery, the Galician provincial presidency submitted a detailed memorandum on June 16, 1820, in which Perl's proposal to reopen separate German schools for Jewish children was enthusiastically supported again. It is worthwhile to review the arguments that were mustered concerning this question by the Galician provincial administration, some truly noteworthy, others, however, dictated by deep-rooted prejudices toward the Jewish population.

The memorandum began with the assertion that the "supreme will" of the Emperor in regard to the Jews was expressed in the decree that Jewish practices and fields of occupation must be rendered innocuous and that Jews must gradually adapt to the practices and occupations of "civil" society for the benefit of the general welfare. As a means of realizing this goal, the imperial decree stipulated that Jewish children attend Christian schools. The provincial authorities, however, contended that in contrast to other Austrian provinces, compulsory education did not apply to Galicia. Therefore, a special ordinance would have to be enacted that would oblige the Galician Jews to send their children to school. It was further concluded that "Jews are on such a low level of intellectual, moral, and even physical culture" and were dominated by superstitions and religious prejudices to such an extent that one could not prevail upon them to send their children to the Christian schools by appealing to their intellect. The governor said that since the German-Jewish schools closed, the Jews had stopped sending their children to public schools altogether. Even if the Jews wanted to change their attitude toward the Christian schools, allowances had to be made for the fact that such schools did not exist wherever there was a Jewish community, and even where such schools did exist, there were neither enough room nor teachers to accommodate all the Jewish youth of school age. It was also pointed out that "The uncleanliness in the dress and in the way of life of the local Jews" was still a hindrance, "even from the hygienic consideration," to Jewish and Christian children's attending the same schools.

Only in the future, when the civil condition of the Jews would be transformed and stabilized, would the Jewish youth be prepared to attend Christian schools. Such a change in the state of the Jews could be expected as a result of the new Jewry ordinance that the Emperor had ordered framed. However, the provincial presidency contended that even then, it would still be advisable to consider Perl's project concerning separate German schools for Jews for the following reasons:

1. Were education to be imparted to Jewish children by "Israelites, people of the same nation," it would not create the impression of being imposed. Indeed, it was from such schools as Perl's in Tarnopol that a "rapprochement between the Jews and civil society" and the "civilizing" of the Jews could best be brought about. The Christian schools, however, would also not be practical for Jewish children because they devoted the greater number of hours to religion and ethics instruction.

2. Were Jewish children to attend the Christian schools they would not only lose much instruction time, since the imperial decree exempted them from religion-related subjects, but also would not have the opportunity to receive the appropriate religious and moral education.[27]

On July 17, 1820, before notice of the rejection of the project had arrived from Vienna, Perl presented a petition to the Galician provincial authorities to open a German elementary school for Jewish children in Brody. He explained that such a school would have great significance for the realization of his broader project of establishing German-Jewish schools throughout Galicia. Inasmuch as all the Jewish communities in Galicia looked upon the Jewish community of Brody as a model for all their activities, the opening of an elementary school in that city would have dispensed with many initial difficulties in the establishment of similar schools throughout the land. Moreover, Brody was in particularly great need of such a school, which would prepare students for its existing *Realschule*.

Perl considered that moment the most opportune for the realization of his project in Brody. He had received information that the Jewish community in Brody was dissatisfied that the local *Realschule* was being supported by taxes paid by *kehillah* members expressly for this purpose, and had complained about this to the Galician provincial presidency.[28]

Therefore, Perl proposed that the governor permit the *kehillah* of Brody to levy a special local surtax on kosher meat. He argued that the consumption of meat by the Jewish community of Brody was so high that such a tax could support not only the projected elementary school but also the local *Realschule*. Even the fanatics "who combat all systematic education of the Israelite youth" would in this case agree to an elementary school in Brody because by doing so they would automatically be doing away with the direct tax for the *Realschule* that was so hateful to them. If the governor agreed to his proposal, Perl promised to persuade the most prominent members of the Jewish community of Brody to submit a request to the provincial authorities to establish an elementary school even before they received permission for a special surtax on kosher meat. Only if this happened before the matter of the meat tax was settled, Perl concluded, could the request for opening an elementary school be passed in the *kehillah* without serious difficulties.[29]

Indeed, from Perl's last remark he obviously understood that the new surtax on meat would not be much more popular than the existing direct tax for the *Realschule*. Perl also knew from his experience with the school in Tarnopol which he directed (the only elementary school for Jewish children in Galicia at that time) that the opposition of the Jewish masses to it[30] was not only because of fanaticism but also because of resistance to the special taxes on kosher meat used to support the school. And yet in the same request Perl had assured the Galician provincial authorities that the fanatics would be relieved that the meat tax would be for the benefit of the planned elementary school in Brody, ostensibly because it would free them from the direct tax for the benefit of the *Realschule*! But Perl had no choice. Under the rule of reactionary absolutism which Perl praised so highly for its "favors" and its "goodwill" toward the Jews, a school for Jewish children could only be established with new taxes on the Jewish population.

But the government rejected the proposal, fearing the dissatisfaction that such new burdens would provoke, and perhaps even more that a new surtax on meat would decrease the consumption of meat and thereby also the state revenues from the regular kosher meat tax. On June 20, 1820, the provincial authorities notified the district office in Tarnopol that despite its fullest recognition of Perl's attempts to disseminate education among his "coreligionists," his proposal concerning an elementary German-Jewish school in Brody could not be accepted. According to the "most supreme" (imperial) instructions that had been recently reiterated, no new tax could be levied on kosher meat.[31] A petition of the same year, 1820, by the managing board of the *kehillah* of Rzeszów, "concerning culture among the Jews and for the establishment of a German-Jewish school like the one in Tarnopol,"[32] was also rejected by the Galician provincial administration, probably for the same reasons.

During this period, the Hasidic movement was persecuted at every opportunity. The instigators of these persecutions were, for the most part, Maskilim who inundated the authorities with their denunciations of Hasidism. In certain cases these denunciations even affected Orthodox leaders who were far removed from Hasidism.

The Concurrent Maskil-Inspired Persecutions of the Hasidim

In 1817 the Galician provincial authorities investigated a certain Kulikower who, together with another Jew, conducted a collection of funds for Palestine among the Jews of Lemberg and used a receipt book that was signed by R. Jacob Ornstein and by the secretary of the *kehillah*, Ḥayyim Ber Modlinger. The investigation was terminated because of lack of evidence.[33] In 1818 the latter was denounced by Abraham Kahane for inducing him and three other Jews to emigrate to Palestine and to transfer money there.[34] Soon afterward an anonymous denunciation was submitted accusing Modlinger and Ornstein of the same violation.[35] It seems that in both cases, just as in 1817, the investigations did not establish the guilt of the accused. The investigation that is mentioned in the records (without an exact date) against Hersh of Żydaczów for collecting money for Palestine also probably took place during the same time. This investigation was also terminated for lack of evidence.[36] In 1818, Hersh was accused of smuggling forbidden Hasidic books from Russia.[37] In August 1822, upon reaching Jarosław on his return from Hungary, Hersh was denounced by a local Maskil, Ungar, seized by the police at the "Third Sabbath Meal," and expelled from the city the following day.[38] He was also arrested once by the district office of Stryj for holding "unauthorized services."[39]

The following police action against Hersh of Żydaczów is gleefully depicted by Nachman Krochmal in his often-quoted letter to the young Maskil, Abraham Goldberg of Rawa:[40]

> The churl and sinner of Żydaczów sits and preaches to a congregation: suddenly all stand trembling in face of the many fortresses that he conquered today in heaven with his prayer, the many worlds that are subject to him and look forward to abundance through spiritual awakening from below and from the water of his apertures. He who sits on high laughs at his insane genius: the word is still on his lips when the city policeman appears in the room with a club in his hand. The rebbe is startled, his face is pale. The policeman raises his hand and he rises from his chair and follows him with great fear. And after he [the policeman] seriously embarrasses and disgraces him beyond description, he drives him out of the city and the worlds are not even shaken and the [heavenly] lights are not extinguished and the earth is as it was. . . .

The conducting of *minyanim* without a permit was the chief offense that was exploited by the Galician administration during this period as a pretext for persecuting the Hasidic rebbes. The question of *minyanim* had been dealt with in several decrees, starting when Galicia first came under Austrian rule.

According to article four of Empress Maria Theresa's Jewry Ordinance of 1776, private religious assemblies were prohibited in conformity with the principle that services should only take place in the synagogue. An exception was foreseen only for such *minyanim* in which the Torah was not read. Under the rule of Emperor Joseph II, this prohibition was repealed, owing to fiscal considerations rather than to the principle of religious toleration. According to a court decree of December 29, 1788, which was later reiterated in paragraph nine of the Edict of Toleration of 1789, a fifty-gulden tax for the benefit of the German-Jewish schools was levied on *minyanim* where the Torah was read. Of course, Jews evaded paying this high tax by telling the authorities that in these *minyanim* only prayers were recited (*Privatandacht*) without a Torah scroll. This was probably the reason that the goverment issued the decree of May 1792—at the suggestion of Herz Homberg, superintendent of all the German-Jewish schools in Galicia—which halved the tax on *minyanim*, but included all *minyanim* without exception, even those where the Torah was not read. In 1793 this decree was incorporated into the charter for the Jews of "West Galicia" (Lublin region), but it was not applied to old Galicia proper.[41]

After the abolition of the German-Jewish schools in 1806, the government no longer even had the pretext that the *minyanim* tax was being used for the school system. Therefore, in 1810, a decree repealing this tax was issued, but a tax of approximately the same amount was imposed in the form of an annual stamp tax amounting to twenty gulden. The meeting of a prayer quorum without such a permit was punishable according to the regulations concerning secret societies.[42]

On July 17, 1823, the decree of 1810 concerning *minyanim* was replaced by a new decree issued by the court chancellery and published on August 22 in the ordinance of the Galician provincial administration.[43] The *minyanim* were no longer to be considered as secret societies, but they could not serve as places of assembly for the Hasidim. The householder on whose premises a *minyan* was held and where the Torah was read would annually have to submit an application and pay the stamp tax. In addition, he was required to prove that the members of the *minyan* could not attend services in the synagogue because of advanced age, infirmity, or great distance. Furthermore, to obtain a permit in the first place it was necessary to establish that both the householder and those attending the *minyan* "are known as law-abiding persons and are not suspected of being religious enthusiasts," that is, Hasidim. For violation of this decree, the leader of the *minyan* was to be punished by a fine or imprisonment.

How the prohibited was distinguished from the permissible in designation of a *minyan* as a *Privatandacht* with a Torah scroll depended somewhat on the obtuseness and malevolence of the Austrian officials, and it was not until 1836 that a gubernatorial decree was issued which, based on the decree of 1823, exempted those unlicensed *minyanim* which were conducted without the reading of the Torah.[44] This situation continued until 1846, when an imperial decree made it clear that not all members of the *minyan* must prove that they were ill, infirm, or lived too far from the synagogue, and that an official permit to conduct a *minyan* should also be issued in cases where the householder alone was forced to worship at home because of one of these difficulties.[45] On the other hand, as late as 1840 an amendment was published by the Galician provincial administration that not only the leader of the *minyan* but also all the participants would be punished if a *minyan* was conducted without a permit from the district office.[46]

The Hasidim generally circumvented the 1823 decree which excluded "religious fanatics" from receiving permission to conduct a *minyan*. According to the report of the Lemberg police directorate in 1838, those Hasidim who wanted permission for a *minyan* would obtain false certificates from district rabbis who were sympathetic to the Hasidim.[47] In any case, the high annual stamp tax was a sufficient reason for the Hasidim to try to avoid legalizing their *minyanim*. The procedure of granting such a permit sometimes took several years,[48] which presented the government with frequent opportunities for reprisals against the Hasidim. However, even those Hasidic *minyanim* that were sufficiently circumspect and legal were not protected against persecution in cases of denunciations.

On October 24, 1823, Judah Leyb Mieses, the prominent Maskil, submitted a memorandum to the district office of Lemberg in which he complained that the managing boards of the *kehillot* were issuing false certificates to Hasidic *minyanim*. He took the opportunity to point out what an obstacle the Hasidim were to the cultural development of the Jews. Immediately afterward, on November 5, a denunciation also was submitted in Lemberg against "the detrimental sect" by two Jews, Marcus Hiller and Moses Rabe.[49]

As a result of Mieses's denunciation, the Galician provincial administration, on October 31, 1823, instructed the district offices "to keep under watchful surveillance people who, under the name Hasidim or hypocritically pious men (*Frömmler*), wander about the country and collect considerable sums from the Jews under all sorts of pretenses and counteract the intentions of the government to spread enlightenment and education among the Jews, to draw them closer to other groups in the population and to suppress their superstitions and fanatical customs." The district offices were to act with the appropriate severity on any report of such offenses.[50]

The provincial government's strictly formulated decree produced immediate results in various localities in Galicia. The district chief of Jasło zealously undertook his mission and dispatched a police commissioner and a military detachment to Dukla. They raided the Hasidic congregation during services, arrested all the worshippers, and all the religious books and Torah scrolls found there were transported in carts to Jasło. The same procedure was repeated in Żmigród. In several other districts of Galicia individual Hasidic leaders were arrested on the basis of denunciations.[51] The following details are related in a document dated January 27, 1824, concerning such a denunciation in the town of Mosty Wielkie in the district of Żółkiew.[52]

Ḥayyim Herbst of Mosty Wielkie charged that a certain Jacob Groynem of Tomaszów in the Kingdom of Poland had entered the district of Żółkiew illegally several years earlier and had been living in Mosty for two years, during which time he had pretended to be the founder of a religion (*Religionsstifter*) and lured Jews into "fanaticism" and illegal acts that were disadvantageous to the imperial revenues: among other things he had cursed the tax lessees and put them under bans, placed alms boxes in the homes to collect money for the city of Jerusalem,[53] instituted an excise on all business transactions for his own benefit, and convinced his adherents to leave the synagogue and to assemble in the house of study for the sake of "religious fanaticism." He also had given his son Simon in marriage without a legal permit.

In the same year, 1824, an investigation was conducted against Hersh of Żydaczów because of a letter he sent to Naphtali of Ropczyce. This letter was forwarded by the provincial presidency to Perl for his judgment, and he expressed the opinion that the Rebbe of Żydaczów had indeed manifested his "wicked intention."[54]

After the Galician administration took increasingly repressive measures against the Hasidim, a more liberal policy was finally instituted. This change was brought about by the energetic intercession of the Hasidim. In his memorandum to the government in 1838 concerning the Hasidim,[55] Perl related that soon after the proclamation of the stringent anti-Hasidic ordinance of October 31, 1823, the Hasidim inveigled the provincial administration into questioning the rabbis about the nature of their sect.[56] When the provincial authorities consented, the Hasidim, in turn, persuaded the rabbis—through terror and various other means—to issue a favorable opinion about their movement. As a result, the provincial administration did not include the anti-Hasidic ordinance which it had sent to the district offices in the official provincial legal code,[57] but issued a new decree in April 1824 which redefined the contents of the previous ordinance in a more moderate spirit.

The decree cited the opinion of the rabbis, who asserted that "the only difference between the 'pious' Jews and other Jews, who are tolerated,[58] has to do with their attitude toward prayers." The ordinance stated that "this difference has as little influence upon the state as their more rigid fasting, wall-beating and other customs." Toleration applied to the Jewish religion, and in accordance with this fact, decrees had been issued in 1788 and in 1814 prohibiting the persecution of "Hasidim or pious Jews."[59] Accordingly, the new decree impressed upon the district officials that they were not to misinterpret the injunction of the ordinance of October 31, 1823, that obliges them "to proceed vigorously in case of denunciations." The district officials "must only see to it that in practicing the tolerated Mosaic religious principles, the existing political regulations must be neither violated nor transgressed in any manner." Only in such cases must the district office act immediately. It explained that the decree of August 22, 1823, was still valid regarding *minyanim,* but a very significant instruction appended as a "comment" essentially invalidated the decree's anti-Hasidic clause: "The government [i.e., the district administrative authorities] is no longer required to investigate whether a Jew [who submits an application for a permit to conduct a *minyan*] belongs to one or another sect, especially since such investigations do not produce any results." Further, when acting on the applications concerning *minyanim,* only the personal qualifications of the applicants were to be considered.[60]

However, severe measures were to be taken against the Hasidic leaders:

> It is a different matter if these Jews are to roam about the country with neither a passport nor an occupation; drag along with them a swarm of other Jews, collect considerable sums of money under the pretense of supporting the poor, attempt, through their teachings and influence upon the lower class of Jewry, to spread superstition and fanatical observances, adversely affect the revenue from the Jewish imposts and otherwise frustrate, by positive action, the intentions and efforts of the government to bring the Jews closer to the rest of the inhabitants of the land through enlightenment, education, and true morality. In these instances that have no bearing on the Jewish religion, but concern actions against specific political regulations, such types of people

who departed from the path of civil order are to be treated with dispatch in accordance with the full severity of the law, since it is a matter of importance to proceed with firmness and decisiveness to oppose such machinations from the outset.[61]

This decree distinguished most clearly between Hasidism as a religious movement and the Hasidic leaders themselves. Hasidism as a religious doctrine would enjoy religious toleration, the principle proclaimed by Joseph II in the edict of 1789, but the Hasidic leaders would be held responsible for all the "offenses" of the Hasidic movement. For they were the ones who spread superstition and fanaticism and resisted the alleged efforts of the goverment to further the education and enlightenment of Jewry; they were to blame for the decrease in state revenues from the kosher meat tax because of the united action of the Jewish masses.

This contrived distinction between the leaders of Hasidism and the Hasidic movement was not just a reflection of the sociology of religion in the Age of Reason, according to which religions were a fabrication of deceitful founders (as in Voltaire's treatment of Mohammed) and a product of the avaricious priests who fanned the flames of fanaticism among the masses for the sake of their own private interests. In pitting the zaddikim against the Hasidic masses, the Galician administration hoped to achieve two goals. The emphasis on the principle of religious toleration was intended to prevent the resentment of the Hasidic masses toward the government from growing into active, antistate opposition. At the same time, the persecution of the Hasidic rebbes was intended to serve as a means of weakening the political aspect of Hasidism, just as the continuing strict prohibition of Hasidic literature was to weaken Hasidic mystic ideology. It was in the light of these considerations that a governor's ordinance of August 22, 1824, was issued in which it was reaffirmed that the government "does not consider its task to influence the various religious rites of the Jews."[62]

Sefer Vikkauḥ *and the Investigation of Hasidism*

A new wave of official investigations of Hasidism and of repressive measures against Hasidic leaders began in 1826, again instigated by the Maskilim. As in 1814 and 1816 the specific occasion was furnished by the censorship of the book *Sefer Vikkuaḥ*.[63]

Almost the entire first edition of this anti-Hasidic pamphlet by the Maggid of Slutsk, Israel Loebl, which was published in Warsaw in 1798, was bought by the Hasidim and burned.[64] Perl, a relentless opponent of Hasidism, decided to find a copy of this work in order to publish a second edition. For this purpose he mobilized his friends, the Maskilim, including J. S. Byk.[65] On January 17, 1825, Perl reported (in German) to his friend Mieses: "The *Sefer Vikkuaḥ* is presently being copied. I hope that it will be completed this week. With God's help I trust that I will have a great effect upon things through it."[66] Apart from the author's preface, the book was supplied with an additional introduction and a list of Hasidic books,[67] which were both probably written by Perl. The book was then presented to the imperial censor for a publication permit by a Jew from Lemberg, S. Rapaport.[68]

The arrival of the manuscript of *Sefer Vikkuaḥ* at the supreme censorship office touched off a three-year investigation of Hasidism by the Austrian officials. It is worthwhile to review the particulars of this inquiry both because of the bungling of the Austrian bureaucratic apparatus that is revealed in the documents and, even more so, because of several interesting official reports concerning the Hasidic movement that were given on this occasion.

On March 15, 1826, Count Sedlnitzky, president of the Supreme Imperial Police and Censorship Office, sent a note to Count von Taaffe, governor of Galicia since 1822, informing him that Rapaport had applied to the chief censor for a permit to print a manuscript in Żółkiew written in the "rabbinic Hebrew" language entitled "Vikkuaḥ Talmudi im Beshtani" (Religious controversy between a Talmudist and a Beshtian). In his written opinion, the censor suggested that permission to publish this manuscript be refused on the grounds that "in the two prefaces to this manuscript the mischief of the kabbalistic sect which is widespread throughout Poland and in Hungary and Wallachia[69] under the name Beshtians or Hasidim is described in a manner entirely unfit for publication."[70]

Sedlnitzky further reported that the censor had noted that fifteen "ringleaders" of this sect were mentioned by name in the book and were depicted as rebels against "His Royal and Imperial Majesty." The members of this sect were accused of swindling and avarice and even of idolatry and the murder of several Talmudists, along with other scandalous deeds.[71] In the appendix to the treatise there is a list of kabbalistic books written by "Beshtians or Hasidim" and published in Lemberg, Żółkiew, and other printing centers in Poland and Russia.

The imperial censorship office had not yet come to a final decision concerning permission to publish *Sefer Vikkuaḥ*.[72] But meanwhile, Sedlnitzky reminded the governor of Galicia of his decree against the Hasidim dated February 11, 1817, and ordered him to investigate all the charges leveled against them in *Sefer Vikkuaḥ* and, regardless of the results of the investigation, to take whatever steps were necessary and report everything to him.[73]

Accordingly, on May 8, 1826, the Galician provincial presidency ordered the book censor's office in Lemberg to secure the names of the fifteen "ringleaders" from the manuscript, which had been transferred from Vienna; to verify the accusation that they were rebels against "His Royal and Imperial Majesty" and whether their adherents were addicted to the vices mentioned therein; to establish whether the books listed in the manuscript as kabbalistic had already been prohibited by the censor; and to find out the names of the printers in Lemberg and Żółkiew who published these works. This entire matter was to be kept strictly confidential.[74]

At the end of June 1826, the censorship office in Lemberg submitted to the provincial presidency the following list of the fifteen Hasidic "ringleaders" mentioned in *Sefer Vikkuaḥ*:

> Levy Isaac aus Berdyczow, Wolf Sitomirer, Josua Dunwitzer, Elimelech Lezaysker, Nachum Tczarnoboler, Marcus Lachowitzer, Salman Lasner, Suszettanepoler, Efraim Rab Maschchis, Israel Magid aus Kozanitz, Isaak Lancuter, Marcus Tczarnoboler, Samuel Amdurer, Mayer Szebser, Marcus Manwer.

The names in this list are exactly the same as those which appeared in the first edition of *Sefer Vikkuaḥ* in 1798.[75] However, it seems that in the manuscript of the planned new edition, Perl corrected several names according to the list in *Shever Posh'im* (or *Zimrat Am ha-Areẓ*) because the Latin transcription of the censor's document agreed with the spelling of the list published in the Mitnaggedic work by David of Maków.[76] The mechanical bureaucracy and the ignorance of the censor's transcription of these names was characteristic. Suszettanepoler[77] was Zushe of Hanipol (Annopol), famous rebbe and brother of Elimelekh of Leżajsk; "the Rabbi of Naskhiz," i.e., the Rabbi of Niesuchojcze in Volhynia was corrupted to read "Efraim Rab Maschis";[78] Mordecai Yonever, that is, from the town of Janów, became Marcus Manwer.[79]

Considering the careless manner of transcribing these names, it is not surprising that the crass Galician censors did not find it necessary to learn something about the men they included in the list. It did not matter to them that except for Mordecai of Chernobyl, all the other Hasidic leaders mentioned had long been deceased, and except for Elimelekh of Leżajsk and Jacob Isaac of Łańcut, none had ever had any connection with Galicia.

On the basis of this "accurate" information from the censor's office, the Galician provincial presidency issued a circular on February 6, 1827, to five district offices and to the municipality of Brody, bringing to their attention the list of the fifteen "ringleaders." The five district offices of Wadowice, Stryj, Zloczów, Przemyśl, and Brzeżany and the city of Brody were chosen, as the circular states, "in consequence of information received" that four of the "ringleaders" resided in the territories of these districts and cities: Marcus Lachowitzer[80] supposedly lived in Lachowice in the district of Wadowice or in Lachowice in the district of Stryj; Samuel Amdurer[81] was indentified with a certain Samuel Hasid of Brody; Meyer Szebser[82] was to be found in Przemyśl or in Przemyślany (district of Brzeżany); and, according to the same source, Marcus Manwer[83] lived in Tyśmienica in the district of Stanisławów.

The circular alluded to the fact that sometime earlier the district offices had received an order from the police directorate to supervise the "religious fanatics" among the Jews who were known as Hasidim or Beshtians. Now the district offices were instructed to determine whether a particular individual designated as a resident of a certain district was an adherent of the Hasidic sect, or a fanatic, or incited Hasidim to violate the law through rebellion against His Imperial Majesty, or whether this individual or other "Israelites" possessed books on the list.[84]

The reports from the district offices reached the provincial presidency in 1827 and the beginning of 1828. According to one such report, filed by the district chief of Brzeżany on March 8, 1827, Meyer Maner of Przemyślany,[85] "nicknamed 'Schabser,'"[86] was denounced by the Maskilim as a member of the Hasidim. Maner, *moreh hora'ah* (a "religious teacher") there,[87] was charged with counterfeiting. After a lengthy investigation, the charge was dropped.[88] The report went on to observe that the Hasidim were a sect of very superstitious Jews and their rabbis had long been suspected of exploiting the foolishness of their adherents in order to collect money from them and send part of it to Jerusalem. An investigation was conducted in Stryj against Hersh of Żydaczów. As for the rest, the district chief said he did not notice any of the vices of the Hasidim alleged in the manuscript of *Sefer Vikkuaḥ*.[89]

The district chief of Wadowice reported on March 2, 1827, that it was proven that Marcus Lachowitzer did not reside in the village of Lachowice in his district "because no Jew is tolerated in the barony of Sucha to which this village belongs." Moreover, no signs of this sect had been noticed in the entire district. He concluded that there were two other villages named Lachowice in the district of Stryj and, therefore, it was possible that Marcus Lachowitzer lived there.[90]

The district chief of Stryj, Hübel, added to his own report that of his commissioner whom he sent especially to Lachowice. This district commissioner learned that neither a Marcus Lachowitzer nor any other Hasidim were there. The few Jews residing there, some paupers and some who supplied rags to the local paper factory, were far removed from any kind of sectarianism or kabbalistic machinations. In his own report, dated March 31, 1827, Hübel asserted that the Hasidim had not yet insinuated themselves into the district of Stryj, and he presented as evidence the fact that the district kosher meat tax lessee had not been the target of any attack to date. The district chief gave the following characterization of Hasidism, based on information he possessed concerning previous investigations in other Galician districts:

The Hasidim are Talmudists but differ from other talmudic Jews in that they tend to lighten the burdens of the talmudic commandments in cases of poverty and need if these commandments hinder the earning of one's livelihood. They call themselves Hasidim, that is, "more pious Jews," because they believe it to be their duty to make life easier and to support their poor and unfortunate "coreligionists." With respect to Christians, they are neither better nor worse than the rest of the Talmudists, and are governed by the same principles of aversion to Gentiles as the other Jews. Therefore, the opinion of the Supreme Imperial Police and Censorship Office that it is the Hasidim who advocate hatred of the government is absolutely false. On the contrary, as long as the Hasidim strive primarily to fortify piety they are less harmful—in the "civil-moral sense"—than the rest of the talmudic Jews who restrict themselves mostly to the ceremonial forms of religion. However, the district chief of Stryj contended that too great an increase in the number of Hasidim would, indirectly, be detrimental to the government. That is to say, if "the Hasidim did not observe the talmudic laws concerning the use of meat and candles as strictly as other Jews, they might cause a decline in the revenue from the kosher meat and candle tax."[91]

This report of the district office of Stryj was characteristic in its blending of fact and fiction. The district chief was correct in noting that the Hasidim were lenient in interpreting laws and customs and in identifying greater piety, charity, and "attention to the poor unfortunate Jews" as chief characteristics of this movement. At the same time, he greatly exaggerated the suspicion that the spread of Hasidism was liable to reduce the consumption of meat and candles. And while his statement that the Hasidim harassed the tax lessees was correct, the inference he drew demonstrated not only his ignorance of what was taking place in his own district but also the lack of continuity and organization in the functioning of the Austrian officials of the time. For example, his predecessor as the district chief of Stryj, Milbacher, said that he had conducted several investigations against Hersh of Żydaczów, considered to be one of the greatest authorities among the Hasidic leaders in Galicia at that time, and even had him arrested once.

The Reports of Mosler on the Hasidim of Brody

The district commissioner of Brody, Mosler, submitted two reports to the provincial presidency, one concerning Hasidim in Brody and the wanted "ringleader," Samuel Amdurer, and the other a detailed memorandum about the Hasidic movement in Galicia in general.

In the report concerning Hasidism in Brody, dated March 19, 1827, he said that a certain Samuel Ostrowski, alias Osterer, alias Shmuelekhl ("Schmulichen"),[92] who had been living in Brody for several years, might be the same Samuel Amdurer mentioned in the governor's edict who held a *minyan* in his residence without a permit. The commissioner listed by name sixteen of Samuel Ostrowski's closest adherents, three of whom also bore the family name Ostrowski. Besides these adherents, he had information concerning four more men suspected of belonging to the Hasidic sect: the district rabbi Lazer Landau, Leyb Te'omim, Alexander Iwiszor, and Michael Kristianpoller. None of these Hasidim in Brody were known to be either rebels against the Emperor or idolators. They were distinguished only by "customary fanaticism" in the matters of fasting and prayer.[93]

Like the district chief of Stryj, the district commissioner of Brody also demonstrated that he knew little about Jewish religious life in the area of his jurisdiction. Four rabbis of Brody who were counted among the greatest talmudic authorities of the time[94] and known as staunch Mitnaggedim were denounced by him as adherents of Hasidism. He altered the name of Alexander Schor to read "Iwiszor" because that is how he garbled the name of Schor's forefather's treatise, *Tevu'ot Shor*. Considering such "erudition," it is no wonder that he, like his superiors, counted Samuel Amdurer among the living and endeavored to prove to them that this man was the same Samuel Hasid in Brody.

The second detailed report by the same commissioner of Brody, a memorandum concerning Hasidism in Galicia dated March 18, 1827, was remarkable for the accuracy of its information and its pointed characterization of the Hasidic movement. This can be explained by the fact that at the end of this memorandum the commissioner recommended the "Mosaist," Joseph Perl of Tarnopol, as someone who could confirm the truth of this report. Apparently, the commissioner had written his memorandum based on information that Perl had provided him during previous official investigations of Hasidism, most recently in connection with the affair of the fifteen "ringleaders" of *Sefer Vikkuaḥ*.

In the preface to his memorandum, the commissioner of Brody cited the following sources: his report of 1815, which he had submitted to the provincial presidency through the mediation of the Lemberg police directorate;[95] copies of the periodical *Sulamith;*[96] official investigations of Hasidism that were conducted in connection with the case of the rebbe of Ropczyce;[97] the second volume of Peter Beer's history of Jewish sects, published in Brünn in 1825. On the basis of these documents the commissioner gave the following characterization of the "sect":

1. The Hasidim were tolerated under an old ordinance from the "highest authority."[98] During the course of his thirty years of service, the commissioner had met Hasidim in many districts of Galicia. It was very easy to recognize them since they went about with bare throat and rolled-up sleeves, and were usually dirtily and shabbily dressed. He had come across many communities of this sect in the district of Miedzyrzec in "West Galicia,"[99] where he had served as district commissioner in 1808 and personally met the local "wonder worker," Rebbe Meyer,[100] to whom many Hasidim flocked. However, since that time the sect had spread quickly in Galicia and even more so in Russia, in Moldavia, and even in Hungary.[101] There was a grave of a rebbe in the town of Leżajsk, in the district of Rzeszów, and also in another city[102] to which Hasidim made pilgrimages.

2. The Hasidim were wholly devoted to one another. Because they prized the zaddikim above all and obeyed them unconditionally, they always quarreled with their brethren, the Mosaists[103] and Talmudists. The Hasidim so irritated the other Jews that they stopped at nothing to get rid of them.

The "commonest" Jews belonged to this sect—the lazy, deceitful, and hypocritical ones who had no profession and were usually common tavernkeepers, swindlers, and "soothsayers." A Hasid had such absolute faith that God did not forsake any Jew who conducted himself in accordance with the ways of Hasidism that he was convinced that he could win a prize even if he had not played the lottery, because with God all things were possible.[104]

3. This sect was unfit for social life, for it was afraid of non-Jews, i.e., Gentiles—called them idolators or unbelievers and persecutors of their religion, and bore feelings of hatred and vengefulness toward them. The commissioner concluded from this that an oath by a Hasid in a suit between a Jew and a Christian was highly suspect, for the Hasid regarded it as a commandment to cheat a Gentile and do him harm.

4. The Hasidim's faith in the zaddik and their veneration of him were unlimited. They contended that one had to renounce one's own rationality and convictions and submit to the zaddik's command. To them, the zaddik was the highest authority; he was a king to whom

God had entrusted dominion over the world.[105] As such, the zaddik had the power to overthrow the monarch and destroy his entire nation.

5. Hence, one had to conclude that this sect was incapable of love of the fatherland or loyalty to the monarch and that it consisted of a closed group of hypocritically pious men.

Inasmuch as this sect was growing progressively more powerful, encouraged idleness, infected others, and was a burden to the people, the government should be concerned with curtailing its activities. However, it would not be advisable to outlaw this sect since this would only strengthen it as a secret organization. The commissioner contended that it would be much more practical to issue three ordinances, which would:

(a) abolish all private *minyanim*, both for the Hasidim and the "Mosaic" Jews, and permit worship only in the synagogues proper; (b) enforce the decree of Joseph II which had prohibited the distinctive Jewish garb;[106] and (c) renew, with all severity, the prohibition against the wanderings of the Hasidic rebbes.

Commenting on these ordinances, the commissioner said he hoped that the prohibition of Jewish garb would bring the Hasidim closer to "civilized" society and help to socialize them. The prohibition against the rebbes would check their activity, weaken their influence, and curtail their amassing fortunes.[107] The commissioner said he had not found it necessary to justify his first proposal to abolish the *minyanim* for reasons he considered to be self-evident. This proposal clearly demonstrates that he was influenced by Perl. A detailed memorandum suggesting the temporary suppression of all *minyanim* and *battei midrash* was submitted by Perl in 1838.

The district chief of Przemyśl reported on November 24, 1827, that neither Mayer Szebser[108] nor any other of the fifteen "ringleaders" of the Hasidim resided in his district. The number of Hasidim in the district, however, was rather high; in that city alone there were more than one hundred Hasidim. He stated that in the religious realm there was essentially no distinction between the Hasidim and other Jews. The Hasidim did not pray in the synagogue but rather in rented *shtiblekh*. During prayer they behaved like madmen, clapping their hands, stamping their feet, shaking their heads continuously and beating against the walls. They could be recognized by their long side curls and bare throats and by their distinctive behavior when eating and drinking. He counted among their "vices" their unusual solidarity, antagonism toward the government's educational measures, and "debauchery," as well as their alms collections, which were purportedly for the Jews in the "orphaned land of Judea," but which were really turned over to zaddikim who preached fanaticism and spent the money on feasts.

In summarizing, the report said that although the Hasidim were not rebels or idolators, they were of dubious value to the state. The report ended with an enumeration of the prohibited books discovered at the Hasidic meeting place in Przemyśl.[109]

The latest report to reach Lemberg was that of the district office of Stanisławów, which arrived on February 16, 1828. The district chief reported that his investigation concerning the "Beshtians" produced no results: no "Marcus Manwer" resided in Tyśmienica, nor were any forbidden books found during the investigation.[110]

As a result of the search for the fifteen "ringleaders," the decrees against the Hasidic rebbes and the *minyanim* were enforced more severely than before. On January 2, 1827, Perl informed the district office at Tarnopol that Hersh of Żydaczów was intending to spend the Sabbath at Zbaraż, whereupon the district office ordered the town authorities to watch secretly for the arrival of the "Irrlehrer" (teacher of false doctrine) and turn him out of Zbaraż.[111]

Prince Lobkowitz's Final Report

Nearly three years later, the Galician provincial presidency completed its report concerning the sensational affair of the fifteen Hasidic "ringleaders," and Prince Lobkowitz, the new Galician governor, sent it to Sedlnitzky in Vienna on January 31, 1829.

The report asserted that according to the Hebrew censor in Lemberg,[112] the Hasidim were not at all portrayed as rebels against His Imperial Majesty in *Sefer Vikkuaḥ*. Such an idea could only have been derived from too narrow an interpretation of a statement in the manuscript in which the Hasidim were accused of introducing innovations into the Jewish religious system against the imperial command.[113]

The governor cited a report, which he enclosed,[114] of the Lemberg police directorate stating that the majority of the Hasidic leaders mentioned in this book had long been dead. Similarly, no prohibited books had been found in Galician Jewish homes. He concluded on the basis of this police report that this sect was not really as dangerous and evil as described in *Sefer Vikkuaḥ*. The governor then characterized the Hasidic movement based on the relevant chapter in Peter Beer's book on Jewish sects, as well as on reports that he had received from various places. He noted that the official reports had confirmed Beer's portrayal of the Hasidim. Moreover, the trustworthiness of Beer's description of the Hasidim was further supported by the fact that he had received his information from Perl,[115] who was himself a Hasid in his youth and only later broke with the sect.[116]

According to the governor's report, the sect had been founded about seventy years earlier in Russia by a certain Israel Besht of Medzhibozh, who was famous as a learned man and a miracle worker. The sect was notable for its exaggerated, meticulous observance of all religious customs and for its hatred of the "Talmudists." Its adherents defied all governmental edicts regarding education and enlightenment, and they put boundless trust in their leaders, the zaddikim.

The zaddikim received huge incomes from their followers, and even after their deaths their children continued to draw this income. The governor contended that the Hasidim were being deceived by the zaddikim, who exercised complete control over them and manipulated them for their own advantage. He also believed that the revenue from the kosher meat and candle-lighting taxes depended to a great extent on the Hasidim. Those tax lessees who came to terms with the zaddikim, both through gifts and exemptions from the tax, collected more revenue than those who did not use such means.

The governor reported that the most important centers of Hasidism in earlier times were Ropczyce,[117] Żydaczów,[118] Bełz,[119] Jarosław,[120] Buczacz,[121] Stratyn,[122] Sambor,[123] Radziechów,[124] Chołojów,[125] and Brody.[126] He stated that at present there were only a small number of Hasidim and that he believed fanaticism had abated because the impoverished Galician Jews could no longer satisfy the avarice of the rebbes.

The fact that Hasidim walked about "with the upper part of their chest exposed" was regarded as a secret sign by which the Hasidim could be recognized, since all other Jews buttoned their shirts up to the neck. And to show that Hasidism still had its adherents here and there, he adduced the example of a zaddik who had recently died in Brody: the Hasidim cut up his clothes into pieces and kept them as relics.[127]

The governor concluded that the Hasidim were a fanatic sect which in certain respects could become a menace to the state. He cited the ordinances concerning the Hasidim about which the provincial presidency had submitted a report to Sedlnitzky after May 8, 1825,[128] but felt that it would be expedient to again point out the most important leaders of this sect to the police departments so that they could take necessary measures if they noticed any suspicious activities among the zaddikim. In the governor's opinion, it would also be expedient to prohibit the Hasidic leaders from leaving their places of residence without adequate reason, and in such exceptional cases they should be obliged to inform the authorities of their destinations so they could be kept under constant surveillance. However, he would postpone the issuance of these decrees until he received the approval and necessary instructions from Sedlnitzky. In his opinion, the surest way to eradicate this sect or, at least, to render it innocuous, was to disseminate among the Jews true enlightenment and education, which had been neglected since the abolition of the German-Jewish schools.[129]

The report of the Galician governor, Prince Lobkowitz, consisted on the one hand of several interesting details concerning the contemporary Hasidic movement in Galicia and, on the other, gave evidence of his extraordinary ignorance of local Jewish life. His assertion that the number of Hasidim had sharply declined was far from the truth, and his explanation of this alleged fact was naïve. The governor knew so little about the social nature of Hasidism that he regarded the impoverishment of the Jewish masses as a factor that would weaken the Hasidic movement. His comment about Hasidic dress demonstrates how superficially the Galician administration studied the reports of its officials. For example, the commissioner of Brody had written in his report about the Hasidim that "one *recognizes* [emphasis added] such a Jew very easily; he goes about with a bare throat. . . ." The governor's office probably interpreted this to mean that the Hasidim actually intended their garb to reveal them only to their comrades, but such a proficient policeman as the commissioner of Brody recognized them at a glance. Thus, on the basis of this interpretation, the governor of Galicia told the police president, Sedlnitzky, that going about with a bare throat was a secret sign by which the Hasidim were recognized!

More important than these examples of the Galician administration's ignorance, however, was the fact that the governor, Prince Lobkowitz, concluded his report just as his predecessor von Hauer had in 1817, with the advice that the most expedient means to combat Hasidism would be to disseminate education and enlightenment among the Jews of Galicia. However, just as it did twelve years earlier, the government now demonstrated that it did not have the slightest intention of taking concrete steps in the direction of raising the cultural level of the Jews.

On September 19, 1829, sometime after the Galician governor had submitted his report, with its conclusion concerning the necessity of educating Jewry, to the supreme censorship office, Count Sedlnitzky sent him a note[130] to the effect that the director of the *Deutsch-Israelitische Hauptschule* in Tarnopol, Perl, had submitted a manuscript of a German brochure entitled "Die Erziehung der jüdischen Jugend in Galizien, wie sie ist und wie sie sein soll" (The Education of

Jewish Youth in Galicia, as it is and as it should be) to the imperial censor for a printing permit. Sedlnitzky noted that although the censor viewed the tendencies of this brochure with favor, he wanted to know the governor's opinion concerning a publication permit because the condition of the Jewish institutions of learning in Galicia was shown in a poor light.

In his reply,[131] Prince Lobkowitz dwelt at length on the contents of Perl's brochure. He believed that everything Perl said in the first part of the brochure concerning the present state of schooling among the Jews was absolutely correct. Despite all the efforts of the government, which originally established German-Jewish schools under Emperor Joseph II and later gave Jewish children access to the Christian schools, Galician Jewry was on a very low moral plane. The Jews were governed by prejudices and the most foolish superstitions, which were the source of their depravity. This condition was fostered by the dominant mode of education of Jewish children, that is, by the *ḥadarim*. The governor noted that even before Perl, many excellent gentile as well as Jewish writers—for example, Friedländer and Calmanson—had attested to the fact that this education deadened the intellect and the spirit and destroyed the morals of men. However, the governor had reservations about the second half of Perl's brochure where he dealt with the question of how Jewish youth should be educated. He said that Perl was correct in appealing to the Jewish population to discard its superstitions and prejudices and to give its children a better education "with its own means," but saw his suggestion of abolishing the existing Jewish schools and introducing new schools patterned after the one in Tarnopol as reflecting badly on the government, since such a project was based on the tacit assumption that its previous efforts had been "fruitless and useless"; therefore it would be ill-advised to publish the brochure. The governor considered Perl's project impractical because Galicia did not have the teachers necessary for Jewish schools, and the Galician Jews had already demonstrated their distrust of teachers from "foreign provinces."

Finally, the governor made this telling remark: "If the government does not refuse the applicant [Joseph Perl] permission to publish his brochure, which essentially does not contain anything that is contrary to morality, religion, and the state, it should be pointed out to him that he should first correct the numerous grammatical errors. . . ." One may conclude from this that the man who devoted his life to the germanization of Galician Jewry did not, it seems, write correct German!

The intensification of the reactionary tendencies of the Galician administration during the course of the previous several years was clearly expressed in this official report by Prince Lobkowitz. Lobkowitz, like his predecessor, Franz von Hauer, proclaimed the improvement of the state of education to be one of the government's most important tasks in regard to Galician Jewry. However, von Hauer at least had been consistent enough to give full support to Perl's project of 1819 to reopen the German–Jewish state schools, while Prince Lobkowitz merely gave Sedlnitzky the answer that his superior desired. He understood Sedlnitzky's insinuation concerning the criticism of schooling among the Jews in Perl's brochure, and therefore endeavored to prove that this brochure indirectly embarrassed the Austrian government's previous educational policy with regard to Galician Jewry. Since he foresaw the government's changing attitude, he advanced the idea that the Jews must supply their children with the necessary education "through their own means." The hypocrisy of his arguments against the plan to establish state schools for Jewish children was quite transparent. He complained that there was a lack of qualified teachers to staff such schools, as if private schools, which he did favor, did not require such teachers. He pretended to forget that instructors can be trained over the course of several years in teachers' colleges. But the slogan of "private education for Jewish children" was actually most admirably suited to the objectives of the national and cultural policy of reactionary Austrian absolutism. In the first place, the government would not have to spend money on German state schools for the Jews. Second, with a private system, education could be prevented from spreading to the masses and thus becoming a revolutionary factor.

Count Sedlnitzky's Decree and Its Aftermath

Only after the exchange of letters concerning Perl's brochure did the president of the Supreme Imperial Police and Censorship Office, Count Sedlnitzky, reply to the Galician governor, on November 11, 1829, concerning his report of January 31 about the Hasidim.

Sedlnitzky related that the Lemberg censor and the Viennese censor, Joseph Berger, were divided over the question of whether the Hasidim constituted a threat. On the basis of the documents they presented and of the Hasidic works which Sedlnitzky forwarded to the governor, he sided with the imperial censor's assessment of the sect as detrimental and "dangerous to the interests of the government administration" because the Hasidim manifested separatism in relation to the "tolerated" Jewish community, that is, the state-recognized *kehillah*; the zaddikim had attained absolute authority in both religious and secular affairs, which could work to the detriment of the Hasidim's loyalty to the monarch; they revered the founder of the sect, the Ba'al Shem Tov, in a superstitious fashion and regarded him as a miracle worker; and they were opposed to any type of enlightenment.

Sedlnitzky again demanded that the governor exercise the greatest severity in the censorship of Hasidic books, and he approved all the suggestions to curtail the pernicious effects of the sect which he had submitted in 1825 and in his report of January 1829. As to the manuscript of *Sefer Vikkuaḥ*, permission to print it was out of the question in light of the evaluation of the sect. The publication of this book would lead to a polemic and arouse interest in this "religious party" which, according to all indications, was in a state of decline.

In conclusion, the governor was instructed to inspect the Jewish printing shops in Lemberg and Żółkiew, and to control strictly their publishing activity.[132]

Sedlnitzky's decree, then, actually reiterated the opinion concerning the Hasidim which the governor had expressed in his report in January of the same year. There, too, it was pointed out that Hasidism was an undesirable movement that was liable to become antistate both because of its blind faith in zaddikim and because of its struggle against "enlightenment," that is, germanization. Sedlnitzky accepted the governor's word that the Hasidic movement was progressively losing its influence.

In accordance with Sedlnitzky's order, on December 18, 1829, the governor, Prince Lobkowitz, issued a new circular to all the district offices concerning the Hasidim.[133] The district offices were again instructed to keep the Hasidic movement under surveillance and "to take immediate concrete measures" if they observed any mischief on the part of the sect. The decree prohibiting the Hasidic leaders from leaving their places of residence "without a significant and adequately proven reason" was repeated. In conclusion, an order appeared which demonstrated, more than anything before, the extraordinary confusion and thoughtlessness of the Austrian bureaucracy. The attention of the district offices was again called to the fifteen Hasidic "ringleaders" in accordance with the list of the decree of 1827! Even the garbled names remained the same, including that of Mayer Szebser. The Galician bureaucrats identified him with Meyer of Przemyślany, whose family name was given by the district office of Brzeżany as Maner. Only the name of "Suszettanepoler" was correctly changed to read Zushe of Hanipole. Marcus Manwer (the corruption of Mordecai Yanever, that is, Mordecai of Janów) was now called Marcus Mamwer, and the district offices were asked to take particular note of the change in the family name! And all of this was written after the provincial presidency had established in its report of January to Sedlnitzky that the majority of the fifteen ringleaders were dead and that the remainder did not reside in Galicia!

On August 30, 1831, the Galician governor submitted a report to Sedlnitzky concerning the ordinances against the Hasidim. The first part of the report—the second part recorded the results of the investigation of the Jewish printing shops—concluded with the following statement: "I believe that hereby everything was done that should have been in this matter if one does not want to go too far and undertake measures that would not be in accord with the laws of toleration sanctioned most supremely by His Majesty."[134]

This explicit citation of the principle of religious toleration actually signified a further change in the Austrian government's policy with regard to the Hasidic movement. Due to political motives, which have already been indicated, the government decided not to suppress the movement completely, but to keep it within fixed bounds. The subsequent episodes in the relations of the authorities with Hasidism in Galicia proved that from then on the government consistently followed this charted course.

In March 1838, Perl informed the authorities about a collection of funds solicited by Hasidim for the benefit of Israel of Ruzhin that was illegally sent out of the country.[135] In the circular issued by the provincial presidency to the district offices,[136] they were requested to investigate the matter; but in contrast to previous occasions, there were no orders for special supervision of the Hasidic movement.

The Sachar Report: The Unintended Turning Point

Sachar, the director of the Lemberg police directorate,[137] took the opportunity of writing a report on the investigation of this matter to submit a detailed memorandum about the Hasidic movement in general.[138] This memorandum, which is the most detailed official report of this period about Hasidism, was partially written in the stereotyped style seen in the previous official reports. However, it did reveal new details about Hasidic practices and about the Hasidic leaders in Galicia at that time, and closed with harsher conclusions than any of the previous reports.

According to this report, the basic traits of Hasidism were as follows:

The Hasidim valued kabbalistic and Hasidic literature over the Bible and the Talmud; they were lenient with respect to the "outdated and often burdensome ceremonies" which weighed heavily upon the people and also involved large expenses. Therefore, the common people eagerly embraced the new teaching. Sachar, after correctly designating Hasidism as "pietistic mysticism,"[139] went on to state that "despite all the mystical absurdities, there is a spiritually vigorous element which gives vitality to Hasidism and which until now has not been successfully combatted."

Sachar regarded the faith in zaddikim as the most harmful element of Hasidism. He called them egoists, swindlers, and deceivers who spread superstitions among the people for their own self-interest. The zaddikim undertook to exorcise dibbuks, and they distributed conjurations, amulets, and nostrums against diseases, or even against punishment in a criminal trial. As examples of such nostrums and amulets, the police president pointed out the material found during a search of the home of a certain Goldsohn and also enclosed a remedy written by the rebbe Judah Hersh of Stratyn for his Hasid Isaac Moyshes in Gołogóry, whose wife had suffered severe pains while giving birth.[140]

He regarded the superstitions which the zaddikim spread among the Hasidim as harmful not only from the viewpoint of the physical and financial well-being of the masses but also from the state's viewpoint. Thus, for example, he told of the Hasidim's belief that the shirt of a deceased zaddik was protection for a murderer, and his pants, atonement for incest, while payment to a zaddik was an atonement for any sin. The absolute discipline of the Hasidim and their unconditional obedience to the zaddik were regarded as a direct threat to the government. The Hasidim were convinced that the government could last only as long as it obeyed the commands of the zaddik; otherwise heaven decreed that the government would fall. Since the Hasidim believed the zaddik ruled the world, transgressing the laws of the state was permissible since a law had no substance if it contradicted the zaddik's will. The Hasidim were also said to deem it a good deed to murder an informer.

The Hasidim, being steeped in superstitions and permeated by fanaticism, were the avowed enemies of science and enlightenment and excommunicated everyone who opposed the spread of their movement. Drunkenness was widespread among them because they regarded it as a good deed to drink when experiencing sadness or melancholy. They also were idlers, hypocrites, and beggars; very few businessmen were to be found among them. Hasidism and its faith in zaddikim were the chief cause of the sorry state of the Jews in Galicia as compared with the Jews in Bohemia and Vienna. The Galician Jews did not want to merge with the rest of the population in regard to customs, rites, and dress. They did not want to become artisans, farmers, artists, and soldiers but to occupy themselves with trade and swindling, which were rooted in their tradition and in accord with their nature.

During the fall festivals, masses of Hasidim converged on the residences of the rebbes, and the director of police asserted that these gatherings were particularly sinister. The landowners tolerated this because such assemblies were a good source of profit to them.

The police director listed the following zaddikim in Galicia:

Simon Mareles in Jarosław, Przemyśl district.[141]
Hersh "the attendant" in Rymanów, Sanok district.[142]
Meyer Mayer in Przemyślany, Brzeżany district.[143]
Isaac Judah in Wybranówka, Brzeżany district.[144]
Ḥayyim N.[145] in Kosów, Kolomyja district.[146]
Osher N. in Rubiszów.[147]
Judah Hersh Brandwein in Stratyn, Brzeżany district.[148]
Hersh Meylekh N. in Dynów, Sanok district.[149]
Sholem N. in Kamionka, Zloczów district.[150]
Meyer Julius in Krakowiec, Przemyśl district.[151]
Isaac N. in Nadworna, Stanisławów district.[152]
Sholem N. in Bełz, Żółkiew district.[153]

These twelve zaddikim were the chief leaders of Hasidism in Galicia, but Hasidim were to be found in almost every Galician town. Even in Lemberg, where there was no Hasidic leader, there were *klayzlekh* (small synagogues) where Hasidim prayed "in accord with their own very noisy ritual." The police director listed six such small Hasidic houses of prayer in Lemberg besides two small synagogues know as "Ḥadushim."[154] He reported that he had ordered these *klayzlekh* guarded so that necessary steps could be taken in the event that something forbidden occurred. According to the information he had received, the sect was spreading rapidly throughout Galicia, Hungary, and Russia.

Given these facts, Police Director Sachar contended that the Galician provincial presidency should reconsider its policy with regard to Hasidism. The provincial presidency ought to reflect upon the question of revising the governor's ordinance of August 22, 1824, according to which the government did not deem it necessary "to influence the various religious rites of the Jews."[155] Since "fanatical enthusiasm" of the Hasidim was said to be based on religious rites, the government ought to intercede in matters of religious practice before this "fanaticism" became too entrenched.

Sachar remarked that his proposal could be averted, pointing out that the assemblies of the Hasidim were prohibited, as were those of other "brotherhoods," and that Jews who wanted to conduct a *minyan* must, in addition to paying the tax, furnish certification that they were not "Hasidim or fanatics."[156] However, in reality such certificates were worthless, for they were issued by the district rabbis who were mostly sympathizers with the sect. As an example, he cited the Rabbi of Lemberg, Jacob Ornstein, who received Israel of Ruzhin amiably and treated him with "unlimited" honor when he was in Lemberg. The Rabbi of Lemberg was known as an adherent of the Hasidim, and their *klayzlekh* would certainly not have been established had he not issued the members of these *minyanim* the necessary certificates. It was the police director's opinion that Jacob Ornstein also had a hand in the events in Tarnopol, where the appointment of a district rabbi (Solomon Judah Rapoport) who did not belong to the sect caused disturbances.[157]

The events in Tarnopol, according to Sachar's opinion, demonstrated that the Hasidic movement excelled in obstinacy and insubordination, which was characteristic of the spirit of all sects. This disobedience had to be crushed at the outset before it grew into a threat.

The police director concluded that a religious movement which had no regard for the laws of the state and for the authorities, and which, moreover, carried within itself the germ of intolerance, could lay no claim to freedom and toleration. Such a movement had to be held in check lest it degenerate to the level of impudence and wantonness. He said he would leave it to the "wisdom" of the provincial presidency to decide, but did suggest that his memorandum be sent to all the district offices and to the police commissions in Podgórze (a suburb of Cracow) and Brody so that they could express their opinions as to whether the sect was as dangerous as he had depicted and "whether false teachings and evil ought not to be combatted with rigorous means." He invited these officials to express their opinions on the basis of both their own experience and observations and their questioning of objective and educated "Israelites."

In a note dated June 17, 1838, the Galician provincial presidency rejected the recommendation of the Lemberg police directorate, citing the following reasons: While it had been established that the Hasidic movement intended in both theory and practice to obstruct the education of the Jewish people and to "fetter the spirit of Jewry in chains of superstition," and that these tendencies were contradictory to the government's objectives, there was essentially no distinction between Hasidism and the spirit of the "blatant form of Judaism which unfortunately still predominates in this imperial province." Therefore, a legal prohibition of the sect would be impractical.[158]

Thus, the government first realized in 1838 that Hasidism was so widespread among the Jews and so closely bound up with orthodoxy that it would be impossible to suppress it completely through a legal prohibition. Undoubtedly, this realization was a factor in liberalizing the government's policy with regard to Hasidism. But the primary reason for this change was that the government had altered its fundamental position toward this religious mass movement.

For the same reasons, the government did not seriously consider Perl's memorandum of March the same year concerning official supervision of the *battei midrash*, the *ḥevrot* (religious societies), and the *mikvot*, let alone the even more far-reaching plan of the district chief of Tarnopol to deal with the *battei midrash* and *ḥevrot* in accordance with the regulations regarding *minyanim*.[159] When, in the same year, Perl submitted a detailed proposal concerning the life-long appointment of rabbis and *dayanim* (the rabbis' assistants who resolved questions of ritual cleanliness and settled minor disputes) and the official supervision of *shoḥatim* and *mohalim*, the government rejected it on the grounds that even according to Perl's information, almost all the rabbis and *dayanim* were adherents of Hasidism and therefore it was impossible to find appropriate, enlightened rabbinical candidates in Galicia.[160]

In rejecting Perl's plan, the government resorted to a pretext similar to that used in rejecting his 1829 plan. Then the authorities acted as if they were unaware of the fact that with the establishment of Jewish teachers' colleges the necessary cadre of Jewish teachers could be trained. In 1838 they disregarded the possibility of educating enlightened rabbis in a rabbinical seminary. In so doing, the government illustrated the hypocrisy of Austrian absolutism.

In the following years occasional local investigations of Hasidic leaders were initiated—by denunciations, as in the past. Thus in January 1839, a denunciation of the "miracle workers" Rebbe Sholem of Bełz and Rebbe Meyer of Przemyślany by Police Inspector Ungar was submitted to the provincial presidency by the Lemberg police directorate.[161] Again, the provincial presidency instructed the relevant district offices in Żółkiew and Brzeżany to "act in accordance with the existing regulations," but there is nothing in the archives to indicate whether or not this was implemented. Similarly, there is no record of the effects of the denunciation in 1841 by Joseph Tepper, a Maskil from Tarnopol, of the Hasidim in Buczacz.[162]

The Revolution of 1848, which brought an end to the disenfranchisement of Galician Jewry, also closed the chapter of police persecutions of the Hasidic movement.

4

The Austrian Censorship of Jewish Books

The Travesty of Sedlnitzky as Chief Censor

The reaction that gripped Austria after the defeat of Napoleon was more keenly felt in the ideological sphere than elsewhere. And it was Prince Metternich who devoted himself to the preservation of the privileges of the absolute monarch, the nobility, and the Catholic clergy against Jacobinism, not only in Austria but throughout Europe. In Austria, this effort was institutionalized in the form of *Die Oberste Polizei und Zensurhofstelle* (the Supreme Imperial Police and Censorship Office). This institution, which controlled the fate of every inhabitant of the monarchy, was headed by Count Joseph Sedlnitzky (vice-president from 1815 to 1817 and then president until the Revolution of 1848). His role in relation to Metternich was characterized best by the epithets bestowed upon him: "the lackey of Metternich," "Metternich's monkey and poodle," and "the dust on the Prince's footsoles."[1]

Of limited intellect, Sedlnitzky turned the censor's office into an institution which became no less notorious for its folly than for its rigor. The history of Austrian censorship during the three decades of Sedlnitzky's presidency was described by his biographer as "an inexhaustible source of humor and crude entertainment."[2] The suspiciousness of Austrian censorship evidently knew no bounds, for even the works of Franz Grillparzer, that most patriotic of Austrian poets, were banned. The performance of Schiller's drama *Wallenstein* was permitted by the censor in 1845 only on condition that the play begin from the fourth act.[3] Schiller's *Fiesco* was "slightly" altered by order of the emperor Francis I in 1827 so that at the end of the play the leaders of the rebellion had to throw themselves at the feet of the Doge and beg his forgiveness![4] In a book which gave a retrospective view of the Napoleonic wars, the sentence "The Austrians retreated" was ordered by the censor to be changed to "The French advanced." When a Viennese newspaper reported of an eminent prince that "he is ill" the censor corrected the sentence to read that "he is indisposed [*unpässlich*]."[5]

The censors demonstrated the same ludicrous fear in expurgating the most innocent passages in works of Hebrew literature. When S. D. Luzzatto wanted to paint an ideal vision of the future in his poem "Emek he-Ḥaruz," the censor ordered him to change the sentence "The kingdom of insolence had ended" to read "The evil of insolence had ended," and "How far shall injustice reign" to "How far shall injustice judge."[6] Evidently, it was clear to the censor that these phrases would unavoidably call to mind Metternich's Austrian monarchy.

These are only a few examples of the ridiculous lengths to which the Austrian censors went in order to prevent the printing of utterances that might be considered disloyal to the reigning absolutism. The censor, however, was no less sensitive in matters which might prove unacceptable to the all-powerful Catholic clergy and to government policy in the religious realm. It was the aim of absolutism to subordinate all expressions of religious life to government regulation and to suppress any religious movement that slipped out of its control.

The attitude toward Hasidism was a case in point. Fear of mysticism, fanaticism, and visionary ideologies greatly influenced Austrian censorship about Hasidic and kabbalistic works, just as it had determined the policy of the Austrian government toward the Hasidic movement proper. As in the case of Hasidism, an additional factor moved the Austrian and later the Russian censors to adopt the severest repressive measures against Hasidic and kabbalistic literature—Hasidism was not just a movement of mysticism and religious fanaticism but a Jewish religious mass movement which hindered the government's program to assimilate the Jews.

For this reason, all religious works in Yiddish were banned, regardless of their content. The Yiddish language, which was officially regarded as a corrupt and corrupting version of German, was considered the greatest obstacle to the germanization of Galician Jewry. The Austrian censors were probably not that well versed in Hasidic literature to know that it explicitly promulgated devotion to the Yiddish language,[7] but they could not help knowing that the spirit of Hasidic and kabbalistic literature strengthened the national consciousness of the Jewish masses and fortified their stubborn resistance against all administrative measures to compel assimilation. Hasidic and kabbalistic books received a particularly hostile reception from Austrian censorship because of their ideas concerning the Messiah and redemption, which formed the basis of this literature's world view. The censors strove to eradicate every trace of these ideas, even in the writings of the Jewish poets and scholars of the time. All the lamentations and devotions whose contents expressed yearning for the Redemption of Israel in S. D. Luzzatto's book *Kinnor Na'im* were expurgated by the censor.[8] In Isaac Samuel Reggio's introduction to *Beḥinat ha-Dat* (Investigation of Religion) by Elijah del Medigo, the censor deleted all passages that emphasized the significance of faith in the advent of the Messiah.[9] The messianism that permeated Hasidic and kabbalistic works could not be expunged by censorship, and these books were thus absolutely banned.

At the end of the period of reaction, the Austrian government's policy toward the Hasidic movement changed noticeably for tactical and political reasons.[10] Nevertheless, germanization remained the dominant feature of the government's Jewish policy. This accounts for the fact that the government constantly maintained its policy of strict censorship of Hasidic and kabbalistic books, both during the early days of the reaction, when the severity toward the Hasidic movement proper was relaxed because of the administration's slackened discipline, and even in the later years, when the policy in relation to Hasidism was intentionally liberalized. Throughout the entire period of reaction until 1848, Jewish printing shops, bookstores, and private libraries of Hasidic rebbes were raided and rigorous surveillance was maintained to halt the smuggling of banned books from Russia.

It scarcely needs to be said that all of the Austrian censor's efforts to suppress Hasidic and kabbalistic literature were doomed to failure. The Hasidic movement was remarkable for the solidarity of its members, and due to its mass base, it was able to offer greater resistance to the government's repressive legislation than all the organized political movements in the Austrian empire. Hebrew religious books were smuggled in by Hasidim from adjacent Russia with the same ingenuity as forbidden books were smuggled in by Austrian booksellers with the aid of their agents from Leipzig and other German cities. The *Shivḥei ha-Besht* (In Praise of the Ba'al Shem Tov), the *Zohar*, and other Hasidic and kabbalistic books found their way into the bookcases of the Jews in Galicia despite official prohibition, just as the forbidden volumes of the *Brockhaus Konversations-Lexicon* adorned the shelves of private libraries of cultured Germans throughout Austria.[11] In both cases, the tried and tested means of outwitting or bribing the border guards were used. In addition to smuggling books from abroad, other, subtler ways were devised by German printers and political movements, as well as by the Hasidim, to deceive the office of the censor. Newly printed books were either antedated to prove that they were published prior to the ban on them or the date and place of publication were omitted. The rigorous measures of censorship resulted, above all, in material loss to individuals due to the sudden search-and-seizure visits of private homes, bookstores, and printing shops. Hasidic literature, however, generally continued to flourish and spread despite the censors, just as the development of the Hasidic movement itself could not be checked by repressive police measures.

The first decree restricting the publication of Hebrew and Yiddish books in Galicia was issued during the reign of Emperor Joseph II. In 1785 a decree was promulgated which forbade the printing of Jewish books that contained "foolish nostrums to exorcise demons and similar things," whether printed in the language of the land, Hebrew, or Yiddish. The reason given for the issuance of this decree was of utmost significance. It was claimed that books of such superstitious contents were handicapping or making completely impossible the education and enlightenment of the Jews.[12] Characteristically, the same justification was repeated in all subsequent orders prohibiting Hasidic and kabbalistic books during the period of reaction, although the actual motive was evidently not "enlightenment and education" but rather germanization without education. Similarly, the government of the Kingdom of Poland in the first half of the nineteenth century used the same phraseology of the past Enlightenment slogans. Strict censorship of Jewish books was instituted in Congress Poland with the justification that many of these books contained teachings contrary to "morality," permeated by superstitions, hatred, and contempt of other peoples.[13] The real motive here, as in reactionary Austria, was to destroy the national culture of the Jewish population.

Herz Homberg's Attempts to Ban All Jewish Books

A provincial censorship office was established in Galicia in 1782, but it is not known when this office first began its campaign against Hasidic and kabbalistic books. Herz Homberg, who acted as a censor of Jewish books from 1787, made several suggestions to the government on the matter of prohibiting certain categories of Jewish books. Thus, in 1791 he proposed that Hebrew books which tend to spread intolerance and disdain toward other nations be forbidden. However, the imperial censorship office rejected his suggestion and stressed in its reply the principle of freedom to print Jewish prayerbooks and other Jewish religious books. Homberg's subsequent suggestion that specific paragraphs be changed rather than that the books be banned was also rejected by the government on the ground that such a procedure violated the principle of tolerance proclaimed by the Edict of 1789. The imperial censorship office added that an authoritative opinion of the rabbis would be obtained whenever doubt arose[14] in such matters.

Enlightened absolutism in Austria showed a much more tolerant attitude toward Jewish religious literature than the later reactionary absolutism. And judging by certain administrative acts and government decrees, one may assume that the Galician government's attitude toward the Hasidic movement in general was also more liberal during the period of absolutism.[15] For enlightened absolutism had hoped to achieve its goal of germanizing Jewry by disseminating German education in German schools for Jewish children; therefore, it did not have to resort to the repression of religious movements and religious literature.

The reaction to Jacobinism that began in Austria in 1790 after the death of Emperor Joseph II, and particularly during the reign of Emperor Francis from 1792, was soon to affect Jewish life. In 1794 a court decree was issued that explicitly forbade publication of books that disseminated superstitions as well as kabbalistic and "casuistic," that is, *pilpul,* books.[16] In 1800 an imperial decree forbade the importing of religious books, whether in Hebrew or Yiddish,[17] as of 1802. Homberg, too, became more audacious in his attempts to compel assimilation and "enlightenment." In 1811, at the request of the government, he drafted a new memorandum concerning the censorship of Jewish books in which he advocated a ban not only on works dealing with demonic activities and "artful notes and commentaries on old passages in the Torah" and on "kabbalistic products" but also on all "new works of talmudic-rabbinic content" and even on "biographies of rabbis who did not achieve anything except in talmudic scholarship."[18] Although these suggestions were in line with the government's explicit tendency to reduce the role of the Talmud in Jewish religious life to a minimum, it is not known whether Homberg's suggestions were completely accepted.

Many of the official documents from 1814 onward concerning the censorship of Hasidic and kabbalistic books were preserved in the state archives in Lemberg.

On July 28, 1814, Haager, the president of the Supreme Imperial Police and Censorship Office, wrote to the governor of Galicia, Baron von Goess,[19] informing him that he had considered the question of the reprinting of a book entitled *Sefer Hasidim,* whose author, Judah he-Hasid, lived in the thirteenth century.[20] It was prohibited because it contained "a lot of tenets and fables conducive to superstition and fanatical flights."[21] Another book, the *Tefillat Nehora,* was also forbidden "on account of its numerous kabbalistic interpolations."[22] Haager requested the governor of Galicia to pay particular attention to the Hebrew printing shops in which other mystic books similar to *Sefer Hasidim* were apparently being printed without the censor's permit and to inform him of any violation.

The Fourteen Forbidden Books

It is not known whether this communication from the Viennese head censor immediately resulted in the confiscation of Jewish books, but control over Hasidic and kabbalistic literature was tightened. For example, after Perl presented the manuscript of his German brochure "Über das Wesen der Sekte Chassidim" to the Galician governor, von Hauer, in 1816, it was referred to the chief censor in Vienna.[23] While examining it, the imperial censor compiled a list of fourteen books which were "bought up eagerly and read by the Hasidim."[24] Count Sedlnitzky, who had recently become president of the imperial censorship office, forwarded this list to the governor of Galicia on February 11, 1817, with the following comment: "Some of these books have already been forbidden by the censors in the past because of their mystic and kabbalistic contents; as to the others, they have not as yet appeared before the chief censor, but there hardly can be any doubt that their contents are similar to the books of the former category." Therefore, Sedlnitzky advised the governor to seize all books mentioned in the list, wherever they may be found, and to submit them for official examination. The publication of Perl's brochure was prohibited on the ground that it would arouse "indignation" against the Jews among enlightened Gentiles.[25]

The list of Hebrew religious books included the following titles:[26] *Shivḥei ha-Besht, Keter Shem Tov, No'am Elimelekh, Toledot Ya'akov Yosef, Likkutei Moharan, Likkutei Moharan Tinyana, Kiẓur Likkutei Moharan, Sefer ha-Midot, Likkutei Yekarim, Likkutei Amarim,*[27] *Iggeret ha-Kodesh, Yisemaḥ Lev,*[28] *Eẓ Ḥayyim,*[29] *Zohar.*[30]

This list corresponds almost entirely with the list of Hasidic and kabbalistic books that was later published in 1823 by Peter Beer in his work about Jewish sects, the only difference being that Beer listed some additional titles.[31] This is not surprising, as Beer admitted[32] he drew his information about the Hasidim from a treatise that Perl sent him, that is, from the manuscript "Über das Wesen der Sekte Chassidim."

In accordance with the directive of the chief censor, the Galician governor issued an order to the *Bücher-Revisionsamt* in Lemberg, that is, the provincial headquarters of Galician censorship, in which Sedlnitzky's instructions regarding the fourteen listed books were repeated and the following new strictures added: (1) None of these books may be printed, imported, or sold in the future; and (2) in case of inheritance, all books of the deceased owner must be duly registered[33] and none of them may be delivered to the heirs without a special permit from the office of the chief censor in Vienna.

The second provision was especially stressed in the governor's order, and all authorities were enjoined to ensure its faithful enforcement under a threat of personal liability. A concomitant order was issued to the police director in Lemberg and to the head of the district office in Żółkiew (both of these cities had Jewish printing shops). They were told to search the Jewish printing shops and bookstores to find out how many copies of each of the fourteen books were on hand and to send one copy of each to the office of the censor in Lemberg.[34]

Archival documents indicate that the order of the Galician governor concerning search and seizure of the banned books was carried out with meticulous accuracy. A report submitted by the *Bücher-Revisionsamt* in Lemberg to the Galician provincial presidency on September 12, 1818, indicates that thirty-six Hebrew and Yiddish books were confiscated. It is most likely that this raid was instigated by Anton Schmidt of Vienna, the well-known "privileged" publisher, who in the same year complained to the authorities that Jewish printers in Lemberg were reprinting and selling books in the "Judeo-German" language without any right to do so.[35] Of the thirty-six books sent to the Lemberg censor he cited seventeen, three in Hebrew and fourteen in Yiddish.[36] His list contained the following titles:

Hebrew books: *Seder ha-Yom,*[37] *Siddur* and *Tikkun Shelomoh,*[38] *Maḥaẓit ha-Shekel.*[39]

Yiddish books: *Kav ha-Yoshor,*[40] *Korbon Minḥoh,*[41] *Seliḥos,*[42] *Prager Gebete,*[43] *Ma'aneh Loshoyn,*[44] *Sheloyshoh She'orim,*[45] *Meẓaḥ Aharon,*[46] *Maḥzor,*[47] *Ẓe'enoh u-Re'enoh,*[48] *Berakh Avrohom,*[49] *Eẓ Ḥayyim,*[50] *Simḥas ha-Nefesh,*[51] *Teḥinos u-Bakoshos,*[52] *Shivḥei Ba'al Shem Tov.*[53]

Concerning the Hebrew books, the censor observed that *Seder ha-Yom* and *Tikkun Shelomoh* were approved by the censor in April 1815, and *Maḥaẓit ha-Shekel* in July 1816; regarding the Yiddish books, he confirmed that the *Kav ha-Yoshor* was approved in July 1800, *Korbon Minḥoh* in January 1810, and *Meẓaḥ Aharon* in 1797;

the *Ẓe'enoh u-Re'enoh,* the *Maḥzor,* and *Simḥas ha-Nefesh* "occur in the oldest list of approved religious books; the *Eẓ Ḥayyim* was once approved here [in Lemberg] in the past." The censor had a negative opinion only about *Shivḥei ha-Besht,* noting that this "objectionable" book of 1816 was probably printed abroad, or at home without the censor's permission. Finally, the censor declared that he knew of no order prohibiting books written in the "verderbte deutsche Sprache" (corrupted German language, that is, Yiddish).[54]

Sedlnitzky proved to be more rigorous than the Galician provincial censor. In an order to the governor of Galicia dated January 29, 1819, he advised as follows:

The *Seder ha-Yom* was forbidden according to an order of the supreme censor of August 9, 1817. *Shivḥei ha-Besht* would not be permitted because "it contains praise of the Hasid and has therefore been recognized to be just as harmful as the Hasidic sect in general." Although *Eẓ Ḥayyim* had been approved for publication by the censor in Vienna on July 1, 1814, the edition of the work that was confiscated in Lemberg might not be sold because it was printed abroad and imported without a permit.

As for the other books in Yiddish, Sedlnitzky deemed it proper to exempt them this time, since the prohibition of books in Yiddish was hitherto unknown to the *Bücher-Revisionsamt* in Lemberg and to the local Hebrew censor. In the future, however, no works in the "corrupted German language" could be printed, "in order to bring the Israelite nation gradually to a better acquaintance with the culture of the German language." He explained that this ruling had been observed by the supreme imperial censor for a long time.

Furthermore, Sedlnitzky approved the ordinance of the Galician provincial administration issued in 1811 to the *Bücher-Revisionsamt* in Lemberg and to the district office of Żółkiew requiring that the title page of all Jewish books indicate the name of the printer, the place and date of publication, and the date of the censor's permit. This information had to appear in German, and in Gothic or Latin characters. Finally, Sedlnitzky announced that he was preparing a list of forbidden Hebrew books similar to the lists which had already been prepared of banned books in German and in other languages. In the postscript, he added that the books sent to him for a decision had been returned immediately by stagecoach.[55]

Both the prohibition against printing books in Yiddish and the injunction concerning German titles for all Hebrew books were carried out strictly by the Galician authorities, as indicated in official documents from 1819 concerning another search of books which took place at the end of 1818.

In July 1818, Hersh Eichenstein, the famous Rebbe of Żydaczów, was investigated on the charge of smuggling forbidden Hasidic works from Russia with the aid of a Russian Jew, Jacob Meyer.[56] No results of this investigation were mentioned in the documents, but it was probably in connection with this affair that a search was made that year of the houses of three Jews in Żydaczów: Naphtali Hersh Eichenstein,[57] Naphtali Herz Labin, and Abraham Baumel.

As a result of this search, a score of books was seized and sent to the head of the Galician censorship office, the *Bücher-Revisionsamt* in Lemberg. In December 1818, the confiscated books were divided into three classes: (1) unobjectionable books were to be returned to their owners (moreover, it was decided that the owners would have the right to dispose of some of these, while others were for personal use only); (2) books positively forbidden were to be kept by the censor in Lemberg; and (3) books with a kabbalistic or Hasidic content that were not known to be banned by the supreme censor were to be forwarded to the imperial censor for a final decision.

Unfortunately, the list of books returned to their owners as permissible was not found among the archival documents. Had it been, we would have a complete picture of a typical library of a leading Hasid at the beginning of the nineteenth century.

The following titles were forwarded to the supreme censor:[58]

Abraham Baumel's books: *Shomer Shabbat;*[59] *Ḥesed le-Avraham;*[60] *Ḥefeẓ Adonai.*[61]

Naphtali Herz Labin's books: *Imerei Ẓerufah;*[62] *Sefer Ḥaredim;*[63] *Likkutei Yekarim*[64] and *Likkutei Amarim,*[65] bound together with *Amarot Tehorot;*[66] *Sefer Yere'im;*[67] *Tefillah le-David;*[68] *Ḥelkat Binyamin;*[69] *Sha'arei Orah;*[70] *Me'or Einayim;*[71] *Ḥesed le-Avraham;*[72] *Reshit Ḥokhmah;*[73] *Kanfei Yonah;*[74] *Ḥefeẓ Adonai;*[75] *Tanna debei Eliyahu;*[76] *Or ha-Me'ir;*[77] *Mevaser Tov,*[78] bound together with *Bat Eini;*[79] *Sefer ha-Ḥayyim;*[80] *Or ha-Ḥayyim;*[81] *Sidduro shel Shabbat;*[82] *Mikdash Melekh.*[83]

Naphtali Hersh Eichenstein's books: *Sefer ha-Kanah;*[84] *Pardes;*[85] *Ḥumash Or ha-Ḥayyim;*[86] *Berit Menuḥah;*[87] *Ma'amar Yonat Eilem.*[88]

The following books were immediately confiscated as forbidden by the censor:

From the home of Naphtali Herz Labin: *Shelah,*[89] *En Ya'akov,*[90] *Be'er Mayyim,*[91] *Zohar, Zohar Ḥadash, Sefer Ḥasidim.*

From the home of Naphtali Hersh Eichenstein: *Zohar, En Ya'akov, Zohar Ḥadash, Tikkunei Zohar.*[92]

The inconsistency and arbitrariness of the Galician authorities were strikingly evident in the way these books were classified—permitted, forbidden, and questionable. The two books *Likkutei Yekarim* and

Likkutei Amarim, which had been strictly forbidden in 1817 as Hasidic treatises, were now listed as questionable and sent to Vienna for a decision.

In an order of March 20, 1819, to the district office of Stryj (to which Żydaczów belonged), the presidium of the Galician government announced that the strictly forbidden books had been kept by the provincial censorship office in Lemberg and the questionable books forwarded to Vienna for a decision. On this occasion, the provincial government sent a directive to all the district offices in Galicia referring them to Sedlnitzky's decree whereby the prohibition of Yiddish books was now extended to Galicia. Mention was also made of Sedlnitzky's approval of the regulation issued by the Galician government in 1811, which compelled the publishers of Hebrew works to print the publication data in German on the title page. The Galician provincial presidency added that this information must be supplied immediately for all Hebrew books now on sale; in the future, all books lacking this information would be considered forbidden and confiscated.[93]

The decision of the supreme imperial censor's office concerning the questionable books seized in Żydaczów has not been found among the archival documents. Nevertheless, we can assume with some degree of certainty that almost all of these books were declared forbidden because of their "kabbalistic and mystic" content. That the suppression of kabbalistic works continued undiminished can be seen from an official note, dated 1820,[94] in which the central authorities reported to the Galician government that in Brünn, Moravia, two forbidden books—*Or Hajoscher*[95] and *Mifalon Elohim*[96]—were "discovered" on sale. The Galician authorities were ordered to investigate whether or not these books had been printed in Lemberg.

The Search for Hidden Books and Illegal Presses

A new wave of repression against Hasidic and kabbalistic literature began in connection with the attempts of Perl and his circle of Maskilim to reprint Israel Loebl's Mitnaggedic treatise, *Sefer Vikkuaḥ.* The manuscript of *Sefer Vikkuaḥ,* which was officially submitted to the Viennese censor for permission to be published by one Solomon Simḥah Rapaport, contained, in addition to two prefaces, a list of Hasidic books at the end.[97] In his note to the Galician governor of March 15, 1826,[98] Sedlnitzky related that these "kabbalistic" books were printed "in Lemberg, Żółkiew, and in other places in Poland and Russia." Actually, this list was a copy of the previously cited list of

Hasidic books which Perl compiled in his manuscript "Über das Wesen der Sekte Chassidim."[99]

The investigations concerning Hasidic rebbes and the Hasidic movement which were now conducted at Sedlnitzky's command were also accompanied by searches for Hasidic literature. That the government searches yielded no significant results can be explained by the fact that the Hasidim had profited from previous experience and hidden their books.

Milbacher, chief of the Brzeżany district, reported to the provincial presidency in the year 1827 that he had heard rumors that some forbidden books were to be found in the homes of the Hasidim. Therefore, a search was made at the home of Isaac Meyer of Kałusz during his visit to his brother Meyer of Przemyślany, but only harmless books, such as the *Mishnayot* printed in Żółkiew in 1816, a Bible printed in Vienna in 1810, and a Pentateuch printed in Lemberg in 1808, were found. The zealous official added, however, that his inquiries pointed to Isaac Meyer's having a large library in Kałusz.[100]

The commissioner of the district of Brody, Mohsler, reported that according to his information, the local Hasidim cited by name were in possession of many forbidden books listed in the ordinance, but he had refrained from raiding their homes in order to avoid creating a great stir.[101]

The district chief of Przemyśl evidently was less meticulous than the commissioner of Brody. In his report concerning Hasidism in the district of Przemyśl, he related that he had searched the Hasidic *klayzlekh* and found some forbidden books named in the decree. He submitted a list of these books to the provincial administration and asked that the banned titles be marked.[102]

The district chief of Stanisławów reported in 1828 that during his search for Hasidic books in Tyśmienica,[103] no book mentioned on the list had been found.[104]

In his report to Sedlnitzky about the Hasidic movement, dated January 1829, the governor, Prince Lobkowitz, asserted that no book specified on the list or any banned book had been found in searches made of the Jewish printing shops in Lemberg and Żółkiew. It was also impossible to determine where all of the forbidden books designated on the list of the Viennese censor as Galician editions had been printed.[105]

However, Sedlnitzky, in a communication dated November 1829,[106] replied to Governor Lobkowitz that he still believed the objectionable Hasidic books were being printed in Galicia. He had received this information from the censor, Joseph Berger,[107] according to whom such works had just recently come from secret printing shops in Lemberg, and even more in Żółkiew, either with a false title page or with the omission of the date, place of printing, and name of the publisher. Therefore, Sedlnitzky advised the governor to conduct the strictest investigations in Lemberg and Żółkiew on the basis of the information provided by the censor.

In compliance with Sedlnitzky's orders, the governor issued a circular to all the district offices[108] in which Sedlnitzky's suspicions concerning the secret printing of Hasidic books were repeated and reference was made to the thirteen Hasidic and kabbalistic books forbidden by the censor.[109] The governor also conducted a thorough investigation of the Jewish printing shops in Żółkiew and Lemberg in October 1830. The results of the search were, again, exceedingly meager.

In the only Jewish printing shop in Żółkiew, that of Saul Majerhoffer,[110] forty-nine Hebrew books were seized and one copy of each title was sent to the censor in Lemberg. After due inquiry, the censor's office returned almost all the books to the owner. There were reservations and objections concerning only two books: (1) *Midrash Aseret ha-Diberot,*[111] printed by Gershon Letteris[112] in Żółkiew in 1800, which was returned to the owner with the restriction that it be for personal use only; and (2) two copies of a *Siddur* which were suspected of having been printed without a censor's permit. The censor inferred this on the following grounds:

1. The printing looked unmistakably new.
2. Neither Rosanes nor Rappaport, the previous printers,[113] had ever received a censorship permit for these books, nor was the issuance of such a permit recorded in the documents of the *Bücher-Revisionsamt*.
3. The *Siddur* no. 46 bore two contradictory dates: one in Arabic numerals (1804) and the other in Hebrew letters (1826), and the censor contended that the latter was more probably correct.
4. The *Siddur* had a title page bearing the name of the publisher, date, and place of printing in German, while the order in question was not yet in force in the year 1804. The order had been promulgated on December 18, 1818.[114]

The Banned Mazal Tov

The search made of the printing shops of Herz Grossman[115] and Aaron Madpis (Mattfess)[116] in Lemberg had similar results. No book in Grossman's shop fell under suspicion. At the printing shop of

Aaron Madpis, the authorities seized 4 volumes of a *Maḥzor* and 120 copies of a broadside consisting of a Hebrew alphabet followed by a prayer known as a *Mazal Tov.* The censor's office in Lemberg returned the *Maḥzor* to the publisher after it established that it had been printed with a censor's permit, but the *Mazal Tov* was confiscated because it was a prayer that "demons might not have control over women in childbirth," in short, "a product of superstition." Since the alphabet was printed on one-half of the broadside and the *Mazal Tov* on the other, the sheets were cut in half by the censor; the half sheets containing the alphabet were returned to the owner; the *Mazal Tov* halves, however, were destroyed.[117] The reason for confiscation that was supposed to have been given the printer by the police directorate was that the prayer had not been submitted to the censor for approval.

Publishing the prayerbook with an antedated year of printing and the kabbalistic *Mazal Tov* camouflaged with the alphabet is an example of the clever means used by the Jewish printers to evade the censor's repressive measures.

In his report to Sedlnitzky, dated August 30, 1831,[118] the governor referred punctiliously to all the details of the searches made in Lemberg and in Żółkiew in order to dismiss any suspicion of neglect that his superior might have had concerning the investigation of the Jewish printing shops. He added that according to the report of the police directorate, there were no secret printing shops at all in Lemberg and that previous investigations had also attested to this. Censor Berger's opinion that the banned Hasidic and kabbalistic books were being printed in Żółkiew was refuted by the "frequent investigations that have not detected a trace of such a transgression." He contended that most of the kabbalistic books had been printed in Russia, principally in Berdichev and in Dubno,[119] where the Hasidic sect had many adherents. In some of these books Żółkiew was designated as the place of publication as a ploy by the publishers to increase the prestige and the sale of the edition, for "years ago Żółkiew had been renowned among the Jews as a residence of rabbis and scholars who were in direct contact with the rabbis of Amsterdam and they were always mentioned by learned and pious Jews right after the latter. Żółkiew was also once a center of ardent Hasidism."

The governor resorted to such explanations in order to veil the fact that the Galician administration was simply too weak to successfully carry out its crusade against Hasidic and kabbalistic literature.

Hasidic literature became the subject again in 1838 of an exhaustive investigation by the Galician authorities, prompted, as in the past, by accusations made by the Maskilim. As a result of Perl's memorandum against Israel of Ruzhin and his adherents in Galicia,[120] the Galician provincial presidency issued an order to the district offices summoning them to watch the Hasidic movement more carefully. The material taken during this investigation consisted of exorcism formulas, quack prescriptions, amulets, and talismans. According to the report of the police director, all of these were found in the house of David Goldsohn, a Hasid, in Lemberg, just as he was about to use them at the request of his "superstitious coreligionists."[121] A letter containing remedies for a sick woman that Rebbe Judah Hersh Brandwein of Stratyn[122] was ready to send by special messenger to his Hasid Isaac Ḥayyim Moyshes in Gołogóry was intercepted.[123] However, when Perl approached the government during the same year with a plan to censor the books in all the *battei midrash,*[124] the Galician provincial presidency again simply called the attention of the local authorities to the prohibition on importing Yiddish and Hebrew books and to the orders of the censors concerning books printed locally.[125]

The following episode illustrates the extent to which the Austrian government still regarded kabbalah, and mysticism in general, as the most harmful elements in the Jewish religion.

During 1844 and 1845, Solomon Judah Rapoport, the Rabbi of Prague, provisionally carried out the functions of Hebrew censor in Bohemia.[126] He then submitted an official request for a permanent appointment to this post, accompanied by a statement of his opinion on several questions from the censorship office. Professor Seidler, whom the Bohemian provincial presidency asked for an opinion about the candidates, suggested that Rapoport's candidacy be rejected for the following reasons: Rapoport did not have any systematic academic education. His written answers to the questions of the censors "about the Kabbalah and mysticism in the rabbinical religion (Rabbinismus), about the progress and further development of Jewry and about liberal culture and tolerance do not at all give the guarantee that Rapoport, an ultraorthodox rabbi, is free enough from prejudices." On the basis of this opinion, Rapoport's candidacy for the post of censor, which he so desired, was rejected.[127]

The Revolution of 1848 interrupted the persecution of the Hasidic movement and the repressive measures against its literature for a short time. A period of reaction set in again in 1851. The tendency toward absolutism and forcible germanization once again prevailed, and as a result the prohibition of Yiddish, Hasidic, and kabbalistic literature was restored.[128] In 1852 the ban against importing these books from abroad was renewed. But in the age of liberalism, which began in 1861, all special restrictions on Yiddish and

Hebrew books were lifted. Thus the censorship carried out during the period of Sedlnitzky and Metternich was dropped along with other outmoded weapons used by reactionary absolutism in its attempt to crush national cultures.

5

Joseph Perl's Struggle against Hasidism

Maskilic Denunciation of Hasidism: Its Nature and Rationalization

For those readers who are accustomed to regard the Haskalah as the "heavenly daughter," not as a movement with a definite program of social and political struggle but as a movement of idealists who devoted their entire lives to the cultivation of a flowery biblical style and to the task of disseminating enlightenment among the Jews, the documentary information presented here concerning Joseph Perl's continuous denunciations of the Hasidim will undoubtedly have a disquieting effect. This will be even more pronounced for the reader who is acquainted with the idealized biographies of Joseph Perl in which he is portrayed in his social activity as an intercessor on behalf of the entire Jewish people who "never overreached himself in his endeavors on their behalf and never took a step that could be interpreted or utilized against the Jews."[1] Even the objective scholar of the Haskalah who proceeds to analyze this movement in the spirit of Spinoza's credo, "Not to lament and not to ridicule but to understand," must feel some qualms about him after perusing the following documents. Nonetheless, the scholar who is free of prejudices and careful not to interject his personal sympathies and antipathies into his evaluation of cultural movements will not be forced, even on the basis of the facts that are documented here, to change his position in principle on the Haskalah movement and even on Perl as a Maskil.

Other prominent Galician Maskilim, such as Judah Leyb Mieses, the author of *Kinat ha-Emet* and publisher of *Tekhunat ha-Rabbanim,* resorted to denunciations and informing to the police in their struggle against the Hasidim and for the enlightenment and europeanization of the Jewish masses. As a result of Mieses's denunciation in 1823, a number of *klayzlekh* and *battei midrash* were raided by government troops and a great number of Hasidim were arrested.[2] Nachman Krochmal also considered it fitting and proper to call in the authorities against the attacks of Hasidic fanatics.[3]

Isaac Ber Levinsohn submitted a proposal to the czarist Russian ministry in 1833 to close all the Jewish printing shops with the exception of three in cities that had censorship offices. Admittedly, the decree concerning the censorship of the Yiddish and Hebrew presses, which was issued in 1836, was a result not only of Levinsohn's intercession but also of earlier similar proposals. It is also true that Levinsohn, as he explained in one of his letters, intended his plan and list of "useful" books not only to suspend the publication of Hasidic books but also to save many rabbinic books which were in danger of confiscation. We may certainly believe him when he states that his "object was exclusively the good of our Jewish brethren and the welfare of our government."[4]

The repressive measures taken by Nicholas I against the wearing of traditional Jewish garb were also not ordered solely in response to the petition to the minister of education submitted in 1843 by the Maskilim of Vilna, Mordecai Aaron Guenzburg, Isaac Benjacob, Mathias Strashun, and others,[5] since these measures had already been planned in 1841. However, this does not alter the fact that the Maskilim of Vilna favored the prohibition (though they asked the minister to keep their names in strict confidence). For they, too, sincerely believed that by the forcible abolition of the traditional Jewish garb the Jew would attain "access to Christian society from which he would gradually begin to adopt cultured manners, and in the course of time he would become a useful man and citizen."[6] Abraham Ber Gottlober was also convinced of this; he submitted a memorandum concerning the "Polish–Lithuanian Jewish garb" which he claimed was "the thickest partition which separates Jews from Christians in social as well as in religious life."[7] This was also suggested by the enlightened Rabbi of Sambor, Samuel Deutsch, in his project of 1851 to reform Galician Jewry.[8] As early as 1789, Mendel Lefin of Satanov advised the Polish government in his French brochure concerning the reform of Jewry not to apply the principle of toleration in regard to Hasidism, which, in his words, was fanatic and superstitious, believing in amulets and cures through miracles.[9]

All of these examples clearly demonstrate that denunciations in various forms and degrees accurately expressed the attitude of the Haskalah toward the absolutist regime in Austria and Russia. Regarding the Russian and Austrian monarchies as gracious regimes, the intention of whose laws and repressive measures was for the good of the entire population, including the Jews, the Maskilim contended that they were allowed to seek assistance from the authorities and to support them with all means in the struggle against Hasidism and the Hasidim. The Maskilim also believed that administrative coercive measures had the most expedient effect in the campaign to elevate the people to well-being and understanding. Advising the government on how to apply these police measures against the "ignorant populace" of Jewry for its own sake and informing the authorities how the "ungrateful" masses boycotted the just and useful laws and ordinances because of their obscurantism did not, therefore, denote any betrayal of the Maskilim's cultural and political ideals. On the contrary, the Maskilim regarded their acts as self-evident cooperation in the interest of mutual "noble" goals.

Nonetheless, there was a fundamental difference between the counsel of the Maskilim in regard to decrees against the Hasidim and fanaticism and individual denunciations against rebbes and Hasidim. For the Maskilim, the carrying out of such projects as the censorship of Jewish books,[10] prohibition of the Jewish garb, closing of *minyanim* (Mieses) and even of *battei midrash* (Perl) simply signified a necessary operation on the organism of the Jewish people. They had neither understanding of nor feeling for the pain in such operations; they only saw the benefit that was supposed to be gained for the material and cultural state of the Jews.

Even in the eyes of the Maskilim, individual denunciations of rebbes, rabbis, and Hasidim must have, however, been considered as neither practical nor permissible. Despite their bitter hatred of the Hasidim, the moral consciousness of the Maskilim prompted them to eschew denunciations of individuals, for they must have realized that the denounced individual would be subjected to harsh punishment by the government. In all fairness to the leaders of the Haskalah, they cannot be reproached with the individual denunciation of rebbes and Hasidim on the basis of the historical information to date. Most of the denunciations against individual leaders of the Hasidim known to us were by the followers of the Haskalah, and their names have been preserved for their less than honorable "achievements."[11] Of course, the leaders of the Haskalah were indirectly responsible because of the blind hatred of the Hasidim which they preached.[12]

The Paradoxical Nature of Perl's Attitude toward Denunciation

As evidenced in the documents to be cited, Perl was an exception to the leaders of the Haskalah. He was not satisfied with presenting proposals to the government concerning the destruction of Hasidism, nor did he stop at personal denunciations against Hersh of Żydaczów, Israel of Ruzhin, and several of his adherents, as well as against rabbis who did not have the proper education required by law for their office.

Ironically, it was none other than Perl who in his program for the moral education of the Jews cited denunciations as one of the greatest plagues of Jewry. In an open letter in *Kerem Ḥemed* in 1838, Perl suggested that this periodical should not only be devoted to science and poetry but also should aid in the dissemination of virtues among the Jews, particularly among the Jewish youth. Specifically, the program should aim toward

> strengthening in their hearts our faith and religion and in turning their hearts to sensible habits and conduct and in purging them of bad habits that have recently been spread among the inhabitants of our country, such as lust for money, extravagance and prodigality, envy of one another, hatred of people, flattery, usury, cheating in weights and measures, deception in word, *denunciations* and *calumnies* [emphasis added].[13]

Perl's personality is highlighted in a special way in light of these denunciations. Joseph Perl, the school director, the man decorated with medals by both despots of eastern Europe, Czar Alexander I and Emperor Francis I, the prominent man in the eyes of the Austrian government, acted in his individual denunciations not only as a Maskil but also as a diligent collaborator with the Austrian state apparatus. All this might lead us to link Perl with a figure in the history of Galician Jewry of a previous period who belongs to the history of Austrian absolutism's repressive measures against the Jews rather than to the history of the Haskalah—Herz Homberg, whose very name would call forth a curse on the lips of the tormented Jews in Galicia.

But it would be a great mistake to overlook the great spiritual gap separating these two figures. Homberg's official function consisted of supplying plans to destroy the very foundation of Jewish culture; his "ideology," whose leitmotif was repugnant careerism, was that of a semiapostate. Both in its positive elements, such as the europeanization of the Jews, dissemination of education and productivization, and in its negative aspects, such as linguistic assimilation and political servility in relation to ruling absolutism, Perl's program was a classic example of the ideology of the contemporary Haskalah. Homberg's "literary" legacy consists of religious catechisms that today are only a tragicomic document of forced germanization. Perl holds a prominent position in the history of Jewish culture and literature as one of the pillars of the Haskalah in Galicia who also influenced the Haskalah in Russia, through both his writings and his personal contact with such men as I. B. Levinsohn, Israel Aksenfeld, Bezalel Stern, and Abraham Ber Gottlober.

The documents concerning Perl's collaboration with the Austrian government in the struggle against Hasidism are, after all, much more than a reflection of his personality; they clarify the political ideology and practice of the Haskalah in general, and illuminate the means, besides propaganda and enlightenment, which were utilized to achieve its goals. If the negative features of this movement which laid the foundation of modern Jewish culture emerge so distinctly here, it is only another demonstration of how past cultural movements cannot be evaluated according to absolute moral criteria. The only criterion that is applicable here is the historical one: the lasting value of the Haskalah consists of those elements of its ideology that were progressive in its time. We can discount the negative elements of this movement, the products of the class limitation of the Maskilim, because of the sociopolitical and national progress we have attained in the course of the past century.

Perl's first contact with the Austrian government, which is recorded in the documents, took place on December 2, 1816, when he sent the Galician governor, Franz von Hauer, the manuscript of his brochure "Über das Wesen der Sekte Chassidim."[14] The manuscript was accompanied by a memorandum explaining why he was requesting the governor's consent to dedicate this brochure in his honor.

Perl said that for quite some time he had had the idea to publish a brochure based on quotations from Hasidic books about the teachings and customs of the Hasidim and in this way to reveal to the world the essence of the Hasidic movement. If he had refrained up until now from executing this project which was meant "to awaken the nation from its deep sleep," it was only because he feared persecution and machinations on the part of the powerful sect. Perl believed the sect was becoming ever more widespread "from hour to hour, like a cancer" that must be extirpated.

It should be noted that both the depiction of the Hasidic movement as a threat that must be combatted before it was too late and the expression of fear of revenge on the part of the well-organized Hasidim reappear in Perl's later memoranda.

Perl went on to say that he had decided to complete this task since he had had the good fortune to be introduced to the governor, and he was convinced that the governor truly desired to disseminate light, truth, and pure piety among the Israelite nation and that in this he had the Emperor's full support. This encouraged Perl and dispelled his fear of persecution by the Hasidim. Perl drew even greater encouragement from the governor's ordinances in connection with two recent events: the ban against the Maskilim proclaimed in the synagogue of Lemberg and the attacks of the zealots of Brody against the local *Realschule.*[15] In these actions the governor had furnished grounds for him to hope for success in this undertaking, and therefore he requested von Hauer's patronage of it.

Perl regarded the publication of his work as only the beginning of a campaign against the Hasidim which the government should undertake. He stated his readiness to organize a plan on "how to curb this evil," adding that he did not want to anticipate the government, particularly when he did not yet know what method in the struggle against Hasidism the government considered expedient. Therefore, he was withholding his proposal until the government requested its submission.[16]

It is clear from the formulation of Perl's request for the governor's permission to dedicate the brochure in his honor that the basic motive was to protect himself against the threat that the Hasidim would destroy the edition of his work just as they did with Mitnaggedic books such as *Sefer Vikkuaḥ, Zemer Ariẓim,* and others. For the same reason, Isaac Ber Levinsohn in 1828 published a letter of thanks to Czar Nicholas I for his subsidy in the preface to his *Te'udah be-Yisrael.*

Perl's brochure and memorandum were forwarded by Governor von Hauer to the imperial censorship office, with an enclosed letter which described Perl as "one of the most educated men of his nation," the founder of the "great synagogue," that is, the temple in Tarnopol, who was recently awarded an "important gold medal of merit" by the Russian czar which the Austrian Emperor permitted him to accept.[17] The governor had informed the imperial censorship office at the outset that he did not consent to the dedication of Perl's brochure in his honor, and the Viennese censor prohibited the publication of the brochure.[18]

In order to make amends to Perl for the refusal to publish his work, Governor von Hauer instructed the district office in Tarnopol to append a comment to the official reply to his memorandum to the effect that the provincial president, despite this rejection, appreciated his efforts on behalf of the "moral and political perfection of his Israelite coreligionists" and that he had given expression to this appreciation in his note to the imperial censorship office.[19]

As a direct result of the Austrian authorities' becoming acquainted with Perl's German manuscript, "Über das Wesen der Sekte

Chassidim," there was an increase in the repressive measures against the Hasidim, including several searches and confiscations of Hasidic books.[20]

Since publication of his anti-Hasidic German brochure was forbidden, Perl decided to continue his anti-Hasidic propaganda in Hebrew. After the publication of his anti-Hasidic satire *Megalleh Temirin* in 1819 created a furor (the manuscript had been submitted to the censor for approval in 1816), Perl tried to republish the old Mitnaggedic treatise by the maggid Israel Loebl, *Sefer Vikkuaḥ*. Perl's efforts had consequences similar to those resulting from his previous memorandum. In 1826 the censor forbade the republication of *Sefer Vikkuaḥ*, which sparked a new series of rigorous police investigations of the Hasidim and inspections of Hasidic books as well as an intensification of the regulations concerning Hasidic *minyanim*. For Perl, this was an opportune moment to present a denunciation dated January 2, 1827,[21] of the famous Hasidic rebbe Hersh of Żydaczów, the substance of which is summarized below.

The Denunciations of Hersh of Żydaczów and the Alms Boxes of Rabbi Me'ir Ba'al ha-Nes

Perl cited his petition of September 27, 1826, to the district office in Tarnopol concerning the designation of a punishment for sabotaging the fund from which the German school for Jewish children in Tarnopol was supported. The funding for this school—of which Perl was the director—was derived from a special tax on *sheḥita* paid by the Jewish community of Tarnopol and the surrounding towns of Trembowla, Skałat, and Mikulińce, and from a regular subsidy from two other neighboring towns, Grzymałów and Zbaraż, 250 gulden a year from the former and 450 gulden a year from the latter.[22] Both because of the burden of these taxes and because Perl's school was hated by the pious masses,[23] the Hasidim agitated against the contribution to the school. Perl referred to his memorandum of the previous year in which he had drawn the district office's attention to the fact that some time ago an "association" had been organized against the school in Tarnopol.

Perl went on to state that "a certain head of the very injurious Hasidic sect" named Hersh Eichenstein, also known as Hersh of Żydaczów, who was then in Podkamień, had been invited to the town of Zbaraż for the coming of the following Sabbath. He was invited by a member of this association opposed to the Tarnopol school who had been in Zbaraż the week before and by two representatives of the *kehillah* of Zbaraż, Sholem Horowitz and Abraham Landesberg. Perl observed that he who was fully aware of this sect's deeds and those of its chief would clearly understand why they chose the Sabbath to propagate their false teachings of superstition and fanaticism, for it was a day when the Jew was free of all labor and surrendered himself completely to idleness.

Perl contended that there could not be the slightest doubt that the arrival of the Rebbe of Żydaczów in Zbaraż, where Jews would probably also come from Tarnopol and its district, would harm "the good cause" of enlightenment, and the positive influence exerted on the Jews by good educational institutions in the course of an extended period was liable "to be stamped out in one Sabbath" by a leader of the Hasidim. Moreover, Perl indicated that at such a gathering, plans would certainly be made thoroughly to disrupt the *Deutsch-Israelitische Hauptschule* in Tarnopol. It could also be assumed that such a leader would extort at least 300 to 400 gulden from the *kehillah*. Therefore, Perl requested the district office promptly to deter Hersh of Żydaczów from coming to Zbaraż. This could be accomplished most expediently if the communal representatives of Zbaraż were notified that bringing the Rebbe of Żydaczów to their town would be contrary to the regulations in a circular of the Galician provincial administration dated February 2, 1824, whereby the leaders of the Hasidim were absolutely forbidden to travel around the country. This would apply especially to Hersh, who in 1818 was accused of entering into an agreement with a Russian Jew, Jacob Meyer, to smuggle into Galicia Hasidic books which were banned in the Austrian Empire. Perl further recalled that in 1824 Hersh had sent a letter to Naphtali of Ropczyce which the government intercepted. The government had turned to Perl for information about it, and he had expressed his opinion that this letter revealed the Rebbe of Żydaczów's "bad intentions."

As a result of this information, Perl recounted, the district office in Tarnopol ordered the detention and expulsion of the "teacher of false doctrine Hersh" on the grounds that he did not have a passport or a certificate issued by the lord of the town from which he came,[24] nor could he prove that he had to settle necessary affairs or business in Zbaraż.[25]

The next step that Perl took in seeking the assistance of the Austrian government in the struggle against Hasidism was related to his efforts to publish a treatise, this time a Hebrew brochure concerning R. Me'ir Ba'al ha-Nes' alms boxes entitled "Katit la-Ma'or," written in 1822.[26] In 1829 he applied to the imperial censorship office for permission to publish the treatise "Katit la-Ma'or." In the request accompanying the manuscript he reported that the "offensive custom" of placing alms boxes in the synagogues for the purchase of oil for the lamps on the grave of R. Me'ir Ba'al ha-Nes was popularized by the Hasidim or "Beshtians." He stated that this work aimed to bring these deeds to a halt. He also mentioned that the Hasidim circulated special printed leaflets in which they agitated for the collection of funds in the name of R. Me'ir Ba'al ha-Nes.

The president of the Supreme Imperial Police and Censorship Office, Count Joseph Sedlnitzky, apparently deduced that Perl's objective was not only to receive a censorship permit for his treatise but also to suggest to the government on this occasion that it ought to investigate the collections of these funds and issue a ban against them. Sedlnitzky asked the opinion of the Galician governor, Prince Lobkowitz, not only on the question of a permit to publish Perl's brochure "Katit la-Ma'or," but also about the issue which is treated in this brochure. He called his attention to the fact that the "offensive custom" exposed in the brochure is related to the "ecclesiastical" customs of the local (Galician) Jews, and that the abolition of this custom would have far-reaching consequences.[27]

The provincial administration's reply to Sedlnitzky concerning the alms boxes is not recorded in the documents. Only a note from the governor to the district chief of Tarnopol has been preserved. The district chief was instructed to ask Perl for a German translation of "Katit la-Ma'or," as well as a copy of the Hasidic appeal for such donations which was mentioned in Perl's request to the Viennese censor.[28] Perl finally published the treatise "Katit la-Ma'or" in *Kerem Ḥemed* in 1836.

The Ushitsa Affair

An investigation which the government asked Perl to conduct in 1837–38 afforded him a new opportunity to make accusations against the Hasidim. Alarmed by the propaganda that a certain Karl Gustav Seyfart, a mystic and adventurer, had been carrying on since 1830 for a Jewish state in Palestine in the name of "Siegfried Justus I, King of Israel and High Priest of Jerusalem," the Galician provincial authorities wanted to know the extent to which the "Siegfried Justus movement" had taken root among Galician Jewry. In October 1837 Perl submitted a detailed statement to the government and in February 1838 a further report concerning this matter.[29] In connection with this investigation, Perl came across a collection of funds which was conducted in Galicia for the benefit of the famous Hasidic leader Israel of Ruzhin "whose scope and purpose astonished and shocked him." On March 6, 1838, Perl submitted a detailed report to the district office in Tarnopol concerning the results of his "discovery."[30]

Perl explained the reason for the delay in reporting to the authorities, saying it had taken time to confirm the results of his investigations with complete certainty. The following is a summary of what he had ascertained.

In the town of Ruzhin in the district of Podolia there lived "a certain Srultshe or Srulenyu" whose real name was Israel Shulimovich Friedman, considered to be the greatest of all the Hasidic rebbes in Russia and Galicia. When several years earlier the Russian government forbade the Hasidic rebbes to travel around the country because this was "extremely detrimental to the Jews who are in this manner enticed, rendered unhappy, and fleeced," the rebbes devised a scheme of registering in the merchant guilds so they could travel without impediment. Thus the Rebbe of Ruzhin registered in the merchant guild in order to be able to travel freely, and in this manner he succeeded in obtaining a passport to Galicia in 1835. He arrived in Lemberg and "carried on so" that the police compelled him to leave the city within three days.

Turning to the essence of the report, Perl told of the Rebbe of Ruzhin's participation in the "Ushitsa affair." Two informers, Isaac Oksman and Samuel Shvartsman of the district of Ushitsa in Podolia, were murdered in accordance with a decision adopted at a conference of the Jewish communities of the district with, as all the evidence indicates, the approval of the Rebbe of Ruzhin.[31] However, Perl stated that the rebbe was accused of having ordered the murder, which Hasidim committed at his command. But because he was registered in the merchants' guild, he was released from detention pending investigation and thus had an opportunity to deceive the court with the aid of his adherents by eliminating all traces of the dreadful murder. Perl related that the Rebbe of Ruzhin had organized the collection of funds in Galicia for this trial, as he had spent his entire fortune for his defense and, in addition, having ceased to travel around the country, lost his ready supply of funds.

Perl justified his inability to ascertain all the details concerning this fund-raising campaign by saying that anyone at all acquainted with this sect would understand that it was not a simple matter to investigate all of its perverse and secret deeds but rather a perilous task. Therefore only the following details concerning the campaign could be established:

The largest collections were conducted in the districts of Sanok, Jasło, and Tarnów with the assistance of the Rebbe of Rymanów, Hersh "the Attendant." In other districts, including Lemberg, much smaller sums were collected; in Lemberg the collection was undertaken with the greatest caution so that even the managing committee of the *kehillah* was unaware of it. In the district of Tarnopol, a certain David Parnas of Janów alone contributed fifty gulden, and in Borszczów, in the district of Czortków, there was a rich Jew, Isaac Fischler-Bodek, who very actively participated in the campaign. Fischler was always the organizer of the collection of donations in behalf of Israel of Ruzhin and he often traveled to visit the rebbe; he was also the one who recruited David Parnas into the ranks of the Hasidic sect. According to Perl's information, it is likely that 40,000 to 50,000 gulden were raised in this collection. For example, a certain village Jew had to give the emissaries of Rebbe Hersh of Rymanów 150 silver rubles; large sums were also contributed by merchants of Tarnów, such as Luxenberg and Fraenkel.

Perl concluded with the greatest revelation. He had found out that "the murderer employed by Srultshe [Israel Friedman]" was hiding somewhere in Galicia and was extorting large sums of money from Hasidim under the threat that he would return to Russia and reveal the whole truth. Several months earlier, this murderer came to the Hasid Fischler in Borszczów and, under the same threat, forced him to send 200 silver rubles for his wife, who had remained in Russia.

Perl ended his note by advising the authorities to investigate the matter thoroughly through the Lemberg police directorate, for an investigation conducted through the normal official channels of the district offices would not be successful. He knew from personal experience that this "accursed sect" had various ways and means to attain its "criminal" goals.

This manifold denunciation by Perl is the most remarkable of all the documents of his activity against Hasidism. This report not only revealed the full names of those punishable for the illegal transfer of money abroad and for alleged extortion, but also explicitly identified Israel of Ruzhin as the real culprit in the murder at Ushitsa and his adherent, Fischler of Borszczów, as the one who gave financial aid to the murderers.

During his investigations, Perl probably learned (but, of course, failed to mention in his denunciation) that the two murdered Jews in the district of Ushitsa were contemptible informers who used to blackmail the impoverished Jewish communities and were a menace to the *ne'lamim,* namely, the great number of young men who went into hiding to escape the brutality of the draft under the cantonist system of Czar Nicholas I. However, Perl was certainly sincere in his indignation over the murders. Like the majority of the contemporary Maskilim, he did not regard the draft as a repressive measure but rather one which was intended for the "civilizing" of the Jews. Accordingly, the murdered informers were viewed as loyal citizens who fell victim to the fanaticism and obscurantism of the Hasidim, whose act was not to be considered one of self-defense but a foul murder which deserved to be punished in accordance with the severity of the law.

Perl's denunciation was forwarded by the district office in Tarnopol to the Galician provincial presidency with the comment that the author requested that his name be kept secret and that the case of Parnas, who participated in the fund-raising campaign, be investigated.[32]

The Galician provincial presidency immediately sent a circular to all the district offices containing an excerpt of the denunciation and describing Perl anonymously as "a trustworthy person." The district offices were instructed to investigate in detail the matter of the "dangerous deeds of the Hasidic Jewish sect," particularly the instances of extorting money and sending it abroad. Moreover, it was indicated that if the explanation of some detail or other by the author of the denunciation was necessary, the district chief of Tarnopol should be notified and he would arrange for contact with the informant.[33]

At the same time, an excerpt of Perl's denunciation was forwarded to the governor of Podolia, von Laschkareff, whose attention was called to the "serious accusations" against the Rebbe of Ruzhin "Shulimovich Friedman," "the head of the Hasidic sect which is widespread in both countries." He was requested "in the interest of both governments" to submit a description of the murderer who committed the crime on the order of the Rebbe of Ruzhin.[34]

The replies of the district offices to the provincial presidency's circular have not been preserved in the archives. One can only presume that thanks to their extraordinary solidarity the Hasidim succeeded in hushing up the matter. The detailed memorandum of the Lemberg police directorate concerning this case is the only one which has been preserved.

The police director, Sachar, first explained why he was not successful in uncovering further details concerning the collection of funds in behalf of the Rebbe of Ruzhin, as well as about the murder case. He argued that if the knowledgeable informant who knew precisely the customs, way of life, and moral and religious principles as well as the devices of the Jew was not able to investigate all the details concerning the matter, it should not be surprising that the police director did not accomplish more. Moreover, he did not have the appropriate assistants with the aptitude to investigate the case, and even those who were equal to the task did not dare to undertake such an assignment out of fear of the Hasidim's fanatic vengeance. His hypothesis was that both the organizers of the collection of funds and the murderer from Podolia were to be found in the provincial areas where the rebbes resided and not in Lemberg, where there was no Hasidic leader.

As for the Rebbe of Ruzhin, the police director confirmed the fact that he had spent some time in Lemberg in 1835. He also contended that the Rebbe of Ruzhin "indeed exerts such a great influence and is as dangerous" as he is depicted in the denunciation. He was kept under strict surveillance during his visit to Lemberg in 1835. At that time the Rebbe of Ruzhin lived quietly, but he did receive Jews "of the better class" such as the Rabbi of Lemberg, Jacob Ornstein,[35] and his son. On account of these visits, the police director ordered him to leave Lemberg within three days. At that moment, however, the Rebbe of Ruzhin presented a certificate from Dr. Rapoport,[36] who, together with several other physicians, was treating him for a bladder ailment. During the two weeks that he remained in Lemberg his house was simply besieged by masses of Jews so that the police director dispatched a special agent to his home in order to keep him under constant watch. The Rebbe of Ruzhin felt so uncomfortable because of the police surveillance that he immediately left the city.[37]

The reply of the governor of Podolia to the note of the president of the Galician provincial administration also has not been preserved. As to the murderer of the informers who escaped to Galicia, it seems that despite Perl's denunciation he was not captured. The verdict of the "Letnevits affair"[38] mentions in addition to the four Jews who were direct participants in the murder—Guterman, Introligator, Hofshteyn, and Fleyshman, who were sentenced to run the gauntlet of 500 blows four times and to hard labor in Siberia—three others directly involved who escaped and were never caught: Shtromvaser, Kreytman, and Shtroyman.[39] It was probably one of these three who fled to Galicia and hid there among the Hasidim, as Perl reported in his memorandum. However, in regard to the Rebbe of Ruzhin, it seems that Perl's denunciation did have its effect.

In his report Perl related that Israel of Ruzhin was implicated in the Ushitsa case immediately upon his return from Galicia but succeeded in avoiding imprisonment on account both of his certificate of membership in the mercantile guild and a great sum of money for bribery. It is known from other sources that the Rebbe of Ruzhin was imprisoned for twenty-two months in the jails of Kamenetz-Podolsk and Kiev in connection with the Ushitsa trial.[40] Since the verdict in the Ushitsa case, in accordance with which the Rebbe of Ruzhin was acquitted, was finally confirmed by Czar Nicholas I on January 18, 1840, and issued on February 28, it appears that the imprisonment of Israel of Ruzhin began no later than March or April 1838; therefore he must have been arrested immediately after the governor of Podolia received the letter from the Galician provincial president dated March 17, 1838, conveying the contents of Perl's denunciation.[41]

The verdict in the Ushitsa trial explicitly mentioned the letter which the Galician provincial president had sent to the governor of Podolia. After the statement that "Rabbi Friedman" had been cleared of the charge of complicity in the murder at Ushitsa, the following passage appeared in the verdict:

> However, in spite of all of this *the Galician governor's statement casts suspicion upon Friedman* as a propagator of the Hasidic sect among Galician Jewry and *as an organizer of a collection of funds for his own benefit* [emphasis added]; yet the first [suspicion] was not essentially proven with the necessary conclusiveness and the second [suspicion] is refuted on the basis of an investigation which was conducted at the places where he resided. Considering the testimony of both Jews and landowners who knew Friedman concerning his praiseworthy life and his readiness to help the poor, regardless of faith, it is difficult to imagine any action taken on his part which was dictated by bad intention. In spite of the rigor in trying this case, the presiding official,[42] not finding any just cause to accuse Friedman, decided to vindicate him of any responsibility, allow him to remain in his previous place of residence and only put him under the supervision of the local police.[43]

On the basis of the formulation of the verdict, it is easy to surmise that the decision to keep the Rebbe of Ruzhin under police surveillance was a result of the suspicion that he was disseminating Hasidism. Due to this police surveillance, Israel of Ruzhin was forced to flee to Rumania and, subsequently, when the Russian authorities demanded his extradition, to settle in Sadagura. Thus history played a trick on Perl: through his denunciation of the Rebbe of Ruzhin he indirectly caused the entrenchment of representatives of the Friedman dynasty of Ruzhin for many years in his own region, of all places, in Husiatyn and Czortków.

Perl's Denunciation of Book, Bet Midrash, *and* Mikveh

Probably encouraged by the great interest which his denunciation of March 6 against the Rebbe of Ruzhin and the Hasidim had aroused among the Austrian authorities, about two weeks later, on March 22, 1838, Perl submitted a new memorandum to the government which was to bring about very serious consequences not only for the Hasidim but also for the Orthodox masses in general. This time Perl suggested that the government confiscate all books which it regarded as harmful, partially or completely close the *battei midrash* and limit the use of the *mikvot*. Perl was undoubtedly motivated to a certain degree in proposing this project by the Russian censorship decree of 1836 in accordance with which all uncensored books were to be submitted to the authorities and the banned ones (according to the regulation of 1837) burned.[44]

Perl's justification of his project[45] was based on the imperial decrees of 1798 and 1799, which forbade reading rooms and lending libraries in all the provinces of Austria. Even university, secondary school, and church libraries were subject to special regulations. Among the Jews, libraries were to be found on open shelves, accessible to everyone in almost every community, namely in the *battei midrash* and *klayzlekh*. These libraries did not have any catalogues, and neither the executive of the *kehillah* nor the wardens of the synagogue exercised any kind of control over them. Books were purchased with the funds of Mishnah and Talmud societies that arranged ceremonial banquets for their members on designated days. Books were also acquired with the revenues of *battei midrash* proper or from inheritances which were donated in accordance with wills even before the courts had taken inventory of these bequests.

Perl stated that he did not deem it necessary to dwell upon the harm which resulted from such unlimited freedom to read books. It was unnecessary, in the first place, because the censorship regulations applied to Jewish as well as to non-Jewish books. Furthermore, the Jewish libraries were even more harmful than the lending libraries because one was neither obliged to lay down a security deposit nor to pay any fee whatsoever. The Jewish book collections in the *battei midrash* and *klayzlekh* generally consisted of harmful literature which "distorts the understanding and corrupts the heart," and the reader would become immoral through absorbing fanatical ideas and demoralizing teachings and prejudices.

Perl stated that the book collections in the *battei midrash* and *klayzlekh* indirectly had another even more harmful effect. On the pretext of coming to the synagogue to study, Jews spent days on end in conversation and smoking. Whoever did not frequent the *battei midrash* or dared to criticize the people who gathered there was slandered and ostracized and lost all of his customers because no one would do business with him. In addition, all of the bans against the Jewish taxes and the tax lessees were devised in the *battei midrash*. These institutions were also "a place of refuge for vagabonds, thieves, and similar types and, as a matter of course, a nest of demoralization and of harmful, often even nefarious, scandalous deeds." As an example, Perl pointed to a case of homosexuality which took place in a *klayzl* in Tarnopol forty-eight years earlier when he still frequented the place.

Perl further contended that this category of forbidden places of assembly also included the *mikvot*, where meetings were held throughout the morning under the pretext of coming only for ablutions.

Perl concluded that the *battei midrash* and the *mikvot* could only be detrimental to the Jew, to society in general, and particularly to the state. Therefore, if the state had allowed such institutions to exist until now, it was because no one as yet had clearly pointed out the evil in them. How is it, Perl asked, that no Christian community has such places of assembly? Why, then, did the Jews have them? Still more puzzling was the fact that even educated Christians were required to request permission to organize a club, register the names of their members, and submit to specified regulations and supervision by the authorities. Why should the Jews not be subject to any restrictions in this respect? Why did only the Polish Jews have such institutions and not the Jews of western European countries?

Perl noted that he did not want to presume to indicate to the government the means it should take to stop the negative manifestations; for he trusted that "the sovereign state in its wisdom" would find the best way to change the situation and yet not prohibit the Jews from reading books or performing ablutions in the *mikveh*. Finally, Perl appealed to the government that it not let itself be convinced by the rabbis that these places of assembly must remain open to Jews, without any restrictions, because of religious reasons. As for the *mikvot* in particular, he deemed it necessary to point out that long ago Jews rarely used them except before the Sabbath and holidays. It was the Hasidim who instituted the custom of going to the *mikveh* every day, not for the sake of ablutions, but to hold meetings and chat.

The intentions of Perl's memorandum and the concreteness of his proposals concerning the *battei midrash* and *mikvot* appeared even more clearly in the Tarnopol district chief's official note which accompanied Perl's memorandum to the Galician provincial presidency.[46] The district chief indicated that the author of the memorandum was the school director, Joseph Perl, who had requested that his authorship be kept secret. The district chief supported Perl's proposal that controls be established over the reading done by the Galician Jews, but for a different reason, namely, the antistate role played by the *battei midrash* and *mikvot*. He pointed out that the neglect in this area was a hindrance to the enlightenment and "reformation" of this "numerous class of the people." He contended that such controls could easily be instituted, and for Tarnopol in particular he proposed this plan: that "the books which the censor regarded as acceptable should be placed in the *public library which Perl is prepared to open* [emphasis added] as part of the school which he directed." The district chief informed the provincial presidency that he would submit an appropriate proposal later concerning this library.

As for the *battei midrash* themselves, the district chief contended that essentially they, like the Talmud and Mishnah societies, should be treated as *minyanim* for limited groups of pious Jews who worshipped outside the synagogue. Therefore they should come under the jurisdiction of the law concerning *minyanim,* in accordance with which they were regarded as secret societies. In Tarnopol there were many *battei midrash* that had libraries, and therefore a provisional decree should be issued banning these institutions both in Tarnopol and in the entire province of Galicia. Then the authorities should carry out the necessary reforms so that these institutions could be maintained. In regard to *mikvot,* he believed that meetings there had to be prohibited and the attendants made responsible for enforcing this decree, especially when in accordance with Jewish law only women were required to go to the *mikveh* at specified times, and then only in the evening and not during the day.

The district chief of Tarnopol concluded his accompanying note with the comment that

> although it was within his own competence to issue such a prohibition for Tarnopol he refrained from doing so because *the Jews of Tarnopol would immediately surmise who was the initiator of this decree and he would then be subject to certain inconveniences* [emphasis added]. These undesirable results could easily be avoided if this decree were promulgated by the higher authorities; that is, by the Galician provincial president.

In light of the district chief's note, which evidently was inspired by Perl, the intentions which Perl did not explicitly express in his denunciation now clearly emerged. Perl wanted to induce the government to close the *battei midrash* and *klayzlekh,* and to have the censor screen the book collections. The permitted books would be transferred to premises where reading would be supervised by government appointees; for example, to the library in Tarnopol which Perl was planning to open. Subsequently, the *battei midrash* should be opened only as houses of prayer which would be designated, like synagogues, only for worship during specified hours for morning, afternoon, and evening prayers. Similarly, the *mikvot* would be open during the week only for women, and men would be allowed to use them only on Sabbath eve and holidays.

If Perl's proposal was consistent with his Maskilic program whereby the Jews should be civilized only through the most rigorous police measures by the absolute monarchy, it may appear at first glance that the reasons he gave for the necessity of such repressive measures exceeded the bounds of the Maskilic ideology. For example, there was Perl's bizarre mention of cases of homosexuality in the *battei midrash* which he remembered not only from his youth, but also from letters from his Maskilic colleagues who used to eagerly inform him about such sensations. One case of this kind that was supposed to have taken place in Rawa Ruska was reported to Perl by Samson Bloch in a letter of 1817, and a similar incident in Radziwiłłów was recounted by Levinsohn in a letter to Perl in 1820.[47] However, did the charge that the *bet ha-midrash* was to blame for such cases of debauchery and that the *battei midrash* were a sanctuary for thieves, vagabonds, and similar riffraff fit into the Haskalah's program? Should not the parallel that Perl drew between the "frequenters of the *bet ha-midrash*" and the ancient "Pharisees" be classified as an example of tasteless fawning on the Christian authorities? Does not Perl's statement that the Jews were privileged compared to the Christians in regard to unlimited freedom to read books sound hypocritical when the Jewish population was burdened with special taxes and entangled in a tightly meshed net of economic repressions?

While this argument may seem repugnant to us, Perl's proposals were an integral part of his view of Jewish life as well as a product of his Haskalah program of reforms.

Exaggerating isolated instances of sexual license and capitalizing on this as an accusation against Hasidism were a weapon, albeit a poisoned one, in Perl's relentless struggle against the "sect" which he regarded as the greatest obstacle to the material and cultural ascent of the Jews. The letters from Levinsohn and Bloch to Perl were pervaded by the same firm conviction that the Hasidic teaching and even the kabbalah (in Bloch's opinion) were responsible for the cases of sexual perversion.[48] When Perl denounced the *battei midrash* as places of refuge for "thieves, vagabonds, and similar riffraff" he expressed the contempt for the Jewish *lumpenproletariat* which was characteristic of all the Maskilim of that period. If the Maskilim, like the absolute monarchy, held the petty bourgeois Jewish masses responsible for their alleged inclination toward unproductive occupations, if they reproached these same masses for their cultural backwardness, they certainly could not tolerate the fact that déclassé elements used to come into the *bet ha-midrash* to warm up or even to spend the night there. Perl believed that closing the *battei midrash* would solve the problem just as the police did when they threw "incorrigible tramps" into jail.

Perl's comparing the "frequenters of the *bet ha-midrash*" with the ancient "Pharisees" is not sufficient evidence to warrant placing him in the extreme wing of the Haskalah, which regarded the Talmud as a harmful fabrication of religious deceivers. (Indeed, such opinions are found among the earliest Maskilim in eastern Europe, among them Jacob Frank of Kreslavka and Hirsh Ber Hurwitz, the son of the author of *Tsofnas Paneakh.)*[49] Perl, however, not only never attacked the Talmud but also cited it with respect even in a memorandum to the government,[50] and he instituted the Talmud as an obligatory subject in his school in Tarnopol. In any case, Perl was sufficiently well versed in Jewish history to know that the Talmud was a product of that tendency in Jewish spiritual and social life which was pioneered by the Pharisees. This contradiction can only be explained if it is assumed that in this case Perl was not consciously fawning on the Christian government.[51] Under the influence of Christianity, Perl identified the Pharisees with hypocrites but did not take this to its logical conclusion, which would have meant the rejection of the Talmud.

As to the contradiction between Perl's desire that the Jewish masses completely submit to all the laws on a par with the Christians and the civil inequality of these same masses, Perl probably resolved it in his own mind as did the other leading Maskilim of that generation. The Jewish masses indeed did not have equality of rights with the Christian population, but only through absolute loyalty to all the government's laws and wishes would they be able to demonstrate that they were worthy to be granted full equality with the rest of the citizens. Like the absolutist regime, the Maskilim also believed that loyalty was a precondition for equal rights and not vice versa.

If these principles of the Haskalah program are crucial for evaluating Perl's memorandum concerning *battei midrash* and *mikvot,* one also cannot underestimate moments of his personal life which undoubtedly determined not only the truculence but also the timing of this as well as the next and last denunciation.

In 1838, the year before Perl's death, events occurred which provoked more hatred of the Hasidim on Perl's part than in the course of his entire lifetime of struggle against this movement. Through the endeavors of Perl, his friend, the famous scholar Solomon Judah Rapoport, was appointed district rabbi of Tarnopol. The appointment of this Maskil as rabbi provoked a great rage among the Orthodox in Tarnopol. They issued satires and bans and organized a boycott against Perl.[52] The headquarters of Perl's and Rapoport's opponents was located in the *bet ha-midrash.*[53] This phase of the struggle of the Orthodox Jews of Tarnopol against Perl was reflected in his memorandum concerning the *battei midrash,* and Perl depicted all of the actions of the fanatics that took place in Tarnopol as a general phenomenon: the *bet ha-midrash* as a center of promulgation of bans, the issuing of lampoons by the Orthodox against their opponents, the boycott against the merchant Maskilim. Indeed, when Perl mentioned that these merchants found no customers for their grain supplies, he was really referring to himself; like his father, Todres, he dealt in grain.[54]

Perl's denunciation yielded quick results. In a circular from the Galician provincial presidency, district offices were instructed to investigate whether the *bet midrash* and *mikvot* were really the scenes of such loathsome deeds as depicted "in a denunciation by a trusted person who is acquainted in detail with the nature of Jewry. Where applicable, appropriate steps are to be taken to still this evil." Again the attention of the district offices was drawn to the censorship regulations concerning Yiddish and Hebrew books. The circular closed with the conclusion that the toleration of Galician Jewry's religious customs was valid only to the extent that they were not in contradiction to the laws of the land.[55] To this, the district chief added that both the large and small *bet midrash* in Tarnopol were to be officially closed.[56] Similarly, other district heads, for example those in Jarosław and Kałusz, hurried to close the *battei midrash* in their cities. Only through the earnest pleas of R. S. J. Rapoport were those in Tarnopol allowed to open for the High Holy Days. We may assume that in the other districts the closed *battei midrash* were also reopened soon after that time.

The Repudiation of S. J. Rapoport and His Tarnopol Synagogue

On July 6 of the same year, 1838, Perl presented the government with a new memorandum which was to be his last project in the campaign against Hasidism. The occasion was again the feud which continued to rage with increasing fury in Tarnopol. The Hasidim and the Orthodox were very upset by an action of Perl's which they considered to be a direct provocation against them. Encouraged by the support of District Chief Sachar, Perl was not satisfied with the fact that S. J. Rapoport, who was despised by the Hasidim, had a pulpit in the new synagogue which he had built near the German school. After the death of the old rabbi, Joshua Babad, Perl appointed Rapoport rabbi in the old synagogue in Tarnopol, which had until then been considered a monopoly of the Orthodox. The Hasidim now declared the old synagogue to be defiled and inscribed the verse "thou shalt utterly detest it, and thou shalt utterly abhor it; for it is a cursed thing" on the wall of the synagogue. On the eve of *Shabbat ha-Gadol* (the Sabbath preceding Passover), they broke open the doors of the old synagogue and smeared the steps of the Holy Ark and pulpit with mud and pitch.[57] In response to the closing of the *bet ha-midrash* by the authorities, the Orthodox proclaimed a state of mourning and bade their wives to remove their *shterntikhlekh* (traditional headcoverings).[58] Their representatives explicitly stated to the authorities that their fight against Rapoport was meant to strike at Perl, who "greatly oppresses the city."[59] One of the leaders of the agitation against Rapoport was publicly flogged by the police, and others were sentenced to jail.[60] The "regrettable excesses" in Tarnopol, as well as "the public announcement [i.e., the flogging]" by the local administration, "which was supposed to have called the ringleaders to order" and "which cannot admittedly serve as an example," were also mentioned by the Lemberg police directorate in its report dated June 7, 1838, as evidence of how far the fanaticism and intolerance of the Hasidim could go.[61]

In his request to the district chief of Tarnopol, in which he bade him to forward his memorandum to the Galician provincial presidency,[62] Perl referred to the "loathsome actions against the district rabbi Rapoport" as an example of the machinations "of this most dangerous sect of Hasidim." Perl also reminded the district chief of what the *mohalim* had done to a certain family named Goldhaber.[63] All the intrigues of this sect, Perl further explained, had one specific goal: to divert the Jews from education and to destroy the government's objectives concerning "the rapprochement of the Jews with the rest of the population on the path of education and true morality." Thus, the Jews would blindly follow the leaders of the "sect," give away everything they owned to them, and obey them at the slightest hint. Perl remarked that he was inclined to believe it was a godsend that these dreadful deeds of the sect took place in Tarnopol, for in other places there were no people who regarded it as their duty "to inform the government in writing or orally of such deeds."

Perl concluded that hitherto it had mistakenly been believed that the chief motives of the Hasidim's actions were only fanaticism and superstition. On the basis of his own experience as a Galician Jew, he asserted that the sect was inspired only by self-interest; the Hasidim endeavored to gain control over Galician Jewry and the rebbes were intent upon power and worldly pleasures. There were no means which they would not use in order to attain these ends. Their power was growing from year to year to the detriment of humanity, and therefore the government had to launch a campaign as soon as possible.

Perl's Most Scathing Denunciation

As for the memorandum itself, it was of book length, covering thirty-two folio pages.[64] The beginning of the memorandum was written in the tone of a confession before death. For over twenty-five years, Perl stated, he had spared neither money nor energy in order to elevate the cultural level of his Galician "coreligionists." He had attached his greatest hopes in helping to attain this objective to the *Deutsch-Israelitische Hauptschule* which he had established in Tarnopol. Now that he had reached old age he derived pride and pleasure from his students. Not only those who devoted themselves to science but also even those who took up commerce or crafts and those "who had to be in another man's service" were much more honest, conscientious, and reliable *"than one usually finds among their kind"* (emphasis added). However, all of this could not set him at ease when he looked on as the dangerous sect of Hasidism, which resisted every attempt to establish friendship between the Jews and the rest of the inhabitants of the state and to render them more useful to society, progressively spread its corrupting power and entrenched itself even in Tarnopol. He feared that soon all his efforts would go to waste and all his hopes would come to naught due to the poor state of his health[65] which prevented him from submitting a detailed description of this sect to the provincial presidency. Therefore it would suffice to enumerate the means by which the sect succeeded in gradually trapping all of Galician Jewry in its net and in ruling over it as it desired:

1. The sect subjugated all the rabbis, even those who were Mitnaggedim at heart. The sect consisted for the most part of idlers who would ferret out all the rumors in the city. A Mitnaggedic rabbi was persecuted and denounced as a heretic until he himself went to the zaddik to beg forgiveness in order to retain his rabbinic post. The other rabbis were thus frightened and renounced any kind of resistance. After the government issued a rigorous decree against Hasidism in 1823, the Hasidim succeeded, through the intercession of the zaddikim, in persuading the authorities to send an official questionnaire to the rabbis concerning the nature of Hasidism. The rabbis were so terrorized into giving a favorable statement of opinion that the government completely changed the interpretation of that decree on the basis of their statements.
2. Almost all the *shoḥatim* were members of the sect or friendly toward it at that time. A candidate for *shoḥet* learned *sheḥitah* only from a Hasidic *shoḥet* and received his license to practice from a Hasidic

rebbe who chose the community where he might be employed. If a *kehillah* or a lessee of the kosher meat tax refused to recognize this *shohet,* the consumption of meat was banned in that community and the *shehitah* of another *shohet* was declared to be nonkosher until that *kehillah* submitted to the will of the rebbe. Contrary to the explicit laws of 1776 and 1789 requiring a *shohet* to obtain certification from a rabbi, the rabbi had no authority whatsoever in the matter, with the exception of the cities of Lemberg, Brody, "and, perhaps, another *kehillah*."[66] The following were the reasons why the Hasidim had so set their hearts on filling the positions of *shohatim* with their own people:

a. The rebbes attained power in the *kehillot* through the *shohatim,* who subjugated the kosher meat tax lessees, the meat purveyors, the rabbis, and the entire community. They pronounced the head of cattle nonkosher when it suited them, they refused to slaughter a fowl for a person whom they disliked on the pretext that they were not well disposed to perform their task, that they must go to the *mikveh* or the *bet ha-midrash* and the like. It even happened that they would break a limb of a fowl in order to make it nonkosher. If the rabbi was a Mitnagged, the *shohet* spread false rumors that he couldn't decide questions regarding *kashrut* (ritual purity), for he judged kosher meat to be nonkosher and vice versa.

b. The *shohatim* were the "janissaries" of the rebbes, their agents and spies. The rebbes' emissaries would always lodge with the *shohatim* on their journeys. The *shohatim* were also responsible for the fact that the revenue from the kosher meat tax had greatly declined for some years. Despite the laws of 1789 and 1810 which only permitted them to live in the cities, the *shohatim* travelled through the villages, or slaughtered in private homes, thereby avoiding payment of the meat tax. The *shohatim* slaughtered tax-free not only for the rebbes and their families, who were exempt from this levy, but also for all the Hasidim who boarded with them on Sabbaths and holidays in the hundreds.

3. The Galician *mohalim*, who were not subject to any control, in contrast to the *mohalim* in Bohemia, were also tools of the sect to dominate the *kehillot*. Cases occurred in which *mohalim* refused to perform a circumcision because one of the parents of the child, or even the *kvater* (godfather) or *sandek* (the man who holds the child while it is being circumcised) was a Mitnagged.

Perl concluded that the Hasidim, controlling the three positions of rabbi, *shohet,* and *mohel* in every community, had the potential to subjugate Galician Jewry without exception.

> If this is allowed to continue, no force on earth will be able to bring about a rapprochement between Jewry and civil society and to *assimilate it* [emphasis added] with the rest of the inhabitants of Galicia. The strict separatism and intolerance of this sect will render impossible from the outset any attempt of this kind.

Perl contended that in order to achieve a radical improvement of the situation the laws regarding rabbis, *shoḥatim,* and *mohalim* in Galicia must be changed.

In accordance with the "Jewry ordinance" of 1789, rabbis were to be engaged in the chief cities of the districts, and in the other towns *morei hora'ah* ("Religionsweiser," or religious teachers) who must be subject to the district rabbis. According to the same charter, district rabbis who could not demonstrate the knowledge equivalent to a German elementary school education could no longer be engaged. The imperial court decrees of 1826 and 1827 required the same of a *moreh hora'ah*, and the candidates were to be tested on the German catechism for the Jewish religion, *Bnei Zion,* by Herz Homberg. According to an imperial decree of 1836, by 1846 a rabbi or *moreh hora'ah* could not be employed who had not completed philosophical and pedagogical studies. The district rabbis and "Religionsweiser" were chosen by the *kehillot*, and it was decided that elections for the post of district rabbi were to be held every three years. The rabbis were assigned a modest wage because they received additional revenues from fees and commissions at certain functions, such as betrothals and weddings.

Perl asserted that although the government undoubtedly had had the best of intentions in instituting all these regulations with regard to rabbis, its objective had not been attained. Almost fifty years had passed since the "Jewry Ordinance" was promulgated and yet only three rabbis satisfied the requirements of the law. These were the rabbis Hirsh Ẓevi Chajes in Żółkiew, Michael Kristianpoller in Brody, and Solomon Judah Rapoport in Tarnopol. The other sixteen district rabbis and over two hundred "Religionsweiser" not only had no learning apart from that of the Talmud but also were the greatest enemies of education.

Even these three educated rabbis had no effect upon the people and had themselves been exposed to persecution by the obscurant fanatics. Rabbi Kristianpoller constantly had to fend off the attacks of the local "Religionsweiser," Kluger,[67] who pronounced him a heretic and an unbeliever and organized all the rabbis of Galicia against him. If not for Kristianpoller's ancestry—his father was the rabbi of Brody and was respected throughout Galicia and, in addition, he himself became connected by marriage with the most prominent families of

Brody, the Nathansohns, Kallirs, and Bernsteins—he would have had to surrender to his opponent, Kluger, long ago. The Rabbi of Żółkiew, Chajes, had to give away the entire fortune which he had inherited from his father "in order to shut the mouths of the enemies of everything that is good." The worst fell to the lot of the Rabbi of Tarnopol, Rapoport, who had neither an influential family nor other means necessary to counter the attacks of his enemies.

Since the government had never yet ousted a rabbi or rejected a newly elected rabbi because he did not have the necessary qualifications, there was no inducement for the educated Jews to make an effort to gain a rabbinical post. The officials were satisfied if a rabbi only perfunctorily adhered to the demands of the law, if he sent another man to take the examination or if he extracted certification of schooling through dishonest means. The rabbis combatted education for the sake of their own egoistic interests because they well understood that Jews who received a normal school education and were permeated by "universal love of one's fellow men" would lose all respect for them. In their struggle against education, the rabbis invoked religion but, in fact, their religion obliged the Jews to educate their "heart and understanding." The new decree of 1836 which required that rabbis take philosophic studies would certainly have no effect if the law concerning German elementary education had been ignored for fifty years. The fanatical rabbis would manage just as they had before. Even the "obscurantists" would want to exploit the new decree as a pretext to depose the only three educated rabbis, because they themselves were not university graduates. Perl noted in passing that in Przemyśl a certain Anshl Tsoyzmir[68] appeared officially as a rabbi because he knew a little German. In fact, he was a merchant and speculator who lived in Stryj all year and sometimes came to Przemyśl for his business. The actual district rabbi was a certain Zaynvl Heller,[69] who was not even registered with the authorities.

In addition to the fact that the government did not enforce the law regarding the educational qualifications for rabbis, Perl enumerated several other reasons why even the three educated rabbis were not able duly to influence the people. The fact that rabbis did not have steady and ample salaries but were dependent on voluntary gifts meant that an educated rabbi who fought against fanaticism and intolerance was condemned to starvation if he was not a wealthy man. In contrast, the rabbis who did find favor with the *kehillah* were provided with large incomes. Despite the fact that a provincial decree of 1825 forbade the levying of an impost on *sheḥitah,* such a tax was instituted in the *kehillot* under the pretext that it was designated for the *shoḥet,* although it was actually for the benefit of the rabbi. There were even *kehillot* that issued a tacit ban against the kosher meat tax lessee who refused to pay a weekly sum for the rabbi. As an example of such illegal imposts on *sheḥitah,* Perl cited the *kehillah* of Zbaraż, where the surtax on *sheḥitah* brought in 400 gulden a year for the local *moreh hora'ah.* There were also *kehillot* that imposed a tax on salt (a kreutzer on a cone of salt) for the benefit of the rabbi.

Perl also regarded the provision of the law that a rabbi should be chosen for only three years as a hindrance to an enlightened rabbi conducting his activity properly. Aside from the fact that in the course of three years little can be done for the education of the people, the rabbi was faced with the threat that after his three-year term expired he would be deposed, and therefore he had to refrain from any action which did not find favor with the people. The fanatics also had another weapon to force a rabbi who was active in behalf of the dissemination of education and enlightenment into submission; namely, they did not accord him the honors customarily due a rabbi,[70] and he was thus disgraced.

The reforms which Perl suggested to the government included the following main proposals:

1. The salaries of district rabbis and *morei hora'ah* should be designated by law to enable them to maintain a suitable standard of living. These salaries should be covered by a direct tax which the *kehillah* should exact from its members in proportion to their means.
2. All the honors which are customarily accorded to rabbis and *morei hora'ah* should be proclaimed to be the legal duty of the *kehillah* so that the "enemies of order and of the good cause" would not have the opportunity to resort to trickery.
3. The *ḥadarim* should be under the supervision of the rabbis; it should also be their duty to examine the *melamedim* and certify them.
4. The district offices should see to it that the newly chosen rabbis and *morei hora'ah* demonstrate proficiency equivalent to the curriculum of a German school through a special exam and that they also be tested on the textbook *Bnei Zion.* Even the rabbis and *morei hora'ah* who had already been installed in office should now be examined, and if they did not pass the examination or if they were known to the government as "ignoramuses and enemies of knowledge," they should immediately be dismissed from their posts.
5. The rabbis and *morei hora'ah* should be appointed for life. They should be deposed only in cases of old age, infirmity, or serious crime and then, however, only by the government authorities and not by the *kehillah.*

6. As long as the position of rabbi or *moreh hora'ah* is vacant, the *kehillah* must pay the salary to the district office, where the money should be reserved as a fund for the future rabbinical school (Collegium Rabbinicum).[71]
7. *Shoḥatim* should receive regular salaries from the *kehillot*, and a tax on *sheḥitah,* salt, and the like should no longer be imposed by the *kehillot.*[72]
8. In the future, not only the salary of *shoḥatim* but all of the *kehillah*'s expenses should be covered by a graduated Jewish communal tax. The indirect taxes did not tally with the meaning of the law and it was also unjust, Perl contended, that a poor man should pay as much as a rich man or even more if he was burdened with many children or if he employed journeymen or apprentices.

If in Perl's last proposal, just as in Levinsohn's *Hefker-Velt,* the character of the Haskalah is revealed as a progressive movement which combatted the feudal exploitation of the masses, the conclusions with which he ends his lengthy memorandum are indicative of the close link between the Haskalah and the absolutist regime.

In order to convince the government that it had to adopt his proposals regarding the rabbis, he asserted that only through the execution of this program would the Jews be supplied with mentors who would instill in them loyalty and obedience to the government. On the face of it, Perl said, one could ask the question why the Galician Jews disobeyed virtually all the state laws which had a bearing on them. The simple answer that Jews were restricted by so many laws that they strove by all means to evade them was a superficial one. Perl contended that this answer could easily be refuted when we considered that the Jews even acted against laws which undoubtedly were intended for their welfare. The Jews did not want to give their children a "practical" upbringing and education because of religious prejudices. But why, Perl asked, did they not care for the poor in each community instead of allowing thieves and vagabonds to beg from door to door and commit thefts? Why was Galicia, and particularly the area bordering on Russia, flooded by thieves and the "dangerous gang"? Why did the Jews of Tarnopol side with every Russian Jew who was apprehended and give false testimony that he was a native of Tarnopol?[73] The only answer, Perl contended, was the influence of the people's teachers, the rabbis, who had only their own interests at heart and the ideas that were born in their one-track minds. If the people only had honest and qualified rabbis as teachers, they would be instilled with respect and obedience even toward those laws which seemed to restrict the rights of the Jews. Thus, for example, they would be able to demonstrate to the people that the restriction of Jewish occupations which was contained in the "Jewry Ordinance" of 1789[74] was dictated only and completely by the wish to lead the Jews to useful labor and to economic enterprise.

In conclusion, Perl assured the provincial presidency that his proposals were motivated exclusively by the knowledge that it was his duty to impart to the government his longstanding experience and observations regarding what was useful for the state and for Jewry.

The reply of the provincial presidency to the district office in Tarnopol regarding Perl's memorandum[75] again demonstrates that the government was more cautious in its policy with respect to the Hasidim than toward the zealous Maskilim. The presidency agreed with Perl concerning the "harmful tendencies of the Hasidic Jewish sect," and recognized that his description of the deeds which the Hasidim committed in order to dominate the rabbis and other members of the Jewish clergy undoubtedly had a practical use and was further proof of his commendable devotion to work in behalf of the "objectives of the state administration."

As to the measures which he suggested to combat those deeds, the government could not agree to adopt them. Particularly regarding his proposals concerning the rabbis, they would have to wait until the promulgation of the imperial decree regarding the Jews in all the provinces which was then in preparation.[76] Moreover, there was no practical reason to institute at that time the reforms which Perl had proposed. Perl himself admitted that for the time being there were not yet any rabbis or rabbinical candidates who were not under the "noxious influence" of the Hasidim. Therefore, it appeared that the government would have to give life appointments to rabbis.[77] The provincial presidency promised to take Perl's proposals concerning the *shoḥatim* and *mohalim* into consideration in the drawing up of new plans.

A year later, on *Simḥat Torah* of 1839, Perl died. His funeral was symbolic of his life's work. His admirers reported that on the instruction of the authorities, the two medals which he had been awarded by the Russian czar and the Austrian emperor were pinned to his shroud. His coffin was followed by the district chief, the mayor, all of the higher-ranking officials of the district office and the municipality, and a large number of officers of the garrison in Tarnopol.[78]

Another report of the funeral, written by one of Perl's opponents, added the following details:[79]

The men in civilian dress who followed the coffin with bowed heads were armed police agents who were dispatched to guard the corpse against an attack by the Hasidim. On Perl's fresh grave the Hasidim let loose in a wild dance.

6

Joseph Perl's Hebrew Almanacs

The Literary Context of the Almanacs

The important part played by Joseph Perl as a pioneer in the Haskalah movement of eastern Europe is generally recognized. The tremendous influence he exerted upon his contemporary Maskilim in Galicia and Russia is by now fully recorded in the histories of Jewish life and literature.

With regard to his literary activities, he is still largely know only as the author of the anti-Hasidic satire *Megalleh Temirin*. Less known and appreciated is Perl's second satire, *Boḥen Ẓaddik*, which was composed in the form of a critique of the *Megalleh Temirin*. The *Luḥot* (Almanacs) which Perl edited in Tarnopol during the years 5574–76 (1813–15) were virtually ignored and unfortunately never analyzed from the cultural point of view.

This oversight by historians of Haskalah literature may be due partly to the rarity of these *Luḥot* and to the fact that they virtually escaped bibliographical notice. Max Erik mentioned, though only in a footnote, that Perl published the yearbook *Ẓir Ne'eman* (Faithful Messenger), which "in the spirit of Lefin's suggestion is made up mostly of popular scientific articles."[1] It is doubtful whether Israel Zinberg ever actually saw Perl's *Luḥot*, for he gave incorrect dates for them (1814–

16 instead of 1813–15), and described them as periodicals intended for schoolchildren.[2] Although I. Weinlös inexplicably called Perl's *Luḥot* the first prose products of the Haskalah in eastern Europe,[3] he was right in saying that "these almanacs never pretended to any great literary value." That is probably why he never took the trouble to penetrate their essential values. Even Joseph Klausner, the only historian of Jewish literature to furnish a list of the articles contained in Perl's *Luḥot*,[4] did not consider them of sufficient importance to analyze their contents. This was probably because they did not seem to be anything more than common almanacs. The fact is, however, that both in form and content, Perl's *Luḥot* reflect the general attitude of the older Haskalah to all spheres of life. And, in addition to supplying well-popularized information on scientific subjects, they presented an example of how the ideas of the Haskalah were spread in a highly original and artful manner.

Externally, Perl's *Luḥot* resembled the general run of *Luḥot* which were issued in various German cities during the eighteenth and early nineteenth centuries: they were pocket size and carried the caption *Luaḥ ha-Shanah*[5] (Annual Calendar). The first part of Perl's *Luḥot*, the actual *Luaḥ ha-Shanah*, was also compiled along the same lines as the other popular almanacs, but the innovations which he introduced were quite remarkable.

Perl's *Luaḥ* typically began with a Jewish calendar for the "days of the week and month, fast days and holidays, four seasons of the year and the like, according to the calculation of the People of Israel, and the deadline for the recitation of the blessing of the moon for each month." This was followed by the Roman Catholic and Greek Orthodox calendars, which included the names of all the saints' days and the genealogy of the Russian czar and his family,[6] which was considered an integral part, just as the genealogy of the German princely dynasty was considered essential in the German *Luḥot*.[7] According to the accepted usage, there also was a table giving the time of daily sunrise and sunset[8] and details for the *minhagim* (customs) of prayers and holidays.

It was only with respect to the general *minhagim* connected with prayers that Perl revealed his departure from the traditional almanac. Here he commented on the practice of expectorating after the words "kekhol hamonam" in the *aleinu* prayer, citing Isaiah Horowitz, who, in his *Shenei Luḥot ha-Berit*, had repudiated this custom as outdated, since there were no longer any idol worshippers (*Akum*) and there was a danger in observing this practice. Perl added that many synagogues posted wooden boards with warnings inscribed on them in large letters, asking the worshippers to refrain from this reprehensible practice.

Taking the Prussian and other German calendars as his model, Perl listed all the fairs during the year but took into account the needs of his readers. First he listed the fairs in Galicia, the Ukraine, and Poland, and then the fairs of Leipzig and of several other cities in Austria, Bohemia, and Hungary. A new feature of Perl's calendar was a list of the days on which the courts in Russia were not in session.

In the oldest extant Jewish almanacs[9] a section is devoted to the chronology of the most important events in Jewish history. They begin with the traditional dates of the deluge, the births of the patriarchs and Moses, and then give the dates of historical events, such as the destruction of the First and Second Temples, the compilation of the Mishnah, the Talmud, the *Alfasi* and the *Yad Ḥazakah*, and finally the dates of various expulsions from western European countries and conflagrations in large Jewish communities, such as Prague, Nikolsburg, Frankfurt-am-Main, Posen, and Lissa.

Perl's chronology, entitled "Zikron Yemot Olam," also contained these traditional religious and historical Jewish dates, but added dates from general history, such as those of the founding of Rome and Vienna, and of various discoveries and inventions, such as gunpowder, the cannon, paper, printing, inoculation against smallpox, and lightning rods.[10]

Perl's Goals and Methods

The calendars printed at that time in Germany included the years of the reign of the rulers of the land (Prussia, Hesse). Similarly, Perl supplied numerous dates from the history of Russia such as the founding of Kiev, Moscow, and Petersburg, when the titles czar and emperor of Russia were instituted, and the year a regular army was organized in Russia.

This expansion of the traditional chronology reflects some of the goals of the Haskalah which Perl aimed to achieve, namely, to spread general knowledge and to identify the readers more closely with the country in which they lived. In his almanac for the year 5576 (1815), Perl became so outspoken in his propaganda as to add at the end not only "the third year of the composition of the *Luaḥ Ẓir Ne'eman*" but also "the second year of the establishment of the School (*Bet ha-Ḥinukh*) in Tarnopol." The calendar part of his *Luaḥ* composed less than half the book; that is, only fifteen of the forty pages. The second part of the *Luaḥ* was entitled *Luaḥ ha-Lev*, after the injunction in Prov. 3:3: "Write them upon the table of thy heart." In the introduction to the *Luaḥ ha-Lev*, which Perl reprinted without any changes in the second and third annual, he admitted that his reason for combining the *Luaḥ ha-Lev* with the calendar proper was that every Jew consulting the *Luaḥ* on a Sabbath or holiday should also glance through the almanac section. The actual *Luaḥ*, then, was but a means of attracting the reader to the almanac.

The introduction is filled with citations concerning fear of the Lord so that the simple reader hardly notices that the new Haskalah notions have been interwoven in the text. Thus Perl started out with a moralizing dissertation concerning the transitory nature of human life, pointing to the lesson that all our striving and pursuit after money was but vanity. Only the Torah and kind deeds could create a lasting memorial, for subsequent generations acquire a love of God and a desire for godly actions only from the zaddikim (righteous) who had lived long ago. In this connection, he introduced the verse from Prov. 10:25: "The righteous is an everlasting foundation"—one of the fundamentals of the Hasidic Torah. Thus, good deeds had to be recorded and preserved for coming generations. Here he casually commented that the reader must not be surprised to find occasional references and stories about Gentiles in the *Luaḥ ha-Lev*. He justified this with such talmudic dicta as "he who cites a wise saying, even from other nations, should be called a sage,"[11] and "the righteous of the nations have a share in the world to come."[12] Perl further stated that he had rendered the talmudic stories in "a lucid and fluent style," intelligible to everybody, and that he had translated all Aramaic expressions into Hebrew. As an authority for such a procedure he cited Rashi, who used to translate talmudic expressions into Hebrew or even French.

What Perl regarded as "lucid and fluent language" (*lashon ẓaḥah ve-kalah*) as compared to talmudic Hebrew may be gathered from the following juxtaposition of an *aggadah* from *Kiddushin* 31a with the version printed by Perl in his *Luaḥ* for 5574:[13]

A comparison of the two texts makes it evident that Perl's argument about making the texts of the talmudic stories which he cites more intelligible was merely a pretext for spreading and promoting the knowledge of "pure" biblical Hebrew. Except for two added sentences, which are entirely superfluous, Perl's variant does not render the original text any clearer. It merely "translates" the flexible language and style of the Mishnah and Gemara into the "lucid language" of the Bible.

PERL'S RECENSION

שאלו לר׳ אליעזר עד היכן כיבוד אב ואם? אמר להם צאו וראו מה עשה כותי אחד לאביו באשקלון ודמא בן נתינה שמו. פעם אחת בקשו ממנו חכמים אבנים לאפוד בששים רבוא שכר, והיה המפתח מונח תחת ראשותי אביו הישן על מטתו ולא רצה להקיצו משנתו. לשנה הבאה נתן לו הקב״ה שכרו, כי נולדה לו פרה אדומה בעדרו, ויבואו חכמי ישראל אליו ויאמר להם הכותי, יודע אני בכם, שאם אבקש כל כספכם וזהבכם, הלא אתם נותנים לי, אולם אנכי לא אבקש כי אם הכסף אשר אבדתי בעבור כבוד אבי בשנה אשר עברה. כאשר שמעו החכמים את דבריו אמרו הן מי שאינו מצווה עושה כן, ומה יעשה כל איש ישראל אשר צוה לו אלהים לאמר: כבד את אביך ואת אמך? ומה יהיה שכרו בעשותו את מצות ד׳?

TALMUDIC TEXT

שאלו את רבי אליעזר עד היכן כיבוד אב ואם. אמר להם צאו וראו מה עשה נכרי אחד לאביו באשקלון ודמא בן נתינה שמו. בקשו ממנו חכמים אבנים לאפוד בששים ריבוא ורב כהנא מתני בשמנים ריבוא והיה מפתח מונח תחת מראשותיו של אביו ולא ציערו. לשנה האחרת נתן הקב״ה שכרו שנולדה לו פרה אדומה בעדרו. נכנסו חכמי ישראל אצלו אמר להם יודע אני בכם שאם אני מבקש מכם כל ממון שבעולם אתם נותנין לי. אלא אין אני מבקש מכם אלא אותו ממון שהפסדתי בשביל כבוד אבא ואמר רבי חנינא ומה מי שאינו מצווה ועושה כך מצווה ועושה כך על אחת כמה וכמה.

Propaganda for the program of the Haskalah was also the purpose Perl had in mind in selecting stories from the Talmud and of the sages of the nations for his *Luaḥ ha-Lev*. This is clearly shown by the kind of morals Perl drew in the introduction and explanatory notes accompanying the *aggadot* and other stories. It is always obvious that not a single *aggadah*, or tale, was introduced for its own sake, but for its moral and ethical content.

In this connection, a very instructive comparison can be made with the periodical *Sulamith*, which began to appear in Dessau in 1806.[14] *Sulamith* contained many of the talmudic dicta and stories which Perl used in his *Luaḥ*, but without the moral that Perl invariably affixed to the end of each story. This was either because the editors were dealing with a more cultured reader who could derive the moral for himself, or because the reader was already so well "enlightened" that all further Haskalah propaganda was considered superfluous. The stories which appeared in Perl's *Luaḥ* were printed in *Sulamith* with different objectives in mind, solely for the purpose of spreading morality (naturally in accord with *Sulamith*'s concept of the Enlightenment) or to prove through examples from the Talmud that the teachings of the Jewish religion embodied the same humanitarian ideals as those presented in modern culture.

The Context of the Almanacs: A Study of the Haskalah Ethos

Let us now examine more carefully the content of the *Luaḥ ha-Lev* in the three annual volumes of Perl's *Luaḥ* and see to what extent they were in accord with the aims of the Haskalah.

The *Luaḥ ha-Lev* for the year 5574 began with a story entitled "Edut Ne'emanah" (Reliable Evidence), which consisted of an excerpt in Hebrew of the report made by Joseph August Schultes, professor at Cracow University,[15] on his journey through Galicia. He found that "Jews are virtually the only merchants, tailors, and shoemakers of that province; they apply themselves extensively to glass and metal products; there are also Jews who till fields, leased from magnates." The professor also remarked on the fine appearance of the Galician Jews. The moral which Perl drew in his lengthy introduction and in a still longer note at its conclusion was:

> We must praise and give thanks to God for the compassionate feeling which he aroused in our behalf in the hearts of scholars and saints, so that they speak well of us. It accrues to our benefit that in place of the evil mongers, who fabricated malign rumors in the past, we now have benevolent spokesmen among the nations who intercede in our behalf with princes and rulers, persuading them to deal kindly with us.

Perl concluded with an appeal to the Jews that they too be compassionate and act kindly toward every human being, for then they would be highly regarded by the sages of the nations and would surely receive the compassion of all the kings on earth.

This may be said to be the essence of the political ideology of the Maskilim. They seem to have been dazzled by the fact that Jews were not as despised under the rule of Austrian absolutism as they were during the Middle Ages. From this, they concluded that the Jews had to improve their relations with the Christians to prove to the rulers that they were deserving of still greater favors.

The same reasoning underlies the second story, entitled "Hakhnasat Orḥim" (Hospitality). Here Perl cited a talmudic *aggadah* about R. Gamaliel:[16] R. Gamaliel was graciously waiting on his guests; R. Eliezer was greatly admiring R. Gamaliel's manner of hospitality, whereupon R. Joshua pointed out to him that even the patriarch Abraham was standing while his guests (namely the angels, whom he believed to be Arabs), were seated. R. Zadok remarked that we must take an example from God, who by sending down rain fructifies the earth and thereby sets a table for everybody. In his introduction, Perl paid tribute to the Jewish people who excel over others in charity, acts of kindness, and hospitality. In a lengthy moralizing lesson at the end of the story, Perl revealed his reason for citing this *aggadah* about hospitality. He emphasized that we must follow in the footsteps of our wise ancestors and take to heart R. Zadok's remark that God feeds sinners as well as saints.[17] It is important, however, to learn from the patriarch Abraham that we are obliged to aid every one who needs our assistance, irrespective of his origin or religion. Here, in the guise of *hakhnasat orḥim*, Perl injected two fundamental ideas of the Haskalah: tolerance toward the nonpious instead of religious fanaticism, and a closer rapprochement with the gentile environment instead of religious and cultural separatism. Perl utilized this indirect method of espousing the principles of the Haskalah in almost all his stories under headings that suggest a different content than the one given.

The idea of tolerance toward the nonpious was the reason for introducing another *aggadah* from the Talmud in the same almanac, under the heading "ha-Ishah ha-Ḥakhamah" (The Wise Woman). Here Perl cited the well-known story of Beruriah, the wife of R. Meir, who chided her learned husband because he prayed for the death of the wicked who made his life miserable.[18] Beruriah defended her position by quoting the verse from Psalms,[19] "Let sinners cease of the earth," reading *Ḥatta'im* to mean "sins" instead of "sinners." Perl concluded with an appeal that we not hate the wicked but his wickedness.

A similar purpose is served by citing the talmudic *aggadah* about R. Elazar ben R. Simeon, who begged the forgiveness of a man he insulted because of his ugly appearance.[20] This story is entitled "Le-olam yehe adam rakh ke-kaneh" (One must always strive to be as gentle as a reed). It concluded with Perl's moralizing paragraph, admonishing the reader to have compassion for one afflicted with a physical or moral defect. For the latter he suggested moral suasion. It is apparent that this is but remotely connected to the *aggadah*, if at all.

The idea of love for the Gentile was directly propounded by Perl when he cited under the caption "Ahavat reim" the well-known *aggadah* about Hillel imparting knowledge of the whole Torah to a proselyte while standing on one foot.[21] Perl did not repeat Hillel's maxim in its original wording: "What is hateful to you, do not to your neighbor." Instead, he substituted the positive formulation of the same principle in the scriptural verse, "Thou shalt love thy neighbor as thyself."[22] Perl concluded that the precept to love one's fellow man is based on the principle that all men are created in the image of God.

The intention of the Haskalah in advocating the idea of *ahavat ha-adam* (love of man) was not merely to do away with the social barrier but also to bring about a cultural rapprochement of Jews with their environment by spreading secular knowledge among them. In Perl's introduction he revealed his intention to cite stories about Gentiles because, according to the Talmud, we may acquire knowledge (Torah) and wisdom from everybody.

This is the theme of the lengthy article "Ahavat ha-Torah ve-ha-ḥokhmah" (Love of the Torah and of Wisdom). It begins with the well-known legend about Hillel, who was frozen in a cold winter night on the roof of the *bet ha-midrash* while trying to listen to the discourse of Shemaiah and Abtalion.[23] It is followed by similar stories concerning Greek scholars "which he had read in Greek books in his youth [*bi-yemei alumai*]." As an apology for such a radical step, Perl explained to his pious readers that the Greeks' actions were somewhat similar to Hillel's "even though they cannot compare with him." He told of Kleontes, who worked at night watering a garden or turning a handmill and studied under the philosopher Zeno by day. There is a story about Euclid, who, during the war between Athens and Megara, used to come to Athens disguised as a woman despite the danger to his life, in order to receive instruction from Socrates. Here Perl took the opportunity to devote a lengthy explanatory note to Socrates, whom he introduced to the reader as the wisest and most righteous man among the Gentiles, a sage who by his own intellect arrived at the idea of the unity of God. Paraphrasing a combination of scriptural verses, Perl concluded his eulogy as follows: "Blessed is he because he died the death of the righteous and his end is a blessing." At the end, he presents Diogenes of Sinope as a persevering student who would not part from his teacher Antisthenes even though brutally abused by him. In this circumspect manner, Perl endeavored to prove to his readers that the rest of the world also had its sages and saints. In any event, he achieved one of the main aims of the Haskalah in acquainting the Jewish reader with the names of Greek philosophers.

The *aggadah* concerning a Gentile, Dama b. Netinah, whom talmudic sages set up as a model of filial piety, was also included in the *Luaḥ* as a vehicle for this same moral lesson, that is, much can also be learned from the Gentiles. Perl added a sermon to this *aggadah* that was twice as long as the story, praising the greatness of the talmudic sages for having been aware of this truth. Perl concluded his moralizing with the following invocation to the Tannaim:

> Oh, Ye saints of God and righteous of the Most High! Look down from your exalted place and behold your children and spiritual descendants. Bestow upon them some of the glory of your spirit and wisdom so that they may know and understand how to follow in your footsteps and emulate your noble deeds. May they love truth and righteousness above all desires and delights of the world. May they bend their ears and make their hearts receptive to words

of truth from every one who utters them. May they not hold in contempt wise sayings that pour forth from the mouth of any sage . . . because it is God who bestows wisdom and all knowledge and understanding proceed from Him.

Thus, Perl subtly reminded his generation of east European Jews that they deviated from the pious Tannaim by their insularity. And as for the Tannaim, "our holy ancestors," Perl found it necessary to emphasize their religious authority by adding that they indeed learned from God Himself, as He poured His "Ruaḥ ha-Kodesh" (divine inspiration) into them so that they might lead us into the paths of righteousness.

In the article entitled "Kibbud Av ve-Em" (Honor thy Father and Mother), there was a striking discrepancy between the length of the story itself and the appended sermon. Perl must have realized this, for he added by way of explanation that he did not consider it necessary to dwell at length on the merit of obeying the Fifth Commandment. He said that it was not out of flattery or blindness to the shortcomings of his people that he asserted that in this respect the Jews excelled all other nations.

In his article "Yegia Kappayim" (Toil of One's Hands), Perl stressed another vital tenet of the Haskalah, namely the necessity of productive occupations for all Jews which he relates to the talmudic statement, "R. Hiyya b. Ammi said in the name of Ulla: 'Greater is he who enjoys the fruit of his labor than one who fears Heaven.'"[24] Perl explained that the Talmud does not refer "to the toil of hands without the fear of Heaven, because 'the fear of the Lord is the beginning and end of everything,'" but to one who toils with his hands *and* fears the Lord. Moreover, Perl pointed out that living by toil is an absolute necessity from both the personal and societal points of view. To show that labor is indispensible for personal happiness and pleasure, Perl cited a long list of talmudic sayings, such as, "Study of Torah along with work is seemly,"[25] "One is bound in respect to his son to teach him a craft,"[26] "Rather flay carcasses in the marketplace than live from handouts,"[27] "Treat thy Sabbath like a weekday rather than be dependent on men,"[28] and "The world is dark to anyone dependent on another's table."[29] From the point of view of society, idleness must be condemned because healthy people who live on alms detract from the support of the impoverished, the aged, the weak, the sick, and the maimed. Since the giving of charity represents the performing of a great *miẓvah*, healthy people who accept alms are committing a grave sin. Such people are also harmful socially, because being forced to court the favor and good graces of their benefactors, they cannot afford to be candid with them. This has a demoralizing effect and thus Jews who live on alms are disgraced in the eyes of other nations.

It is quite evident that this article expressed through proverbs couched in the popular idiom the attitude of the Haskalah toward productive occupations. In the name of social betterment, the Haskalah had launched an attack against this form of idleness and the nonproductive livelihoods just as Humanism and the Enlightenment had done in the past. For the Maskilim, however, there was the additional motive of the rising Jewish bourgeoisie, whose motto of class prestige was formulated in terms of "avoiding disgrace for Jews in the eyes of other nations." This article also revealed the outlook of the Haskalah on the general social questions. For example, it believed poverty had ceased to be a punishment from heaven or the outcome of a game between mystic forces, the *midat ha-ḥesed* and the *midat ha-din*, as Hasidic tradition would have had it, but the result of laziness and idleness, except for those who were physically unfit. This social theory was expounded in a clearer and more systematic fashion in the *Luaḥ* for the year 5575 (1814), in an article entitled "Da Mah she-Tashiv."

The rather transparent allusion in this article to the Hasidic rebbes constitutes about the only attack against Hasidism in the three issues of Perl's *Luaḥ*. The zaddikim living from *Pidyonot* (intercessory offerings) were virtually the only ones who fit the characterization of "poor people living from donations, currying the favor of the rich and therefore afraid to spread admonishing words." In general, however, Perl did not consider it good policy openly to attack any Jewish group, especially the Hasidim. He thought it better to introduce Haskalah notions through stories dealing with morals, the fear of God, and kindly deeds.

Although every story and article in Perl's *Luaḥ* is a vehicle for a central element in the program and ideology of the Haskalah, side issues of the movement are also interwoven. Thus, in the above story about Hillel, entitled "Ahavat ha-Torah ve-ha-ḥokhmah," Perl said it was a "disgrace for any intelligent man to remain idle" and live off alms. In telling about the diligent Kleontes, he praised the laws of Athens which punished idleness, because, as Perl explained parenthetically, "idleness," which is the translation for *rifeyon yadaim*, is the father of every sin and misdeed.

The article "Ẓedakah la-aniyim" (Charity for the Poor) is even more characteristic of Perl's tactics. It begins with the talmudic story about Mar Ukba, who each day used to place four "zuz" in his poor neighbor's door-socket.[30] This is followed by a lengthy story about B. M. Cohn, the well-known philanthropist from Berlin who had died seven years earlier. Before his death, Mr. Cohn had requested that a sack be placed in his grave containing receipts from the poor and destitute to whom he had distributed all that money. It would be puzzling to consider why Perl, the Maskil, devoted a whole article to charity were it not for the inclusion of the following epigram which he attributed to Cohn: "I pity those poor fellows who married rich women, because I am not in a position to support them."[31] Perl explained that Cohn was referring to those women who, regarding themselves as aristocrats, were forced to eat and dress luxuriously. "Brothers and friends," Perl intoned, "be on your guard because this is a rotten well from which a great evil comes to Israel." Clearly this warning against luxury, though presumably incidental, was the reason for this lengthy story's being introduced. The fight against waste and luxury was the logical consequence of the Haskalah's belief in productive occupations and essential to the accumulation of capital. Hence it was a popular subject for all the writers of the Haskalah.

The Second Almanac: Issues of Language and Politics

The *Luaḥ-ha-Lev* for the year 5575 (1814) begins with the same introduction as the one in the preceding year. Perl explained that the publication of the previous year's *Luaḥ* had been delayed for various reasons and therefore had not been adequately circulated.

The first article in this volume, entitled "Halakhah ve-Aggadah," was a kind of editorial in which Perl stressed the need of *divrei mussar* (ethical teachings). He quoted the well-known rabbinic parable about R. Abbahu and R. Hiyya b. Abba,[32] in which the aggadist is compared with a seller of cheap needles for which there is great demand, while the Halakhist is like a dealer in precious stones who counts on very few customers. After the word "aggadah," Perl inserted the comment "divrei mussar" parenthetically and thus applied this talmudic parable to his own moralizing tales. He believed that his "divrei mussar" were accessible to and necessary for everybody, while "Halakhah" could be comprehended only by the few. Evidently Perl's tactic was to interpret a given passage in a way that would best serve his own purpose.

In the subsequent articles, Perl presented those principles of the Haskalah which hardly were touched upon in the preceding volume. The second article, "Daber Ẓaḥut" (To Speak Lucidly or Eloquently), deals with one of the fundamental slogans of the Haskalah, one which had already been stressed in Naphtali Herz Wessely's *Divrei Shalom ve-Emet* (Berlin, 1782). As a starting point, Perl took this statement of Rab Judah: "The Judeans who cared for [the beauty of] their language retained their learning, but the Galileans who did not care for [the beauty of] their language did not retain their learning."[33] Perl applied this not only to Hebrew but also to the language used in daily discourse. He did not dare openly to advocate German over Yiddish, but he clearly intimated his preference, as can be seen in the following verse he cited from Nehemiah: "And their children spoke half in the speech of Ashdod, and could not speak in the language of the Jews, but according to the language of each people."[34] He argued either for pure Hebrew ("for God in our prayer") or for pure language ("the language of each people") in our daily life. In order to give his demand for "daber ẓaḥut" a moral sanction, Perl subtly introduced the injunctions against falsehood and evil speech.

Perl related the subject of guarding against uncouth expressions to the problem of "ẓaḥut ha-lashon" in another article, entitled "Lashon nekiyah" (Clean Language), which draws on the familiar dictum of the school of R. Ishmael: "One should always discourse in decent language."[35] "Daber Ẓaḥut" is also the moral of the fourth article, "Tehillah, Neḥamah u-Tefillah" (Praise, Consolation, and Prayer). Perl cited the prayers uttered by the sages on several occasions when they came to console mourners,[36] and drew three conclusions: (1) we must emulate the sages by performing acts of kindness and consoling mourners; (2) the sages did not recite any set prayers but were in the habit of pouring out their hearts to God as the occasion demanded; (3) those responsible for the fiction that the sages were not masters of Hebrew and could not speak it correctly should be truly ashamed of themselves. For the sages used a cultured language in their prayers[37] and spoke in the vernacular only when addressing the people so that they would learn to follow in the paths of the sages.

Perl's articles were written in precisely the same form as the spoken homilies of popular *maggidim*, except that where the homilies close with an expression of hope for the Redemption, "and a redeemer will come to Zion," all three issues of the *Luaḥ* omit such reference. However, a special addendum to the introduction for the 5575 edition, where the new title of the *Luaḥ, Ẓir Ne'eman*, is explained, does conclude with the following prayer:

> To serve as a loyal messenger . . . that should be a sign through days, months, and seasons, for the People of Israel and all nations according to their speech and faiths. May the Lord God turn all to one tongue and heart to serve him in truth and sincerity. May he send us the redeemer of truth and righteousness. Amen.

It is quite obvious that this invocation is intended only to give the notion of redemption a universal, cosmopolitan twist!

The fifth article, entitled "ve-Da Mah she-Tashiv le-Shoalkha Davar" (And Know What to Answer an Inquirer), is a parody of the talmudic dictum, "And know what answer to give an unbeliever."[38] Perl expatiated on a subject which he only casually touched upon in the article "Yegia Kappayim" in the *Luaḥ* for 5574. The point of departure in this instance is supplied by the following *aggadah*:[39] Turnus Rufus asked R. Akiba, "If your God loves the poor, why does he not support them?" R. Akiba replied, "In order that we may be saved through them from the punishment of Gehinnom." In this connection, Perl raised the question of where the poor came from, and replied that there were two kinds of poor people. The first were those who lost their wealth through their own doings, namely, through wastefulness, luxury, card-playing, or just through laziness and idleness. A careful investigation would easily have shown that most poor people belonged to this category. The second kind consisted of the unfortunate, the sick, and the crippled who were made so by God, either because they would have abused their riches if they had had them, or to develop noble qualities in men. Thus compassion and loving kindness were the noble qualities of the rich, while trust in God and gratitude to the rich were those of the poor. Perl concluded that this was the real meaning of R. Akiba's reply.

Given such a social philosophy, it is no wonder that the Maskilim shared the views of the absolute rulers. Like them, they believed that the miserable condition of the Jewish masses was brought on by themselves; that is, by their refusing to abandon dickering, bartering, and crafty practices for productive occupations. Perl's attitude toward this problem is also reflected in his other articles.

The article "Orekh Yamim" (Length of Days) began with a statement of R. Jochanan, "Woe to lordship which buries its possessor."[40] In confirmation of this maxim, Perl adduced the findings of an investigation conducted by the scholar Hufeland[41] which asserted that kings and great princes did not live to a ripe age, as a rule, either because of their strenuous labors or because they spent their lives amidst riotous escapades. From this Perl deduced the following morals: (1) one should not strive for power; (2) one should not indulge in excessive pleasure but lead a simple life, enriched with Torah and hard work; and (3) one must love kings and princes with all one's heart and carry out all their orders, because the heavy responsibility they bear enables others to lead a peaceful and undisturbed existence.

There can be no doubt that Perl was sincere about his first two conclusions. He preached against luxury on other occasions, and the slogan of modesty and refusal of power were in accord with the general system of political absolutism. The main purpose, however, of this article was to teach the third lesson, namely, to instill loyal submission toward the ruler and his officials. This is reinforced by another article, entitled "Hitpalel bi-Shelom Malkhut" (Pray for the Welfare of the Government), which takes for its starting point the familiar injunction of the prophet Jeremiah to the exiles in Babylon, "And seek the peace of the city whither I have caused you to be carried away captive . . . for in the peace thereof shall ye have peace,"[42] as well as the scriptural verse, "Thou shalt not abhor an Egyptian because thou wast a stranger in his land."[43] From these verses, Perl deduced the following:

> If prophets like Moses and Jeremiah enjoin us, respectively, to love the Chaldeans who destroyed our Sanctuary and laid waste Jerusalem and Judaea, or the Egyptians who tortured the Hebrews, how much more so should we love the nations among whom we live and offer prayers in their behalf. We are living peacefully in the shade of our just and lawful kings, who not only would not do us any injustice but made equal laws for all inhabitants of the land without any differentiation. Therefore we must render praise and thanksgiving to God and pray for our kings.

If Perl, in his appeal for loyalty, referred to equal rights enjoyed by Jews of all lands, he was merely repeating the conviction of all Maskilim of his day. Basing their opinion on the rights and opportunities granted to Jews under the regime of absolute monarchy, the Maskilim believed that the other legal disabilities affecting the Jews in Austria and Russia would be removed as soon as the Jews were qualified for this by becoming "europeanized" and by other "improvements." Details in the program of "improvements" were stressed in the next article, entitled "Mi hu Ḥakham be-emet u-betamim"(He Who Is Truly and Sincerely Wise). Perl paraphrased Abaye's comment on the precept "and thou shalt love the Lord thy God"[44] in which the qualifications of a true "Talmid Ḥakham" are enumerated: He must be a student of the Torah and Mishnah, speak calmly to his fellow men and be honest in business. For the Maskilim, "honest business" meant a substantial business, organized in a European manner, as opposed to hassling, innkeeping, brokering, and other such insubstantial activities.

The idea of productive work is also the theme of the subsequent story, "Do Not Judge Your Neighbor until You Have Been in His Place."[45] It tells of a woodchopper and his wife who were complaining that because of the sin of Adam and Eve they must toil with the sweat of their brow and eat dry bread. The king, while hunting in the forest, chanced to hear their complaint and invited them to his palace. But, like Adam and Eve, they disregarded his warning against displaying curiosity, and as a result they were chased out of the palace. The king tells them to live from their toil just as they had before and convinces them that they have no just claims against Adam and Eve. Thus labor was not regarded as a curse by those who believed in productive occupation.

To the last story, entitled "ha-Dayag ve-ha-Oreiaḥ" (The Fisherman and the Guest), Perl added the German title "Der Fischer und der Reisende" in parentheses in order to show that it was derived from a German story. Essentially this story also reechoes the clamor of the Haskalah for productive occupations. A fisherman who was invited by his guest to the big city soon began craving wealth and luxury. An angel appeared before him and told him that he would fulfill any three wishes. In compliance with the fisherman's three requests, his hovel was transformed into a palace, his lake into an ocean, and his little fishing smack into a gorgeous ship. Then a hurricane broke loose and the fisherman was drowned together with his ship. On the basis of verses from Proverbs concerning wisdom and folly, Perl arrived at the following moralizing reflection: "Such is the end of those, who chase after honor and have lustful desires."

The Haskalah had not yet appropriated from capitalist ideology the notion that engendering a desire for more and more creature comforts is necessary in order to create a greater demand for goods and thus enlarge the market. The Haskalah still held fast to the ideology of thrift and simplicity of life which accompanied the beginnings of modern capitalism. However, one must not lose sight of the fact that the idea of making the masses more productive, a particularly pressing need in the Jewish environment, could only be spread by idealizing the simple life.

The Third Almanac: Enter the Sciences

The *Luaḥ ha-Lev* for the year 5576 repeats the same introduction. It is followed by an article entitled "How Good and How Pleasant It Is for Brothers to Dwell Together in Unity!"[46] It contains a description of the twelve branches of culture and civilization: agriculture, architecture, geometry, medicine, natural science, astronomy, rhetoric, logic, morals, painting, music, and dancing. The list is neither systematic nor complete, even according to the concepts of the early nineteenth century. Astronomy and medicine are listed apart from natural science; geometry is the only branch of mathematics cited; and history, poetry, drama, and sculpture are not mentioned at all. Even here, Perl moralized, dwelling on agriculture and using talmudic aphorisms, such as "A man who owns no land is not a man," "No flour, no Torah," to show that this constitutes the foundation of human society, culture, and civilization. Hence, it is our duty to love the peasant who feeds us. The whole article is imbued with the spirit of Herder's ideas on the philosophy of history and the constant progress of mankind on the path to culture and civilization.[47] The political tendency of the Maskilim reappeared in the closing section of the article: "May God, who gives wisdom to the sages, open our hearts and enlighten our eyes in Torah and Wisdom, that we may become wise and cultured and remove from us the reproach of the nations, so that we need not feel ashamed when they happen to discuss matters with us in public." "Reproach of the nations" is a recurring motif in all the writings of the Maskilim urging the Jews to study languages and sciences and to enter the field of productive labor.

As in all his articles and stories, Perl sought to gain the confidence of the reader by intertwining aphorisms from the Talmud, verses from the Scriptures, and moralizing preachments about the fear of God. He began his article with Ben Zoma's tribute to "Adam ha-Rishon," who had to toil so hard in order to have bread to eat and a garment to wear.[48]

In his description of architecture he began with Jabal the son of Lemech. With regard to medicine, he sententiously observed that disease descended upon mankind as a punishment from God when men strayed from the straight path and began to follow their lustful inclinations; and in speaking of natural science, he quoted verses from Job which extol God for His great wonders of nature. In connection with astronomy, he cited the scriptural verse, "Lift up your eyes on high, and see who has created these."[49] In discussing music and dance, he mentioned the verse from Psalms, "Let him praise His name in the dance; let them sing praise unto Him with the timbrel and the harp."[50] Sheltering himself constantly behind such fortifications, he found many opportunities to inform the reader about the part the nations of the world played in the history of civilization; for example, the Egyptians were masters of medicine and geometry.

The second story, entitled "The Earth Is the Lord's, and the Fulness Thereof,"[51] is about Canute, king of Denmark and England, who chided his courtiers when they sought to flatter him by saying that he was the king of the land and the seas. To this the king replied: "God alone is the King of Kings." A rather lengthy scientific explanation for the expression "tide of the sea" was added. The explanation concluded with a verse from Job about the omniscience of God.[52] The whole story was related primarily to introduce this scientific explanation.

Perl's article "Charity and Loving Kindness" is related to the talmudic passage "In three respects the practice of kindness is greater than charity"[53] in order to disseminate the Haskalah notion of love and sympathy for our fellow men.

All eight sentences in the chapter "Musar Ḥokhmah" are directed against laziness. Even the eighth sentence, which parodies the first chapter of the Book of Psalms in comparing man with a tree, is also essentially nothing but propaganda for productive occupations. A man who dwells permanently in one place may be compared with a "tree planted by streams of water that brings forth its fruit in its season"; but not so the man who is tossed by the wind from city to city and from land to land. Perl, the Maskil, was an adherent of stability and permanent habitation, which are necessary conditions for agriculture and handicraft. He cited without comment the *aggadah* about Eleazar of Bartota,[54] who gave all he had to the poor, probably to show that he too advocated charity when it was justified.

In "Gedol Ḥemah" Perl cited the Gemara[55] to prove that one should not be angry, a moral lesson in line with his pleas in preceding almanacs for tolerance.

Almost half the *Luaḥ ha-Lev* for the year 5576 is devoted to the lengthy story about the grave danger of the Jews who refused to obey Caligula's decree to place his statue in the sanctuary. Aside from the fact that Perl wanted to acquaint the reader with a rather important and interesting episode from Jewish history,[56] the main purpose of relating this story was purely political, as is clearly evident from the long introduction and the still longer explanation at the end. In the introduction, he attributed to Plutarch, whom he referred to as "a Roman Sage," a story about a music teacher who wanted to give a practical demonstration to his pupils of the difference between good singers and bad ones. He used to take his pupils to the theater, where he would sharpen their critical sense using the performance of the artists as an example. The lesson of the parable was revealed by Perl in the closing explanation. He drew the attention of the reader to the vast difference between the attitude toward Jews of emperors like Caligula and that of the "upright and righteous kings" of Europe.

As in the previous *Luaḥ*[57] there follow a tribute to God, "who has given us grace and mercy in the eyes of kings, sages and saints who fulfill His will," and a prayer to God in behalf of their greatness. Perl did not fail in any of his almanacs vigorously to advocate loyalty and unconditional submission to the absolute rulers. This political attitude was as essential a part of the ideology of the Haskalah as were the clamors for education in languages and sciences and for productive occupations.

In all the articles and stories of the three issues of the *Luaḥ* the moralizing tone peculiar to the Maskilim is transparent, but not in the "mishlei musar" at the end of the *Luaḥ ha-Lev*. These are partly in poetic form and partly in the form of fables which teach the proper way of life. Very few of them promote the aims of the Haskalah as such.

The first of the two, the end of the *Luaḥ ha-Lev* for 5574, "Absalom between the Thick Boughs of a Terebinth," is an exhortation on parental honor, although the motif of rebellion could easily have been linked with the moral preachment concerning those who rebel against royalty. The lesson of the second, spelled out in the heading "Not Learning but Doing Is the Chief Thing,"[58] is directed against moral defects such as conceit, gambling, and lying. All these defects are displayed by a father who wanted to give moral training to his son.

Four parables are presented in the *Luaḥ ha-Lev* for 5575. In the first we are told about a pact between "emet" (truth) and "mashal" (parable) which was concluded because people usually do not listen to truth alone; they like amusement, sophisticated sayings, and puzzles. Here he articulated the theory of propaganda which he had applied in the literary section of his almanacs and in his two satires, *Megalleh Temirin* and *Boḥen Ẓaddik*. The observation made in the second parable, "The Raven and the Dove after the Flood," that "it is better to be a slave of a kind man than to be free in the company of the ungodly," is a moral lesson that fit in well with the political philosophy of the absolute monarchs, who described the fighters for liberty as "demagogues." The third parable, "The Stargazer in the Pit," poked fun at an astronomer who fell into a pit while he was looking up at the skies. The lesson of the story is, Why climb to heaven, you fool, when the earth is still a strange sight to your eyes? The quotation from the Gemara which follows, about the prohibition to seek counsel from an astrologer,[59] is a veiled attack upon the Hasidic rebbes who presumed to foretell the future and soar in the skies without even knowing what was going on here on earth. The last in this volume is the familiar fable "The Ape and the Mirror," signed Sh. L. R. [Rapoport],[60] in which truth is compared with a mirror.

The three fables in the *Luaḥ* for 5576 are (1) "The Wolf, a Shepherd," about a wolf who disguised himself as a shepherd; (2) "The Wolf and the Lamb" (apparently copied from LaFontaine); and (3) "The Lion and the Fly," the lesson of which is that even the most insignificant enemy is able to do harm.

In the three *Luḥot* there also are riddles ("ḥidot"), the answers to which are furnished in the *Luaḥ* for the next year, evidently introduced to keep alive the readers' interest in the *Luaḥ*. One of the puzzles in the *Luaḥ* for 5575 is signed Sh. L. R. [Rapoport]. Another puzzle in the *Luaḥ* for 5576 is signed B. Z.—Sh, "talmid be-vet ha-ḥinukh," that is, Bezalel (Basilius) Stern (1798–1853), at that time still a pupil and afterward a teacher in Perl's school in Tarnopol. The fact that signatures of writers appear only in connection with the *ḥidot* indicates that the other parts of the *Luaḥ* were all compiled by Perl himself.

About one-third of the *Luaḥ ha-Lev* (twenty-two pages in the *Luaḥ* for 5574) is devoted to the section containing natural science data under the heading "Beḥinot ha-teva." It is rather peculiar that about sixteen years after the appearance of the well-known *Sefer ha-Berit*, by Phinehas Elijah Hurwitz,[61] which contained a large section on the natural sciences, Perl found it necessary to write a seven-page introduction justifying its inclusion. He emphasized the importance of natural science from the viewpoint of "reverence for God" and cited verses from Psalms and Job to convince the reader that one must study nature in order to appreciate more fully the Powers and Providence of the Creator. He adduced proof from the Talmud[62] that by observing the nature of beasts and cattle we may learn good qualities; for example, patience and diligence from an ox, courage from a horse, etc. He pointed out that the sages had practical knowledge of natural science (a description of the symptoms of rabies is given in *Yoma*, pp. 83–84) and a comment that such sages as Bahya, Maimonides, Nachmanides, and Ibn Ezra were well versed in natural science.

Following this introduction, he offered a sketchy description of minerals, plants, and animals, and mixed in some geography, indicating where the enumerated animals were to be found. There was never a shortage of didactic explanations. For instance, in the description of the vine there is a strong warning against drunkenness. The interest of the reader was aroused by his emphasis on exotic plants and animals and strange natural phenomena. The entire description is permeated with teleology and theodicy: "God did not create anything large or small in the world, unless it could be useful to man, his faithful servant." Included is the observation that there are fewer wild beasts than useful domestic animals. It is hard to discern whether Perl was sincere about the medieval teleology or whether it was only a clever propaganda ploy.

After this general introduction and classification of the natural sciences in the *Luaḥ* for 5574, the succeeding *Luḥot* furnish a systematic and detailed description of the various fields. The *Luaḥ* for 5575 concerns itself with worms, insects, fish, and amphibia. The *Luaḥ* for 5576 is devoted exclusively to birds. The names of all the species are also supplied parenthetically in German. The use of German is connected to the effort of the Haskalah for "ẓaḥut ha-lashon."

Thus Perl utilized the form of the traditional *Luaḥ* in a manner and spirit entirely contrary to what it had been until then. In addition to remarks about repentance, saints, and sinners, the traditional *Luaḥ* also contained a "didactic section" which told the reader the things which may or may not be done on certain days because of the evil forces holding sway then.[63] Perl transformed the *Luaḥ* into a real almanac whose function was to disseminate the ideology of the Haskalah and to popularize science among the Jewish masses. His almanacs are of great importance to the history of Jewish culture and to the study of Jewish literature because they represent a striking example of the ideology of the Haskalah and its propaganda methods. They virtually contain the whole program developed later in the *Te'udah be-Yisrael* by Isaac Ber Levinsohn, but in a more popular and more circumspect form. The program of the Haskalah is permeated by the pious preaching of "Yireat Shamayim" (the fear of heaven) and is in complete accord with the spirit of a popular almanac. The literary influence exerted upon Perl's *Luaḥ* by the German periodical *Sulamith*, especially in the selection of talmudic legends and other stories, indicates the whole trend and extent of the Jewish Enlightenment movement and its spread from Germany to Austria, Galicia, and Russia. Perl, the protagonist of the fight against Hasidism, is now revealed as the tireless propagandist of the Haskalah and the popularizer of science.

II

POLAND

7

The Socioeconomic and Political Status of the Jews in Central Poland

Urban Industrialism; Rural Feudalism

Although there were many common elements in the Hasidic movements of central Poland and Galicia, a distinct Hasidic doctrine was fashioned in Przysucha (Pshiskhe) and Kock (Kotsk) which differed from that fostered at the courts of the zaddikim in Ropczyce and Żydaczów, Rymanów and Bełz. The socioeconomic, political, and cultural conditions out of which this Hasidism grew were also marked by definite and distinctive characteristics.

The overwhelming majority of Jews in Poland were concentrated in central Poland, which was known as the Kingdom of Poland or the Congress Kingdom because the Congress of Vienna proclaimed it an independent kingdom under the rule of the czar of Russia. The Jewish community was one of the largest in the entire Diaspora, second only to that in the Ukraine. There were almost twice as many Jews in the Kingdom of Poland as in nearby Galicia. In 1827 there were 377,754 and in 1843 there were 523,396. In those sixteen years the percentage of Jews in the total population rose from 9.1 to 11.1.

The specific economic significance of the Jews in Congress Poland reflected the fact that they constituted a large part of the urban population. According to the census taken in 1843, the Jews accounted for about 41 percent of the total urban population. In three of the eight districts—Lublin, Podlasie (Siedlce) and Augustów— the majority of the total urban population were Jews. By 1827 the Jews were the majority in four of the nine largest cities in the state: Lublin, Hrubieszów, Zamość, and Kalvarya. In the remaining five (Warsaw, Kalisz, Płock, Częstochowa, and Ozorków) at least 20 percent of the population were Jews; and even in Warsaw, the capital city, the Jews, despite restrictions, accounted for 23 percent of the total population (30,702 out of 131,484).[1]

The situation of the Jews in the Kingdom of Poland was determined not only by the economic and social development of the country but also to a great extent by the particular policy of the government toward them.

When the Kingdom of Poland was first established, the regime was still a feudal one. In 1816 the urban population accounted for only 19 percent of the total population.[2] However, from an economic viewpoint, most of the urban centers, even in their external appearance, resembled the villages. For example, in 1827, of the 80,239 houses, only about 10 percent were stone; the remainder were wooden houses or thatch-covered clay huts.[3] Most of the Christian residents earned their livings by farming and only some of them were artisans, taverners, shopkeepers, and traders. Among the latter, most traded in pigs and many in horses and cattle. According to an official report of the "inspector of the cities" in the Lublin district in 1820, "the majority of the Catholics in the cities are engaged in agriculture and there is no other national group able to engage in trade except the Jews."[4] According to a report of the same year issued by the inspector of the cities in the district of Płock, the Gentiles in the cities of Ciechanów, Mława, and Maków earned their livings solely from agriculture.[5] Even in Kalvarya, one of the larger cities in the state, there was a correlation between religion and occupation. According to an official report in 1820, all 1,315 of its Catholic inhabitants were farmers, a number of the 237 Lutherans were artisans; while the majority of the 2,426 Jews were engaged in "skilled work," and the minority were traders.[6]

By the 1820s capitalism had already developed considerably in this backward country, and it gathered momentum in the 1840s. In contrast to Galicia, important industrial centers kept springing up, thus allowing for the penetration of capitalism even into the field of agriculture. The discovery of coal and iron, as well as zinc and lead, in the southern section of the country was exploited to establish industrial enterprises. In 1840 more than seven hundred workers were engaged in coal mining.[7] A number of the large metal-smelting enterprises which were to become well known in the twentieth century, such as Huta Bankowa and Strachowice, had already been established by the 1830s. With the establishment of factories for agricultural machinery, which was accelerated by the development of farming estates, the need for iron grew ever greater. In 1829 there were more than one hundred workers in the largest of these factories, that of the government in the Solec quarter in Warsaw; by 1839, their number had increased to five hundred.[8]

The main industrial product in the field of agriculture continued to be alcoholic beverages, but here, too, the means of production were improved. Also, the use of potatoes and rye as raw materials became widespread. The first sugar factories were established in the 1820s and by the end of the 1840s there were more than thirty of them.[9]

Textiles, the main industry in Poland, was concentrated in the provinces of Kalisz and Mazovia. A very considerable factor in its rapid development was the open market with Russia, the result of political ties between the two countries. In 1822, for example, the tariff border between the Kingdom of Poland and the Russian Empire was abolished, and all of Russia was opened up to the export of Polish textiles. Among other factors which furthered the development of this industry were the imposition of high tariffs on goods imported from the West, the imperial army's great need for textiles, and the immigration of expert weavers from Germany and Silesia. Besides the many small workshops—some independent, others dependent upon contractors for credit—large factories sprang up, each employing hundreds of workers. By 1829, 35 million zlotys' worth of woolen textiles was being manufactured. In this same period a cotton factory was established which, by 1825, was supplying one-fourth of the country's needs; and in the four following years, its production increased more than fourfold (from 848,000 yards to 3.7 million yards). In 1832, after the failure of the Polish insurrection, the tariff border between Poland and Russia was reestablished, and consequently the manufacture of woolen textiles declined. In contrast, the production of cotton textiles flourished. At that time, it was concentrated in and around Łódz: Zduńska Wola, Ozorków, and Pabianice. The number of looms increased between 1836 and 1850 from 7,300 to 61,300. The linen output also increased with the development of the large center in Żyrardów, south of Warsaw.[10]

This industrial development was accompanied by a major shift of the urban and peasant populations. Between 1816 and 1855, the urban population more than doubled, from 527,332 to 1,116,768 persons, and its percentage of the total population of the country rose from 19 to 24.[11] This process of industrialization and urbanization was directly linked to the social changes in agriculture. Just as industry increased and capitalism developed, so the power of feudal relations in the village declined and the proletarianization of the peasants deepened. Moreover, the peasants who were dislodged and uprooted from their soil were converted into an industrial reserve force, a condition essential for the development of industry.

Capitalism was introduced into the villages by means of a paragraph in the constitution of the Duchy of Warsaw of 1807 which abolished serfdom. But this rescission was interpreted merely to mean freedom of movement, allowing the peasants to leave the village and estate owners to drive the peasants from their farms. Not only did it never occur to the authorities to adopt a program of reforms such as the proposal of Kościuszko of 1814, regarding the granting of ownership of the farmsteads to the emancipated peasants, but even the substitution of forced labor by payment of a crop tax to the owners of the estates was not implemented except in a few of the large estates and under conditions imposed by the owners. Indeed, the very government which had proclaimed this plan desirable sabotaged it in various ways: it increased the payments of the peasants settling on royal land ("the national estates"); and, on the eve of the rebellion of 1830, it initiated the sale of estates belonging to the treasury, thereby making the plight of many of these peasants as bad as that of the peasants on private estates.

The majority of the peasants remained serfs like their forebears and the yoke of servitude, both in labor and payments, became even heavier than in the past. The government itself intensified the exploitation of the peasants by imposing special taxes which replaced the *corvée* (road repair tax) and by raising the price of the monopolies on salt, tobacco, and liquor. In their memoirs, the nobles confessed that the peasants became steadily impoverished and were unable to buy even those necessities which were available in the eighteenth-century village. But the worst evil for the peasants was the wholesale eviction from their land by the landowners. By 1827 the number of landless peasants reached 800,000, or 30 percent of the total village population. Many of the evicted peasants remained in the villages, increasing the legions of hirelings on the estates which had adopted the system of intensive farming. Those who wandered off to the cities were not readily absorbed into service, handicraft, or factories. The number of vagabonds, paupers, and beggars multiplied dramatically.[12] The sorry spectacle of the early accumulation of capital in the England of Shakespeare's time was a recurring phenomenon here as well, and cruel measures were decreed by the government against paupers, including the penalties of expulsion and hard labor. To be sure, there was also a novel aspect to these decrees characterizing the absolutism of the government: by its order of 1840, mendicant children were penalized by being turned over to the army as cantonists.[13]

Government as the Instrument of Oppression

This essentially feudal socioeconomic system found its appropriate instrument in the political regime of the Kingdom of Poland. According to the Constitution of 1815, which was patterned after that of the Duchy of Warsaw of 1807, the right to legislate was given to the *Sejm*, which consisted of the czar-king, the Senate and the Chamber of Deputies. The Senate was composed exclusively of the upper aristocracy, the clergy, and the castellans. The Chamber of Deputies consisted of seventy-seven members elected by the nobles in the *Sejm* and fifty-one chosen at communal assemblies. In addition to the nobles, estate and factory owners, merchants, and skilled workers could participate in these assemblies.

In the *województwo* (provincial councils), the nobles, emissaries of the *Sejm*'s members, were also assured of a decisive majority. The executive power was placed in the hands of the Administrative Council (*Rada Administracyjna*), composed of ministers and councillors, over which the viceroy presided.

The nobility, which held power together with certain financial magnates, was compelled to keep the reins of government in its own hands. Thus, in the Administrative Council, the decisive vote was given by the constitution to the viceroy. Furthermore, the viceroy, Prince Józef Zayonczek, did not move without the approval of the czar's brother and the commander of the army, Grand Duke Constantine, and particularly, without the approval of the czar's commissar, Senator Nicolai Novosiltzev. After the death of Prince Zayonczek in 1826, no new viceroy was appointed, and Novosiltzev, assisted by the czar's brother, remained the supreme authority.

Just as the political regime of the Kingdom of Poland was essentially a continuation of that of the Duchy of Warsaw, the policy toward the Jews was dictated by the same aims but was far more discriminating than before. Decrees against the Jews which had not been fully implemented by the Duchy of Warsaw, either because it was short-lived or out of consideration for the constitutional principle of civil equality, were now implemented in the Kingdom of Poland. Indeed, all the hypocrisy and cant of the Holy Alliance of the Metternich era, the alliance of the three reactionary powers of Europe which pretended to act in the name of "the principles of Christian love for man," became evident in the government's policy toward the Jews.

It is well known that, in order to discharge its obligations in connection with its professed statements of principle, the Congress of Vienna in 1815 decided to include in the constitution for the Federation of Germany a paragraph regarding the Jews. Paragraph 16 of the final draft required the German Federation to show regard for the improvement of the civil status of the members of the Jewish faith and to confirm the rights already granted to them by the individual states of the federation. Parallel to this resolution of the Congress, Czar Alexander—in the basic guidelines of the constitution for the Kingdom of Poland, elaborated by Prince Adam Czartoryski in paragraph 36 concerning "the members of the Old Testament faith"—proclaimed that "those civil rights which had already been assured to the Jewish people through existing statutes and enactments shall be preserved. Special ordinances shall determine the conditions by which it will be made easier for the members of the Old Testament faith to attain a greater share in the common welfare."[14]

From the outset, both decisions confirming the existing rights were significantly undercut by the particular wording in the Congress's resolution concerning the Jews of Germany: the preposition "of" ("of the Federated States") was substituted for "in" ("in the Federated States"), which served to nullify all the rights granted the Jews of Germany by the governments established by Napoleon, such as those in the Kingdom of Westphalia, in Frankfurt, and in the Hanseatic cities. These governments were not recognized by the Congress, and thus the rights of the Jews were not regarded as granted "by the states." Similarly, the granting of "civil rights" for the Jews of the Kingdom of Poland was intended expressly to deny what was seemingly being affirmed, namely, civil rights. For ten years, the government of the Duchy of Warsaw had suspended the political rights of the Jews which had been granted them by the paragraph in the constitution regarding the equality of all natives. The "basic guidelines" of the new constitution of 1815 nullified these rights permanently.

In those basic guidelines, the paragraph relating to the Jews was preceded by the one concerning "the numerous and useful class of peasants." They were guaranteed "the protection of the law," "true justice," and "paternal concern," with the aim of advancing them gradually toward attaining "a good and improved status." However, in the constitution itself, which was signed by the czar (acting as king of Poland) on November 27, 1815, all mention of obligations toward peasants was omitted, as was any mention of the Jews. In order to dispel any misunderstanding regarding the rights of the Jews, paragraph 11 of the constitution expressly stated that all *Christians*, irrespective of differences in their beliefs, were to benefit from equal rights, both civil and political.

The blatant violation of the principle of civil equality as it concerned the Jews was particularly evident in the area of taxation. In addition to the burden of direct and indirect taxes carried by the entire populace, the Jews bore special taxes, some having come down as a legacy from the Duchy of Warsaw and some having been newly decreed. The kosher meat tax, decreed by the Duchy of Warsaw in 1809, amounted to six grosz per pound, which together with payments to the community increased the price of meat to double that of nonkosher meat. It goes without saying that this was especially burdensome to the poor Jewish population. Similarly, a "recruits' tax," which had been introduced in 1812 as compensation for the exemption of Jews from military service, remained in effect until 1844. Special new taxes in the Kingdom of Poland were the *Billet*, or "ticket tax," needed for admission to Warsaw by Jews from outside the city; and the "*consens* tax," or the taverner's license fee, which was required only of Jewish innkeepers. The extent of the discrimination in these taxes can be appreciated by comparing them with the kingdom's income from general indirect taxes. At a time when the kingdom's entire income from the monopoly on tobacco in the beginning of the 1820s did not exceed one and one-half million zlotys,[15] the Jews paid that same amount in kosher meat taxes and also for the *consens* tax.

But the goal of the two new taxes—the *Billet* and the *consens*—was not merely fiscal; rather, the taxes were from the beginning intended as an instrument of the government's economic policy toward the Jews. With respect to the village Jews, this policy was motivated by the interests of the ruling class of nobles; and with respect to the urban Jews, by the aim of strengthening and fortifying the competitive position of the dominant middle class.

A Case Study: The Elimination of Jewish Innkeeping

These two aims of government policy were combined in the decrees against the Jewish tavernkeepers which deprived myriads of Jewish families of their livelihoods. In 1812, the last year of its existence, the government of the Duchy of Warsaw succeeded in issuing a decree prohibiting Jews in the cities and villages from being tavernkeepers. In the cities, the purpose of this decree was to transfer the liquor business from the Jews to the Polish townsmen. As for the Jews in the villages and the private towns, the edict had a twofold aim: (1) to concentrate the management of all aspects of the economy of the estate in the hands of the estate owners and to raise the level of its efficiency along capitalist lines; (2) to demonstrate that the government was concerned with improving the lot of the peasants; that is to say, by making liquor less accessible, it was helping to allay the acute problem of drunkenness among them.

These goals were a guide also to the government of the Kingdom of Poland, but it decided to implement them gradually out of consideration for the landed estate owners. In 1814, when the edict of 1812 was to be implemented, certain officials called to the attention of the provisional government the losses which would accrue to the owners of the villages and towns if the edict were to go into effect immediately; the landlords would not be able to establish distilleries or set up the necessary equipment.[16] It was also possible that the taverns would not be frequented. These considerations were more effective than the efforts of the Jewish representatives (who continued throughout to send "gifts" to Senator Novosiltzev),[17] and in 1814 the edict concerning liquor was postponed for a year and in 1815 for an additional year.

In 1816, with a postponement in effect for still another year, an edict was issued by the viceroy prohibiting Jewish taverners from providing liquor to peasants on credit or in exchange for produce. This prohibition, which was intended to appease the peasants, was modeled after the law promulgated in western Galicia in 1804 by the Austrian authorities, but with this essential difference: The Austrian law included in the prohibition gentile as well as Jewish taverners, whereas the prohibition issued by the authorities in Poland affected only the Jewish taverners.[18]

From this time on, the implementation of the prohibition against Jews' dealing in liquor was postponed annually, but as of 1814 this postponement was contingent upon the Jews who continued to engage in the sale of liquor, innkeeping, or tenancy obtaining a *consens*, the fee for which varied according to the size of the village or city. This fee was continually raised so that by 1824 it was eight times higher and by 1830, it was almost twelve times more.[19]

As a result of this oppressive fiscal measure leveled against the Jewish taverners (gentile taverners were exempt from both the *consens* requirement and the payment attached to it) the government gradually attained its goal. The Jewish taverners and innkeepers in the villages worked unsparingly to eke out their meager livings: Their wives assisted them in the inn, their children served the wayfarers for a few grosz and the men themselves also worked as coachmen.[20] But with all this, it was hard for Jews in both cities and villages to meet the high *consens* fees; thus the number of taverners compelled to seek other sources of livelihood grew. As though the *consens* edict were not enough, the dispossession of the Jews from innkeeping in the villages—at the instigation of the estate owners—also increased. The Jewish innkeepers on government property had been evicted in accordance with the edict of 1812, and by 1822 the number of those evicted amounted to 649 families. By that year, 5,797 Jewish families had been expelled from the estates of the nobles. During the first eight years in which the Kingdom of Poland was in existence, a total of 28,985 Jews had been driven from the villages. Similarly, between 1814 and 1822, the overall number of Jews in the cities and villages engaged in the production and sale of liquor declined from 17,561 to 3,996 heads of families. Even this remnant of the Jewish innkeeping class was viewed with disfavor by the government, and during the next eight years restrictions on obtaining the *consens* were gradually increased so that by 1830 only 2,088 Jewish heads of family possessed a *consens*.[21]

The fate of the few remaining Jewish innkeepers who survived in the villages was sealed by the government's decree of 1844: as of June 18, 1845, Jews engaged in the manufacture and sale of liquor were forbidden to dwell in the villages. In 1848, village Jews were prohibited from engaging in the liquor business, which included mead, beer, and wine.[22] Thus, by the middle of the nineteenth century all Jewish innkeepers, except for a few farmers in the Jewish agricultural settlements who clandestinely engaged in the liquor business, were cleared out of the villages.

Although the absolute ban on innkeeping did not apply to the urban Jews, the already small number of Jewish innkeepers dwindled, and in 1850 only 1,675 heads of Jewish families made their livings in this way.[23] Instead of issuing a total ban, the government carried out its scheme, as it had in the earlier period, by constantly increasing the fee on the *consens* as well as making it more difficult to obtain. Some of the lords of the towns demonstrated the same harshness toward their Jewish subjects as they did toward the Jewish taverners in the villages. Thus, in their memorandum to the viceroy Paskevich in 1832, the Jews of Końska Wola complained that after the death of Prince Czartoryski, his son and heir removed all thirty Jewish innkeepers from their inns in the town.[24]

The Ghetto

While the restrictions on innkeeping mainly hurt the Jews of the towns and villages, the decree of the *revir* (the Jewish quarter) hurt urban Jews. Just as the decree on innkeeping was intended to take the manufacture and sale of liquor away from the Jews, so the *revir* decree was to give the Polish burghers advantageous conditions for competing in the areas of trade, handicrafts, and manufacture. Again it was the government of the Duchy of Warsaw which took the first steps. It decreed a special Jewish quarter, initially in the city of Warsaw (1809) and later in such cities as Wschowa (Fraustadt), Płock, Maków, and Przasnysz, in addition to the existing Jewish ghetto in the city of Lublin. This government also kept in force the ban on Jewish settlement in the cities privileged "not to tolerate Jews" from the time of ancient Poland. The provisional government which was constituted in the duchy after Napoleon's defeat continued along the same lines, establishing *revirs* in additional cities such as the one in Radom in 1814.[25]

The institution of *revirs*, which, under the rule of the Duchy of Warsaw, had been limited to only a number of cities, was systematically developed by the government of the Kingdom of Poland. In the controversy over the Jewish question which had started in 1816 in the newspapers and in special pamphlets, many venerable statesmen came forth with plans for concentrating the Jews in special cities and quarters. None of those who proposed these plans concealed the economic reasons behind them. The most liberal among them, Ludwig Lentowski, the author of the pamphlet about the Jews in Poland (which he dedicated to the viceroy Zayonczek), called for the assignment of special cities to the Jews which only they would inhabit after the Gentiles had left; that is they would be permitted to reside only in the suburbs of Warsaw and Lublin. In his opinion, this was the only way to stave off the danger of the total domination of trade and industry by the Jews.[26] In a newspaper article that same year, Raymond Rembielinski, who was later appointed head of the *województwo* of Mazovia (the province of Warsaw), argued for the setting up of *revirs* for the urban Jews "as an urgent need to remove Jews from the urban markets, which are the most likely sites for trade and innkeeping."[27] The veteran diplomat and member of the government Stanislaw Staszic could see only one option to rescue the nation from the "peril" of the Jews, whom he depicted as dominating all branches of the urban economy: "Either expel them from the country . . . but it is now too late for us to do this, or assign to them within the cities residential areas, set completely apart."[28]

Not many years passed before these demands, expressed by prominent statesmen in the kingdom and intimates of royalty, became government policy.[29] Again, the first to feel it were the Warsaw Jews, whose continued growth was seen by the authorities as representing a danger: the judaization of the capital city. In 1821 the area of the city in which Jews were permitted to reside was further restricted, by adding about ten streets in the center of the city to those which had been forbidden by the edict of 1809. These included Żabia, Graniczna, Nowy Świat, Leszno, Marszałkowska, Chłodna, and Electoralna. The new Jewish quarter of Warsaw was established in the northern section of the city, in the neighborhood of Nalewki and Franciszkańska streets. On May 7, 1822, the czar issued an edict which stated that in the future special Jewish quarters should be established after the pattern of Warsaw in other cities in the Kingdom of Poland. The decision regarding each individual city was to be made by the viceroy in accordance with the suggestion of the Committee for Internal Affairs. As if to add irony to the plight of the deprived Jewish population, the stated reason for the decree was the government's concern about urban overcrowding which might increase the danger of contagious diseases, fires, and other troubles. Accordingly, it was decreed that in Jewish houses no more than one family could reside in each room; in all district towns and other larger towns permission to build new houses would be granted to Jews only if the houses were built of stone and not of wood, the roof made of slate and not thatched.[30] Thus, the government sought to attain two goals at the same time: to isolate the urban Jews in special quarters, and to expand construction in the cities at their expense, since they perforce would have to build houses for themselves.

By this decree, the Jews were thrust into *revirs* over the next eight years, up to the rebellion of 1830, in many of the larger cities throughout the kingdom, such as Łowicz (1820), Włocławek (1823), Suwałki (1823), Zgierz (1824), Sieradz (1825), and Częstochowa (1829)[31] and even in some of the small towns. For example, by 1830, *revirs* were established in nineteen towns in the *województwo* of Mazovia.[32]

The hypocrisy of the government's justification for the decree establishing the ghetto was exposed by the Advisory Chamber of the Committee for the Affairs of Old Testament Believers (which consisted of Jews and was headed by a Pole). In its 1826 memorandum to the committee, it points out that while the government pretended to be preventing overcrowding in the cities by this decree, it was precisely within the *revirs* that the overcrowding of the Jews had reached unbearable proportions. To aggravate the suffering, the authorities insisted on bringing the decree into effect at its designated time even in cities where the new section allocated to the Jews did not have a minimum number of dwellings to house them or did not have any houses at all. In the city of Bodzentyn (in the province of Kielce) the mayor, in a humane gesture, requested that the authorities of the *województwo* postpone the implementation of the decree lest those expelled be left without roofs over their heads.[33] His request was rejected with the threat of a penalty for each delay in the implementation of the decree. Such pleas were routinely dismissed as being nothing more than "customary Jewish moanings and groanings."[34]

As for Warsaw, the decree of the *revir* was not considered sufficient by the government. In order to block the increase of Jews in the city through immigration and to further limit their ability to compete in trade, a decree was issued in 1824 renewing the *Billet*. Like the decree issued in the last decade of the existence of the old Kingdom of Poland, every nonresident Jew entering Warsaw was obliged to pay the *Billet*, which permitted him to stay in the city for one twenty-four-hour period. The payment was fixed at twenty grosz per diem, plus ten grosz for the stamp.[35] This decree obviously made it especially difficult for the impoverished—peddlers, petty traders, and laborers—to come to the capital in order to provide bread for their households.

The Polish revolutionary government abolished the humiliating *Billet* decree over the objections of the municipal authorities, mainly because of the demand for Jewish craftsmen to supply the needs of the revolutionary army. However, the government did not abolish the decree concerning the *revirs*. On the contrary, even though the government had decided against establishing new *revirs* before the uprising of July 14, 1830, the revolutionary government nevertheless complied with the suggestion of the authorities of the *województwo* of Kalisz and introduced a *revir* in the city of Szadek.[36] After the collapse of the uprising, even the institution of the *Billet* was restored in Warsaw.

The Pale of Settlement of the Jews in Congress Poland became even more restricted with the Border Zone decree of 1823 which ordered the expulsion (as of the beginning of 1824) of all village Jews living within a three-mile zone along the borders of Austria and Prussia. The reason given for the decree was the prevention of smuggling and only craftsmen, laborers, farmers, and dairymen were exempt.[37] In 1834 and 1836 this decree was extended to include the village Jews living in the border zone between Poland and Russia.[38]

The observations of Count Anton Ostrowski, written in exile after the failure of the Polish rebellion, give a vivid picture of the harsh conditions under which the Jews of Congress Poland lived:

> Everywhere [in every part of Poland] they were allowed to sustain themselves under duress. . . . The laws and regulations of the administration constantly and ubiquitously militated against them and the lot of the Jews depended

upon the arbitrary machinations of the rulers. They were harried out of the villages into the cities and from the small cities to the big ones, and within the cities proper—from street to street. [The authorities] scrutinized minutely the number of families and persons allowed to occupy this dwelling or that and set all kinds of conditions in permitting them to engage in certain occupations for their livelihood. Everywhere they harassed the Jews and terrified them so that they knew no rest. . . .[39]

The Consequences of Ghettoization: Poverty, Plague, and Polarization

The initial development of capitalism in central Poland caused a deepening social polarization within the Jewish population similar to that within the general population. The accumulation of wealth by holders of large estates, manufacturers, merchants, and bankers was also a factor in the growing misery of the Jewish shopkeepers, traders, and artisans. The large numbers of Jews who depended for their existence on the owners of estates were especially affected by the changes in the economy of the state. For the impoverishment of some of the estate owners, who were unable to incorporate the new farming methods, in turn brought the impoverishment of the Jewish merchants, middlemen, and shopkeepers who were their business agents. The decline in the export of wood, grain, and other crops in the wake of high tariffs (of neighboring Prussia, as against the Polish tariffs on the import of manufactured products) indirectly affected the Jews, who marketed the yield of the estates. But beyond all the economic factors, there were the discriminatory decrees coupled with the heavy burden of special taxes that steadily ground down Polish Jewry.

The severest of these decrees, the one ordering the expulsion of the Jewish innkeepers from the villages, not only brought suffering to the families involved; but also, having been uprooted from their villages, they streamed into the cities and towns and added to the already overcrowded conditions of their fellow Jews. All too soon the inevitable consequences of such miserable living conditions became evident—hunger, and in its wake, contagious diseases. In the early 1820s, the government was alerted by the authorities of various districts of Poland about the danger of plagues spreading from the Jewish quarters to the entire country. The direct initiative for the introduction of *revirs* in 1822 came as a consequence of such a memorandum by the commission of the *województwo* of Cracow in Kielce. In 1820 this commission informed the government's Committee for Internal Affairs and Religions that the many adherents of the Old Testament, who migrate to take up residence in other towns after losing their taverns in the villages, may readily cause the spread of plague among themselves which will even become infectious among the Christians. When reports reached the Committee that in the cities of Chęciny and Będzin a disease had appeared which the doctors referred to as typhus, doctors were sent promptly to those locations.[40]

In the fall of 1822 such alarming reports arrived from Siedlce about the plague which had erupted among former Jewish innkeepers who had been driven out of the villages that both the government and the commander in chief, Grand Duke Constantine, found it necessary to deal with the situation with particular urgency. It is worth noting that in an exchange of letters with Viceroy Zayonczek, the duke expressed the opinion that the Jewish innkeepers did not deserve to be in this grievous situation, as they were no worse than the Christian innkeepers. Later, in its report of November 15, 1822, the Committee for Internal Affairs allayed the concern of the viceroy, asserting that the situation in Siedlce was not so perilous, for only 76 of the 2,388 Jews in the city were stricken with the plague.[41]

The center of the gravest distress was the province of Augustów, on the Lithuanian border. In 1819 the commission of the *województwo* of Suwałki had urged the committee to begin settling the evicted innkeepers on royal lands, since "every delay in this matter will lead to heavy outlays for the support of any vagrants seized, or . . . will beget many criminal acts, brought on by the hunger and deprivation endured by these people, who remain without any means of sustenance or roof over their heads. . . ."[42]

The hunger of the innkeepers who had been uprooted from the villages brought attention to the distress of the multitudes of Jews in the cities and towns who were engaged in small business, trade, handicrafts, and brokerage. In 1826, when the Committee for the Affairs of Old Testament Believers took up the question of establishing schools for Jewish children, it received a plan from its Advisory Chamber accompanied by this pessimistic comment: "For the time being there is no hope that members of the Jewish faith will be able to maintain the schools from their own financial resources, inasmuch as nine-tenths of them are sunk in poverty."[43] This estimate was not greatly exaggerated, as demonstrated by other testimony from parties having no concern in the matter. For example, at the session of the revolutionary *Sejm* on May 26, 1831, the delegate Jakób Klimontowicz declared, "We are aware that in the cities the Jews constitute the majority of the population, of which three-fourths are without a means of livelihood and sustain themselves by questionable kinds of small trade and by acting as middlemen." On the basis of this estimate, the delegate demonstrated that the imposition of the conscription tax on the entire Jewish population was a crying injustice to the poor, and he suggested imposing the full tax only on those who were richer, that is, on one-fourth of this population.[44] However, Klimontowicz was incorrect in saying that the decisive and impoverished majority in the Jewish population was that engaged in "questionable kinds of small trade and acting as middlemen." According to the official census of 1843 no less than one-third of Jewish heads of family in the Kingdom of Poland were artisans or were engaged in other kinds of productive work. However, his estimate of the number of poor Jews was based on contemporary sources.

Corroboration of Klimontowicz's estimates can be found in the reflections on the Jewish question by Count Ostrowski, "That which we define as an ample livelihood implies whatever is necessary for proper living, without too much difficulty, and in tranquillity. Now, it is my opinion that I do not err in asserting that four-fifths of the Jews of Poland do not have it within their means to live in this fashion, and they must perforce engage in questionable small trade."[45] He went on to observe:

> It is indeed true that the Jews of this status, really the *lazzaroni* of the north, garner, by their deceit and trickery, only very meager profits; they can barely satisfy their hunger and with difficulty provide the payment of one-fifth and at most one-third of the rent money; they are pressed into one room, in which, for the greater part, a number of families crowd together, an atrocity to the eye and to the sense of smell. One actually behólds a picture of human deterioration, shocking poverty, all black, sad, gloomy. Lacking everything, dirty, naked in part or altogether, the children cry. . . . Properly, only one should be eating what has been prepared for five and as a result Jews on this level are emaciated, without a healthy glow on their faces, and they have neither desire nor strength for any sort of work. They keep themselves alive from day to day with a slice of bread. . . .[46]

He then remarked on the fact that those who cry out for bread are clad in rags

> . . . holes upon holes and holes on top of patches; this is the dress of the poor among the Jews, while the rich go about in silk caftans . . . often a delight to the eye; but for the rest, the simple folk—in the full sense of the term—they are an offense to the eye and even provoke a sense of shame. What poverty! The heart is rent apart from a sense of pity.[47]

The depth of the poverty of the Jews in the towns is similarly depicted in the *Yearbooks of the Economy of the State* (1842), an organ of the aristocrats and the nobles:

Let us look into the terrible habitations of the Jews in the towns, which are stricken with contagious diseases. Let us recognize them in all their details and we will then be convinced that the clothes of all the members of the family are, for the greatest part, merely filthy rags, and their daily food—some onions, bread and potatoes. It is deemed a sign of plenty if to all this is added, in the summertime, a goat in the marketplace which is overgrown with grass. . . . A Jew who could afford to own a cow is thought to be one of the notables.[48]

The most shocking picture of the abject poverty of the Jews was drawn in the beginning of the 1840s by the most prominent nobleman in the district. In his anonymous pamphlet *On the Reform of the Jews*[49] he proposed the establishment of a Jewish state in the steppes of the southeast of European Russia:

Surely there is no wretched race under the sun such as the poor Jewish people who dwell in our towns. To convince oneself of this, it is enough to visit some of the towns—Pińczów, Daleszyce, Działoszyce and the like. With the minor exception of a few with greater means, there dwell in one small room which is stricken with a plague-ridden miasma, over a dozen Jews, begrimed, half-naked, who lie down at night in actual layers one over the other in hammocks, engaged in an almost incessant struggle with hunger, illness, and all too often even with death, without help or hope in this world, save for the courage imbedded in the heart by reason of strong faith despite all the many afflictions which bedevil them. There is indeed no uglier sight than these towns ridden by this plague; nothing touches one's heart more than the poverty of this people over whom the curse holds unrestrained sway in a manner so plainly visible. Observing the multitude of gloomy faces of Jewry wending its plodding way in our towns, the thoughtful person will ask, perforce, on what does this poor people sustain its life?

In the writer's opinion, one cannot compare this terrible poverty with the poverty of the peasants. For "our peasant, although he is poor, does have for the wintertime, some grain, a store of potatoes or other vegetables; he has his hut, a small piggery or a barn. At the same time more than half of Poland's Jews have none of this; inasmuch as in their wretched dwellings they do not even have a breath of clean air."

The pamphlet concludes that "the entire Jewish population, with some very minor exceptions, subsists among us in grinding poverty, without any certainty of a daily livelihood and without any future whatsoever."[50]

At the other extreme were the wealthy Jews who accumulated their capital mainly through trade. Indeed, most of the large wholesalers and merchants in the provincial towns were Jews. Even within Warsaw, the majority of merchants were Jews. For example, in 1849, of the 441 merchants, 231 were Jewish.[51] Some of the agents of the nobles also had amassed great wealth. According to the testimony of Count Ostrowski, there was hardly a landlord who was involved in business dealings without the participation of "his court Jew, as it were; Levek, Itzik, Hershik, or Moshke." The agent would provide the landlord with whatever merchandise he needed, and it was he who marketed the farm produce.[52] According to the official reports of a number of the country's districts in the early 1840s most of the export of grain, cattle, hides, wool, textiles, and wood was concentrated in the hands of Jewish agents and merchants.[53] As in earlier centuries, the Jewish merchants had almost complete control over the overland export of goods. Hundreds of Jews would journey from Poland to the Leipzig fairs, whereas the number of Christian merchants from the entire Kingdom of Poland attending those fairs amounted to less than fifty, and in the 1830s dwindled to about twenty or even a mere dozen.[54]

Owing to their diligent business activities, the Jews also played an important role in the development of manufacture, particularly of textiles. Jews exported Polish textiles to Russia, and through collaboration with Russian merchants, these textiles went from there to China.[55] The owners of the textile mills would get the wool from abroad, mainly through Jewish merchants. An even greater role was played by the Jewish merchants in importing cotton yarn, which was brought directly from England or from Hamburg and Breslau. In 1844 there were fifty Jewish merchants among the sixty-one owners of large cotton warehouses in Poland.[56] By virtue of their dealings in raw materials, the Jewish merchants, like the Christian manufacturers, hired home laborers for the manufacture of textiles on a credit basis. They would provide the weavers with cotton on credit which would be applied against what they produced. These Jewish contractors were to be found in Łódz and a number of other cities in the region—Pabianice, Zduńska Wola, Konstantynów, Kalisz, and Częstochowa.[57]

There were also Jewish capitalists, especially in the 1840s, who invested all or part of their money in establishing factories. Members of the Epstein family were among the first to establish sugar, paper, and candle factories. Members of the Bergson family owned textile mills in Warsaw. In 1829 an Austrian Jew, Ignatz Bondy, set up a cotton mill in Ostrołęka. The factory which had been established in 1823 in the village of Kuchary, in the Płock district, by Solomon Posner, one of the leaders of the Warsaw community, employed 150 laborers at the beginning of the 1840s. Unlike the other factories owned by Jews, all its workers were Jews. During those years, Jews established about six textile mills in Łódz, among them the large cotton spinning mill owned by the merchant from Kalisz, David Landau.

In the beginning of the second half of the nineteenth century, the banking establishments of Kronenberg and Rosen were already well known for their industrial activities. In addition, scores of Jews were engaged in small-scale manufacture. According to a census taken in 1843, the overall number of Jewish factory owners in the Kingdom of Poland was 115, of whom 41 were in the paper industry (including 8 lessees of factories), 32 were in textiles, 20 in glass, 18 in iron, 3 in chinaware and 1 in the production of silver and gold objects.[58]

The Great Jewish Banking Families

As against industry, which Jewish capitalists were just beginning to penetrate, private banking was a major area of activity. To be sure, both Christian and Jewish capitalists lent money at interest. According to an 1840 listing, among 275 Warsaw capitalists lending money at interest, less than one-half were Jews. However, among the well-known banking houses in Warsaw, only a few, such as that of the active industrialist Piotr Steinkeller, were under Christian ownership. All the rest were in Jewish hands, though these included converts to Christianity. Aside from their own capital, the Jewish bankers in Warsaw also availed themselves of the funds of Jewish banking houses in western Europe with which they maintained business ties. The banking houses of Frankel, Laski, and Epstein had ties with the Berlin houses of Mendelssohn and Magnus, and at the end of this period the banker Leopold Kronenberg was collaborating with the Parisian bankers Pereira, James Rothschild, and Fould. These large Jewish banking establishments in Poland would provide loans to the government in time of need, mostly with the participation of banks from abroad. In 1835 a loan of this kind in the amount of 150 million zlotys brought Joseph Epstein alone—he was a partner in the banking house of Frankel—a profit of several million zlotys.[59]

The capital of the Jewish banking houses, which originated in commerce, increased tenfold through dealings with the government, either as purveyors, or through acquiring monopoly rights and leases for the collection of taxes. Samuel Zbitkower of the surburb of Praga, the patriarch of the Bergson family which controlled five of Warsaw's large banks, was a purveyor both to the armies of Poland and to Poland's enemies in the days of Kościuszko's insurrection. His widow, Judith, and son Berek continued to augment the already considerable fortune by providing supplies for the army. Judith's son-in-law, Samuel Frankel, who converted to Christianity and changed his name to Leopold Antoni, founded a banking house which, over the years, surpassed all the banking houses of Warsaw and the rest of Poland. In 1816, after the establishment of the Kingdom of Poland, Samuel's son, Berek, together with four Jewish partners, paid over five million zlotys for a five-year lease of the state salt monopoly. After the abolition of the general lease of this monopoly, a lease on the tobacco monopoly provided another prime source of wealth for the lessees. In the initial years of the Kingdom of Poland, this lease had been held by the former Maskil Judah Leyb ben Noah Nevakhovitch of Russia, who, after converting, changed his name to Leon. In the 1840s, when the government revenue from this monopoly reached almost ten million zlotys, the lease, which had previously been in the hands of another convert, Koniar (Moritz Cohen), was given to the young banker Leopold Kronenberg, in partnership with a few merchants. In the provincial towns as well (such as in Kielce, Łódz, and Siedlce) there were Jews who leased monopoly rights on excise taxes applicable within their borders. A considerable number of Jews amassed great wealth by supplying materials for government mines and factories, and in particular, in the Duchy of Warsaw, by provisioning the army. Berek ben Samuel Zbitkower's partner, the merchant Neumark, supplied the army of Duke Constantine with textiles which he imported. During the insurrection of November 1830–31, nearly all supplies to the revolutionary army were provided by Jewish purveyors, the majority of whom were from Warsaw, a situation which apparently vexed the members of the *Sejm*. From the memoranda they submitted to the government after the revolt was crushed, it became clear that there even were several Jewish purveyors to the Russian army.[60]

Just as the Jewish financiers made a great deal of money by leasing various types of monopolies which involved social exploitation and oppression of the population at large, they also increased their fortunes by collaborating with the government in collecting the discriminatory taxes from the masses of their impoverished coreligionists. Indeed, in 1818 there were several lessees of the kosher meat tax—including Aaron Michael Ettinger and Solomon Posner, the very active communal leaders in Warsaw. In 1820 the general lease of that tax was awarded to R. Ḥayyim Davidson, who was later to occupy the post of Chief Rabbi of Warsaw; and Jacob Epstein, the head of the dynasty of prominent bankers. The two were quickly appointed to the three-member Synagogue Supervisory Board which was set up by the government in place of the suspended community council. In this matter, too, there was no difference between converts (such as Leon Nevakhovitch, the general lessee of the kosher meat tax in the *wo-*

jewództwo of Mazovia), scholars, leaders of the Mitnaggedim, and "enlightened" persons (Jacob Epstein) or supporters of the intellectuals (Michael Ettinger). Theodore Teplitz, who acquired one of the leases for the kosher meat tax in the Mazovia *województwo*, was at once a friend of the Haskalah and an outstanding supporter of Maskilim as well as a "supervisor" of the community and a philanthropist. He had obtained the lease at the end of 1831 by increasing his bid to 523,055 zlotys. His way of "oppressing the poor" in collecting the tax served as the official reason for his being deprived of the lease in 1834.

The complaints, which have been preserved in the archives of the Ministry for Internal Affairs of the Kingdom of Poland, demonstrated the oppressive acts of the lessees. The lessees frequently went "beyond the strict letter of the law" during the entire period of the existence of this discriminatory tax. In 1836 malfeasances in the collections of the kosher meat tax were uncovered in the city of Maków, near Warsaw. In 1837 Moshe Amshiovitch (the son of Anshel) presented a complaint about oppressive acts in the Grzybow quarter of Warsaw by Ḥayyim Lote (a partner of Solomon Posner), who was a lessee for the collection of the kosher meat tax. In 1847 the authorities reinstituted an investigation of oppressive acts which had been uncovered in the lesseeship of Jacob Epstein.[61]

The wealthy lessees did not hesitate to use their authority and influence within the community in order to invoke, in the name of the rabbis, a ban on those who evaded the payment of the discriminatory tax. A number of bans were declared in Warsaw. For example, in November 1817 a ban was proclaimed in all the synagogues of Warsaw and Praga in the name and under the seal of the *bet din*, ten rabbis and officials of the *Ḥevra Kadisha* (burial society), and the Society of the Visiting of the Sick and the Hospital. The lessees of the kosher meat tax in Warsaw and the administrative district at that time were Michael Ettinger, Wolf Michelson, and five more partners who won the lease after raising their bid to 56,000 zlotys. This time, however, the ban involved the leaders of the community in a dispute. The *parnas*, Moses Aaron Fuerstenberg, came out strongly against the ban, citing the Prussian regulation of 1797 which abolished the imposition of a ban as a penalty by the community, and deeming it sufficient to impose an oath on those suspected of circumventing the tax. Michael Ettinger, Solomon Posner, Loeb Shaulson, and Solomon Eger (the son of Akiba Eger, the rabbi of Posen) supported the ban. On December 16, 1817, the government's Committee for Religions and Education issued a statement which leaned toward those imposing the ban, but the president of Warsaw intervened in the matter and, on the basis of the 1797 regulation, nullified the ban. After Ettinger and his associates appealed this ruling, the committee turned to the viceroy on January 2, 1818, for his decision. Later that year the Administrative Council decided to leave the ban in force until the lease expired. In 1820 a government order abolished the right to impose a ban, which in any case was contrary to the aim of the authorities. This became clear at the end of the year with the liquidation of the community council and the establishment of the Synagogue Supervisory Board.[62]

Due to their connection with the authorities and their influence "in high places," the lessees of the meat tax succeeded in frustrating all plans for the nullification of the tax. For example, after the revolt of 1830, the authorities considered a plan to levy a tax on woolen textiles in place of the kosher meat tax. Those proposing the plan wanted to alleviate the tax burden on the poverty-stricken Jews, since, unlike meat, woolen textiles were to some extent luxury goods. However, the lessees of the kosher meat tax were able to get the viceroy to oppose the plan.[63]

The *Billet* tax on entry into Warsaw was also frequently leased to Jewish capitalists. It is ironic that among the lessees of the tax were leaders of the Warsaw community as well as renowned philanthropists. In the 1850s this tax was leased by the banker Matthias Rosen, who was the head of the "community supervisory body" of Warsaw during 1856–58. He contributed to Jewish and Christian charitable institutions and was a patron of Polish literature. In the first year of his lesseeship, his profit amounted to approximately one-quarter of a million zlotys.

The lessees of the *Billet* tax as well as the kosher meat tax remained on guard lest the source of their profits be cut off. At the end of 1824, when the levying of the *Billet* was impending, the wealthy Jewish capitalist David Bauerertz wrote a detailed memorandum to the Committee for Religions and Education proposing that he and his partners be the lessees for this tax. He supported this proposal with the following arguments: It is worthwhile for the government to collect by lease, rather than by its functionaries, inasmuch as the collectors, "men of low station," were likely to become lax in fulfilling their obligations as collectors, especially when the "emotion of pity" would be added to "their self-interest," that is, in taking bribes. And moreover, it was important that the lessee and his staff of collectors be Jews, since it could be assumed that they were familiar with those who were exempt from this payment and therefore more likely to assure that the payments due the royal treasury were made. Some weeks later, Bauerertz, after having learned that several members of the Synagogue Supervisory Board had requested that the decree be postponed for several months, presented a second memorandum in which he warned that a postponement was likely to cause an irreparable loss of *Billet* revenue. The authorities, disregarding Bauerertz's claim that the revenue from the kosher meat tax had increased considerably in the *województwo* of Mazovia, decided to appoint Gentiles for the collection of those taxes imposed on Jews. This they did on the assumption that gentile collectors would be more trustworthy than Jewish ones and would enforce the decree rigorously. However, several years later Jewish capitalists succeeded in acquiring this source of wealth, initially as partners of gentile lessees and later as official lessees.

In 1843 a memorandum was submitted petitioning for the liquidation of the *Billet* in the name of the destitute Jews of the provincial towns, but it had no effect. As the authors of the memoranda observed, and as even the magistrate in Warsaw testified, the Jews of Warsaw, that is, the affluent among them, were themselves interested in the maintenance of the tax in order to prevent an influx of Jews which would increase competition in trade and commerce.[64]

Thus there was a thin upper stratum of Jews, mostly from Warsaw, who had grown wealthy from big business and provisioning, from contracting in construction of factory buildings and factory enterprises, banking, and the lease of monopolies and taxes. According to the list of those paying the recruit tax to the Jewish community, in 1825 there were in the capital city about 12 men with property worth more than a million zlotys[65] and about 120 with worth less than one million.[66] In the 1830s and 1840s affluent Jews could also be found in the manufacturing centers of Kalisz and Łódz.[67]

The Privileges of Wealth

The wealthy Jews did not suffer from the discrimination endured by the masses of their brethren; on the contrary, they enjoyed extensive privileges. For example, the kosher meat tax was hardly felt. According to a description of the situation in a complaint against the burden of that tax, the case of the rich man was different: "He can enjoy fish, asparagus and costly vegetables and if he has a craving for meat, he—as a more cultured person—does not buy from the Jewish butchers but from the Christians. As a matter of course, the rich man is thus excluded from the onus of the tax, while the poor, noncultured are obliged to pay in his stead."[68] A number of memoranda written to the Warsaw magistracy by individuals and groups of enlightened persons requesting exemption from the payment of the kosher meat tax inasmuch as they did not observe *kashrut* have been preserved.[69]

In addition, this wealthy class was exempt from the decree of the *revir*. In accordance with the terms already established in 1809, the right of residence anywhere in the capital[70] was given to those wholesale merchants, factory owners, physicians, practitioners of the other free professions, and builders of new stone houses provided they had property worth 60,000 zlotys or more, wore European clothes, were literate in Polish, French, or German, and sent their children to the public schools.[71]

In the provincial towns, a lesser amount of property was required to reside outside the *revir* than in Warsaw; in Łódz the sum was 20,000 zlotys.[72] Wealthy merchants were also accepted as members of the Merchants Association of Warsaw, albeit with reservations: in 1817 it decided that only those Jews invited by the Board of Elders could participate in the association's meetings. In 1829 two representatives of the Jewish merchants (Herman Epstein and Theodore Teplitz) were proposed for the Board of Elders. They were to serve as liaisons through which the association could inform those merchants who were "Old Testament Believers" about the government's instructions. This limited access was given to the Jewish merchants so that they would collaborate in restraining competition from the multitude of Jewish petty merchants and middlemen. In 1818 lists of Jewish merchants in the city were given to the heads of the Jewish associations. Subsequently (in 1823 and 1828), the association turned to the authorities with complaints against "the Jews who make the rounds of the streets and the houses with their merchandise" and against the Jewish agents and petty traders.[73]

The Jewish bankers collaborated in a similar way with the Christians against the petty Jewish moneychangers who carried on business negotiations in the hall of the bourse. In 1840 a complaint was made about this matter to the heads of the bourse both by Polish bankers and by the Jewish banker Matthias Bersohn; the only difference in the complaints was that the Polish bankers referred expressly to "a rabble of Old Testament Believers," whereas Bersohn merely characterized them as "a rabble of moneychangers."[74] Like the merchants and bankers, some Jewish house owners did not hesitate to act in concert with gentile house owners against the general welfare of their own people. In 1850, when the extension of the limits of the Jewish *revir* in Łódz was under consideration, a number of Jewish house owners presented a memorandum to the authorities of the gubernium protesting this plan and recommending that the Jews living in the city be expelled. When this memorandum failed to gain attention, a new one was presented in 1852 signed by the house owners within the *revir*—twenty-five Christians and twenty-four Jews. This time there was no demand for expulsion, but apprehension was expressed that the price of dwellings would fall if additional streets were included in the *revir*.[75]

Over the years, particularly during the period following the rebellion of 1830, a Jewish elite developed consisting of those granted certain limited rights and privileges for service rendered to the Russian army and the empire during the Polish rebellion, for service in the prerevolutionary Polish army, or for civilian acts of heroism and charitable deeds. Most of these privileges merely granted permission to engage in innkeeping within the city and the maintenance of horses for the post. Persons who had been granted broader privileges were exempt from the special tax imposed upon Jewish innkeepers or were permitted to lease estates. Those who had served in the army of the Kingdom of Poland before the rebellion were also exempt from having to purchase the *Billet* for entering Warsaw and from the kosher meat tax. The wealthy who had adopted modern European ways—bankers, merchants, and factory owners, all of whom wore European clothes, knew the Polish language and sent their children to schools (including the Rabbinical School in Warsaw)—were granted permission to reside outside the Jewish *revir* and also were given broad economic privileges. Some were permitted to engage in any kind of trade and occupation, including dealing in liquor throughout the land, and others were allowed to own property (houses and lots) within the cities. The wealthy magnates were especially privileged in that they and their children were permitted to acquire estates and even entire villages. In 1824 the legacy of Berek Samuel Sonnenberg included, besides cash, mortgages in the amount of 350,000 zlotys, six stone houses in Warsaw, and an estate in the district of Czersk. By the end of the 1840s, there were about forty Jews who owned estates in the Kingdom of Poland, including Jacob Epstein and his sons, Abraham Simeon Cohen and his progeny, Solomon Posner, and Simeon Rosen and his son Matthias. The highest privileges were those derived from the title "honorary citizen," which was bestowed by the office of the czar in St. Petersburg. The recipients were virtually full citizens, for they had the right to elect and to be elected to municipal offices and were exempt from service in the army and from the recruit tax as well as from corporal punishment.[76]

With these privileges, particularly the right to possess estates, the new Jewish bourgeois upper class in Poland, along with the gentile financiers, approached the level of the ruling nobility in the land in its social status and life style.

In the 1840s only one-fifth of all the Jews engaged in commerce, or one-tenth of the total Jewish population in the capital city, could be considered wealthy. There was the same proportion of fairly well-to-do in the city, while the rest of those earning their livelihoods from commerce and brokerages were shopkeepers, petty traders, peddlers, and middlemen. In the 1840s, as in the previous era, according to the register of 1831, the majority of Warsaw Jews were exempt because of poverty from all payments for the needs of the Jewish community. A similar social stratification existed in the small community in the manufacturing center of Łódz, where in 1838 about half the heads of families were exempt from community taxes because of poverty, and in 1850 about two-fifths.[77]

The social polarization of the Jewish population in the capital city and its surrounding environs is reflected to some extent in the list of Jews paying the recruit tax which was drawn up for the *województwo* of Warsaw in 1842. The percentage of Jews in the six social classes into which they had been divided for tax purposes is as follows: Of the first four classes (17.92 to 213 rubles per family), 16 percent; the fifth class (0.78 rubles), 54 percent; while 30 percent were exempt from payment of the tax because of poverty.[78] In reality, the proportion of downtrodden poor among the Jews was greater than indicated by the percentage of those exempt from this tax. This is indicated in the account by Klimontowicz of the May 26, 1831, session of the revolutionary *Sejm*, in which he dwelt in detail on the method of apportionment of the recruit tax practiced in the provincial towns. He said the apportionment in Warsaw "is fair, since each one is concerned for his own safety; however, in the provincial towns those who have means are wont to foist everything upon the poor to such an extent that the first-born of the poor pay two zlotys each, and even the invalids and the maimed pay that tax."[79]

Persecution and the Paradox of Assimilation

The impoverishment of the majority of the Jewish population was checked somewhat by a partial reorientation in the direction of increased productivity. As in Galicia and Russia, the authorities of the Kingdom of Poland were interested in directing part of the Jewish population to agricultural work as some slight compensation for the eviction of Jewish innkeepers in cities and towns. However, the viceroy's edict of 1823 regarding agricultural settlement had so many restrictions as to deprive it of any real substance. Even the directive issued in 1843 had little effect due to the top-heavy bureaucracy and its ill will toward the Jews. The move toward agricultural settlement was given slight impetus. Later that year an edict was issued which abolished the recruit tax but obliged Jews to serve in the army. Agricultural settlers were promised exemption from military service for twenty-five or fifty years, according to the size of the village. Only a small number of families were involved in this spontaneous settlement, with no sizable assistance from the Jewish community leaders. According to the census of 1843, only 104 heads of families among the Jews in the entire Kingdom of Poland, 4 percent of Jewish breadwinners, were engaged in agriculture, half of them as dairy farmers. Even after about twelve years, when settlement had reached its zenith, there were only about 400 Jewish families scattered over sixty villages in the entire kingdom and the total proportion of those who earned their livelihoods from agriculture amounted to merely 5 percent of all the Jews in Poland.

The tendency of the Jewish population toward productive labor proved incomparably more effective than that toward agriculture. The increase in the number of Jewish artisans was greatly facilitated by the royal edicts of 1816 and 1823 while the discrimination against the Jews concerning the privileges of the members of the Artisans' Assemblies (the erstwhile guilds) remained in force. In 1843, according to the official census, almost one-fourth of breadwinners in the Jewish population were artisans. The number of Jews seeking their livelihoods in manual labor grew as innkeeping and leasing became closed to them. Yet most of the Jewish artisans gravitated toward the traditional trades—becoming tailors, furriers, butchers, and bakers. The only occupation new to the Jews as a result of the abolition of the monopoly of the guilds was shoemaking.

This tendency of the multitude of Jewish artisans to concentrate in the traditional trades was one of the reasons for the impoverishment of the entire class, just as the concentration in small trading and brokerage limited the livelihood of storekeepers and others engaged in commerce.[80]

The abnormal socioeconomic structure of the Jewish population which resulted from the discriminatory decrees was the root cause of the grave Jewish problem in the Kingdom of Poland. The government's policy on this problem was assimilation, which it tried to implement by a number of new decrees directed against the Jewish national culture and tradition, and even the Jewish religion itself. In the Kingdom of Poland this was an even more glaring contradiction than in the neighboring states. In czarist Russia, the special levies imposed on the Jews had already been repealed in the period of the Napoleonic wars. In Galicia no special quarters were designated for the Jews except in Lemberg (Lwów), the capital, and in a few other cities; and as for the decree relating to Jewish innkeepers, the authorities were not too rigorous in its implementation. Unlike its neighboring countries, the government of the Kingdom of Poland (before the rebellion in 1830, almost in its entirety; and after it, within a framework of broad autonomy) was in the hands of the ethnic majority living in that land who exploited their political status to oppress the Jews more than elsewhere.

Like the despotic governments of Austria and Russia, the Polish authorities felt constrained to justify the contradiction between the oppression of the Jews and the alleged goal of integrating them into the dominant nation and its culture. The official doctrine was that the Jews must first "mend their ways," turn to useful employment, "cease their isolation and . . . raise the level of their culture," and only then would they be worthy of the benevolence of the kingdom, including equal rights with other inhabitants of the country.

The first step taken by the government toward ending the "separatism" of the Jews was the removal of the community's autonomy. This step was accelerated by the complaints of those who were discriminated against in the autonomous regime, especially by the actions of the "enlightened" Jews in the assimilationist faction. The autonomous Jewish community in the Kingdom of Poland was abolished by authority of the royal edicts of 1821 and 1822 and was replaced by the Synagogue Supervisory Board, which was subject to the strict control of the municipal authorities.

The Crusade against the Talmud and against Jewish Garb

The Polish authorities started to deal with the reform of the Jews on a wider scale after they established the Committee for the Affairs of Old Testament Believers. However, none of the proposals for involving Jews in agriculture and handicrafts developed by the committee was acted upon. Nor were requests granted for the mitigation of a number of the harsh decrees. The government did respond favorably to a number of the committee's proposals relating to the "moral improvement" of the Jews and the eradication first of their national individuality and then of their religious unity.

The real attitude of the authorities toward the Jewish religion was revealed in their crusade against the Talmud, which, under the inspiration of the Committee for the Affairs of Old Testament Believers, continued until the outbreak of the Polish uprising and kept the Jewish population in a state of tension and anxiety for four years. In accordance with the suggestion of the committee, the government supported the publication of the Abbé Chiarini's diatribe against the

Talmud in 1829 under the title *A Theory of Judaism*, as well as his translation of the Babylonian Talmud into French, of which two volumes were published in 1831. The only reason the committee's program for spreading Polish education by means of special schools for the Jews did not materialize was the government's reluctance to provide the necessary funds from the royal treasury; the government contented itself with the maintenance of Polish schools for Jewish children in Warsaw. These schools, which in time numbered five, were funded by revenue from the *Billet*. In order to raise the status of these schools, whose pupils were recruited from among the most destitute, an obligatory registration of the *ḥadarim* in Warsaw was ordered and a test was required of those who taught in them. In accordance with the committee's program, a Rabbinical School was opened in Warsaw at the end of 1826 which was also funded by the *Billet*. As if to symbolize the aim of this school, the Abbé Chiarini was appointed its supervisor and the extreme assimilationist Anton Eisenbaum was appointed its director. Despite the opposition of the Advisory Chamber, Abraham Buchner, who had assisted the Abbé Chiarini in the preparation of *A Theory of Judaism*, was chosen for the post of teacher of Hebrew and Bible. The course of studies per se demonstrated the role which the authorities had assigned to this institution. That is, secular studies were given priority over Jewish studies, which, in addition to Hebrew and the Bible, included Talmud and the *Shulḥan Arukh*.

Supervision of the Jewish religion was carried out by the authorities chiefly by means of the censorship of Hebrew books, which had already begun in 1818. In 1822 the Minister for Religions and Culture established the Committee for the Censorship of Hebrew Books, headed by the ubiquitous Abbé Chiarini. Prompted by demands of the Committee for the Affairs of Old Testament Believers which Chiarini initiated, the authorities closely scrutinized Hebrew books, the majority of which were brought in from Russia (Vilna and Slavuta in Volhynia). They also decreed that all Hebrew books in the country must be registered with the censorship office in order to receive a stamp of approval. But the greatest harassment from censorship occurred after the committee was abolished in 1837. From then until 1843, Polish Jews lived under the threat of implementation of a decree requiring the deletion of certain passages from the *Ḥoshen Mishpat* of the *Shulḥan Arukh* which were said to contain "harmful views" with regard to Gentiles and the observance of the laws of the kingdom. Although the decree was never implemented as such, it did provide a pretext for searches of *battei midrash* and private homes, and in the district of Kielce police officers even confiscated a number of copies of the book.

The most draconian of all the measures for bringing about the acculturation of the Jews was the campaign waged against Jewish garb.

In the days of the Duchy of Warsaw, the Polish authorities had already adopted a system of granting special privileges to those who abandoned the traditional Jewish dress. This was one of the requirements for permission to reside in any of the sections of the capital. This requirement was extended to all the cities where Jewish *revirs* had been established and at the same time was made a condition for granting special privileges, such as obtaining an innkeeping license without the payment of the *consens*, the right of acquiring real estate in the cities, the leasing and even the purchasing of landed estates.

In addition to removing "any distinguishing difference in dress," the beard and earlocks were to be shorn. The punctiliousness of the authorities in this regard is attested to by the fact that they rejected the request of David Bauerertz to be exempt as long as his seventy-two-year-old mother was alive.

In 1844, when a special levy was imposed in Russia on those who wore Jewish garb as a first step toward its total prohibition, the government of Poland acted speedily to adjust the legal status of the Polish Jew to that of his brethren in Russia. In accordance with this aim of coordinating the legislation regarding the Jews in the two parts of the empire, obligatory military service had been imposed upon the Jews of Poland a year earlier. According to the edict issued in 1845, as of July 1 (later extended to October 10), 1846, the Jewish mode of dress was forbidden in Poland, because "it sets apart the members of the Old Testament faith from the other inhabitants of the country in an unseemly fashion, and constitutes one of the chief causes for the curbing of the progress of civilization of that people." Until January 1, 1850, Jewish dress was permitted those who paid the annual *consens* of three to fifty rubles, set according to the six professional classes mentioned above. No one was exempt from the payment except people over sixty and children under ten.

The majority of the Jewish population could not comply with this decree for economic reasons. It could neither meet the payment of the *consens* nor afford to acquire the new obligatory clothes. But beyond that, the decree struck at the Jewish people's religious feelings. For aside from the fact that the adoption of "the alien mode of dress" was considered a transgression of the biblical injunction against the imitation of gentile customs (Lev. 18:3), the decree forbade males growing earlocks and married women shaving off their hair, both considered inviolable religious imperatives.

Indeed, when the edict went into effect in the autumn of 1846, a chapter of martyrdom began in the history of the Jews in Poland which was to last for many years. It became a daily occurrence for the police or army detachments to attack Jews in the streets of the cities and towns, and anyone found with earlocks or a beard was brutally shorn; some were lashed and imprisoned. This maltreatment continued for the more than twenty years it took for the adoption of modern garb to spread throughout the Jewish population.[81]

However, all of these coercive measures to assimilate and civilize the Jews failed. The marked national instinct for survival based on a tradition dating back thousands of years was reinforced by the specific socioeconomic structure of the Jews.

Hasidic Leadership of Jewish Passive Resistance

Because of the strong sense of national solidarity, the masses of oppressed and persecuted people succeeded in overcoming the decree abolishing the autonomy of Jewish community organization. All the Jewish societies, the most important among them being the *Ḥevra Kadisha*, continued to exist despite their prohibition. To cope with budget curtailments, the Synagogue Supervisory Board employed the device of keeping two account books—one official and one secret. And it need scarcely be said that despite the abolition of the juridical authority of the *bet din*, the devoutly observant, who accounted for a decisive majority of the Jewish population, regarded those who brought disputes into "the courts of the Gentiles" as transgressors.

With regard to the Rabbinical School, it merely served to prepare one for entering the schools and universities, or for careers as accountants and business managers for the big Jewish merchants and bankers in Warsaw. Throughout its thirty-seven years of existence, until 1863, this institution did not produce a single rabbi, since there was not a community in the country which would agree to accept a student of "Eisenbaum's school" as its rabbi. As to the rigorous law of censorship, people contrived to evade it by circumventing the office of the censor and its seal and by smuggling books from abroad.

Even in the matter of the legal prohibition of Jewish garb, the government did not achieve its goal except in relation to women. They were compelled to desist from the age-old custom of cutting off their hair before their weddings, since it was incumbent upon the rabbis, under threat of severe punishment, to look after this in officiating at a marriage. However, the Orthodox men maintained their distinctive garb. To be sure, the earlocks were cut short or thrown back behind the ears; but growing a beard had from the beginning been allowed by law, it being in keeping with the garb of "Russian merchants." This compulsory Russian dress, which the devout chose over European dress, became the external distinguishing mark of their Jewishness. And, in the course of time, this style of dress—the long coat and the cap, later referred to as "the Jewish cap"—became sacred to the devout, having the force of religious tradition, and anyone who did not observe it was ostracized.

Thus, in Poland, as in Russia, the "dress decree" resulted in nothing more than that the old Jewish garb was replaced by a new "Jewish" mode of dress.

The Hasidic movement took the lead in mobilizing the people's passive resistance to the oppressive measures against its national and religious unity. For example, when the authorities abolished the autonomy of the community, the Hasidim responded by marshaling their consolidated groups in the cities and towns. They declared a ban against the Rabbinical School in Warsaw. At the first rumor of any impending decree directed against the Jews or their tradition, the Hasidim immediately tried to intercede and mounted fund-raising campaigns in order to "appease with presents" the powers that be. It is no wonder that the Hasidim stood out even in the milieu of the devout masses for their desperate stubbornness in resisting the decree on the compulsory "gentile" dress. According to official sources, in the early period of the decree, the era of the *consens*, the Hasidim were the ones who most frequently paid the high fine imposed on those who objected to the required mode of dress. Even later, when the option to pay was abrogated, the Hasidim, according to reports of the local authorities, were the rear guard of those who persisted in zealous disobedience.

These decrees affected the political balance between the two polarized camps—the Hasidim and the Maskilim. The Hasidim, who placed their trust in faith and in salvation from heaven, became more dominant in relation to the Maskilim, who, like the upper echelon of the "enlightened" assimilationists, enthusiastically endorsed the official phraseology concerning the civilizing and productivity programs and put their trust in "the benevolent royalty" and its "lofty government."

8

Brooks of Assimilation and Buds of Enlightenment

The Haskalah Fails to Take Root in Poland

In Poland, the Haskalah movement was not very successful; it is as though the Haskalah bypassed this country on its way eastward from Germany to Galicia, Volhynia, and Lithuania. In those neighboring countries the Haskalah flourished in the first half of the nineteenth century, after having faded in Germany; but within Poland proper, it produced only a few isolated Maskilim. The factors behind the Haskalah's fate in Poland lay in the socioeconomic structure of the country and its political regime, as well as the specific circumstances of the geographical and historical development of Polish Jewry.

Because of Poland's socioeconomic backwardness even at the outset of its industrial development, the bourgeois class, which was the bearer of modern culture in the industrialized countries in the West, did not emerge. The inhabitants of the Polish towns were culturally no more sophisticated than the rural population, and most of them engaged in the same agricultural occupations. The thin stratum of Polish industrialists, bankers, and leading merchants, mostly of German origin, did not form a class of its own, but gradually merged with the nobility, whom it also took into partnership in its business enterprises. The acquisition of estates by the bourgeois financial magnates was a major step toward this integration. But the social character of Polish culture remained unaltered, and the stamp of the *Szlachta*, the ruling class, was impressed upon it as before. This culture had no attraction or influence except for the elite of the financiers.

Unlike Galicia and the Pale of Settlement in Russia, Poland lacked that class of enlightened government officials who brought the Jewish well-to-do and their clerks closer to the ideas of European enlightenment. The Russian official in the area of White Russia, Lithuania, and the Ukraine and, even more, the German official in Galicia were closer to the Jewish population with respect to language and preferred the society of the Jews to that of the peasant and provincial Ukrainian or White Russian. In contrast, a wall of strangeness separated the Polish official from the Jewish people. Furthermore, lower-rank Polish officials were intellectually limited and permeated by a religious and national hatred of the Jew. The higher officials, except for enlightened liberals, had nothing but contempt for the Jew—a contempt shared with the nobility. In their eyes every Jew was a lowly innkeeper who existed solely to serve them and who was expected to cringe before them in abject subservience. Certainly, no cultural contact was thought possible.[1]

In light of Poland's distinctly aristocratic culture, it is understandable why the few Maskilim in Poland were attracted to and influenced by German culture, and not at all by Polish culture. Moreover, the very closeness to Polish culture was in itself a conspicuous indication of a tendency to extreme assimilation, which was a far cry from the aims of the Haskalah movement. The contact with German culture, as with western European culture in general—and at a much later period, with Russian culture—had a marked influence upon the Jewish intelligentsia. It was a source of literary ideas which spurred national creativity in both Hebrew and Yiddish. In contrast, polonization, for the few Jews who were involved, signified a rise in social status as they became integrated in the dominant class and, by this very fact, held themselves aloof from their people, usually to the point of estrangement. Thus, this class of Jews who were drawn into the maelstrom of Polish patriotism, especially in the stormy days of the uprising of November 1830, became assimilationists.

This assimilationist tendency of the new plutocracy among the Jews of Poland—the leading merchants, the bankers, and the industrialists—a tendency inherent in the social order prevailing in the land, was also encouraged by the authorities in the form of special privileges. These privileges were very appealing because they progressively opened up to those who possessed them all the opportunities withheld from their brethren: from the right of residence in the capital city and in any other city and on every street, to permission to buy houses, building lots, and estates, and beyond that, "honorary citizenship" or citizenship *de jure*. This upper stratum of "enlightened ones" was created ostensibly by virtue of the termination of "their segregation" from the Polish nation but actually was a reward for keeping aloof from their own people. Thus, "enlightened" assimilationists could not serve as a social basis for the Haskalah movement among the Jews of Poland.

In the annals of the Haskalah, it was the communities in the capital cities that provided its social basis. This was the case in Berlin in the eighteenth century and in Vienna, Lemberg, and Vilna in the nineteenth century. Why it did not happen in Warsaw is partly explained by the role of the assimilationists and partly by the specific development of the Jewish community there.

The Jewish community in Warsaw was the largest among the communities of Poland, and by 1827 numbered 34,000 people.[2] The main growth of the community had occurred in the first quarter of the century. Up to the last division of Poland, that is, until the end of the eighteenth century, the Jews had lived in Warsaw illegally, but because they were already there they were tolerated *de facto* under the protection of the nobles. Many of them resided there only temporarily in connection with their business or work while their families remained in their place of origin. Nonetheless, in 1784, expulsion of the Jews from the city was decreed and rigorously implemented. It was only during the years of the "Quadrennial *Sejm*" (1788–92) that the Jews could reside in the city legally, and during those few years, their number increased to 7,000.[3] However, the authorities did not recognize any organized Jewish community until the period of Prussian domination. Thus, the Jewish community of Warsaw was typical of those Jewish immigrant communities which lacked the social and cultural tradition of a Torah center.

In old, deeply rooted communities, the Haskalah developed organically as a modern continuation of talmudic scholarship. It was only much later, when extremist wings broke away from the Haskalah camp, that the movement took an assimilationist turn. When the Haskalah appeared in Warsaw, it was mainly as an imported trend in its final stages of extreme assimilation. In the decade of Prussian rule (1796–1806), Jews from Prussia and Austria settled in Warsaw; and more arrived during the era of the Duchy of Warsaw and in the beginning of the Kingdom of Poland. These German Jews—important merchants, purveyors, and bankers—brought the brand of assimilation propagated by David Friedlaender and his followers along with their wealth. This group of magnates did not miss any opportunity to demonstrate to the authorities that they were not to be confused with the other Jews in Poland, and that they deserved all civil rights.

Following the edict of 1808 suspending the political rights of the Jews for ten years, a memorandum was presented to the ruling duke in the beginning of 1809 in the name of the thirteen signatories and of "the other German families who were born, or who settled in this city." While acknowledging the legitimacy of the decree in relation to the Jews of the duchy in general as an educational measure, they requested exemption from its provisions on the grounds that they already were close to the "most enlightened among the nations" both "in their ethical conduct and in their mode of dress," and had also acquired the "polish and the knowledge which were needed for participation in human society."[4] It was not in vain that the assimilationists, who regarded themselves as being above their brethren, stressed the merit of the "polish" and the European mode of dress, since even the "knowledge" of which they boasted was no more than the knowledge of a non-Jewish language and the manners which prevailed within the plutocracy. Trusting in the merit of these advantages of civilization, the representatives of the "enlightened," Joseph Wolf and the publisher Nathan Gluecksberg, presented memoranda to Senator Novosiltzev in 1815, and later to Czar Alexander I at the time of his visit to Warsaw, in the name of twenty-six heads of families who were signatories and in the name of the forty "meritorious members of the Jewish faith," or "the *distingués*," in Warsaw and the many others in the provinces. They lay "in utter subservience at the feet of His Majesty" for him to bestow upon them the privileges of citizenship. It is true that in order to discharge their obligation toward the entire Jewish community in Poland, they pleaded in behalf of the majority of the people—"those who preserve their mode of dress and their customs"—for economic rights and for freedom to reside anywhere in the city.[5]

In boasting about the difference between themselves and the rest of the nation, the *distingués* indeed fulfilled the aims of the government, and as a reward for their "civilized state" were granted most of the rights necessary for accumulating wealth; some were even granted the rights of full citizenship. Their superior attitude toward their deprived brethren did not change over the years, after their group had grown to a substantial class in Warsaw and the provincial towns. According to a report of 1840, there were 300 "German" families in the community of Warsaw, and the number of Jews there who wore "German-style" clothes amounted to 2,500 males, with an equivalent number dressing that way in the provincial towns.[6] To be sure, those who wore this respectable apparel outside the capital city were merely 1 percent of the total Jewish population, and even in Warsaw they constituted only 10 percent of the community.

In Warsaw, the "enlightened" assimilationists—by virtue of their wealth and closeness to government circles—contrived to seize important positions in the management of the community, namely, to be appointed to the Synagogue Supervisory Board; the wealthy banker Matthias Rosen even served as its chairman at the beginning of the 1840s and during the 1850s. Those "enlightened ones" did communal work for the hospital, the orphanages, and the homes for the aged. Their philanthropic activity was rewarded by the authorities with certain privileges, including the rank of "honorary citizen." When Czar Nicholas visited Warsaw in 1845, he was pleased to receive the directors of the Jewish hospital among those who presented themselves before him, and he also informed them of his wish to issue a decree prohibiting the Jewish mode of dress.[7]

The complaint presented in 1845 to the viceroy by Moses Jerózolimski, an eighty-four-year-old resident of Warsaw, throws light upon the deep chasm between the "enlightened ones" who exercised control over the community and the simple folk. Not only were the former a source of vexation to the devout Jews because of their public desecration of religion; they were also hardhearted and indifferent to the poor man's troubles, for "in their veins flows cold blood and malice." If one of the needy came with a complaint to the Synagogue Supervisory Board, he was turned away empty-handed, his plea rejected, and he would leave "silenced, his eyes full of tears." To compound the evil, since the board held its sessions in the town hall during the late evening hours, the poor and the invalids never even got to see the board members, for the poor were driven away by the police.[8]

From Assimilation to Apostasy

The circumstances which account for the extreme assimilationist movement among the upper echelons of the Jewish bourgeoisie and intelligentsia in Poland also explain the widespread phenomenon of conversion. For baptism was a means of becoming totally integrated in the dominant class of nobles. Many of these apostates attained the rank of nobility because of their wealth and economic activity, and many more, like their gentile counterparts, merged with the nobility through marriage, thus overcoming the stigma of their "plebeian" origin. Just as the families of the Jewish magnates were connected through marriage, it was also customary to make matches among their offspring who had become converts. Also, some were adopted by the nobility, mostly among the second generation, after they had acquired estates, for aside from the fact that acquisition of an estate was an inexhaustible source of wealth, it also carried with it the crowning seal of having reached the highest rung in the social hierarchy.

The number of conversions in Poland was unusually high for eastern Europe. While there were only isolated instances of conversion in Galicia and in the Pale of Settlement in Russia, in Poland, and particularly in Warsaw, apostasy eroded many families of the "enlightened" Jewish bourgeoisie, and some completely broke away from Judaism. The great extent to which greed and career figured in conversion can be seen by the fact that there were very few conversions during the period of liberal reforms in the Polish political system, when the Jews obtained broad civil rights, including permission to buy estates and hold office. The number of conversions began to increase in the 1880s when the reaction took place in Poland, thus closing off the road to careers for the Jewish intelligentsia in particular.[9] In the first half of the nineteenth century, when the number of Jewish professional intelligentsia was still small, the converts were from wealthy families.

Apostasy among the moneyed families had begun in the days of the Duchy of Warsaw with the Frankel-Laski family, by the conversion of the daughter of Samuel Zbitkower, Ita Athalia Laski, her children and her second husband, Samuel (Leopold Antoni) Frankel, the founder of the Frankel Banking House, one of the largest banks in Warsaw.[10] In the ensuing decades, sons and daughters of the following "enlightened" affluent families in Warsaw also converted: Bloch, Bondy, Brunner, Flatau, Fraenkel (Adolf, the son of David), Gluecksberg, Hirszendorf, Wertheim, Jakobowski, Kronenberg, Loewe, Wiener, Janasz, and Epstein. At various times, many of the converts' fathers served as heads of the community in Warsaw, including: Nathan Gluecksberg, Samuel Kronenberg, Ḥayyim Jonah-Józef Janasz, and Jacob Epstein. The Gluecksberg family had built a good reputation throughout Poland as publishers and supporters of Polish literature. Leopold Kronenberg, the son of the banker, Samuel, was famous for his extraordinary initiative in the areas of banking, industry, and railroads. His younger contemporary and competitor, Jan Gottlieb (Bogumil) Bloch, the son of the owner of a textile factory in Warsaw, Shalom Bloch, had a reputation not only for his initiative in setting up industrial enterprises and building railroads but also as an outstanding economist, diplomat, and writer. The members of the

Epstein family were very active in the paper and sugar industries. Among the Jewish physicians in Warsaw in that era, Dr. Leopold Leo (the father-in-law of Leopold Kronenberg) and the two Wolff brothers converted to Christianity.

In the 1850s and 1860s, assimilation resulted in apostasy in the following families of the Jewish haute bourgeoisie in Warsaw: Brauman, Fajans, Goldstand, Haller, Lesser, Loewenstein, Rosen, Rosenthal, and Salinger. At the end of the century, there were conversions in other distinguished families: Ehrlich, Bauerertz, Berson, Davidson, Kunitz, Lande, Orgelbrand, Osser, Nathanson, Rotwand, Teplitz, and Wawelberg.[11]

The frequency of apostasy among the enlightened assimilationists was harmful to the Haskalah movement in Poland for a number of reasons. In the consciousness of the devout and in the conviction of the simple folk who were concerned for the religious and national existence of Judaism, the dividing line between the "civilization" of the assimilationists and the Haskalah as a movement of cultural rebirth became blurred; therefore, they placed the blame for the desertion from the camp and for the disloyalty on both. The waves of apostasy also washed away the choice social soil which would have nourished the roots of the Haskalah movement in Poland, that is, the new Jewish bourgeoisie. Thus the superior cultural resources and outstanding talents among the Jewish people were lost to the centrifugal forces of extreme assimilation.

The Instruments of Assimilation

The aims and ambitions of the assimilationist financial magnates were expressed by the group of Jewish intelligentsia in Warsaw who were connected to the instruments and institutions designated by the government for spreading assimilation among the Jewish population: censorship of Jewish (Hebrew) books, the Rabbinical Seminary, and the elementary schools for Jewish children. The literature of this group was mainly limited to two categories—textbooks on religion and ethics for Jewish youth and apologia in behalf of the Jewish faith. They were printed in Polish, usually with the original Hebrew text. As might be assumed, this vapid, hollow literature reflected the threefold slogan of loyalty to the kingdom, love of the "fatherland," and acculturation. At times, the young would be encouraged to engage in handicrafts and agriculture as vocations useful to the fatherland and the kingdom.

The censor Jacob Tugendhold (1794–1871) was the most prolific and influential of the authors of these books. A native of Działoszyce, he had received a traditional education in the Talmud, and his knowledge of the Bible and Hebrew grammar came from his father, the Maskil Isaiah Tugendhold. After studying for a while at the lycée in Breslau, he went to Cracow, where he eked out a living as a private tutor for a wealthy family. When he was unable to obtain a position in the office of the Austrian censor in Lemberg in 1817, he left for Warsaw, where he tutored in the house of the wealthy Jacob Epstein.[12] In 1818 he was acclaimed by both the Jewish and Polish public for his Polish pamphlet *Jeruba'al,* a polemic against an indictment of the Jews entitled *A Device against Jews* which advocated the expulsion of the Jews to the land of the Tatars. In 1819 he founded a private school for Jewish children, a year later he was appointed by the government to establish elementary schools for Jews in Warsaw, and for a few years he served as executive secretary for those schools. In 1820 he was appointed to a post in the office of the censor for Jewish (Hebrew) books, where he stayed until his last years, except for a brief period during the Polish uprising in November 1830.

His access to government circles and to the all-powerful Senator Novosiltzev paved the way for his appointment as secretary of the Synagogue Supervisory Board which was established in Warsaw.[13] Before long he was hated by the community leaders, and even the assimilationists complained in a letter to Israel Jacobson in Berlin that he "perpetrates much evil against the Jews." He tried to defend himself against this accusation in letters to the community leaders Joseph Ḥayyim Halberstam, Solomon Posner, and David Friedlaender.[14] Afterward, Tugendhold kept aloof from the community to such an extent that in the introduction to his Polish edition of Menasseh ben Israel's *Teshu'at Yisrael* (Hope of Israel) in 1831 he cited this as evidence of his objectivity in a blood libel case: "All who know me better are well aware that except for the main principles of the faith, I have practically no contact with my coreligionists, but I at all times associate with estimable Christians."[15]

In the 1840s[16] and 1850s[17] he served as an honorary member of the Synagogue Supervisory Board. In that period, he was active in the community's philanthropic organizations and sat among the businessmen as a member of the directorate of the orphanage and the home for the aged. His honor and importance reached their peak in 1852, when the government appointed him to the post of director of the Rabbinical School upon the death of Anton Eisenbaum.

To reinforce his status among the community leaders, Tugendhold cited the fact that he differed from his assimilationist associates in his devout conservatism in religious matters. He maintained that there was an analogy between his religious conservatism in which he renounced the heresies of his youth[18] and his Russian superpatriotism through which, in the eyes of his masters, he atoned for his sins of Polish republican patriotism which he had expressed in the Polish uprising. This Polish patriotism is reflected in his pamphlet *Reflections of a Member of the Jewish Faith Standing Guard*, which was published in the beginning of 1831 while he was a member of the democratic "Patriotic Society" headed by Lelewel.[19]

The fact that his associate in the censorship office was the Maskil Abraham Jacob Stern (1762–1842), an indisputably wholehearted and pious believer, further enhanced his status in the eyes of the community leaders. Stern, however, was so completely a Mitnagged in his outlook that in his proposal for a rabbinical school which he presented to Count Potocki in 1816, he asserted that one of the main functions of the institution's director was to wage war against Hasidism "to the bitter end."[20] In contrast, Tugendhold, out of political considerations, regarded rationalism as more dangerous than superstitious beliefs and religious zeal and was therefore inclined to censor every sharp criticism against the Hasidic movement. In his report of the year 1852 to the authorities in St. Petersburg, he wrote, "It is an irrefutable truth, which finds its confirmation in point of fact over the centuries, that any rationalism, no matter how slight, has consequences both to monarchism and society which are evil and harmful in a far greater measure than exaggerated zeal or superstitious belief which are linked with any religion whatsoever."[21] In 1833, Tugendhold, in his memorandum to the Committee for Internal Affairs and Religions concerning the Rabbinical School, had proposed that the study of French be abolished, inasmuch as the students of the institution were led astray by their reading of writers such as Voltaire and Volnay. This proposal was accepted by the authorities and put into effect.[22] With all of his admiration for Mendelssohn—whose book on the immortality of the soul, *Phaedon*, he published in Polish—he nevertheless omitted in the Polish translation of his introduction to Menasseh ben Israel's *Teshu'at Yisrael* the words of his mentor against the community's right to impose a *ḥerem* (excommunication) or any kind of coercion in religious matters. It seems that this view was too liberal for him. It is therefore not surprising that Tugendhold rejected religious reforms "as innovations which, by a complete abolition of practices hallowed over many centuries, undermine the roots of religion."[23]

The sacrosanct character of his religious observance notwithstanding, Tugendhold did not shrink from deleting some of the chief tenets of Judaism—the belief in the coming of the Messiah and the Return to Zion. In his tract *Jeruba'al* he deleted from his translation of the prayer for the peace of the ruling monarch, "May He who gives salvation," the traditional ending, "In his days and in ours may salvation come to Judah and may Israel dwell securely." In the translation of that prayer, which he introduced into the Polish section of his book *Kosht Imrei Emet* (The Certainty of the Words of Truth), he retained only the verse which is also susceptible to a purely religious interpretation: "And may the redeemer come unto Zion, Amen."[24] Wherever it was necessary to explain the Jewish belief in the Messiah, this opponent of the Reform movement did not hesitate to adopt that given by it, namely, that the Messianic Era merely denotes the millennium of world peace, the brotherhood of nations, and a time when "the earth will be full of knowledge."[25] Even when he cited the words of Maimonides in the *Mishneh Torah* concerning the Messianic Era,[26] he followed the practice of the German-Jewish periodical *Sulamith*,[27] deleting all the passages in the "Laws Relating to Kings" regarding the earthly and political significance of the Redemption—for example, the phrase "to restore the Kingdom of the House of David to its pristine status as the first government." This was also his practice in the religious textbooks for the young. When he published the catechism of Herz Homberg, *Ben Yakir* (Precious Son), in Hebrew characters supplemented by a Polish translation, he saw no reason to change the author's interpretation of Maimonides' twelfth article of faith, which restricted the role of the Messiah to that of teacher and guide of the Torah and the love of mankind and to establishing the Temple as a house of worship for all people.[28] Adhering to this approach, Tugendhold even found fault with the expression "the hope of salvation" at the conclusion of the romantic tale of knighthood *Bovo Ma'aseh* (the Story of Bovo), which appeared in Warsaw in 1849, and he replaced the phrase "and may salvation come" with "and may our Temple be rebuilt."[29]

Allegiance to the Monarchy: The Work of Abraham Buchner and Jacob Tugendhold

It is only natural that worship of the absolute monarchy was the mainstay of the political and religious philosophy of the government's supervisor over the *kashrut* of Judaism, taking *kashrut* in the double sense of the word: Free of all unorthodox views and unsullied by any liberal ideas. Even the well-known talmudic dictum that the "Kingdom on earth is like the Kingdom of heaven" *(Berakhot* 58a) was not sufficiently monarchistic for Tugendhold, and in an appeal in 1845 in behalf of the orphanage and the poor of the community, he translated the quotation with an added flourish for the earthly king: "The reigning authority which rules in this land is the shining luster of the Supreme Ruler in heaven."[30] The avowed loyalist was not even perplexed in the days of the uprising, when Poland routed the government of the czar. In his introduction to *Teshu'at Yisrael*, which he published during that turbulent period, he declared that "there is a good and beneficent God Who sees all, there is the just administration of the government, which serves as His regnant authority on earth."[31] It is not surprising that in censoring the manuscript of his friend Solomon Ettinger he replaced the word "monarch" with "man of wealth," and "freedom" (which had no political significance whatsoever here) with "pleasure"; he even considered *frayheyt* (free) in the compound word *foygl-frayheyt* (to be abandoned and ostracized) as posing a threat to the monarchy, and he replaced it with a word similar in sound alone, *erfreyung* (gladdening).[32] And, out of consideration for the honor of royalty, he modified every title of king in the aforementioned edition of *Bovo Ma'aseh* to pasha, every prince to a son of a pasha, the kingdom to a *pashalik* and the "crown" merely to "glory."[33]

Tugendhold's attitude toward Christianity was also obsequious. In his introduction to the Polish version of *Kosht Imrei Emet*, he admonished his coreligionists: "The dark clouds which, in the Middle Ages, covered the benevolent sun of Christianity, have been scattered for a long time now. At present, we are equal before the law, benefiting from the prevailing security and the paternal protection of the Christian governments." And since the status of the Jews in the Christian kingdom indeed was one of equality, they were obligated not only to respect the Christians, but also to harbor "sentiments of gratitude for the benefactors of our people," ". . . appreciation and thanks to the Christians."[34]

This pronouncement of equality notwithstanding, even he was at times compelled to acknowledge reality; namely, that the assimilationists' love for "their neighbors of other faiths" was not mutual, that the Gentiles were contemptuous of them and preferred keeping them at a distance. In a "Word to the Teachers" of the Jewish schools which he included in the Polish edition of *Prayers*, he called upon the teachers to educate Jewish youth with a view to a social and linguistic rapprochement with the native population: "Let but our young people follow this path which is deserving of praise and let them not flinch in the face of any obstacle, any scorn from others, any oppression no matter how distressing," since the commandment to love one's neighbor is obligatory to all mankind, "irrespective of religious differences and regardless of their conduct toward us." He charged them to remember "that particularly in this way people who are most downtrodden and despised are apt to arouse at least the grace of compassion, if not of mutual sentiments of brotherhood."[35] It is no wonder that the government's Council for Public Education described this book as "appropriate for the desired goal and very useful."

Tugendhold's social views are analogous to his opinions on the "reverence of God and king." Not only were his speeches on various occasions infused with humility and flattery, and full of praise of the magnates, but also he wrote special pamphlets to glorify their philanthropy as "deserving of blessings and praise."[36] The bankers and the "speculators," that is, those who were involved in big business, were also, from an economic aspect, the central pillars of society, for they resembled "that marvelous spring which provides the impulse, nourishment, and uplift to farming, manual labor, and all other branches of production in the state."[37] True, Tugendhold did see the need for the productivization of the Jewish population through industrialization and agricultural settlement. In 1836 he proposed a program to the Ministry for Internal Affairs for the establishment of a school to teach skilled labor and manufacturing to Jewish youth. In regard to the Edict of Jewish Agricultural Settlement of 1823, in addition to his expression of the "moving gratitude of the poor class of my coreligionists," he even ventured a comment about the need to improve upon that "kindness" by facilitating matters for the settlers.[38] However, he held the generosity of the wealthy on behalf of "their impoverished co-religionists" to be the main route in the implementing of this objective.[39] As for the pupils of the Jewish elementary schools who had no clothing or shoes, he urged the teachers "not to be ashamed to gather donations for modest aid in [their behalf]."[40] Thus was philanthropy woven into the ideology of the censor of his imperial majesty Czar Nicholas I—Jacob Tugendhold.[41]

In contrast to Tugendhold, who wrote all his books—except the bilingual *Kosht Imrei Emet*—in Polish, his rival, Abraham Buchner (1789–1869), wrote mainly in Hebrew, publishing only his last works in a foreign language.[42] Like Tugendhold, he was a second-generation Maskil. In dedicating his pamphlet *Doresh Tov* (Seeking the Welfare) to his father, Samuel Buchner, "of the Feltz family of Cracow," he expresses his heartfelt gratitude for his education: "You did sate me from the streams of Eden, from the fountains of Holy Scriptures and the Talmud. . . . You inspired me, and day by day prevailed upon me to dedicate myself to the study of the Hebrew language, and yet not to refrain from studying other languages nor to stand aloof from knowledge which is beneficial to him who possesses it." He, too, started his career in Warsaw as a private teacher in the homes of the wealthy, and it was only in 1826 that he obtained a post which could provide a livelihood, having been appointed to teach Hebrew and Bible at the Rabbinical School. Aside from Hebrew grammar and the Bible—subjects he never really mastered—he studied medieval Jewish religious philosophy, the writings of the early Maskilim, such as R. Israel Zamość and Mendelssohn, and the German philosophers Leibnitz and Herder. In his biblical studies he depended on the German sources, such as Michaelis and Gesenius.

Like his colleague Tugendhold, Buchner focused the propaganda in his pamphlets around ideas of loyalty to the government and the attitude of "brotherhood" toward all mankind. He also tried to awaken the young people to the importance of productivity and the benefits of labor and agriculture, citing biblical passages and wise sayings of the talmudic and midrashic sages to support his propaganda.

Despite his emphasis on reverence for God and principles of faith—even to the point of entering into a polemic against the doctrine of the eternity of matter—Buchner, in contrast to Tugendhold, avidly espoused the concepts of rationalism and condemned ignorance and superstition. In his pamphlet *Doresh Tov*, he preached religious toleration not only toward members of other faiths but also toward "trangressors against one of God's commandments." He attacked the Hasidim, but without mentioning them by name: "I will not deny that currently visionaries and [false] expounders multiply, an unruly and mad person is called a prophet, insofar that he who is blind says, 'I see.'" He went on to say that those "who stray and mislead the people" write "words which do not speak peace to other nations . . . they distort Scripture with vapid commentaries" and with "false commentaries which violate the rules of the Hebrew language." But now, "the sun of knowledge sent forth its arrows" and "among ethically minded nations" only a few still cling to superstitious beliefs.[43]

The Hebrew-Polish catechism *Yesodei Ha-dat u-Musar ha-Sekhel* (The Foundations of Faith and Discipline of Wisdom), which Buchner published in 1838 for the government's Committee for Religion and Education, stressed one's duty toward the government and "obligation toward all mankind." This ethic also pervades his book *Ha-Moreh le-Ẓedakah* (The Teacher of Righteousness), a compilation of excerpts from the *Moreh Nebukhim* (Guide of the Perplexed) on the reasons for the commandments, accompanied by comments. At the end of his introduction, Buchner proves that Maimonides, the author of the *Guide of the Perplexed,* "did not differentiate between Jews and Gentiles in all those obligations which lie between one person and another."[44] However, Buchner also took this as an opportunity to disseminate his rationalist beliefs.

This rationalism is very moderate, and—no doubt in order to demonstrate religious propriety—does not deviate from the views of Maimonides. "The Torah and Reason," declared Buchner, "have one progenitor, and God, who gives the Torah, instructs mankind, imparting knowledge to it." He also saw fit—and this for tactical reasons—to disagree with the views of Mendelssohn, "who holds that Judaism does not obligate one to believe in dogmas, being a religion of performance consisting solely of *miẓvot*, since this view is contrary to that of Maimonides as well as the sages of Israel."[45] Despite these reservations, Buchner praised to excess *or ha-sekhel* (the light of reason), his Hebrew translation of *Aufklärung*, and even alluded to the deistic concept that the essence of religion is its ethical teachings, "for without ethics even religion cannot be the foundation for the establishment of a social order among mankind." He also complained about the attitude toward the Maskilim among the Jewish public, saying that "many reject the light of reason and he who walks by this light is a reproach in their eyes and it has become a byword among the Jews to so designate the man who travels an improper road." He went on to clarify, in the vein of the eighteenth-century Enlightenment, what kind of person walks in the light of reason: "Neither the sum of one's knowledge, nor the type of knowledge are the standard of what constitutes being enlightened," since it is even possible for a person to study the Holy Scriptures intelligently "if he does not depart from the straight path based upon the rules of grammar and other types of knowledge." The main thing is the desire to acquire any knowledge that is beneficial for society. This is practical wisdom, the understanding of human ethics, whereby "man has learned to know that whoever walks in righteousness with all mankind and seeks the welfare of society, and observes the laws of the king of the land and his princes—such a one is a good man, worthy of entering into the community of the inhabitants of the state and being as one of the native-born." Due to the spread of this "light of reason," the Jews in some states enjoy total civil equality, "and even in those places where the rulers distinguish between the Jews and Gentiles, it is not so because of religious hatred," and the "light of reason" is progressively spreading even there. He declared that one who still errs because of religious hatred is ashamed to admit it, "because a generation of reason now prevails." And if this is the "effect of reason," then "let also us, the Jewish people, walk in its light."[46]

Buchner's limiting the "light of reason" to a rationalist Weltanschauung, loyalty, and integration into the life of the state was unusual for the Haskalah movement. There is no mention in his program of the Haskalah of slogans for the fostering of the knowledge of Hebrew and the Bible nor of the study of "languages and wisdom." Like Tugendhold, Buchner was first and foremost a spokesman for the government, but he was also a rationalist who endeavored to win adherents to his views. However, Buchner's writings made no impression, not only because of his dry style and lack of literary ability but also because the author's character was justifiably suspect. Buchner's beginnings foreshadowed his end, even as his end reflected his beginnings.

As early as 1818, Buchner, together with Hirschorn, had presented a memorandum to the government suggesting that the *ḥadarim* be closed, that the study of the Talmud be prohibited, and that Jewish youth be obliged to study in public schools.[47] It is possible that the Jewish public at large was unaware of the memorandum, but nobody could fail to notice his slighting of religious matters,[48] which contradicted the teachings in his catechism. The community knew of his association with Abbé Chiarini, whose name appeared among the subscribers to his book *Doresh Tov* in 1822. Thanks to the support of the Abbé, Buchner was appointed instructor in the Rabbinical School over the objections of the Warsaw community. In gratitude to his benefactor, Buchner helped Abbé Chiarini by translating the excerpts from the Talmud and rabbinical literature which the Abbé needed for his book of indictment. Buchner was remunerated for this under an agreement approved by the government.[49] Ostensibly, he was no more than Chiarini's appointee as instructor for "rabbinic Hebrew," and even Tugendhold, in the introduction to *Teshu'at Yisrael*, referred to a critique of Chiarini's book which was about to be published by Buchner but never was. In 1842 Buchner published a book in Polish, *Kwiaty Wschodnie* (Blossoms of the East), which was a compilation of sayings of the Sages and the legends of the Talmud and Midrash designed to illustrate the lofty thought and exalted ethics of the men of the Talmud. He prefaced this compilation with an introduction explaining that the Oral Law supplements the Bible and clarifies any ambiguities. Buchner pointed out that the book was intended mainly to correct erroneous opinions Gentiles had about the Talmud and thereby to contribute to the progress of brotherhood between members of both faiths. It is possible that another of Buchner's intentions in publishing the book was to improve his standing in the eyes of the leaders of the community. Abraham Stern, the censor, had died that year, 1842, and Buchner wanted to be appointed to the vacant post; for this he surely needed the backing of the heads of the Warsaw community. But his candidacy was rejected, and the convert Christian Czersker was appointed to serve as censor along with Tugendhold.[50]

The Attack on the Talmud and Jewish Books

What had occurred in Buchner's family that year did not make the community more confident of his religious integrity. His son Joseph converted to Catholicism and in 1861 a second son, Franciscus, followed in his footsteps. Also, the son of another teacher in the Rabbinical School, Centnerszwer, converted.[51] It is most probable that at the time of Moses Montefiore's visit to Warsaw in 1846, he received a complaint that Buchner himself had converted while continuing to serve in his post at the Rabbinical School, for it appeared in his memorandum to Minister Uvarov in St. Petersburg which he wrote after returning to London.[52]

The fact is that Abraham Buchner never did convert, but his opportunism and hypocrisy lent plausibility to the report. These traits were expressed in his views on the Talmud. Later that year (1846) Buchner published a second book in Polish praising the Talmud, *The True Judaism*, and two years later a German translation of it, *Der Talmud in seiner Nichtigkeit* (The Worthlessness of the Talmud), was published in two small volumes in Warsaw.[53] In the main, Buchner's purpose here was to prove that the Talmud had distorted the meaning of the Bible rather than explicating it, that the hermeneutic methods used by the Tannaim and Amoraim to expound the Torah contradicted logic and common sense, and that there is no foundation in the Bible for the laws of the Talmud. Even though he discussed this notion like a true Karaite, he did not refrain from denigrating those views which he had praised so strongly in his earlier books. He referred to the talmudic Sages as "Pharisees," an epithet used in the New Testament to signify hypocrisy and dissembling piety. "The Pharisees," Buchner argued, "are the ones who pave a path of deceit and cunning for the pieties of religion." "The state of mind of the men of the Talmud and their ethics are the product of the baneful influence of a decadent intellect. . . ." "The entire Talmud is permeated by a spirit of intolerance." ". . . The barren interpretations" in rabbinic literature are manifestations of "rooted prejudices, perversity, absence of humanitarian sentiment, and concepts of God which are a desecration of God's name."[54] To further support his arguments, he cited illustrations from the Kabbalah and from a secondhand source (the *Zohar* according to the *Sh'lah*—R. Isaiah Horowitz—*Tola'at Ya'akov*), in order to create the impression that it came from the talmudic literature.

It may be assumed that one of Buchner's motives in writing an indictment of the Talmud was his desire to take revenge against the Orthodox who spoke ill of him to Montefiore and through him, to the government. His contemporaries had even accused him of being commissioned to write the book by English missionaries.[55] Indeed, the title page noted that it was published in the printing house of those missionaries.[56] The extent of his corruption is not revealed by his negative attitude toward the Talmud alone, for he had already adopted this point of view in his youth, when he proposed to the authorities that the study of the Talmud be prohibited. His dissimulation was much worse. For a quarter of a century he wrote books in praise of the Talmud and the Oral Law. He also lied in contrasting himself to "Jews who wrote against the Talmud in European languages." Even the extremists among the initiators of religious reform such as Holdheim, who negated the Talmud as an authoritative source of the faith, never stooped so low as to heap calumny upon the ideas of the Talmud and its ethics. Furthermore, the author of *The Worthlessness of the Talmud* paid tribute to his patrons by including an evaluation of the New Testament in which he said it "complements, develops, and broadens the scope of the Old Testament."[57] In this propaganda for the New Testament, Buchner, in effect, removed the dividing line between himself and Christianity. But he was restrained from converting because of his teaching post in the Rabbinical School.

In this respect, much more candor was demonstrated by the colleague of Buchner and Tugendhold, Ezekiel Stanislaw Hoge, who also was the author of Polish-language textbooks for Jewish youth on religion and prayer. He, at least, did not publish his book on the Jewish question, *Tu Ḥazy* (Come and See), until 1830, some seven years after he had converted. And even then he did not condemn the Talmud in its entirety, acknowledging that it contains ethical teachings which deserve to be compiled in a textbook for Jewish youth.[58] It is characteristic both of Hoge's nature, as well as of Tugendhold's attitude toward him even after he converted, that this childhood friend presented him in the preface to *Teshu'at Yisrael* "as a man known for his character and his familiarity with the theology of the Mosaic faith."[59]

Anton Eisenbaum (1791–1852) was the fourth in this group of government-appointed teachers and educators.[60] He was the director of the Rabbinical School from the time of its founding until his death. Unlike his colleagues, he only had an elementary Jewish education. He studied at the lycée in Warsaw and knew a number of languages.

He had literary ability, having already published in his youth articles in the Polish press, as well as a talent for organizing, which he clearly revealed as director of an educational institution. In 1823 he submitted an essay to the monarch, "On the Status of the Jews in Poland and on the Means to Turn Them into a Useful People," which was written in French.[61] During 1823–24, he published—with financial assistance of the government—a bilingual (Polish and German written in Hebrew characters) Jewish weekly, *Der Beobachter an der Weichsel* (Observer on the Vistula). Besides local and foreign news, the Jewish content of the periodical was limited to a few historical articles and biographies of famous Maskilim. The publication lasted less than a year, and its editor then devoted himself fully to work in the field of education.

Eisenbaum, unlike his rival, Tugendhold, did not pretend to be God-fearing and therefore was involved in a constant struggle with the majority of the community. He was an ardent Polish patriot who imparted this patriotism to his students, many of whom, like him, volunteered to serve during the Polish uprising in the National Guard. The spirit of complete assimilation which he instilled in the school where he taught found its clearest utterance in the ideological declarations of his students.

In 1850 Tugendhold's disciple and son-in-law, Abraham Paprocki, an instructor in Jewish history at the Rabbinical School, published a textbook on Jewish history, a succinct abridgment in Polish of Jost's assimilationist *History*. Even the sparse data on neo-Hebraic literature cited at the end was culled from Tugendhold's Polish article, "An Abridged History of the Hebrew Language and Literature," which was incorporated in his introduction to the Polish edition of *Beḥinat Olam*.[62] He added his own personal touch to Jost's doctrine of assimilation in a formulation that was both extreme and vulgar. Jost viewed the history of the Jews after the destruction of the Second Temple as the history of "the spirit which was regenerated after the death of the body."[63] In his introduction, Paprocki explained the lesson to be derived from Jewish history: "From this it is demonstrated that only in their obligations to God do the Jews constitute one body, but with respect to society they constitute neither a nation nor a particular social group, but each one is what he must be according to the laws and customs of the land . . . people, subjects of the king, and inhabitants of the country." And in justifying all the suffering endured by the nation in the Middle Ages he surpassed even his master, Jost: "The sorrowful annals of our forebears were in the main a consequence of ignorance, of a lone and isolated posture among the nations, and of their way of earning a living which was directed solely toward trade and the acquisition of wealth and not toward labor and creative work. . . ."[64]

Another distinguished disciple of Eisenbaum, A. J. Cohn, kept in view the words of the noted sociologist, the apostate Ludwig Gumplowicz: "The fact that the Jews had a history was their misfortune in Europe and indeed their lot will improve only when their history is obliterated. For their history inevitably presupposes an isolated life, severed from that of the nations in whose midst they live. . . ."[65]

Paprocki submitted slanderous information to the authorities against the book *Shevet Yehudah*, which had been published in Warsaw in 1841 by permission of the censor, because it allegedly contained a blasphemy with regard to Jesus of Nazareth and Christianity and desecrated the honor of kings, and particularly the czar of Russia.[66] There is no doubt that this was in retaliation against the censor Tugendhold, who had tried to discredit Eisenbaum in the eyes of the authorities and cause him to be removed from the directorship of the Rabbinical School. But in terms of Jewish self-esteem, the slandered censor was not much better than his calumniator, just as he was on the same level of servile assimilation. When he and his associate and superior in the censorship office, the apostate Czersker, were called to St. Petersburg in 1852 to give an accounting of the activities of this office, Tugendhold declared that he and Czersker "were always of one mind in their work" and that he agreed in advance to his associate's responses in censorship matters.[67] Indeed, all the official educators of Jewish youth and preachers of morality in the service of Czar Nicholas—Tugendhold, Hoge, Buchner, Paprocki, and their followers—were alike, differing only in the extent of their estrangement from their people for the sake of their careers.

Besides these professional assimilationists who wrote in Polish, there were also several Maskilim in the Warsaw community who wrote poetry and prose in Hebrew. But none of them was a native of Warsaw; they all came to the capital from provincial towns, mainly in Poland, and from neighboring Lithuania and the Duchy of Posen.[68]

As with Haskalah literature in other countries, the concept of loyalty to the monarchy is central in the writings of the Polish Maskilim. In their attitude toward loyalty, the leaders of the Mitnaggedim were of one mind with the Maskilim. The approbation profusely bestowed in 1844 by the rabbi of the Warsaw community, R. Ḥayyim Davidson, upon Tugendhold's book *Kosht Imrei Emet* illustrated well this attitude, as did the approbation of R. Judah Bachrach from the city of Seiny, who described him in such laudatory terms as "the wise and perfect talmudic scholar" and a magnificent master of style. In his statement, R. Davidson, after referring to the talmudic Sages who urged that the "ruler and his ministers be honored because he is the Lord's chosen one and dominion had been bestowed upon him by Him Who makes kings," went on to cite the verse in Proverbs: "My son, fear the Lord and the king." Then he commented, "Here the people are exhorted that even in their bedrooms and in their thoughts they should reverence the honor of the king even as they fear the Lord, from Whose eyes nothing is hidden." Unlike the Mitnaggedim, the Maskilim were not passive in this matter, but like the assimilationists, they considered it their special role to disseminate propaganda about loyalty.

The writings of the Maskilim honoring rulers and ministers, such as Isaac Kandia's elegy on the death of Czar Alexander I (1826), A. J. Stern's *Rinah u-Tefillah* (Song of Joy and Prayer) for the coronation of Nicolas I as King of Poland (1829), or the translation from Polish to Hebrew of *Devar Gevurot* (A Story of Mighty Acts) of the Russian viceroy in Poland, Duke Paskevich, by Feivel Shiffer (1855), were not merely the discharge of an obligation. The idea of monarchy was a keystone of the Maskilim's political thought in Poland, as well as in Galicia and Russia. Indeed, abhorrence of the French Revolution as a "schooling in bloodshed" for all rebellions, which found utterance in that book on Paskevich,[69] expressed the spirit of all the Maskilim. Even the Yiddish folkwriter Solomon Ettinger called upon his people to serve in the czar's army, and praised the rulers:[70]

> . . . Take an example from other faiths,
> Look at the Jews in other lands!
> Joyous and gay
> They serve the king.
> . . . You just only obey the officers
> And diligently learn military maneuvers.
> . . . Always be ready
> To run into the face of gunfire,
> To execute the king's plans.
> For the good men who wear the crowns
> Well know how to reward everyone.[71]

Moshe Tannenbaum and the Maskilic Philosophy of Monarchism

One of the leading Maskilim in Warsaw, Moshe Tannenbaum (1795–1849), supported the doctrine of monarchy with a theological and sociological theory to the extent that it became the keystone of his philosophy. A native of Terespol, Tannenbaum acquired a secular education while still a student in the *bet ha-midrash* with the help of the town's Maskil, R. Samuel Monat. When he moved to nearby Brest, he was supported by affluent men.[72] After settling in Warsaw in 1831, he became moderately wealthy through business dealings, and his house became a meeting place for the local Hebrew writers and Maskilim.[73] Tannenbaum was the only one among Warsaw's Maskilim who did not collect subscriptions for his writings, but he would never have been able to publish even one book without the help of benefactors. His book *Mataei Moshe*, which appeared in 1838, was dedicated to "the esteemed man of affluence, a prince and benefactor" who had allotted him a "double portion" of his "generous benefaction."[74]

Earlier, in the years 1835 to 1837, Tannenbaum published a new edition of the Pentateuch with Mendelssohn's German translation and commentary (the *Biur*). The publication was financed by Theodore Teveli Teplitz, the lessee of the kosher meat tax, a community leader and enlightened assimilationist, as well as the merchant and Maskil from Vilna, Hirsh Klaczko (the father of the well-known Polish author Julian Klaczko), who had become friendly with Tannenbaum when he visited Warsaw on business. Wanting to profit from his investment, Teplitz suggested to the government that it obligate the Synagogue Supervisory Board to purchase sets of the German Pentateuch. Apparently his suggestion was accepted.[75] Tannenbaum also wrote a book in Hebrew defending the Talmud against the denunciator Buchner; after his death, the manuscript was translated into German by his son-in-law, Hilary (Hillel) Nussbaum, and was published in Germany in 1849.[76]

Like most of his contemporary Maskilim in eastern Europe, Tannenbaum awakened to the problems of philosophy when he read *Moreh Nebukhim*.[77] He did not put it aside even after he had familiarized himself with eighteenth-century rationalism and had become influenced by the ideas of Mendelssohn and his contemporaries. Consequently, his opinions were a mixture of medieval theology and modern philosophy. That is, he espoused the Kantian notion "that *belief* is only belief, and its truth is not determined by any proof"[78] while disputing the view about the primordiality of matter.[79] He reiterated the deistic concepts that "the new religions all proclaim the praises of the Lord" and "the principles of faith are the same for all" and that "they all have good statutes and laws to spur love and brotherhood between all men whatever their faith," for they do not differ from each other "except for some varying customs and commandments wherein they are unlike and separate from each other."[80] Nevertheless, he still held that theology surpasses all the sciences, saying that "the study of

Divinity is, as it were, the drawingroom, while the study of the nature of man is its anteroom."[81] Moreover, all of mankind's progress is concerned only with "the expansion of knowledge of matter," while theology, which is "the queen of all the sciences," had already been perfected and completed in ancient times, leaving no room for innovations. As proof, he noted that the ancients enjoyed longevity, which attests "to their perfect temperament and even disposition to the extent that they could study and observe all branches of wisdom and science with a clear mind, refined sevenfold more than we who are not a mighty people."[82]

Tannenbaum considered Maimonides' greatness as consisting in his synthesis of knowledge and faith, in accordance with the well-known aphorism of the Sages: "Where there is no wisdom, there is no fear of God; where there is no fear of God, there is no wisdom." And just as true faith is "pure and free of the slightest blemish" of idol worship and vanity, so wisdom is "refined and purified from the consequences of rebellion and treachery which might conceivably rear themselves upon it." Wisdom is a remedy which prevents the dross of superstitious belief from mixing with religion; and faith, too, stands guard to ensure that wisdom does not lead to "insurgency."[83] Were it not for the restraints afforded by the prevailing religions, "faith would be utterly destroyed, and revolts would now have multiplied throughout the earth and the fullness thereof, and as a result of this state of freedom (emancipation), throughout the tumultuous cities each man would have torn asunder the head of his fellow man."[84]

The chosen are those with a proper understanding of true freedom and liberty "which is achieved by one who believes in God and honors his king." A third element, loyalty, is "bound together as a threefold cord, so interdependent that without any single one, the other two would fall." Wisdom is in the center of this intertwined cord; it is the "mother of all the world's delight, the birthplace of belief in God and the love of kings."[85]

Monarchism is founded upon the history of the universe and man's nature. Echoing the Neoplatonic doctrine found in medieval philosophic literature, Tannenbaum asserted that it is the human intellect which restrains lustful impulses and directs man's will toward desirable goals. This order of man's soul is but the mirror reflecting the way God orders the world; that is, "one simple substance, exalted and lofty, which links all the hosts of the universe and their fullness, both by their nature and character, so that they may all run toward one goal which is designed for a purpose beneficial to us and yet hidden from us. . . ." "The kingdom on earth is similar to the Kingdom of Heaven." Moreover, "this exalted substance brought this splendor yet lower, placing within the hand of each one, the scepter of dominion over the portion allotted to him." The lowest rung in this ladder of authority is "the master of the house, the man who, in his house, rules over its persons and those born therein, supervising their affairs . . . [and] subdues them altogether under the rod of terror and fear . . . in order to hold the reins of peace and quiet in their midst." At the top is the king, "who bestows strength and power upon all his officials and leaders . . . in order that they establish justice and righteousness throughout the land. . . ." All dominion emanates from God, and "as for the rulers of the earth and its judges . . . , a portion of divine wisdom is in their hearts." The state and the soul of man are under the same regime: "for all acts that are performed, that are prompted by thought—for all there is need of one supreme authority." Also, the ultimate goal of monarchy and human beings is the same, since the entire hierarchy of the monarchy is directed toward achieving the end of the intelligent soul; it is the government that instructs man "in his studies to grow wise and become intelligent"; and "not to be swept away in the eddies of the sea of desire, nor scalded by the searing fire of lust."[86]

The tyrant Nicholas I and his partners in the Holy Alliance, the rulers of Austria and Prussia, found a willing advocate of absolutism and the clergy in this retrograde Jewish intellectual.

The propaganda for monarchism and loyalty in the writings of the Maskilim is full of enthusiasm about the equality of rights which the Jews were said to have attained under the rule of absolutism. Like the Maskilim of Galicia and Russia, the Maskilim of Poland not only disregarded the oppression suffered by the Jewish masses under such a regime but also were enthusiastic about the economic privileges enjoyed by their social patrons—the bankers, merchants, lessees for the collection of taxes, monopoly holders, and purveyors. They viewed their epoch as the continuation and acme of the Age of Enlightenment which had begun in the eighteenth century, and which essentially consisted in the abolition of bigotry and showing tolerance toward all faiths. Moshe Tannenbaum, for one, expressed his praise and thanks to God that in his time, unlike the "days of Egypt" or the Middle Ages, "wisdom has let its splendor illuminate the entire earth, love of the Lord and love of one's neighbors buds and flourishes, and the Lord has implanted in the heart of the rulers and the ministers who give them counsel benign statutes and just laws prompting them to establish courts of law, to execute acts of justice and righteousness among all men without regard for religious differences or distinctions of belief. . . . A covenant of brotherhood among all nations and tongues bears fruit."[87]

Isaac Kandia also extolled the new epoch as the era of the supremacy of wisdom and righteousness and the brotherhood of members of all faiths. In a song which he composed in 1840 "for the day of the dedication of the house of worship and the school for the study of Torah" on Iron Gate Place [88] in Warsaw, the soloist sings:

> Before a curtain separated nation from nation
> Different faiths were held apart from the pact of friendship
> Until wise rulers set righteousness as a plumbline
> So that peace reigned throughout the earth and nations were united.

The chorus responds:

> Under the rule of knowledge, peace blossoms in the land.
> There is no adversary, no affliction, no outcry, no breach of peace.

The soloist continues:

> Truly with wisdom's supremacy, salvation sprouts forth.
> Envy among nations departs, no man coerces his brother.
> The earth is tranquil, the sun of righteousness shines forth.
> They are separated no more, nor divided in their hearts.
> . . . Jacob is no longer put to shame, nor Israel an object of contempt.
> There is none who deride and heap scorn, nor condemn a man
> in his labor,
> To them applies the law of the native, with respect to inheritance
> and possessions,
> And to the sanctuary of God, so that men may seek Him and His faith.[89]

Eliezar Thalgruen, born in Posen but an old-time resident of Warsaw,[90] was one of the devout Maskilim in the city. His introduction to *Tokhaḥat Musar* (Chastisement for the Sake of Betterment), a commentary on Psalms with a German translation, which he published in 1854, included a "Mikhtav Tehillah" (A Laudatory Epistle) from the Rabbi of Warsaw, Ḥayyim Davidson. In this introduction he displayed strict conservatism regarding all customs, including the various practices related to mourning for the Temple. He complained about the neglect of the customs of wearing different clothing on Shabbat Ḥazon (the Sabbath before Tishah B'av): "Why should there not be some indication of the loss of our Temple in this respect if we do make a distinction in the accoutrements of the ark [which contains the scrolls of the Torah]?"[91] Nonetheless, he inveighed against cantors who chant the prayer "Umipnei Ḥataenu" (And because of our sins) on the Sabbath "in a melody which induces weeping," and against those preachers who came to Warsaw to give Sabbath sermons "reminding the people of ancient tales, of the travails which we suffered, using them to draw a parallel to our own times, and provoking therewith much weeping." The practices of cantors and preachers were "very foolish" since it is improper to weep on the Sabbath. In contrast, Thalgruen entreated,

> Let us thank and praise the Lord for His great mercy toward us, for our times are not like the days of old; all the rulers of Europe are righteous kings, who dispense justice and righteousness; they will not forsake us to the masses to wreak their will upon us, as in ancient times. Turn your gaze to the tales in *Shevet Yehudah* and see the tribulations which befell us, but thanks to God, blessed be His name, they have disappeared, never to be heard of again.[92]

It is not at all surprising that the Maskil Thalgruen demanded redress from the preachers for the unfairness done to just royalty, for he even assigned the blame for the *revir* decree of 1809 to the Jews themselves, not to the royal government, saying, "And why have we been driven from the streets within our city? Only because of the despicable deeds which we have done very insolently and wholly devoid of good manners, in plain view of the nations; open your eyes and see the decree of the King of Saxony, the Duke of Warsaw, and you will realize that I am not uttering any falsehood."[93] He went on to explain that the expulsion of the Jews from the center of the city stemmed from their "uncleanliness, disorder, and lawlessness," which resulted from their having crowded into small quarters.[94] But apparently it did not occur to him that the confinement in ghettos could only exacerbate the situation.

Another major goal of the Haskalah movement—that Jews draw closer to their neighbors, in "love for their fellows" and "in love for all mankind"—occupied an important place in the propaganda literature of the Maskilim of Poland, just as it did in the literature of the assimilationists. One of the distinct signs of "true civilization," according to the teaching of Tannenbaum in *Mata'ei Moshe*, along with love of God and loyalty to the king, is love "for all mankind who were made in His image."[95] In his introduction to *Tokhaḥat Musar,* Thalgruen asserted "that there is no difference between the Jews and any other nation insofar as commandments on relations between man and his fellow man are concerned," and that the commandment "thou shalt love thy neighbor as thyself" applies to the "whole of mankind," and consequently obligates every person to observe the commandment of alms-giving to the poor, and forbids cheating in weights and measures, et cetera.[96] The author saw this principle as being so important that he concluded his book with it.[97]

Agricultural Settlement of the Jews

The parallel between the Maskilim's ideological horizon and that of the Polish regime, particularly in its policy toward the Jews, also accounts for the fact that the idea of agricultural settlement of Jews was far more prominent in the Haskalah literature of Poland than in that of the neighboring countries. The authorities in Poland twice announced programs for the transfer of the Jews to agricultural occupations; first in the edict of 1823, and a second time in the decision of the viceroy in 1843. Both were well received by the Maskilim.

Two years after the edict of 1823, the Maskil Moses ben Meir Laski wrote a tract entitled *Siaḥ Ha-sadeh* (Field Meditations) which was never published.[98] The concept of productivization is based on his system of political economy, and on talmudic aphorisms that praise labor and agriculture. In his economic exposition, Laski demonstrated expert knowledge of the physiocratic system and of mercantilism.[99] He explained the transfer of Jews to manual labor and agriculture in terms of the need to improve both their inferior socioeconomic status and the welfare of the state. While Tannenbaum had persisted in using the term "loyalty to the king" in his political theory, Laski based his program on the concept that the state is the "homeland" and therefore the individual is concerned with the welfare of society, "for its welfare is his own." The Kingdom of Poland deserved the love of the Jews because it had treated them well over a long period of time. Even the lack of civil rights was not a sufficient reason for the Jews not to seek the welfare of the state, which was synonymous with their own good. With this unqualified loyalty, the author even defended the restrictions of the edict of 1823 as being intended for the welfare of the Jews.

This pamphlet is unique to Haskalah literature in that it is based on principles of political economy and begins and ends with poems dealing with this theme. In 1840 Laski published a poem, *Ḥuldah Va-Bor* (The Weasel and the Well), based upon a talmudic legend, and in 1844 he published *Nefesh Ḥayah* (A Living Being), a book on the immortality of the soul.

The renewal of the government program for the agricultural settlement of the Jews in Poland in 1843 moved the prolific Haskalah writer Feivel Shiffer to compose a rhymed idyll in praise of farming. It was printed in Warsaw that year under the title "Mata le-Shem" (The Plantations of Jews). He remained faithful to the idea of a Jewish peasantry to the end of his life, and even his book *Mahlkhim* (Of Conduct), published in 1866, contained passages depicting the felicity and charm of the Polish peasants' life: "O, Israel! Can you rejoice and be glad as is this nation? Do you know the joy of the harvest? . . . Will the threshing-floor and the wine press feed you and will you rejoice over new wine and oil and over young sheep?—Alas! Since you have turned aside from this labor and have forsaken it, your joy has been destroyed!" Among the Jews, farming was only a memory of an ancient past, and Shiffer, in the vein of Abraham Mapu in *Ahavat Ẓion* (Love of Zion), aroused memories of that golden age:

> O remember the sound of your harps, the strumming of your lyres, when the songs of Jerusalem rang to the sound of those who came to the House of God, bringing all the first fruits of the soil on the backs of the horned bulls. . . . Remember your joy at all the good, and how you caused the Levite and him who dwelled with you to rejoice—and now as for us, what do we have to bring and present as a sacred offering?[100]

Yiddish, Hebrew, and German: Political Dimensions of Language

Just as there was no essential distinction between the Maskilim and the assimilationists in their espousal of loyalty, "love of fellow men" and productivity, there also was little difference—except for a group of Maskilim outside Warsaw—in their contemptuous attitude toward Yiddish. Moses Tannenbaum, for example, railed against Yiddish, describing it as "the absurd language which has become attached to our jaws like a malignant leprosy," and which was derived "from the conversations of women with each other, and from the speech of a maidservant with her mistress in the embroidery shops and in the kitchens."[101] Similarly, Thalgruen criticized the Yiddish language not only as "a highly corrupt, confused and garbled form of German" but also as the language of "the lowly and the rustics." He also complained that "there is none who can speak the language of his people, the language of the country in which we live,"[102] that is, Polish. Like Naphtali Herz Wessely when he spoke out against Yiddish in *Dvar Shalom ve-Emet* (Words of Peace and Truth), the Maskilim of Poland contrasted Yiddish to the purity of the Polish language, and Tannenbaum explained that the mark of a "pure" language is "the preciseness of its expression, which is customary among the élite of the nation and its sages, its scholars, and those who understand rhetoric"; in a word, the language of the higher class.[103]

The main difference between the Maskilim and the assimilationists lay in their respective attitudes toward Hebrew. For the Maskilim, Hebrew was not only the sole language of their literary creativity but also the language which held the nation together in its dispersion and maintained its ties to its splendid past. For example, in the introduction to his book on grammar, *Darkhei ha-Lashon*, which he published in Warsaw in 1822, Dov Berish Kahana urged every Jew to study grammar not only in order "to understand the Sacred Scriptures" but also "to enable him to understand our holy tongue as completely as possible, for it is all that has remained to us of all that we cherished from ancient days."[104]

J. L. Paradisthal, a Maskil from Suwałki who settled in Warsaw, explained in the introduction to his book *Ma'arekhet Mikhtavim* (A Series of Letters) that rabbinic statements of approbation were superfluous since the great talmudic scholars themselves urged the study of Hebrew, as, for example, R. Akiba Eger, who noted that each nation speaks its own language and loves it.[105] Although most of the Maskilim complained about the decline and neglect of "the Hebrew language" from its ancient glory while praising each other highly for rejuvenating it,[106] only Feivel Shiffer, in the introduction to his book of poems, offered a historical explanation for its revival in the Diaspora. According to him, the language "declined greatly" because the nation's leaders "carried upon themselves the heavy burden of the people" and "put all their efforts into instruction in the law." He dated the revival as 1840; that is, when "the Maskilim among our people voluntarily came to the aid of our language." Then some of the most outstanding Jews saw that "this had been brought about by God," but even their hands grew weak when they were attacked by "the wrath of the unruly of the nation," namely, by the zealots, "and to this very day the rage has not ended." Therefore, the poet called upon "those who seek the welfare of the Hebrew tongue . . . to bend their shoulder to bear with us the labor in behalf of the language."[107]

The Maskilim were divided over the place of Hebrew in the contemporary culture. The devout Abraham Stern, Tugendhold's friend in the censorship office, was a well-known mathematician and inventor[108] who also wrote a number of poems which are noted for their fine meter and originality of language.[109] Stern expressed his displeasure with those poets who translated "the thoughts of aliens," composed love poetry, and "made no distinctions between the sacred and the profane."[110]

David Loewenthal was a minor Hebrew poet who wrote in the style of the Psalms. He was a conservative Jew, but this did not prevent him from praising the modern rabbis in Germany whose sermons in German he regarded as an answer to the needs of the times. As for the role of Hebrew, he contented himself with the modest desideratum that it be preserved as the language "principally of prayer and of sermons" and that its study by the young be begun "somewhat earlier."[111]

Moshe Tannenbaum, whose sober realism was masked by his florid rhetoric, attempted to clarify the status, role, and prospects of Hebrew in the Diaspora. At the end of his book *Mata'ei Moshe* he complained that in the Diaspora, Hebrew is different from the languages of other nations inasmuch as it is only a literary language and is not spoken by the people:

> Now in this alone the lot of the Hebrew language is diminished from all the languages of the nations, for in all of them the mouth speaks and the hand writes and both together have made a covenant, and united, they take delight . . . , and each instructs the other in the utterance of pleasant sounds as though they were twin sisters. . . . But Hebrew, that refined tongue, alas! it brings pain to our heart! It must perforce abide among a people of stammering tongue without understanding—and between the beautiful phrasing of our literature and the mixed language in our mouths there is no association whatsoever.

Not only does the vernacular differ from the language of Hebrew literature, it is also a different species because it is utterly lacking in literary style: "Can a garbled and corrupt tongue reveal the mysteries of a purified and refined language?"

Tannenbaum proposed two methods to be used separately or together to foster the Hebrew language and help it take root in the nation's soul: The first, which had already been expressed by pioneers of the Haskalah, such as Naphtali Herz Wessely, was to study the style, similes, imagery, and figures of speech of a foreign language and "by means of them to understand the value of the rhetorical passages which are stored up in the breadth of our sacred literature," namely, the language of the Bible.The second proposal was more original, "to train ourselves from our youth to study the sacred books day and night . . . until that holy tongue implants . . . in our souls all the thoughts expressed by its lofty phrasing, as if it were our spoken language. . . . It will then in turn reactivate itself within us . . . to the extent that we and the prophets, the seers of old, will seem to be at one point in time . . . the living present."[112] In short, by diligent study of the Bible, Hebrew could be restored as a language of thought, even though it was impossible to restore it as a spoken language.

Tannenbaum did not see any way of reviving Hebrew as a spoken language in the Diaspora. This could only come with the nation's return to its land; then the language of literature and the spoken language would be one:

This evil cannot be healed, until God looks down and sees, zealously acts in behalf of His land, and shows pity to His nation; He will set His hand again the second time to recover the remnant of His people from Assyria and from Pathros and from all the places of their dispersion, and He will give them a pure language [which they will accept] unanimously; then like a phoenix, the youthful character of the Jewish language will be restored; and its dry bones will be revived in all the smoothness of its expression; then the words of our lips and the writing of our hands in the powerful embrace of love, will cling together. . . .[113]

This prospect of the revival of the language, as well as the Return to Zion, was also a beacon for other Hebrew writers among Warsaw's Maskilim. In the letter to his son, Moses, about "the value of the sacred language," which he published in his book *Mahlkhim*, Feivel Shiffer concluded with the hope "that it will become a pure language for all the nations, for it will return to its pristine state when the Lord will bring us back from our captivity."[114] Even the assimilationist Tugendhold alluded to the connection between the Hebrew language and hopes for the future in his letter to Feivel Shiffer, which he sent with the censor's permits for his book *Ḥaẓrot ha-Shir* (Courts of Song):

. . . Would that all the Lord's people would know its sacred tongue, would that they should understand it perfectly, for the worth of every nation lies in its language and its writing; would that they who please themselves in the brood of aliens alone would understand quite thoroughly, that we who are exiled from our land, we who are scattered throughout all the corners of the earth—although it is incumbent upon us to speak the language of the people in whose shadow we live—nevertheless, one Hebrew language is the heritage from our forefathers to us. Into it, all the unique treasures of our sacred faith are absorbed; all the bands of brotherly love are fastened by means of it; within it are stored the treasures of solace for our souls which are bowed down and our spirits which are sorrow laden; and by it our exalted hope is engraved with the finger of God.

He was deliberately vague about the content of this exalted hope, for in his writings he repeatedly stressed the universal pan-humanistic explanation of that hope.

In contrast to the assimilationists, the Maskilim saw no contradiction between their unqualified loyalty to the throne and their hope for the Restoration of Zion and the Ingathering of the Exiles, for this was an article of religious faith. Indeed, the Maskilim were only following their political principles in refraining from mentioning—in connection to the Restoration of Zion—anything related to servitude or suffering in the Diaspora. Traditionally, it is held that every synagogue erected in the Diaspora is, as it were, "a little sanctuary" until the Temple itself is rebuilt. Isaac Kandia expressed this in his ode on the occasion of the dedication of a synagogue in Warsaw:

> It is sacred to the Lord, to Him we raise our hands
> He will lead us erect to His sacred precincts . . .
> Renew within us a firm spirit from on high
> Until the holy mountain and Jerusalem are firmly established.[115]

The foreword to Feivel Shiffer's *Ḥaẓrot ha-Shir* had as its motto, "If I forget thee, O Jerusalem, may my right hand forget its cunning," while every stanza of the poem began with the prayer of "Do not forget me."

Similarly, Solomon Ettinger, in his poem "A Confession of Faith," declared:[116]

> I believe that You strongly love the holy site
> And Jerusalem is Your choicest place. . . .
> I believe that our redemption from exile
> Has been a matter[117] of concern for hundreds of years. . . .

In this, Ettinger and Shiffer were joined by their contemporaries and fellow countrymen.[118]

Zamość: Meeting Ground of Polish and Galician Haskalah

In general, the literary works of the Warsaw Maskilim were artistically inferior to those of the Maskilim in Galicia, Lithuania, and Volhynia.[119] But more important was the lack of social standing of the Warsaw Maskilim in their community. Haskalah writers in the neighboring countries, even where they were few in number, were considered spokesmen of a social movement, but the Maskilim in the capital city, in addition to being isolated from all social classes, had neither influential leaders nor avid followers. This explains their emphasis on drawing closer to the gentile neighbors and on loyalty to the authorities. The drive to disseminate knowledge among the people, which was a hallmark of the Haskalah in the other East European countries, was virtually absent here. Even the propaganda for the establishment of elementary schools was not conducted by the Maskilim but by assimilationists who spoke in behalf of the government.

The isolation of this group of Maskilim from the people is most clearly reflected in the absence of any fighting spirit. The Haskalah in eastern Europe, like its counterpart in Berlin, struggled for a new order in the Jewish community, courageously exposing ignorance and bigotry. The Maskilim of Galicia and Volhynia waged a bitter war against Hasidism, regarding it as a stumbling block to the spread of the Haskalah among the people. But the Maskilim of Warsaw were careful not to challenge Hasidism, as though they concurred with Tugendhold's tactics. It was at the end of that period, in the early 1860s, that the moderate Maskil Eliezer Thalgruen, in his *Tokhaḥat Musar,* dared to rebuke Hasidim openly, lumping them together with others who pretended to piety.

There was, however, one district which could be said to have constituted an active center of the Haskalah movement—the city of Zamość and its environs. By virtue of its character and aim, it was a branch of the movement of regeneration and renascence among the Jews of nearby Galicia. The historical reasons for its uniqueness are readily apparent.

Zamość was a small city, but from the time it was founded by the count Zamoyski in the late sixteenth century it developed into an important commercial and cultural center. After Armenians and Greeks settled in this city, Sefardic Jews settled there on the basis of a broad privilege granted by the lords of the city in 1588.[120] This group quickly disintegrated, like the small group of Spanish exiles in Lemberg from which it had emerged. However, the Ashkenazic community within the city grew and flourished, and in the beginning of the eighteenth century the "Ordynacya Zamoyska" was separated from the district of Chełm and organized as a special district within the central autonomy of the Council of the Four Lands. According to the official census of 1764, the Jewish community in the city of Zamość and its environs numbered 1,905 people. By 1827, Jews constituted a majority within the city proper—2,874 out of a total of 5,414 inhabitants.[121]

At the end of the old Kingdom of Poland, the community of Zamość had already been singled out in the culture of Poland's Jewry as a center of Torah where the first buds of secular Haskalah burgeoned. The city's rabbi, formerly the Rabbi of Chełm, R. Solomon ben Moses Khelma, was the author of the book *Merkevet ha-Mishneh*. One of the teachers in the Yeshivah in Zamość was his contemporary, R. Israel ben Moses Zamość, the author of *Neẓaḥ Yisrael* (Eternal Israel), who was a distinguished mathematician and a teacher of the Maskilim in Berlin and Brody.[122] The Jews of Zamość were no doubt aided by the European culture which reached them through the enlightened nobles living in the city since the Renaissance and Humanist periods. They were influenced even more, like the Jews in other commercial centers of Poland and Lithuania at that time—such as Shklov, Vilna, Brody, Lemberg, Dubno in Volhynia, and Satanov in

Podolia—by the Haskalah of their German brethren with whom they maintained commercial ties. During the era of the Partitions of Poland, the groundwork had been well prepared in Zamość to absorb the roots of the Haskalah which had originated in eastern Europe.

Even more than the entire cultural tradition of the community, Zamość's place in the Haskalah movement was determined by its political conditions. The district of Zamość was the only portion of what was to be Congress Poland which had been annexed to Galicia under Austrian rule in the first Partition in 1772. While the whole eastern part of central Poland had not been conquered by Austria until the third Partition, in 1795 (and then abandoned by 1809), the district of Zamość was under continuous Austrian rule for thirty-seven years.[123] This period of Austrian rule and attachment to Galicia was sufficient to implant the seeds of Haskalah in the Jewish population of the district of Zamość. The German-Jewish schools, which existed in that district as in all of Galicia until 1806, were a major factor in the spread of knowledge of the German language and of secular knowledge. The commercial and cultural ties of the district with the Galician cities of Lemberg and Brody were also factors; the ties were strengthened during this period and continued even after the demarcation of political boundaries between the two adjacent areas.

A group of Haskalah writers prominent in the annals of Hebrew and Yiddish literature and tied by proximity among themselves and with the Maskilim of Galicia arose in the Zamość area of central Poland, which was within the political sphere of the adjacent Haskalah center for a long time.

Abraham Jacob Stern was a native of Hrubieszów in the district of Zamość. He was not ten years old when the city of his birth passed over to Austrian rule. The childhood and youth of the prolific writer Feivel Shiffer were spent in the cities of Laszczów, Józefów, and ultimately, Szczebrzeszyn—all in the district of Zamość—except for an interval of three years, which he spent in Brody with the help of the city's generous benefactors of the Haskalah. Shiffer related his life story in his introduction to *Ḥaẓrot ha-Shir*:

> In Laszczów my mother conceived me . . . and to Józefów my father sold [delivered] me. . . . To Brody my God sent me; there I dwelt for three years in the company of kindhearted men of wealth. . . . From there I went to Szczebrzeszyn, the city in which I dwell, that city in which there are those whom I love, the rich Szper brothers, the wealthiest of them Yehuda! Piles of gold you set upon my book.[124]

The "kindhearted men of wealth," the members of the Szper family, were not the only ones with whom Feivel Shiffer associated during his stay in Szczebrzeszyn. The renowned Maskil, Jacob Reifmann, who was one of the distinguished pioneers of Jewish studies, settled in the district of Zamość soon after his marriage and spent the rest of his life there. It is characteristic of the Haskalah tradition in Szczebrzeszyn that this scholar, about whom the poet Y. L. Gordon wrote the laudatory poem "How Many Jacob Reifmanns Are There in the Marketplace?"[125] read the *Guide of the Perplexed* for the first time in his father-in-law's house in that city.

Among the well-known Haskalah writers, the following were natives of Zamość: the poet Aryeh Leib Kinderfreund (1798–1837), a man of broad learning and author of articles on meter in poetry, who went to Galicia at an early age; Ephraim Fischel Fischlsohn,[126] the author of the biting anti-Hasidic satire in Yiddish entitled *Teyator fun Khsidim* (The Theater of Hasidim), which was written in 1839 but not published until the twentieth century. The renowned Yiddish author Solomon Ettinger settled in Zamość immediately after his marriage, at age fifteen, and became known to the Maskilim of Galicia in Lemberg, where he studied medicine at the university. But each of the three writers received his initial education in the spirit of the Haskalah among the Maskilim in Zamość.

Two well-known Haskalah writers, natives of Galicia, were also influenced by the group of Maskilim in Zamość. Samson Halevi Bloch was twenty years old when he married in Zamość, where his brother, the Maskil Solomon Zev Bloch, lived.[127] Jacob Eichenbaum, the famous poet and mathematician, also arrived in Zamość when he was young and was married there.[128]

The literary work of the Maskilim of the district of Zamość reflects, in microcosm, the Haskalah literature in Galicia. While Jacob Reifmann followed in the footsteps of Solomon Judah Rapoport in the sphere of Jewish studies, Ephraim Fischl Fischelsohn and Solomon Ettinger were influenced by the Galician writers Joseph Perl and Isaac Erter in both Jewish studies and their commitment to the spread of enlightenment among the masses. These two Yiddish writers employed satire to depict the negative phenomena in Jewish public life.

While Fischelsohn's satire is directed entirely against Hasidism, there are only a few instances in Ettinger's writings in which the rabbi of the Hasidim is held up to ridicule as a wonder worker; for example, in *Der Hoylekh-rokhil* (The Talebearer) and in *Di Sheydim* (The Demons). As a spokesman for the folk ethic, Ettinger (1803–56) lashed out in his satire mainly at those social transgressors most hated by the people: the sanctimonious men and women who exacted exorbitant rates of interest from widows and from the poor under the pretext of the *heter iska* (a legal device to circumvent the Torah prohibition of taking interest). These types recur in many of his parables, which charm by the light touch of their language: *Dos Likht* (The Light or Candle), *Vitele*, *Der Kholem* (The Dream). The triumph of fairness and righteousness and the downfall of sanctimonious people, hypocrites, scoundrels, and swindlers is also the moral of Ettinger's humorous satirical play *Serkele* (Little Sarah), which was very popular and was presented many times after the author's death. In Ettinger's fables, the popular social ethic is bound together with the traditional social outlook of the middle class in that he gave an undue measure of praise to being content with one's lot (*The Dog with the Meat*), and condemned those who envy the wealthy (*Envy*) and those who rebel against their masters, forgetting that the "master provides their food" (*The Two Horses*).

An undertone of Haskalah lore can be heard in those fables of Ettinger where he mocked foolish customs, such as *Kapores* (expiatory slaughter of fowl on the Eve of the Day of Atonement) in *Dos Likht*; superstition, in *Di Sheydim*; and barren casuistry in the excellent satire *Di Tsvey Hener* (The Two Hens). Prompted by the noblest aims of the Haskalah—the spreading of knowledge among the people—Ettinger began writing a book in Yiddish, *Mythology, Natural History, and the History of the World.*[129] Ettinger saw it as the writer's duty to stimulate the people to productive work, a most fundamental point in the program of the Haskalah. The distress and disgrace of poverty could be remedied only if the people could remove the traditional false pride from their hearts. In *Di Shmates* (The Rags) he wrote that hucksters pound the pavement from morning to night, and though they scarcely earn their meager bread with all their rushing around, they despise labor, which sustains those who engage in it. And prejudice keeps young people from military service though it is a secure and dignified livelihood. *Dos Katshkele* (The Duckling) describes the system of education where every father teaches his son Gemara and *Posekim* (Codes) in the hope that he will grow up to be a rabbi even when the child demonstrates proclivities and talents for work and craftsmanship. As a rule, the lad is left with nothing. He neither attains the rabbinate nor does he have any profession or source of livelihood.

As for *Dos Panele* (The Young Lady), his propaganda in praise of farming, the doctor-Maskil practiced what he preached. He acquired a hundred-acre estate in the suburbs of Zamość, and for a number of years earned his livelihood solely from farming.[130] It would seem that the writer was influenced to take this step by the initiative of the wealthy Szper family. Leyb Szper had already leased a number of farmsteads from Count Zamoyski and employed Jewish farmers to work on them.[131] It may, of course, be conjectured that in settling Jews on their estates the wealthy benefactors combined their interest in the public good with their self-interest: the right to acquire estates granted to individual wealthy Jews[132] was generally qualified by the condition that the new estate owner employ only Jewish labor. At any rate, the enterprise of the Szper brothers was hailed by the Maskilim in the entire region.

Ettinger was not the only one in the district of Zamość to personally respond to this call to return to the soil. Caught up in the enthusiasm of that idea, a group of Maskilim banded together and settled on the land. Feivel Shiffer, in his memoirs of the 1860s, reports, "For a long time I and my beloved companions were settled on a parcel of land."[133]

Unfortunately Shiffer did not tell why this group separated and what prompted him to forsake agriculture and move to Warsaw. In any event, his many books, which he published with the help of wealthy benefactors, did not provide him with a sufficient livelihood, nor did the several professions in which he engaged simultaneously—matchmaking and tutoring in the homes of the wealthy. In the following lines he epitomizes the lot of the writer: "His lack was his recompense and his distress as great as the destruction of the universe." Thus Shiffer asked with mordant irony: "Is he not rightly named *meḥaber* (writer; lit., one who combines) because in him are joined together judgment and shame?" As if he were intentionally paraphrasing Abraham Ibn Ezra's satire, "I rise up early to go to the house of the prince," Shiffer, on the basis of his own experience, urged the *meḥaber*—to whom he refers parenthetically as "a man who shall not prosper in his days"—to be cautious in intercourse with wealthy patrons:

> Writer, if you happen . . . to come to the wealthy man at a moment when he is angry and he rebukes you, make haste and flee, thereby sparing your dignity . . . , for the man of wealth lives according to a fixed schedule, and if he is not prepared to receive you at this moment, then when you come on the next day, his scowl will have gone and he will be at ease with you!

Moreover, he advised the writer not to greet his rich patron in the street, lest the benefactor be offended by this demonstration of familiarity. "The rich man might be slighted by you, since someone might ask him, 'What has this pauper to do with you that he greets you?' "[134]

The Subscription Lists and the Story They Tell

The limited public support for Haskalah literature within the Kingdom of Poland is demonstrated by the lists of subscribers for these books. Up to the early 1840s, the number of subscribers for a book of poetry or prose in Hebrew amounted to little more than 100. In the following decade, the number of subscribers for the books of Shiffer and Thalgruen reached 250, but this increase must also be ascribed to the content of those books. It is reasonable to assume that Shiffer had almost that number of subscribers (243) for his 1849 book *The History of Napoleon* because he was reputed to be a person close to the authorities by virtue of his previous book *Devar Gevurot Paskevich* (The Story of the Heroic Deeds of Paskevich), published in 1845; just as Thalgruen was helped by the fact that his work, *Tokhaḥat Musar,* was just a preface to his translation (German in Hebrew characters) of the Book of Psalms. In the previous year, 1853, Paradisthal had a mere 60 subscribers for his book *Ma'arekhet Mikhtavim*.

Almost all the subscribers were inhabitants of Warsaw. Of 951 persons (1,415 subscriptions) who subscribed to one or more of eleven secular Hebrew books which appeared from 1822 to 1854,[135] no more than 110 lived outside Warsaw. It may be assumed that even those few subscribers from the provinces were acquired mainly because the author had lived there. Thus, in 1838 Buchner had 18 subscriptions in Częstochowa, in addition to 92 in Warsaw, for his book *Moreh le-Ẓedakah* (Teacher of Righteousness). Shiffer, a native of the district of Zamość, made the rounds for subscriptions to publish in 1840 *Ḥaẓrot ha-Shir,* not only in Warsaw, but also in Zamość and Lublin. However, he did not specify any figures. Lewenthal, a native of western Poland, added to 49 subscribers from Warsaw 20 from Kalisz and 26 from Włocławek. In contrast, Thalgruen, a native of Poznan, numbered among his 257 subscribers only 10 from outside Warsaw, including 7 from the germanicized city of Wielun (Filehne). Paradisthal found 23 subscribers in his native town of Suwałki and 37 in Warsaw. However, the disproportion in relation to Warsaw notwithstanding, even these numbers testify to the initial awakening of the Haskalah spirit in the larger provincial towns. In Lublin, whose subscribers Shiffer mentioned favorably, Shalom Hacohen in 1838 had 13 subscribers for his book *Koreh ha-Dorot* (He That Called the Generations), "a chronicle of our people, the seed of Jacob," still less than one-sixth of his 82 subscribers in Warsaw.

The occurrence of the two designations "R." and "Herr" preceding the names in the lists of subscribers reflects the progress of the

Haskalah. It is no coincidence that, in the subscription list of 1822 for the book *Doresh Tov* by Buchner, all the subscribers were referred to by the designation "R." Seven years later there appear in the list of subscribers for Isaac Kandia's *Toldot Moshe* 89 with the appellative "R." and 10 with "Herr." From mid-1840 to the 1850s, between one-third and two-fifths of the total number of subscribers for a book were designated as "Herr." It need hardly be said there were two categories of supporters for Haskalah literature: on the one hand the wealthy, whose classification as Mitnaggedim or Maskilim is a moot point; and on the other hand Maskilim, who even in their life style and appearance, especially in their mode of dress, were among the "enlightened." In 1854 almost all the subscribers with the appellative "Herr" had Polish or German surnames. The wealthy communal leaders from Warsaw, R. Solomon Posner and his sons, R. Abraham Vinaver, and R. Joseph Ḥayyim Halberstam, were typical examples of the first group. Those on the list designated as "Herr" were members of the banking families of Rosen, Epstein, Janasz, Teplitz (some subscribing for 5 or even 10 copies). The same is true of physicians: in 1838, seven Warsaw physicians subscribed for Buchner's *Moreh le-Ẓedakah*.

The boundary dividing Mitnaggedim in general and those sympathetic with the Haskalah was not rigid, and there were several names among the subscribers for Haskalah books with the designation "R.," which also appeared on the lists of subscribers to homiletical works.[136] Even the Rabbi of Warsaw, R. Ḥayyim Davidson, subscribed to Haskalah books. He, as well as the rabbis of Zamość and Lublin, subscribed to Shiffer's book, *The Story of the Heroic Deeds of Paskevich*, no doubt as a mark of loyalty to the throne. However, R. Ḥayyim Davidson was the only one among the rabbis also to subscribe in 1854 for *Tokhaḥat Musar* by Thalgruen. The sons and the son-in-law of R. Solomon Eger appeared—with conspicuous reference to their distinguished lineage—in the lists of subscribers to a number of books by Maskilim which were published in Warsaw.

Joseph Schoenhack's *Toldot ha-Areẓ* (The History of the Earth. Part 1: The History of Life), which appeared in Warsaw in 1841, had a large number of subscribers, most of whom were not on the lists of subscribers to Haskalah books. The list of Schoenhack's subscribers includes 361 names, of which 129 were from Warsaw and the remainder from provincial towns. The rabbinical approbations displayed at the front of this book on zoology written in Hebrew contributed to its extraordinary success in circles far removed from Haskalah literature. In addition to the presiding judge of the rabbinical court of Königsberg (R. Jacob Zvi Mecklenburg), the rabbis of

Suwałki, Tykocin, Kalvarya, and Sejny[137] recommended it unanimously, stressing its value in reinforcing piety. In the description of animals by their species, the author adds his comments to those mentioned in the Gemara. It is not surprising that there were 30 subscribers from Tikocin, the birthplace of the author, and 87 from Suvalki, where he resided. The other provincial towns in the list of subscribers to Schoenhack's book were all centered in the northeastern district of the Kingdom of Poland bordering on Lithuania, far from the influence of the Polish centers of Hasidism, or across the border, in Lithuania proper: 24 subscribers in both Kalvarya and Szaki and a number in Wolkowysk and Augustów. One-third of those listed as subscribers from Warsaw were persons from provincial towns, classified as "visitors" in the capital. It is reasonable to assume that Schoenhack's work found acceptance among those who were not influenced by Haskalah slogans, the majority of them Mitnaggedim, and those who, lacking knowledge of foreign languages, needed a Hebrew book for information in the field of the natural sciences. In recommending this book, Tugendhold observed, "For there are many among our coreligionists who do not understand the languages of the nations, who yearn to slake their thirst for the mathematical and the natural sciences." The fact that these readers belonged to groups who observed the traditional way of life is also confirmed by the subscribers' appellatives: not only are all the subscribers in the provincial towns listed by the designation "R.," but also, even among the subscribers in Warsaw only 11 are designated by the title "Herr."

As to the titles of the subscribers from the few provincial towns[138] for books of a pronounced Haskalah bent, the picture varies according to the particular situation in each town. In the cities near the Prussian border—Kalisz and Włocławek—all the subscribers in 1843 were designated as "Herr." In Kalisz, the list included all the men of considerable wealth in the city, members of the families of industrialists such as Redlich, Mamroth, Lande. In the manufacturing city of Częstochowa, the division of the meager group of subscribers in 1838 into Mitnaggedim and Maskilim on the one hand and "the enlightened" on the other was similar to the division in Warsaw (10 "Rabbi" and 8 "Herr"). By contrast, in Lublin in 1838 and in Suvalki in 1853, all the subscribers bore the designation "R." except for one "Herr" in Suvalki.

Comparison of the lists of subscribers confirms the fact that a third category existed—those who did not subscribe to any Hebrew book. However, their representation among the subscribers to the rare books on Jewish subjects in the Polish language was considerable: for example, Buchner's Polish book *Kwiaty wschodnie*, a collection of selections from the ethical lore of the Talmud; and *Beḥinat Olam* (The Test of the Universe) by Yedaiah ha-Penini, in Tugendhold's Polish translation (1846). Of 304 Jewish subscribers for both of these books, 121 names did not appear on any list of subscribers to Hebrew books published in Poland until that time. Except for a few who just belonged to the extremely Orthodox, like R. Isaac of Warka, who consented to subscribe for "the sake of peaceful coexistence," there were instances here of assimilationists, who were far removed from any contact with Jewish culture. More than a dozen of them were members of families who had been baptized or who would convert in the next generation—Bondy, Brunner, Fajans, Kunitz, Kronenberg, Loewenstein, Levi, Reichman, Rotwand, Wawelberg. Leopold Kronenberg subscribed to Buchner's Polish book three years before he converted, and one year after his conversion ordered nine copies of the translation of *Beḥinat Olam*. This is not at all surprising considering that scores of Gentiles, all high officers and royal dignitaries, agreed to be included in the list of subscribers to a book written by the censor of his Royal Majesty.

The Effects of the Haskalah's Failure in Poland

Complaints about Poland's abandoning the Enlightenment were repeatedly voiced in the German-Jewish weekly *Allgemeine Zeitung des Judenthums*, from the time of its appearance in Germany in 1837. Protests were held against Hasidism, which was spreading throughout the provincial towns—such as Lublin, where the *battei midrash* of the Hasidim drew more worshippers than all the other synagogues in the city.[139] According to the calculations of one reporter, the Hasidim constituted two-thirds of the population in every community.[140] Similarly, complaints were voiced that in the provincial towns there were no Jewish community schools because the initiative of the enlightened toward the establishment of a school, such as that of the wealthy Mamroth family in Kalisz, ran into the vigorous opposition of the rabbis and the zealot communal leaders.[141] By way of contrast, the reporters found solace in the cultural achievements of the Warsaw community. In the field of education, they cited the Polish schools for Jewish children, although the total number of pupils in all five schools never reached more than 238. The reporters stressed that all the pupils were children of the downtrodden, that is, those poor who were drawn to the school in the hope of receiving clothes for the winter and other forms of assistance, or the worst mischief-makers with whom parents could not cope at home.[142] In 1840 there were about 150 Jewish students in the lycées of Warsaw. According to the reporter's explanation, the pupils in the lower grades were the children of German Jews, that is, the enlightened ones, but those in the higher grades had transferred from the Rabbinical School, which served as a springboard to general secondary education.[143] The Rabbinical School was the delight of the enlightened reporters, and they praised its achievements, just as they noted every sermon in German in the "German" synagogue on Danilowiczowska Street, which was established during the time of the Duchy of Warsaw. They also pointed to the increase in the number of those wearing German garb in the capital city of Warsaw.[144]

It did not occur to the spokesmen for the "enlightened" that this veneer of civilization could not really raise the cultural level of the Jewish populace throughout the country. Thus, Hasidism grew even within the capital city itself.[145]

The absence in Congress Poland of a genuine Haskalah movement had an indirect effect on the character of Hasidism. Depite numerous obstacles, rationalist tendencies were already apparent in that period, as indicated, for example, by the interest in Maimonides' philosophy in certain circles of Orthodox youth.[146] And inasmuch as this interest in rationalist thought could not be satisfied by the Haskalah, rationalist elements having no other means of expression were at work within Hasidism itself. This gave to the Hasidism of Poland one of its unique traits, especially the Hasidism of the school of Przysucha-Kock.

9

Two Schools of Hasidism in Poland

The Centrality of the Zaddik

As in Galicia in the period of European reaction, Hasidism spread very swiftly through the Kingdom of Poland, albeit with differences both in its stage of development and in the conditions for its growth. On the one hand, Hasidism in central Poland was younger than its Galician counterpart, so that at the start of that epoch all the strongholds of the Mitnaggedim had not yet been captured by it, especially in the big cities, including the capital. On the other hand, this movement in Poland, at its very outset, was characterized by the faith of the simple folk in which the zaddik (the righteous one), the all-powerful helper, divinely inspired performer of wondrous deeds, figured prominently. In its early stages, a reaction set in against the vulgar element of Hasidism, and an effort was initiated to reform and dignify it.

In the first decades of the Kingdom of Poland, there still existed centers of Hasidism whose leaders, possessing little that was original, reiterated in their sermons the teachings of the zaddikim of the previous generations. They drew mainly on the teachings of the great men of the movement's golden age, the Napoleonic era in Poland. Thus, the Rabbi of Stopnica and Opatów (Apt), R. Meir Halevi Rotenberg, fostered the teachings of his master, R. Jacob Isaac, the

"Seer" of Lublin, and R. Moyshele of Kozienice followed the lessons of his father, the renowned R. Israel, from whom he had also inherited the post of *maggid* (preacher) in his city.

The teachings of the Hasidic leaders of Kozienice and Opatów invariably centered on the enhancement of the zaddik's status. One of the obligations toward the zaddik, a term considered synonymous with the true scholar, was providing for his maintenance. Understandably, the material circumstances of those who were engaged professionally in the study of Torah and in prayer were greatly reduced because of the impoverishment of the Jewish population; nor could they maintain their dignity or social status while continuously exhorting their flock to support them. R. Moyshele of Kozienice chided his contemporaries for the sorry lot of the scholars by citing Ps. 19:11: "More to be desired are they than much fine gold." He explained,

> the word "desired" is an allusion to the scholars and those who study, because they are constantly occupied with the holy Torah which is an esoteric delight, and it is beyond a doubt proper that they be honored by all who behold them. . . . But alas! because of our sins, they are held as naught and accounted as nothing in the eyes of the ignorant and the ordinary people. It is, alas! because of our sins, that they are without means of a livelihood and in great distress, need, and poverty. And this is the plea of the *sweet singer of Israel* in behalf of this generation which is practically in the wake of the Messiah[1]. . . . They will be full of gold and much fine gold and will wax rich in silver and gold. Then they will surely find themselves held in esteem. . . .[2]

To be sure, in consonance with Hasidic lore, the *maggid* stipulated that for the scholars to be considered zaddikim, it was necessary "that they occupy themselves with the study of the sacred Torah in the greatest measure of perfection,"[3] that is, that they act with the intent to sanctify God's name, "and that all their contemplation be directed to God, blessed be His Name." He also cited the opinion of Alshekh that when "the men of perfect faith" possess "all that is good," then also "all other men will be prompted to emulate their conduct so that they too may merit the same reward."[4]

R. Meir of Opatów repeatedly required of his Hasidim that they be among the "supporters of the Torah," namely, that they be concerned for the scholars, the zaddikim, that they provide for them. These supporters were likened to the olive leaf in the Noah episode, "for even as the leaves cover and protect the fruit, even so do those who support the Torah protect the scholars by giving in abundance to them."[5] It is an obligation to give support to the zaddik "so that he should not be burdened by mundane concerns,"[6] and thus can devote himself tranquilly to the study of Torah and the worship of God. In line with the teaching of R. Jacob Isaac of Lublin, his disciple explained that the observance of the Torah calls for a "goodly abundance" so he can observe such commandments as "to build a *sukkah* and obtain a *lulav, etrog* and the like."[7] Rabbi Issachar Ber of Radoszyce, known as the "Holy Grandfather" and one of the most popular Hasidic leaders in Poland, went further than his mentor, "the Seer" of Lublin. According to him, not only does the fulfillment of the commandments require a good living but even with respect to devotion to God, affluence is a beneficial factor. Accordingly, he alters the simple meaning of the scriptural verse, "Lest when thou hast eaten and art satisfied, and hast built goodly houses . . . thy silver and thy gold is multiplied—then thy heart be lifted up, and thou forget the Lord thy God"[8] to read: "If you multiply all this and your heart be lifted up, that is, that your heart will be exalted in the paths of the Lord, if Israel will have all that is good, then you will forget [*v'shakhaḥtah* literally means "and you will forget," but in Aramaic it has another sense: ". . . then God will be with you in your heart, for the *Shekhinah* does not dwell . . . except through joy and expansiveness"].[9]

"The Holy Grandfather" also explained that giving a present to the zaddik is an essential expression of cooperation with the one who prays in his own behalf. The commandment "thou shalt surely release it with him"[10] is obligatory, according to the Gemara,[11] only when the owner of the ass which is prostrate under its burden does not refrain from participating in the effort of loading and unloading. Similarly, "when a person comes to the zaddik to pray in his behalf that person must also give aid to the zaddik . . . , and this consists in giving him money."[12] In the view of R. Meir of Opatów, this is even a matter of justice, since it is the zaddik "who causes plenty to flow from the source of all blessings, and it is fitting that he too should not lack anything, and that sustenance come to him in abundance." This is also the explanation of the commandment in the Torah that one "should not muzzle the ox while he threshes," inasmuch as "the zaddik is called *shor* [an ox], for he deems himself an ox bearing a burden."[13] R. Jacob Isaac said, "The Holy One, blessed be He, Himself remunerated the zaddik for acting as a mediator."[14] Of course, the zaddik himself must always set before his eyes his own duty to bring abundance to his people and not just to be concerned with the perfection of his own soul "in ever rising and higher degree."[15] "The zaddik must forget his own self, all his labors being directed only toward the flowing of abundance to Israel," who will then "know no lack, but will constantly have only all that is good."[16]

But the mere provision of material assistance to the scholars and zaddikim is not enough. Faith in the zaddik is the basic article of faith, without which worship of the Creator is inconceivable. For an ordinary Jew does not have it in his power to draw close to God except by being close to a zaddik. The constant need to reiterate this principle, which had been enunciated initially by R. Elimelekh of Leżajsk, was in itself evidence of the incipient erosion of faith among the people. Obviously, the Hasidic leaders of the courts of Opatów, Kozienice, Radoszyce, and others regarded the buttressing of faith in the zaddik as the main way to strengthen religion against the peril of heresy, which had already cast its first shadows. The great-grandson of R. Issachar Ber of Radoszyce praised his "Holy Grandfather," whose wondrous deeds had checked the rise of "heresy" which had begun in many places. "Since the time he became famous . . . as a performer of deeds of salvation, even men in whom the spark of Jewishness had become extinguished, now were prompted to visit him. . . ."[17] R. Moyshele of Kozienice vented his wrath on the nonbelievers, whom he mentions in the same breath as "the wicked who devise evil decrees against Israel."[18] Undoubtedly, he had in mind the extreme assimilationists who were close to the government and who had prepared a program for the polonization of the Jewish population. R. Meir of Opatów demanded that they "be separated from the Jewish community so that they will not, God forbid, lead Israel astray." According to his interpretation of the verse "Shall one deal with our sister as with a harlot?"[19] this ostracism is a precondition for the establishment of the *Shekhinah*: the word *hakhezonah* (as with a harlot)—as he interprets it—is a compound of two words, *hakh* and *zonah,* hence, "it is incumbent upon us to strike with a fist the wicked who deny any belief in the God of the universe." They are referred to as harlots, "for he who has a false belief is called a harlot." The subsequent restoration of the *Shekhinah* is alluded to in the end of the verse, "He will deal with our sister."[20]

There are many ways in which the zaddik acts as intermediary between the Creator and His people, Israel.

According to R. Moyshele of Kozienice, the "light is sown for the righteous" means that the zaddik "draws light down to this world for his brethren, the children of Israel, in order to elevate them to the worship of the Blessed One."[21] R. Meir of Opatów, expounding on the meaning of "The Holy One, blessed be He, is near to him who cleaves to the zaddik,"[22] asserted that in order "that the Torah and prayer be acceptable to the Omnipresent, blessed be He, it is necessary to participate with the zaddikim, and by means of this collaboration with the zaddikim everything one does will be clear and pure. . . ."[23] It is impossible for man to improve and illuminate his soul except by means of the zaddik, "for God has so ordained that all the integrations and emanations shall occur by means of the zaddik."[24]

The merit of those who go to the true zaddikim and gather together with them is great, for they restore the *Shekhinah,* and advance the Redemption and Ingathering of the Exiles.[25] The ordinary folk who draw close to the zaddik must thereby learn to occupy themselves with the Torah and the service of God, although they cannot attain the level at which he performs those acts. To be sure, the zaddikim can instill in these people the love of God only on condition "that they will believe in them with a strong faith, without any disparaging thoughts whatsoever concerning them."[26] For just as it is forbidden to be critical of the Torah, even with regard to certain commandments, such as that of the red heifer, "so it is forbidden to criticize the zaddik in a given generation if at times he performs vague deeds, for he is just in all his ways and his deeds are for the sake of Heaven."[27] According to the exposition of another disciple of "the Seer," R. Ezekiel of Kazimierz (Kuzmir),[28] who was also close to the Przysucha (Pshiskhe) school, if one does so he would bring about a separation between his master and himself which is like the separation between the Holy One, blessed be He, and the *Shekhinah.* Only by linking one's prayer with that of the zaddik can one attain the high virtue of reverence for God. Even when a man comes to the zaddik for help, he should first pray for the zaddik, so that he will gain God's compassion.[29]

Since the ordinary person cannot compare himself with the zaddik, he must be satisfied with his own level and must not concern himself with matters that are too great for him. "He should not do more than lies within his capacity, but act within the limits with which God favored him."[30] Only the extraordinary person knows how to cause emanations to be drawn down to the world, and the main purpose of his prayer is to restore the integrity of the upper worlds. For one who is not in this position, it is fitting that he pray even for a livelihood, provided that he believes "that the matter which he asks for also concerns the upper worlds."[31]

The role of the zaddik in the world has no measure or bounds. Creation itself was for their sake,[32] since, as the Talmud states, God desires the prayers of the zaddikim. The zaddik in each generation has the aspect, as it were, of God, and it lies within his power "to draw down a flow of great benevolence and good to the world,"[33] for by reestablishing a union with God, he causes *midat ha-ḥesed* to predominate over *midat ha-din* and thereby changes justice into mercy. The power of the zaddik extends so far "that whatever God does, it is also within the capacity of the zaddik to do."[34] "The eyes of the Lord are toward the righteous" means that "though all the children of Israel are vessels for the *Shekhinah,* the eyes of the Lord mainly watch over the zaddikim, and from the blessings bestowed upon them, the rest of the nation is also blessed."[35] Angels are created from every utterance of the zaddik about Torah and in prayer.[36] It is a matter of course that all the needs of the Jewish people—spiritual and material—are fulfilled by means of the zaddik. The zaddik brings down a spiritual flow to "the holy flock, the holy people of Israel" to implant in them reverence for God so that they "will grow wise in the service of the blessed Name."[37] The zaddik does this because he grieves over "what concerns God, in that they are unable to serve Him with complete perfection; and because of the distress and exile of the holy *Shekhinah.*"[38] And by sharing in the pain of all Jews and every single Jew, he makes abundant whatever their desire. R. Moyshele, the *Maggid* of Kozienice, usually formulated this abundance as comprising: "children, life, sustenance, and healing and wealth and honor and all good for the House of Israel."[39] The zaddik spurs the holy celestial beings on to "drive away the *kelipot* [the shells; the forces of evil which veil the Light], so that they will not be able to hold back abundance from the Jews."[40] It is he who brings about the union of the Holy One, blessed be He, with the *Shekhinah,* which is at the same time His union with the people of Israel. Indeed, according to R. Meir of Opatów, it is fitting that the Holy One, blessed be He, in His love for the people of Israel, "first bestows His blessing upon His children, the Jews who are His holy people," even before that union is accomplished; this is analogous to the statement of our Sages of blessed memory[41] about the rules dealing with the interrelationships of human beings, which require that one conciliate before coming together in union.[42]

One of the principles of Hasidism was that throughout the period of Exile since the destruction of the Temple, the flow of abundance had been reversed, and this is the reason for the difficulty the Jewish people had encountered in earning a livelihood. Earlier, "during the time the Temple existed," abundance flowed mainly to the righteous, that is, to the Jews, and only from the remainder could the wicked, namely Esau, find a livelihood. This is in keeping with Isaac's blessing to Jacob: "Be a *gevir* [lord] over thy brethren," that is, be an actual *gevir,* a rich man.[43] According to R. Ezekiel of Kazimierz, improvement depends on the quality of worship of the Creator; that is, "the *very* choicest of the celestial abundance is for the most holy among the Jews."[44] This same Ezekiel explained that according to the blessing of Isaac, "Let peoples serve thee and nations bow down to thee," the Jewish people in the Diaspora also could benefit indirectly from the abundance of the nations. For even after the nations have become wealthy, they will give money to the Jews so that they may serve God and study His Torah, on the analogy of Zebulon providing the sustenance for Issachar. The relationship is a mutual one: "If the nations will so contrive it" that the Jew should be free from the burden of making a living and devote himself to the service of God, "then they will also have abundance," inasmuch as abundance is brought down to the world only through the service of God.[45] But this theory of ideal symbiosis was based on a division of social functions—economic and spiritual—and was merely a reflection of the dependence of the Jews in Poland for their livelihood upon their gentile clientele, especially upon the benevolence of the Polish squires, the estate owners who paid the "court Jews" their brokers' fees from their economic abundance. Generally, it was the impoverishment of the Jewish community that was reflected in the then-current kabbalistic-Hasidic doctrine concerning the sufferings in Exile, whereby the Gentiles had the preponderant share of the good things. It was the zaddik who was to reverse this situation. Indeed, R. Meir of Opatów never wearied of reiterating in his homilies that the zaddik must direct his prayer in a way that the abundance which he draws down from on high should not be squandered during its descent, and not "wander away," that is, outside, to the Gentiles, but that it mainly reach the Jews, the holy people, with only a residue flowing to the Gentiles, who are "the other side" (Satan's camp).[46]

The Message of the Zaddikim: Consolation and Approbation

The zaddik, the channel of sustenance and abundance, also has it in his power to nullify "all the harsh and evil decrees," inasmuch as "the zaddik rules in the fear of God."[47] According to R. Meir of Opatów, this power over the gentile nations is assured in the verse "The Lord brings to naught the design of the nations."[48] To be sure, it was no coincidence that what was being referred to was not the nullification of existing decrees but the bringing to naught of "the evil designs" for new decrees which were being prepared against the Jews.[49] Hasidic legend also tells of the wonders performed by the zaddikim in nullifying the plans for new decrees. Evidently, the decrees which had already been in effect for a long time were considered to be an evil connected with oppression in the Diaspora which would cease only with the coming of the Redemption. And, indeed, the bitterness of the Jewish population, which sighed and groaned under the yoke of the tyrannical absolutism of the Kingdom of Poland under the overlordship of the czar of Russia, found clear expression in the homilies of the Hasidic leaders, especially those of the school of the "Seer."

The sermons of R. Meir of Opatów reverberate with indignation at the humiliation of the Jewish nation: "The Jews are now despised and scorned in the eyes of the gentile nations."[50] He related the question asked by the sons of Jacob, "Shall one deal with our sister as with a harlot?" to the sorry status in the Diaspora, "for during the Exile the Jews must make themselves acceptable in the eyes of the princes and authorities." The reproach of the Jewish people is also, as it were, the shame of the *Shekhinah,* for it is stated that "you are My servant, in whom I will be glorified,"[51] that is, that "the main principle should be," were it not that the *Shekhinah* is in exile, that "then it would come to pass that my glory is on me, and His on Him." The question put by the sons of Jacob thus alludes to astonishment "that the upper worlds declare and state their surprise." R. Meir ended with a prayer: "Let it be His will . . . that there be a complete redemption" and the glory of Israel be restored.[52] The Redemption will be the compensation for enduring the prolonged shame: "for the zaddik lifts up Israel's desires, as well as the shame they are put to by the gentile nations, to the summit of all yearnings and draws redemption from there to Israel."[53] The Redemption is also a reward for observing the *mizvot* even in the midst of the torment of Exile. R. Meir of Opatów interpreted the Torah's commandment "The Feast of Unleavened Bread you shall keep" as follows: "By means of the observance of the unleavened bread which Israel keeps throughout this bitter Exile in want and oppression, we will quickly merit in our own day the fulfillment of the observance of the Three Pilgrimage Festivals . . . and go up to Zion in song."[54]

R. Moyshele of Kozienice also complained about the humiliation of the nation in exile in his generation, finding solace for himself and offering the comforting thought that despite it all Israel had not ceased to be the chosen of God, His treasured people, "His delightful children." Thus he expounded on the verse, "For the Lord has called Jacob unto Himself":[55] "For Jacob, although downtrodden and humiliated as at the present time during our Exile—for we are despised and lowly—was nevertheless chosen by God."[56] He bemoaned the fate of the Jews in their "cruel and bitter Exile," saying that "each year we hope and look for redemption and salvation, but it is remote from us, and because of the multitude of our sins the yoke of Exile is protracted for us, and the burden of subjugation is beyond our capacity to endure; and time and again the yoke of servitude is made heavier upon us and the burden of the Exile grows quickly. . . ."[57] In one of his sermons for Yom Kippur, the *maggid* poured out his bitter heart against their lot: ". . . for because of our many sins we have been visited by the decrees of the gentile nations, who have made enactments against Jews in the matter of their livelihood and have laid a heavy yoke upon them through the imposition of taxes. And they have placed in particular a heavy onus upon the residents of the villages, the lessees of inns, by the amount of taxes they must pay, so that they cannot bear it."[58]

All the decrees were designed to strike at the religion of the Jews, for in depriving Jews of their bread, they were distracting them from the single-minded worship of God. This is alluded to in the words of Mordecai in the Scroll of Esther:

> For our enemy oppressors confuse our minds with their evil designs, constantly devising cruel decrees against us to take from each Jew his means of sustenance, so that nothing remains to us in this bitter Exile with which to make a living and keep one's wife and children alive. And, we cannot set our thoughts in order that we be able to pray with intent as is proper, because of the great oppressive yoke of the Exile which bears down upon us so that we are unable to endure it.[59]

It goes without saying that the impoverished Jews were not able to engage in the study of the Torah.[60] Moreover, the gentile nations induced the Jews "to forsake the Jewish religion" by granting those who did so immunity "from all taxes, burdens, and persecutions."[61] The *maggid*, who understood quite well the clerical politics of the reactionary absolutism in Russia and Poland, expressed his distress over the fact that there were some individuals who did not resist temptation. But he used one set of terms for "the impious who change their religion and are tranquil and at ease without any trouble or sorrow, lacking nothing whatsoever,"[62] namely, those careerist, ambitious financial barons, and another set of terms for those "villagers who were compelled to change their religion because of their poverty."[63] But all those who forsook their people and their faith were exceptions, and the *maggid* spoke with pride of "the simple Jewish folk who proclaim themselves to bear the name of Jacob . . . [and who] are already known for the soundness of their hearts and greatness of their sincerity, for they have suffered much severe and bitter agony in order to remain within the Jewish faith." For the *maggid*, the meaning of "You shall show faithfulness to Jacob and mercy to Abraham"[64] was "that this faithfulness and great uprightness of the congregation of Jacob will abide with them forever, and then, as a matter of course, mercy will be granted to Abraham."[65]

The *maggid* R. Moyshele quite often gave vent in his sermons to his anger at those who oppressed and mocked his people. He called for vengeance like that wreaked upon Pharaoh and his servants, "so even now, as in the time of our departure from Egypt, He will show us His wondrous deeds, bringing judgment upon our enemies."[66] When the Redemption comes "He will be your God," namely, "He whose name is blessed will be manifest to you also in the aspect of *Elohim,* the aspect of strength and justice, when you will need the quality of strength to bring justice upon the enemies of Israel and be avenged of those that persecute them."[67] "Then the Holy One, blessed be He, will don a cloak of zeal and vengeance, to bring justice upon our foes and repel all our enemies before us. And he will cast them down . . . before us until there will no longer abide in them any strength to make any decrees against Israel."[68] In a sermon for Ḥanukkah, the *maggid* prayed that "He whose name is blessed, grant that the great illumination and fervor enter into the hearts of our brethren, the Children of Israel, leading them to His service. Thus the kindling, the burning, and the flames which issued forth to distribute themselves[69] among the wicked Gentiles who plan evil designs against us shall bring a conflagration of God to consume them like thorns which have been cut down. . . .[70]

In spite of all these outbursts of pent-up anger, the *maggid*, being imbued with the ethical tradition of the Bible and the Talmud, cannot disregard the doctrine of the Prophets as reflected in the passage, "I have no pleasure in the death of the wicked . . . but that he turn from his way and live."[71] Nor could he disregard the famous statement of R. Meir's wife: "Let *sins* cease out of the earth . . . does it then say *sinners*? It states rather—*sins.*"[72] Moreover, the kabbalistic-Hasidic doctrine which is based on the mystical principle of the predominance of *midat ha-ḥesed* over *midat ha-din* in both the upper and lower worlds did not hold much store in *midat ha-din,* for if it were to prevail for even a brief moment in the world there was the real danger that even the people of Israel would not be judged righteous. It is therefore not surprising that the angry cry for vengeance against the willful and evil kingdom was moderated. Thus, the *maggid*'s goal was the salvation of the Jews and not the destruction of the wicked.

It is in this light that the *maggid* interprets the verse in the Sabbath hymn, "O, continue thy loving kindness to those who know Thee, zealous and vengeful God," saying that "this in itself, which is for the good of Israel, will be a form of vengeance upon our foes, being, as it were, a matter of inflicting a blow and a healing."[73] Enlarging upon this theme, he explained that

> . . . the zaddik may desire to bring judgment upon Israel's enemies and to deal them a grievous blow. But it is not the zaddik's wont to harm any creature in

the world, especially so because he does not want to arouse *midat ha-din* in the world; the zaddik therefore wraps his action in the aspect of mercy, so that it may come to help Israel to rid itself of the yoke of subjugation to the wicked. And this will, of course, compel the wicked man to turn away from his wickedness, so that he will not do any more harm to anyone among the Children of Israel.[74]

To be sure, the *maggid* could not entirely restrain his vengeful impulses; in another exposition he contended that bringing justice to the tyrannical and dominant nation would by itself bring all manner of blessings to the Jewish people: "For lo, there will descend [punishment] on Edom and a whirlwind will come down upon the heads of the wicked, and through this judgment all kinds of good will accrue to Israel."[75]

Redemption through Repentance

With all the yearning for the Day of Judgment and the Redemption, a program for satisfying the minimal daily needs of the people held an important place in Hasidic doctrine as long as the nation languished under the yoke of Exile. This program was reflected in the doctrine of the *Yiḥudim* (actions designed to restore the true unity of God) and bring abundance down to the earth. It was articulated in the sermons of the disciples of the "Seer" of Lublin and the *Maggid* of Kozienice. The son of the *maggid* applied the verse, "And his king shall be higher than Agag,"[76] to the activities of the "perfect zaddik," through whom

the Kingdom of the blessed One will be elevated and exalted throughout the whole world, and all the decrees which they want to issue against the Jews will be annulled, and He whose name is blessed, in the multitude of His mercies, will implant good within the heart of kings and princes so that they will do us good with all manner of loving kindness and good that abound in the world.[77]

In another place he says that "in our own time the counsel of the nations of the world 'who devise decrees against Israel' shall fail and their designs will be thwarted," while for Israel, "He will issue decrees of beneficence, salvation, and solace." This is alluded to in the verse, "The same day came they into the Wilderness of Sinai,"[78] as well as in the passage from the Song of Songs, "Let him kiss me with the kisses of his mouth," that is, "we seek in this cruel Exile . . . to merit even now that state of delight and pleasure which prevailed at the time of the creation of the world for Israel."[79] In this theory of Hasidism, even temporary succor from the wicked lies within the power of the zaddik.

As R. Moyshele of Kozienice explained, the superiority of the zaddik over the angels consisted in his power to cause children, life, and nourishment to be bestowed upon Israel, and power and justice upon those who hate the Lord, whereas each of the angels is only in charge of a particular matter—for example, Michael is responsible for grace; Gabriel, for power; and Raphael, for healing. "The sacred kingdom," the *maggid* goes on to explain, has a scale, "and that which for Israel is *midat ha-ḥesed,* is *midat ha-din* for the oppressive kingdom."[80] The zaddik "mitigates all the judgments at their very roots to convert them to mercy . . . so that they [the Children of Israel] will be able to endure the Exile—until our Messiah comes." As it is stated in the blessing of Jacob to Issachar, "And he bowed his shoulder to bear and became a servant under taskwork," that is, until the Redemption, "so that Esau will be under taskwork and we will be free men."[81]

In line with his colleague from Kozienice, R. Meir of Opatów commented on "She rises while it is yet night,"[82] saying that "Israel in Exile will be saved and rise up expansively and in comfort, and it is toward this end that we pray and this is implied in redemption."[83] But in contrast to the zaddik of Kozienice, who saw temporary deliverance mainly as the nullification of the oppressive edicts, R. Meir conceived of it in terms of "expansiveness," "sustenance in comfort," and "great wealth and much honor." It is for such a redemption in the midst of tranquillity that the zaddik prays, even though it lies within his power to annul the evil decrees against Israel, as well as being "able to exert influence that they be saved from the Wars of Gog and Magog before the complete Redemption."[84]

The fulfillment of this yearning for redemption while in a state of ease seemed to grow even more remote as the condition of the Jewish multitudes in Poland worsened. Therefore, R. Meir of Opatów added an explanation to the doctrine of salvation based on the juxtaposition of two prophecies heralding the Redemption, "Ye shall go forth with joy,"[85] and "They shall come with weeping, and with supplications will I lead them."[86] R. Meir explained that "the Redemption will no doubt proceed in the midst of joy only by virtue of the weeping of Israel out of its anguish." It is out of these tears, together with those shed by the zaddikim out of their joy in cleaving to God, that "Israel will deserve redemption."[87] From this it may be concluded that the era of expansiveness in Exile will in itself be a sign of the Redemption to come.

In full accordance with the tradition of the Prophets, and Sages of the Talmud and Kabbalah, the leaders of the Hasidim in that generation taught that complete redemption depends upon repentance. In the words of R. Ezekiel of Kazimierz, "all redemptions must come through repentance."[88] And although everything is in God's hands, and even repentance depends on His will, yet "the Lord thy God will turn thy captivity and have compassion upon thee," that is, "although He whose name is blessed will induce you to repent, He will nevertheless love you."[89] Similarly, R. Moyshele of Kozienice taught "that it is impossible that the Redemption and the advent of our righteous Messiah will come but through repentance at the end of time." It is therefore incumbent upon Israel to pray to God that "the spirit [of the Lord] be poured from on high" upon him, "to bring him near to perfect repentance," and "that He implant it in our hearts to return in perfect repentance." Even the fact that servitude in Exile is ever more severe and "the yoke of the Exile is increasingly heavier" demonstrates God's intent to bring the nation to perfect repentance in order to hasten the Redemption. In the name of R. Abraham Joshua of Opatów, the author of *Ohev Yisrael* (Lover of Israel), the son of the *Maggid* of Kozienice stated "that before the coming of the Messiah, the Jews will be driven out of the villages."[90] The "Holy Grandfather" of Radoszyce found support for the idea that redemption comes about through increased suffering in the verse, "And the sons of Dan: Hushim."[91] He said, "If the children are judged"—namely, if the principle of justice is dominant and evil decrees multiply—then the Redemption will come "quietly."[92]

Even according to the doctrine of the Kabbalah, repentance is an indispensable condition for Redemption, for in its view the Messianic Era depends upon the completion of the purification of the souls. It is not only that the Messiah is the last soul, whose descent from heaven is delayed as long as the souls of all Jews have not yet been purified, but also that He is "a composite of the souls of all of Israel," so that the blemish of any single Jew is also His own. R. Moyshele of Kozienice and R. Meir of Opatów found in Isaiah 53 an allusion to the idea that repentance is a *mizvah* calling for compassion for the Messiah in that He suffers for the sins of all Israel, lovingly taking upon himself the afflictions which should have come upon the nation of Israel. This suffering of the Messiah is in itself enough to arouse "reflections of penitence in the hearts of sinners in Israel . . . to the extent that there should be no need for afflictions to beset the Messiah of God." According to the *maggid* R. Moses ben Israel, this commandment regarding both compassion and acceleration of the Redemption is alluded to in the verse "If thou at all take thy neighbor's garment to pledge, thou shalt restore it to him by the time that the sun goeth down."[93] R. Meir of Opatów infers this *mizvah* from the verse "Thou shalt not muzzle the ox when he treadeth out the corn"[94] on the ground that "Messiah, the son of Joseph, is called *shor* [an ox]."[95]

The zaddik also served an important function in the matter of repentance. R. Moyshele of Kozienice explained that from the fervor of the penitent, "radiance is increased in the zaddik," which is the meaning of the verse, "And the angel of the Lord appeared to him in a flame of fire in the midst of a bush. . . ."[96] R. Meir of Opatów elevated the rank of the zaddik even more than any of his contemporaries. He also urged his listeners to speed the coming of the "two Messiahs," Messiah ben Joseph and Messiah ben David, by worshipping the Creator;[97] yet in his teaching, it is the repentance of the zaddik that is stressed, as in his explication of the words of Joseph "I seek my brethren. Tell me, I pray thee, where they are feeding the flock." The *maggid* said that "this is what the Holy One, blessed be He, says to the zaddik, . . . 'Speak to Me, confess your wicked deeds to Me, and do penitence in My presence in behalf of all Israel and I will accept it as if they had done penitence and I will forgive them.'"[98]

Unity of Israel: The Hasidic Path to Redemption

One of the chief ways of hastening the Redemption is the unity of Israel, a fundamental tenet of Hasidic doctrine from its beginning. R. Ezekiel of Kazimierz explained the connection between unity and redemption according to the tradition of the Talmud concerning the cause of the destruction of the Temple, "The Redemption will result mainly from the unity of the Children of Israel; for since the destruction of the Temple was caused by baseless hatred, to mend matters there must be selfless love, that is, every Jew should love his fellow Jew gratuitously, inasmuch as he worships the Lord like him, and through this means the Redemption will come to pass. Amen! May this be His will!"[99] R. Meir of Opatów chided his contemporaries who were worthy of witnessing the advent of the Messiah by dint of their knowledge but not in their "disregard for the total community of Israel." "The essential improvement is that amity, fraternity, and close attachment prevail throughout the Jewish nation."[100] When there is no union "the word of God is in exile," and conversely, "when there is union below, then there is also union on high."[101]

It can be seen from the above formulation that the unity of Israel consisted of "amity, fraternity, and close attachment," that is, a solid front against the oppression of the dominant nation, as well as mutual assistance, a quality in which—according to all official documents—the Hasidim excelled.[102] At times, the call for union even conveyed a hint of social solidarity among the classes. R. Ezekiel of Kazimierz preached not only "that every one should feel concern for the welfare of his neighbor and pray over his neighbor's distress more than over his own," but also that "when he sees good redounding to his neighbor, even if because of this he will be deprived, let him not have any misgivings whatsoever."[103] To be sure, just as the poor man is forbidden to envy one who is richer than he, a person who has attained "importance, wealth, or wisdom" must conduct himself with modesty, which is a sign that his superiority was bestowed on him by God for his good and not by Satan for his harm.[104] This Hasidic leader ascribed to the matter of unity a meaning which is both individualistic and realistic: Israel (Yisrael) may be compared to the Torah, as is demonstrated by the acronym for the phrase *Yesh Shishim Ribo Otiyot Latorah* (the Torah contains 600,000 letters), which in turn is equal to the number of Israelites who went out of Egypt. Thus each man in Israel has "a root and a letter in the Torah." The levels of unity and its essence follow from this: "And just as in each scroll of the Torah there must be parchment around it so as not to touch the Torah, so must the [divine] service of each Jew be singled out unto him without touching that of his fellow. And just as no letter of a word in a Torah scroll may be far from its neighbor, so people who are close to each other must not grow far apart; and just as every Torah scroll must be stitched together in order to possess the sanctity of a Torah scroll and not that of a *Ḥumash* [a book of the Pentateuch], so must all Jews be united together . . . and the people who are closest are like one word and others like a *parashah* [a chapter] and others like a *seder* [a section] and yet others like a *sefer* [a book]."[105] This unity that does not exclude the personal way of worshipping the Creator is compounded of concentric circles, from the inner circle, of those who are closest, to the outer circle, which encompasses the whole nation of Israel.

The "Holy Grandfather" of Radoszyce gave the precept of union a Hasidic folk character, as, for example, in his assuring his devotees that the fact that "they eat a meal together leads to their associating with each other" and "then there need be no apprehension that they will not know how to pray with proper intent, because their very association is reckoned by God as equivalent to introducing all the appropriate intent in our prayers"; moreover, "through this, He will save them from their distress."[106]

It is natural that in their discourses, the Hasidic leaders did not overlook the talmudic tradition based on the prophets' views of the importance of charity for redemption. R. Meir of Opatów, particularly, taught the obligation to be charitable and gave a mystical explanation of how charity brings about salvation. He claimed that the statement in the Gemara, "Great is charity, for it brings Redemption close,"[107] was intended to indicate actual union of the (kabbalistic) Spheres, as "when a poor man comes to the door, he brings the left close to the right and the letters of *Mashiaḥ* will be completed."[108]

It is self-evident that the significant role assigned to the zaddik by the schools of the "Seer" of Lublin and the *Maggid* of Kozienice included his mission to accelerate and actually bring about the Redemption. The son of the *Maggid* of Kozienice concluded, from the verse "Ye shall grant a redemption to the land,"[109] that the zaddik had the power to bring it about. The initial letters of the verse "**G**eulah **t**itnu **l**a-areẓ are "Gimal Lamed Tav," and the meaning of the verse is "that the true zaddik alters the combination of the letters **GLT** and converts it into a combination meaning *geulah* [redemption]."[110] R. Meir of Opatów, a disciple of the "Seer," taught that Redemption is dependent on the "worship of the zaddikim": they "extend the will of God to the limits of each level, and then all judgments will be mitigated and there will be a perfect Redemption." The zaddik "draws down the soul of our Messiah, the Righteous One, to the world" and by means of his *repairs* in the upper worlds he "will speed the Ingathering of the Exiles."[111]

In their sermons about the Redemption, the Hasidic leaders reflected the state of mind of the masses of Jews in Poland, "whose eyes failed" while waiting for the end of their distress and emergence into freedom. The frequency of these sermons points to the aim of the Hasidic leaders to strengthen the spirit of the nation and to encourage its hope for Redemption.

Despite the disappointment of their expectations during the epochal days of Napoleon, the disciples of the "Seer" and the *Maggid* of Kozienice remained confident that the Redemption was at hand. It was not just for rhetorical effect that R. Moyshele said, "Each year we hope and look for salvation but it is remote from us. . . ."[112] He warned his audience against accepting his explanations about the Redemption as nothing more than fine preaching; his sermon about the two Messiahs—the son of Joseph and the son of David—who, he maintained, are alluded to in the verse, "And of all thy cattle thou shalt sanctify the males, the firstlings of ox and sheep"[113] (*peter,* firstling, that is, the start of the complete Redemption; a *shor,* ox, Messiah, the son of Joseph; and *seh,* sheep, Messiah, the son of David). He concluded with the assertion, "And as Heaven is my witness, that I have come not for preaching but for action," namely to urge greater "intensity in the worship of the blessed One" and more good deeds in order to accelerate the Redemption. And he goes on to pray:

> May it be pleasing before the Creator of the universe, the Lord of hosts, and may it be a time of favor from the blessed One to speed for us the hour of

Redemption and salvation and, as in the days of our departure from the land of Egypt, may He show us wondrous deeds, sending us our righteous Messiah speedily in our own time. And may Judah and Jerusalem be saved before our very eyes and may He grant us everlasting Redemption so that we may live to go up to Zion in song. . . .[114]

The expounders of Hasidism were fully aware of the stringent exhortation in the Talmud "not to force the end," that is, the coming of the Messiah; the very fact that the Jews remained faithful to this exhortation, enduring persecution with forbearance, meant—as R. Moyshele of Kozienice pleaded and hoped—that the Redemption would soon come. In a discourse for Hoshana Rabba (the seventh day of Sukkot), he expounded upon the text, "she who is scattered among those who vex her" as follows:

For our Sages have stated that one of the three oaths with which God adjured Israel requires that they will not force the end.[115] And for some time now we have been fulfilling our oath and do not at all force the end, but we endure whatever is decreed, as long as we have the strength to suffer. And this is the significance of the verse in question. For now we are scattered unto every corner among wicked idolaters and heretics who are like an *akhs'a* [adder] or like vipers who sting us so very much that we no longer have strength to bear it. And it is therefore fitting and proper that you soon deliver us out of their hand.[116]

R. Meir of Opatów viewed his contemporaries as "a generation near to our righteous Messiah," as is intimated in the verse "This day ye go forth in the month Aviv,"[117] as well as in the verse "And it came to pass that on the sixth day they gathered twice as much bread,"[118] which is "an allusion to the sixth millennium." Consequently, there is no longer a need in his generation for many *repairs* in order to elevate "the sparks which had fallen below." In earlier generations, there had been a need for asceticism "in order to break up the shells and to set aside the curtains from the souls," whereas now it was sufficient that "they believe in the God of the universe and in their belief they shall live." Of course, "whatever in former years was corrected over a long period of time, will now be repaired . . . almost instantly in order to bring near the time of Redemption. . . ."[119]

In this view of Redemption, Ereẓ Yisrael was considered as the nation's homeland which awaited the return of its children. At times, the Hasidic leaders of this school strongly emphasized the historical right of the Jewish people to return to its land. Thus R. Moyshele of Kozienice expounded on the verse, "In the year of the jubilee the field shall return to him of whom it was bought, even to him to whom the possession of the land belongeth,"[120] saying, ". . . For everything in the heavens and on the earth is His and He gave us for our inheritance the Holy Land, and perhaps the time and season to lead us to our land has arrived and you are the one who detains it."[121] R. Ezekiel of Kazimierz went into a political and juridical discourse to prove that Ereẓ Yisrael is destined to return to the Jewish nation. The point of departure of his homily is the verse "For ye are not as yet come to the rest and the inheritance."[122] He went on to explain that since Ishmael, the son of Hagar, the maidservant of Sarah, was the servant of Israel and since, according to the law, a servant's property becomes the property of his master, then Ereẓ Yisrael, which is under the dominion of Ishmael, does not pass out of the authority of the nation of Israel. And in His kindness, God has pledged to the people of Israel "that it will yet come under the control of Israel."[123] It is likely that the zaddik heard reports of the rivalry among the great powers of Europe with regard to Turkey and its claims to Palestine by right of possession.

In addition to the political aspect of the Redemption, R. Ezekiel also gave the term *naḥalah* (inheritance, possession) the meaning of "heritage," in keeping with the well-known notion of the "little sanctuary" in the Diaspora: "a heritage unto Israel, His servant."[124] This was to teach us that "he who serves Him of the blessed name also has a heritage in his own home," that is, "in *his* dwelling he had—in a certain sense—Ereẓ Yisrael."[125]

In contrast to this school of Hasidism, the outstanding representatives of which were the disciples of the "Seer" of Lublin and the *Maggid* of Kozienice, faith was indentified as casting one's burden upon the omnipotent zaddik. At the same time there was widespread throughout Poland an extreme form of folk Hasidism which brought heaven down to earth for the multitudes of devotees and also brought the zaddik down to the level of a wonder worker. While theoretical Hasidism was still being fostered in the courts of Kozienice, Opatów, and Kazimierz, the Hasidism which flourished in the courts of the "wonder workers" was exclusively practical Kabbalah.

Zaddikism Taken to Its Extreme: The "Wonder Workers"

Among the many "wonder workers" who were active in Poland in that era, the following became famous: R. Yeraḥmiel of Przysucha, the son of "the Holy Jew"; R. Joseph Barukh of Neustadt, "the Good Jew," the son of R. Kalman of Cracow and author of the commentary on the Torah *Maor Veshemesh;* R. Ḥayyim Meir Jeḥiel of Mogielnica; R. Ḥayyim David "Doktor" of Piotrków; and above all, the "Holy Grandfather," R. Issachar Ber of Radoszyce.

The biography of R. Issachar Ber, mainly a legendary account, before "he became revealed" as one of the zaddikim of the age faithfully reflects this firm belief of the multitude of Hasidim in miraculous salvation for those who trust wholeheartedly in God. The youth and early manhood of R. Issachar Ber were spent in poverty and want. Like the Ba'al Shem Tov, with whom his Hasidic devotees compared him, he started out as a *melamed* (after marrying a woman in Chęciny, near Kielce). Unsuccessful in this profession, he peddled small wares in the villages. But after his pious wife took upon herself the burden of earning a living, as did many wives of Hasidim, he devoted himself entirely to Torah and prayer. Yet he was like the pious man in the hymn sung on the termination of the Sabbath who had neither food nor sustenance . . . nor clothing to wear. The Hasidic legend about the Passover Seder which was prepared for him by the angels Michael and Gabriel in the likeness of two *daytshn* (German Jews)[126] later served as a basis for the story by I. L. Peretz, "Der Kuntsn-makher" (The Magician). In the meantime, he wore out his feet going to the courts of the great Hasidic leaders of his generation, such as R. Moses Leyb of Sasów, R. Abraham Joshua Heschel of Opatów, R. Jacob Isaac, the "Seer" of Lublin, R. Israel, the *Maggid* of Kozienice, and *ha-Yehudi* from Przysucha. As he himself later boasted, he succeeded in "serving and studying under one hundred twenty sages, all of them divinely inspired."[127] It is apparent that at this period in his life he was one of the vagrant wayfarers who were depicted by his biographer as "zaddikim who wandered and drifted from city to city as was then their fashion."[128] Even after he moved to Chmielnik, there was no improvement in his highly straitened circumstances, and he was still regarded by people as "Berel Batlan" (Berel the Ne'er-do-well) when he settled in Radoszyce, where he subsequently occupied the post of rabbi. In this tiny town, there were 476 Jews out of a total of 1,626 inhabitants in 1827.[129]

Various legends concerning the way the "Holy Grandfather" of Radoszyce "revealed himself" are recounted by his disciples and in turn, by their disciples.[130] The most plausible of them is the account in which he, as the central character, tells about a *melamed* without a post, who, before being revealed, eked out a meager living by healing the sick through his prayers. Once, when "all hope was fled . . . and his wife and children were crying for bread and there was none," the *melamed* tearfully poured his heart out before God: "Master of the universe, what will you lose if some sick person should be cured instantly and give me something in order to keep my soul alive? I do not mean to be presumptuous, God forbid,[131] but I am in great peril and my life hangs by a hair. Master of the universe, take pity on me and the souls of my household, for their lives are not worth living." The Zaddik of Radoszyce ended by saying that

When the *melamed* ended his prayer, God[132] helped him, and all the people of the town came running to him; this one came telling him that his wife was having difficulty giving birth, God forbid,[133] and gave him a certain sum, and this one came because his son had fainted, God forbid, and that one came because an evil spirit[134] had attached itself to his house, and the daughter of yet another . . . had disappeared, so that the poor man now had the wherewithal to supply all his needs. . . .

And as the legend has it, the Rabbi of Radoszyce had hardly ended his story when the house in which he was staying was virtually besieged by men, women, and children crying for his help in alleviating their suffering or curing the maladies besetting the members of their families or because their wives were having difficulty giving birth.[135]

One important detail about the zaddik is to be found in another story which also was reported in the name of the Zaddik of Radoszyce, but told as a true story rather than a fable. The "Holy Grandfather" tells one of his disciples that a marked change for the good in his distressed existence came when, by means of his prayer, the daughter of one of the notables of Radoszyce was healed: "Thenceforth Jews began to flock to me and reward me generously, so that I would pray in their behalf and they would be blessed for my sake."[136] These two complementary stories reflect the precarious status of local rebbes who were "zaddikim in their towns only," and who earned their meager livings by saying prayers for the sick when the opportunity offered itself. There were times when they were compelled to pray that a sick person should chance their way so that he would be delivered from his illness and they from their bitter poverty. At the same time, these stories explain how this kind of "healer of the sick" rose to the level of "wonder worker," for his reputation would spread beyond the boundaries of his town if he succeeded in performing "a great miracle" which aroused wonder and admiration.

The fame of the "Holy Grandfather" of Radoszyce after he "revealed himself" did indeed spread throughout Poland, and according to the Hasidic tradition, in the course of a few weeks some four hundred sick people came to him for help.[137] Also many mentally ill people from all corners of the land were brought to him, and in two years "he exorcised some fifteen evil spirits and *dibbukim*."[138] His method of healing the sick consisted mainly of remedies, but there were instances when it was only through physical contact. His remedies were a mixture of the sacred, the magical, and folk medicine, the "pharmacy" being made up of the

> remains of jars, the residue of oil from Hanukkah lamps, the left-over wine from the Kiddush and Havdalah [benedictions ushering in the Sabbath and bidding it farewell] and of the *Afikoman* [the last morsel of matzoh eaten at the Passover seder] and of the four species [of the *lulav*] and the willows and Hoshanahs [yellow twigs held at the Hoshana prayer], the remains of myrtle leaves and the drippings from the Havdalah candles, the wax from the candles for Yom Kippur, and other such residues of objects used in performing a *miẓvah*.[139]

Besides these remedies, the wonder worker of Radoszyce also used a most simple nostrum for healing the sick: drinking water from the well in the rebbe's yard was deemed a sure cure for all kinds of ailments.

In an emergency, when the number of sick was too large for the Zaddik of Radoszyce to give his personal attention, he would heal all of them in a group. It is reasonable to assume that he learned this collective treatment from his teacher, "the lover of Israel" from Opatów, who did not hesitate to pile all the slips, each bearing the name of a person seeking help, together and to pray for the deliverance of all of them. When about four hundred sick were assembled at the home of the Zaddik of Radoszyce, he ordered his attendant to announce in all the synagogues and inns that they should come at a specified time the following day to the well in his courtyard. At the appointed time they all assembled "and many who could not walk had to be brought there in small carts." Two strong men drew water from the well and apportioned it to the sick, telling them whether to drink it or to wash in it. The narrator ended his account by noting that all for whom waters from the "well of salvation" were drawn were healed. This strange scene brings to mind a picture of Lourdes when it first became famous as a holy spring, but there is a distinct difference. According to this account, the miracle occurred mainly by virtue of the "Holy Grandfather's" prayer: "He sweetened the waters for me for one hour, so that I would be able to heal by means of them . . . so that I would not need to spend my time and cancel my [Torah] lesson"; moreover, those who did not have faith in him and did not take water from the well were turned away.[140] The zaddik and wonder worker R. Ḥayyim David "Doktor" of Piotrków, although a skilled physician, nonetheless placed his trust in prayer. In his approach to healing the sick, he applied the verse "He creates remedies. He is revered in praises. He is the Lord of wonders."[141] If a prescribed remedy was ineffective, he would order the sick person's household to recite psalms, and if the danger was imminent, he placed his hope in the wonders of the Creator.

Aside from healing the sick, which included exorcising evil spirits (dybbuks), the Zaddik of Radoszyce was a helper in all kinds of trouble. He gave succor to lessees in the villages whose rents for their inns had been increased by the estate owners; to rich lessees in the cities who had lawsuits with the lord of the city; to moneylenders who were dunning the noblemen for the payment of debts; to artisans, such as bakers, who were troubled by gentile competitors. And it need scarcely be stated that pleas for help came to him from unfortunate *agunot* (abandoned wives). The tales about those in a predicament most frequently involved village Jews seeking vindication in lawsuits in the courts.[142] These village Jews and simple folk were the source of the wonder worker's store of abundant humor and of his knowledge of Polish expressions which served him as a basis for his puns.[143]

The "Holy Grandfather" of Radoszyce was confident that his help extended to anyone coming into contact with him, however indirectly, be it no more than touching the knob on his door. Even one traveling to him or merely intending to visit him could be helped.[144] In an unwitting confirmation of Aksenfeld's anti-Hasidic satire, the following *aggadah* preserved in his family tells of his marvels: It happened that the zaddik promised rainfall to a Hasid who wanted to bathe while on the road, and some moments later he promised the opposite to a Hasid who requested that there not be any rain. When the first Hasid expressed astonishment at this contradiction, he replied: After all, he worships Him whose name is blessed, "who is all-powerful and is capable of providing for the needs of all."[145] It is true that even in boasting of his numerous miracles, which greatly exceeded the number of miracles wrought by the Ba'al Shem Tov, he knew "his place as one of the epigones of Hasidism." He explained the difference between himself and the Ba'al Shem Tov in this way: "Miracles were wrought for the Ba'al Shem Tov on the strength of his righteousness and holiness, whereas for me, they were wrought only because of God's compassion."[146] He also was conscious of the blessing he received from the "Seer" of Lublin, according to which his strength would lie only in wonders and not in Torah and prayer, nor in "serious matters" generally: "God will provide you with Jews who will tear you away from Torah and prayer."[147] It was in this spirit that he explained his role in Hasidism to his disciple R. Solomon of Radomsko, the author of *Tiferet Shelomo* (The Grandeur of Solomon). That is, he was sent into this world to propagate the divinity of Him whose name is blessed throughout the world, but not merely "to praise and glorify His holy name."[148] R. Isaac Meir of Ger (Góra Kalwaria), the distinguished disciple of R. Mendel of Kock (Kotsk), properly defined the contrast between the two extremes in Hasidism—the refined and the vulgar. The difference is that in Kock they brought the hearts of the Jews closer to their Father in heaven, while in Radoszyce they brought their Father in heaven to dwell within the hearts of the Jews.[149]

A New Branch of Hasidism Emerges

The opposition to the Hasidism of the Lublin school broke out in the camp of Hasidim in Poland during the lifetime of the "Seer" of Lublin, and was organized at his "court" under the banner of R. Jacob Isaac of Przysucha, *ha-Yehudi* (the Jew). The counterpart in the history of the Hasidic movement in the Ukraine was the activity of R. Naḥman of Bratslav.[150] As in the Ukraine, the aim of the opposition was the regeneration of Hasidism and the refurbishing of its tarnished prestige. The common factor in both branches of Hasidism was also apparent in the content of the regeneration: Contrary to the system of miracles and assistance, the reformers—each in his respective area—called for a deepening faith in Hasidism, praising highly the virtue of absolute faith while negating every element of naturalism in its philosophy. Both the system of Bratslav and the system of Przysucha-Kock emphasized a pronounced proclivity to negate "this world" and all material concerns and to affirm the ascetic way of life. Both schools enjoined their devotees to punctiliously avoid sin and urged them to enter the road to penitence. Again, like the Hasidim of Bratslav, the Hasidim of Przysucha-Kock stood apart from the common mass of Hasidim. And just as the Hasidim of Bratslav mocked and derided R. Aryeh Leyb, "the good Jew," the savior of the masses, the "Grandfather of Shpola," the elitist Hasidim of Kock made the "Holy Grandfather" of Radoszyce the object of their scorn. In view of this similarity, it is not at all astonishing that the Hasidim of Kock esteemed, over all the Hasidic literature, the writings of the leader of the Hasidim of Bratslav.[151]

Nevertheless, with all their common elements, there was also a great difference between the two systems in both their doctrinal and their social bases. The Bratslavian Hasidism remained an isolated sect, with no marked influence among the masses of Hasidim in the Ukraine, whereas the doctrine that emerged from Przysucha struck deep roots in Hasidism in Poland and continued to exert a strong influence on later generations.

The Hasidism of Przysucha-Kock, while professing the principle of the duty to attach oneself to the zaddik, conceived of the role of the zaddik in a new light. The zaddik is, first and foremost, the guide who leads his Hasidim to a way of life of Torah and faith. The obligation of perfecting one's virtues and ascending from level to level in the service of God is incumbent not only upon the zaddik, but on every individual. In a declaration of war against all the superficiality and externality in the observance of the faith, and in the wake of the aspiration to deepen religious feeling and to purify it of all the dross of material "motives," the virtue of truth was stressed as one of the highest principles; this deepening of spiritual life was linked with the individualism that ran through the doctrine of Przysucha-Kock. This individualism reflected both the social standard of the middle-class well-to-do Hasidim of Przysucha and the self-exaltation of this class over the multitude of simple folk who were accustomed to the traditional religious practices and absorbed in the routine of daily life.

Hasidism, as established in Przysucha, was distinguished from the very start by the elevation of the study of the Gemara to a central place in the Hasid's way of life. This was carried out to such a degree that even in the time of *ha-Yehudi,* his Hasidism was defined by his Galician contemporary, Uri, the *Saraf* of Strelisk, as "the worship of the Lord through Torah and prayer together."[152] The leaders of the Hasidim were scholars who had thoroughly studied Talmud and *Posekim* at the Yeshivot in Poland and abroad. At their meetings they would engage in casuistic interpretations of the Gemara and the commentaries, and their homilies were interlaced with their own interpretations of the Gemara. According to Hasidic tradition, R. Ḥayyim of Płońsk praised the disciples of R. Simḥah Bunem, saying, "R. Isaac of Warka is a scholar; R. Isaac Meir of Warsaw [who founded the dynasty of Ger] is brilliant; as for R. Menaḥem Mendel of Tomaszów [who later moved to Kock], his colleagues are unable to comprehend his thoughts."[153] They also urged their Hasidim to devote themselves to the daily study of Gemara. In the name of *ha-Yehudi* of Przysucha, it was reported that in the study of the Torah every morning were encompassed all the virtues enumerated in the Talmud concerning *pat shaḥarit,* i.e., "the morning bread."[154] An allusion to this is to be found in this same tradition in that *pat* has the same numerical value as *Talmud*.[155] R. Isaac of Warka said that the desire to study Torah is a real desire only when a person does not want to do anything but study. It is reported that his last words before his death were, "The Gemara is the greatest purification."[156] The Hasidic rebbes also gave lessons in the Talmud to groups of their Hasidim. Simḥah Bunem of Przysucha required everyone in his group to develop some new interpretations of the Halakha.[157] R. Isaac of Warka studied Mishnah and Gemara with his Hasidim.[158] The Hasidim of the Przysucha fraternity would gather in their respective cities for study sessions on the Gemara; and there were some who even shortened their prayer services on Rosh Hashanah and Yom Kippur to devote more time to the study of Gemara.[159] R. Mendel of Kock required the merchants who visited him but did not belong to his group of Hasidim "to rob themselves of at least one hour every day for the study of the Gemara."[160]

Whereas the dignity of the Talmud was elevated, that of the Kabbalah was lowered. The system of mystery in general no longer held a significant place in the doctrine of the school of Przysucha; obviously, those subjects which constituted the main preachments of the earlier Hasidic leaders, that is, the prevalence of *midat ha-ḥesed* over *midat ha-din,* reunion in the upper spheres, combinations of letters, bringing down the flow of Divine Grace, were rare or altogether absent. No wonder that the role of the zaddik as the conduit of the flow of grace and the foundation of the universe was no longer emphasized. R. Simḥah Bunem found it necessary to supply a reason for limiting one's preoccupation with the Kabbalah; namely, that in his generation there was a decline in the number of those who could grasp it properly or plumb its depth.[161] This restrained attitude toward the Kabbalah was bound up with the modification in the essence of Hasidism which took place in the school of Przysucha. With the abolition of the zaddik's function as a savior and wonder worker, and the limiting of his role to that of a guide and a teacher, it had little interest in the entire mystic apparatus, whose central prop and stay was the zaddik. The decline in the study of the Kabbalah was also a natural result of the restoration of the Talmud to its pristine status. Diligent study of the Talmud was not consistent with the study of books dealing with Kabbalah and Hasidism, the spirit of which was alien to the talmudic mode of thought sharpened by dialectic reasoning. For the same reason there was less interest in the study of the Midrash, which, in the past, had been popular with the Hasidic communities. In this respect, two *aggadot* of the Hasidim of Przysucha-Kock are characteristic. The first is about two "very sharp and keen-witted" scholars, Hasidim of Przysucha, who studied with the Gaon R. Jacob of Lissa, and who "discontinued the study of **GFT** [Gemara, the commentary of Rashi, and *Tosafot*] and applied themselves to the study of Midrash and *Zohar,* and the Gaon of Lissa wrote a letter to Przysucha, complaining about them."[162] According to the second, R. Mendel of Kock "made a great outcry" when he learned from the Rabbi of Biała, the father of his son-in-law Abraham (who was to become famous as the Rabbi of Sochaczew), that the latter was studying a great deal of Midrash. He was apprehensive lest he become familiar "with the pious language of the Midrash," and therefore vigorously demanded that he first be imbued with a knowledge of the Gemara, and then he would also understand the Midrash in all its profundity.[163]

In the view of the Rabbi of Kock, understanding and knowledge should not only be the end but also the means of studying the Talmud. Taking exception to the original conception of Hasidism, which regarded devotion to God as the sole criterion for the study of Torah for its own sake, R. Mendel taught that of all manner of devotion to the Creator "the most proper is achieved through studying the Torah," but it is fitting to confine it to preparation alone and disengage one's mind from it while studying, lest it hinder concentration on the subject. "When a man sits at his studies, he must cleave unto God, so that he is aware before Whom he is engaged in study; but if during the time he is studying he constantly applies his thoughts to such cleaving, he will not grasp what the rabbis are saying; therefore, while learning, he should devote his thoughts to the matter being studied." He found an allusion to this in the verse (Ps. 1:2) "But his delight is in the law of the Lord," which refers to the devotion at the start of the study session; whereas later, during the time he is studying, the operative clause is "and in His law he doth meditate."[164]

How far the Hasidism of talmudic erudition had moved from folk Hasidism can be seen clearly in the following two *aggadot* which together reflect the contemptuous attitude of the Rabbi of Kock to the "Psalm-reciting" Hasidim. One tells of R. Mendel's early manhood, when he went for the holiday of Shavuot to his rabbi in Przysucha, R. Simḥah Bunem. At dawn he saw R. Jeraḥmiel, the son of *ha-Yehudi,* standing near the window of the *bet ha-midrash* reciting psalms, and he slapped him on his back and said derisively, "Well, Jeraḥmiel, so you are saying *Tehillim*?"[165] The second occurred after he was already a well-known rabbi in Kock. He told one of his Hasidim who was not a scholar, "My friend, someone like you need not travel to see me but ought to sit in back of the stove reciting psalms."[166]

The New Hasidism's Social Appeal and Its Relation with Mitnaggedim

Above all, the greater emphasis on the study of Gemara marked a turning point in the social aspect of Hasidism. In contrast to Hasidism based on theoretical and practical Kabbalah, which still vexed the scholars (even though the spirit of opposition had been weakened for some time now), the exhortation to study the Torah won over new social classes (especially the scholars among them), thus bridging the rift between Hasidism and the Mitnaggedim. The revival of the study of the Torah was designed to strengthen faith, especially among those classes to whom Hasidism of the popular type could neither appeal nor satisfy spiritual needs.

One of the clear indications of this development and of the rapprochement of the Hasidism of Przysucha with the Mitnaggedim was the involvement of the rebbes in Jewish community life. Not only were the Hasidic leaders deemed worthy of entering the inner circles of the communal leadership but they were also the initiators of rabbinic enactments for the strengthening of religion as well as of interventions with the authorities to nullify decrees which were injurious to religion and tradition. R. Simḥah Bunem of Przysucha was appointed by the government commission of the *województwo* of Sandomierz as one of two fellow correspondents of that district to the Advisory Chamber of the Committee for the Affairs of Old Testament Believers. When Abbé Chiarini's project made it clear that the goal of the committee was to undermine the Jewish faith, the Hasidim, headed by the disciple of R. Simḥah Bunem, R. Isaac of Żarki (later Warka), were the most active organizers of a vigorous campaign about the imminent danger from the committee. Earlier, in 1826, it was the Hasidim who mobilized the community against the committee's plan to establish a Rabbinical School.[167]

The enactments of the rabbis in 1837 (the 19th of Ḥeshvan, 5598) for the buttressing of the faith as a remedy against repetition of "the weakness" (i.e., the plague) were signed by R. Solomon Zalman (Lifschitz), the Rabbi of Warsaw, and R. Isaac, president of the court of the community of Warka.[168] This same R. Isaac of Warka used to come to Warsaw frequently on matters relating to intercessory actions and would consult with R. Isaac Meir Alter, like himself a disciple of R. Simḥah Bunem, and his colleague R. Mendel of Kock.[169] Both he and the Rabbi of Warsaw were signatories to an appeal at the end of December 1841 regarding agricultural settlement, and R. Isaac of Warka was a member of the delegation of eight rabbis who presented themselves before the viceroy at the end of December 1843 to request the abrogation of obligatory military service.[170] He interceded with Moses Montefiore during his visit to Poland to obtain a repeal of the royal decree against the traditional Jewish garb,[171] and according to Hasidic tradition it was he who, in consultation with R. Isaac Meir Alter, worked to nullify the strict censorship imposed on the *Ḥoshen Mishpat*.[172]

A big factor in building the bridge with the Mitnaggedim was the social composition of the Przysucha Hasidim. Unlike their rival, the

"Holy Grandfather" of Radoszyce, the Hasidic leaders of Przysucha were themselves members of the well-to-do and middle classes. R. Simḥah Bunem, the son of the *Maggid* of Wodzislaw, R. Ẓevi ben Judah Leyb, author of the homiletic works *Ereẓ Ẓevi* and *Asarah le-Meah* in his early manhood, was a businessman who mingled with merchants, served for a time as a clerk with the lessee of the consumption tax in Siedlce,[173] was a grain dealer in Danzig,[174] and later was a certified pharmacist in Przysucha. R. Mendel of Kock, the son of R. Aryeh Leybush, one of the notables of the community in Goraj, was a dealer in hides—though an unsuccessful one—after he married the daughter of one of the important men in the community of Tomaszów,[175] where he led a congregation of Hasidim before moving to Kock. His second wife, the sister of the wife of R. Isaac Meir, was the daughter of an extremely wealthy man. This brother-in-law, R. Isaac Meir, the son of the Rabbi of Magnuszew, was the proprietor of a textile shop managed by his wife; a manufacturer of prayer shawls; and later the owner of a vinegar factory until he was appointed judge in the *bet din* in Warsaw (1843). He was assisted with the necessary funds for his business dealings by his brother, a successful businessman and contractor of government projects.[176] R. Isaac of Warka was the lessee of the monopoly of tobacco in the town of Żarki and in the surrounding district before he became the rabbi and leader of the Hasidim in Warka.[177] R. Yeḥiel Meir, also the disciple of R. Mendel of Kock, was the proprietor of a tobacco shop before his appointment as Rabbi of Gostynin.[178]

These Hasidic leaders were intimates of the very rich family of Sonnenberg-Bergson in Warsaw, having ready access to their home, and some of them also received their training in management of business enterprises as officials of their patrons' large mercantile banking firm. R. Simḥah Bunem was engaged in supervising the floating of logs to Danzig for R. Berke, the son of Tamar.[179] For some time R. Isaac of Warka managed the properties of "the wealthy lady Temerl of Warsaw,"[180] who was mother and matron to the fellowship of Hasidim of Przysucha. When she came from Warsaw, she presented each man in the fellowship who required assistance "every necessity, as was her wont."[181] In times of financial distress she appeared as a redeeming angel for R. Simḥah Bunem and his disciples.[182]

Those who "journeyed" to the rebbes of this school, as reflected in the *aggadah* of Hasidim, were people of means. Of those journeying to R. Simḥah Bunem, "a wealthy man" who brought "a sum of three silver rubles" is mentioned along with a "certain Hasid, a merchant, who was wont to stay in Leipzig a number of weeks."[183] To be sure, from the sayings transmitted in his name it may be deduced that it was primarily to middle-class Hasidim that the Rabbi of Przysucha was speaking when he foresaw that "at the time of the coming of the Redeemer" the laws of nature would be altered: "There will be scholars without knowledge of the Torah, Hasidim lacking Hasidic qualities, moneyless men of wealth, summers without warmth, winters without cold, and produce that will sprout without rain."[184] On another occasion, "as he grasped the Havdalah cup in his hand" he solemnly described what was to be anticipated "before the advent of the Redeemer": "A Jew will not make a living from his shop; everyone will be forced to have a source of livelihood on the side; my hair and my nails stand on end at this prospect."[185]

A certain *aggadah* tells of the Rabbi of Kock that "one man provided his living, for he was unwilling . . . to accept [help] from just anyone."[186] To be sure, this account is to be assigned to the period in which the Rabbi of Kock had not yet become famous as a preeminent Hasidic leader. The following highly instructive *aggadah* has been preserved concerning the inordinate demands he made upon his affluent supporters during the period of his fame: "Our master, of blessed memory, asked R. Nathan of Czyżew why R. Shmelka did not journey to Kock. And R. Nathan replied with a touch of effrontery, Because he feared you. It is said that you take money from the rich. At which our rebbe thundered, And in your opinion what else am I to do?"[187] Among his intimates were the wealthy Hirsh Leyb Kotsker[188] and Isaiah Prywes of Warsaw. The period of his self-imposed "imprisonment" (when he would isolate himself in his room) was especially hard for "wealthy merchants among his Hasidim," who were in a hurry to get back to their businesses but were compelled to wait around for a long time until the secluded rebbe was willing to give them a farewell blessing. To provide for the needs of R. Mendel's court, prominent men such as R. Wolf of Stryków would go as envoys to gather "money for Kock"—self-imposed taxes—from his Hasidim thoughout the country.[189]

Those who came to the court of R. Isaac of Warka were villagers[190] as well as extremely rich men. To be sure, a number of those rich men happened to be mentioned in tales about him, but only to demonstrate the extent to which the rabbi's blessing was fulfilled, whether because of a favor they had done for him or because they had obeyed him.[191] However, the Zaddik of Warka was also on good terms with the wealthy men of Warsaw, from whom he would receive "large contributions" for the needs of the community and for the prevention of "evil decrees."[192] One of his admirers was R. Mottel of Kałuszyn, who held the "lease of Kałuszyn, including all its income from the lord of the town."[193]

The Transformation of the Hasidic Categories in Przysucha-Kock

As a consequence of the social status and the scholarly level of the new community of Hasidim, and in consonance with the new outlook on the role of the zaddik in matters of religion and faith, even the aid to his visitors in material concerns was really nothing more than good counsel, although there also was an element of blessing involved in it. This can be seen in the story of two young men who came to R. Simḥah Bunem asking his advice as to "what business to undertake and what occupation to engage in." He advised them to engage in "yokhtn," which meant tanned hides and a yoke, but the "yoke" might have referred to that of the Kingdom of Heaven.[194] At any rate, his outstanding disciple, R. Mendel of Kock, was esteemed by his Hasidim as a counselor in business matters. When he was once asked how he knew "what advice to give in all sorts of business affairs, inasmuch as he had secluded himself from worldly matters," he replied that it was precisely for that reason that he had a proper perspective, for "whoever is outside an object can look inside that object."[195] However, this did not prevent his Hasidim from pressing him, at times, to pray for anyone in trouble.[196]

Merchants would ask R. Isaac of Warka to write a deed of partnership for them,[197] and a trader in oxen from Hungary was even privileged to get from the rebbe a list of all the market days on which it was worth his while to do business.[198] His advice was sought even about whether to buy a lottery ticket.[199] Giving advice in making matches was so accepted as the rebbe's function that R. Mendel of Kock expressed astonishment at a certain Hasid who failed to turn to him for counsel in this matter. The Hasid's reply, as well as the rebbe's observation, are indicative of the new conception of the zaddik's function. The Hasid replied "that on matters of matchmaking even his rebbe is not informed," to which R. Mendel countered, "But the rebbe could, in any case, offer good counsel."[200] Indeed, this practice of turning to the rebbe as a counselor in business and family matters, which had been initiated at Przysucha-Kock, spread throughout all the reaches of Hasidism in Poland.

Although the social doctrine of the school of Przysucha was founded upon principles common to the entire Hasidic movement in that generation, the stamp of the new class which provided its base was clearly impressed upon it. R. Simḥah Bunem reiterated the idea which had already been articulated in *Toldot Ya'akov Yosef*[201] concerning the obligation of the wealthy to be among the supporters of the Torah, to be near those engaged in the study of the Torah and to provide for their sustenance.[202] He also quoted an adage of *ha-Yehudi* of Przysucha "that it is a very great service to cleave to the true zaddik and this is even harder than to be the zaddik himself."[203] Furthermore, he said that each of the classes has its own duties: the poor man, if he is learned, is obliged to occupy himself with the study of Torah and with service, which is prayer, and as for the man of wealth, "his service consists mainly in charity and benevolent deeds in order to save the poor man from those who oppress and exploit him." In his opinion, it was the ambition to ascend to an inappropriate level that was the main sin for which the Second Temple was destroyed.[204] Following in the wake of the tradition which evolved from the Talmud,[205] his disciple, R. Mendel of Kock, also taught that "God placed wealth in the world so that the glory of Heaven should be enhanced"; that is to say, the rich person is blessed with wealth not for his own benefit but in order to do the will of heaven.[206]

This doctrine of the division of social functions is to a certain extent a reflection of the Hasidic milieu, which was also preserved in the school of Przysucha-Kock. Aside from the Hasidim who journeyed to the rebbe for festivals and holidays, the rebbe was also surrounded by his "Hasidim in residence," who were engaged in the study of Torah.[207] This "congregation of Hasidim" was dependent for its livelihood, as was the zaddik, on the offerings of the benefactors "who give support to the Torah." As Hasidism spread, the number of those journeying to the rebbe from among the *ba'alei battim* (householders) class increased beyond the limited circle of the Hasidim proper. The turning point occurred when R. Isaac Meir inherited the "throne" of the Rebbe of Kock. Concerning this, an *aggadah* of Ger relates that "after the death of the holy Rabbi of Kock, with the increase in the gatherings of people, many of the *ba'alei battim* began journeying to the holy rebbe, R. Isaac Meir; and the question was asked, What need has he for such a large gathering among whom are many *ba'alei battim,* whereas the rebbe exists principally for the sake of Hasidim?" R. Isaac Meir replied with a saying from the Midrash, "A thousand enter upon the study of the Bible . . . , but only one emerges to study Mishnah."[208] In view of the continuous change in the composition of the Hasidic community, the positive view of the rebbes on the combination of Torah and commerce may easily be understood. One Hasid apologized to R. Mendel for being compelled to engage in trade, inasmuch as he was burdened with a large family and consequently no longer had any time to engage in the study of Torah and Hasidism as was his wont previously. The rebbe put his mind at ease: "One can also fulfill the Torah and the commandments through trade, by exercising care in weights and measurements, by refraining from cheating and deception, by abstaining from staring at women, and by letting one's yea be a righteous yea and one's nay be a righteous nay."[209] To be sure, the rebbe also cautioned anyone engaged in trade to devote himself to Torah and prayer as soon as he rises in the morning, otherwise it will become "very difficult to return to a state of sanctity." A young man who was being supported by his father-in-law asked R. Isaac Meir whether "it might be proper for him to engage a little in trade while being supported by his father-in-law." The rebbe jokingly cited the example of the Patriarch Jacob, who was "even a greater deceiver than Esau, and yet he engaged in the study of Torah day and night."[210]

What was new in the social doctrine of Przysucha was its individualistic outlook on wealth and poverty and, stemming from it, the elevation of wealth to the point where it endows its possessor with merit. According to a trustworthy Hasidic *aggadah*, R. Simḥah Bunem held "that every poor person will have to justify being poor," that is, it must be because of his sins that he became poor.[211] In a similar vein, his disciple, R. Mordecai Joseph Leiner of Izbica, taught "that God is concerned about man's bread since it affects the life of the Jew, for should he, God forbid, be lacking bread, he will then be lacking in the service of God. . . . Therefore a person should reflect upon his deeds and return unto God that He may have compassion upon him. . . ." The general rule was "that when a man is more successful than his neighbor, it is because he holds within him a greater measure of worship of God and good deeds." This view was based on his kabbalistic doctrine about the dependence of the flow of spiritual and material grace on man's readiness to receive this flow. "For God does not give a blessing except in a brimming vessel; that is, provided man, for his part, prepares himself, and to the extent that he is a receptive vessel, so God fills him, and the receiving vessel is called purity, and through this vessel sanctity is received. Therefore, when one receives sanctity, he also obtains the flow of grace bearing all the good things of this world. . . ."[212]

According to R. Mordecai Joseph's master, R. Mendel of Kock, "Man's place below is his root in the upper spheres."[213] This same R. Mendel expressed his indignation that in the house of a certain zaddik (of Zaklików), the apartments were rented out to tailors, they being classed as "unworthy people."[214] This social outlook is far removed from the advocacy of the simple folk that can be seen in the doctrines and deeds of the Ba'al Shem Tov.

A rule of thumb in social conflicts was provided by R. Isaac of Warka, namely, tolerance. Thus R. Mottel of Kałuszyn, the Hasid of the Rebbe of Warka, admonished his children in his will, "Do not enter into a dispute, flee from a quarrel, and be numbered among the persecuted. . . ." To show that he followed these precepts he related:

At the time that I held the lease[215] of Kałuszyn, together with its various incomes, from the lord of the city, a dispute developed and the whole city conspired against me and the people . . . complained; this was the counsel of our master and teacher, the holy rabbi[216]—that we should be counted among the tolerant; and the fires of dispute died down, for he had charged me not to quarrel with them, nor to display a strong hand, for God seeks him who is persecuted. And so it came to pass that all those who rose up against me fell and even perished.[217]

No less characteristic than the counsel to refrain from "displaying a strong hand" was the rabbi's stand in support of the lessee against the men of the insurgent community. Perhaps this incident has some relation to the rebellion of the community of Kałuszyn against its rabbi in 1842, concerning which the mayor submitted a report to the Committee for Internal Affairs to the effect that on August 7, many Jews in Kałuszyn whose occupation consisted of "idleness and plotting rebellions" assembled at the synagogue. An uproar arose within the synagogue and around it, and the leaders of the insurgents extinguished the candles inside the synagogue and committed "improper acts" against the rabbi of the city.[218]

From the old social doctrine of Hasidism there remained in the school of Przysucha the glorification of the *mizvah* of charity. R. Simḥah Bunem gave twice a fair sum as alms to a decent, needy man, the second gift following immediately upon the first. He explained it thus: The first time he gave out of a feeling of pity, but that was not enough, because we must give alms out of a sense of obligation to fulfill the Torah's commandments.[219] He also explained, with his own unique brand of witticism, the problem raised by R. Solomon ben Adret: Why is it that, unlike the other positive commandments, no blessing is required when giving alms? The reason he gave was that if a man were to make preparations, as for other commandments, by ablution, or by reciting the formula "For the sake of the sanctification," the poor man would die of hunger in the meantime.[220] In the same vein, the clever rabbi explained the reason for the absence from the Torah of a prohibition against miserliness, although it is such a reprehensible quality: "Because it is a stumbling block to all the other commandments . . . , therefore it is unnecessary to put it in writing." And he found an allusion to it in Ps. 119:165: "Great peace have they that love Thy Torah; and there is no stumbling for them."[221] R. Mendel of Kock interpreted the verse "If thou lend money to any of My people, even to the poor with thee"[222] on the basis of the saying of the talmudic Sages:[223] "For in the hour of a man's departure, neither silver nor gold accompany him . . . but only Torah and good works." For "if a man's silver accompanies my people, you may know that it is only what you will give to the poor that you will take with you."[224] R. Isaac of Warka, a follower of Dovidl of Lelov in the quality of compassion and renowned as a charitable person[225] who dispensed justice on behalf of the poor,[226] explained that the well-known principle of the Sages, "He who wants to be liberal must not give away more than one-fifth,"[227] applies only to a squanderer and not to one "who is parsimonious as regards himself, being content with little and giving alms."[228]

The school of Przysucha-Kock also did not differ from the general Hasidic movement of its time with regard to Jewish solidarity, that is, the attachment of the individual to his people and the love of Jews. R. Simḥah Bunem also stressed the obverse; namely, the ban on association with Gentiles.[229] According to his interpretation, the commandment to love Jews obligates one to love all those who have no other virtue but the fact that they recite *Shema Yisrael.*[230] His explication of the phrase "See whether it is well with thy brethren" was that one should plead the cause of the Jews "so that he can behold them in a state of perfection and not in a defective state."[231]

In the same vein, he took the sentence of the Sages, "All Israel has a share in the world to come," to mean that "they have nothing in and of themselves except as they are within the totality of Israel."[232] His disciple, R. Mendel, interpreted the verse "Ye shall be holy" in this spirit, saying that it is only possible for the collective to be holy but not the individual.[233] He even found confirmation of this in the rearrangement of the letters of the word *sheker* (falsehood) to read *kesher* (a tie), as if to say that he who does not tie himself to the totality of Jewry is dominated by falsehood.[234] The reward of unity, according to R. Simḥah Bunem and R. Isaac of Warka—they being in consonance with the Hasidic doctrine of the school of Lublin and Kozienice—is the acceleration of the Redemption, the coming of the end, that is, the Messianic Era, before its fixed time.[235]

The conception of Przysucha-Kock concerning the doctrine of redemption was based on the tendency to deepen religious life which distinguished this school within the Hasidism of Poland. Just as the Hasidim of Przysucha negated the miracles and wonders of the zaddik as a way to the transitory salvation of the individual, so they rejected the belief that redemption came as a consequence of a sudden miracle and not by virtue of repentance and a determined effort in the worship of the Creator. For this reason, *ha-Yehudi* of Przysucha had expressed his indignation against "those zaddikim who reveal the end of time, signaling the advent of the Messiah," even though he himself believed that the Redemption was at hand.[236]

The contrast between the two schools of Hasidism in Poland in this matter grew sharpest in the atmosphere of messianic expectancy in the year 5600 (1840). This expectancy relied upon the passage in the *Zohar* that in the six-hundredth year of the sixth millennium the gates of wisdom on high and the fountains of wisdom below would be opened, and the world would prepare itself to enter the seventh century, just as a man readies himself at sunset on Friday to enter the Sabbath.[237] The masses of eastern European Jews as well as the Hasidic leaders and great scholars were all seized by this belief. It is no surprise that the "Holy Grandfather" of Radoszyce, the wonder-worker, was among the zaddikim in Poland who were enthralled by this hope.[238] R. Mendel of Kock and his disciples, however, were not swept along by that flood of messianic expectation. R. Mendel himself, together with R. Isaac of Warka, brought the statement of the *Zohar* concerning the year 5600 (1840) to bear upon the revival of secular knowledge: "Except that then the Jews were undeserving of it, so science was handed over to the secularists," that is, the gentile nations. His disciple, R. Isaac Meir, explained this passage as a necessity for the repair of the blemish in the covenant.[239] However, his own disciple, R. Mordecai of Izbica, who had deviated from him, saw in it an allusion to, and thus an encouragement to reveal, precisely in that year, his kabbalistic doctrine pertaining to Hasidism.[240]

As for R. Mendel of Kock, not only did he reiterate the admonition of his teacher, *ha-Yehudi* of Przysucha, with reference to the ban against revealing the end of time, the advent of the Messianic Era,[241] but he also expressed his fear lest the disappointment would bring on the rise of a new Shabbatean movement. This is the only way one can understand his saying, which was handed down in his name by his son-in-law, R. Abraham of Sochaczew,[242] "In the period preceding the coming of the Messiah" the wearers of white robes "will need the mercy of Heaven, lest, God forbid, they fall under the influence of heresy."[243] His view, that repentance was the only way, albeit a prolonged one, to hasten Redemption was expressed in the following conversation with one of his disciples: Once, when R. Jacob David, the *dayan* of Mezhirech, who was later known as the Rabbi of Kozienice, came to him, R. Mendel inquired after the welfare of his teacher, R. Hershel of Łęczna, remarking, "I love him dearly, but why does he cry out to God to send the Messiah; why doesn't he cry out that the Jews should repent? For this is what is inferred in the verse,

Wherefore criest thou out to Me? Speak unto the children of Israel, that they go forward."[244]

Because he considered the improvement of the soul and character to be the main purpose of the Hasid, R. Mendel of Kock was almost indifferent to *aliyah* (immigration) to Ereẓ Yisrael. In his opinion, there was no benefit in *aliyah* if it was not preceded by an *aliyah* (ascent) in the perfection of the worship of God. On the contrary, it was bound to delude the immigrant and to assuage his conscience so that in appearance he would have discharged an obligation which in actuality was only the outer part of the commandment. To one who wanted to journey to Ereẓ Yisrael to spare himself the pain caused by the "rolling of the dead underground" (on their way to Israel for the Resurrection), R. Mendel said sarcastically, "Do you so love your body that you are afraid of bodily pains even after death?"[245] According to another Hasidic *aggadah*, he advised someone to refrain from making a trip to Ereẓ Yisrael because "it is better to travel to the Jew of the land than to the land of the Jew."[246]

R. Mendel saw no contradiction between his passivity regarding *aliyah* to Ereẓ Yisrael and his stress on the obligation of the people to be attached to their homeland. The following *aggadah* attests to R. Mendel's concern for the suffering of the people in Exile: When R. Jacob of Amshinov (Mszczonów) told him that he dreamt he saw his deceased father, R. Isaac of Warka, "standing by a river and leaning on his staff as if he were looking into the river," R. Mendel replied, "Do you know what this river is? This river consists of the tears of weeping Israel."[247] Following in the footsteps of his teacher, the *Maggid* of Kozienice, R. Israel,[248] he interpreted the verse "The land whereon thou liest, to you I have given it" as "the land with which you are inextricably bound up, I will give you,"[249] and to this interpretation he added, "and Jacob lay down in this place"—namely, that "Jacob became inextricably bound up with the land at this place."[250] His teacher, R. Simḥah Bunem, who, according to the tradition of his Hasidim, never lay down to sleep even in the daytime without placing his *talit* and *tefillin* under his head (as provision for the road, should the Messiah come), taught that abroad "there cannot be an aptitude for worship as that which prevails within the land."[251]

In keeping with his teaching that it is man's duty to ascend ever upward on the ladder of perfection, the Rabbi of Przysucha interpreted Ps. 37:34, "Wait for the Lord, and keep His way, and He will exalt thee to inherit the land," as signifying the necessity to reach an exalted state of knowledge in order to hope to inherit the land.[252] In this verse he also found support for the view that "before the land is inherited it will be good for the Jews and their glory will be enhanced ever more."[253]

With regard to the difficulties of making a living in the period preceding the advent of the Messiah, R. Simḥah Bunem explained the verse "they will mingle themselves with the nations and learn their works" (Ps. 106:35) as meaning that the gentile nations will learn from the Jews how to conduct business and thus deprive them of their livelihoods.[254] It is therefore reasonable to assume that in his doctrine regarding the End of Days he made a distinction between the period preceding the advent of the Messiah and the actual time of the Redemption, which is destined to come at a time of plenitude and ease. Similarly, his disciple, R. Isaac of Warka, on the basis of a clever combination of Ps. 147:2, "The Lord restoreth Jerusalem, He gathereth together the dispersed of Israel," with the midrashic interpretation of that verse and the law in the Gemara in reference to partners in a house and attic—distinguished between the time of the Ingathering of the Diaspora and the time of the building of the Sanctuary. ". . . If, Heaven forbid, the Jews would not do penance, God would build up the earthly Jerusalem and have the option of not allowing them to rebuild the Temple; nevertheless, He would gather together the dispersed of Israel."[255] It appears that even the yearning expressed in the strong belief in the Redemption of the *Shekhinah* and the restoration of the Service in the Temple accorded a priority to the longing of that generation for redemption in an earthly sense, emancipation from the servitude of the Exile, the Return to Zion and the rebuilding of the land from its desolation.

A Sustenance of Faith: Cornerstone of the New Hasidism

Faith more than any other element of the original doctrine of Hasidism was stressed in the school of Przysucha-Kock. This emphasis is sufficient in itself to indicate the tendency to combat the naturalistic outlook on the world, which already was at the threshold of middle-class consciousness. It is related that R. Simḥah Bunem, as he was strolling with his followers, lifted a grain of sand and then returned it to its place, saying, "Whoever does not believe that this grain of sand must lie precisely in this spot because it is so appointed by God, is—Heaven forbid—a skeptic."[256] He also taught, in accordance with the doctrine of his predecessors, that even in the matter of earning a livelihood man is forbidden to rely on material causes and his own efforts, but must trust in God alone.[257] R. Mendel of Kock likened to the eaters of manna those Jews who have enough for the day's needs and are not concerned about tomorrow.[258] There was a story about a man "who was very diligent at devising all manner of industrial designs, yet he was a ne'er-do-well." R. Mendel interpreted Eccles. 9:11, "The wise have no bread," as "The Holy One, blessed be He, says, 'If you are so wise, go seek out a livelihood for yourself,'" that is, he derided him for turning to all manner of schemes instead of trusting in God.[259] He also viewed "the giving of the Torah" (the Sinaitic Revelation) as closed to inquiry and as barring the comprehension of the Creator by intellectual means.[260]

All this notwithstanding, a sprinkling of rationalism is still discernible in the Hasidism of Przysucha because of the special position of the Hasidic movement in Poland. Since the Haskalah movement had no real social impact, the strong rationalist trends in Poland perforce attained some sort of expression within the most liberal wing of the devout. The rejection of the belief in miracles and wonders of the zaddik was mainly a consequence of the new mode in the worship of God. The well-known epigram was told in the name of *ha-Yehudi*: "What mastery is there in being a wonder worker? Any man of a certain achievement [in God's service] has in his power to turn heaven and earth topsy-turvy; but to be a Jew—that is really hard."[261] This view also expresses the awareness of the superiority of the new Hasidim over the masses who were addicted to superstitious beliefs. In line with this view, the Rabbi of Kock, relying on Maimonides, explained that demons do not exist at present, although they did abound before, since they are mentioned in the Gemara. He was also angry at those who prayed at the graves of the zaddikim in the Lublin cemetery, "for they are no longer there." In light of this, we can understand his well-known statement to R. Isaac of Warka when they met at the grave of their master, R. Simḥah Bunem, on the anniversary day of his death, "I did not come to observe the anniversary day, I am not a Jew who recites prayers at a grave [for others], I have come to see you."[262] R. Mendel of Kock even encouraged the study of the *Yad Ḥazakah,* recommended the writings of the *Maharal* (of Prague), "which provide intelligence and reason for the understanding of the Gemara and the *Posekim,*" and saw the perusal of the *Guide of the Perplexed* as beneficial to those who had already had their fill of studying *Shas* (the Talmud) and *Posekim.*[263] Indeed, following in the footsteps of their masters from Przysucha and Kock, the Hasidim would study Maimonides, the *Kuzari,* the works of *Maharal* and other writings in religious philosophy. In keeping with the theosophy of the author of the *Tanya,* R. Mendel also taught "that there is not in the entire reality of the world any reality but that of God alone, for all that man sees with his eyes of the flesh is not reality at all, since only that which he beholds with the eyes of the intellect is reality."[264] His leaning toward rationalism is also reflected in his epigrams in praise of wisdom and about the reward of knowledge in matters of religion. He interpreted the talmudic aphorism "The sage is superior to the prophet"[265] to mean that intelligence *is* prophecy.[266] Similarly, he changed the simple meaning of the verse "He that increaseth knowledge increaseth sorrow" (Eccles. 1:17) to agree with his interpretation of the text: Although one increases sorrow, one should still increase knowledge; and he juxtaposed it with Hos. 4:6, "Because thou hast rejected knowledge, I will also reject thee."[267]

Despite the rationalist tendency which marked the Hasidism of Przysucha-Kock, there was a marked contrast with the Weltanschauung of the Bratslavian opposition[268] among the Hasidim of the Ukraine. Both opposition trends were far from the original Hasidism in their denial of corporeal needs and in their lack of concern for all mundane affairs. Simḥah Bunem comforted his weeping wife as he lay near death, saying, "The only purpose of my life has been to learn to die."[269] Similarly, his disciple, R. Mendel, stated, "Death is nothing at all; we transfer from one abode to another, choosing a more beautiful dwelling."[270] Displaying the same contempt for death as did Socrates, R. Naḥman of Bratslav, in the face of the approaching end, expressed his eager anticipation of being delivered from his corporeal bonds, "I yearn to remove my garment, for I cannot remain on one level." R. Mendel of Kock went to the greatest lengths in his denial of worldly life. His attitude is summed up in his well-known saying, "The entire world is not worth even one sigh."[271] No doubt the tragic circumstances of his life contributed to this pessimistic attitude, as in the case of the Zaddik of Bratslav. It is well known that R. Naḥman of Bratslav suffered from tuberculosis and died before he had even reached "the age of understanding" (forty years old); and as for the difficult personal life of the Rabbi of Kock, it is clearly marked by the fact that he lived apart from his first wife for twenty-five years.[272]

Yet in an even more pronounced manner than in the Hasidism of Bratslav, the Przysucha-Kock doctrine was interlaced with a negation of life in this world and of worldliness as a way of worship.

The doctrine that the Jewish way of life involved bearing the yoke of the Kingdom of Heaven through the study of the Torah and the strict observance of its commands was espoused by *ha-Yehudi* of Przysucha, passed to his disciples and in turn, by them to their disciples. He was wont to say—as is stated in his name by R. Isaac Meir of Ger—that he would give all of this world and the world to come "for a hairsbreadth of *Yiddishkeit*" (Jewishness).[273] Similarly, his disciple, R.

Mendel, spoke of the insignificance of this world and the vanity of worldliness in his aphorisms. "A Hasid rejects the world, and he who rejects the world is a Hasid";[274] "only take heed to thyself, and keep thy soul diligently"[275] (the word "only" is a qualifying term); "give little heed to your physical self and pay great heed to your soul";[276] and "I can take a young man who is absorbed in the lusts of this world and cause him to despise them . . . to the extent that whenever he but hears of them he will spew forth his food."[277] As for "Rashi's interpretation of 'Thou shalt not commit adultery' as always referring to a married woman, this can refer only to one's own wife."[278]

This is not asceticism in the sense of corporeal mortification; it is rather inner asceticism based upon disregarding one's bad inclinations and dedicating one's life to Torah and the worship of God. This sense of asceticism he expressly stated in many of his aphorisms: "Jacob said, 'In the day the drought consumed me, and the frost by night' [Gen. 31:40]—that is, the fervor during the daytime was engendered by the frost of the night";[279] "Walking in the paths of the Torah constitutes the greatest mortification of the body";[280] and "it is easier for the body to endure all manner of mortification and torment than to bear the yoke of the Kingdom of Heaven."[281] Finding satisfaction in the Torah and the commandments does not entail any abnegation, for there is no delight comparable with spiritual delight. Accordingly, the Rabbi of Kock was astonished at the saying of the Sages, "He who enjoys the Sabbath through pleasurable acts is granted his heart's desires."[282] He responded with such aphorisms as "Since there is nothing greater than joy, what else does one lack?" and "this is the glory of royalty, for because of one's joy that he is king, he lacks for nothing."[283] He even said of himself[284] that "if it were not that he needed to speak to people, he would not find it necessary to eat, since the vitality he derived from the holy Torah would suffice for him." The delight over the fulfillment of the Torah as well as its study lasts until one gives up his breath; moreover, it is "a great joy to be sentenced to death by the *bet din,* since this death is in accordance with the law of the Torah."[285] Consistent with this doctrine was his harsh attitude toward those Hasidim who besought him to pray for their sustenance. For example, to one who explained apologetically that he did not know how to pray "before a great and awesome king," he retorted, "If so, you have more to worry about than the worry of making a living, namely, that you do not know *how* to pray." When it was recommended that he pray on behalf of a certain Hasid who had become impoverished, he replied, "If that man is indeed a Hasid and God-fearing, he lacks for nothing."[286] As against devotion to God, all mundane affairs are as vanity of vanities, and man must even render as nothing in his heart all troubles relating to the material sphere. By giving added point to the Yiddish folk saying, R. Mendel summarized that principle in a formulation of the commentary on the verse in Ps. 37:3, "Dwell in the land and cherish faithfulness": *Lig in der erd un pashe zikh mit emune* ("No matter how dire your circumstances, find your sustenance by means of faith.")[287]

This strict doctrine regarding a way of life is somewhat similar to the principles of stoicism in respect to man's overcoming his desires and schooling himself to be indifferent to all that befalls him, in order to stand firm against all of life's afflictions. The Rabbi of Kock used to say—and it is possible that therein he reiterated the words of his master, *ha-Yehudi* of Przysucha:[288] "When one snaps his thumb at himself,[289] he can snap it against the whole world."[290] This constant self-discipline is also related to rationalism, which marks the Weltanschauung of the Hasidim of Kock. They regarded the rule of supremacy of intellect over impulse and of purposefulness over arbitrariness as one of the principles which set them apart from the other Hasidim. As R. Mendel stated, "A Tomaszów Hasid is one who asks himself, in all things, 'What do I want in this matter?'"[291] But the main root of negation of material concerns is inherent in that goal of the reinforcement of religion and faith which required the restoration of the study of the Gemara to its original high status. With respect to the fundamental Hasidic doctrine relating to the elevation of the material world to a spiritual level, there is clearly a certain retrogressive tendency.[292] Still, the form itself of the compromise with the old philosophy of life should be viewed as a vestige of the original Hasidic trend toward ethical monism: In order to escape a dualistic conception of ethics, the Hasidism of Przysucha-Kock did not accept the notion of a struggle with the *yeẓer ha-ra*ʿ (Evil Inclination) as regards lusts and worldliness, but of their complete negation within the mind and heart.[293]

However, in order to plumb the conceptual depth of Przysucha-Kock Hasidism, one must see both fronts on which this school fought for the regeneration and strengthening of Judaism. One front of this war of ideas was directed against the shallow miracle-working type of Hasidism, and in this struggle the old values of Judaism—the study of Torah and the rigorous way of life—were revitalized. Simultaneously, this school, with all its energy and freshness of ideas, led the battle on the second front against the petrified orthodoxy and on behalf of the liberalization of the worship of God. The impact and driving force of Przysucha-Kock Hasidism came mainly from its aggressive war on this second front.

The Distinctly Hasidic Mode of Prayer and Piety

As was the case with the more pristine Hasidism, the leaders of Przysucha-Kock and their disciples elevated "worship amid gladness" to one of the main principles in their way of life. Thus R. Simḥah Bunem explained the verse "Let the saints exult in glory; let them sing for joy upon their beds" as "Hasidim rejoice in great glory; even when their spirit weakens, they nevertheless pray enthusiastically."[294] He also said that one should learn from a child how always to be in a state of joy and not to know melancholy.[295] R. Mendel taught that "joy is sanctity disembodied," and that the "quality of melancholy is a very inferior one," for it is the attribute of Cain.[296] Optimism as an important rule of conduct was expressed by R. Simḥah Bunem in his well-known aphorism which he stated in reference to the merchants of Danzig: "Lose money, and you lose nothing; lose courage,[297] and you lose everything."[298] To be sure, on the strength of this psychological dialectic, R. Naḥman of Bratslav was able to reconcile worship amid joy and the dispelling of gloom with the doctrine that "at a particular moment, man may be beset by a broken heart."[299] Neither did the zaddikim of Przysucha-Kock refrain from enlarging upon the virtue of brokenheartedness. Ps. 89:16, "Happy is the people that know the joyful shout; they walk, O Lord, in the light of Thy countenance," is explained by R. Mendel of Kock as, The Jews "are holy, yet their hearts are broken within them."[300] His master, R. Simḥah Bunem, explained it thus: "The hurting of a soul and a broken heart are deemed equal to one who falls from an upper storey and breaks his bones."[301]

In their mode of life, the Hasidim of Przysucha-Kock did indeed maintain a marvelous synthesis of profound earnestness and abundant *joie de vivre*. They who burned the midnight oil in their zealous study of the Gemara were also wont to refresh themselves at frequent intervals by partaking of brandy in fellowship, joining in dancing and rejoicing in song, or even playing cards.[302] The Rabbi of Kock, who cast fear upon his Hasidim "as if he were a king" merely by his appearance (he had bushy eyebrows),[303] valued music very highly. This is reflected in his saying that "he who plays wholeheartedly, with no ulterior motive for doing so, can hasten the Redemption, for the Temple of Melody is close to the Temple of the Messiah."[304] As for the place of strong drink in the life of the Hasidim, it is attested to in the saying of R. Isaac of Warka: "When our Messiah, the Righteous Redeemer, will come speedily in our time, the Jews will go forth to meet him, holding a flask of brandy in their hand to show him how they gave themselves courage during the bitter and dark exile."[305]

The requirement for rendering the worship of God more profound by basing it on emotion was a distinct mark in the regeneration of Hasidism in the schools of Przysucha-Kock. "Prayer," as R. Simḥah Bunem explained, "is acceptable precisely if it issues from the depths of the heart and one prays with the very essence of his soul. . . ."[306] And this rule applies to every *mizvah,* "for everything that is done for God must have in it an inner vitality, and if it lacks an inner vitality, it cannot ascend heavenward. . . ."[307] Worship without feeling is no more than superficial imitation, and this is primarily what sets the Jews apart from the gentile nations, such as the Philistines, who wanted to go in the way of our father Abraham.[308] Mind without heart also characterizes the gentile nations, for "Esau's mind possessed great potentialities, but he guarded his heart so that no illumination could enter into it, therefore the blessings were taken away from him."[309] Apparently, this explanation was also intended to deal with the actual situation, namely, to point up the anomalous contradiction between the highly civilized state of the rulers and their hardheartedness in the suppression of the Jews. R. Mendel of Kock held the essence of the Hasidic doctrine to consist of what "the Ba'al Shem Tov sought to correct, that is, that observance of the commandments should not be a matter of rote, but that God should be worshipped in a heartfelt manner," and he also prompted his disciple, the Rabbi of Szczuczyn, "to draw the Lithuanian Jews close to this manner of observance."[310] He gave a penetrating interpretation of "heartfelt worship" (prayer) in his explanation of the statement in the Midrash, "Open for me one window of penitence, be it as small as an eye of a needle, and I will open many gates for you."[311] "What is required of man is an opening and a spiritual awakening, no matter how slight in value, provided that it truly stems from the very depth of the heart, without any ulterior motive or reservation. . . ."[312]

Just as prayer and observance of the *mizvot* must be done with a depth of feeling, so the study of the Torah can be of no value without discharging one's ethical obligations. An echo of the holy war waged by the Ba'al Shem Tov's disciple, R. Jacob Joseph of Polonnoye, against the conceited scholars is discernible in the sarcastic sayings of R. Mendel of Kock which express his deep contempt for scholars of this type: "They go about with ugliness in their heart and fondle their bellies with a few pages of Gemara."[313] He defined the difference between a Hasid and a Mitnagged in a similar vein: "A Hasid fears God and a Mitnagged fears the *Shulḥan Arukh.*"[314] The main goal in studying the Torah is to learn a proper way of life, and only then does it become the study of Torah for its own sake; the very meaning of the word Torah—R. Mendel expounded in etymological terms—is "that it instructs man."[315] The Rabbi of Kock asked of an eminent scholar who had told him he had *studied Shas to the end:* "To what end?"[316]*

Regarding the role of the Torah from that standpoint, the school of Przysucha-Kock also stressed the principle of fundamental Hasidism in the matter of people's ordinary conversation, as well as in respect to the value of observing the world around one. R. Simḥah Bunem expounded the Midrash which likens the Jews to a bee "which, whatever it gathers, does so in behalf of its owner" (*Midrash Rabba D'varim* 1:5), as follows: What is under consideration is the bee's wax, apart from its honey; the analogy is that "Whatever Jews acquire, that is, even fine conversation . . . it is all precious and beloved by our Father in Heaven."[317] This is also the meaning of the saying in the tractate *Avot* (4. 1): "Who is wise? He who learns from all men." For all tales about mundane matters he deems to be Torah, namely, even what inferior men have to say in the mundane sphere.[318] On the basis of Ps. 104:24, "The earth is full of Thy creatures," his disciple, Rabbi Mendel, deduced that "from every single thing man can learn how to worship God."[319] To be sure, the very formulation of the words points to a marked retreat from the original doctrine of the Ba'al Shem Tov and his disciples. The latter, the pioneers of Hasidism, deemed ordinary small talk with people in the street to be the very essence of worship, raising it to the level of the professing of "The Union of God and the *Shekhinah*"[320]; in the revised Hasidism of Przysucha-Kock, it was no more than material for instruction in the worship of God.

A logical consequence of the principle concerning wholehearted worship was the negation of the rigid formalism in prayer and fulfillment of *mizvot,* and in this the Hasidim of Przysucha-Kock far outstripped the Hasidism of the Ba'al Shem Tov. In this regard, the conversation between a Chernobyl Hasid and R. Mendel of Kock is highly illustrative. The Hasid told the Rabbi of Kock about some of the Chernobyl principles of conduct: "They stay awake the entire night of the eve of the Holy Sabbath and on Friday they give alms according to their ability and on the Holy Sabbath proper they recite the entire book of Psalms." To this R. Mendel replied scornfully, "In Kock, this practice is not followed; they do however stay awake *every* night, and they give alms *whenever* they come upon a needy person and at *all* times when they have money, and as for the Psalms, they haven't the strength to recite the entire book at one time, seeing that

*In the Yiddish original the play on words is based on the double meaning of the word *oysgelernt*: first time—studied to the end; then—taught.

King David (may he rest in peace) required seventy years for it. But they do recite *devoutly* a few Psalms, or a few verses."[321]

Believing that intent is the essential thing in prayer, the Hasidim of Przysucha-Kock were not at all strict regarding the time of the recitation of the *Shema* and of prayers and on occasion would recite the morning prayer in the evening and the afternoon prayer at midnight.[322] And it need not be said that their Hasidic opponents could hardly forgive them for this arbitrariness, for they even deemed it a sin that they did not recite the prayer of supplication (*Taḥanun*) every day.[323] R. Mendel himself did not recite *Tikkun Ḥaẓot,* explaining that "for him *Tikkun Ḥaẓot* consisted in his saying 'Uvneh Yerushalayim' after the evening meal during the recitation of *Birkat Hamazon.*"[324]

Consistent with the principle of disregard for externals and appreciation of inner feelings, the votaries of Przysucha and Kock abolished bodily movement (swaying to and fro) during prayer—which was practiced, as it were, to give reality to the phrase "All my bones shall proclaim"—a characteristic practice of Hasidism from the very beginnings of that religious trend. R. Simḥah Bunem used to say, "When we pray, it is only the soul which should pray, and the body's role should be that of a bundle of straw which is being dragged along from behind."[325] As if pointing intentionally at the Ba'al Shem Tov's doctrine of the need for swaying during prayer in order to clear away "alien thoughts," his disciple from Kock interpreted the verse, "And if you will put away your detestable things out of My sight, and will not waver" (Jer. 4:1) thus: "If you will remove your filth from your thought, you will not need to move your body [during prayer]."[326] The verse "And when the people saw it, they trembled, and they stood afar off" (Exod. 20:18) teaches us that "it is possible to see and shake and yet stand at a distance" (far from God).[327] According to one *aggadah*, even the rabbi "prayed on Rosh Hashanah in his own room near the *bet ha-midrash* without movement or agitation" save that "his face, which burned as if lit up by torches," testified to his feelings.[328]

In clear opposition to the "practice of religion by rote," the Hasidim of Przysucha-Kock rejected every manifestation of routine in the worship of God. In the verse "If thou turn thy foot away because of the Sabbath" (Isa. 58:13), R. Mendel found support for his view of the way in which to worship the Creator—"that it should not be an act of habit."[329]* This was the way of Aaron the priest: "And Aaron did so" (Num. 8:3), which Rashi explained as meaning "that he did not change," to which the Rabbi of Kock added his interpretation, "It never became old [habitual] for him; he would worship each day anew,

*This is based on a play on words in Hebrew; *regel* means both foot and habit.

and not routinely as if it were something old."[330] This manner of conduct R. Mendel observed in his teacher, *ha-Yehudi* of Przysucha, who, each day, on reciting the blessing "for not having created me a Gentile," felt anew within his soul that he had been changed, "as it were, from a Gentile into a Jew."[331] Negation of routine practice obligates a person not to depend on tradition in his worship of God; rather, he must consciously seek his own particular way. In this matter, the Rabbi of Kock reiterated the doctrine of the Ba'al Shem Tov, that each person must pray "at his own urging and not at that of his father." In this vein, the Ba'al Shem Tov explained the phrase "God of Abraham, God of Isaac" to signify that "each one learned to know the Creator on his own initiative," and in support, R. Mendel added the verse, "And the house of Jacob shall be a fire and the house of Joseph a flame," explaining "that in the case of Joseph, we note [in the Midrash] that he 'curled his hair and acted childishly'; he did not pattern his conduct on that of his father, but acted after his own fashion. . . ."[332] In the view of the pioneers of Hasidism, the absence of intent in the worship of God is sheer idolatry, the *actual* worship of idols; R. Mendel put in the same category the sin of routine worship and brought the point home with a homily on the verse "Take heed unto yourselves, lest ye forget the covenant . . . and make you a graven image, even the likeness of any thing which the Lord thy God hath forbidden thee" (Deut. 4:23). He said, "We should take heed not to make anything of what 'the Lord thy God hath forbidden thee' an idol or a likeness. . . . A person's worship without clear intent is as great an abomination in the eyes of the Lord as an idol and a likeness."[333] On the strength of that appreciation of inner intent over and above all the minutiae of ritual law, the Hasidism of Przysucha-Kock esteemed quality and not quantity in the observance of the Torah. R. Mendel would say, "The sanctimonious person makes the essential subordinate and the subordinate he makes to be the main thing."[334]

If by their negation of "mundane vanities" and physical pleasure the Hasidim of Przysucha-Kock demonstrated a point in common with Stoicism, then surely in their scorn for all outer appearances and routine behavior patterns they attained—and this was especially true of the followers of R. Mendel in Tomaszów and Kock—the level of the ancient Greek Cynics. More than all the principles of the Hasidism of Przysucha, these manifestations in the way of life of the new Hasidim indicate that with the resurgence of Hasidism in Przysucha-Kock, there was a new wave of Sturm und Drang which was like a repetition, in another form, of the deeds of the Hasidim in the era of its growth. The riotous actions of some of the Hasidim of the school of the *Maggid* of Mezhirech and his disciples is defined by an eyewitness, the philosopher Solomon Maimon, as the behavior of "actual cynics": At the court of R. Dov Ber of Mezhirech, Hasidim lashed themselves to induce mirth, and his disciples in the Ukraine, in Lithuania, and especially in White Russia (Kolisk, Lyozna) would perform somersaults, that is "they would turn over, head down and feet in the air" both in the synagogue before the Holy Ark and in "the marketplaces and streets"; there were among them those who—in the words of Solomon Maimon—"offended against all the rules of good manners, running naked in the main streets, relieving themselves in public and the like." According to the descriptions in works by Mitnaggedim, there were Hasidim whose boisterous "laughter and derision" was expressed in public. And they even dared "to mock the scholars and to heap all manner of humiliation upon them." Besides being an expression of religious enthusiasm, this "unbridled behavior" was also a manifestation of scorn for the hauteur and proper behavior of sedate *ba'alei battim,* an expression of rebellion against the rule of the moneyed magnates and scholars in the community.[335]

This "unbridled behavior" was a common occurrence among the Hasidim of Przysucha,[336] but the Hasidim of Kock were most noted for it. After the death of R. Simḥah Bunem in Elul 5587 (September 1827), the way of life of R. Mendel's fellowship in Tomaszów assumed an aspect of "bohemianism": They lived from hand to mouth and spent whatever they earned for brandy and for modest meals which were eaten communally. With utter disregard for the slightest show of pride, they did not refuse even hard physical labor, such as the job of building the synagogue in the city.[337] To be sure, this way of life lasted no more than about two years, that is, until R. Mendel took the position of rabbi of Kock, thus becoming the leader of thousands of Hasidim who flocked to him not only from Poland but also from Greater Poland (the Duchy of Posen) and from Lithuania. However, even in the era of his glory, the Hasidim of the Rabbi of Kock were still known for their contempt for anyone who put on airs, such as scholars. The usual way of expressing this was to knock off their *shtrayml* (the fur-trimmed hat worn on the Sabbath and Festivals), or even to strip them of their white *kitel* on Yom Kippur.[338] In order to demonstrate their vilification of titles of renowned scholars, they called the grandson of R. Akiva Eger, who had become a Hasid of Kock, simply "Leybl, the son of Solomon, the son of Akiva."[339] It was deemed by them to be a mark of modesty to go about in torn and ragged clothes.[340] The Hasidim of Kock were so careful to be free of any taint of "arrogance" that they even tried to give the impression that they did not observe the commandments, lest they err on the side of pride in their Hasidism. It was this that gave rise to the well-known saying among the Hasidim of Kock, "What is the difference between the Hasidim of Kock and the rest of the Hasidim? The latter perform the *miẓvot* openly but commit transgressions in secret, whereas the Hasidim of Kock commit transgressions openly and perform the *miẓvot* in secret."[341]

R. Mendel himself would vent his scorn upon the *shtraymlekh* and the *vayse yupitses* (white robes),[342] namely upon both the arrogant rabbis and the sanctimonious zaddikim. In this regard, he interpreted the verse in the episode of the spies (Num. 14:6), "And Joshua, the son of Nun, and Caleb, the son of Jephunneh, who were of them that spied out the land, rent their clothes" by referring to the "leaders of the thousands of Israel" who don *shtraymlekh* and *yupitses* but spread an evil report of the land. Joshua and Caleb did not tear their own clothes, but those of the spies, saying to them, "Why do you still wear *shtraymlekh*?"[343] To the emissary of a certain zaddik who claimed that the zaddik was "so big that he reaches to the seventh heaven," R. Mendel retorted sharply, "This demonstrates that he is so small that they must force all the seven heavens down to him. . . ."[344] A residue of this scornful attitude toward men of esteem and courtly behavior was still preserved among some of his distinguished disciples. R. Yeḥiel Meir of Gostynin was contemptuous of the practice which prevailed in the houses of the wealthy of having spittoons; he told R. Moshe Aaron of Kutno that when he came to collect alms in the house of a poor person he was promptly given money, but when he came to the house of a certain rich man he was given a cuspidor to spit in. To this, R. Moshe Aaron replied that it was his custom when he came to the house of a poor person to spit on the ground; however, in a rich man's house he was not permitted to spit on the ground; "he is therefore compelled to spit in the rich man's face."[345]

Truth and Individualism: Components of the Hasidic Personality

The aim of deepening religion and ethics as to matters of heart and purifying them of the peripheral and external was expressed within resurgent and reformed Hasidism in the elevation of truth to a supreme principle. Rabbi Simḥah Bunem demonstrated the gravity of the sin of falsehood by pointing out that all precepts relating to *harḥaka* (keeping at a distance) and restrictions to help keep a person from transgressing derive from rabbinic authority, while in the matter of falsehood *harḥaka* stems directly from the Torah,[346] which enjoins us to "keep . . . far from a false matter."[347] It is necessary that falsehood be considered "by the masses" to be as great a transgression as adultery, and then the Messiah would come.[348] His disciple, R. Mendel, commenting on the statement in the Gemara that "the seal of the Holy One is truth,[349] said that the "seal must be in writing which does not lend itself to forgery, and it is indeed impossible to falsify the truth, since falsified truth is not truth."[350] Like his teacher, he included in the sin of falsehood not only the spoken lie but also facial expressions which reflect insincerity and lack of personal integrity. Among his gemlike aphorisms are: "When a man does not show his real face it is idolatry."[351] The statement in Ps. 60:13, "For vain is the help of man," means "The duplicity with which a person covers up his abominable acts is a falsehood."[352] The commandment "Thou shalt not steal" was interpreted to mean that one should "not even engage in self-deception."[353] The abhorrence of aping and mimicry is transparent in the following saying then current among the Hasidim of Kock: "If I am I because I am I, and you are you because you are you, then I am I and you are you; but if I am I because you are you, and you are you because I am I, then I am not I and you are not you."

The school of Pryzsucha-Kock also considered it necessary to make certain innovations in its conception of Judaism, which was done by modifying and even formally changing values. The exponents of the new concepts were not content with the method prevalent in Hasidism since its beginnings, that consisting of seeking support in the Torah by distorting the real meaning of the verses and interpreting them homiletically; rather, they strove to establish a general formal principle. In the school of the "Seer" of Lublin, the verse "And they judged the people at all seasons" (Exod. 18:26) was interpreted to mean that "according to the season and the time, so shall they judge the *Halakha*." This was further expounded by R. Meir of Opatów: ". . . God delivered two Torahs, the Written and the Oral, to each generation, so that by means of them the zaddikim of the generation should expound the Written Law as their intelligence will allow according to the season and the time."[354]

In a similar fashion R. Simḥah Bunem taught that "truly the principle and the basis of the Torah is to be stated 'According to the law which they shall teach thee' [Deut. 17:11], and so in every generation, even as the zaddik decides the law according to the holy Torah, so shall it be established." Thus he infers from the exact wording of "the time of the giving of the Torah" and not the time when we received the Torah "that the Torah is given to us as a gift to the zaddikim and the Sages."[355] But R. Simḥah Bunem and his disciples regarded this as more than just a formal principle. For them it denoted the essential way of life. The very fact that those qualities are not mentioned in the Torah was cited as incontestable proof of their supreme importance. They are to be considered unwritten rational precepts, for they are the main prop of the entire Torah and a necessary condition for its observance. It was in this light, as was mentioned above, that R. Simḥah Bunem explained the fact that the prohibition against miserliness is not mentioned in the Torah. In keeping with this doctrine, R. Mendel of Kock regarded man's lack of personal integrity and tendency to presume to have attained an eminence not really his as vices which are graver than ordinary transgression and tantamount to idol worship. He reiterated the saying in the Midrash[356] "Good manners take precedence over the Torah," explaining that this is the "introduction which God made for his book," in accordance with the popular adage "A book without an introduction is like a body without a soul."[357] In addition, he interpreted the verse "And ye shall be holy men unto Me" (Exod. 22:30) to mean that "you shall be holy unto Me in terms of human qualities."[358] In line with this view, his disciple, R. Isaac Meir, taught that "a lack of proper human qualities is equivalent to a grave transgression."[359]

This revisionism found particular expression in their view of the characters in the Torah. For example, the sympathy they felt for the rebel Koraḥ can be seen in the comment ascribed to R. Mendel in the name of his master, R. Simḥah Bunem, on the verse "And Koraḥ took . . .": "Koraḥ wanted to take action for himself, therefore it did not succeed."[360] Speaking for himself, R. Mendel of Kock explained that Koraḥ's mistake was that "when he saw that he had attained a high level of importance when he stood upon the dais, he thought if he were to stand in the sanctuary proper, he would reach even higher levels of importance, but he did not realize that his attainments sprang from that man who stood in the sanctuary."[361] At any rate, R. Mendel pointed out that "Koraḥ was not a person from the marketplace" and that "Moshe Rabbenu revealed to us an inkling of this: 'And will you seek the priesthood also?' Is it enough merely to demand?"[362] A more far-reaching change in appraisal of Koraḥ was given in the comment of R. Mendel's disciple, R. Mordecai Joseph Leiner of Izbica, who had split with him and attracted some of his master's Hasidim. He saw Koraḥ as an example of himself in that Koraḥ knew that everything is in the hand of heaven, even the fear of heaven, and he therefore was sure that he was doing nothing but the will of God. He was right about the essence of the principle of equality when he argued "that all the congregation are holy, every one of them. . . . Wherefore then lift yourselves up above the assembly of the Lord?" But he disregarded the elevation of his own tribe, the tribe of Levi. In the same way, Koraḥ saw only the outer garb of the soul of Moses which was the reverse of the inner aspect of meekness.[363] The spies, as R. Mendel explained, were not liars, "for they really told the truth," but their sin was "that they did not want to penetrate by this means to the truth of God's word, as was done by Joshua and Caleb."[364]

R. Isaac of Warka found in the episode of the spies support for the new doctrine of Hasidism, that is, that the Hasid should not depend upon his rebbe to improve everything but that he is obliged to pray fervently himself. Joshua prayed for himself, therefore Moses uttered a prayer for him (as the Gemara puts it:[365] May God save you from the counsel of the spies), "but the other spies displayed no fervor, nor did they pray in their own behalf."[366] The men of the generation of the desert, expounded R. Mendel, knew why they complained and demanded flesh, even though they could find every taste in the manna, because "they wanted substance and not merely taste."[367] He also explained why Balaam did not become a Jewish proselyte even after "he beheld the favorable circumstances of Israel in the end of days." According to the statement in the tractate *Avot* 5. 19, the disciples of the wicked Balaam were arrogant, and "ger" (proselyte) derives from the term "magrir garir," that is, one who is drawn after others, whereas Balaam "wanted to be the chief and leading person."[368] Just as the Rabbi of Kock appreciated the trait of pride even in Balaam the wicked,[369] so he praised Adam (the first man) for his candor, even after he had sinned. According to the Midrash, Adam replied to God, "I have eaten and am eating" (*Breshit Rabba* 19). As R. Mendel expounded it, there was no insolence toward God in this, but rather that Adam answered candidly that he had not yet suppressed his lust, "and this is a great lesson for man in that he should know himself."[370]

R. Simḥah Bunem explained that even Cain was not an ordinary transgressor, "for in the natural course of things we cannot understand how a brother would kill his brother," except that he was certain that he was doing the Creator's will. Hence his reply, "Am I [*anokhi*] my brother's keeper?"; that is, "I [*anokhi*] the Lord your God" know all that he did.[371] Even R. Mendel defended Cain, who said to God, "My punishment is greater than I can bear," that is, it was decreed that he be a fugitive and a wanderer and he would be unable to do penance if God would not forgive him.[372] R. Mendel's disciple, the Rabbi of Izbica, also held Zimri to be guiltless of the sin of adultery, not only on a formal basis—"for God would not set aside for the adulterer a section in the Torah"—but also according to his kabbalistic line of thought: Zimri "really did keep himself from all the evil lusts" in all the ten counts relating to harlotry; therefore he was confident that the Midianite woman was his predestined mate and that he was fulfilling the will of God, and basically he was right. Phineas, who in the externality of his soul was a zealot in his love for Israel, regarded Zimri "with the eyes of the human intellect and no more," and therefore he slew him, to be sure, only his body and not his soul; and in consideration of this, God gave him "His covenant of peace."[373]

R. Mendel of Kock found a new formal basis not only for the teaching of the Torah "according to the season and the time" by the zaddikim and *geonim* of the generation but also for the grading of the obligation to worship God by each man according to his level and depth of perception. This finds support in the verse "Judges and officers shalt thou make thee in all thy gates" (Deut. 16:18), which is set down to teach us a great principle: "You shall make judges and officers, precisely, 'for yourself'; with every measure of your capacity which you can conceive (*leshaer*) to be in you; and this is the sense of the word 'bisharekha.'"[374]* This principle is a clear manifestation of the trend of individualism which characterizes the doctrine of the Hasidism of Przysucha-Kock.

Individualism is characteristic of both the original Hasidism and its offshoot at Przysucha-Kock, that is, in their negation of "rote performance of the *mizvot*" and of routine behavior and the demand for depth of feeling and pure intention in the fulfillment of the *mizvot.* But the Przysucha-Kock Hasidism explicitly stressed each man's obligation to seek his own way in the worship of God and, similarly, that each individual should feel it incumbent upon himself to attain perfection. Consequently, as R. Simḥah Bunem taught, not only was the role of the zaddik reduced from being a wonder worker and savior to giving guidance, but even in this very guidance he merely makes people aware of those failings which were concealed from them.[375] R. Mendel formulated this principle positively and with greater clarity when expounding on his doctrine of Hasidism to his new disciple, R. Yeḥiel Meir of Gostynin. "We do not produce any innovations whatsoever, but we do bring into the open whatever qualities a man does possess."[376] In the same vein, he said of himself that he did not want to quicken the dead but rather "to reanimate the living."[377] R. Simḥah Bunem held that "every Jew who sets out to worship God should dig a well out of his own essence by means of which he will be able to cleave to his Creator."[378] In this spirit, R. Mendel expounded the verse "For . . . the Lord hath chosen thee" (Deut. 7:6; 14:2): "The letters *bet, ḥet, resh* [which constitute the word *baḥar,* meaning chosen] are the abbreviation for *bokea ḥalonei rakia* [cleaves to the windows of the firmament], indicating that each Jew can cleave to the windows of the

*Literally "in your gates," but used here as "your measure."—Tr.

firmament and repent his misdeeds."[379] He even went further than his teacher in requiring a person's self-involvement in the worship of God. "He said of his teacher from Przysucha, that he raised up and helped all who came to seek refuge in his shadow, but his desire is that each person raise himself up by himself."[380]

From this personal obligation of each individual to worship God in his own particular way, there also followed the recognition of the singular value of the personality. R. Simḥah Bunem admitted that "when he has a large congregation on the holy Sabbath, then it is difficult for him to 'say' a lesson on the Torah, for each individual needs Torah, so that in his Torah lesson each single person would be included, and each individual would receive his share."[381] Similarly, his disciple, R. Mendel, was of the opinion that with regard to the *giving* of the Torah, everyone was equal, but in the *receiving* of it, each individual did in accordance with his own ability.[382] With this in mind, he explained the phrase "Behold, I set before *you* . . . [the plural form is used in the Torah]" (Deut. 11:26). He objected that the verse starts in the singular and ends in the plural and went on to explain that "in the matter of giving all are included together, because each is given in like measure, but in respect to seeing and feeling, all do not fall into one category . . . for each person can only see by means of *his* endeavor and *his* understanding."[383] His teacher, R. Simḥah Bunem, concluded from this principle "that the soul of every single person has one style in the worship of God so that it fulfills the Torah and the commandments without any difference; it is only in the matter of qualities and conduct that people are divided." For if he were asked, "How much would you give so that you could exchange your quality with our Father Abraham, may he rest in peace, so that he would be like you and you like him, I would not even give a farthing."[384] This appraisal of the worth of the personality also implied that each one must be content with his own worth "and not exercise himself in things too great, and not within the measure of his worth."[385] But his disciple, the Rabbi of Kock, demanded the maximum of aspiration from each individual. He inferred from the differences among persons the necessity for tolerating the opinions of each individual. "Even as you can tolerate the fact that the visage of another person does not resemble yours, so you must be tolerant if the opinions of another are not like your opinions."[386]

Another consequence of this doctrine of individualism was man's obligation constantly to perfect himself. R. Simḥah Bunem concluded from the verse "And the children of Israel *went up* armed" that "Jews are obligated *to go ever upward.*"[387] He also read the verse "Turn ye not unto the ghosts, nor unto familiar spirits" (Lev. 19:31) as meaning that man should not stand in one place or remain still in the worship of God until he reaches the desired aim, nor should he rest content with what he knows or ever think "that he has already reached the degree of real knowledge."[388] Unlike the Hasidism of the Ba'al Shem Tov's school, here knowledge is regarded as important in the attainment of perfection as devotion to God. R. Mendel interpreted the saying in Prov. 22:6, "Train a child in the way he should go, and even when he is old, he will not depart from it," to mean that "even in old age one should not desist from educating himself further."[389] In this spirit, he also explained Gen. 24:1, "And Abraham was old, well stricken in age," to mean that "he continually perfected himself throughout his days."[390] As for the obligation to perfect oneself, he explained Prov. 14:14, "The dissembler in heart shall have his fill from his own ways; and a good man shall be satisfied *from himself*," as follows: "Whoever is sated from his own ways and has no desire to rise ever higher at all times is a person with a heart of dross and refuse, while if he *from himself* knows that he must rise ever higher at all times, he is a good man."[391]

R. Mendel also taught that everything must come to a man through his own effort; whatever does not come "through knowledge, labor and effort from within" will not endure, and even deeds of righteousness which are performed without consciousness have in them the aspect of "arbitrariness."[392] The meaning of the verse "Yet thou hast not called upon Me, O Jacob, neither hast thou wearied thyself about Me, O Israel" (Isa. 43:22) is that God says to man, "If you have become weary, it is a sign that your intentions are not directed toward Me, for no person grows weary through My Torah."[393] As for the saying of the Sages, "I have toiled and have not achieved—do not believe" (*Megillah* 6b), it means, "If you have not achieved, do not believe that you have toiled"; and this is also the meaning of Prov. 2:4–5, "If thou seek her as silver, and search for her as for hidden treasures; then shalt thou understand the fear of the Lord, and find the knowledge of God." That is, "if a person knows that in a given place the treasure is indubitably hidden, then even if he does not find it, he will not despair but will continue to search and will not go from there until he finds it; so it is with the Torah and the *mizvot*. . . ."[394]

The doctrine of the perfection of man implied the obligation to strive to be humble, to achieve inner profundity and to be free even of the slightest tendency toward ostentation—all this even to the point of isolation from other people. Commenting on the verse "How beautiful are thy steps in sandals" (Song of Songs 7:2), R. Mendel asserted that "the pulsating of the heart and feelings of love and reverence shall be locked up and one's soul shall weep in secret only[395] and pour out its complaints before God."[396] This tenet was also included among the three rules of conduct which he formulated in the following terms: "What do I want from them? Only three things: Not to look beyond one's own self, not to look into another [not to obtrude oneself upon the secrets of another], and not to be concerned with oneself."[397] The third tenet was customarily expressed by the Hasidim of Kock in a popular formulation: "One should be concerned for the person of his fellow man and for one's own soul." In keeping with the principle of the inwardness of emotion, he explained that "when a person has—God forbid—reason to cry out and cannot, this is the greatest outcry."[398] Refraining from idle talk was also considered meritorious. For example, with regard to a person who has a joke to tell "but swallows it and doesn't let it get out," Prov. 21:14 is cited: "A gift in secret pacifieth anger."[399] This restraint applies to writing and publishing: "Not every thought that we harbor is proper to tell, and not everything we say is appropriate to write, and not everything we write should be printed."[400] It is quite obvious that the principle of humility even applies to seclusion: "There may be a man—as R. Simḥah Bunem makes plain—who wants to separate and sequester himself within faraway woods in order to worship God, but he really hopes that somebody will learn about his self-seclusion; such a person is very inferior."[401] And since seclusion is a matter of the inner heart, R. Mendel believed that "it is very wise on the part of a man that when he mingles among people, he nonetheless remains aloof from them." His colleague, R. Isaac of Warka, said of himself "that he is most alone precisely when he is among people."[402]

The doctrine of the perfection of man's personality also gave rise to the remarkable principle of maximalism, which was peculiar to the school of Kock. While this trend of regeneration within Hasidism had absorbed elements of rationalism, which had bypassed Polish Jewry in the absence of proper conditions for a broad Haskalah movement,[403] it gave full expression to Romanticism, then current in the literature and philosophy of Europe. Yet this unique literary form did not detract in any way from the élan and impetus of Hasidic romanticism. True, Hasidic literature had its particular pattern which consisted of the traditional manner of the interpretation of biblical verses or the new style of conversation amid a gathering of the Hasidim and the utterance of aphorisms. That same middle class, which among the gentile nations sought through a spiritual revolution to give vent to its rebelliousness against a degenerate feudalism and a despotic absolutism as well as to express its aspiration for the emancipation of the individual, also provided the patrons of the Kock school of Hasidism. Moreover, upon the Jews—that people which was the most downtrodden of nations, and which hoped for deliverance and yearned over the generations for a messianic redemption—the distress of soul lay heavily to the point of suffocation, and therefore they had a deep yearning for a beautiful world. "Mete out your strength in accordance with the objective!" cried the Polish romanticist Adam Mickiewicz in his "Ode to Youth." At the same time, the distinguished leader of the Hasidim in Kock raised a difficult question: "About Pharaoh's daughter, it is written, 'And she sent her handmaid' [but here the word *amah* is given the meaning of "forearm"]; now this poses a problem; how could she stretch out her hand? Did she not stand at a distance? However, if one desires to attain any goal whatsoever, let not his thoughts linger upon the obstacles standing in his way, but let him stretch forth his hand and it will lengthen itself even by several cubits."[404] Like "the small improvisation" of the greatest of the Polish poets in his play *Dziady*, the Rabbi of Kock exclaimed: "Let the matter cost blood, but let man be a holy person," and as was his wont, he found an allusion to his words in the Torah. The portion *Kedoshim* opens with "Ye shall be holy" and concludes with "their blood shall be upon them."[405] He created his "great improvisation" with an outburst of the bitterness of his heart on that very eve when Rosh Hashanah was over, as he emerged suddenly from his private room and went to the nearby *bet ha-midrash*, where he aroused his sleepy Hasidim with a loud shout, "Faces! Tell me, does any single countenance exist which is comparable to the countenance on high?" And when they arose trembling, he continued in a loud voice, "Do you know what I want? I want this, that even if the heavens bend down to the earth and the earth is split apart, man should not desist from his own [truth]—that's what I want." Still, it was only natural that the concluding words of the Hasidic leader were quite different from the blasphemous conclusion of the "Improvisation": He repeated the words of Deutero-Isaiah, "Seek ye the Lord while He may be found,"[406] and then, together with his Hasidim, raised his voice in song.[407]

The verse "Give ear, ye heavens" was interpreted by the Rabbi of Kock to mean "give ear on a heavenly level";[408] and in the name of his master from Przysucha he taught that man was created "to elevate the heavens."[409] Here R. Mendel raised himself to a higher conceptual level than that of his disciple, R. Isaac Meir of Ger, who said of the verse "The heavens are the heavens of the Lord, but the earth hath He given to the children of men"[410] that it was given "to make of it a heaven."[411] In Polish Romanticism, this was the point of view of Slowacki, who was second in rank to Mickiewicz, and who bequeathed in his poem "My Testament" the power that would not rest until "I will transform you, eaters of bread into angels." The imperative of aspiring to lofty ideals was also expressed by the Rabbi of Ger in a comment on the folk saying "If you can't get across from above, you have to get across from below": "And I say on the contrary, if you can't get across from below, you must get across from above." As his disciples explained it, "One should always set himself sublime goals, and thereby one will renew his strength."[412]

This theme in the doctrine of Kock is epitomized by R. Mendel's marvelous parable, which makes clear his principle in both religion and ethics on exertion of the will beyond the limits of possibility, as well as his basically optimistic conception of activism, which triumphs over every onset of despair and discouragement:

> Let us imagine that God made a ladder by which the souls descended from the upper world to this world and the ladder was removed, and the souls were called upon from heaven to return upward: there were some who would not even begin to do anything to ascend, since they believed that it was not possible to ascend to heaven without a ladder; and there were some, who began to jump upward and fell down a number of times until they desisted from jumping anymore. But there were some prudent people who said that since there was no ladder there was no other way but to keep on jumping upward; although we know of those who fell, we must perforce continue to jump upward until God—blessed be His Name—has mercy upon us and brings us up to the heavens.[413]

Elitism and Profundity as Byproducts of the New Hasidism

The extreme individualism, which was expressed in romantic perfectionism and maximalism, also developed naturally into élitism. According to this school, R. Simḥah Bunem already had inclined toward this view and R. Mendel received it from him. It was R. Simḥah Bunem who said to his disciple, "Of what use to me is a multitude of Hasidim like this? A few Hasidim are enough for me."[414] Many of R. Mendel's sayings have been recounted which demonstrate the consistency of his doctrine and its development in this matter. The pride in his Hasidim should be ascribed to an earlier period of optimism: "I have Hasidim who can make a gesture with a finger toward heaven and say, This is my God, and I will glorify Him."[415] Of his steadily deepening disillusionment, he said, "I had thought that I would have three hundred Hasidim, most divine in their sanctity."[416] He told R. Wolf of Stryków that he had thought "he would have fifty or one hundred fifty Hasidim, who would stand upon the roofs and attain the level of the prophets."[417]

He found no comfort in the fact that multitudes of ordinary Hasidim who were not men of achievement flocked to him. On the contrary, he regarded this popularity as beneath his dignity and as a mark of a weakening of his character. Thus, pointing to the large crowds in his room, he said to his son-in-law R. Abraham (who later became the Rabbi of Sochaczew) with disdain, "In my earlier years, the likes of these would not have had access to me, but what a low pass I have come to today!"[418] And during another conversation he explained apologetically, "In my youth, when I could look inside myself, Hasidim such as these would not have been able to become attached to me."[419] Just as Horace expressed his contempt for the "profanum vulgus" in poetry, the rabbi, who was a spiritual aristocrat, was fond of the talmudic saying, "How numerous are the men named Joseph in the marketplace,"[420] to which he gave an added derisive turn by a free translation into Yiddish, "There are enough *yosiflekh* [little Josephs] in the streets."[421] Finally, in his old age, suffering a severe bout of melancholy, a sense of despair brought on by abandonment overcame him. This despair burst forth when he suddenly opened the door from his room to the *bet ha-midrash* and cried out, "O, did I ever imagine that there would be with me only a *minyan* of men dressed in white garb and no more?"[422]

The original thoughts propounded by the school of Przysucha-Kock as a result of its outspoken trend of religious individualism not only paralleled many leading ideas of romantic literature of its generation but also partly even presaged the new extreme, individualistic philosophy, particularly that of Nietzsche. In their effort to achieve profundity of religious thought and religious feeling, the spokesmen of this regenerated Hasidism also reached a penetrating psychological power of observation. Their aphorisms are marked by a pungent wit and folk humor. R. Simḥah Bunem, himself a witty conversationalist and man of the world, extolled the virtue of wisdom and stigmatized folly. "A person can be a righteous, yet foolish man." This he proceeded to demonstrate: "For it is decreed concerning man whether he shall be wise or foolish, but not that he shall be righteous and wicked, for whether one is righteous or wicked depends on man's choice. And if it has been decreed concerning one that he be a fool, and he chooses to be righteous, then he is both a fool and righteous."[423] It need hardly be said that the cutting edge of the satire lies in the dual meaning of the term "zaddik." He saw the perfection of man as being a compound of three qualities—goodness, piety, and wisdom—for each one by itself suffers from a deficiency. The man who merely displays goodness may be an adulterer; if only devout, he may be a thief; and if merely wise, he may be a skeptic. For this too he found biblical support (Lam.

3:26): "It is good that a man should wait quietly for the salvation of the Lord."[424] The following interpretation of the verse in Proverbs (17:28) "Even a fool, when he holdeth his peace, is counted wise" was attributed to the Rabbi of Kock: "Even if the fool holds his peace, still the wise man will be counted; the wise person will in any event be recognized."[425]

R. Mendel demonstrated a profound psychological, as well as intellectual, understanding of the many paradoxes which have confounded man. On the subject of laziness he had this to say: "The difference between the lazy man and the cautious man is that the latter acts with composure and not hastily, whereas the lazy person is quite the contrary, being too lazy even to think anything over."[426] With the insight of a psychoanalyst, he explained that "the evil inclination toward pride occurs mainly among men from whom all other desires have already departed."[427] Although not in harmony with the formulae of the new psychology, yet with a great deal of psychological acumen, he maintained that "envy is inborn in man, while lust results from experience and being reared in it."[428] In explanation of a statement in the Midrash (*Tanḥuma, Parashat Pekudei* 3)—"the seventh age is like that of an ape"—he defined one of the essential characteristics of old age: "It would appear that man at the time of old age, being bereft of his vitality, does nothing of his own volition in the matter of worshipping God but what he sees others do, or what he himself did already."[429] He expressed with terse pungency his opinion on the psychology of the intimate relations of a man and his wife when a young man complained to him that "his wife dominates him." He answered, "It is written 'And thy desire shall be to thy husband and he shall rule over thee'; but if the reverse is the case, then also in this matter, the reverse prevails."[430]

Culmination of the New Hasidism in Izbica

A particular strain in the Hasidism of Poland, the doctrine propounded by R. Mordecai Joseph Leiner of Izbica, was an offshoot of the Przysucha-Kock school of Hasidism. Here also extreme religious individualism was very prominent, but it was based, as was the entire doctrine of Izbica, on a definite kabbalistic foundation. The concept advanced by his teachers—R. Simḥah Bunem of Przysucha and R. Mendel of Kock—regarding man's duty constantly to perfect himself and correct his imperfections, was the cornerstone of Mordecai Joseph's doctrine of Hasidism. In this doctrine, there also were some of the elements of predestination, divine grace, and submission to

God's will that are found in Calvinism. In asserting religious individualism, it was said that "no two persons are like each other, since each is an individual by himself; for they all branch out from one root, yet each individual shines in one aspect in greater measure than does his fellowman in his aspect."[431] The twelve sons of Jacob are illustrative of this individualism: For example, Reuben's nature was such "that in all things which were his concern, the start should always be very good—but he could never bring the action to a conclusion. . . ." Gad, on the other hand, "was born small, hence he was given the name 'Gad' which is philologically derived from the term meaning a small grain."[432] It was Ephraim's nature "in respect to every deed, to look always at the aspect of law and *Halakha* without departing from it . . . ," while it was the very "source of life of Judah to look always to God in connection with every deed . . . and not to perform a religious act in merely routine fashion."[433] Indeed, just as each individual differs from his fellow in the good qualities assigned to him from the time of his birth, so there is "implanted in man a particular shortcoming from the day of his birth."[434] Also in the matter of the words of the Torah, each person understands them according to his level, and to the degree that a man stands higher than his fellowman, they shine with greater clarity.[435] And, similarly, in the matter of sanctity "which evolved from God by way of the Patriarchs reaching unto us," "every individual Jewish soul receives from God the sanctity which pertains to his particular soul."[436] However, with regard to goodness itself, God allocated to each person a certain measure of goodness as well as a certain deficiency. Therefore, goodness cannot be activated until a person corrects his deficiency, and it will not help him no matter "how much he prays or indulges in self-mortification" unless he clarifies for himself what he lacks.[437] Thus, the Torah was given to render complete that lack which is implanted in man.[438] But "at the beginning of Creation God caused a portion to emanate to each individual soul, through which he would endeavor to worship God in this world."[439]

Since everything is foreseen from the beginning, and there is no change in God's will, it is the cardinal principle of faith to understand and "to feel" that everything originates from His will, including the measure of each man's reverence for God, as well as the measure of man's striving in the worship of God. At times, after God has helped a man, "he can fall into error and imagine that by his own actions he has removed illusions from his heart, when in actuality man's actions do not at all help him, for only God helps him." Indeed, it is "the mark of the scholar that he recognizes that he has no power which stems from himself, but only from God—even the power to pray." The meaning of *vaetḥanan* (and I besought) is "that no person has any claim upon

God, except by way of supplication." It is "like winning a large sum of money in a lottery without having made any effort for it."[440] This does not signify that man is destined to passivity. On the contrary, man is obliged "to determine initially by a number of tests" each action in order to ascertain whether it stems from the will of God which He bestowed upon him; then, having determined that this *is* the will of God, "he must be resolved not to allow any such will to pass away to no purpose"; the very force of this will is itself proof that this is "certainly the will of God."[441] But, on the other hand, when it happens that a man is unable to reach a decision by himself on some matter, "and does not know where to turn," he is advised to act on the principle of "sitting still and doing nothing" until he himself feels what is the will of God.[442] As with the worship of God, the words of the Torah are given by God "only to him who is aware that he lacks them and needs them to make up what he lacks."[443]

Just as one is obligated to clarify every action from the aspect of God's will, so should he establish the order of his personal conduct on the basis of the clarification of his personality. "Every Jewish individual must probe his soul to establish what is his character and his level."[444] Here too he will receive help from God. If out of good intention "he sometimes takes a step above his station," exceeding that portion which God imparted to him at the beginning of Creation, then "God will enlighten him so that it too will become his portion," that is, He will raise him to a station higher than that fixed for him at the beginning.[445] So, too, God will provide the individual with the occasion to perform a deed by means of which he will distinctly see a shortcoming which had not come to his attention because it was hidden deep within his heart; through this deed the person will come to understand that he must pray for help, and then God will help him.[446] The very punishment which befalls a wicked person is likely to stir the upright man to search inwardly to see whether this shortcoming is not found within him, thus "leading him to repent and make perfect that in which he was deficient."[447]

This individualism, as well as the complete submission to God's will, are both essentially contrary to "a religion of rote." The verse "Ye shall not make with Me gods of silver, or gods of gold" (Exod. 20:23) was taken to mean that one should not do "as you have seen your teacher and your forebears in the matter of reverence and love." Not only must one not follow in the footsteps of his forefathers' tradition, but also he should not even rely upon himself or do today what he did yesterday, "since God will show him His will." From this R. Mordecai deduced the extreme conclusion that "a person is at times obliged to act contrary to the *halakha*," indeed even against the rules enunciated in the Torah, if it has been made clear to him that this is God's will. . . .[448] In support of this radical opinion, he cited the well-known verse in Psalms (119:126) in the homiletical version of the Sages:[449] "When it is a time to work for the Lord, one should break Thy Torah."

Those two principles—religious individualism and the manifestation of the Creator's will in all that is done in the world—also provided the basis for the social outlook of the Rabbi of Izbica. This outlook constitutes a complete justification of social differences[450] and differences in communal status. A person is prohibited from being envious of "his friend or neighbor—who is endowed with all that is good"—even if he himself has only a "limited livelihood," since the Creator allots to each one his portion, but the rabbi's advice is that "one should pray to God that he [too] may have an ample share of the flow of God's grace." A lack of livelihood should be attributed by a person to a lack within himself in the worship of God, it being his own fault that he did not examine his soul adequately.[451] Thus it is not permissible for one to speak ill of any "Jew to whom God has accorded eminence, even though he thinks him unworthy," since if that one has been elevated over others, it is a sign "that God delights to honor him and that he is surely worthy to be given eminence."[452]

To be sure, this social and religious individualism was held in check by the concept of the unity and solidarity of the Jewish people, which also was maintained as a cardinal tenet in the doctrine of Izbica. A person is obliged to link his lot with that of the entire nation, "to include himself as being equally a part with all Jews"; and inasmuch as "Jewish souls, in their totality, are all linked in one chain," it follows that when "a person prays for welfare, he intends it for all Jews."[453] In addition, this solidarity constitutes a remedy for the deficiency inherent in each person, that is, the lack of perfection. Thus Gad, who was born to an inferior status, "was blessed by Jacob with [belonging to] a group: 'A troop shall troop upon him.' That is, he will have a predilection for a group, and so, as a matter of course, when he associates with the many, he will attain perfection, for all benefits and power and strength are implicit in the act of association and in peace and unity."[454] In the doctrine of the Rabbi of Izbica, there are also recognizable vestiges of the democratic tradition of Hasidism which make it obligatory to accept even simple folk for the worship of God. For example, in the incident of the bitter waters it is written, "And the Lord showed him a tree" (Exod. 15:25). "By this God shows us that man should not bring near to Him only scholars and men of great learning, but even simple people—who are compared with the bitter waters—who want to entreat God; for even to them the ways of God will impart instruction to direct them into straight paths."[455]

These principles also apply to the Rabbi of Izbica's teaching with regard to the Jews and the gentile nations and to the Redemption. Just as God chose individuals from among the Jews in accordance with His will, bestowing the light of His Torah upon them in greater abundance than upon others, as it is written, "I will be gracious to whom *I* will be gracious" [emphasis added] (Exod. 33:19), so did He select the Jews to be His chosen people.[456] And just as each individual differs from his neighbor in the personality traits inherent in him, so "each of the gentile nations possesses its own singular quality, this one having wealth, that one power," and if "one nation is abundantly endowed with a certain good, it will lack some other good, and the reverse will be true for another nation."[457] But all these differences among the gentile nations with regard to each other are as nothing when compared with the abyss which exists between them and the Jews. Even "the good qualities and the beneficent knowledge" of gentile nations, which are reflected in their wealth and possessions, are there in exile, since idol worshippers do "the reverse of God's will"; but when the Jews have one of these qualities, then God's will is fulfilled through it, for the Jews are the "instrument by which God's will is implemented."[458] It is Benjamin's mission to be "a wolf that raveneth . . . [and] divideth the spoil," for if he should see a worthwhile thing among the Gentiles, "he will snatch it from them and pass it on to the Jews."[459] So beloved are the Jews in the eyes of God that even if they do deeds like those done by the Gentiles, they are good precisely because they are the deeds of Jews. Even the wicked among the Jews have goodness at the root of their lives, for it is only their acts which are not good, and those can be amended through penitence. However, the root of the Gentiles is bad and their acts are evil, even though they seem good "in their outer guise," as in the outer shell of Amalek, who "stretches forth his cloven hoof, as if to say, I am a clean animal." The quality of the Jewish people is that of Aaron, kind and peaceful, whereas the quality of Edom is one of murder, as it is written (Gen. 27:40): "And by thy sword shalt thou live." It is true that it is stated (in Mal. 1:2): "Was not Esau Jacob's brother?"—but this resemblance is merely external, for "God is aware that they are not equal." Also, "it seems that Esau and Jacob hated each other in the same way; but Esau's hatred of Jacob is a deep-rooted hostility, since he hates him in his very essence," whereas Jacob dislikes Esau for "the evil of his nature, because he is irate and cruel." Similarly, "the hearts of the children of Israel are filled with joy," while "the gentile nations appear happy, but their hearts are really filled with grief." In this world, "the idol worshippers . . . are called rich" and "the Israelites are called poor," even though the gentile nations subsist only from the waste matter of life which flows abundantly to the Jews. The gentile nations do all sorts of things in order to maintain themselves, for they conduct themselves according to the laws of nature, but the Israelites understand that all of life is the reverse of nature, since everything is a manifestation of God's will.[460]

In his dialectical analysis of these contrasts between truth and appearance in relation to the Jews and the gentile nations, the Rabbi of Izbica proceeds to distinguish between the "essence of reality and the semblance of diversity," between "the inner essence" and "the outer garb," and between that which is "concealed" and that which is "revealed." In line with this principle of contrasts, he depicts the characteristics of people who are, at the root of their being, the reverse of the "garb which covers": Thus the Patriarch Isaac, in terms of outer garb alone, had the quality of power, but considered from the aspect of his inner essence, he was destined to be the source of all salvation;[461] according to his nature Jacob was a quiet man, yet Esau testified concerning him that "he has supplanted me these two times"; concerning Moshe Rabbenu, the Torah states that "the man Moses was very meek" (Num. 12:3), yet Datan and Abiram reproached him to his face: "Must thou make thyself also a prince over us?" (Num. 16:13). This contrast between outer garb and inner essence in the nature of man was considered a necessity with regard to the worship of God: In order to clarify his nature, he must continually refine "his garb" and thus get to his true root, for if he were to be remiss in the work of this refinement, it is likely that the outer qualities would penetrate to his heart and turn into his very root.[462]

The influence of R. Mendel's doctrine on this psychological-dialectical analysis of his rebellious disciple is obvious. Even the very example of inwardness and its opposite on the surface—for example, meekness which appears as haughtiness—derives from the environment of the Hasidim of Kock, who covered up their inner modesty with a breach of manners. Paralleling his admonition that no one should reach the point where his garb becomes the very root of his soul, the Rabbi of Kock gave a homiletical interpretation of the verse "This is the statute of the law . . . a red heifer, faultless." He explained that "red" precedes "faultless," yet "red" is merely the color, whereas "faultless" refers to the animal itself. However, when the color penetrates the essence, then the color also becomes part of the essence.[463] Like the parable of the Rabbi of Izbica concerning the complaint of Datan and Abiram against the pride of Moses, the following saying had been transmitted in the names of both the Rabbi of Kock and his teacher, the Rabbi of Przysucha: If a man is stripped entirely of a bad trait and has no contact with it at all, there will then be found adversaries who will hold him suspect of the very thing of which he was stripped.[464] The distinguished disciple of Przysucha-Kock, R. Isaac Meir of Ger, was of the opinion that every "good Jew" (zaddik) has his own disguise. For example, "the disguise of *ha-Yehudi* of Przysucha consisted in his being a scholar, and that of the Rabbi of Lublin ["the Seer"] consisted in his being inspired by the Holy Spirit.[465] But the leader of the Hasidim of Izbica developed the doctrine of qualities promulgated by his teachers into a system of psychology and even elevated the kabbalistic concept concerning "what is concealed" and "what is revealed" to a major principle in the doctrine of the Redemption.

In his teaching about the Redemption, the Rabbi of Izbica returned to the concepts of the Kabbalah, which were propagated by the Hasidic movement but which did not yet occupy a place in the system of Przysucha-Kock. The Exile continues as long as the sparks of holiness which are scattered in a state of defilement among the gentile nations have not been purified and collected.[466] The prolongation of the Exile is beneficial for the Jews, for if all the sparks are purified, the Jews will become even more exalted, as they will take possession of all the wealth of the gentile nations. True, "God can bring the time and the salvation nearer, for time is in God's hand alone." Thus the Jews are obligated "to thunder and cry out to God because of the Jews' anguish at being in exile." But it is God who gives Israel the strength to endure the oppression of the nations, and this endurance is a sign of their "resoluteness," their reliance upon their Rock and their belief that He will not forsake them. Although the Jews suffer in Exile, they are not cut off from their root, and even if they sin, there is no break in God's love for them. The main thing is that Jews in Exile "utterly devote their lives and thoughts to the belief that God is always engaged in behalf of the welfare of Israel."[467]

The basis of the Exile is that although God's will is not alterable, it is covered with a garb as long as the Jews are not redeemed. Therefore, it seems to the gentile nations that the Jews are subservient to them, that the power is in their hands; and the Jews themselves are also "slightly" influenced by this delusion, "and this is the essence of their being in exile."[468] When the Redemption comes, it will be clear to all that the power resides in God; then He will also clarify the thoughts of the Jews, and it will be demonstrated that their "alien thoughts" were only a cloak, "for all their desire and their wish was only for the good that inheres in anything." The example is given of a

Gentile who sold a bar of tin to a Jew assuming it to be tin, and later it was discovered that inside it was solid silver.[469] The verse (Isa. 25:9) "Lo, this is our God, for whom we waited" alludes to the notion that "God confers deliverance even upon the past, and makes it clear that He has not caused any part of His will to turn aside even by a hair's breadth": "Then God will show us that we never were in exile and that no nation whatsoever held sway over us, save God alone."[470]

Just as God's love for Israel, which had been concealed, will be revealed at the time of Redemption, so will His vengeance upon the gentile nations be manifested "because of the Redemption of Israel," although "He is good and all the garbs in which He arrayed Himself, as it were, are good." And as the deliverance is extant throughout the days of the Exile, albeit in a state of concealment, so "the main part in the rebuilding of Jerusalem is done during the time of the Exile," when the Jews are scattered among the Gentiles "so that they may receive all the benefits from them in order to bring them to sanctity." Accordingly, the verse in Psalms should have read: "The Lord doth build up Jerusalem, He scattereth the dispersed of Israel." However, King David introduced as a scribal emendation the word *yekhanes* (gathereth together) in place of *yefazer* (scattereth); that is, the time of the Redemption should come in order "to gather the dispersed of Israel, so that then the rebuilding of Jerusalem will be completed."[471] And since God does not cease from delivering the Jews "and is always prepared to help them," "the Jews likewise must be prepared and always wait for God"; and just as God indicates to each individual what his deficiency is so that he may be cleansed of it, so "doth He declare His word to Jacob," that is "He tells them the sin, the deficiency which is found in them, for thereby the gentile nations are endowed with the power to have dominion over them to the end that they will be brought to repentance."[472]

When the sanctification is completed and the curtain of separation and all "the garbs" come off, then the explicit words of the Torah will become visible and the "depth of their importance" will stand revealed, "for it is the very root of the earth's existence that on it the words of the Torah are rendered explicit"; the Torah which seems "like a yoke and a burden" will stand revealed as pure love of the Jewish people. Then the curtain of separation in prayer will also be done away with: "All the prayers which we recite as they were arranged by the Men of the Great Assembly only provide the means of revealing that all things stem from God"; but only then, when His Kingdom manifests itself, "will there be prayer coming from the hearts of the Jews with regularity."[473]

And thus in its own singular way, through the dialectic method of the Kabbalah, the Hasidism established in Izbica strove toward that lofty goal which was a beacon for all the schools of Hasidism: to reinforce the nation in its unity against its oppressors, buttressing its faith and encouraging its hope for Redemption.

Crystallization, Contention, and Decline: The Career of Rabbi Isaac Meir of Ger

Despite their common goals, the antagonism between the rival schools was most conspicuous and gave rise to prolonged quarrels. By the beginning of the nineteenth century, two camps of Hasidim had crystallized: that of the adherents of "the Seer" of Lublin and that of *ha-Yehudi* of Przysucha. According to an *aggadah* of the Hasidim of Kock, R. Meir of Opatów, who carried on in the ways of his Lublin master, did not refrain from cursing the Hasidim of Przysucha; and the Hasidim of Kozienice used to say that daily one should say the prayer giving thanks "that He did not make me a Hasid of Przysucha."[474] A kind of coalition of rebbes in Galicia and in the Kingdom of Poland who followed in the footsteps of the old system of Hasidism banded together against Przysucha. In order to forestall any trouble, R. Simḥah Bunem sent a delegation to the wedding in Ustilug (in Volhynia) of the grandchildren of R. Abraham Joshua Heschel of Medzhibozh (who became famous as the Rabbi of Opatów) and R. Meir of Opatów, where "four hundred rebbes wearing white *kapotes* [caftans]" were assembled. Although the astuteness of R. Isaac Meir of Warsaw—a disciple of R. Simḥah Bunem—was helpful in preventing a "holy war" against his master and his Hasidim,[475] the mutual opposition continued.

After the death of the Rabbi of Przysucha in 1827, the controversy between the Hasidim of his successor, R. Mendel of Kock, and the other Hasidic factions became sharper and the feud intensified. There are grounds for conjecture that the Hasidim of Kock were the ones who provoked the strife and their opponents were compelled to defend themselves. According to an *aggadah* of those in opposition to Kock, the Hasidim of R. Mendel did not shrink from carrying out acts of terror against them.[476] The dispute in the camp of Hasidism turned into enmity and hatred to the extent that those who had been close became distant. After R. Mendel of Kock had fallen ill with melancholia around 1840,[477] and his disciple, R. Mordecai Joseph, had left him and established his own "court" in Izbica, the Hasidim of Kock and Izbica harassed each other mercilessly. The Rabbi of Kock, in particular, could not forgive the disloyalty of his former adherents and criticized them severely.[478]

The death of R. Mendel of Kock in 1859 marked a decisive turn in the history of Hasidism in Poland. To be sure, there still existed many factions of Hasidim, almost as many as courts of the rebbes and their dynasties. The "throne" of R. Mendel was occupied by his son, R. David, and the tradition of the doctrine of Kock was ably fostered by his son-in-law, the distinguished scholar R. Abraham Bornstein, the Rabbi of Sochaczew. R. Isaac of Warka, who died in 1848, similarly had established his own dynasty in his town and in Mszczonów. Centers of Hasidism of the disciples of R. Mendel arose during the lifetime of their teacher in such sites as Ciechanów, Biała, Stryków, Gostynin, Mogielnica. Also, the descendants of the *Maggid* of Kozienice, "the Holy Grandfather" of Radoszyce, as well as other grandchildren led communities of Hasidim in their respective "courts" who were loyal to the Hasidic schools of their forebears. But the predominant figure in the Hasidism of Poland was the disciple of the Rabbi of Kock, R. Isaac Meir (known by the initials RIM) of Warsaw, who quickly moved to the town of Ger (Góra Kalwaria) east of Warsaw. Only after his death, in the beginning of 1866, did there arise a rival court to Ger that was established in the town of Alexander, near Łódz, that of R. Yeḥiel ben Feivel Danziger, one of the disciples of R. Isaac of Warka. Most significantly, despite the rivalry among the "courts" the doctrinal division in the Hasidism of Poland came to a halt. In that era, R. Isaac Meir of Ger put his stamp on Polish Hasidism, and it was he who charted its course for the future. While his master from Kock repelled Hasidim of various schools both in his radical doctrine and in the arrogance and loftiness of his conduct, his distinguished disciple attracted them by his moderation both in doctrine and in temperament.

One of the prominent traits in the system of Ger which won over the Hasidim of Poland was the establishing of the study of the Talmud and the *Posekim* as a fundamental way of life. In the synthesis of Torah and piety, his master from Kock stressed the element of inner perfection, while his disciple elevated the study of the Torah above all the other commandments. Indeed, he himself viewed the development of the doctrine of Przysucha as a three-stage process. "R. Simḥah Bunem led the community through love, the Rabbi of Kock led it through reverence, and I lead it through the Torah."[479] It was not for nothing that his colleague, Ḥanokh Henekh of Alexander, was wont to observe that for R. Simḥah Bunem there were "two commentaries, the first, our master and teacher of Kock; and the second, our master and teacher of Ger."[480] This goal of R. Isaac Meir indeed drew close to him the camp of constantly diminishing opponents.

The rapprochement of the camps of the Hasidim and the Mitnaggedim was facilitated by the inflexible and extreme conservatism of the Hasidism of Ger, no less than by the strengthening of the pillars of the Torah. "Anything new is forbidden by the Torah" was a saying current with the Hasidim of Ger, on the basis of the verse (Lev. 26:10) "And ye shall bring forth the old from before the new." During the lifetime of his teacher from Kock, R. Isaac Meir of Ger made every effort to oppose any modernization in the life of the people. He mobilized all the pious in the community of Warsaw against the plan of the enlightened to require the teachers in the *Ḥadarim* to undergo an examination. In this he was very successful: even though the tests were required of all the teachers by law, only a few tried to obtain certificates. Similarly, he organized a successful opposition to the establishment of new schools for Jewish children in Warsaw, in addition to the few schools already in existence.[481] R. Isaac Meir also was the leader of those in both camps who campaigned against the decree requiring the adoption of the gentile mode of dress.

In the spring of 1846, when it became known that an edict banning the Jewish mode of dress was being prepared, R. Isaac Meir, in collaboration with his colleague R. Isaac of Warka, sought to enlist the aid of Moses Montefiore, who was then visting Poland, but to no avail. When the decree was issued some months later, he organized an attempt to intercede with the authorities for its annulment. It is true that in 1849, when a manifesto in the name of Warsaw's rabbinate was issued urging the members of the community to obey the royal statute in the matter of the change in dress, this Hasidic leader also signed it as a member of the community's *bet din,* a function he had been performing since 1843. But later he was the moving spirit in the opposition to the decree, and as a penalty for this he was arrested by the police, although he was freed the following day because of the popular feeling aroused by the news of his arrest. According to a Hasidic *aggadah*, it was as a result of the propaganda of R. Isaac Meir that the pious chose the Russian and not the German style of dress, for it included permission to grow a beard; moreover, the coat was longer than that in fashion in western European dress.[482]

The strong insistence and strictness of R. Isaac Meir of Warsaw regarding the preservation of the traditional Jewish mode of dress were in themselves characteristic of the development of Hasidism along conservative lines. Nor was his colleague and teacher R. Mendel of Kock—like R. Simḥah Bunem the teacher of both of them—fond of close contact between Jews and their neighbors, considering it to be dangerous to the self-preservation of the Jewish people. R. Simḥah Bunem interpreted the verse "And their laws are diverse from those of every people" (Esth. 3:8) as meaning "that this is their law that they shall be different from every other people."[483] He also commented on the verse dealing with the covenant of Abraham and Abimelech "And they two made a covenant" (Genesis 21:27), saying that "they two, and not one [means that] there shall be no unity between them, they should never be joined together to be alike in their deeds."[484] R. Mendel of Kock interpreted the prophecy of Balaam (Num. 24:14) "what this people shall do to thy people in the end of days" as relating to the days when "this people will be your people, to the extent that they will, God forbid, be alike in all their manners and customs."[485] But this same Rabbi of Kock was agitated to the very depth of his being when he was told that R. Abraham of Ciechanów, in concert with R. Isaac Meir of Warsaw, held that Jews are obligated to risk their lives regarding the decree on the mode of dress. Not only did he ridicule this judgment, which, in his opinion, was not in accord with Jewish law, but also, displaying an understanding of history, he recalled that the Jews had changed their mode of dress more than once.[486]

The conservatism of the disciples of Kock continued to increase as the Haskalah appeared, and also spread among Poland's backward Jewry. R. Isaac Meir composed special poems to warn against the "plague" of the Haskalah, which gives its devotees "the accursed waters, gall and wormwood" to drink.[487] During the service in the synagogue, the zaddik R. Yeḥiel Meir of Gostynin sought forgiveness from the Holy Torah when he learned that ordinary householders and youths were reading "books of romance" and "poems and love stories" on the Holy Sabbath, and he moralized at great length on the desirability of reciting from the Book of Psalms and reading from the *Kav Hayashar* instead.[488] In the early 1880s the son-in-law of R. Mendel of Kock, R. Abraham of Sochaczew, issued proclamations against "those who read in the books and periodicals of the free thinkers."[489] Thus the circle of the devout, who viewed all social and cultural progress among the people with hostility, became ever smaller. The refreshing and invigorating concepts of the Hasidism of Przysucha and Kock in the period of Sturm und Drang steadily evaporated, and nothing remained of them but memories.

10

The Policy of the Polish Government toward Hasidism

The Influence of the Galician Policies

When one considers the similarity in the economic and cultural policies of the absolute monarchies toward the Jews in both Galicia and Congress Poland, it is not surprising that the political policies toward the Hasidic movement were also quite similar. The principles of absolutism were in themselves reason enough to predispose the authorities at the outset against this developing movement in which mysticism and superstition were rife. Also, the essentially spontaneous character of this movement was in opposition to the absolutist principle of the strict supervision of every detail in the life of its subjects; it certainly would contradict the maxim of Frederick II: "Everything *for* the people, nothing *by* the people." Hasidism particularly, with its religious fanaticism and extreme stand on national exclusiveness, was viewed as a serious obstacle to the government's programs for the dissemination of "civilization" among and the gradual assimilation of the Jews. Nor was the government of Poland superior to its neighbor as far as its heavy, dull-witted, bureaucratic apparatus was concerned; here, too, the authorities gave credence to the initial reports of provincial officials, according to which Hasidism was a totally insignificant sectarian movement which had no influence over the general Jewish population.

The fact that decrees concerning Hasidism were issued in both countries during the very same years, 1823 and 1824, was a mere coincidence. But this is not to say that Galicia's nullification of the decree against the Hasidim did not influence the Kingdom of Poland's policy in this regard. The instructions of the gubernium in Galicia stating the principle of tolerance toward Hasidism and permitting Hasidim to maintain *minyanim* was issued on April 26, 1824;[1] in the Kingdom of Poland, the viceroy's directive to the Committee for Internal Affairs permitting the existence of Hasidic synagogues was issued on August 30, 1824. The latter decision was based on the opinion of a subcommittee of the Committee for Religions and Education which convened in June and finished its deliberations by the beginning of August. It is highly likely that this subcommittee knew of the gubernium's directive in Galicia. It is also reasonable to assume that in their effort to nullify the decree, the Hasidim of Poland called attention to the action taken in Galicia.

This favorable turn in the attitude of the Polish authorities toward Hasidism resulted from a number of factors. Bribes, the tried and tested means used by the Jews in that era to mitigate harsh decrees and even to have them nullified, had even better results in Poland than in Galicia, for Count Novosiltzev, the pivotal figure in setting the kingdom's policy, never rejected "gifts." The Hasidim in Poland were also helped by the fact that the government would reach decisions in matters affecting the Jews only after asking the opinion of the Committee for the Affairs of Old Testament Believers. Since Jacob Bergson, a representative of the Hasidim, was a member of the Advisory Chamber of the committee, the Hasidim could obtain information concerning the activities of the government and benefit from his intercession.

The main reason for the favorable decisions toward Hasidism—in Poland as in Galicia—was the general religious policy of strengthening religion and faith as a shield against the spread of liberal ideas which would undermine the foundations of both "the royal throne and the altar." Despite its dislike of mysticism and superstition, the government preferred them to the "harmful views" of deistic rationalism and to the utter heresy of atheism. Thus the government preferred Hasidism to the Haskalah and correctly saw the Hasidic movement as a counterbalance to the activities of the Maskilim and the "enlightened ones." And therefore decrees were issued against the Hasidim only occasionally.

Hasidism in Poland benefited from greater tranquillity than its counterpart in Galicia. As discussed, it was the Maskilim, headed by Joseph Perl, who initiated attacks against the Hasidim; whereas in the

Kingdom of Poland, the handful of Maskilim had no support within the Jewish community and therefore did not dare to mount an offensive against the Hasidim, especially since the government disapproved of the dispute between the two groups. "The enlightened" assimilationists turned their backs on both the Maskilim and the Hasidim, while the spokesman of the assimilationists, the censor Jacob Tugendhold, completely accommodated himself to the position taken by the authorities, that is, that the real danger to the regime came from rationalism and not from religious fanaticism and superstitious beliefs.[2]

Hence it happened that in Galicia, even after 1824, inquiries and investigations concerning Hasidism were initiated, and Hasidic leaders were even persecuted sporadically, while in Poland no questions were asked about Hasidism except during discussions within the government.

A Report of "Hussites"

As in Galicia, the Polish government's interest in the Hasidic movement was first aroused by a local incident.

At the end of the summer of 1823, the police chief in the town of Parczew in the *województwo* of Podlasie, Colonel Dalfus, informed the central government about a "Hussite sect which is being founded by young Jews" in this town. He reported that the members of this sect did not worship in the synagogue but in private homes, where they gathered until late into the night, making a great deal of noise and commotion. They recruited members from various communities who lived with them secretly and without certificates of residence.[3]

In the eighteenth century, Parczew was still one of the small communities in Poland. According to the census of 1764, when the town belonged to the *województwo* of Lublin, the number of Jews aged one year and older came to no more than 303, and, including the settlements in the 29 villages in its vicinity, to 454.[4] By 1827, four years after it attracted the special attention of the authorities as a cell of Hasidism, the number of Jews had risen to 1,079, amounting to 37 percent of the total population of 2,922.[5] Parczew did not occupy a prominent place in the history of Hasidism in Poland except in the period of the decline of the movement at the end of the nineteenth century, when the post of rabbi was held by grandchildren of *ha-Yehudi* of Przysucha.[6] The fact that the Hasidic sect had already struck root in this community at the beginning of the nineteenth century is indicated in the literature of Hasidism. The Hasid R. Barukh Leybush of Parczew was one of the intimates of R. Simḥah Bunem, and later he also became an intimate of R. Mendel of Kock.[7] When R. Mendel was at his peak, he maintained close relations with the Rabbi of Parczew, the author of *Ḥeshek Shelomo*.[8]

The chance discovery of Hasidism in Parczew was the immediate cause of the decrees against the Hasidic movement in Poland, which were to continue for nearly a year.

The Parczew police chief's report was forwarded by the viceroy, Prince Josef Zayonczek, on September 26, 1823, to both the Committee for Internal Affairs and the central Police Department, with an order to investigate the matter and to take appropriate measures. Three days later, the Committee for Internal Affairs asked the Committee for Religions whether the sect was a new one and whether it belonged to the category of sects which are not tolerated in the country; it also asked for an opinion about measures for implementing the viceroy's order. When the Committee for Religions did not reply by mid-January, the Committee for Internal Affairs, spurred by the viceroy's request for the report, asked the other committee to expedite its report.

The delay on the part of the Committee for Religions was caused by its efforts to obtain detailed information about the Hasidim from various sources. Its main source was a memorandum entitled "Information concerning the Sect of the Hasidim." The name of its author was withheld by the committee for fear that the Hasidim would wreak vengeance upon the informer.

The memorandum opens with a definition of the term "Hasid." A Hasid was defined as one who observes the ceremonial and ethical *mizvot* even more scrupulously than required by the law and is distinguished by his modesty, humility, love of his neighbor, and generosity in charitable donation. The memorandum went on to say that several decades ago there appeared in Medzhibozh, Podolia, a man named Israel, a native of Wallachia, who proclaimed himself "Ba'al Shem," that is, one who performs miracles through the Kabbalah and by means of the various names of God and the angels. He claimed to be able to send his soul aloft to God at any time. On the strength of this relationship no secret was hidden from him, and he was thus able to heal the sick and help barren women. This "Ba'al Shem" attracted a number of disciples from various places who told of his wonder workings. In order to enhance the importance of their innovations, he and his disciples instituted a different prayer ritual from the one customary among the Jews of Poland, Lithuania, Bohemia, and Moravia, namely, a variant of the Sefardi ritual. That is, in the recitation of prayers they would clap their hands in a strange fashion and engage in wild leaping and earthshaking shouts, arguing that only this mode of worship would open the gates of heaven. The proclivity of simple folk and those of limited intellect toward superstitious beliefs resulted in people flocking to them with incidences of illness and other family troubles. After they became famous for their wonder-working, kabbalistic acts, fervid prayers, and devotion to God and the angels, they called themselves Hasidim. All this notwithstanding, the Jewish communities regarded both them and their doctrines with such scorn that the very name "Hasidim" became a derisive term. In some places they were called "Kitayowcy" (men of silk) because, being apprehensive of linsey-woolsey (a mixture of linen and wool or cotton cloth forbidden by the Torah), they wore silk instead of woolen clothes.

The memorandum went on to say that after the death of the Ba'al Shem his disciples dispersed and each proclaimed himself the successor of his master by virtue of his talismanic power to perform wonders and also obligated those who came to visit him to offer a sum of money called *pidyon*, meaning redemption, that is, the redemption of the soul, as a condition for his plea for help's being fulfilled. Each sought to draw into his fold the youth and those of limited intelligence, and even more, the rich and women. To this end, they tried to mobilize adherents in every city and town who would worship in their manner in a *shtibl* (a small room used for worship) after their fashion, and that this *shtibl* would also serve as a meetingplace. Upon the death of one of the group leaders, several would arise in his place who followed in his way and designated themselves as leaders, and thus they multiplied.

They conducted themselves as follows: They would spread reports among the multitudes that in a specific city there could be found a man endowed with the divine spirit who foresaw everything and, by virtue of his soul's devotion to God, was qualified to alter the course of the world by his word alone, and by way of proof they would tell of his spurious wonders. The ignorant, especially women, asked him various questions, personally or by messenger, such as whether to enter into a particular business undertaking, whether or not to make a specific marriage match, or whether a couple would remain married. They also made requests such as for their sons' success in business, for the sick to be healed, for deliverance from trouble, for the restoration of what was stolen, for the exorcism of a dybbuk, for the granting of a request submitted to the authorities, or for a favorable judgment in a lawsuit. At times, a sheet of paper on which the request was to be written was brought by the supplicants or submitted through a messenger so that it would be blessed by the holy man, the leader (*herszt*). Each request was accompanied by a *pidyon*, but the Hasidim constantly emphasized that the condition requisite for a favorable decree was that the giver of the *pidyon* have complete faith in the Hasidim and their leader. For the most part, the leader of the Hasidim assured the fulfillment of the request, but in the event of a negative outcome, the Hasidim invented all kinds of excuses, such as that the giver of the *pidyon* did not have enough faith in the zaddik or that he later became an even greater sinner than he had been previously.

For a yet greater degree of deception and spread of superstitious belief, the Hasidim inaugurated a custom of placing petition slips on the graves of their leaders, the intermediary being the son of the deceased or his successor; this also was done with a *pidyon*. Recently, the number of Hasidic leaders had multiplied, each one with followers who elevated him over the others. Furthermore, despite their common goal of disseminating vanities and rebelling against enlightenment, it sometimes happened that the leaders would quarrel among themselves, each claiming that everyone except himself was a charlatan.

They engaged in all kinds of licentious acts in their meeting-houses, and idleness was second nature to them. During the *Shalosh Seudot* (the third Sabbath meal), they would eat, drink, and sing *Zemirot* (Sabbath hymns), thus affording an opportunity for their leader to inculcate in them vain beliefs by vapid interpretations of the Scripture. Then they would recite the evening prayer, and then the *Melaveh Malkah* (literally, accompanying the Queen, that is, the Sabbath), and drink, sing, and dance until midnight, and sometimes even through the entire night. In their opinion, this was the way to attain a state of closeness to God.

The great assemblies of the Hasidim took place in the courts of their leaders. They came there from far and near on the festival days and sometimes on the Sabbath. At times, young people came without asking their parents or even against their wishes with slips bearing petitions, bringing *pidyon* for themselves and others. The Hasidim believed that every word uttered by their leader was divinely inspired and had the force of a heavenly decree. Many young people spent several weeks there and educated themselves to a life of idleness and superstitious beliefs. Their conduct, as well as the doctrines inculcated at their meetings and assemblies, had one purpose—to keep the youth removed from any learning and knowledge and to bring them into close contact only with mystical doctrines. The reading of any book in a foreign language or a book written in a foreign alphabet was considered sinful.

The memorandum concluded with the following apologia: "It is true that the Jewish people in Poland regret that these deceivers and instigators continually spread worthless and vapid beliefs and endeavor to keep the young generation far away from enlightenment; but it cannot summon strength to devise any schemes against this evil."

This banal essay on "the superstitious beliefs" of the Hasidim contains nothing new compared with the polemical writings of the Mitnaggedim but is inferior to them because of its superficial historical description and its hollow generalizations. Indeed, it is reasonable to believe that the author of this memorandum never even saw one of the polemical works. His account of the zaddik's cleaving not only to God but also to angels, as well as his account of the wondrous works achieved through combinations of the names of angels, indicates his ignorance of both the doctrine of Hasidism and the teachings of the Kabbalah. The only fragment in this work which sheds more light on Hasidism is the detailed account of the matters on which people in his generation seeking help would turn to the leaders of the Hasidim. He consistently refers to them as *herszt*, that is, leader of a band or a gang of liars, thieves, or murderers. Of particular interest is the description of the practice customary in those matters, namely, the request for the zaddik's blessing over the paper on which a petition to the authorities was to be written.

Just who was the author of this memorandum? The Polish terms used by the author to define the practical and ethical *mizvot* reflect the influence of the German Haskalah, which denigrated the religious tradition, viewing it as within the compass of ceremonial law. Some of the expressions and phrases, such as "oszuści i zwodziciele" (deceivers and instigators) suggest a Hebrew influence. There is thus no doubt that the author belonged to the tiny group of Maskilim in Warsaw, and, within that group, to the handful of extremist Maskilim who were close to government circles.

Within that group, Jacob Tugendhold must be ruled out at the very beginning, since he had already been serving for a number of years in the office of the censor for Hebrew books, and Tugendhold wrote Polish perfectly, while the memorandum contained a number of grammatical errors. Similarly, the second Jewish censor, Abraham Stern, has to be discounted although he had clearly demonstrated his hostile attitude toward the Hasidim. In his program for the Rabbinical School which he submitted to the government in 1818, he stated that one of the principal functions of the director of the school was to wage war to the hilt against Hasidism and the Kabbalah.[9] As to the other two men who were close to the authorities—Anton Eisenbaum, the future superintendent of the Rabbinical School, and the apostate

Ezekiel Stanislaw Hoge—the latter wrote pure Polish and Eisenbaum did not know Hebrew very well.

There is, however, good evidence to believe that the author of the memorandum was Abraham Buchner, who also was a *persona grata* with the authorities and one of the friends of the censor Tugendhold. Not only was Buchner weak in Polish (in those years he wrote only in Hebrew), but also he was the sole person in his group who interlaced his writings with condemnatory comments about the Hasidim, although he was careful not to mention them by name.[10] In 1822, about a year or more before the memorandum was written, Buchner published his book *Doresh Tov*, a compendium on ethics for youth, which contains a brief description of the Hasidim's "worthless explanations" of the Torah which appeared later—almost word for word—in the memorandum.[11]

The Committee for Religions was not satisfied with the memorandum about the Hasidim, especially as to the question whether the sect of "Hussites" described in the report from Parczew was identical with the Hasidic sect depicted in the memorandum. Therefore, on December 20, 1823, the committee turned to the Synagogue Supervisory Board (the body recently established to manage the community) in Warsaw requesting a detailed report concerning "the sect of Hussites, which they had recently encountered in several locations in the *województwo* of Podlasie and in the *województwo* of Cracow." According to the committee's findings, the members of the sect were no different from other Jews except that they assembled for worship in private houses rather than a public synagogue, were more devout than the others, and in certain communities would sing and dance during the prayer service. The Synagogue Supervisory Board was requested to explain the rules of this sect; whether its name, "Hussites," was a modification of the name Hasidim; and in what respects it was different from other Jewish groups. The board was asked for a report which would include detailed information as well as its own opinion of the sect.

The board, which included a Hasid, Jacob Sonnenberg-Bergson, among its three members, avoided giving its opinion of the sect, and in its special session on February 1, 1824, decided to discharge its obligation with the following brief philological explanation:[12] The "Hussites" are not a new sect, but are the Hasidic sect which has been known throughout the land for some time. The modification in its name was to be explained by the fact that in Polish, the plural form of "Hasid" is "Husyci."[13]

The board's reply satisfied the Committee for Religions, since it definitely established that the "Hussites" and the Hasidim were the same sect, and thus the committee needed no further explanation. On February 12, 1824, the reply of the Committee for Religions to the Committee for Internal Affairs was issued, accompanied by the memorandum. It reported that the "Hussites" and the Hasidim were indeed one and the same, and that the Hasidim had already attracted the attention of the government several years earlier. They were characterized by their superstitious beliefs, strange mannerisms, sorcery, and most important by the fact that the Hasidic leaders tried to keep the masses subservient to them and in a state of ignorance. They were to be found in all the provinces, except the *województwo* of Augustów near Lithuania. The city of Przysucha in the *województwo* of Sandomierz was their main center. In order to extirpate or at least weaken this sect, the Committee for Religions instructed the *województwo* committees to forbid Jews to worship in private houses where the Hasidim were accustomed to assemble, and to prohibit pilgrimages or gatherings in the houses of Jews suspected of being leaders of the sect or associated with it.

Clearly, the Committee for Religions had come across the question of the Hasidim before, but apparently had turned its attention away from it until the matter of the "Hussites" came up for consideration as a result of the report by the police chief in Parczew. From other sources, the committee learned that Hasidism had spread throughout Poland, except in the *województwo* of Augustów, which remained a citadel of the Mitnaggedim. The committee was also aware of the fact, not mentioned in the memorandum, that Przysucha was the center of Hasidism for the entire country.

The Committee for Religions Acts

Relying on the opinion of the author of the memorandum, the committee determined that Hasidism was harmful because it was steeped in superstitious beliefs and because its doctrines led to ignorance among the people and dependence upon zaddikim. The decision to prohibit *minyanim* and Hasidic gatherings at the rebbes' was based on the memorandum's depiction of the *minyanim* as organized cells and the courts of the zaddikim as the bulwarks of Hasidism.

On the basis of the communiqué of the Committee for Religions, an order was issued on February 24, 1824, by the Committee for Internal Affairs to the *województwo* committees. Apart from the prohibition on *minyanim* and all Hasidic gatherings—formulated precisely in accordance with the order of the Committee for Religions—the *województwo* committees were ordered to instruct the local authorities to supervise the Hasidic sect and prevent its spread "wherever they see its traces." The order included the *województwo* of Sandomierz, which encompassed the town of Przysucha, and the *województwo* of Podlasie, which included the town of Parczew, where according to the police chief's report a new cell had been established. The obligation to inform the Committee for Internal Affairs of the measures they would take against the sect was imposed on both *województwo* committees.

The viceroy did not content himself with the decrees regarding the *minyanim* and the Hasidic gatherings which had been issued by the Committee for Religions and the Committee for Internal Affairs. In his letter of March 15, 1824, to the Committee for Religions, he defined Hasidism as a harmful sect not only because it agitated against enlightenment, but also because its tenets were contrary to good order and hindered the government's plans for reforming the Jews; and although the violent deeds of the Hasidim and their vigorous propaganda to win adherents to the sect did not violate the law, they were considered harmful to the state. Therefore, the Committee for Religions was called upon to appoint rabbis who were "the usual Old Testament Believers" in Parczew and wherever else the sect of the "men of silk" maintained cells. These rabbis were to see to it that members of the sect worshipped in the city's synagogue and to persuade them, through sensible reasoning and the teachings of the Torah, to see the error of their ways and eschew their sect. The rabbis were also required to inform the committee of any violations on the part of the members of the sect. The Rabbi of Przysucha was expressly prohibited from collecting "payments" and giving advice or reporting "imaginary visions" to members of the sect. It was incumbent on the police generally to prevent gatherings of Hasidim in private homes; the Hasidim were permitted to pray only in the synagogues of the other "Old Testament Believers."

In conformity with the viceroy's order, the Committee for Religions sent a circular to the *województwo* committees on March 26, 1824, but it tempered the instructions for appointing rabbis in Hasidic centers, formulating them as follows: "These positions are to be filled to the extent that it is possible with more enlightened rabbis." In a special order to the *województwo* of Sandomierz, its committee was called upon to prohibit the rabbis in Przysucha and Kozienice (although the latter was not mentioned in the viceroy's letter)[14] from collecting payments and giving advice to their Hasidim. On that date, the Committee for Religions sent a transcript of the viceroy's letter of March 15 to the Committee for Internal Affairs and urged it to order the police to take heed that the Jews gather for worship in "public synagogues, and not in private houses." In its reply of April 7, the Committee for Internal Affairs informed the Committee for Religions about its circular to the *województwo* committees dated February 24 and about its special order to the *województwo* committees of Sandomierz and Podlasie, attaching a transcript of those orders.

Before two months elapsed, the policy of the authorities toward Hasidism changed, and the decrees against it were nullified. There are grounds for conjecture that some *województwo* committees had already implemented the decrees. For instance, the *województwo* committee of Płock had issued a decree closing all the *minyanim* where Hasidim assembled.[15] The local authorities were unaware that the government had changed its mind. On June 2, 1824, an order was sent by the viceroy to the Committee for Religions "to investigate whether in truth the Jewish sect of the Hasidim does not hold harmful principles which are contrary to good order and if it will indeed be shown that the sect only wants its own synagogues in order to hold itself apart from the rest of the Jews, then no decree would be issued against their existence," that is, against the *minyanim*.

In carrying out the order of the viceroy, the Committee for Religions appointed a special subcommittee to investigate Hasidism, composed of the following: Minister Staszyc,[16] the Senator and Chancellor;[17] State Counsellor Szaniawski,[18] and two members of the Committee for Religions, Lipinski[19] and Surowiecki.[20] Immediately after its establishment, this special subcommittee obtained the names of the leaders of the Hasidic movement throughout the entire country, as is evident in the letter circulated by the Committee for Religions to the *województwo* committee, dated July 8, 1824. The letter informed them of the viceroy's new order concerning the Hasidim, and they were instructed to summon the particular Hasidic leaders to appear at the office of the Committee for Religions "in order to answer questions . . . and to give the required explanations and clarifications." The letter went on to say that in the meantime (that is, until the government reached a decision) the *województwo* committees were urged to make sure that the authorities refrained from carrying out the orders of the Committee for Religions against the Hasidim, dated February 12 and March 26 of that year, "and no persecutions or rigorous treatment should be meted out to the members of this faith." During this time they should also be allowed to gather for worship in private houses, "while, of course, maintaining a proper order."[21]

On that same date, July 8, 1824, the Committee for Religions informed the Committee for Internal Affairs about the viceroy's letter of July 2 concerning both the establishment of the special subcommittee to investigate Hasidism and the order to the *województwo* committees to summon the Hasidic leaders before the subcommittee. Although the minutes of this subcommittee have not been preserved among the documents of the Committee for Religions, there are grounds to assume that the Hasidic leaders did appear before this committee. In a memorandum that the Committee for the Affairs of Old Testament Believers submitted three years later to Senator Novosiltzev, mention is made, as one of the reasons for the subcommittee's nullifying the decrees against the Hasidim in 1824, of the fact that "the Hasidim themselves admit that the dancing, the feasting, and shouting during their gatherings are no more than excesses on the part of some individuals."[22]

In the collection of documents of the Committee for the Affairs of Old Testament Believers relating to the Hasidim, there is a memorandum on which the opinion of that committee, as well as the government's decision to grant freedom to the Hasidic movement, was apparently based.[23] The main points of the memorandum, entitled "Comments concerning the Jewish Sect Called Hasidim," are:

The Jewish people are divided, as a result of changes which took place in the previous century, into three "groups": (1) ordinary Jews; (2) Jews holding liberal opinions; (3) Hasidim. Each of these groups is hostile to the others, though Hasidim are more thoroughly disliked by the two others, on the ground that the Hasidim have been affecting their membership.

The Hasidim are particularly superstitious; their superstitions did not originate with them, but were inherited from their Jewish forefathers, and since they are more zealous than other Jews in all matters, they have fostered these beliefs even more. They believe that the souls of the dead, the good as well as the evil, attach themselves to people. This provided the basis for the many foolish customs, such as conjuring the spirits of the dead, consulting the dead,[24] praying to the dead to intercede before God, carrying a talisman, and healing the sick through various folk remedies. These have been practiced by Jews since ancient times, but are more widespread among the Hasidim. The Hasidim believe they are walking in the footsteps of the ancient Hasidim; that the Patriarchs themselves were none other than proper Hasidim; and even David, the King of Israel, who, according to the biblical account, danced while bringing up the Ark of the Covenant, was seized with a holy devoutness similar to that of the late *Maggid* of Kozienice. They choose leaders from their midst whose fear of God they hold in such esteem that they blindly believe in whatever they say; they view them as seers who have in their power through their intercession with the Creator to nullify every evil and to bestow all manner of good. Their advice is sought in all matters, and their decrees are like those from heaven. They also regard them to be knowledgeable about the Kabbalah, but this is untrue, for only a few are familiar with this doctrine, which is beyond man's understanding, so that at the present time none can be found who know the Kabbalah.

These leaders of the Hasidim are not impostors but are themselves deluded, being endowed with vivid imaginations, and encouraged by their adoring followers. Also, they are detached from mundane realities, given to contemplation of mysteries, and are sure that they are divinely inspired and have the gift of prophecy. The Hasidim observe all the *mizvot* of the Jewish religion and do not differ from other Jews except in regard to certain opinions and customs. Although some of them know the Talmud, they do not honor the traditional rabbis, considering them hypocrites and insufficiently pious. They place greater value in the miracle tales of their leaders than in talmudic disputes. The main difference between them and other Jews is that contemplation of pious matters is held to be more important than the observance of *mizvot*.[25] To be joyful, to immerse oneself daily in a spring or a river, to give alms, to share everything with one's friends,[26] to pray fervently and with inner excitement and energy, to gather on the Sabbath with the leader, to listen to his teaching (Torah), to sing the Sabbath hymns, to eat and drink with pleasure, and to enjoy sitting among one's associates—all of these are elevated over the *mizvot*. For them, prayer is the greatest *mizvah*; there are some who spend consecutive days in prayer, while others do not pray at all for several days, claiming that they cannot pray because their prayer is not free of "alien" (improper) thoughts. They even accept sinners in their midst, arguing that repentance through sincere prayer rather than fasting is sufficient for becoming a good man.

The "Comments" advised the government not to destroy this sect so as to avoid an increase in the number of free-thinking Jews. It suggested that the government exploit this sect, as the holder of the balance of power between the two other Jewish groups, for its own purposes. Thus, if they were handled with understanding, these zealots could be a powerful instrument for removing any obstacles impeding the government's program for the reform of the Jews.

The "Comments" had a different spirit from that expressed in the memorandum submitted to the Committee for Religions in early 1824. The author of the "Comments" demonstrated a proper understanding of such tenets of Hasidism as sincerity, devoutness, worship in a spirit of joy, and negation of asceticism, and even understood that superstitious beliefs were not the invention of the Hasidim but were rooted in the historical tradition of the Jewish people. There even was ground for his opinion that the Kabbalah is no longer intelligible to the Hasidic community. For R. Simḥah Bunem had voiced a similar opinion in his explanation and justification of the fact that in his generation few Hasidim occupied themselves with the Kabbalah.[27]

The consistent line followed in the "Comments"—namely, to judge the Hasidim rather favorably—a priori precludes the possibility that it was drafted by one of the Maskilim. The author's conclusions indicate that he did not approve of the spread of the Haskalah, or, in his terms, "the sect of Jews holding liberal opinions." In conclusion, he advised the government to support the Hasidim so that they would hold both the Maskilim and the Mitnaggedim in check. Therefore, it is reasonable to assume that the author of the "Comments" was one of the high officials of the Committee for Religions and drew his information from the censor for Hebrew books or from some other Maskil who had connections with the government but reached his own conclusions independently.

It is no wonder then that the special subcommittee's opinion favored the Hasidim. In stating its reasons, the "deputation" formulated its descriptions of Hasidism in line with the "Comments": It was convinced that the Hasidim differed from the rest of the Jews in the following respects: they believed that meditation was a more important part of their prayers; they were more devoted to mysticism and Kabbalah; and they had no regular rabbis, but put their faith in leaders who were graced by sanctity and inspiration through which they were able to cleave to the angels. The main point of the "Comments," namely, the belief that Hasidism should be considered as a safeguard against the spread of the Haskalah—was not mentioned by the subcommittee at all, and for good reason. Were it to make such an admission, it would expose the fraud in all the government's high-flown declarations regarding its declared goal of raising the cultural level of the Jewish population. The subcommittee recommended "the cessation of any persecution of the Hasidim, that they be treated with unconcern, except that in the future the local authorities should eliminate shouting, noises, and nocturnal gatherings."[28]

Relying upon the subcommittee's opinion, on August 16, 1824, the Committee for Religions submitted a proposal concerning the Hasidim to the viceroy. On August 20, a letter was sent by the viceroy to the Committee for Internal Affairs declaring, on the basis of the opinion of the Committee for Religions, "that the sect of the Hasidim or the wearers of silk garb do not . . . hold any principles which contravene virtuous conduct, and that it desires special houses of worship only for the purpose of keeping itself apart from the rest of the Jews; therefore no obstacles should be placed in the way of maintaining public worship in private houses." On September 3, the Committee for Internal Affairs notified the *województwo* committees of the viceroy's letter and explicitly rescinded its decree of February 24 against the Hasidim. It submitted a report to the viceroy regarding the nullification of this decree, and the Committee for Religions was also informed of it.

Rabbi Meir Halevi Rotenberg's Defense of Hasidism

The cumbersome bureaucratic machinery of the local authorities did not accommodate itself immediately to the dramatic reversal in attitude toward the Hasidic movement. Persecutions continued for two months after the issuance of the order, as can be seen from the official documents of the inquiry which was conducted on complaint of the Hasidic leader in the city of Opatów.[29]

The leader of the Hasidic community in Opatów was R. Meir Halevi Rotenberg of Stopnica, author of a commentary on the Torah, *Or la-Shamayim* (A Light to the Heavens), and one of the disciples of the "Seer" of Lublin. He was an avowed rival of R. Simḥah Bunem of Przysucha and a vigorous opponent of his doctrine. After the proclamation of the royal order of August 30, 1824, the friends of the Hasidim in the capital apparently hastened to inform the Hasidic communities throughout the land about the annulment of the prohibition of the *minyanim* and the granting of permission for Hasidim to move about freely and hold gatherings. However, the letter of September 3 from the Committee for Internal Affairs to the *województwo* committees notifying them about this permission did not reach the local authorities very quickly. When the decrees against Hasidism continued in Opatów, R. Meir sent a memorandum to the government in Warsaw requesting an explicit directive. In response to his request, the secretary sent him a copy of the viceroy's letter to the Committee for Religions of August 30 granting permission for the *minyanim* of the Hasidim. But the local authorities in Opatów remained unaware of this order and continued to oppress the Rabbi of Opatów and his Hasidim.

According to the police chief's report during the investigation which was conducted later on, his intervention was confined to examining the passports of the Hasidim who came to R. Meir for the Sabbath and holidays. He stated that some two hundred Hasidim would gather at the rabbi's for the Sabbath, and five hundred to six hundred for the festivals; and that the Hasidim who came from abroad were required to show their passports. R. Meir testified that sometimes a policeman would come to his house and ask the assembled Hasidim whether there were Jews from abroad among them, "which caused them some uneasiness." But there is no doubt that the oppressive measures of the local authorities went beyond the details submitted at the investigation, and this explains the second daring step by the Rabbi of Opatów. On November 22, he submitted a complaint against the police to the Committee for Internal Affairs through the wealthy patron of the Hasidim in Warsaw, Jacob Bergson.

The complaint by R. Meir has not been preserved among the documents of the Committee for Internal Affairs, but its contents can be inferred from the letters exchanged between the two committees. On November 24 the Committee for Internal Affairs sent R. Meir's letter to the Committee for Religions and asked for its judgment in the matter. The former regarded it as a matter within the jurisdiction of the Committee for Religions, since the complainant had referred to the obstacles placed by the local police against the religious practices of the Hasidic sect.

It was incumbent upon the local authorities to decide whether the decree of August 30 by the viceroy authorizing the Hasidim to pray in private homes and the order of the Committee for Internal Affairs of September 3 based on that decree implied that the Hasidim were allowed to come to their rabbi from various places. But the attempt of the Committee for Internal Affairs to pass off the responsibility for making this decision onto the Committee for Religions failed. On December 23, 1824, the Committee for Religions returned R. Meir's letter to the Committee for Internal Affairs with the following explanation: In view of the fact that the leader of the Jewish sect of Hasidim, Meir Rotenberg, complained that the police had prevented those of his adherents living some distance away from assembling with him for the worship of God, the issue was not so much a matter of freedom to observe the precepts of religion but freedom to congregate. Therefore, the problem for consideration had to be solved by the police, which was within the jurisdiction of the Committee for Internal Affairs.

Even after receiving this reply, the Committee for Internal Affairs did not rush to decide on the question of its own responsibility. On January 20, 1825, it sent R. Meir's complaint to the *Województwo* Committee of Sandomierz and charged it to investigate the matter and to submit its opinion about it. The *województwo* committee in turn charged the Commissary of the District Chief of Opatów, J. Pomianowski, to investigate the matter. On February 13, R. Meir Rotenberg was summoned to clarify his complaint; minutes of the meeting were recorded.

R. Meir's replies at this investigation were obviously influenced by the new state of affairs. Having achieved his main goal—to call the government's attention to the oppressive acts of the local police—he now wanted to tone down his complaint and not provoke the representatives of the local authority, who might take revenge against him or even put him on trial for making a false charge.

According to R. Meir's testimony, reports had reached him that the police had received an order prohibiting Hasidim from coming to his gatherings. The police, in fact, had come to his home twice to inquire whether there were Jews from abroad without passports at his place, and informing him that "it is forbidden to assemble in large numbers." They had conducted themselves properly. But to avoid any possible "unpleasantness" in the future, he had written to the Bergson family in Warsaw recounting what had happened. In his letter, he had not asked that a complaint be submitted against the police and its chief, but he did request that Bergson make an effort in his name to expedite the publication of the order of August 30, 1824, on behalf of the Hasidim, and to bring it to the attention of the local authorities. Because of a misunderstanding, Bergson, in R. Meir's name, had submitted to the Committee for Internal Affairs a complaint against the police chief of Opatów. R. Meir's reply to the question of why he referred to himself as the leader of the Hasidim was that there were rabbis who were not leaders of the Hasidic sect, but he was both the local Rabbi of Opatów and a Hasid, namely one who was well versed in the principles of Hasidism, and was therefore considered a leader.

The police chief in Opatów, W. Butrymowicz, received the minutes of the investigation of R. Meir and was asked for an "explanation." In his written reply he made it clear that the police had never received an order to disturb the Hasidim or their gatherings. They had only been charged to keep an eye on those suspected of smuggling—inhabitants and aliens alike—and to check their passports. He said the supervision of an open city, such as Opatów, populated by Jews was very difficult since the Hasidim who came to the city by the hundreds on the Sabbath and the festivals did not stay at inns but entered the city by various roads and paths, some by carriage, some on foot, most often at night, and stayed in private Jewish homes for several days, thus eluding the supervision of the police. Obviously, smugglers and suspects moved among the large number of Jews streaming in from abroad, and it therefore was proper for the government to give this matter its attention and to instruct the police to operate under stringent rules.

On April 5, 1825, the *Województwo* Committee of Sandomierz sent the results of the investigation—the minutes and the report of the District Chief of Opatów—to the Committee for Internal Affairs. The Committee for Internal Affairs replied to the *województwo* committee that inasmuch as the minutes showed that the Hasidim had not been disturbed by the police chief during their worship and that the complaint was submitted by mistake, the Committee for Internal Affairs regarded the matter as resolved, and the *województwo* committee was ordered to apprise "the Old Testament Believer," R. Meir Rotenberg, the Rabbi of Opatów, of this decision.

Not only was the Hasidic movement recognized as legal in every respect from then on, but the advice of the author of the "Comments"—namely, to use this movement to help stem the spread of the Haskalah and as a wedge into the large camp of the Mitnaggedim—was accepted by the government. This stand was reflected in the establishment of the Committee for the Affairs of Old Testament Believers in 1825. Jacob Bergson, one of the notables among the Hasidim, was appointed to the Advisory Chamber of this committee along with four Mitnaggedim and Maskilim. Among the delegates of the committee from the provincial towns—of whom two from every *województwo* were proposed by the *województwo* committees—was R. Simḥah Bunem of Przysucha, and his appointment was confirmed by the *województwo* of Sandomierz.[30] This friendly treatment of the Hasidic sect by the authorities contrasted sharply with the government's mistrust of any group which did not fit into the rigid framework of the Synagogue Supervisory Board, which defined Jewish community life. In 1826, for instance, during an investigation involving smuggling among the Jews in the city of Kolno, in the vicinity of Łomża, the log of the "Ner Tamid" society was confiscated and sent to be scrutinized by the Committee for Internal Affairs. The Committee for Internal Affairs sent it to the Committee for Religions, which gave the following reply: The society was in itself harmless, but as a "subsidiary" society it might open the door to abuses; therefore the *Województwo* Committee of Augustów was ordered to disband it.[31]

The legal status of Hasidism was summed up in a report by the Committee for the Affairs of Old Testament Believers written in 1827. On November 1, Senator Novosiltzev directed a number of questions to the committee concerning the Jewish population within the state, and among the questions was one regarding Hasidism. On November 3, the committee replied to his questions and presented a review of the authorities' position with regard to the Hasidim:

"Nearly all the Old Testament Believers living within the Kingdom belong to either the rabbinic or the talmudic sect; there are very few Hasidim." In the official documents gathered by the committee, the Hasidim were first mentioned in 1798. On June 28, 1799, a directive was issued by the authorities permitting the Hasidim to hold their services, with the proviso that they be conducted in public synagogues.[32] The report described the way the Hasidic problem was treated by the authorities of the Kingdom of Poland up to the viceroy's order of August 30, 1824, which declared the Hasidic movement legal.

What is surprising in this report is that the Hasidim were viewed as an insignificant minority in contrast to the overwhelming majority in the "rabbinic group," namely, the Mitnaggedim. Evidently, the committee did not even take the trouble to read the material of the Committee for Religions which had been placed at its disposal. Otherwise they would have noticed that the author of the "Information concerning the Sect of the Hasidim" had already described the rapid growth of the sect as an evil which the Jewish people could not arrest.

Isolated incidents against the Hasidic *minyanim* occurred even in this period, apparently because the central and local authorities had not understood the connection between the organizing of special houses of worship and the Hasidic movement itself. In 1828 a Jew from Łomża, Liwenter, in the name of the Synagogue Supervisory Board in his city, requested that the Committee of the *Województwo* in Augustów prohibit the organization of religious services in private homes. The leaders of this community—which, like all the cities of that region near Lithuania, were strongholds of the Mitnaggedim—wanted to avail themselves of the power of the authorities in order to nip in the bud the growth of any Hasidic group in the city. The *województwo* committee sent the memorandum from the community leaders in Łomża to the Committee for Internal Affairs, and received the following reply on October 11, 1828: "While the gatherings in private homes are likely to bring in their wake a number of undesirable phenomena," it was proper that the *województwo* committee clarify the proposals of the Synagogue Supervisory Board and give a directive to the local authorities in Łomża for the purpose of assuring order in this matter. The Committee for Internal Affairs also informed the Synagogue Supervisory Board in Łomża of this reply through Liwenter.[33]

In the Wake of the November Insurrection

Within the framework of the curtailed autonomy of Poland after the failure of the November insurrection in 1830–31, the Committee for Internal Affairs and the Committee for Religions were amalgamated into the Committee for Internal Affairs, Religions and Public Education. This committee apparently forgot about the deliberations concerning the Hasidim which had been conducted by the Committee for Religions and in its special subcommittee in the 1820s. Its attention to the Hasidic movement was aroused by information it received from the censor's office about books which the Hasidim were printing without permission or bringing in from abroad. It can also be assumed that the committee was spurred to deal with the problem of Hasidism because the heads of the Warsaw community were informing against the Hasidim. In 1834 the Synagogue Supervisory Board, which consisted of four Mitnaggedim and one assimilationist,[34] submitted the following memorandum to the chief of police:[35]

> Several years have passed since the factional split between the Hasidim of Kock and the Hasidim of Przysucha. Lately, "charlatans" belonging to these Hasidic factions have been coming to Warsaw from the provincial towns and from neighboring countries and have found admirers to publicize their doctrines and their ability to help. They have bilked the gullible simple folk by assuring them of complete recovery from whatever ails them, and they promise fertility to barren women, a happy family life, and all that is good in the world. Matters have gone so far that women surreptitiously bring their husbands' money to them, and young men gather at the houses of these charlatans, wasting both their money and their time. The Synagogue Supervisory Board relies on the police chief to put a stop to these activities which impoverish many families, and impede the collection of taxes. And even though fundraising or alms collecting is forbidden without the permission of the police or the Synagogue Supervisory Boards, these men collect money on various pretexts; and they do not even inform the Board of their arrival in the city. Finally, the Synagogue Supervisory Board welcomes any directives on this matter, so that it will know how to proceed.

The reasons advanced in this complaint against the Hasidim indicate that the Warsaw community leaders were less interested in doctrinal matters than political and economic ones; that is, the Hasidim had evaded the supervision of the community's administrators, and they did not pay taxes to the community (explicit mention was made here only of government taxes). The consequences of this memorandum are not known, but there is no doubt that the chief of police deemed it necessary to bring the complaint to the attention of his superiors, that is, to the Committee for Internal Affairs, instead of assuming responsibility for the matter.

On June 17, 1834, the Department of Religions and Culture of the Committee for Internal Affairs and Religions wrote to the Committee for the Affairs of Old Testament Believers requesting that it gather information "with the utmost accuracy" concerning the

Hasidic sect so that it could reply as soon as possible to the following questions:

1. Is the Hasidic sect widespread among Old Testament Believers throughout the Kingdom, and to what extent?
2. What are the sect's principal doctrines?
3. How many Old Testament Believers belong to this sect? Who are its leaders and how can their identities be ascertained?
4. Do the Hasidim distribute any books; and if so, which ones, and where and how are they distributed among their coreligionists?
5. What measures would be effective for finding those books and removing them from circulation; and how can the sect be destroyed or at least its spread be prevented?

The committee replied as follows:[36]

1. The Hasidic sect has no adherents except in the provinces of what was formerly Poland and is now the Kingdom of Poland.
2. The difference between the articles of faith of the Hasidic sect and those of the rabbinic sect consists in the fact that the Hasidim's are derived not only from the teachings of the Talmud but also from commentaries on the Talmud, known by the general name of "Kabbalah." The Hasidim—in keeping with the meaning of the term "Hasid" itself, namely, one who is God-fearing—deem themselves to be more God-fearing than the Rabbinists, and believe that the man chosen from their midst because of his piety and virtue has the power to perform wonders, that is, whatever he decrees, God confirms. In all other matters relating to the Mosaic faith they concur, and in matters of conscience they ask the advice of the rabbis, the Rabbinist leaders.
3. The number of Hasidim in the Kingdom of Poland can only be approximated, but they clearly do not amount to even one-twentieth of the members of the Jewish religion within the Kingdom, although recently there has been a marked increase in the number of followers.

This sect has practically no permanent leaders. The leaders of the Hasidim, like those of the Rabbinists, depend upon the people's opinion of their piety and virtue, and their authority rises and falls according to this opinion. Currently, the Rabbis Mendel of Kock and Jeraḥmiel of Przysucha are most esteemed among the Hasidim.[37] The government can ascertain the state of things through contact with Maskilim who have never refused to provide it.

4. The books used by the Hasidim are for "the most part commentaries on the Talmud"; they are printed in Lithuania and then circulated in the Kingdom of Poland after being examined by the censor.

Whether other religious books are distributed throughout the country is a matter for police investigation, not the committee.

5. As for finding banned books and removing them from circulation, only the police authorities of the *województwo* committees are in a position to do this. It would be difficult, if not impossible, to prevent the spread of Hasidism, since it is no more than a religious belief and since freedom of religious belief is guaranteed by the "organic Statute."[38] What can be done is to unite the two sects with the aid of scholarly Rabbinists, which is what scholarly men among the Old Testament Believers are continuously trying to do.

Of all the memoranda submitted to the authorities since 1823, when the problem of Hasidism was placed on the agenda of the government, this report was the most uninformed. Without going into the strange division of the Jews into four "sects," which besides the Maskilim, Mitnaggedim, and Hasidim no doubt included the Karaites, there is the committee's ill-conceived explanation of the Kabbalah, the study of which the committee believed to be a distinguishing mark of the Hasidim. Its misconceptions can only be explained by the fact that the "experts" who held the highest rank in the committee confused the two concepts of the Kabbalah—"Kabbalah" as a term for the tradition of the Oral Law and "Kabbalah" as a mystical doctrine. Similarly, the experts were confused by the fact that the Hasidim, like the Mitnaggedim, recognized the authority of the rabbis in matters dealing with *kashrut*, so they stated that the Hasidim asked the advice of the rabbis in "matters of conscience." Similarly, they misunderstood the fact that many of the great rebbes also occupied the post of rabbi in their communities, and thus inferred that Mitnaggedim also turned to the rebbes in matters of conscience. Nor did the committee make any effort after 1827, when it had submitted its report to Senator Novosiltzev, to find out how far the Hasidic movement had spread among the people. The committee was absolutely sure, as it had been seven years earlier, that the Hasidim were a negligible minority among the Jewish population, only this time it estimated their number to be no more than one-twentieth of the Jewish population, while admitting, however, that they were continually increasing.

The committee recommended that the government refrain from any punitive measures against the Hasidim. This, the committee explained, was based on the fact that religious freedom was guaranteed by the fundamental laws. In addition, there was insufficient evidence of the negative character of this sect to warrant its persecution or suppression, aside from the above legal difficulties involved in doing so. Nevertheless, the committee took a position far from that of the author of the "Comments concerning the Sect of the Hasidim," who in 1824 had advised the government to leave the Hasidim alone so that they would serve as the balancing force between the Mitnaggedim and the Maskilim. The committee, however, saw the organizational and ideological unification of the Jewish population as advantageous to the government, since the existence of a special sect was likely to obstruct the authorities in supervising the affairs of the Jews—as, for example, controlling the books which circulated among them. The committee expressed the hope that the government would succeed in uniting the two camps, the Mitnaggedim and the Hasidim—an aim shared by the Jewish scholars.

In this conclusion, the committee did reflect the historical situation. For at that time, a process of rapprochement between the Mitnaggedim and Hasidim leading to their consolidation into one camp of Orthodox Jews was already at an advanced stage.

Notes

The Appendix citations refer to the appendix in the Hebrew edition of this book.

All the documents cited here, as well as the documents published in the appendices, were taken from the Polish Government Archives (Archiwum panstwowe) in Lwów (Lemberg). For the most part the documents cited are taken from the volume entitled *Chassiden-Judensekte 1814–1838 (Acta praesidialia, Rectificatum praesidiale* 129), and these are designated in the notes in brief as *Chassiden* with the relevant numeration. Others are scattered in various volumes of documents pertaining to the former praesidium of the Galician provincial government (*Acta praesidialia*). Documents from other collections are listed as "S. A., Lemberg" (State Archives, Lemberg) with the appropriate catalogue number.

Chapter 1

1. S. A., Lemberg, *Acta Gubernialia Publ. Polit.* i/j 11. no. 8201.
2. J. Wertheimer, *Die Juden in Oesterreich* (Leipzig, 1842) 1:300–310.
3. A. F. Pribram, *Urkunden und Akten zur Geschichte der Juden in Wien* (Vienna, 1918), 2:279–306.
4. I. Schiper, "Die galizische Judenschaft in den Jahren 1772–1848 in wirtschaftsstatistischer Beleuchtung," in *Judische Monatshefte* 9–10 (1918): 23; cf. F. Friedmann, *Die galizischen Juden im Kampfe um ihre Gleichberechtigung* (Frankfurt, 1929), p. 9.

5. M. Stöger, *Darstellung der gesetzlichen Verfassung der galizischen Judenschaft*, 1:263–66. According to Stöger, only 1,172 Jews had their own commercial firms in 1826.
6. Ibid., pp. 202–8.
7. Friedmann, *Die galizischen Juden*, p. 89.
8. Wertheimer, *Juden in Oesterreich*, p. 304.
9. Schiper, "Die galizische Judenschaft," p. 23.
10. Schiper arrived at this conclusion on the basis of the figures cited (ibid., p. 229); cf. Stöger, *Darstellung der gesetzlichen*, p. 15.
11. Piller, *Galizische Provinzialgesetzsammlung*, 1823, no. 42077.
12. *Chassiden* 18g, 1827; cf. document 16.
13. Ibid., 4553/838; cf. appendix: document 9e.
14. Most of the Hasidim described in Perl's satire *Megalleh Temirin* (Lemberg, 1879) are tavernkeepers, whereas the wealthy merchant appears as an exemplar of the worthy Maskil.
15. Solomon Judah Rapoport, "Ner Mizvah," in *Naḥalat Yehudah* (Cracow, 1868), p. 15.
16. This letter was published by Philip Friedman in his article "Di ershte Kamfn tsvishn haskole un khsidizm," in *Fun Noentn Over* 4 (1938): 265.
17. Moses of Sambor, *Tefilah le-Moshe* (Lemberg, 1858), Torah portion *Lekh lekha*, p. 9a.
18. *Kerem Ḥemed* 2 (1836): 35.
19. Perl, *Megalleh Temirin*, p. 75a, letter 101.
20. Joseph Perl, *Boḥen Ẓaddik* (Prague, 1838), p. 53.
21. Published by Letteris in *Mikhtavim* (1827), letter 5; *Zikkaron ba-Sefer* (Vienna, 1868), pp. 65 ff.; *Kerem Ḥemed* 1 (1833): 90 ff. (letter is signed "Peli"); *Moreh Nevukhei ha-Zeman* (Lemberg, 1863), p. 24, and in Rawidowicz, ed., *Kitvei Rabbi Naḥman Krokhmal*, p. 417.
22. Perl revealed this geographical map in *Megalleh Temirin*, p. 22a, letter 16 ("Among residents of Poland, Wallachia, Moldavia and part of Hungary almost all are our people").
23. Ephraim Fischl Fischelsohn, *Teyator fun Khsidim,* in *Historishe Shriftn fun YIVO* 1 (1929): 649–93.
24. Isaac Ber Levinsohn, *Emek Refa'im* (1867), pp. 3, 4, 9.
25. Isaac Ber Levinsohn, *Divrei Ẓaddikim* (1867), pp. 28, 31.
26. *Be'er Yiẓḥak*, p. 127. A play on words in the Hebrew original: "baẓal kenafei ha-ḥasidah."
27. Naphtali of Ropczyce, when once advised that his *gemaṭria* did not tally, replied that basically the zaddikim were worthy of hearing their teachings from heaven and the *gemaṭriot* are no more than a hint and are subsequently sought out in the Torah; if the *gemaṭria* did not tally, he explained, one only had to use another system of computation, such as comprehension or minor value; see his *Ohel Naftali* (Warsaw, 1911), p. 138.
28. See, for example, Menaḥem Mendel of Kosów, *Ahavat Shalom* (Czernowitz, 1883); the works of Hersh of Żydaczów; Simon of Dobromil, *Naḥalat Shim'on*; Naphtali of Ropczyce, *Ayalah Sheluḥah*; Abraham David of Buczacz, *Birkat David*. These works all appeared after 1848 because of the rigid Austrian censorship of Hasidic-kabbalistic books.
29. Hersh of Żydaczów, *Sur me-Ra va-Aseh Tov* (Munkacs, 1901), p. 71.
30. Moses of Sambor, *Tefilah le-Moshe, va-Yeẓe*, p. 18b.
31. Menaḥem Mendel of Kosów, *Ahavat Shalom*, p. 15b.
32. Ibid., p. 88b; see also Simon of Dobromil, *Naḥalat Shim'on*, on the portion *Koraḥ*.

33. Wachstein also emphasized the close relationship between the precarious existence of the majority of Galician Jewry, tradesmen, and tavernkeepers, and the Hasidic tenet of faith that in his opinion served as a means to maintain the "psychic balance" of these economically insecure masses; see B. Wachstein, *Die hebräische Publizistik in Wien* (Vienna, 1930), p. lv.
34. A. B. Gottlober, *Zikhronot mi-Yemei Ne'urai, ha-Boker Or*, 5:24.
35. See R. Mahler, *Divrei Yemei Yisrael be-Dorot ha-Aḥaronim* (Merḥaviah, 1954) 1:3:198–99; appendix 22, p. 238.
36. Gottlober (see note 34).
37. Fischelsohn, *Teyator fun Khsidim*, p. 654; cf. episode mentioned in Dov Shtok (Sadan), *Zikhronot mi-Mekhoz Yaldut*, p. 12. The author's great-grandfather, Reb Yossi, a Hasid of Bełz, was removed from his ritual slaughterer's post in Żółkiew because "his main enemies were the artisans of the city" who forced him to sign a certificate ceding his rights to his brother, a Mitnagged.
38. Fischelsohn, *Teyator fun Khsidim*, p. 651.
39. *Makkel No'am*, the satire "Der khosid mit zayn vayb um shabes."
40. Naphtali of Ropczyce, *Ayalah Sheluḥah* (1903), p. 22.
41. Mendel of Rymanów, *Menaḥem Ẓiyyon*, pp. 54–55, 185.
42. In the original: *ak'vata d'moshicha*; according to the Talmud, the impudence of the gentile nations would be intensified before the advent of the Messiah (*Sotah* 49).
43. Hersh of Żydaczów, *Sur me-Ra*, p. 15a.
44. *Pe'er Mikdoshim* (Lemberg, 1865), pp. 53–54. Naturally, the legend ignores the fact that the special Jewish taxes were not rescinded until the Revolution of 1848 and that Hersh of Żydaczów died during the cholera epidemic of 1831. The historical facts presented on the following pages prove that Hersh really had a concessive attitude in relation to the government and the tax lessees regarding the Jewish taxes.
45. *Ateret Zekeinim*, referred to in Michael Braver, *Ẓevi la-Ẓaddik* (Vienna, 1931), p. 60.
46. Mendel of Rymanów, *Menaḥem Ẓiyyon*, p. 43
47. *Hosafot Meherẓa* (initials of Ẓevi Elimelekh) to Hersh of Żydaczów, *Sur me-Ra*, p. 22.
48. Ibid.
49. On the basis of a litigation which was later conducted against abuses of the tax lessees it evolved that Herz Homberg, who, as an expert, expressed his opinion that the candle tax is in accord with the Jewish religion, had previously concluded an agreement with the future tax lessees giving him 2 percent of the net income of the lease; cf. M. Balaban, *Żydzi w Galicyi* (Lemberg, 1914), p. 77.
50. Berger, *Eser Kedushot* (Piotrków, 1906), pp. 38–40.
51. Cf. Mahler, *Divrei Yemei Yisrael*, p. 285.
52. Simon of Jarosław, *Imrei Kedosh Yisrael*, in "Ma'amar Kadishin," addendum to Naphtali of Ropczyce, *Imrei Shefer* (Lemberg, 1884), Torah portion *va-Yakhel*, p. 15a.
53. It is told, for example, that during the cholera epidemic of 1831, on leaving the *bet ha-midrash*, Hersh of Żydaczów put his hand on the mezuzah, saying, "I am the expiatory sacrifice for all the Jews." His brother, Moses of Sambor, allegedly stated when several hundred Hasidim arrived to celebrate the High Holidays with him, "I do not know what to do with such a large crowd . . . but I take upon myself the suffering of Jewry" (Berger, *Eser Kedushot*, pp. 20, 48).
54. Mendel of Rymanów, *Menaḥem Ẓiyyon*, p. 37a.
55. Simon of Dobromil, *Naḥalat Shim'on*, Torah portion *Naso*.

56. Levinsohn, *Emek Refa'im*, p. 12; cf. *Dover Shalom* (Przemyśl, 1910), p. 37, about Sholem Rokeakh of Bełz: "Even Gentiles came to his Holy Eminence of Bełz"; see also p. 152.

57. Fischelsohn, *Teyator fun Khsidim*, p. 686.

58. Naphtali of Ropczyce, *Ayalah Sheluḥah*, p. 22; Simon of Dobromil, *Naḥalat Shim'on*, Torah portion *Toledot*.

59. Simon of Dobromil, *Naḥalat Shim'on*, Torah portion *va-Yeḥi*.

60. Mendel of Rymanów, *Menaḥem Ẓiyyon*, pp. 46–47. Yitskhok Ayzik of Żydaczów used to say that the *bet ha-midrash* of his uncle Hersh of Żydaczów stood on a strap of the phylacteries of Ereẓ Yisrael and that all of the prayers of the Diaspora which were turned toward the land of Israel passed through this *bet ha-midrash* (Berger, *Eser Kedushot*, p. 20).

61. Mendel of Rymanów, *Menaḥem Ẓiyyon*, pp. 56–57.

62. Mendel of Kosów, *Ahavat Shalom*, p. 9b; Hersh of Żydaczów, *Sur me-Ra*, p. 1b; Naphtali of Ropczyce, *Ayalah Sheluḥah*, pp. 6–7; Simon of Dobromil, *Naḥalat Shim'on*, p. 8.

63. The glosses to Hersh of Żydaczów's *Sur me-Ra*, written by Ẓevi Elimelekh of Dynów, p. 4; this passage is taken from *Sanhedrin* 97b.

64. *Dover Shalom*, p. 41.

65. Moses of Sambor, *Tefilah le-Moshe*, Torah portion *va-Etḥanan*, p. 27a.

66. Cf. Mahler, *Divrei Yemei Yisrael*, bk. 4, app. 28, app. 29.

67. Ibid., pp. 245, 256, the citations from the Talmud.

68. Mendel of Kosów, *Ahavat Shalom*, p. 37b.

69. Naphtali of Ropczyce, *Ohel Naftali*, p. 38.

70. This is related in *Seder ha-Dorot le Talmidei ha-Besht* (Lemberg, 1865).

71. Simon of Dobromil, *Naḥalat Shim'on*, Torah portion *Ḥukat*.

72. *Pe'er Mikdoshim*, pp. 58–60.

73. Thus, for example, Hersh of Żydaczów interpreted the verse *Ma'aleh gerah u-mafris parsah* ("cheweth the cud and parteth the hoof"): *Ma'aleh gerah* (he who brings up and contributes a *gerah* [coin]), and *mafris parsah* (he who breaks [*pores*] his bread for the hungry) (Berger, *Eser Kedushot*, p. 26); Meyer of Przemyślany interpreted the rituals of the Passover Seder, "*kadesh* (sanctify) *u-reḥaẓ* (lave) *karpas* (greens), *yaḥaẓ* (divide)" in the following manner: If a Jew wants to sanctify himself and cleanse himself of his sins, he must share his bed and bread, *kar-pat*, with the poor (Bartfeld, *Divrei Me'ir* [1909], p. 20).

74. *Babylonian Talmud, Ketubot* 50a.

75. *Imrei Kadosh ha-Shalem*, glosses, p. 40; a similar interpretation of the reform of the Academy in Usha was reported in the name of Rebbe Isaac of Warka.

76. Hersh of Żydaczów's account of Moses Leyb of Sasów (*Sefer Ma'asei Ẓaddikim im Divrei Ẓaddikim*, n.p., n.d., p. 40) was adapted by I. L. Peretz in his famous short story, "If Not Still Higher"; Peretz transferred the tale to the Rebbe of Nemirov.

77. Hersh of Żydaczów gave forty orphans in marriage. Every time he married off one of his own children he would do the same for an orphaned girl and provide the couple with its keep. His nephew Yitskhok Ayzik of Żydaczów did the same (Berger, *Eser Kedushot*, pp. 21, 74) . It is told of Naphtali of Ropczyce that his Hanukkah menorah was pawned all year for a loan which he would take for the poor (Naphtali of Ropczyce, *Ohel Naftali*, p. 135). The Rabbi of Nowy Sącz, Ḥayyim Halberstam, pointed out the generous philanthropy of the Rebbe of Ropczyce as an exemplar in contrast to the profligacy of the Sadagura dynasty (*Keneset ha-Gedolah* [Rohatyn, 1869], p. 21).

78. See *Pe'er Mikdoshim, Seder ha-Dorot, Divrei Me'ir*. Solomon Rubin, one of the last Galician Maskilim, also related in his memoirs that Meyer of Przemyślany

used to distribute the payments he received among the poor, and he himself lived in dire need (Horodetzky, *Ha-Ḥasidut ve-ha-Ḥasidim* 4:110).

79. Levinsohn, *Emek Refa'im*, p. 5.

80. Cf. appendix: document 6e.

81. Berger, *Eser Kedushot*, pp. 41, 44, 46; Braver, *Ẓevi la-Ẓaddik*, p. 75.

82. Uri of Strelisk, *Imrei Kadosh ha-Shalem*, p. 29.

83. Berger, *Eser Kedushot*, p. 50.

84. Cf. appendix: document 6f.

85. Cf. appendix: document 6g.

86. Ibid., 4553/838; see appendix: document 9.

87. B. Weinryb, "le-Toledot Rival," *Tarbiẓ* 5 (1934): 204.

88. Friedmann, *Die galizischen Juden*, p. 93.

89. Balaban, *Żydzi w Galicyi*, p. 72 ff.

90. The first denunciation of this activity was made against the secretary of the *kehillah* in Lemberg, Modlinger, in 1818.

91. The denunciation by Ḥayyim Herbst of Mosty Wielkie in 1824, by Joseph Tepper of Tarnopol against the Hasidim of Buczacz in 1841. Like Joseph Perl, Joseph Tepper accused the Hasidim of keeping the money for themselves; see appendix: documents 4, 12.

92. See appendix: document 4. The style of this denunciation (against "fanaticism") indicates that the informer was a Maskil.

93. See appendix: document 12.

94. See appendix: document 6.

95. Balaban, *Żydzi w Galicyi*, p. 80.

96. See M. Jost, *Neuere Geschichte der Israeliten*, vol. 10, pt. 3, p. 87.

97. *Chassiden*, 5611 ex. 838.

98. Mendel of Kosów, *Ahavat Shalom,* p. 61b.

99. Levinsohn, *Emek Refa'im*, p. 3.

100. Joseph Perl delivered this report in response to the government's inquiry concerning Galician Jewry's reaction to Siegfried Justus's proposal for a Jewish state. The report was published by N. M. Gelber in his book *Vorgeschichte des Zionismus* (Vienna, 1927), pp. 258–62.

101. *Hosafot Meharẓa* to Hersh of Żydaczów, *Sur me-Ra,* p. 35b.

102. Jost, *Neuere Geschichte*, p. 89.

103. Levinsohn, *Emek Refa'im*, p. 4.

104. *Zemir Ariẓim ve-Ḥarabot Ẓurim* (published by Dubnow) in *Ha-Avar,* vol. 2. It is well known that Hasidim used polished knives; supervision was lightened due to the appointment of persons from their own circles; cf. H. Shmeruk, "Social Implications of Hasidic Ritual Slaughter" (Hebrew), in *Ẓiyyon* 20:1955.

105. Levinsohn, *Emek Refa'im*, p. 5

106. Concerning the role played by the low status of talmudic scholars in the intellectual deficiency of Hasidism, cf. Graetz, *Geschichte der Juden* (1870) 11:114; S. Dubnow, *Toledot ha-Ḥasidut*, sect. 12; B. Dinur, *Reishitah shel ha-Ḥasidut be-Mifneh ha-Dorot* (Jerusalem, 1955), pp. 139–47; Mahler, *Divrei Yemei Yisrael*, n. 107.

107. Gottlober, *Zikhronot mi-Yemei*, pp. 1035–36.

108. Fischelsohn, *Teyator fun Khsidim*, p. 685.

109. Levinsohn, *Emek Refa'im*, p. 15.

110. This refers to tax lessees for community revenue, e.g., the meat tax.

111. Those who furnished the Russian government with military recruits.

112. Brokers. "Faktoyrim" specifically refers to those in the steady employ of the nobility.

113. Tax lessee for indirect communal taxes, especially for the tax on kosher meat, known as the *Korobka*.

114. Officials in charge of quartering soldiers in civilian homes.

115. Cf. n. 33.

116. Levinsohn, *Emek Refa'im*, p. 10.

117. I. B. Levinsohn, *Di Hefker-velt* (Warsaw, 1902), p. 36.

118. *Imrei Kadosh ha-Shalem le-Rabeinu Uri ha-Saraf mi-Strelisk* (Lemberg, 1871), "Kuntres Or Olam," pp. 12–13; Braver, *Ẓevi la-Ẓaddik*, p. 32.

119. I. Weinlös's introduction to *Yoysef Perls Yiddishe Ksovim* (Vilna: YIVO, 1937), p. lix.

120. N. Horowitz, in "Joseph Perl," *Kalender und Jahrbuch der Israeliten* 5 (1846): 214.

121. The same *aggadah* is also used in later Hasidic works in order to substantiate the position of the zaddik as a mediator of abundance; see, for example, Simon of Dobromil, *Naḥalat Shim'on* on the biblical portion *be-Shalaḥ*.

122. *Divrei Me'ir*, p. 23a.

123. Berger, *Eser Kedushot*, pp. 152–53. His letters to the Rabbi of Bóbrka, which are published in this book, treat the same matter. S. J. Rapoport told S. D. Luzzatto in a letter written at the end of 1833 that he had a difficult struggle with the lessees of the meat tax until they reinstated him in his office as secretary. He explained their opposition to him on the grounds that "they sided with the wicked Hasidic sect" (B. Dinaburg, *Iggerot Shir*, collection 1–2 [Jerusalem, 1927], p. 49, quoted by Joseph Klausner, *Historyah shel ha-Sifrut ha-Ivrit ha-Ḥadashah* [Jerusalem, 1937] 2:233).

124. M. Balaban, *Historja Żydów w Krakowie* (1936) 2:566–72.

125. Cf., for example, Mendel of Kosów, *Ahavat Shalom*, pp. 2b, 29b; Simon of Dobromil, *Naḥalat Shim'on*, Torah portion *Ḥukat*.

126. *Hosafot Meharẓa* to Hersh of Żydaczów, *Sur me-Ra*, pp. 4, 16.

127. According to Hasidic tradition, Hersh of Żydaczów came together with R. Jacob of Lissa in Kałusz. After the Hasidic rebbe offered a legalistic talmudic discourse the rabbi spoke on Kabbalah. This brought Hersh to comment that the two men "made peace in the world." He had proved that Hasidim are "well grounded in *GeFet*"—a Hebrew acronym for Talmud and the commentaries of Rashi and the Tosafists—and his partner-in-dialogue that scholars are also well versed in Kabbalah: cf. *Ẓevi la-Ẓaddik*, p. 47.

128. *Imrei Kadosh ha-Shalem*, pp. 29, 34. Nevertheless, in contrast to Przysucha-Kock, Uri stressed the prayer in "Torah and Prayer" (ibid., p. 41). It was no mere coincidence that Uri also expressed individualistic ideas in the spirit of Przysucha-Kock (cf., ibid., pp. 9, 32).

129. The "Ḥadushim" are also mentioned in the memorandum of the Lemberg police directorate of 1838 regarding Hasidism (*Chassiden*, 4553/838); see appendix: document 9e.

130. Participating in the rabbinical assembly which was convoked in Lemberg in 1830 to excommunicate those who evaded payment of the meat and candle taxes, in addition to the Orthodox rabbis like Jacob Ornstein of Lemberg, Ẓevi Hirsh Chajes of Żółkiew, Jacob of Lissa, and Landau of Brody, was the same Hersh of Żydaczów who in his books bemoaned the heavy burden of the Jewish taxes and who himself had suffered persecution by the Austrian police in past years. Among the matters about which the Galician administration solicited the opinion of the district rabbi of Żółkiew, Ẓevi Hirsh Chajes, is the following question: "Should the Hasidic rebbes be called in to participate in the renewal of the bans regarding the evasion of taxes [on kosher meat and candle-lighting]?" See Jost, *Neuere Geschichte*, p. 81.

Chapter 2

1. S. A. Kempner, *Rozwój gospodarczy Polski* (Warsaw, 1924), p. 156.

2. The commerce of Brody in the eighteenth and nineteenth centuries is fully discussed in Tadeusz Lutman, *Studja nad dziejami Brodów* (Lemberg, 1937).

3. In 1840 seven Christian commercial firms in Brody concentrated a capital of 349,000 florins, i.e., almost 37 percent of the entire commercial capital of all of the 573 merchants and tradesmen registered in Brody, which amounted to nearly 941,000 florins (calculated according to the figures given by Lutman, *Studja*, p. 137).

4. Calculated according to Lutman.

5. Meyer Letteris enumerated among the first Maskilim in Galicia only two very moderate Maskilim who came from western Galicia: the well-known Hebrew grammarian Judah L. Ben Ze'ev of Cracow and Shevaḥ Pinsker of Tarnów, the father of the scholar Simḥah Pinsker and grandfather of the author of *Autoemancipation*; see *Toledot Gershon Halevi Letteris* (Vienna, 1864), p. 3.

6. G. Wolf, *Geschichte der Juden in Wien* (Vienna, 1876), p. 113.

7. Samson Bloch, *Shevilei Olam*, vol. 2 (1828), introduction.

8. M. Letteris, preface to Isaac Erter's *Ha-Ẓofeh le-Bet Yisrael* (Vienna, 1864), p. 7. In the same words, Krochmal praised the city of Brody in his letter to Samson Bloch (Bloch, *Shevilei Olam* [1822] 1:3).

9. S. Rawidowicz, ed., *Kitvei Re'Na'K*, p. 248.

10. The acronym of R. Moses ben Menaḥem Mendelssohn.

11. Abraham Ber Gottlober, "Ha-Gizrah ve-ha-Biniah," in *Ha-Boker Or*, 3:642.

12. M. Letteris preface to Erter, *Ha-Ẓofeh*, p. 8.

13. *Chassiden*, 5611/838; cf. chap. 5.

14. M. Letteris, *Mikhtevei Benei Kedem* (Vienna, 1865), p. 154.

15. Bloch, *Shevilei Olam*, 1:4.

16. Lutman, *Studja*, p. 137.

17. Berish Goldenberg, *Ohel Yosef* (Lemberg, 1866), p. 6.

18. Max Erik has correctly pointed this out in his *Etyudn tsu der geshikhte fun der haskole* (Minsk, 1934), p. 179.

19. Isaac Ber Levinsohn, *Emek Refa' im* (1867), p. 3.

20. M. Letteris, *Zikkaron ba-Sefer* (1868), p. 37.

21. Rapoport himself, in a letter to S. D. Luzzatto dated 12 Tevet 5592 (1832), told expressly of his partnership in that business (letter 8, *Levanon* [Mainz, 1882], no. 35).

22. Cf. Perl's letter to Krochmal of September 11, 1826 (I. Weinlös's introduction to *Yoysef Perls Yidishe Ksovim* [Vilna: YIVO, 1937], p. xli).

23. In the Lemberg State Archives there is a record of an accusation from the year 1820, signed by four Jews, against Todres Perl, "the lessee of the mills," concerning "oppression" (S. A., Lemberg, Index of *Acta praesidialia*, 1820, no. 3448). It appears that Perl took over this lease from his father, because in his sermon of 1838, during the feud concerning S. J. Rapoport's rabbinical appointment, he related that his opponents complained to the authorities that he "greatly oppresses the city." (Weinlös, in *Yoysef Perls*, p. lxiii).

24. Rawidowicz proposed the hypothesis that Krochmal's accepting the position there as head of the Jewish community stemmed from his holding the liquor monopoly, because the community often had to guarantee the incumbent (*Kitvei Re'Na'K*, p. 46).

25. Wertheimer, *Die Juden in Oesterreich* (Leipzig, 1842) 1:287.

26. Concerning the Maskilim-teachers Michael Monyes, Z. Plohn, and Bezalel Stern, see Philip Friedman, "Di ershte kamfn tvishn haskole un khsidizm," *Fun Noentn Over* 4 (1938).

Barukh Ẓevi Neu, who had a great influence upon Nachman Krochmal, was a teacher in the German-Jewish school in Żółkiew. Isaac Erter was for a time a teacher of German and Hebrew and principal of the *Realschule* in Brody.

27. Meyer Letteris was for a time a private teacher in the Lemberg home of a wealthy woman from Odessa and he later went with his student to Vienna. I. B. Levinsohn in his *Emek Refa'im* spoke of teachers of German in Brody who were anathematized by the Hasidic rebbes. In Vienna, too, prominent Maskilim, like Judah Jeiteles of Prague and Ber Oppenheimer of Pressburg, were private teachers in the homes of the wealthy. G. Wolf, the historian of the Jews in Vienna, was of the opinion that the Haskalah in Vienna had its beginnings with private teachers of the type of Jeiteles and Oppenheimer (Wolf, *Juden in Wien*, pp. 128–29). A. B. Gottlober first read Mendelssohn's *Biur* in the Moldavia home of a young man from Lemberg who was engaged in giving lessons in wealthy homes (A. Fridkin, *Avrom Ber Gotlober un zayn Epokhe* [Vilna, 1925], p. 149).

28. Other Jewish physicians in Brody of that time were Drs. Chaim Friedlander, Levinstein, Goldschmidt, and Karmin; see N. M. Gelber, "Brody," in *Cities and Mothers of Israel* (Hebrew) (Jerusalem, 1956), 6:176.

29. The physician Dr. Chaim Friedlander, who settled in Brody in 1801, lectured to local Haskalah circles on the philosophy of Kant, which he had heard from the philosopher as a student in Königsberg (from Gelber, "Brody").

30. Joseph Perl, *Boḥen Ẓaddik* (Prague, 1838), p. 63.

31. Letteris, *Mikhtevei Benei Kedem*, p. 145; see also *Zehav Shebah* (Bloch, *Shevilei Olam* [Lemberg, 1855] 3:25–26). I. B. Levinsohn, the Mendelssohn of the Russian Haskalah, was also dependent for a great part of his life on the grace of "benefactors," "wealthy men"; cf., for example, his letter to the Warsaw censor Jacob Tugendhold in 1838 in which he asked him to intercede with the "benefactors and wealthy men" of Warsaw in his behalf (B. Weinryb, "le-Toledot Rival," *Tarbiẓ* 5 [1934]: 206).

32. Maskilim without means of a livelihood who eagerly awaited teaching positions and placed their hopes on Lilienthal's campaign turned to I. B. Levinsohn in a letter in the name of a group of young men in Dubno (*Be'er Yiẓḥak* [1899], p. 60). Jacob Eichenbaum, too, asked Levinsohn for a teaching post, complaining that he was burdened with seven children (idem, p. 93). In the same letter to the wealthy Daniel Hartenstein of Radziwiłłów, in which I. B. Levinsohn noted ironically the Hasidic poor who flocked to the rebbes, he complained of the fate of "the few Maskilim of our people, the poor who cry for food just as I do" (idem, p. 127).

33. S. J. Rapoport and N. Krochmal, too, had gone through periods of great economic distress, the former after he lost his position with the association of kosher meat tax lessees in Lemberg (see n. 21) and the latter after he had given up the tax leasing for the liquor sale monopoly and had moved to Brody in 1836, where he engaged, it seems, in teaching or in bookkeeping (see Rawidowicz, *Kitvei Re'Na'K*, p. 55).

34. Erter, *Ha-Ẓofeh*, p. 60.

35. Goldenberg, *Ohel Yosef*, p. 19.

36. Letteris, *Zikkaron*, p. 9. However, the same Gershon Letteris still prevented his son Meyer from reading German books, such as Lessing and Dohm; see Joseph Klausner, *Historyah shel ha-Sifrut ha-Ivrit ha-Ḥadashah* (Jerusalem, 1937) 2:368.

37. Bloch, *Shevilei Olam* 1:3.

38. Erter, *Ha-Ẓofeh*, p. 79.

39. Ibid., p. 34.

40. Perl, *Boḥen Ẓaddik*, p. 47. Concerning the identification of Briks as Tarnopol, cf. Ḥ. Shmeruk, "Matters as They Were in Reality and in the Imagination in *Megalleh Temirin*," in *Ẓiyyon* 21:93.

41. Letter from S. J. Rapoport to a friend, M. O., in 1822 in *Bikkurei ha-Ittim* (1828), p. 9. According to Klausner's supposition, M. O. was Mordecai Ornstein, the son of the Rabbi of Lemberg, Jacob Ornstein; see Klausner, *Historyah* 2:235.

42. *Di Genarte Velt*, ed. M. Viner (Moscow, 1940), p. 78.

43. Max Lilienthal, *Maggid Yeshu'ah* (1842); M. Letteris, *Mikhtevei Ivrit* (1894), p. 157.

44. A. B. Gottlober, *Ha-Niẓanim* (Vilna, 1850), p. 87.

45. *Tekhunat ha-Rabbanim* (Lemberg, 1879), p. 15. The question whether the author of *Tekhunat ha-Rabbanim* is really J. L. Mieses himself (as Graetz and W. Zeitlin contend) or the Maskil of Posen, David Caro (Zinberg's opinion), does not essentially change anything, because Mieses identified himself with this work in any case. In light of the disputed authorship, subsequent references in the text will be given as "the author."

46. Weinlös, in *Yoysef Perls*, p. xxxi.

47. Menasseh ben Israel, *Teshu'at Yisrael* (Vienna, 1813).

48. Erter, *Ha-Ẓofeh*, p. 159.

49. Perl, *Boḥen Ẓaddik*, p. 60.

50. *Tekhunat ha-Rabbanim*, p. 48.

51. Bloch, *Shevilei Olam* 1:22.

52. S. Bloch in *Teshu'at Yisrael*.

53. See n. 41.

54. *Bikkurei ha-Ittim*, 5588 [1828], p. 11; see n. 41.

55. J. L. Mieses, *Kinat ha-Emet* (1828), p. 177. Klausner (*Historyah*, p. 273) thought that "in the language that is now spoken" refers to German or French; in any case, not to Yiddish, because Mieses was an emphatic opponent of Yiddish. Opposition to Yiddish was also voiced by Perl, Levinsohn, and other prominent Maskilim, and yet they wrote in Yiddish in order to disseminate enlightenment. The quoted passage by Mieses is correctly interpreted by Max Erik in *Etyudn*, p. 198.

56. Z. Kalmanovich, in Weinlös's introduction, *Yoysef Perls*, p. lxxx.

57. See Joseph Perl's letters in Weinlös's introduction to his Yiddish writings, as well as his letters to I. B. Levinsohn in *Be'er Yiẓḥak*; see also the letters of J. S. Byk to Mendel Lefin, published in Friedman, "Die ershte Kamfn," in *Fun Noentn Over* 4:259–74.

58. Nachman Krochmal wrote in German to his son-in-law Dr. Horowitz (*Zikkaron*, p. 63), to his son Abraham in Hebrew and German (Rawidowicz, *Kitvei Re'Na'K*, p. 448); Solomon Judah Rapoport's son David wrote to his father in German with Hebrew letters; his son-in-law Bodek and his brother from Lemberg wrote to him in Hebrew; his daughters and grandchildren wrote to him only in German; See M. Balaban, "Aus der Korrespondenz S. J. Rappaports," *Jewish Studies in Memory of George Alexander Kohut* (New York, 1935), p. 47.

59. *Tekhunat ha-Rabbanim*, p. 43; see also Mieses, *Kinat ha-Emet*, p. 9, where he inveighed against those who cast aside the kernel of religion together with its husk, the superstitions.

60. S. J. Rapoport, *Tokhaḥat Megulah* (1845), letter 3, p. 34.

61. The fact that Maskilim like S. J. Rapoport and Joseph Perl maintained friendly relations with Naphtali Herz Homberg and even with converts was derived not only from the characteristic tolerance, a tenet of the Haskalah world view, but also from their loss of zeal in matters of piety. Among the broader circles of the Maskilim, discipline in the observance of the traditional Jewish religion was

much more lax than among the leaders. A. B. Gottlober related in his memoirs that when he visited Perl's school in Tarnopol as a boy in 1828, he met the teacher Bezalel Stern, who was not only dressed in the European fashion but also clean-shaven ("Zikhronot," *Ha-Boker Or* 6:163).

62. Rawidowicz, *Kitvei Re'Na'K*, p. 414.

63. Ibid., p. 439.

64. *Harkavy Jubilee Volume* (St. Petersburg, 1908), p. 485.

65. Goldenberg, *Ohel Yosef*, pp. 10, 14.

66. "Masa Ẓafon," p. 44.

67. See appendix: document 10a.

68. *Historishe Shriftn fun YIVO* 1:684. Fischelsohn mistakenly cited the statement in the name of R. Hamnuna instead of R. Abbahu (*Shabbat* 119b).

69. *Di Genarte Velt*, p. 84.

70. *Di Genarte Velt*, p. 60.

71. Cf. J. L. Mieses' letter to S. Goldenberg in *Kerem Ḥemed* 2 (1836): 36; also, B. Wachstein, *Die hebräische Publizistik in Wien* (Vienna, 1930), p. 44.

72. See Graetz, *Geschichte der Juden*, 2d. ed., 2:415, for his opposition to the *Grenzpfahlpatriotismus* (patriotism of boundary posts).

73. Concerning fundamentals of Humanism found in the Haskalah, see R. Mahler, *Divrei Yemei Yisrael be-Dorot ha-Aḥaronim* (Merḥaviah, 1954), 1:2:81–82.

In contrast, however, to the Humanists, who had conclusively begun to create a literature in their own national languages (Italian, French, Polish, etc.) modeled after the classical Latin language and the forms of Latin literature, the Galician Maskilim did not transfer the refined style to Yiddish, for they did not consider it a language.

The disparaging attitude toward Yiddish was derived from the contempt not only of the language proper but also of the culture of the common people, as exemplified by the passages in the introduction by S. J. Rapoport to his *She'erit Yehudah*, where he condemns the Ahasuerus plays as "a great infamy among the Jews" because of their "wantonness," "indignity," "obscenity," etc.; see *Bikkurei ha-Ittim*, 5588 [1828], pp. 179, 180, 183.

The Galician Maskilim who wrote Yiddish (e.g., Perl) did so for purposes of propaganda and enlightenment only and therefore thought it necessary to write all the more "plainly"; they did not make an effort to elevate Yiddish to the level of a literary language.

Of the Maskilim outside Galicia, Khaykl Hurvits, Aksenfeld, and Ettinger had already transferred their literary proficiency from Hebrew to Yiddish. Those in Russia, the Ukraine, and Poland where German did not play the role of a state language and knowledge of this language was less widespread, tended to have a more positive attitude toward Yiddish. Mendel Lefin, who came from Podolia and later settled in Galicia, with his translation of parts of the Bible (also in a "common" language), indeed occupies an intermediate position between the Ukrainian-Polish and the Galician Maskilim.

74. Rawidowicz, *Kitvei Re'Na'K*, p. 452.

75. I. B. Levinsohn, *Te'udah be-Yisrael*, sect. 1, chap. 11.

76. *Ẓiyyon* 1 (1840).

77. Levinsohn, *Te'udah be-Yisrael*, chaps. 9–10.

78. S. J. Rapoport, "Letter to a Close Friend," in *Bikkurei ha-Ittim*, p. 281.

79. *Tekhunat ha-Rabbanim*, p. 53.

80. Mieses, *Kinat ha-Emet*, p. 119, note.

81. See N. M. Gelber, *Vorgeschichte des Zionismus* (Vienna, 1927), pp. 260–61.

82. *Mishneh Torah, Hilkhot Melakhim*, chaps. 11–12.

83. *Sanhedrin* 99a.

84. Ephraim Fischl Fischelsohn, *Teyator fun Khsidim*, in *Historishe Shriftn fun YIVO* 1 (1929): 651.
85. *Sefer ha-Ikkarim*, art. 1, chap. 1.
86. Cf. the description of Hasidim rising at midnight for study and prayer in commemoration of the destruction of Jerusalem in Fischelsohn, *Teyator fun Khsidim*, p. 651.
87. *Tekhunat ha-Rabbanim*, p. 45. Klausner (*Historyah* 2:282) mentions in connection with this passage that other Maskilim, like J. L. Gordon, also argued against the recitation of *Tefillat Geshem* on Shemini Azeret.
88. A. B. Gottlober, "Zikhronot," *Ha-Boker Or* 4:9.
89. Quoted in Gelber, *Vorgeschichte*, p. 261.
90. A. B. Gottlober, *Ha-Niẓanim*, p. 87.
91. *Mikhtevei Ivrit*, p. 110.
92. Rawidowicz, *Kitvei Re'Na'K*, p. 439.
93. See chap. 8.
94. *Bikkurei ha-Ittim*, pp. 244–45. Klausner rightly calls attention to this in his *Historyah* (2:233).
95. Rapoport, *Tokhaḥat Megulah* (1845), p. 21.
96. *Ketubot* 111a.
97. I. B. Levinsohn, *Bet Yehudah* (1839), pp. 332–35.
98. I. M. Dick, *Ha-Oreaḥ* (Königsberg, 1860), p. 13.
99. Rawidowicz, *Kitvei Re'Na'K*, p. 248.
100. Perl, *Boḥen Ẓaddik*, p. 47.
101. Levinsohn, *Bet Yehudah*, p. 319.
102. See n. 41.
103. Erter, *Ha-Ẓofeh*, the end of the satire "Tashlikh."
104. *Bikkurei ha-Ittim*, pp. 133–39.
105. *Tekhunat ha-Rabbanim*, p. 26; cf. also pp. 13, 68.
106. Meyer Letteris, *Mikhtevei Benei Kedem* (Vienna, 1866), p. 27.
107. *Mikhtevei Ivrit*, p. 117.
108. Mieses, *Kinat ha-Emet*, pp. 118–23.
109. *Tekhunat ha-Rabbanim*, p. 64.
110. *Mikhtevei Ivrit*, p. 115.
111. Eliezer Sinai Kirschbaum, "La-menazeah be-hitkadesh ḥag ha-pesaḥ shir," *Yalkut Shirim u-Meliẓot* (Berlin, 1820), pp. 7–8.
112. Klausner, *Historyah* 2:378.
113. Wolf, *Juden in Wien*, p. 128.
114. See chap. 8.
115. Jacob Eichenbaum, *Kol Zimrah* (Leipzig, 1836), pp. 15–22.
116. I. B. Levinsohn, *Te'udah be-Yisrael*, sect. 3, chap. 67.
117. Gottlober, *Ha-Niẓanim*, pp. 199–201.
118. David Luria, *Omer ba-Sadeh* (Vilna, 1853), pp. 120–21.
119. *Mikhtevei Ivrit*, p. 123. According to the address of the letter, Kulików, it appears that the addressee is Samson Bloch.
120. A. A. Harkavy, *Zikkaron la-Rishonim ve-gam la-Aḥaronim*, pt. 2 (Vilna, 1881), pp. 47–48.
121. See Bloch's letter to Krochmal in his *Shevilei Olam*, vol. 1, and his letter to Joseph Perl in ibid., vol. 3.
122. Letter of Bloch to S. J. Rapoport in *Shevilei Olam*, vol. 2.
123. S. J. Rapoport in his letter on the Hasidim "Ner Miẓvah," in *Naḥalat Yehudah* (Cracow, 1868), p. 19; Nachman Krochmal, too, in a letter to Abraham Goldberg of Rawa quoted this saying (Rawidowicz, *Kitvei Re'Na'K*, p. 418).

124. S. Bloch, introduction to Menasseh ben Israel, *Teshu'at Yisrael* (Vienna, 1813).
125. I. Zinberg, *Geshikhte fun der literatur bay Yidn* (Vilna, 1936) 8:2:209.
126. Letteris, *Zikkaron*, p. 9.
127. *Tekhunat ha-Rabbanim*, p. 31.
128. Fischelsohn, *Teyator fun Khsidim*, pp. 659, 675.
129. Letter to Rapoport in introduction to Bloch's *Shevilei Olam*, vol. 2.
130. In the article "Toil of One's Hands" in the *Almanac for 1814* and "Da Mah she-Tashiv" in the *Almanac for 1815*; see chap. 6.
131. "Divrei Re'Na'K" in Rawidowicz, *Kitvei Re'Na'K*, p. 456.
132. *Tekhunat ha-Rabbanim*, "Ha-Mevi le-Beit ha-defus," p. 31, note.
133. In the letter to his friend M. O. (*Bikkurei ha-Ittim*, p. 23), S. J. Rapoport speaks of the necessity for every educated Jew to know those passages in the Talmud that speak of the importance of handicraft and farming "in order to remove from us the disgrace and to roll away the libels that we are lazy"; see also the anonymous *Di Genarte Velt*, p. 78.
134. This motive did not prevent Perl from ridiculing, in his *Boḥen Ẓaddik* (p. 65), those merchants who were anxious to shift as many Jews as possible to handicraft and farming in order to decrease competition in business.
135. See Mieses, *Tekhunat ha-Rabbanim*, p. 24, note.
136. *Di Genarte Velt*, p. 100.
137. R. Mahler, *Divrei Yemei Yisrael* 4:74.
138. N. M. Gelber, *Aus Zwei Jahrhunderten* (Vienna, 1924), p. 105.
139. *Tekhunat ha-Rabbanim*, p. 67, note.
140. Perl, *Boḥen Ẓaddik,* p. 83.
141. *Di Genarte Velt*, p. 100.
142. Perl, *Boḥen Ẓaddik*, p. 65.
143. *Di Genarte Velt*, pp. 100–101.
144. See B. Shlosberg, "Tsvey oysgabes fun Hirsh Reitmans poeme, 'Der Kitl,'" *Yivo Bleter* 9 (1936): 143–49; see also bibliography there.
145. Abraham Goldberg, "Masa Ẓafon," stanza 71.
146. Benjamin Mandelstamm, *Ḥazon la-Moed* 1:13.
147. "Ner Miẓvah," p. 14.
148. A. B. Gottlober, "Zikhronot," *Ha-Boker Or* 6:164.
149. This letter was published by Weinryb in "le-Toledot Rival."
150. A. B. Gottlober, *Toledot ha-Kabbalah ve-ha-Ḥasidut* (1869), pp. 12, 14.
151. Especially characteristic in this case is J. S. Byk's letter to S. J. Rapoport, Elul 1829, published in *Oẓar ha-Sifrut*, vol. 3, "Orot me-Ofel," pp. 26–28.
152. "Ner Miẓvah," pp. 15–17, 22.
153. Rawidowicz, *Kitvei Re'Na'K*, p. 429.
154. A. B. Gottlober, "Zikhronot," p. 529.
155. A. Pories in *Ha-Shaḥar* (1869), p. 26.

Chapter 3

1. Thus, for example, the Austrian government instructed its ambassadors in the German provinces in 1817 not to issue a passport to Madame von Krüdener to enter Austria because she "was a religious enthusiast"; see H. Srbik, *Metternich* (Munich, 1925) 1:763.
2. In accord with an Austrian governmental decree of 1812 all books preaching Socinianism, deism, and materialism were banned, and at the same time the pub-

lication of books tending to further superstition was forbidden; see H. H. Houben, *Der gefesselte Biedermeier* (Leipzig, 1924), p. 68.

3. In 1788 the district office of Rzeszów received instructions "not to persecute the Hasidim or pious Jews"; see Piller, *Galizische Provincialgesetzsammlung* (1823), no. 42077.

4. In the other provinces of Austria where Jewish youth also attended the general elementary schools, the German-Jewish schools, as is known, remained open after 1806 and even after 1820, despite the imperial decree which decided that they should gradually be eliminated. As early as the eighteenth century the Jewish community in Vienna sabotaged the government's plan to establish a separate elementary school for Jewish children because it saw in this separatism an obstacle to cultural assimilation and to social rapprochement with the Christian population (see G. Wolf, *Geschichte der Juden in Wien* [Vienna, 1876], p. 127, as well as Salo Baron, "Le-Toledot ha-Haskalah ve-ha-Ḥinukh be-Vinah," *Sefer Turov* [1938], pp. 167–83). Wishing to stop the process of assimilation among the Jews in those German-speaking Austrian provinces, the clergy therefore presented the demand that Jewish children be prohibited from attending Christian schools. After the death of Emperor Joseph II, the bishops of Austria complained to the government that Jewish children in the general elementary schools were liable to influence the Christian students in the spirit of Judaism. The supreme chancellor Count Kolorwrat had to assure them that such a case of the religious influence of Jewish children on Christian children had not yet occurred (see Wolf, idem, p. 95).

5. His correspondence with the police president concerning Austrian Jewry's reaction to the call of the Sanhedrin in Paris demonstrates the extent to which the emperor Francis I viewed with suspicion the teachers of the German-Jewish schools in Galicia as disseminators of atheism. The emperor commented on the report of the police president of October 22, 1806, that he had initially foreseen that the "proceedings in Paris" would not make a good impression on the "strict adherents of the Old Testament"; in return, however, "some of the German-Jewish school teachers in Galicia and other newer ones who are closer to deism" would have to be kept under surveillance (see Wolf, *Juden in Wien*, p. 116).

6. General compulsory education which was instituted in other provinces of Austria did not apply at all to Galicia because, it seems, of similar considerations of fear of the national awakening of the Polish and Ukrainian populations.

7. See, for example, the report of the imperial chancellery on the Jewish question, dated December 29, 1818, in A. F. Pribram, *Urkunden und Akten zur Geschichte der Juden in Wien* (Vienna, 1918) 2:279–306.

8. I. Zinberg (*Geshikhte fun der Literatur bay Yidn*) (Vilna, 1936, vol. 8, pt. 1, p. 43) correctly points out that the German officials in Galicia, living in the midst of the Polish and Ukrainian populations, naturally felt attracted to the wealthy Jews who had a German education.

9. See n. 3.

10. In Loebl's German pamphlet about the Hasidim *Glaubwürdige Nachrichten* . . . published in Frankfurt in 1799 and reprinted in 1807 in the periodical *Sulamith*, vol. 1, bk. 2, no. 5.

11. Piller, *Galizische Provincialgesetzsammlung* (1810), pp. 145–46.

12. Ibid. (1823), no. 42077.

13. *Chassiden* 3203/814; see appendix: document la.

14. S. Dubnow points out in his *Geshikhte fun Khsidizm* (YIVO, 1933) 2:142 several examples of how both Mitnaggedim and Maskilim of the end of the eighteenth century used to compare the Hasidim with the Freemasonic Order of Illuminati or with Freemasons in general. In his autobiography (chap. 20) Solomon Maimon compares the Hasidim with the Illuminati of Bavaria, according to both their objectives and the means which they used but chiefly on the basis of the

same conspiracy of the leaders of both movements. In the Mitnaggedic book *Shever Posh'im* (*Zimrat Am ha-Areẓ*) the Hasidim are compared with the "people" "mnistin . . . or Freemasons." The Russian poet and senator Derzhavin recounts that he heard from "several enlightened Jews that the Hasidim are similar to the *Illuminati*" (Dubnow).

15. Such a decree was issued based on Governor Hauer's 1817 report to Sedlnitzky (see chap. 4, n. 114).

16. The names of the four Maskilim are given by Meyer Letteris in his "Toledot R. Nachman Krochmal," preface to *Moreh Nevukhei ha-Zeman* (Lemberg, 1863). For the episode of the excommunication, see S. Bernfeld, *Toledot Shir* (Berlin, 1899), p. 17.

17. The German-Jewish *Realschule* in Brody was given its charter on July 10, 1815, but was not opened until 1818; cf. Balaban, *Żydzi w Galicyi* (Lemberg, 1914), p. 93. Joseph Perl in his application of 1816 to the governor mentioned the attacks of the "zealots" upon this school and expressed his enthusiasm for the subsequent measures taken against them by the governor.

18. It is well known that the Rabbi of Lemberg, Jacob Ornstein, was forced by the authorities publicly to revoke the ban in the synagogue. In the introduction to *Yoysef Perls Yidishe Ksovim* (Vilna, 1937), pp. xxxi–xxxii, I. Weinlös published an interesting letter by a Maskil fully describing this revocation of the ban.

19. *Chassiden*, 4006/816; see appendix: document lb.

20. See appendix: document 2a. Various hypotheses have been advanced concerning the author of this pamphlet, which was extensively used by Peter Beer and M. Jost in their works on the Jewish sects; see S. Dubnow, "Der ershter Kamf fun haskole Kegn Khsides," in *Yivo Bleter* 1 (1931): 4–9; I. Weinlös, idem, 2 (1932): 89–90; Zinberg, *Literatur bay Yidn*, vol. 8, pt. 2, p. 283; and Philip Friedman, "Die ershte Kamfn tsvishn haskole un Khsidizm," in *Fun Noentn Over*, vol. 4 (1938). The archival materials cited here put an end to this dispute, making it clear that Perl himself was the author. A copy of this pamphlet has been preserved in the National and University Library in Jerusalem. A detailed analysis of its content, though biased in the conclusion, has been published by A. Rubinstein in *Kiryat Sefer* 38 (1963): 23; 39:1.

21. *Chassiden*, 4860/816; see appendix: document 2b.

22. *Chassiden*, 689/817; see appendix: document 2c.

23. Concerning these raids and their results, see chap. 4.

24. *Chassiden*, 689/817; see appendix: document 2d. Imperial Chancellor Count Ugarte made excuses to the Emperor on June 27, 1812, saying that "the preparation of a new Jewry ordinance must still take a lot of time because this is a complicated and important matter that demands long deliberation" (see Balaban, *Żydzi w Galicyi*, p. 137). Actually this "deliberation" continued right up until the outbreak of the Revolution of 1848, which gave the Jews civil equality in the place of a new "Jewry ordinance."

25. See chap. 1 for these repressive measures of germanization. The decree is published in Pribram, *Urkunden und Akten*, p. 305.

26. See appendix: document 3.

27. S. A., Lemberg, *Acta praesidialia* 2928/820.

28. The financial consideration formally submitted in the accusation was probably not the only one. The struggle between the Orthodox and the Maskilim concerning the *Realschule* in Brody was sharply intensified just at that time. Desiring to weaken the influence of the *Realschule* on the youth, in 1817 the local Orthodox opened a large yeshivah headed by Hersh Heller (known as R. Hersh *Ḥarif*), whom they brought from Hungary. The leaders of the *Realschule* in Brody saw in this yeshivah a threat to their institution, informed against it that it did not have a concession from the government, and denounced Heller himself for teaching

according to prohibited books. As a result of this denunciation Heller was administratively expelled from Brody in 1818; see M. Jost, *Neuere Geschichte der Israeliten*, vol. 10, pt. 3, pp. 80–81.

29. See appendix: document 4a.

30. See chap. 5. concerning Joseph Perl's denunciation of Hersh of Żydaczów in 1827.

31. See appendix: document 4b.

32. S. A., Lemberg, *Index Acta praesidialia* 1820, no. 3450.

33. See Balaban, "Aus der Korrespondenz S. L. Rappaports," *Jewish Studies in Memory of George Alexander Kohut* (New York, 1935), p. 101.

34. S. A., Lemberg, *Index Acta praesidialia* 1818, no. 306.

35. Ibid., no. 17778/825.

36. *Chassiden*, 15g/1827; see appendix: document 6b.

37. Cf. Perl's memorandum of 1827 in chap. 5.

38. See Friedman, "Die ershte Kamfn," pp. 265–67.

39. *Chassiden*, 15/1827; see appendix: document 6b.

40. In the original version of this letter (editions of 1863 and 1868; see chap. 1 n. 20) the text explicitly states "from Żydaczów." However, the version published in *Kerem Ḥemed* reads "from Berdichev," and Rawidowicz uncritically reprinted this mistake in his edition of *Kitvei Re'Na'K*, p. 417.

41. All of these decrees regarding *minyanim* were cited in an ordinance of the Galician provincial administration on the subject dated April 21, 1836 (Piller, no. 14388).

42. See n. 11, Piller, *Galizische Provincialgesetzsammlung* (1810), no. 33776.

43. Ibid. (1823), no. 44076.

44. Ibid. (1836), no. 14338.

45. S. A., Lemberg, *Acta Gubernialia Publ. Polit.* 11h/i no. 45730.

46. Piller, *Galizische Provincialgesetzsammlung* (1840), no. 53081.

47. *Chassiden*, 4553/838; see appendix: document 9e.

48. The processing of an application by a certain Jacob Glanzer of Lemberg for a permit to conduct a *minyan* lasted from 1843 to 1848! S. A., Lemberg, *Acta Gubernialia Publ. Polit.* 11h/i no. 4573.

49. Balaban, "Aus der Korrespondenz S. L. Rappaports," p. 101.

50. Piller, *Galizische Provincialgesetzsammlung* (1823), no. 60718.

51. Balaban, "Aus der Korrespondenz S. L. Rappaports," p. 104.

52. See appendix: document 5. This is the same town mentioned with scorn as a nest of Hasidism in the letter from Nachman Krochmal to Abraham Goldberg.

53. Of course, the R. Me'ir Ba'al ha-Nes's alms boxes are referred to here. For the struggle of the Maskilim against these alms boxes, see chap. 5.

54. See chap. 5. The district commissioner of Brody mentioned in this report of 1827 "a defense of the rebbe of the Ropczyce Hasidim through official channels" which occurred before 1825. It is possible that this negotiation had a bearing on the letter from Hersh of Żydaczów concerning which Perl issued an unfavorable statement.

55. *Chassiden*, 5611/838. This memorandum is treated in detail in chap. 5.

56. Such official inquiries addressed to the district rabbis concerning various matters, including Hasidism, also often took place in the later years. Jost (p. 81) recorded ten statements of opinion (*Gutachten*) which were delivered at the government's demand by Ẓevi Hirsh Chajes from 1829, when he became the district rabbi of Żółkiew.

57. This is the collection of laws for Galicia, published by Piller, which is often cited in this chapter.

58. Tolerated Jews, i.e., the community of Jews which enjoyed religious toleration.

59. Concerning these two decrees, see previous references in this chapter.

60. In practice, the officials continued to uphold the previous decree, and they would demand certification from those applying for a permit to conduct a *minyan* that they were not Hasidim. As late as 1838 the Lemberg police directorate mentioned the obligation to furnish such certificates.

61. Piller, *Galizische Provincialgesetzsammlung* (1824), no. 23819.

62. This ordinance was quoted in the report of the Lemberg police directorate of 1838. Since the number of the ordinance was indicated there, it is hard to imagine that the police director would have made a mistake in the date and that he had in mind the detailed ordinance of April 26 of the same year, 1824.

63. Israel Loebl, *Sefer Vikkuaḥ* (Warsaw, 1798).

64. See S. Dubnow, *Geshikhte fun Khsidizm*, p. 180.

65. See Friedman, "Die ershte Kamfm," p. 270.

66. See Weinlös's introduction, *Yoysef Perls,* p. xlii.

67. In the letter by Sedlnitzky cited below, two prefaces to the book, as well as an appendix which lists Hasidic books, are mentioned.

The brilliant Haskalah scholar Simḥah Katz conveyed to me in his letter dated June 16, 1939, the following details regarding the manuscript of *Sefer Vikkuaḥ*, which he saw in Perl's library in Tarnopol. Appended at the end of the book is a list of Hasidic books (similar to the list at the end of *Megalleh Temirin*). The content of the manuscript is quite different from that of Israel Loebl's book of 1798. Here the Talmudist engaged in polemics in the spirit of the Haskalah. Katz contends that this is not the version of *Sefer Vikkuaḥ* which was forwarded to the censor in Vienna in 1825/26 because it is indicated in the manuscript catalogue in the Tarnopol library that this manuscript is from 1831.

Both Katz's information and the fact that the censorship office explicitly refused permission in 1829 to publish *Sefer Vikkuaḥ* contradicted Weinlös (*Yoysef Perls*, p. xlii), who wrote that the manuscript of *Sefer Vikkuaḥ* which was in Perl's archives was "recopied for publication with the consent of the censor in Vienna." It is not likely that Perl would have sent *Sefer Vikkuaḥ* to the censor again after its rejection in 1829, and it is even more far-fetched that the censorship office would later have revised its position and permitted the publication of the book. It seems that the book was examined by the censor in Vienna, and Weinlös mistakenly interpreted this to mean that a permit was granted by the censor. However, in this case, the date of the manuscript in the catalogue is not correctly indicated, and it is the same manuscript which was forwarded to the censorship office in Vienna in 1825/26.

68. In the letter to the Galician governor, cited below, Sedlnitzky gave only the first initial of Rapaport's name, "S." The identification of this Rapaport with the famous Solomon Judah Rapoport is controverted by the full name Solomon Simḥah found in a document of the provincial office from 1829. It is not to be assumed that the official scribe mistook Judah or Leyb for Simḥah.

69. Approximately the same countries where Hasidism spread are mentioned in the preface to the manuscript "Über das Wesen der Sekte Chassidim": "Approximately within half a century this sect spread in all of the provinces which belonged to the former Kingdom of Poland, in the principalities of Moldavia and Wallachia, and it appears that from the imperial province of Galicia it took root in a part of adjacent Hungary" (see Dubnow, "Der ershter Kamf," p. 5). Dubnow correctly pointed out that Nachman Krochmal, in his apologetic letter of 1816 regarding the Karaites, also enumerated approximately the same lands as the area of diffusion of Hasidism. It must be added that in Krochmal's letter to his young friend Abraham Goldberg of Rawa, the description of the spread of Hasidism resembles even more closely the formulation in the preface to Perl's manuscript "Über das Wesen": "and taken root [cf. "it took root"—"Wurzel gefasst zu

haben"] among the villagers dwelling on the Hungarian frontier, in the Wallachian hideouts of robbers and in the distant Ukrainian steppes, all of them new communities recently established by refugees and exiles from the adjacent countries . . ." (Letteris, *Mikhtavim* [1827], letter 5; S. Rawidowicz, ed., *Kitvei Re'Na'K*, p. 417). Dubnow presents the first analogy as another piece of evidence to support his hypothesis that the manuscript "Über das Wesen" could have been a collective work by several authors. However, the archival documents cited above regarding Perl's authorship of the manuscript were unknown to Dubnow. The almost identical phraseology about the spread of Hasidism in Perl's brochure and in Krochmal's two letters can therefore be explained only by the fact that Krochmal read Perl's manuscript and adopted the relevant passage. That approximately the same version is found in the new preface to *Sefer Vikkuaḥ* strengthens the hypothesis that Perl himself is indeed the author of this preface, too.

70. Because of similar considerations, the censorship office in Vienna refused permission to publish the manuscript "Über das Wesen" in 1816. The final consideration for refusing to permit the printing of *Sefer Vikkuaḥ* in 1829 is slightly modified in comparison with the above-cited formulation.

71. All these outlandish accusations against the Hasidim are indeed to be found in Israel Loebl's preface to *Sefer Vikkuaḥ*; See Dubnow, *Geshikhte fun Khsidizm*, pp. 139, 177.

72. See n. 69.

73. *Chassiden*, 186g, 826; see appendix: document 6a.

74. Ibid.

75. See the list of zaddikim according to *Sefer Vikkuaḥ* in Dubnow's *Toledot ha-Ḥasidut ve-ha-Ḥasidim*, vol. 3 (Tel Aviv, 1932), app.

76. Thus Joshua Dunwitzer is listed in *Sefer Vikkuaḥ* as Yeshayah Dadinitz but in *Shever Posh'im* as (Donawitzer) Yeshayah Donatzer; Marcus Manwer is called (Yanover) Mordecai Yanever. Dubnow (*Geshikhte fun Khsidizm*) lists the names in parentheses as variant readings.

77. In the document of 1829, the name was correctly recopied as Susze Hanepole. The first copyist corrupted the letter *H* to read as double *t* (*tt*).

78. The error is to be explained in this manner: Ha-Rav Daskhizh from the printed edition of *Sefer Vikkuaḥ* was probably copied in Perl's manuscript with the Hebrew preposition instead of the Aramaic, i.e., Ha-Rav Maskhizh. However, it is difficult to understand why the censor called him Ephraim since the Rabbi of Neskhizh, the friend of the *Shpoler zeyde*, was named Mordecai (see Dubnow, *Geshikhte fun Khsidizm*, p. 233).

79. The Hebrew text that the censor saw probably read Mordecai mi-Yanove, i.e., of Janów.

80. Mordecai of Lachowicze (Lekhevitsh), a town near Baranowicze, died before 1821 (Dubnow, *Geshikhte fun Khsidizm*, chap. 33).

81. Samuel of Amdur, a town in the district of Grodno, died c. 1798 (Dubnow, *Geshikhte fun Khsidizm*, chap. 33).

82. Meyer of Sheps, the Yiddish name of the township of Sierpc, north of Warsaw; Dubnow regards him as an insignificant Hasidic leader and does not even attempt to identify the name of the town by which he is called.

83. Mordecai of Janów. Dubnow did not find anything about him either in Hasidic literature. In this case the identification is very difficult because there are many towns named Janów (Yanove or Yonev in Yiddish) in Poland. In *Seder ha-Dorot le-Talmidei ha-Besht* (Lemberg, 1865) two rebbes of the town of Yaniv (i.e., Yonev, Yanove) are mentioned. One is Isaiah of Yaniv, a student of the Ba'al Shem Tov, and the second is Moses of Yaniv, a student of Jacob Isaac of Lublin.

84. *Chassiden*, 410g, 826.

85. All the evidence indicates that the famous Hasidic rebbe Meyer of Przemyślany was referred to here.

86. In the denunciation of the Hasidim by the Rabbi of Pinsk, Avigdor ben Ḥayyim, in 1800, they were depicted as followers of the Sabbatians and Frankists (Dubnow, *Geshikhte fun Khsidizm*, p. 152). Later the Hasidim themselves would designate people whom they suspected of heresy as Sabbatians ("Shabse-tsvinik").

87. As mentioned above, in accordance with the Charter of 1789 only those rabbis of the chief cities of the districts had the title "Rabbi" (*Rabbiner*). In the smaller towns they were known as "Religionsweiser," i.e., *morei hora'ah*.

88. The records of that investigation are in the archives in the same collection as the documents about the Hasidim.

89. *Chassiden*, 15g, 1827; see appendix: document 6b.

90. *Chassiden*, 16g, 1827.

91. *Chassiden*, 29g, 1827; cf. appendix: document 6e.

92. R. Shmuelekhl Ostrover, author of "Torat ha-Adam," is mentioned in *Shem ha-Gedolim he-Ḥadash, Ma'arekhet Sefarim*, letter 39.

93. *Chassiden*, 28g, 1827.

94. See Jost, *Neuere Geschichte*, p. 91. Jost was referring to the information given by the famous Rabbi of Żółkiew, Ẓevi Hirsh Chajes.

95. See the Galician governor's circular of 1814, which instructs the officials to turn to the commissioner of Brody for information regarding the Hasidim.

96. Israel Loebl's treatise on Hasidism was printed in the periodical *Sulamith*.

97. See above, as well as chap. 5.

98. Undoubtedly this referred to the decree of 1788 concerning toleration toward "Hasidim or pious Jews" which was issued in connection with an inquiry from the district office of Rzeszów.

99. "West Galicia" was the designation of the Lublin region which Austria occupied during the third Partition of Poland in 1795 and retained until 1809.

100. Difficult to identify; the literature about Hasidism does not refer to any Rebbe of Międzyrzec (Mezritsh, in the region of Podlasie) during that period.

101. The same list of the succession of countries in which Hasidism spread, as in the letters by Krochmal, in Perl's brochure "Über das Wesen," and in his preface to the planned new edition of *Sefer Vikkuaḥ*, is characteristic. It is possible that the commissioner of Brody took these facts from Peter Beer's work *Geschichte, Lehren und Meinungen der religiösen Sekten der Juden* (Brünn, 1823), which was based, as is known, on Perl's manuscript "Über das Wesen."

102. The name of the city is illegible.

103. The commissioner of Brody probably labelled the Maskilim as "Mosaists," while he called the Mitnaggedim "Talmudists." At the end of the memorandum he referred to Perl as a "Mosaist." However, he then completely forgot these details and designated all opponents of the Hasidim "Mosaists."

104. This was not intended as an exaggeration of the status of faith among the Hasidim. According to the tradition of Strelisk Hasidim—that after a certain Hasid received a blessing from his rebbe, Uri, he would receive 80,000 gulden—he returned home to learn he had won that amount in a lottery, although he had never played the lottery. As a result of this news the landowner leased his property to him (*Imrei Kadosh ha-Shalem*, "Or Olam," p. 24). Dov Shtok (Sadan) related that his great-grandfather, Yossi, a Hasid of Bełz and a *shoḥet* in Brody, was told as a trick that he had won the lottery, which he believed despite never having played the lottery. He even celebrated with a banquet (Dov Shtok, *Mi-Meḥoz ha-Yaldut*, p. 23.)

105. This is explicitly stated in *Keter Shem Tov*, a book which the commissioner had enclosed with his report on the Hasidim in 1815. In the original, a comment is here added that this book was published in Żółkiew in 1798. According to *Seder*

ha-Dorot, the first part of *Keter Shem Tov* was published in Żółkiew in 1784, the second part in 1795.

106. The ban on Jewish garb promulgated by Emperor Joseph II in 1789 was revoked shortly thereafter in 1790 by his successor, Emperor Leopold II.

107. *Chassiden*, 18g, cf. appendix: document 6f.

108. On the basis of the misinformation supplied by the censorship office in Lemberg, the provincial presidency identified Meyer Szebser with Meyer of Przemyślany and the town of Przemyślany with the district of Przemyśl and therefore sent the circular to the district office of Przemyśl. The district chief of Przemyśl further corrupted the name Szebser to read "Szebsen."

109. *Chassiden*, 243g, 827; cf. appendix: document 6g.

110. *Chassiden*, 72g, 828.

111. See chap. 5.

112. The Hebrew censor in Lemberg at the time was the well-known Maskil Joseph Tarler, the teacher of Isaac Erter, who converted and received the Christian name Peter. He is further cited by this name in a document from 1838. Concerning him, see M. Weissberg, "Die neuhebräische Aufklärungsliteratur in Galizien," in *Monatsschrift für die Geschichte und Wissenschaft des Judentums* (1928), p. 185.

113. In the preface to *Sefer Vikkuaḥ* (p. 8) Israel Loebl speaks of the changes in the tradition of prayer which the Hasidim introduced without the permission of the authorities.

114. Unfortunately, a copy of this police report has not been preserved in the records.

115. Peter Beer also mentioned (p. 205), in addition to Perl, a preacher, Nieschke, as a source of his information.

116. This fact is related by all of Perl's biographers, beginning with the first, Dr. Nathan Horowitz.

117. Naphtali of Ropczyce died in 1827.

118. Hersh of Żydaczów died in 1831 during the cholera epidemic.

119. The founder of the "court" of Bełz, Sholem Rokeakh, died in 1855.

120. Simon of Jarosław, a student and friend of the Rebbe of Bełz, author of *Naḥalat Shim'on*.

121. Abraham David Kru of Buczacz, author of the kabbalistic commentary on the Torah *Birkat David*, died in 1840 (see the denunciation by Joseph Tepper, appendix: document 12).

122. Judah Ẓevi of Stratyn, student of Uri of Strelisk, "the Seraph."

123. Moses of Sambor, author of *Tefillah le-Mosheh*, and a brother of Hersh of Żydaczów.

124. A town near Kamionka Strumilowa. As far as we know, no Rebbe of Radziechów is mentioned in Hasidic literature.

125. The Rebbe of Chołojów was Yehoshua Heshl Efrati, author of *Naḥlat Yehoshua*. We are indebted for this information to R. Ze'ev Leiter of Pittsburgh, Pennsylvania.

126. The commissioner of Brody tells of a Samuel Hasid or Samuel Ostrowski of Brody in his report; see n. 92.

127. It was impossible to discover the name of this rebbe.

128. A copy of this report was not preserved in the records.

129. *Chassiden*, 72g, 828; cf. appendix: document 6h.

130. S. A., Lemberg, *Acta praesidialia* (1829), no. 7347; see appendix: document 7.

131. Ibid. On the copy which was preserved in the State Archives in Lemberg, the exact date is not indicated, only the year, 1829.

132. *Chassiden*, 9141/829; see appendix: document 6i.

133. *Chassiden*, 9141/829.
134. *Chassiden*, 5079/831; see appendix: document 6j.
135. Appendix: documents 9a and b.
136. Appendix: document 9c.
137. He was the father of the famous writer, Leopold von Sacher-Masoch; see *Allgemeine Deutsche Biographie* 53:681.
138. *Chassiden*, 4553/838; see appendix: document 9e.
139. In connection with the investigation which the Austrian government conducted in 1806 concerning the Jews' reaction to the call for the Sanhedrin in Paris, the Galician governor compared the Hasidim in his report with other sectarians, namely with the Quakers and Moravian Brethren; see Wolf, *Juden in Wien*, p. 113.
140. See appendix: document 9f.
141. Simon of Dobromil, rabbi in Jarosław, student of Sholem of Bełz, author of the book *Naḥalat Shim'on*.
142. Popular rebbe in central and western Galicia who happened to be an attendant in the service of Rebbe Mendl of Rymanów in his youth and succeeded him as zaddik after his death. According to the testimony of Solomon Rubin, he was quite an ignorant and avaricious person. He would charge fifty gulden for promising the birth of a son, half of which was to be paid in advance (see S. A. Horodetzky, *Ha-Ḥasidut ve-ha-Ḥasidim* 4:110). He became connected by marriage to Israel of Ruzhin, and died in 1858.
143. Meyer of Przemyślany, famous rebbe-philanthropist, one of the most interesting personalities among the Galician rebbes in the first half of the nineteeth century. His teachings are collected in the book *Divrei Me'ir*. A. B. Gottlober referred to him as insane and to his teachings as nonsensical and ridiculous (see A. Fridkin, *Avrom Ber Gottlober un zayn Epokhe*, pp. 148–49). In contrast, Solomon Rubin spoke with respect about his charitable acts (ibid.). In the report of the district chief of Brzeżany from 1827, his family name was given as Maner but his brother in Kałusz was correctly called Mayer (Isaac Mayer).
144. According to *Seder ha-Dorot*, Judah Isaac of "Barnifka" was a student of Hersh of Żydaczów.
145. Police Director Sachar designated with an "N" those rebbes whose family names he could not find out.
146. Ḥayyim of Kosów, son of Menaḥem Mendel of Kosów, died in 1854.
147. The city of Hrubieszów in Congress Poland was known as Rubishoyv in Yiddish.
148. Student of Uri of Strelisk, who was himself a student of Solomon of Karlin.
149. Ẓevi Elimelekh of Dynów, student of Hersh of Żydaczów, author of *Benei Yissakhar* and of several other books, zealous enemy of the Haskalah. Legends have been preserved about his relation to Joseph Tarler, the Maskil and later apostate and censor in Lemberg (see Naphtali of Ropczyce, *Ohel Naftali* (Warsaw, 1911), p. 99. Solomon Rubin said of him that he was a very sagacious person (Horodetzky, *Ha-Ḥasidut*, p. 110).
150. Student and contemporary of Sholem of Bełz (see *Seder ha-Dorot*).
151. Difficult to identify.
152. Yitskhokl of Nadworna, popular rebbe in eastern Galicia.
153. Sholem Rokeakh of Bełz, student of Jacob Isaac of Lublin, founder of the dynasty of Bełz.
154. See the end of chap. 1. The police director translated "Ḥadushim" as "new small Hasidic houses of prayer"; actually, this was the designation of those Hasidim of the new movement which combined the Hasidic teaching with the principle of diligent study of the Talmud.
155. As mentioned, it is not likely that the police director would have made a mistake in the date, in this case, having in mind the decree of April 26 of that year.

156. In accord with the decree of April 26, 1824, the decision, which demanded certification that the members of a *minyan* were not Hasidim, was revoked. Therefore, it appears that this concession was not carried out in practice.
157. For the feud in Tarnopol, see chap. 5.
158. *Chassiden*, 4553/838; appendix: document 9g.
159. *Chassiden*, 2889/838; cf. appendix: document 10b; more detailed treatment of this project is given in chap. 5.
160. *Chassiden*, 5611/838; see appendix: documents 11a, b.
161. S. A., Lemberg, *Acta praesidialia* 7263/839.
162. *Chassiden*, 7692/841; see appendix: document 12.

Chapter 4

1. See H. Srbik, *Metternich* (Munich, 1925) 1:492.
2. L. Wurzbach, *Biographisches Lexicon*, vol. 33, quoted in F. M. Mayer, *Geschichte Österreichs* (Vienna, 1909) 2:623. Sedlnitzky's procedure was described in precisely the same way in *Allgemeine Deutsche Biographie* 33:528–31.
3. Mayer, *Geschichte Österreichs*, p. 623.
4. See H. H. Houben, *Der gefesselte Biedermeier* (Leipzig, 1924), p. 228.
5. The democrat Held, who related this episode, finished his story: "What's the difference if these lords pronounce themselves as being ill or 'indisposed,' the devil will take them in any case" (ibid., p. 228).
6. See Shalom Spiegel, "Tashlum ha-Hakdamah le-Sefer Kinnor Na'im le-Shadal," in *Jewish Studies in Memory of George Alexander Kohut* (New York, 1935), p. 133.
7. Cf. the quotes from Mendel of Rymanów, *Menaḥem Ẓiyyon,* and from Ẓevi Elimelekh of Dynów's glosses to Hersh of Żydaczów, *Sur me-Ra va-Aseh Tov* (Munkacs, 1901), in chap. 1.
8. See Spiegel, "Tashlum ha-Hakdamah," p. 134.
9. See *Yalkut Yashar*, quoted in Joseph Klausner, *Historyah shel ha-Sifrut ha-Ivrit ha-Ḥadashah* (Jerusalem, 1937) 2:99, n. 47.
10. See chap. 3.
11. See Houben, *Biedermeier*, pp. 74, 87.
12. Published in A. F. Pribram, *Urkunden und Akten zur Geschichte der Juden in Wien* (Vienna, 1918) 1:554, n. 234. The original text of this decree reads as follows:

> Damit die Judenschaft, welche alle albernen Teufelsbanereyen und ähnliche Dinge begierig auffast, wenigstens nicht durch neue Schriften in ihren Irrthümern genähret und dadurch ihre Bildung und Aufklärung entweder verzögert oder ganz unmöglich werde; so ist künftig allen Büchern worinnen dergleichen Ungereimtheiten vorkommen, sie mögen in der Landessprache oder jüdischen und hebräischen geschrieben sein, der Druck mit Typum non meretur zu versagen.

13. See Natalia Gąsiorowska, "Cenzura żydowska w Królestwie Kongresowem," in *Kwartalnik Historji Żydów w Polsce* 1:2 (1912): 55–64.
14. See G. Wolf, "Zur Geschichte jüdischer Buchdruckereien in Oesterreich," in *Hebräische Bibliographie (Ha-Mazkir)* (1865) 8:58–60.
15. See chap. 3.
16. See Heinrich Ritter von Kopetz, *Versuch einer systematischen Darstellung der in Böhmen bezüglich der Juden bestehenden Gesetze und Verordnungen* (Prague, 1846), p. 166.

17. See Pribram, *Urkunden und Acten*, p. 71, n. 296. It is very probable that this order was suggested by Anton Schmidt, the famous printer of Hebrew books in Vienna, who enjoyed great influence at the court of the Emperor. Meyer Letteris (in his article "Devarim aḥadim ha-Noge'im le-Toledot Melakhat ha-Dafus be-Vien," in N. Keller, ed., *Bikkurim* (Vienna, 1865) 2:25, remarked that the prohibition on importing books contributed to the enormous enrichment of the printer A. Schmidt, who thereby secured a virtual monopoly on Hebrew books in the entire Austrian monarchy. The few Galician printing houses in Lemberg and Żółkiew were of such limited scope that they could hardly be considered competitors.

18. See G. Wolf, *Geschichte der Juden in Wien* (Vienna, 1876), p. 123; see also M. Balaban, "Zur Geschichte der hebräischen Druckereien in Polen," *Soncino Blätter* 3 (1929): 27–28.

19. *Chassiden*, 3203/814.

20. B. Friedberg's *Bet Eked Sefarim* records an edition of *Sefer Ḥasidim* at the turn of the nineteenth century which was published without a declaration of place and date of printing. It is not unlikely that a copy of this edition was seized by the head censor in Vienna in 1814. However, Friedberg also lists an edition of *Sefer Ḥasidim* printed in Żółkiew in 1805.

21. Because of its marked anti-Christian tendency, *Sefer Ḥasidim* was already severely expurgated by Catholic censorship in its second edition, Basel, 1582; see I. Zinberg, *Geshikhte fun der Literatur bay Yidn* (Vilna, 1936), vol. 2, supp. 1, p. 315. It is characteristic that the Russian censors, too, subjected this book to severe examination. In the edition of Sudilkov, 1832, many paragraphs were deleted and expressions such as *shmad, hegmon, komer, goy* were struck out (cf. L. Zunz, "Die Zensur hebräische Werke," in his *Gesammelte Schriften* 3:239–41, as well as Zinberg, *Literatur bay Yidn*, p. 316.

22. Ben-Jacob, in his *Oẓar ha-Sefarim*, mentions an edition of *Tefillat Nehora* from Ostrog (1810). Only one edition for this period, Berdichev (1811), is mentioned in *Kiryat Sefer* 9 (1932–33). Most probably the Vienna censor had to deal with this edition since the latter one was not published until 1817 in Hrubieszów.

23. Cf. chap. 3.

24. *Chassiden*, 689/817.

25. Simon Dubnow contended that there is a connection between the censors' statement of opinion concerning the list of Hasidic books in Perl's brochure and the ban on the brochure itself. He wrote to the author about this in a letter dated July 9, 1939:

> I found an answer to my question of why Perl's pamphlet "Über das Wesen der Sekte Chassidim" was not published. Your archival materials show that the "smart" Austrian police prohibited the printing of this anti-Hasidic work and used it in the confiscation of such later Hasidic books as the *Vikkuaḥ Talmudi u-Veshtani*."

However, the fact was unknown to Dubnow that, along with the list, Perl's manuscript was also sent back by the censorship office in Vienna to Lemberg and from there to the author in Tarnopol. Therefore, there must have been some substance to the reason adduced by Sedlnitzky.

26. The titles of these books are given here in their correct form. In the original German transcription they are generally corrupted, sometimes to be unrecognizable. Not only is *Shivḥei ha-Besht* called "Schwuche Beschet," and *Iggeret ha-Kadosh* "Ageres Hakodesch"; but also *Sefer ha-Midot* by Naḥman of Bratslav is referred to as "Sepher Hameor," *Likkutei Yekarim* "Lekute Jekorun," and *Likkutei Amarim* was corrupted to read "Lekol Hamorim"!

27. The *Likkutei Amarim*, also entitled *Maggid Devarav le-Ya'akov*, referred to here is that by Dov Ber, Maggid of Mezhirech (Międzyrzec). *Iggeret ha-Kodesh* is

the letter appended to *No'am Elimelekh*. These titles have been identified through the manuscript of Perl's "Über das Wesen der Sekte Chassidim," a copy of which is in the Archives of the National and University Library, Jerusalem (cf. A. Rubinstein, "The ms. 'Über das Wesen der Sekte Chassidim,'" *Kiryat Sefer* 38:270, nn. 60, 61.

28. A treatise by Naḥum of Chernobyl.

29. The famous book by Ḥayyim Vital.

30. The strictness of the Austrian censorship of kabbalistic literature is responsible for the fact that no edition of either *Ez̧ Ḥayyim* or the *Zohar* was published in Galicia during the period of reaction. The first Galician edition of *Ez̧ Ḥayyim* appeared in Lemberg in 1865. The *Zohar* was printed in Żółkiew in 1793 but was not reprinted again in Galicia.

31. It is possible that Beer learned about the other Hasidic books from the preacher Nieschke, whom he thanked for the information received. Peter Beer listed the titles of the books correctly, except for *No'am Elimelekh*, which he corrupted to read "No'am ha-Melekh." Apparently, he had not actually seen the Hasidic books.

32. See Peter Beer, *Geschichte, Lehren und Meinungen, der religiösen Sekten der Juden* (Brünn, 1825) 2:205.

33. Cf. H. Von Kopetz, *Versuch*, p. 167, where a decree of 1812 is cited which required that lists of books left as an inheritance be drawn up by sworn appraisers.

34. *Chassiden*, 689/817.

35. S. A., Lemberg, *Index Acta praesidialia* (1818), no. 1755.

36. *Chassiden*, 685/819. The censor enumerated seventeen books, but numbered in such a way that the title of the last one was designated "36." Apparently the remaining nineteen books presented no cause for the censor to deal with.

37. Author, Moses ibn Makir; contains religious ordinances for every occasion, arranged chronologically for the whole year. *Editio princeps* (Safed, 1586). Editions which appeared in Poland and the Ukraine until then were: Slavuta, 1802; Żółkiew, 1805; Polonnoye, 1816 (see Friedberg, *Bet Eked Sefarim*, p. 450).

38. Actually *Siddur Tikkun Shelomoh, Editio princeps* (Amsterdam, 1737) (Friedberg, *Bet Eked Sefarim,* p. 687). This prayerbook, *Tikkun Shelomoh*, is listed by Beer, *Geschichte, Lehren und Meinungen,* p. 236, as a kabbalistic work.

39. The famous supercommentary on *Magen Avraham*, a commentary on the first part ("Oraḥ Ḥayyim") of the *Shulḥan Arukh*. Earliest edition, Vienna, 1807; 2d ed., Vienna, 1817; Poryck, 1812.

40. The first edition of the *Kav ha-Yashar* by Z̧evi Hirsh Kaidanover, with a Yiddish translation, appeared in Frankfurt a. M. in 1709. A Yiddish edition without the Hebrew text was first published in Sulzbach in 1724. At the end of the eighteenth century, three editions appeared—one of 1773, one of 1793, and one without date of publication—all, significantly, bore no place of printing (Friedberg, *Bet Eked Sefarim*, p. 531). It may be assumed that the edition of 1773 was antedated because of the decree of 1785 against books which disseminated superstition, and that the place of publication was missing in all three editions for the same reason.

41. Popular prayerbook.

42. About the various editions of *Seliḥot* with a Yiddish translation (Luneville, 1799; Vienna, 1799), see Friedberg, *Bet Eked Sefarim*, p. 459; A. Freimann, "Die hebräischen Druckereien von Prag," in *Soncino Blätter* 3 (1930): 210, mentions a Prague edition of 1784.

43. Difficult to identify.

44. Prayers for the dead. Editions printed only in Yiddish: 1688, 1709, 1718, all in Germany. The Hebrew text with the Yiddish translation was published much later: Lemberg, 1808; Vienna, 1815 (Friedberg, *Bet Eked Sefarim*, p. 395).

45. A collection of devotions (*teḥinot*) by Sarah Bas Toyvim from the beginning of the eighteenth century. Zinberg (*Literatur bay Yidn* 6:288) records an undated edition from the beginning of the nineteenth century.

46. *Targum Rishon* and *Targum Sheni* to *Megillat Esther*, in Yiddish. First edition, Frankfurt a. M., 1718; early nineteenth-century editions: Slavuta, 1810; Vilna, 1812; Berdichev, 1814 (Friedberg, *Bet Eked Sefarim*, p. 406).

47. With Yiddish translation, Żółkiew, 1806 (ibid., p. 358).

48. This was probably the Żółkiew edition of 1793 (ibid., p. 519).

49. A collection of legends from the Talmud and the *Zohar* and stories from moralistic books by Abraham ben Yeḥiel Michael. First edition, Wilhermsdorf, 1731; reprinted in Żółkiew, 1795; Shklov, 1799; Ostrog, 1815 (Friedberg, *Bet Eked Sefarim*, p. 100; see also Zinberg, *Literatur bay Yidn* 6:243–45).

50. Isaiah Horowitz, a Yiddish summary of *Shenei Luḥot ha-Berit (Shelah)* (Lemberg, 1785, 1786; Żółkiew, 1807) (Friedberg, *Bet Eked Sefarim*, p. 489).

51. By Elḥanan Kirchhan. First edition of the first part, Frankfurt a. M., 1707; of the second part, Fürth, 1727. No edition published in Galicia is recorded in the bibliography.

52. All hitherto-known editions were issued in Germany (Friedberg, *Bet Eked Sefarim*, p. 668).

53. *Shivḥei ha-Besht*, Yiddish edition, Ostrog, 1816 (see S. Dubnow, *Geshikhte fun Khsidizm* (Vilna: YIVO, 1933) 2:382, 415–16.

54. *Chassiden*, 685/819.

55. Ibid.

56. Cf. chap. 5, where Perl mentioned, in his memorandum regarding Hersh of Żydaczów, the investigation which was conducted against this rebbe in 1818. In the State Archives in Lemberg a note was preserved about an investigation concerning the smuggling of Jewish books in 1818 (S. A., *Index Acta praesidialia* [1818], no. 1816). It is not unlikely that this note indeed referred to the investigation against Hersh of Żydaczów, mentioned by Perl.

57. In Hasidic literature, the Rebbe of Żydaczów was always cited as Ẓevi Hirsh, and the official documents also list him only by the name Hersh and the family name Eichenstein. It is possible that the police mistakenly replaced the name Ẓevi Hirsh with Naphtali Hersh (in one place in the list he is called Naphtali Hershek) or that his full name was not given to them deliberately. However, it is also possible that this Naphtali Hersh Eichenstein was not the rebbe Hersh of Żydaczów. In that case, we must assume that the search and seizure of Jewish books in Żydaczów had no connection with the investigation of smuggling but was conducted in connection with an inheritance (cf., the decrees of 1812 and 1817 regarding obligatory lists of books from a bequest).

58. The records of this raid are designated by catalogue number *Chassiden*, 1610/819.

The titles listed here have been corrected. Those titles so corrupted in the German transcription as to make them difficult to identify are discussed below.

59. Treatise by David Lida, printed in Żółkiew in 1804, and in Zhitomir without declaration of the year of publication (Friedberg, *Bet Eked Sefarim*, p. 588).

60. A kabbalistic work by Abraham Azulai. Nineteenth-century editions prior to 1818: Żółkiew, 1802, and one edition without date or place of publication.

61. In the original, *Cheiser Haschem*. It probably was mistranscribed from *Ḥefeẓ Adonai*, a treatise by Ḥayyim ibn Attar, reprinted in Żółkiew in 1805. It is less probable that it was *Ḥasdei Adonai*, a kabbalistic work by Moses Mordecai Margoliot (Cracow, 1589) (Friedberg, *Bet Eked Sefarim*, p. 238), since that was an old and rare book.

62. In the original it was mistranscribed *Imres Cerife. Imerei Ẓerufah* (Berlin, 1756), a halakhic work; Abraham Yehiel Fishl of Trembowla (cf. B. Wachstein, *Catalogue* 1:16, and Friedberg, *Bet Eked Sefarim*, p. 52).

63. In the original, mistranscribed *Choraidem*. Eleazar Azkari, *Sefer Ḥaredim*, (Żółkiew, 1796, 1804; Radziwiłłów, 1818); one edition from this period was printed without place and date of publication (Friedberg, *Bet Eked Sefarim*, p. 242).

64. This time the title of this famous Hasidic book was mistranscribed *Lekuta Ekurem* (cf. the list of 1817 n. 26).

65. Cf. n. 28.

66. Among the many books bearing the title *Amarot Tehorot* (mistranscribed *Imros Theores*), there were three published before 1818: (1) by Abraham ben Nissim Ḥayyun, Constantinople, 1518; Saloniki, 1595; (2) by Benjamin Wolf Leitmeritz, Lublin, 1645; (3) Menaḥem Azariah da Fano. It is quite probable that the third book was referred to here. Two editions appeared at that time, in Mohilev in 1819 and in Żółkiew without date of printing (Friedberg, *Bet Eked Sefarim*, p. 49). The very fact that a copy of this kabbalistic work was bound together with two Hasidic works which also appeared at that time seems to confirm the assumption that Fano's book was referred to here.

67. A moralistic book by Eliezer ben Samuel of Metz, last edition (Żółkiew, 1804) (Friedberg, *Bet Eked Sefarim*, p. 275).

68. A treatise of about one hundred blessings by David Amar (Saloniki, 1777) (ibid., p. 681).

69. Commentary on the Passover Haggadah by Benjamin ben Aaron (Lemberg, 1794) (ibid., p. 159).

70. Well-known kabbalistic work by Joseph Gikatilla, latest editions Żółkiew, 1782 and 1804 (ibid., p. 626).

71. In the original, mistranscribed as *Moser Eneim*. It is either the commentary by Josaiah Pinto on *En Ya'akov* (Amsterdam, 1754), or, more probably, the Hasidic treatise on the Torah by Naḥum of Chernobyl, published in Slavuta, 1798; Polonnoye, 1816, and Hrubieszów, 1818 (ibid., p. 323).

72. Cf. n. 60.

73. In the original, surprisingly, it was in a French transcription *Reiches Chochmo*. This popular moralistic work by Elijah de Vidas was published in Poland: Żółkiew, 1740, 1791; Lemberg, 1800; Zhitomir, 1804; Lemberg, 1811 (Friedberg, *Bet Eked Sefarim*, p. 562).

74. Probably the kabbalistic work of Menaḥem Azariah da Fano, published in Korets in 1786 (ibid., p. 292).

75. In the original, unconsciously corrupted into a blasphemy, *Chaifer Heschem*; cf. n. 61.

76. This is either the work on religion and ethics by Elijah Pines, Żółkiew, 1753, or the well-known Midrash collection *Tanna debei Eliyahu,* which was published in Żółkiew in 1796; Lemberg, 1799 and 1805 (Friedberg, *Bet Eked Sefarim*, p. 676).

77. In the original, mistranscribed as *Or Hamoer.* This is the Hasidic book by Wolf of Zhitomir (Korets, 1798; Poryck, 1815) (ibid., p. 30).

78. Friedberg (ibid., p. 360) mentions a treatise by this title as an appendix to *Maḥloket Ani ve-Ashir,* one edition Constantinople, 1515, and an earlier one without date or place of publication.

79. In the original, corrupted to read *Bassaine.* A halakhic work (Dubno, 1798) (ibid., p. 106).

80. A moralistic work by Ḥayyim ben Bezalel, last editions Lemberg, 1804; Medzhibozh, 1817 (ibid., p. 228).

81. The popular commentary on the Pentateuch by Ḥayyim ibn Attar, 2d ed. Żółkiew, 1799 (ibid., p. 27).

82. By Ḥayyim of Mohilev (Mohilev, 1813; Żółkiew, 1815; Poryck, 1818).

83. Mistranscribed in the original as "Mikolesz Mẹlech." A commentary on the *Zohar* by Shalom Buzaglio, published in Poland: Żółkiew, 1717, 1795; Kopys (Kopust), 1810 (Friedberg, *Bet Eked Sefarim*, p. 408).

84. In the original, *Saifer Hakine*, but this is certainly *Sefer ha-Kanah*, a familiar kabbalistic book, printed in Korets in 1784.

85. Moses Cordovero, *Pardes Rimonim*; editions published in Poland: Korets, 1780, 1786 (Friedberg, *Bet Eked Sefarim*, pp. 570–71).

86. Cf. n. 81.

87. In the original, *Pris Menicha*. Abraham ben Isaac of Granada, *Berit Menuḥah* (Berdichev, 1807) (Friedberg, *Bet Eked Sefarim*, p. 99).

88. In the original, *Jones Ilem*. A second edition of *Ma'amar Yonat Eilem* by Menaḥem Azariah da Fano appeared in Żółkiew in 1756.

89. Isaiah Horowitz, *Shenei Luḥot ha-Berit*, Ostrog, 1804; Poryck, 1817 (Friedberg, *Bet Eked Sefarim*, p. 622).

90. In addition to the edition of *En Ya'akov* published in Slavuta in 1812, another edition of Lemberg, 1818, is recorded despite the fact that it was listed among the absolutely forbidden works. It is possible that the Lemberg edition was a later one and was antedated.

91. Probably the commentary *Be'er Mayyim* on the Passover Haggadah by Joseph Moses of Zaloshits (Zalośće) (Medzhibozh, 1817).

92. In the original *Tekinum*. If Naphtali Hersh Eichenstien was Rebbe Hersh of Żydaczów, who was the author of kabbalistic works, it is amazing that very few kabbalistic books were found during the search of his home. It must be assumed that a great part of his library was concealed before the search-and-seizure action or that Naphtali Herz Labin assumed responsibility for most of the kabbalistic books belonging to his rebbe in order to protect him from any penalty.

93. *Chassiden*, 1610/819.

94. S. A., Lemberg, *Index Acta praesidialia* (1820), no. 1974.

95. *Or ha-Yashar*, a prayerbook with a kabbalistic commentary interpreting the liturgy according to the teaching of Isaac Luria. Friedberg (*Bet Eḳed Sefarim*, p. 28) records only the editions of Amsterdam, 1709; Fürth, 1764; Żółkiew, 1849; Vilna, 1877. However, from the above report it is evident that this book was also reprinted in the early years of the nineteenth century.

96. A corrupt transcription of *Mif'alot Elohim*, a treatise on the practical Kabbalah by Joel Ba'al Shem Heilperin, Żółkiew, 1810; Lemberg, 1812 (Friedberg, *Bet Eked Sefarim*, p. 403).

97. Cf. chap. 3.

98. *Chassiden*, 186g, 1826; cf. appendix: document 6a.

99. Cf. chap. 3. The fact that the lists are identical is substantiated by the equal number of banned books. In a document which is discussed below the number of thirteen books is explicitly mentioned.

100. *Chassiden*, 15g, 1827; see appendix: document 6b.

101. *Chassiden*, 28g, 1827; see appendix: document 6f.

102. *Chassiden*, 243g, 1827 (see appendix: document 6g); the list of the confiscated books in Przemyśl has not been preserved in the records.

103. The search was conducted in Tyśmienica because this was the alleged residence of Marcus Manwer (mistranscribed from Mordecai mi-Yanove), who is mentioned in *Sefer ha-Vikkuaḥ* (cf. chap. 3).

104. *Chassiden*, 72g/828; see appendix: document 6h.

105. *Chassiden*, 72g/828.

106. *Chassiden*, 9141/829; see appendix: document 6i.

107. M. Letteris tells, in his article "Devarim Aḥadim," that in 1833 Gabriel Berger was the Hebrew censor in Vienna. A well-known Maskil, contributor to *ha-*

Me'assef, and later an apostate (see S. Spiegel, "Tashlum ha-Hakdamah," p. 135), G. Berger, together with the famous maskil Judah Jeiteles, worked on a commentary and German translation of the Prophets and Hagiographa which were later included in Anton Schmidt's new (fourth) edition of the Bible with German translation (Letteris, ibid.). It is probable that the censor Joseph Berger was Gabriel Berger and that he had two names because he had converted.

108. *Chassiden*, 9141/829.

109. The names of the thirteen were not specified. The difference of one book compared with the list of 1817 can easily be explained when it is remembered that *Likkutei Moharan* appeared in that list three times: *Likkutei Moharan, Likkutei Moharan Tinyana*, and *Kiẓẓur Likkutei Moharan*. This time, probably one of these three editions was omitted.

110. About Saul Dov Majerhoffer, see B. Friedberg, *Le-Toledot ha-Dafus ha-Ivri be-Polonyaḥ* (Antwerp, 1932), pp. 55–56. Friedberg also mentions a contemporary printer in Żółkiew, Mordecai Rubinstein. But the governor, in his report to Sedlnitzky, stressed that Majerhoffer's was the only printing shop left in Żółkiew, as other printers, especially the recently active Gershon Letteris, were going out of business.

111. In the original it was mistranscribed *Midrash Aseres Habidros*. Friedberg mentions two editions of this book, Żółkiew, 1798 and 1810. It is unlikely that the censor made a mistake of ten years in the date; rather, one may assume that another edition was also published in 1800 which is not listed in the bibliography.

112. Gershon Letteris, father of the scholar and writer Meyer Halevi Letteris; cf. M. Letteris, *Toledot Gershon ha-Levi Letteris* (Vienna, 1864) and *Zikkaron ba-Sefer* (Vienna, 1868).

113. Hersh Rosanes and Solomon Rappaport (Jares), printers in Lemberg in the late eighteenth century. See M. Balaban, "Druckerein in Polen," p. 19, and Friedberg, *Le-Toledot*, p. 65.

114. As mentioned above, Governor von Hauer, in his order issued in 1818, stated that this rule had already been instituted by the Galician government in 1811.

115. After the death of Naphtali Herz Grossman in 1817, the printing shop was run by his widow; see Friedberg, *Le-Toledot*, p. 65.

116. According to Balaban ("Druckereien in Polen," p. 17) and Friedberg (*Le-Toledot*, p. 64), the publisher Aaron Madpis died in 1815. Apparently the heirs continued to run the printing shop under the same name.

117. Among the matters about which the Galician administration asked the opinion of the district rabbis on various occasions was this question: Is it permitted according to the "rabbinical" laws to burn Hebrew books that have been confiscated because of their prohibited contents? See Jost, *Neuere Geschichte der Israeliten*, vol. 10, pt. 3, p. 81.

118. *Chassiden*, 5079/831.

119. For the Jewish printing shops in Berdichev and Dubno, see Friedberg, *Le-Toledot*, pp. 81, 95. Among the publications listed by Friedberg as having been printed in these two cities during this period, there is not a single Hasidic book! (See Friedberg, bibliography.)

120. Cf. chap. 5.

121. *Chassiden*, 4553/838; see appendix: document 9e.

122. See chap. 3.

123. See appendix: document 9f.

124. Cf. chap. 5.

125. *Chassiden*, 2889/838; see appendix: document 10c.

126. See M. Balaban, "Aus der Korrespondenz S. L. Rappoports," in *Jewish Studies in Memory of George Alexander Kohut* (New York, 1935), p. 50.

127. See G. Kisch, "Die Zensur jüdischer Bücher in Böhmen," in *Jahrbuch der Gesellschaft für Geschichte der Juden in der Čechoslovakischen Republik* 2 (1930): 477.

128. Concerning the Austrian government's germanization policy toward the Galician Jews during this period, see F. Friedmann, *Die galizischen Juden in Kampfe um ihre Gleichberechtigung* (Frankfurt, 1929), pp. 100–108.

Chapter 5

1. Quote from I. Wenlös's introduction to *Yoysef Perls Yidishe Ksovim* (Vilna: YIVO, 1937), p. xlix; cf. also R. Mahler, review of Weinlös's introduction, in *Jewish Social Studies* 1:4 (1939): 487–88. The same one-sided elucidation of the personality of Joseph Perl is given by his earliest biographers, Nathan Horowitz in *Kalendar und Jahrbuch der Israeliten* 5 (1846): 211–32; Berish Goldenberg, *Ohel Yosef* (Lemberg, 1866).

2. Cf. chap. 3.

3. Cf. Krochmal's often-quoted letter to the young Maskil Abraham Goldberg, whose books were burned by the Hasidim; Rawidowicz, ed., *Kitvei Re'Na'K*, p. 417 ff. Krochmal offered his assistance in bringing this case to the attention of the authorities.

4. *Shorashei Levanon* (1842), p. 295, cited by I. Zinberg, *Geshikhte fun der Literatur bay Yidn* (Vilna, 1936) 8:84.

5. See *Perezhitoye,* vol. 1, documents, pp. 11–14.

6. Translation based on S. Ginsburg, "Redifes oyf yidishe malbushim," in his *Historishe Verk* 3:290.

7. Zinberg, *Literatur bay Yidn*, supp. 3.

8. N. M. Gelber, *Aus Zwei Jahrhunderten* (Vienna, 1924), p. 105.

9. R. Mahler, *Divrei Yemei Yisrael be-Dorot ha-Aḥaronim* (Merḥaviah, 1954) 1:4:74.

10. During the period of intensified censorship, after 1836, denunciations of Hasidism and Hasidic books by rabbis also took place. From 1839 there were two such denunciations, submitted by the Rabbi of Rowne, Berenson, and the Rabbi of Verkhne-Dnieprovsk, Moses Katzenellenbogen; see "Voskhod" (Russian), vol. 1, documents, pp. 11–14.

11. Of these informers in Galicia, M. Balaban (*Żydzi w Galicyi* [Lemberg, 1914], p. 102) mentioned a certain Jacob Silberstein of Oleszyce; P. Friedman recorded the denunciation against the Rebbe of Żydaczów by the Maskil of Jarosław, Ungar, in "Di ershte Kamfn tsvishn haskole un Khsidizm," in *Fun Noentn Over* 4 (1938): 252 ff. New archival materials concerning such denunciations in Galicia are published here in the appendices.

12. It is worth noting that in moments of intensified struggle the Hasidim themselves did not refrain from denunciations against opponents even in their own camp. In the controversy with the Mitnaggedim in northwestern Russia, they were indeed the attacked and not the attacking side, and the initiative in submitting denunciations in all cases stemmed from the Mitnaggedim. However, in the feud between Nowy Sącz (Tsandz) and Sadagura which broke out in 1869, in connection with the "Rebbe Berenyu affair," the truculence of the two Hasidic factions went so far as to employ denunciations against individuals. In his letter to the *kehillah* of Rzeszów, the Rabbi of Nowy Sącz, Ḥayyim Halberstam, wrote concerning the local Hasidim of Sadagura: "Above all, you should reject and expel them from your community with the power of the laws of the land. . . . And therefore it is your duty to inform in the courts and expel them from the city and

their *melamedim* should be banished at once. . . ." (*Keneset ha-Gedolah ve-Divrei Ḥakhamim* [Rohatyn, 1869], pp. 17–21).

13. *Kerem Ḥemed* 3 (1838), letter 4, signed Obadiah (Perl's pseudonym).

14. See appendix: document 2a.

15. Concerning these events, see chap. 3.

16. *Chassiden*, 689/817; see appendix: document 2a.

17. *Chassiden*, 4860/816; cf. appendix: document 2b.

18. See chap. 3.

19. *Chassiden*, 689/817.

20. Concerning this, see chaps. 3, 4.

21. The document of this denunciation was published by J. Nacht under the title "Ein unveröffentliches Aktenstück von Joseph Perl," in *Monatsschrift für die Geschichte und Wissenschaft des Judentums* 71 (1927): 308–11.

22. See Goldenberg, *Ohel Yosef*, pp. 15–16, as well as Weinlös, *Yoysef Perls*, p. xxii.

23. When Perl erected a separate structure for his school in 1815, the Hasidim attacked this building and smashed the windows; see Goldenberg, *Ohel Yosef*, p. 4.

24. During that period Jews in Galicia could not travel without passports.

25. According to the circular of February 2, 1824, which Perl mentioned in his memorandum and which was a repetition of a circular regarding *minyanim* and Hasidim dated August 22, 1823, the rebbes were forbidden to travel not only in those cases where they did not have a passport but also if they could not prove that they had a permanent occupation.

26. This is the date indicated in "Katit la-Ma'or," which was subsequently published in *Kerem Ḥemed* 2 (1836).

27. See appendix: document 8.

28. S. A., Lemberg, *Acta praesidialia* 7348/829.

29. See N. M. Gelber, *Vorgeschichte des Zionismus* (Vienna, 1927) pp. 117–24.

30. See appendix: documents 9a, b.

31. The verdict of the Ushitsa trial was published by S. Dubnow in *Perezhitoye* 1 (1908) under the title "A Case of Jewish Summary Justice in Podolia"; see also Saul Ginsburg, "Mayse Ushits," in his *Historishe Verk*, vol. 3 (1937).

32. See appendix: document 9a.

33. See appendix: document 9c.

34. See appendix: document 9d.

35. Balaban related (*Żydzi w Galicyi*, pp. 128–29) an interesting tradition concerning the meeting of Israel of Ruzhin and Jacob Ornstein, the author of *Yeshu'ot Ya'akov*. Because the Rebbe of Ruzhin was not a learned Talmudist, the conversation was a strained one. He was said to have asked Ornstein what was used to cover the roofs in Lemberg. Ornstein answered that tin was used. The Rebbe of Ruzhin then asked why tin was used; Ornstein replied that this was a protection against fire. To this, the Rebbe of Ruzhin asked why tiles were not used as roofing, whereupon Ornstein impatiently broke off the conversation. Balaban stated that Israel of Ruzhin visited Ornstein, but from the police report it appears that the opposite is true. Balaban also erred in giving 1839 as the date of the visit by the Rebbe of Ruzhin in Lemberg and connects it with the Ushitsa affair. Both Perl's denunciation and the report of the police directorate of 1838 list the date as 1835, before the trial in Ushitsa. A second visit of Israel of Ruzhin to Galicia in 1839 could not have been possible, because he was imprisoned at the time as one of the accused in the Ushitsa affair (see S. A. Horodetzky, "The Sadagura Dynasty," in *Yevreiskaya Starina* 1 [1909]: 47–51). It was not until 1840 that he fled to Jassy and from there to Austria.

36. It appears that this is the same Dr. Jacob Rapoport who later treated Joseph Perl in 1839, as is indicated by Weinlös in *Yoysef Perls*, p. lxix.

37. See appendix: document 9e.

38. Novaya Ushitsa was once known as Letniowce (Letnevits), and therefore the frightful episode of Ushitsa was preserved in folk tradition as "the Letnevits affair"; see S. Dubnow, "Jewish Summary Justice."

39. Ibid.

40. See S. A. Horodetzky, "Sadagura Dynasty," pp. 47–51.

41. Horodetzky related that Israel of Ruzhin's arrest in 1838 was a direct result of the fact that partners of the murdered informers, who lived in Berdichev, informed the police that the murder was committed by Hasidim "with the approval of the zaddik of Ruzhin." However, it is highly improbable that this denunciation would have been a sufficient reason to arrest the Rebbe of Ruzhin, because the authorities had previously known of such an accusation against him. In the verdict of the Ushitsa trial it is stated that one of the direct participants in the murder, Guterman, revealed that the *parnasim* who persuaded him to take part in the murder invoked the approval of the Rebbe of Ruzhin. On the basis of Perl's denunciation the accusation was more serious, for he stated that the Hasidim committed the murders at the command of the Rebbe of Ruzhin. Moreover, Perl's memorandum presented new accusations of clandestine activity and the illegal collection of funds among the Hasidim in Galicia.

42. The Ushitsa murder case was tried in a military court.

43. The translation is based on the document published in Dubnow, "Jewish Summary Justice."

44. His letter of 1833 to I. B. Levinsohn demonstrated the extent to which Perl was interested in the fate of the projected ban of Hasidic literature. In the postscript he wrote to Levinsohn, "How is it going with the ukase regarding Hasidic books which, as is understood, will ban them from the earth?" (*Be'er Yiẓḥak* [1899], p. 41).

45. See appendix: document 10a.

46. See appendix: document 10b.

47. See the letters to Joseph Perl in Simḥah Katz, *Mo'znaim* 10:2–3 (Shevat, 1940), pp. 266–76.

48. Thus I. B. Levinsohn explained why he informed Perl of a case of homosexuality in Radziwiłłów: "When I learned that it is suitable to make known such things as these in public I did not desist from also telling my master." In connection with a case of homosexuality in Rawa Ruska and a case of sodomy which allegedly took place in Brody, Bloch ridicules certain passages in the *Zohar* (Katz, *Mo'znaim*, pp. 270, 275).

49. Cf. Mahler, *Divrei Yemei Yisrael*, pp. 58–60; also appendix: document 32.

50. See the memorandum by Perl regarding the Siegfried Justus affair in Gelber, *Vorgeschichte*, p. 261.

51. A. B. Gottlober went to such lengths in his servility and flattery in relation to the dominant religion that in his memorandum concerning a prohibition of the traditional Jewish garb he stated that it was the wish of the majority of the Jews "to adopt European ethics and Christian morality"! See Zinberg, *Literatur bay Yidn*, supp. 3, p. 256.

52. See S. Bernfeld, *Toledot Shir* (Berlin, 1899), pp. 85–86; Weinlös, *Yoysef Perls*, p. lvii.

53. In his sermon on the Torah portion *Niẓẓavim,* in 1838, Perl said of the *bet ha-midrash* that it had become a "den of violent men" (Weinlös, *Yoysef Perls*, p. lxii).

54. See Goldenberg, *Ohel Yosef*, p. 6. He related that Perl used to travel to Vienna in his father's service to sell agricultural products.

55. See appendix: document 10c.

56. See Perl's sermon on the Torah portion *Nizzavim* in Weinlös, *Yoysef Perls* (p. lxiii), as well as Bernfeld, *Toledot Shir* (pp. 85–88). Of course, neither Bernfeld nor all the other biographers of S. J. Rapoport and Perl hitherto knew that Perl was responsible for the closing of the *battei midrash*. In a letter to the Hungarian maskil Shelomo Rosenthal (25 Tishrei 5599 [1838]) Rapoport wrote of such closings outside Tarnopol, "in other districts like Jarosław and Kałusz."

57. See Samson Bloch's letter to Rapoport of Rosh Ḥodesh Iyyar 5598 (1838), "Zehav Shebah," *Shevilei Olam* 3:2. Perl, too, mentioned these deeds, although not in such detail, in his above-cited sermon on the Torah portion *Nizzavim* in Weinlös, *Yoysef Perls* (p. lxv).

58. Perl's sermon, Weinlös, *Yoysef Perls*, p. lxiii.

59. Perl himself tells about this in the cited sermon. How Perl, being a merchant, "oppressed the city" is not clear. He probably took over the lease of the mills in Tarnopol from his father. As mentioned (see chap. 2), it is recorded in the State Archives in Lemberg that in 1820 four Jews complained to the authorities about "oppression" on the part of the lessee of the mills, Todres Perl.

60. Bernfeld, *Toledot Shir*, pp. 86–87.

61. See appendix: document 9e.

62. See appendix: document 11a.

63. The *mohalim* did not want to circumcise a child of the adherents of Rapoport; see Bernfeld, *Toledot Shir*, p. 90; cf. also Joseph Klausner, *Historyah shel ha-Sifrut ha-Ivrit ha-Ḥadashah* (Jerusalem, 1937) 2:237. The date of Perl's memorandum shows, however, that these events did not take place around Rosh Hashanah but at the latest at the beginning of July 1838.

64. *Chassiden*, 5611/838; the entire document has been published by the author in the Jubilee Volume in honor of N. M. Gelber; see R. Mahler, "Tazkir shel Yosef Perl le-shiltonot bi-devar shitat minui rabbanim, shoḥatim u-mohalim," *Sefer ha-Yovel likhvod Dr. N. M. Gelber* (Tel Aviv, 1968), pp. 85–104.

65. Perl became seriously ill in 1838.

66. Perl probably was referring to the city of Tarnopol, where S. J. Rapoport was then the rabbi.

67. Solomon Kluger, famous author of many halakhic works, was at that time the preacher in Brody.

68. Actually a prominent talmudic scholar. According to R. Ze'ev Leiter, he was called Reb Enzil, wrote responsa, and glossed the *Avnei Milu'im* written by his teacher, author of the *Kezot ha-Ḥoshen*.

69. Also a well-known scholar; brother of the Hirsh Ḥarif mentioned in chap. 3.

70. Perl probably referred here to such customs as honoring the rabbi by calling him up to read the most prestigious section of the portions of the Law, such as *Shishi, Shelishi*.

71. In 1832 S. J. Rapoport had already mentioned in a letter that Perl planned to open a rabbinical seminary in connection with his school in Tarnopol and he hoped to receive an appointment as a professor; see B. Dinaburg, *Iggerot Shir* (Jerusalem, 1927) 1:50–51; quoted in Klausner, *Historyah*, p. 232.

72. Perl took such great precautions to eliminate any additional income for the *shoḥatim* apart from their salary that he enumerated as "extortions" no longer to be tolerated the custom of the *shoḥet* appropriating the feathers and feet of geese and certain parts of the slaughtered cow, etc.

73. Just as in Tarnopol, there were many Jewish refugees from Russia in the second Galician border town of Brody during this period; see *Wiener Blätter* 29 (1850), cited by Friedman, "Die ershte Kamfn," p. 6.

74. Perl was referring to the prohibition of Jews in the villages from engaging in tavernkeeping, leasing rural industries and privileges, and, in general, any trade other than agriculture.

75. See appendix: document 11b.

76. As mentioned, the projected new "Jewry ordinance" was never completed.

77. An analysis of these excuses of the Galician administration was given at the end of chap. 3.

78. See *Allgemeine Zeitung des Judenthums* (1839), p. 606; see the report by S. J. Rapoport in *Kerem Ḥemed* 5 (1841): 163.

79. This report, which appeared in a German newspaper, was hotly condemned by Rapoport in his cited report in *Kerem Ḥemed*.

Chapter 6

1. M. Erik, *Etyudn tsu der geshikhte fun der haskole* (Minsk, 1934), p. 170.

2. I. Zinberg, *Geshikhte fun der literatur bay yidn* (Vilna, 1936), vol. 7, pt. 2, p. 284.

3. I. Weinlös, introduction to *Yoysef Perls Yidishe Ksovim* (Vilna: YIVO, 1937), p. xxv. It is evident that this statement of Weinlös is a gross exaggeration in view of the fact that the *Kol Shavat Bat Yehudah* by Judah Leyb Nevakhovich and also the Hebrew works of Mendel Lefin appeared much earlier.

4. Joseph Klausner, *Historyah shel ha-Sifrut ha-Ivrit ha-Ḥadashah* (Jerusalem, 1937) 2:300–301.

5. The second and third almanacs carry a title page with the caption *Ẓir Ne'eman* before the title page *Luaḥ ha-Shanah*.

6. The district of Tarnopol was under Russian rule from 1809 until 1815.

7. Cf., for example, the *Luaḥ* of Cassel for the year 5562 (1801–2) (in the library of the Jewish Theological Seminary of America, New York City) or the *Luḥot* of Berlin for the same period, which since 1744 had appeared with the approval of the Prussian Academy of Sciences (some of these *Luḥot* are in the New York Public Library).

8. Daily Calendar for Sunrise and Sunset.

9. Cf., the *Luaḥ* of 5486 (1725–26) published in Sulzbach (in the New York Public Library).

10. It appears that it was only by following Perl's example that the compilers of the popular *Luḥot* in Germany also included in the chronological section significant dates from general history. Thus, for instance, prior to the year 5575, not a single date of a general event was recorded in the Berlin almanac, which in 1744 received from the Prussian king a monopoly for its distribution in all Prussian provinces. In 1815 there began to appear in the chronological section of that almanac the dates of such events as the discovery of America, the invention of gunpowder and printing, the Thirty Years' War, the French Revolution, and the burning of Moscow.

11. *Megillah* 16a.

12. *Sanhedrin* 105a.

13. All of Perl's variants of the talmudic text are indicated in italics. As for the term *Kuti*, no edition known to the author uses this term instead of *Nokhri* or *Goy*.

14. See the interesting study by Siegfried Stein, "Die Zeitschrift Sulamith," in *Zeitschrift für die Geschichte der Juden in Deutschland* (Berlin, 1937) 7:193–226; also L. Horwitz, "'Die Sulamith,' ein Beitrag zur Geschichte der Jüdischen Journalistik" in *Populär-wissenschaftliche Monatsblätter* (Frankfurt a. M., 1896) 16:49–

55, 77–80, 106–8; cf. also R. Mahler, *A History of Modern Jewry, 1780–1815* (London and New York, 1971), pp. 218–20.

15. Joseph August Schultes, born in Vienna 1773, died 1831, professor of botany in Wiener Neustadt, in Cracow, and later in Innsbruck (see *Allgemeine Deutsche Biographie* [1891] 32:691). The same report of Schultes is given by Judah Jeiteles in *Sulamith* 1:2 (1807): 182–88, quoted from *Annalen der Litteratur und Kunst des oesterreichischen Kaisertums*.

16. In *Kiddushin* 32b. In indicating the sources of his quotations in his *Almanac for 5575*, Perl never supplied references to page or chapter. The same *aggadah* about R. Gamaliel, but without any moralizing lesson, is given in *Sulamith*, 1:2, p. 78.

17. In the original text of the Talmud, R. Zadok made no mention of the "reshaim"; he spoke only of "each and every one" (*Kol eḥad ve-eḥad*).

18. *Berakhot* 10a.

19. Ps. 104:35.

20. *Ta'anit* 20b.

21. *Shabbat* 31a.

22. Lev. 19:18.

23. *Yoma* 35b.

24. *Berakhot* 8a.

25. *Avot* 2. 2.

26. *Kiddushin* 29a.

27. *Pesaḥim* 113a. This saying is also cited in *Sulamith*.

28. *Shabbat* 118a.

29. *Beẓah* 32b.

30. *Ketubot* 67b.

31. This story is printed in *Sulamith* 1 (1806): 88–90.

32. *Sotah* 40a. In the *Luaḥ ha-Lev* for 5575, Perl supplied his quotations with the chapter of the tractate but did not indicate the folio.

33. *Eruvin* 53a.

34. Neh. 13:24.

35. *Pesaḥim* 3a.

36. *Ketubot* 8b.

37. The prayers referred to actually excel in originality and freshness of style.

38. *Avot* 2. 19.

39. *Baba Bathra* 10a.

40. The original text in *Pesaḥim* 87b reads, "Woe unto the *rabbanut*, that buries its ruler." Perl, however, correctly renders the meaning as *memshalah*.

41. Christoph Wilhelm Hufeland (1762–1836), one of the famous physicians of his time and professor at the University of Prussia. His book *Die Kunst das Menschliche Leben zu verlaengern* (1st ed., 1796; 3d ed., 1805) has been translated into several European languages: see *Allgemeine Deutsche Biographie* (1881) 13:286–96.

42. Jer. 29:7. This verse was frequently quoted by assimilationist leaders of the reform movement.

43. Deut. 23:8.

44. *Yoma* 86a. Perl's quotation is incomplete and varies from the Talmud.

45. *Avot* 2. 5.

46. Ps. 133:1.

47. Most likely Perl was acquainted with the article entitled "Früheste Culturgeschichte des Menschengeschlechtes," by Friedrich Murhard, in *Sulamith* 3:2 (1811): 152–70.

48. *Berakhot* 58a.

49. Isa. 40:26.

50. Ps. 149:3.

51. Ps. 24:1.
52. Job 38:4.
53. *Sukkah* 49b.
54. *Ta'anit* 24a.
55. *Shabbat* 105b.
56. Klausner (*Historyah*, p. 304) greatly admired Perl's familiarity with Jewish history but held that he was not acquainted with the primary sources of this episode, in Philo and Josephus, and obtained the story from Jost. But this assumption is not warranted, since M. Jost's *Neuere Geschichte der Israeliten* did not appear until 1820–29. Klausner apparently did not read Perl's introduction and note, as he offered no explanation why Perl included this story in his almanac. Moreover, Klausner made no effort to ascertain to what extent the contents of Perl's *Luḥot* mirror a particular ideology and evidently were meant as propaganda.
57. Cf. "Orekh Yamim" and "Hitpalel be-Shalom Malkhut."
58. *Avot* 2. 17.
59. *Pesaḥim* 113b.
60. Evidently Solomon (Judah) Leyb Rapoport.
61. The first edition of *Sefer ha-Berit* appeared in 1797.
62. *Eruvin* 100b.
63. Cf., for example, the *Luaḥ* for the year 5487 (1726) published in Sulzbach.

Chapter 7

1. The figures for the year 1827 are given in B. Wasiutyński, *Ludność żydówska w Polsce w Wiekach 19 i 20* (Warsaw, 1930), pp. 37–38; the list of the large cities in Poland is found in Ryszard Kołodziejczyk, *Kształtowanie się burżuazji w Królestwie Polskim (1825–1850)* (Warsaw, 1957), p. 50; the census of 1843 is given in A. N. Frenk, "The Number of Jews and Their Occupations in the Kingdom of Poland in 1843," *Bleter far Yidisher Demografye, Statistik un Ekonomye* vol. 3 (Berlin, 1928), in table 1; the percentages were computed by Ignacy Schiper, *Dzieje handlu żydowskiego na ziemiach polskich* (Warsaw, 1937), p. 394.
2. Kołodziejczyk, *Kształtowanie*, p. 65.
3. Ibid., p. 50, quoted by Rodecki, table 2.
4. Archiwum Glówne Akt Dawnych, Komisja Rządowa Spraw Wewnętrznych (hereafter A.G.A.D., K.R.S.W.), 3195, p. 8.
5. A.G.A.D., K.R.S.W., 4206, pp. 50, 84, 90.
6. A.G.A.D., K.R.S.W., 4761.
7. Kołodziejczyk, *Kształtowanie*, p. 25.
8. M. Orlowski, *Zelazny przemysl hutniczy na ziemiach polskich* (Warsaw, 1931), pp. 28–93; Kołodziejczyk, *Kształtowanie*, pp. 31–32.
9. Jan Rutkowski, *Historja gospodarcza Polski* (do 1864 r.) (Warsaw, 1953), p. 355.
10. Ibid., pp. 354–55; Kołodziejczyk, *Kształtowanie*, pp. 13–23.
11. Rutkowski, *Historja*, p. 280; Kołodziejczyk, *Kształtowanie*, p. 65.
12. According to the report of the governmental Committee for Internal Affairs and Police, 6,946 "floaters," lacking identification documents, were caught and imprisoned in 1823 throughout the entire country; see in Kołodziejczyk, *Kształtowanie*, p. 72.
13. For the condition of the peasants in that period, see Z. Kirkor-Kiedroniowa, *Włościanie i ich sprawa w dobie organizacyjnej i konstytucyjnej Królestwa Polskiego*; A. Brückner, *Dzieje Kultury Polskiej* (Warsaw, 1946) 4:252–56; Kołodziejczyk, *Kształtowanie*, pp. 70–74.

14. For the Congress of Vienna and the Jewish question in Germany, see Salo Baron, *Die Judenfrage auf dem Wiener Kongress* (Vienna, 1920): "The Basic Lines of the Constitution of the Kingdom of Poland" was published by M. Handelsman, in *Trzy Konstytucje* (Warsaw, 1915), pp. 34–40. It is true that the "basic lines" of Poland's constitution were signed by Czar Alexander in Vienna on May 25, 1815; however, the constitution of the German Federation was not approved by the Congress until June 10 of that year. But the analogy between the two documents is evident even in the combination of the approval of existing rights and the assurance of an improvement in the situation for the future. There is therefore no doubt that Prince Czartoryski and his master, the czar, took for themselves as a model the stand of the Congress toward the Jews of Germany. Despite the many different versions, this attitude found expression in the deliberations concerning the constitution of Germany which had already begun in the autumn of 1814. At all events, Czar Alexander himself was not only well versed in the deliberations of the Congress regarding the Jews of Germany but also had a positive influence on those deliberations. This was prompted by his financial ties with the House of Rothschild and other Jewish bankers in Germany, as well as by his desire to appear in the eyes of European Jewry as a kindly, liberal ruler preferable to Napoleon. For this role of Alexander at the Congress of Vienna, see S. Askenazy, "Ze spraw żydowskich w dobie Kongresowej," *Kwartalnik . . . Żydów w Polsce* 1:3:14.

15. Rutkowski, *Historja*, p. 454.

16. Such memoranda were submitted to the Supreme Council of the government *pro tem* in 1814 by the Prefect of the Department of Warsaw, as well as to the Ministry of the Interior by the Central Committee (A.G.A.D., K.R.S.W., 6708).

17. Askenazy, "Ze Spraw," p. 14.

18. A.G.A.D., K.R.S.W., 6634, pp. 10–11, 16.

19. See Rutkowski, *Historja*, p. 454.

20. *Rzut oka na stan Izraelitow w Polsce, czyli wykrycie bjednego z nimi postępowania* (Warsaw, 1831), p. 38.

21. From the report of the Committee for Internal Affairs of November 15, 1822, to the viceroy, A.G.A.D., K.R.S.W., 6629, pp. 112–19; A.G.A.D., K.R. Prz. i. k. 1849, p. 85 (Tabelle Starozakonnych familiy trudniących się zarobkami propinacyinemi od. r. 1814 do 1830 r.).

22. J. Kirszrot, *Prawa Żydów w Królestwie Polskim* (Warsaw, 1917) pp. 110–16.

23. B. Weinryb, *Neueste Wirtschaftsgeschichte der Juden in Russland und Polen* (Breslau, 1934), pp. 154–55.

24. A.G.A.D., K.R.S.W., 6744.

25. See R. Mahler, *Divrei Yemei Yisrael be-Dorot ha-Aḥaronim* (Merḥaviah, 1954) 1:3:87.

26. Ludwig Lętowski, *O Żydach w Polsce* (Warsaw, 1816), pp. 24–25, 28.

27. R. Rembielinski, *O miastach* (Warsaw, 1816), pp. 180–81; F. Friedman, *Dzieje Żydów w Lodzi* (Łódz, 1935), p. 48.

28. Stanislaw Staszic, *O przyczynach szkodliwości Żydów* (Warsaw, 1816; Lwów, 1857) (Zgubne Zasady Talmudyzmu. Dodatek), pp. 94–113.

29. Rembielinski agreed to concessions in this matter regarding the Jews of Łódz in 1822; see Friedman, *Dzieje Żydów,* pp. 48, 349.

30. A.G.A.D., K.R.S.W., 6634, p. 176; Kirszrot, *Prawa Żydów*, p. 101.

31. According to J. Shatzky, "Yidn in Czenstochowa," in R. Mahler, ed., *Czenstochower Yidn* (New York, 1947), p. 14, a Jewish *revir* existed in this city in 1818; however, J. Hessen fixed the year of the decree of a *revir* in Częstochowa as 1829 (see *The Russo-Jewish Encyclopedia* 15:848).

32. Friedman (*Dzieje Żydów*, pp. 95–96) justifiably concluded from this that a total of thirty-one *revirs* in the entire kingdom, as maintained by L. Wolski, is less

than the actuality. According to Wolski, there were throughout the country ninety cities having the "privilege not to tolerate Jews," and the Jews dwelt there illegally.

33. Wasiutyński, *Ludność żydowska*, p. 55.

34. *Rzut oka*, pp. 4–5.

35. Ibid., pp. 30, 50; Kirszrot, *Prawa Żydów*, p. 226; I. Warszawski, "Yidn in Kongres-Poyln," in *Historishe Shriftn-Yivo* 2:326.

36. Warszawski, "Yidn in Kongres-Poyln," p. 328, and at some length in his article "Yidn in di nay-oysgeboyte shtet in Kongres-Poyln," *Yivo Bleter* 3:30–32.

37. A.G.A.D., K.R.S.W., 6634, p. 218.

38. Kirszrot, *Prawa Żydów*, pp. 104–7.

39. A. J. Ostrowski, *Pomysły o potrzebie Reformy Towarzyskiej przez Założyciela miasta Tomaszowa Mazowieckiego* (Paris, 1834), p. 45.

40. A.G.A.D., K.R.S.W., 6634, p. 170.

41. Ibid., 6629, pp. 101–19.

42. Ibid., 6634, pp. 101–2.

43. *Rzut oka*, p. 29.

44. *Djarjusz Sejmu z roku 1830–31 wyd. M. Rostworowski* (Cracow, 1910) 4:20.

45. Ostrowski, *Pomysły o potrzebie*, p. 47.

46. Ibid., p. 98.

47. Ibid., p. 47, n.

48. *Roczniki Gospodartswa Krajowego* 1 (1842): xxxiii; Kołodziejczyk, *Kształtowanie*, pp. 98–99.

49. *O Reformie Żydów, Projekt podany w r. 1841* (Poznan, 1854). The anonymous author has been indentified as the statesman and philosopher Józef Gołuchowski; cf. N. M. Gelber, *Tokhniyot shel Medinah Yehudit* (Knesset, 1939), p. 20.

50. A. N. Frenk was the first to cite an excerpt from this highly valuable pamphlet in his study "Tsu der geshikhte fun der yidisher kolonizatsye in Kongres Poyln," *Bleter far Yidisher Demografye, Statistik un Ekonomye* (Berlin, 1925) 5:17–18; also see 3:192 for the statement of opinion of Matthias Rosen to the government in 1845, in which poverty is defined as a general phenomenon of the Jews in Poland.

51. Aleksander Kraushar, *Kupiectwo Warszawskie* (Warsaw, 1929), p. 100.

52. Ostrowski, *Pomysły o potrzebie*, p. 45.

53. Weinryb, *Neueste Wirtschaftsgeschichte*, p. 9.

54. R. Markgraf, *Zur Geschichte der Juden auf den Messen in Leipzig, von 1664–1839* (Bischofswerden, 1894), pp. 24–35.

55. Ostrowski, *Pomysły o potrzebie*, p. 165.

56. Kołodziejczyk, *Kształtowanie*, p. 83.

57. Ibid., pp. 80–83, 143–44; Friedman, *Dzieje Żydów*, pp. 214–15.

58. Kołodziejzyk, pp. 17, 23, 34, 36–37, 105, 130–44, 212; Friedman, *Dzieje Żydów*, pp. 225–56; Schiper, *Dzieje handlu*, pp. 385–86, 400–409; A. N. Frenk, p. 187. B. Weinryb, "Tsu der geshikhte fun yidishn onteyl in der poylisher industrye," *Ekonomishe Shriftn* (Vilna: YIVO, 1932) 2:36–39.

59. Adolf Peretz, *Żydzi w bankowości polskiej, Żydzi w Polsce Odrodzonej* (Warsaw, 1933) 2:432–41; I. Schiper, *Dzieje handlu*, pp. 400–404; R. Kołodziejczyk, *Kształtowanie*, pp. 122–23.

60. A.G.A.D., K.R.S.W., 6603 (passim); Peretz, *Żydzi w bankowości*, pp. 432–41; Schiper, *Dzieje handlu*, pp. 367–69; Kołodziejczyk, *Ksałtowanie*, pp. 88–89, 97–98, 144–59; Mieczysław Ajzen, *Polityka gospodarcza Lubeckiego* (Warsaw, 1932), pp. 34–40, 57, 68, 168, 230; Friedman, *Dzieje Żydów*, pp. 71–77.

61. A.G.A.D., K.R.S.W., 6910, 6911; I. Schiper, *Żydzi Królestwa Polskiego w dobie powstania listopadowego* (Warsaw, 1932), pp. 38–39, 43, 100–101; Kołodziejczyk, *Kształtowanie*, p. 92.

62. A.G.A.D., K.R.S.W., 6634, pp. 82–87; Hilary Nusbaum, *Z Życia Żydów w Warszawie* (Warsaw, 1881), pp. 44–50; J. Shatzky, *Geshikhte fun Yidn in Varshe* (New York) 1:275; 2:38, 39, 131, 283.

63. D. Kandel, *Żydzi w Królestwie Polskim po 1831* (Warsaw, 1910) 3:549–50.

64. A.G.A.D., K.R.S.W., 5628, pp. 2–26; Kołodziejczyk, *Kszałtowanie*, pp. 123–24; Shatzky, *Geshikhte fun Yidn* 2:38–39.

65. *Prośba czyli usprawiedliwienie się Ludu Wyznania Starego Testamentu w Królestwie Polskim zamieszkałego* (Warsaw, 1820), p. 17; Schiper, *Dzieje handlu*, pp. 387–88. S. Kieniewicz, ed., *Przemiany społeczne i gospodarcze w Królestwie Polskim (1815–1830), wybór tekstów żródłowych* (Warsaw, 1951), p. 26.

66. Schiper, *Dzieje handlu,* pp. 387–88.

67. Friedman, *Dzieje Żydów*, pp. 74–77, 171–74, 245–56, 300–301.

68. D. Kandel, *Żydzi w Królestwie*, pp. 549–50.

69. A.G.A.D., K.R.S.W., 6910.

70. In contrast, even a man of property, if he had not been a resident of the capital city before 1825, was not exempt from the *Billet* for each day's stay in Warsaw, except in isolated instances, as is seen in the stipulations of lease-contracts (A.G.A.D., K.R.S.W., 6528, p. 72); the concessions cited by Kołodziejczyk (*Kszałtowanie*, p. 90), according to another archival source, were apparently established at a much later period.

71. Kirszrot, *Prawa Żydów*, pp. 99–100.

72. Friedman, *Dzieje Żydów*, pp. 48–49.

73. Kraushar, *Kupiectwo Warszawskie*, pp. 50, 62, 64–65, 77, 81. Schiper, in *Dzieje handlu*, was not precise in establishing that in 1829, at the request of the Jewish merchants, two of them were elected to the Office of the Heads of the Christian Guild of the Merchants (p. 387); the truth is that only in 1856 were two representatives of the Jewish merchants accepted to the Office of the Heads (still only in an advisory capacity and only in matters relating to salespeople and Jewish apprentices); cf. Kraushar, idem, p. 110.

74. *Stulecie Giełdy Warszawskiej 1817–1917*, p. 54; Kołodziejczyk, *Kszałtowanie*, p. 246.

75. Friedman, *Dzieje Żydów*, pp. 61–62.

76. A.G.A.D., K.R.S.W., 6601–5, 6628, 6636.

77. Schiper, *Dzieje handlu*, pp. 397–98; *Żydzi Królestwa Polskiego*, p. 8; Friedman, *Dzieje Żydów*, pp. 293–98.

78. Weinryb, *Neueste Wirtschaftsgeschichte*, p. 9.

79. *The Journal of the Sejm*, pp. 20, 58 (see n. 44).

80. The archival sources and the historical bibliography concerning the problem of agriculture, work, and the professional composition of the Jews in Poland in that period are specified in R. Mahler, *History of the Jews in Modern Times* (Merḥaviah, 1970), vol. 5.

81. The policy of the authorities in Poland toward the Jewish culture and religion and its legislation in this respect are discussed at length in Mahler, *History of the Jews*.

Chapter 8

1. The views expressed by W. Szokalsky, the agent of Prince Adam Czartoryski for emigration, are characteristic of the Polish aristocracy's outlook on the Jews. In his eyes, the Jews were identical with "shopkeeping and underhanded dealings which provoke repugnance"; only after they turned to labor and agriculture (with

the status of tenant farmers on the estates of the nobles!) would they merit the privileges of citizenship; see M. Handelsman, *Adam Czartoryski* (Warsaw, 1948) 1:311, 316–317.

2. B. Wasiutyński, *Ludność żydowska w Polsce w wiekach 19 i 20* (Warsaw, 1930), p. 37; the figures are based on data found in A. Rodecki.

3. R. Mahler, *Tsol un tseshpreytung fun di yidn in Varshe in akhtsetn yorhundert*, Landkentenish (Warsaw, 1934), pp. 40–50.

4. *Kwartalnik Żydów w Polsce* 1:3:174–76; also see Mahler, *Divrei Yemei Yisrael be-Dorot ha-Aḥaronim* (Merḥaviah, 1954) 1:3:86–87.

5. *Kwartalnik*, pp. 27–31.

6. *Allgemeine Zeitung des Judenthums* (1840), no. 7; the correspondent from Warsaw who signed his name Dr. J. B. was apparently Dr. Bernhard, who also served as a member of the Synagogue Supervisory Board.

7. A.G.A.D., K.R.S.W., 6643, p. 22.

8. Ibid., 6630, pp. 83–89.

9. Teodor Jeske-Choinski, *Neofici Polscy* (Warsaw, 1904), p. 115.

10. A. N. Frenk, *Meshumodim in Poyln* (Warsaw, 1923), pp. 31–37.

11. Besides the book by Jeske-Choinski, see also Kazimierz Reychman, *Szkice genealogiczne* (Warsaw, 1936); Mateusz Mieses, *Polacy chrześcijanie pochodzenia żydowskiego* (Warsaw, 1938); Ludwik Korwin, *Szlachta polska pochodzenia żydowskiego* (Cracow, 1933).

12. In one of Tugendhold's letters to his nephew Joseph Mohr, he gives him the biographical details; Tugendhold, *Divrei Yeshayahu* (Cracow, 1896), pp. 78–81.

13. Ibid., p. 79.

14. Ibid., pp. 72–82.

15. J. Tugendhold, *Obrona Izraelitow przez Rabbi Manasse ben Izrael* (Warsaw, 1831), p. iv.

16. In 1842 he was mentioned by the title of "Member of the Synagogue Supervisory Board in Warsaw" in the list of the subscribers to the Polish book of A. Buchner, *Kwiaty wschodnie*; in 1844 he was a signatory to the Warsaw community's letter to Montefiore, together with the communal heads—Matthias Rosen, Meyer Berson, and Abraham Winawer; cf. *Kwartalnik* 1:93.

17. J. Shatzky, *Geshikhte fun Yidn in Varshe* (New York) 2:177.

18. In one of the letters his father chides him:

> For they have heard the words of your mouth and have seen the work of your fingers which you have written to your brethren, and they are tokens and fabrications which make a mockery of many of the laws of our faith, and you esteem yourself a wise man in your own eyes, for you have a discerning heart . . . How then do you dare risk standing in judgment over them? (Tugendhold, *Divrei Yeshayahu*, p. 24.)

19. Ignacy Schiper, *Dzieje handlu żydowskiego na ziemiach polskich* (Warsaw, 1937), pp. 116–17, 149–51.

20. A. Sawicki, *Szkoła Rabinów w Warszawie, Miesięcznik Żydowski* (1933) 3: 247–48.

21. B. Weinryb, in his article on censorship in *Monatsschrift für die Geschichte und Wissenschaft des Judentums* (1933), p. 294; see also the opinion expressed by Tugendhold in 1857 concerning the role of a Polish-Jewish periodical, J. Shatzky, "Der kamf arum geplante tzaytshriftn far Yidn in Kongres Poyln," *Yivo Bleter* 4 (1934): 75.

22. H. Nussbaum, *Szkice historyczne z życia Żydów w Warszawie* (Warsaw, 1881), p. 157.

23. J. Tugendhold, *Skazówki prawdy i zgody* (Warsaw, 1844), p. ii.

24. Ibid., p. 37.

25. Ibid., pp. 11–12; also see his introduction to the translation of Menasseh ben Israel, *Teshu'at Yisrael* (Vienna, 1831), p. xc.
26. Tugendhold, *Kosht Imrei Emet*, Polish section.
27. See R. Mahler, *Divrei Yemei Yisrael be-Dorot ha-Aḥaronim* (Merḥaviah, 1954) 1:164.
28. J. Tugendhold, *Ben Yakir*, 2d ed. (Warsaw, 1834), chap. 8.
29. N. Prilutzki, "Vi azoy di Rusishe Tsenzur hot gebalabatevet in der Bovo-Maase," *Yivo Bleter* 3 (April–May 1932): 366.
30. J. Tugendhold, *Słowo w swoim czasie* (Warsaw, 1847), p. v.
31. See his introduction to *Teshu'at Yisrael*, p. vii.
32. Max Weinreich, introduction to Dr. Shlomo Ettinger's *Kesovim* (Vilna, 1925), p. 35.
33. N. Prilutzki, "Vi azoy di Rusishe," pp. 359–71.
34. Tugendhold, *Kosht*, Polish introduction, pp. i–ii.
35. J. Tugendhold, *Modły* (Warsaw, 1837), pp. 87–89.
36. Tugendhold, *Słowo*, p. 14.
37. J. Tugendhold, *Rys myśli poważnych* (Warsaw, 1848), pp. 7–8.
38. Tugendhold, *Modły*, p. 76.
39. Tugendhold, *Skazówki*, p. 92.
40. Tugendhold, *Modły*, pp. 93–94.
41. Tugendhold, *Skazówki*, p. 79.
42. Adolf Jakob Cohn, *Szkoła Rabinów, Z dziejów Gminy Starozakonnych w Warszawie* (Warsaw, 1907) 1:72–73.
43. A. Buchner, *Doresh Tov* (Warsaw, 1822), pp. 16a, 25a, 37, 39, 54.
44. A. Buchner, *Ha-Moreh le-Ẓedakah* (Warsaw, 1838), p. 6a.
45. Ibid., p. 19b.
46. Ibid., pp. 2–3.
47. Sawicki in *Szkoła Rabinów*, p. 245.
48. A. J. Cohn in *Szkoła Rabinów*, pp. 72–73 on the Rabbinical Seminary.
49. Schiper, *Dzieje handlu*, p. 76.
50. J. Shatzky, *Yidishe Bildungs-Politik in Poyln fun 1806 biz 1866* (New York, 1943), p. 200.
51. Jeske-Choinski, *Neofici Polscy,* p. 124; Mieses, *Polacy chrześcijanie* 1:68.
52. L. Loewe, *Diaries of Sir Moses and Lady Montefiore* (Chicago, 1890) 1:379. The correct view—that A. Buchner is meant—was expressed by Shatzky in his *Yidishe Bildungs-Politik*, p. 200.
53. A. Buchner, *Der Talmud in seiner Nichtigkeit* (Warsaw, 1848).
54. Ibid., 2:91, 98, 103, 121, 123.
55. In a correspondence from Warsaw to *Orient* for the year 1850 (37:148), it was reported that "a society of English missionaries allocated to Buchner . . . 10,000 gulden so that he would write against the Talmud; this he had already fulfilled in three pamphlets."
56. *Gedruckt in der Missions-Druckerei*, Eisengasse, no. 2449.
57. Buchner, *Der Talmud*, p. 84.
58. S. Hoge, *Tu Chazy czyli Rozmowa o Żydach* (Warsaw, 1830), pp. 12–14.
59. Tugendhold, in *Teshu'at Yisrael*, in Polish, p. lxv.
60. Cohn, in *Szkoła Rabinów, Z dziejow*, p. 71.
61. Sawicki, in *Szkoła Rabinów w Warszawie*, p. 241.
62. J. Tugendhold, "Krótki rys historyi języka i literatury hebrajskiej," *Bechynot Olam* (Warsaw, 1846).
63. M. Jost, *Geschichte des Judentums und seiner Sekten* (Leipzig, 1857) 1:1.
64. A. Paprocki, *Krótki rys dziejów Ludu Israelskiego* (Warsaw, 1850).
65. Cohn, in *Szkoła Rabinów, Z dziejow,* p. 1.
66. B. Weinryb, his article in *Monatsschrift*, pp. 289–90.

67. Ibid., p. 292.
68. No information about the origin of Isaac Kandia could be located.
69. Feivel Shiffer, *Devar Gevurot* (Warsaw, 1845), pp. 72, 86.
70. *Ettingers Kesovim*; *Di Shmates*, pp. 203–4.
71. Translated from the Yiddish original by the author.
72. Tannenbaum, in *Mataei Moshe* ([Warsaw, 1838] pp. 23, 227), mentions as his benefactors the deceased Judah Leib Lubliner Warhaftig of Brest, in whose business establishment he worked, as well as Jacob Kahana-Shapiro of Brest, commonly called *Livorner* because he used to import sandalwood and citrons from Livorno; that benefactor, possessor of a large library which he had gathered abroad, rebuilt the synagogue in Terespol after the fire of 1726.
73. H. Nussbaum, *Szkice historyczne*, pp. 73–74; H. Nussbaum, biographical list in *Allgemeine Zeitung des Judenthums* 28 (1849).
74. The benefactor is identified as "Judah Yudel Epstein, a native of the fortified city Bobruiski, now sojourning in the fortress city of Brest in Lithuania" (see Tannenbaum, *Mataei Moshe*).
75. B. Weinryb, "Vegn der ershter oysgabe fun di Khumoshim mit mendelsons iberzetsung in polyn," *Yivo Bleter* 8 (1935): 85–88; P. Kon, "Yulyan Klatshko un zayn foter hirsh" *Historishe shriftn, YIVO* (1929) I:777.
76. "*Der Talmud in seiner Nichtigkeit*, nach einem hebraeischen Manuscript von M. Tannenbaum, bearbeitet von H. Nussbaum zu Warschau" (Magdeburg, 1849).
77. See Tannenbaum, *Mataei Moshe*, p. 14:

> I am the man that has seen affliction like all the young sons of my people, and like all the many of my colleagues in the house of my beloved teacher and instructor, with a dry switch was I beaten and engaged in studies without any special order. . . . Much did I learn . . . until I reached that estimable book *Moreh Nebukhim*.

78. Ibid., p. 166.
79. Ibid., pp. 105, 107.
80. Ibid., pp. 72, 104.
81. Ibid., pp. 17, 200.
82. Ibid., pp. 78, 89, 113.
83. Ibid., pp. 4–5, 14.
84. Ibid., p. 71.
85. Ibid., pp. 52, 61, 68–69.
86. Ibid., pp. 59, 69, 82, 185.
87. Ibid., p. 158.
88. Plac Żelaznej Bramy.
89. I. A. Kandia, *Shir le-Yom Ḥanukat Bet Tefillah* (Warsaw, 1840), pp. 2–3.
90. In the introduction to his book *Tokhaḥat Musar,* which came out in 1854, he related (p. 2b): "It is now fifty-seven years that I reside here in Warsaw," that is, he settled in the city in 1796 and was numbered among the "ninety-sixers," who had special privileges because of seniority of residence in the locality.
91. Thalgruen, *Tokhaḥat Musar*, p. 22a.
92. Ibid., p. 21b.
93. Ibid., p. 18a.
94. Cf. Mahler, *Divrei Yemei Yisrael*, 3:87:72.
95. Tannenbaum, *Mataei Moshe*, p. 51.
96. Thalgruen, *Tokhaḥat Musar*, pp. 15a, 28a.
97. Ibid., p. 231.
98. B. Weinryb published the contents of the manuscript in his article "Letoldot hadeot hakalkaliyot vehaḥevratiyot etzel ha-Yehudim bameah hatesha-esrei," *Tarbiẓ* 7:57–73.
99. See Weinryb, "Letoldot," p. 69.
100. Feivel Shiffer, *Mahlkhim* (Warsaw, 1866), pp. 78–82.

101. Tannenbaum, *Mataei Moshe*, pp. 212, 214.
102. Thalgruen, *Tokhaḥat Musar*, p. 27.
103. Tannenbaum, *Mataei Moshe*, p. 212.
104. D. B. Kahana, *Darkhei ha-Lashon* (Warsaw, 1821), introduction.
105. J. L. Paradisthal, *Ma'arekhet Mikhtavim* (Warsaw, 1853), introduction.
106. See I. Kandia, *Toledot Moshe* (Warsaw, 1829), p. 7. A panegyric from one of the friends of the author J . . . . P . . . . A . . . : "A skillfully wrought poem by my esteemed friend, the flowery stylist, R. Isaac Kandia," in honor of *Ḥaẓrot ha-Shir* by F. Shiffer (Warsaw, 1840).
107. F. Shiffer, *Ḥaẓrot ha-Shir*, introduction.
108. Cf. the biography of A. Stern in *Allgemeine Zeitung des Judenthums* (1842), no. 13; in another biographical sketch which was published in that weekly in 1840 (no. 35), it is mentioned that he was born in 1769.
109. A number of Stern's poems were printed at the end of *Shirei Musar le-Rav Hai Gaon*, which was published in Warsaw in 1835 by Alexander Zusha Gazan.
110. Cf. A. Stern's poem in praise of Feivel Shiffer at the beginning of *Ḥaẓrot ha-Shir*.
111. D. Leventhal, *Ayelet ha-Shaḥar* (Warsaw, 1843), introduction, p. 2.
112. Tannenbaum, *Mataei Moshe*, pp. 215, 216–17.
113. Ibid., p. 217.
114. Shiffer, *Mahlkhim*, p. 168.
115. I. Kandia, *Shir le-Yom*, pp. 3, 8.
116. *Ettingers Kesovim*, pp. 80, 81.
117. It is reasonable to assume that in this formulation in the past tense, the author does not have in mind the Egyptian exile, and it can therefore be surmised that the hand of the censor fell upon this verse: past tense instead of present tense.
118. As is explained by M. J. Landau, the publisher of Moshe Laski's *Ne-emanei Ereẓ o Ḥuldah va-Bor,* 2d. ed. (Lemberg, 1860), in "A Word to the Reader," the deceased author intended in that poem to strengthen the hope for Redemption and a Return to Zion: "For the hap of Shulamit was the lot of the daughter of Judah, and what ye see in Shulamit, ye behold in the house of Jacob." An allusion to regeneration in Zion can also be drawn from Laski's poem "Mah Kiviti," which was printed at the end of his poem "Nefesh Ḥayah" (Warsaw, 1833).
119. Cf. the destructive criticism leveled against Feivel Shiffer's *Ḥaẓrot ha-Shir* by Victor Goldbaum of Lublin, in *Orient* 39 and 41 (1841).
120. Shatzky copied the *Privilege* in its Polish original in an appendix to the book *Zamość bi-Geonah ube-Shivrah* (Tel Aviv, 1952).
121. Wasiutyński, *Ludność żydowska*, p. 33.
122. For details about him, see Mahler, *Divrei Yemei Yisrael* 1:4:26–30.
123. It is very strange that no Jewish historians paid any attention to that highly significant political and geographical fact; some of them (Balaban, Wischnitzer) did not even trouble to consult the map of the First Partition of Poland and stated erroneously that Zamość and the district were not annexed to Austria until the Third Partition of Poland, as a part of "Western Galicia."
124. Shiffer had in mind a panegyric by Judah Szper concerning *Ḥaẓrot ha-Shir* which was printed at the beginning of the book.
125. I. Zinberg, *Toldot Sifrut Yisrael* (Tel Aviv, 1960) 6:287.
126. According to J. Shatzky, "Haskalah in Zamość," *Yivo Bleter* 36:45, Fischelsohn was born in the town of Krushnevitz but resided in Zamość for many years.
127. Joseph Klausner, *Historyah Shel ha-Sifrut ha-Ivrit ha-Ḥadashah* (Jerusalem, 1937) 2:352.
128. Zinberg, *Toldot Sifrut Yisrael,* p. 229.

129. Cf. Weinreich's introduction to *Ettingers Kesovim*, p. xxvi and the excerpt from the year 1833, ibid., p. 547.

130. Weinreich's introduction, *Ettingers Kesovim*, pp. xl–xli; J. Shatzky, in a review article of this edition of Weinreich, *Pinkas* (New York, 1928) 1:3:282.

131. J. Shatzky, "Tsu der geshikhte fun der yidisher Kolonizatsye in Kenigraykh Poyln," *Yivo Bleter* 6 (March–April 1934): 215–16.

132. Kołodziejczyk, *Kształtowanie się burżuazji w Królestwie Polskim (1825–1850)* (Warsaw, 1957), p. 137; among twelve members of the Szper family, whose names appear in the lists of subscribers for Feivel Shiffer's books, Isaac-Judah-Itshi-Yudel Szper is mentioned twice, in 1840 (*Ḥaẓrot ha-Shir*) and in 1849 (*Napoleon*). It is possible that he is identical—because of his first name—with Itzik Szper, who is mentioned commendably in the Polish press as a very active industrialist and man of property and, in view of his second name, he is that same Judah Szper who published a panegyric to the author at the beginning of *Ḥaẓrot ha-Shir*.

133. F. Shiffer, *Mahlkhim*, p. 82.

134. Ibid., pp. 70–73.

135. Books published without any lists of subscribers whatsoever, such as *Darkhei ha-Lashon* by Dov Berish Kahana (1822), or books whose publication was made possible by individual benefactors, such as *Mataei Moshe* by Moshe Tannenbaum (1838), have not been included. Schoenhack's *Toledot ha-Areẓ* (1841) has also been excluded, for reasons explained above, pp. 240–241.

136. Six of the subscribers to the book of sermons *Olat Ḥodesh* (Warsaw, 1847), by the *Maggid* R. Sinai Sapir of Brezhin, appear in the list of subscribers to Thalgruen's *Tokhaḥat Musar* in 1854.

137. This rabbi from Seiny, R. Judah Bachrach, gave—as did R. Ḥayyim Davidson, the Rabbi of Warsaw—his approval in 1844 to the Hebrew-Polish book of the censor Tugendhold, *Kosht Imrei Emet*.

138. One hundred of the subscribers to the book of sermons *Olat Ḥodesh* are distributed, apart from Warsaw, among twelve provincial towns, of which not even one is mentioned in the list of subscribers for books of the Haskalah.

139. *Allgemeine Zeitung des Judenthums* 31 (1841) . This press report contradicts the earlier one of June of that year (ibid., no. 28), according to which the Mitnaggedim are dominant in the community of Lublin, whereas the Hasidim have no foothold at all in this city.

140. Ibid., 1840, no. 23.

141. Ibid., no. 37.

142. Ibid., no. 23.

143. Ibid.

144. Ibid., no. 7.

145. Cf. Thalgruen, *Tokhaḥat Musar*, pp. 9, 15.

146. Cf. the press report from Lublin in *Allgemeine Zeitung des Judenthums* (1841), no. 28.

Chapter 9

1. The reference here is to the popular talmudic saying: "In the Messianic era insolence will prevail" (*Sotah* 49b; *Sanhedrin* 97a); with a slight modification, "impudence will increase."

2. *Be'er Moshe* (Jozefów, 1883), p. 390 (*Likkutim*).

3. Ibid., p. 4.

4. Ibid., *Toledot*, pp. 20–21.

5. R. Meir of Opatów, *Or la-Shamayim*, undated (the statements of approval are from the year 1849), p. 13a; cf. also *Vayelekh, Ha-azinu*, p. 62a.
6. Ibid., p. 6a.
7. Ibid., p. 8a.
8. Deut. 8:12–14.
9. Reuben Ḥayyim Alexander Cherniḥa, *Niflaot ha-Saba Kadisha* (Piotrków, 1929), p. 93.
10. Exod. 23:5.
11. *Baba Meẓia* 32a.
12. Cherniḥa, *Niflaot ha-Saba Kadisha*, p. 97.
13. R. Meir of Opatów, *Or la-Shamayim*, p. 60a.
14. Ibid., pp. 35a, 45a.
15. Ibid., p. 31a (*Mishpatim*).
16. Ibid., p. 42a (*Bamidbar*).
17. Cherniḥa, *Niflaot ha-Saba Kadisha*, p. 117.
18. *Be'er Moshe*, p. 110 (*Mishpatim*), p. 392 (*Likkutim*).
19. Gen. 34:31.
20. R. Meir of Opatów, *Or la-Shamayim*, p. 15a (*Vayishlaḥ*).
21. *Be'er Moshe, Toledot*, p. 23.
22. R. Meir of Opatów, *Or la-Shamayim, Yitro,* p. 29.
23. Ibid., *Vayikra*, p. 33a.
24. Ibid., *Metzora*, p. 35a.
25. Ibid., *Bamidbar*, p. 42b; *Niẓavim,* p. 61b.
26. *Kohelet Moshe* (Lublin, 1924), p. 72; *Be'er Moshe*, pp. 4, 10.
27. R. Meir of Opatów, *Or la-Shamayim, Ḥukat*, p. 48a.
28. R. Ezekiel of Kazimierz, *Neḥemad mi-Zahav* (Piotrków, 1909), p. 29.
29. R. Meir of Opatów, *Or la-Shamayim*, p. 9b, 32a.
30. Ibid., *Shemot*, p. 20b.
31. Ibid., *Vayikra*, p. 33b.
32. *Kohelet Moshe*, *Vayeḥi*, p. 48.
33. *Be'er Moshe, Vayishlaḥ*, p. 40; cf. also R. Meir of Opatów, *Or la-Shamayim*, p. 20a (*Shemot*): "And *Elokim* is an appellation of the zaddik who holds sway by reason of his reverence for God."
34. *Be'er Moshe, Vayeshev*, p. 48.
35. *Kohelet Moshe*, p. 43.
36. *Be'er Moshe, Vayishlaḥ*, p. 34.
37. *Be'er Moshe, Vayeẓe*, p. 27.
38. *Be'er Moshe, Toledot*, p. 19.
39. *Be'er Moshe, Bo*, p. 95 passim; cf. a similar version by R. Meir of Opatów: "Abundance of blessing and prosperity and health, children, life and sustenance, healing and deliverance for all Jews" (R. Meir of Opatów, *Or la-Shamayim*, *Aḥare*, p. 35b).
40. R. Meir of Opatów, *Or la-Shamayim, Vayakhel.*
41. *Erubin* 100b.
42. R. Meir of Opatów, *Or la-Shamayim, Vayikra*, p. 33b.
43. *Be'er Moshe, Toledot*, p. 23.
44. Cherniḥa, *Neḥemad Mizahav, Koraḥ*, p. 64.
45. Ibid., *Toledot*, p. 36.
46. R. Meir of Opatów, *Or la-Shamayim, Noaḥ,* p. 6a; *Beshalaḥ*, p. 28b; *Yitro*, p. 29a; *Mishpatim*, p. 30b; *Behar*, p. 39b.
47. 2 Sam. 23:3; *Be'er Moshe, Vayishlaḥ,* p. 37.
48. R. Meir of Opatów, *Or la-Shamayim, Emor,* p. 38b; the cited verse is Ps. 33:10; *Balak*, p. 3b.
49. *Be'er Moshe, Yitro,* p. 104; *Balak*, p. 290.

50. R. Meir of Opatów, *Or la-Shamayim, Bereshit*, p. 5a.
51. Isa. 49:3.
52. R. Meir of Opatów, *Or la-Shamayim, Vayishlaḥ*, p. 15a.
53. Ibid., *Bamidbar*, p. 42b.
54. Ibid., *Mishpatim*, p. 30b.
55. Ps. 135:4.
56. *Kohelet Moshe, Shemot,* p. 54; cf. also *Be'er Moshe,* p. 385: "Your splendid abode, for inasmuch as we are in the bitter exile in great poverty, actually like trodden down rubbish. . . ."
57. *Be'er Moshe,* p. 392, *Likkutim.*
58. Ibid., *Likkutim,* Omission for Yom Kippur, p. 394.
59. Ibid., Sermon for Yom Kippur, p. 373.
60. Ibid., pp. 381, 382 (Sermon for *Hoshannah Rabbah*), *Shemini*, p. 181; *Kohelet Moshe, Shemot,* p. 61.
61. *Be'er Moshe*, p. 383; cf. ibid., *Vaera*, p. 85.
62. *Be'er Moshe, Vaera*, p. 85.
63. Ibid., p. 394.
64. Mic. 7:20.
65. *Be'er Moshe*, p. 385.
66. Ibid., *Shemini*, p. 180.
67. Ibid., *Ki Teẓe*, p. 329.
68. Ibid., Sermon for Yom Kippur, p. 373.
69. A play on words according to the *halakhah* of R. Nathan in an interpretation of the verse "Ye shall kindle no fire": "The law about kindling a fire on the Sabbath is specified to intimate that each transgression involved in the kindling *was* to be atoned for separately." (Thus in *Yebamot* 7b, in *Sanhedrin* 35b, the version is given in the present tense: *is* to be, etc.)
70. *Be'er Moshe*, Sermons for Hanukkah, p. 59; *Vayeshev*, p. 41.
71. Ezek. 18:23, 32; 33:11.
72. *Berakhot* 10a.
73. *Kohelet Moshe*, p. 232 (*Likkutim*); the verse in the Sabbath hymn is a combination of fragments of Ps. 36:11 and Naḥ. 1:2.
74. *Be'er Moshe, Shemot*, p. 83.
75. *Kohelet Moshe, Ḥukat*, p. 179 (in an explanation of the verse [Num. 21:19] "and from *Mattanah* to *Naḥaliel*; and from *Naḥaliel* to *Bamoth*").
76. Num. 24:7.
77. *Be'er Moshe, Balak*, p. 290.
78. Ibid., *Yitro* (Exod. 19:1), p. 104.
79. Ibid., *Rimzei Shir Ha-Shirim*, p. 164.
80. *Kohelet Moshe, Balak,* p. 180.
81. Ibid., *Vayeḥi*, p. 48.
82. Prov. 31:15.
83. R. Meir of Opatów, *Or la-Shamayim, Beḥukotai,* p. 41a.
84. Ibid., *Behaalotekha,* p. 44b; *Ḥukat,* p. 49a; *Balak,* p. 50b; *Vayakhel.*
85. Isa. 55:12.
86. Jer. 31:8.
87. R. Meir of Opatów, *Or la-Shamayim, Emor*, p. 37b; in the course of the statement a really erotic and sexual interpretation is given to the opinion that the sufferings of the Jewish people and the weeping are likely to increase God's love for His people.
88. R. Ezekiel of Kazimierz, *Neḥemad Mizahav, Toledot*, p. 37.
89. Ibid., p. 73, a sermon on *Niẓavim,* Deut. 30:3.
90. *Be'er Moshe, Parashat Ki Teẓe*, p. 329; ibid., p. 392 (*Likkutim*), *Kohelet Moshe*, p. 235 (*Likkutim*).

91. Gen. 46:23.
92. Cherniḥa, *Niflaot ha-Saba Kadisha*, p. 97.
93. Exod. 22:25.
94. Deut. 24:4.
95. *Be'er Moshe, Mishpatim*, p. 112; R. Meir of Opatów, *Or la-Shamayim, Ki Teẓe,* p. 80a.
96. *Kohelet Moshe, Shemot*, p. 61.
97. R. Meir of Opatów, *Or la-Shamayim, Beḥukotai*, p. 40b: a comment on the verse "and keep My commandments and do them."
98. Ibid., *Vayeshev* (Gen. 37:16), p. 16a.
99. R. Ezekiel of Kazimierz, *Neḥemad Mizahav,* p. 77 (sermons on the Psalms).
100. R. Meir of Opatów, *Or la-Shamayim, Ekev*, p. 55a.
101. Ibid., *Vaera,* p. 20b.
102. Cf. chap. 1.
103. R. Ezekiel of Kazimierz, *Neḥemad Mizahav, Vayigash,* p. 41.
104. Ibid., *Beshalaḥ*, p. 46.
105. Ibid., *Bamidbar*, pp. 61–62.
106. Cherniḥa, *Niflaot ha-Saba Kadisha*, p. 97: As a scriptural proof, R. Issachar Ber interpreted the verse "I pray you, my brethren, do not so wickedly" by means of his own peculiar analysis: "Do not" (namely, "if they cannot pray and achieve by means of the prayers") "my brethren *become companionable*." . . . "It is advisable . . . to join in friendly fellowship and take a repast together—in love and fraternity." In similar fashion he expounded: "And they journeyed from *Ḥaradah*, and pitched in *Makhelot*" (Num. 33:25): "If a person is seized with a trembling of the heart because of the troubles which, Heaven forbid, beset him, then it is good counsel to pitch in *Makhelot*, that is, to join together with his companions in fellowship."
107. *Baba Batra* 10a, with reference to Isa. 56:1: "Thus saith the Lord, Keep ye justice and do righteousness; for My salvation is near to come, and My favor to be revealed"; *Ẓedakah*, having the sense of righteousness and justice, is here given the meaning of aid to the poor.
108. R. Meir of Opatów, *Or la-Shamayim*, p. 63a (selected passages); cf. there also pp. 19b (*Shemot*), 31a (*Terumah*), 37b (*Emor*); Sermons of R. Moshe of Kozienice on the role of *Ẓedakah* in bringing down to earth the flow of grace from on high; *Be'er Moshe, Vayeẓe*, p. 28, *Bo*, p. 95.
109. Lev. 25:24.
110. *Be'er Moshe, Behar*, p. 222.
111. R. Meir of Opatów, *Or la-Shamayim*, *Vaera,* 20b; *Ki Tisa; Shelaḥ,* 46b.
112. Cf. pp. 252–255.
113. Exod. 34:19.
114. *Be'er Moshe, Ki Tisa,* pp. 128–29.
115. *Ketubot* 111a.
116. *Be'er Moshe,* Sermon for *Hoshannah Rabbah*, p. 387.
117. Exod. 13:4.
118. Exod. 16:22.
119. R. Meir of Opatów, *Or la-Shamayim, Bo*, p. 22b; *Beshalaḥ,* p. 28b.
120. Lev. 27:24.
121. *Kohelet Moshe, Beḥukotai*, p. 157.
122. Deut. 12:9.
123. R. Ezekiel of Kazimierz, *Neḥemad Mizahav, Re'eh,* p. 71.
124. Ps. 136:22.
125. R. Ezekiel of Kazimierz, *Neḥemad Mizahav, Re'eh,* p. 71.
126. Cherniḥa, *Niflaot ha-Saba Kadisha,* p. 5.
127. Ibid., p. 3.
128. Ibid., p. 50.

129. B. Wasiutyński, *Ludność żydówska w Polsce w wiekach 19 i 20* (Warsaw, 1930), p. 56.

130. A number of these legends are cited by I. Alfasi in his book *Ha-Saba ha-Kadosh me-Radoszyce* (Tel Aviv, 1956), chap. 3 of Solomon Gabriel Rosenthal, *Hitgalut ha-Ẓaddikim* (Warsaw, 1927), pp. 69–77.

131. *Ḥas veshalom* (God forbid).

132. *Ha-Shem Yitbarekh* (He whose Name is blessed).

133. *Raḥamana litzlan* (May the merciful One save us).

134. *Ruaḥ Ra'ah* (an evil spirit).

135. Cherniḥa, *Niflaot ha-Saba Kadisha,* p. 14.

136. Rosenthal, *Hitgalut*, p. 35; quoted by Alfasi, *Ha-Saba*, p. 72.

137. Cherniḥa, *Niflaot ha-Saba Kadisha,* p. 45.

138. Ibid., p. 78; see also p. 117.

139. Ibid., pp. 15, 23, 31.

140. Ibid., pp. 45–46.

141. *Siaḥ Sarfei Kodesh* (Łódz, 1926) 2:233:72; concerning him cf. also Cherniḥa, *Niflaot ha-Saba Kadisha,* pp. 53–54.

142. Cherniḥa, *Niflaot ha-Saba Kadisha,* pp. 39–40, 42, 47–50, 57, 65, 70–71, 82, 115.

143. Cf. ibid., p. 109: On Purim at the *Maggid*'s place in Kozienice, he would strike with an axe upon stubble for a long time, until he would be covered with sweat; he explained: "I wanted to break up and render null the falsehood which exists in the world" (axe in Polish is *siekiera*, which somewhat resembles the sound of the Hebrew term for "falsehood"—*sheker*); ibid., p. 113; he gives the reason for eating honey on Rosh Hashanah, because *devash* (the Hebrew word for "honey") has the initial letters for *Daj Boże szczescie* (a Polish phrase meaning "God give good luck," which is a benediction bestowed by the wayfarer on those who toil in the field).

144. Ibid., p. 78.

145. Ibid., p. 85.

146. Ibid., pp. 87–88.

147. Ibid., p. 16.

148. Ibid., p. 74.

149. Ibid., p. 43.

150. Cf. R. Mahler, *Divrei Yemei Yisrael be-Dorot ha-Aḥaronim* (Merḥaviah, 1955) 3:121; "*Ha-yehudi" mi-Pshiskha v-Shitat ha-Ḥasidut ha-Metukenet,* pp. 304–7.

151. Cf. Aaron Marcus, *Ha-Ḥasidut* (Tel Aviv, 1957), p. 160; cf. also Moses Menaḥem Walden, *Ohel Yiẓḥak* (Piotrków, 1914) 173:68: On the day that R. Isaac of Warka received the book *Likkutei Moharan,* "it was as though it were a festival day for him because of his great joy."

152. R. Uri of Strelisk, *Imrei Kadosh ha-Shalem* (Lemberg, n.d.) 68:34.

153. *Siaḥ Sarfei Kodesh, Yo'etz Kim Kadish Rakacz* (Piotrków, 1923; Łódz, 1928) 1:276:60.

154. *Baba Meẓia* 107b.

155. *Siaḥ Sarfei Kodesh* (Łódz, 1927) 2:253:78.

156. M. Walden, *Ohel Yiẓḥak* 211:92; 259:107.

157. Ibid., 164:64; also cf. Z. M. Rabinowicz, *Rabbi Simḥah Bunem mi-Pshiskhah* (Tel Aviv), p. 37.

158. M. Walden, *Ohel Yiẓḥak* 88:37.

159. A. Marcus, *Ha-Ḥasidut*, p. 133; Rabinowicz, *Rabbi Simḥah Bunem*, p. 69.

160. *Siaḥ Sarfei Kodesh* 4:110.

161. Shmuel of Shinavi, *Ramatayim Ẓofim*, commentary upon *Tanna de-Bei Eliyahu* (Warsaw, 1881), p. 227; also cited in Rabinowicz, *Rabbi Simḥah Bunem*, p. 47.

162. Shmuel of Shinavi, *Ramatayim Ẓofim,* p. 195.

163. Ẓevi Yehudah Mamlak, *Abir ha-Ro'im* (Piotrków, 1935) 1:23; also cf. there R. Mendel's complaint to his daughter's father-in-law, that his son-in-law Abraham "prays overmuch"; he therefore fears lest this bring harm to "his mental powers."

164. Aaron Walden, *Mikdash Me'at* (Warsaw, 1890), p. 27; *Siaḥ Sarfei Kodesh* 3:18:25.

165. A. Marcus (Verus), *Der Chasidismus* (the original edition, in German) (Pleschen, 1901), pp. 300–301.

166. *Siaḥ Sarfei Kodesh* 3:18.

167. D. Kandel, *Komitet Starozakonnych, Kwartalnik . . . Żydów w Polsce* 1:2:89, 95–96, 100–103.

168. The appeal was published in full in M. Walden, *Ohel Yiẓḥak,* pp. 93–97.

169. Ibid., p. 79.

170. See A. N. Frenk, "Tsu der geshikhte fun yidisher Kolonizatsye in Kongres-Poyln," *Bleter far Yidisher Demografye, Statistik un Ekonomye* (Berlin, 1925) 5: 17–27.

171. M. Walden, *Ohel Yiẓḥak,* pp. 14, 97; *Siaḥ Sarfei Kodesh* 1:31–32.

172. M. Walden, *Ohel Yiẓḥak,* pp. 7, 79.

173. *Siaḥ Sarfei Kodesh* 4:15.

174. Ibid., 1:33.

175. Ibid., 1:271:59.

176. Abraham Issachar Alter, *Meir Einei ha-Golah* (Tel Aviv, 1954) 1:38–39, 125; 2:83–84.

177. M. Walden, *Ohel Yiẓḥak* 130:54.

178. *Siaḥ Sarfei Kodesh* 1:41.

179. Ibid., 2:24:15; see Jonathan ha-Levi Eibeschütz, *Ḥedvat Simḥah* (Warsaw, 1930), p. iii.

180. M. Walden, *Ohel Yiẓḥak* 16:10; 56:25.

181. *Siaḥ Sarfei Kodesh* 4:73.

182. M. Walden, *Ohel Yiẓḥak* 293:125; according to that story Temerl "herself, in person, washed their shirts."

183. Shmuel of Shinavi, *Ramatayim Ẓofim,* pp. 68, 215.

184. *Siaḥ Sarfei Kodesh* 1:653; the rhyme in the original in Yiddish (*Negidim on gelt . . . vinter on kelt* [plutocrats without money . . . winter without cold] is a trustworthy mark of the antiquity of the adage which may, perhaps, even have been culled by R. Simḥah Bunem from current folklore.

185. Ibid., no. 654.

186. Ibid., 384:74; also cf. there, 3:9.

187. Ibid., no. 662.

188. *Siaḥ Sarfei Kodesh* 2:321:93; *Emet ve-Emunah,* no. 745; *Meir Einei ha-Golah* 1:78.

189. Ibid., 4:33.

190. M. Walden, *Ohel Yiẓḥak* 146:59; 189:79.

191. Cf. ibid., 18:11; 145:59: It is told of Reb Itchi Blass that at a time when the Rabbi of Warka was in straitened circumstances, he presented him with money, "and from then on he was successful insomuch that he was one of the few wealthy men of Poland"; ibid., no. 146: It is told of a Jewish villager that he treated the rebbe with a great measure of hospitality and was blessed "with very much wealth"; ibid., no. 96: It is told of one who became wealthy in virtue of having made a concession in the matter of a debt which he was to have collected in Warsaw.

192. Ibid., 128:53.
193. Ibid., 25:14.
194. *Siaḥ Sarfei Kodesh* 4:90.
195. *Emet ve-Emunah,* no. 734.
196. Ibid., no. 731.
197. *Siaḥ Sarfei Kodesh* 2:248:75.
198. M. Walden, *Ohel Yiẓḥak* 85:36.
199. *Siaḥ Sarfei Kodesh* 3:7:24.
200. *Emet ve-Emunah* 91:17.
201. Cf. R. Mahler, *Divrei Yemei Yisrael* 3:226.
202. Shmuel of Shinavi, *Ramatayim Ẓofim,* p. 61 and elsewhere.
203. Ibid., p. 61.
204. *Siaḥ Sarfei Kodesh* 1:434:50; also cf. *Kol Simḥah, Parashat Ḥayei Sarah, Matot, Masaei;* M. Walden, *Ohel Yiẓḥak* 186:77 (R. Isaac of Warka in the name of R. Simḥah Bunem).
205. *Baba Batra* 10a.
206. *Emet ve-Emunah* 479:75.
207. Cf. ibid., no. 664.
208. *Siaḥ Sarfei Kodesh* 1:96; in the midrashic source (*Koh. Rab.* 7:49): 1,000 people enter upon the study of *Mikra* (Scripture), of whom 100 go on to the study of the Mishnah; of these, 10 continue on to the study of Talmud; of these, 1 emerges to be a religious teacher (i.e., 1 qualified to decide questions of law).
209. *Siaḥ Sarfei Kodesh* 3:12, 26; a similar opinion on the observance of the Torah in the course of conducting business transactions had already been voiced by R. Levi Yiẓḥak of Berdichev; cf. *Kedushat Levi* (Berdichev, 1908), p. 209 (*Likkutim*) on the *Avot.*
210. *Siaḥ Sarfei Kodesh* 1:666:131.
211. *Shem mi-Shemuel, Sefer Vayikra* (Tel Aviv, 1957), *Parashat Be-Har,* pp. 343–44; the author is the son of the son-in-law of R. Mendel of Kock, R. Abraham of Sochaczew; also cf. *Kol Simḥah, Parashat Matot,* p. 51b.
212. *Mei ha-Shiloaḥ* (Lublin, 1922), pt. 2, *Vayetze,* p. 14; ibid., *Lekh-Lekha,* p. 10; ibid., *Be-Har,* p. 141 (supplements).
213. *Shem mi-Shemuel, Sefer Bereshit* (Tel Aviv, 1949), *Vayishlaḥ,* p. 52; cf. also *Emet ve-Emunah,* no. 180: man needs three things: good birth, personality, and help from God.
214. *Siaḥ Sarfei Kodesh* 1:272:59; to be sure, there has also been preserved a tradition, according to which R. Mendel ordered a fiddler to "play at weddings," explaining that "whoever benefits from the toil of his own hands is an eminent Hasid"; cf. *Siaḥ Sarfei Kodesh* 3:12.
215. In Polish, "leasing."
216. R. Isaac of Warka.
217. M. Walden, *Ohel Yiẓḥak* 25:13.
218. A.G.A.D., K.R.S.W., 6636, pp. 134–35; cf. appendix: document 20.
219. Shmuel of Shinavi, *Ramatayim Ẓofim,* a commentary on *Eliyahu Zuta,* p. 4; also cited in *Siaḥ Sarfei Kodesh* 2:279:84.
220. *Siaḥ Sarfei Kodesh* 1:657.
221. Ibid., no. 253.
222. Exod. 22:24.
223. *Avot* 6. 9.
224. *Emet ve-Emunah,* no. 391.
225. M. Walden, *Ohel Yiẓḥak,* no. 56: because of his generosity in philanthropy, he owed R. Hirsh Leyb Friedman of his city, his future relative by marriage, 10,000 zlotys.

226. Ibid., no. 144: To those who argued that it was forbidden to take pity on a licentious woman who claimed the wages of her deceased husband, he replied, "If such is the case, that she became so impoverished as to be compelled to become licentious, it is surely all the more reason to take more pity on her"; in like manner, he showed mercy to the thief who had broken into his son's shop because he had not slept for two nights (ibid., no. 142).

227. *Ketubot* 50a.

228. M. Walden, *Ohel Yiẓḥak,* no. 286; an explanation similar to that kind of restriction on philanthropy was transmitted in the name of R. Uri of Strelisk, "the *Saraf*"; cf. *Imrei Kadosh ha-Shalem,*" supplements, p. 40. According to another explanation of that principle in the Gemara, *ha-Yehudi* of Przysucha permitted a man who wanted to atone for his sins even to distribute all his money to the poor; cf. *Tiferet ha-Yehudi* (Warsaw, n.d.), p. 3.

229. *Siaḥ Sarfei Kodesh* 3:11, 46.

230. Shmuel of Shinavi, *Ramatayim Ẓofim,* p. 49.

231. *Kol Simḥah, Vayeshev,* p. 20a.

232. Shmuel of Shinavi, *Ramatayim Ẓofim,* p. 127.

233. *Shem mi-Shemuel, Vayikra, Kedoshim,* p. 277; cf. A. D. Zigelman, *Ohel Torah* (Lublin, 1909), p. 30: Each and every person must perform all sacred acts in association with the entire community of Israel.

234. *Siaḥ Sarfei Kodesh* 4:171; 109.

235. *Ḥedvat Simḥah, Vayeḥi,* commentary on the verse "Gather yourselves together, that I may tell you," pp. 87–88; M. Walden, *Ohel Yiẓḥak* 170:67.

236. *Tiferet ha-Yehudi*, p. 40.

237. *Zohar, Vaera,* p. 117; the Hebrew translation is by the author.

238. Alfasi, *Ha-Saba ha-Kadosh,* pp. 86–91.

239. See ibid., p. 88, concerning R. Isaac Meir; concerning the opinion of R. Isaac of Warka and R. Mendel, cf. *Emet ve-Emunah,* no. 263.

240. *Mei ha-Shiloaḥ* 2:5, introduction.

241. R. Mendel of Kock, *Siaḥ Sarfei Kodesh* 1:636; 125.

242. Ibid., 4:106.

243. An epithet containing an element of ridicule, directed against the zaddikim, who wear white garments.

244. Exod. 14:15; cf. *Siaḥ Sarfei Kodesh* 3:285; Yeḥiel Moshe of Jadimów, *Niflaot Ḥadashot, Parashat Be-shalaḥ* (Piotrków, 1897), p. 35.

245. *Emet ve-Emunah,* no. 126.

246. *Siaḥ Sarfei Kodesh* 1:356:71.

247. Ibid., 3:73:227.

248. R. Hanokh Henekh of Alexander, *Ḥoshvah Le-tovah* (Piotrków, 1929), p. 10; cf. Z. M. Rabinowicz, *Ha-Maggid Mi-Koznitz* (Tel Aviv, 1947), p. 134.

249. In the Yiddish: *farleygn*—to seize hold of something and not let go.

250. *Emet ve-Emunah,* no. 420.

251. *Kol Simḥah, Vayishlaḥ,* p. 18a.

252. Ibid., *Likkutim*, p. 56a; also cf. *Siaḥ Sarfei Kodesh* 2:282:85.

253. Ibid., 27:16.

254. Ibid., 350:98.

255. M. Walden, *Ohel Yiẓḥak,* p. 97.

256. *Siaḥ Sarfei Kodesh* 1:234:50; this same statement is also cited in the name of R. Mendel of Kock; cf. *Emet ve-Emunah,* no. 801.

257. *Ḥedvat Simḥah, mi-Keẓ,* pp. 77–78; this doctrine is also handed down in the name of his disciple, R. Mendel; cf. *Emet ve-Emunah,* no. 769; R. Isaac of Warka was also of the opinion that Joseph the Righteous was punished, "even though he was a person who put great trust [in God], but held that . . . some action

should be taken and therefore spoke to the butler"; cf. M. Walden, *Ohel Yiẓḥak,* 271.

258. *Emet ve-Emunah,* no. 625.

259. The end of the anecdote: The man remained—"may it not befall us"—a pauper, that is, he was punished for his lack of faith in God; ibid., no. 617.

260. Yeḥiel Moshe of Jadimów, *Niflaot Ḥadashot,* p. 90.

261. *Siaḥ Sarfei Kodesh* 4:17:67.

262. *Emet ve-Emunah,* nos. 123, 670; *Siaḥ Sarfei Kodesh* 3:430:118.

263. Ibid., nos. 710, 762, 819; to be sure, his master, R. Simḥah Bunem, did not allow the *Moreh Nebukhim* to be read consistently, but it was to be perused intermittently, in order to find an answer before the question arose, for "the moment the question precedes the answer, it follows that for that moment he is not a Jew. . . ."; cf. Shmuel of Shinavi, *Ramatayim Ẓofim,* p. 134.

264. Ibid., no. 486.

265. *Baba Batra* 12a.

266. *Siaḥ Sarfei Kodesh* 2:325:93.

267. Shmuel of Shinavi, *Ramatayim Ẓofim,* p. 99.

268. R. Naḥman of Bratslav, in his doctrine of perfect faith—"without any speculation whatsoever"—reached the point of admonishing against any study, not only of the *Moreh Nebukhim* but even of *Hilkhot Deot* (laws relating to the knowledge of God) and *Hilkhot Yesodei ha-Torah* (laws relating to the fundamentals of the Torah) in the *Yad ha-Ḥazakah* (Maimonides' *Mishneh Torah*); cf. *Shivḥei Moharan,* p. 13a.

269. Shmuel of Shinavi, *Ramatayim Ẓofim,* pp. 243, 246.

270. *Siaḥ Sarfei Kodesh* 2:326:94.

271. *Emet ve-Emunah,* no. 337.

272. Ibid., no. 708.

273. *Siaḥ Sarfei Kodesh* 1:46:14–15.

274. Ibid., 390:67.

275. Deut. 4:9.

276. *Emet ve-Emunah,* no. 484; cf. ibid., no. 887: "He said to his entourage, 'I ask no more of you than this—that you abhor the body as Reb Moishele of Lutomiersk abhors it.'"

277. Ibid., no. 666.

278. Ibid., no. 612.

279. Ibid., no. 302.

280. Ibid., no. 51.

281. *Shem mi-Shemuel, Sefer Vayikra, Ẓav,* p. 89.

282. *Shabbat* 118b.

283. *Shem mi-Shemuel, Sefer Bereshit, Vayera,* pp. 152, 166.

284. In a conversation with the Rebbe of Alexander; cf. *Emet ve-Emunah,* p. 286.

285. *Siaḥ Sarfei Kodesh* 1:671:132.

286. Yeḥiel Moshe of Jadimów, *Niflaot Ḥadashot,* p. 92; *Emet ve-Emunah,* no. 731.

287. *Siaḥ Sarfei Kodesh* 3:342:69; in the book of Yeḥiel Moshe of Jadimów, *Niflaot Ḥadashot* (p. 82, *Tehillim*), this saying is cited in the name of R. Simḥah Bunem.

288. *Tiferet ha-Yehudi,* the letter *ayin-vav.*

289. In Yiddish, a "fig"; a *fico.*

290. *Siaḥ Sarfei Kodesh* 3:12.

291. *Ḥashovah le-Tovah* (new interpretations by Ḥanokh Henekh from Alexander) (Piotrków, 1929), pp. 56, 61.

292. Cf. Rabinowicz (*Rabbi Simḥah Bunem,* p. 64), who rightly points out that the way of lifting up "alien thoughts" seemed to the School of Przysucha a dangerous one; however, the author had not grasped the social nature of this new tendency, the significance of its retreat from the ethical monism of original Hasidism, and its compromise with the Mitnaggedic system of ethics.

293. The "annulment" or effacement of alien thoughts is expressly discussed in the teaching of R. Simḥah Bunem; cf. the quotation in Rabinowicz, *Rabbi Simḥa Bunem* (p. 64). In the name of R. Mendel of Kock a remark on this matter has been related with some variation. It is precisely the verse "In all thy ways acknowledge Him" (Prov. 3:6), which had become a prop for the doctrine of the Ba'al Shem Tov concerning the worship of God even in a material way, that he interprets, "even in a matter of transgression, for in virtue of one's knowledge of the name of God . . . will arise the ardor to separate oneself from a transgression." See *Siaḥ Sarfei Kodesh* 2:291. In contrast, R. Mendel also spoke of the negation of existence ("that one should forget his own essence and be null and void in actuality, insomuch that there will be fulfilled in him that the Lord God is Truth" (ibid., 1:328).

To be sure, as against the doctrine of the nullification of transgressive thoughts, there has been handed down in the name of R. Simḥah Bunem a tenet that one must be incessantly on the defense against the evil inclination: "Against the evil inclination," he stated, "one must always imagine it to be as if a man stood opposite him, holding an axe in his hand to decapitate him; and if he does not have this in his mind, it is a sign that his head was already cut off" (*Siaḥ Sarfei Kodesh* 1: 214:46).

294. Ibid., 2:348.

295. Ibid., 1:246; the same saying is also transmitted in the name of R. Isaac of Warka.

296. *Emet ve-Emunah,* no. 244; *Siaḥ Sarfei Kodesh* 3:215:60.

297. You lost your courage, i.e., you became depressed.

298. *Shem mi-Shemuel, Parashat Yitro,* p. 268.

299. Cf. Mahler, *Divrei Yemei Yisrael* 3:290.

300. *Siaḥ Sarfei Kodesh* 2:290:86.

301. Shmuel of Shinavi, *Ramatayim Ẓofim,* p. 216.

302. Marcus, *Ha-Ḥasidut,* p. 134; cf. the German original, p. 305: The Hasidim of Kock go forth in dance to a Polish song (*Hopcy, chłopcy, kudry szudry*).

303. *Emet ve-Emunah,* no. 402; *Siaḥ Sarfei Kodesh* 4:29:68.

304. Yeḥiel Moshe of Jadimów, *Niflaot Ḥadashot*, p. 79; R. Mendel found support for his opinion in that verse "And it came to pass, when the minstrel played, that the hand of the Lord came upon him" (2 Kings 3:15), and according to Solomon Maimon, it was interpreted in similar fashion by the *maggid* R. Ber of Mezherich: The divine spirit does not rest upon a man except on condition that he hold himself to be a mere vessel for the reception of influence; cf. Mahler, *Divrei Yemei Yisrael* 3:232.

305. M. Walden, *Ohel Yiẓḥak* 168:66.

306. *Kol Simḥah, Parashat Vayigash,* p. 24a.

307. Ibid., *Parashat Toledot,* p. 14a.

308. Ibid.

309. *Shem mi-Shemuel, Sefer Vayikra,* a sermon for Passover, p. 107.

310. *Emet ve-Emunah,* no. 699; cf. also no. 503.

311. *Shir ha-Shirim Rab.* 5:2.

312. Yeḥiel Moshe of Jadimów, *Niflaot Ḥadashot,* p. 95.

313. *Siaḥ Sarfei Kodesh* 1:322:67.

314. *Emet ve-Emunah,* no. 645.

315. *Siaḥ Sarfei Kodesh* 2:46:22; 3:7:24; 22:26.

316. Ibid., 1:364:72: The word play hits home with greater force in the language of the conversation, Yiddish: The one who is asked, said, "I learned (*oysgelernt*) the entire *Shas,*" to which R. Mendel replied, "And what did the *Shas* teach you?", employing the expression *oyslernen* in a second sense—to teach something perfectly, to teach the way of life.

317. *Kol Simḥah, Parashat Devarim,* pp. 53–54.

318. Ibid., *Parashat Vayeẓe,* p. 17.

319. *Siaḥ Sarfei Kodesh* 1:332:68.

320. Thus the Ba'al Shem Tov expressly interpreted the passage in the Mishnah (*Ketubot* 13a): "They saw her speaking with someone in the marketplace"; cf. Mahler, *Divrei Yemei Yisrael* 3:218.

321. *Emet ve-Emunah,* no. 172.

322. Ibid., no. 109; Rabinowicz, *Rabbi Simḥah Bunem,* p. 69.

323. Cherniḥa, *Niflaot ha-Saba Kadisha,* p. 42.

324. *Siaḥ Sarfei Kodesh* 2:59:25.

325. R. Ḥanokh Henekh of Alexander, *Ḥashovah le-Tovah,* p. 18.

326. *Siaḥ Sarfei Kodesh* 2:293:87; cf. his interpretation of the verse "And Aaron did so" in the *Parashat Be-ha'alotekha*; ibid., 3:23.

327. *Emet ve-Emunah,* no. 870.

328. *Siaḥ Sarfei Kodesh* 3:453:124; *Abir ha-Ro'im* 1:32, 42.

329. *Siaḥ Sarfei Kodesh* 2:291.

330. *Emet ve-Emunah,* no. 643.

331. Ibid.

332. *Rimzei Esh,* p. 149; *Siaḥ Sarfei Kodesh* 3:25.

333. Shmuel of Shinavi, *Ramatayim Ẓofim,* on *Eliyaho Zuta,* p. 39.

334. *Siaḥ Sarfei Kodesh* 1:386.

335. Cf. regarding this episode from the aspect of the growth of Hasidism: R. Mahler, *Divrei Yemei Yisrael* 3:233–34.

336. Marcus, *Ha-Ḥasidut,* pp. 127–36; cf. in the German original (Pleschen, 1901), p. 300: R. Mendel, when he was in Przysucha, derided R. Yeraḥmiel, the son of *ha-Yehudi*; also cf. *Me'ir Einei ha-Golah* 1:124: the Hasidim of Przysucha snatch the phylacteries of R. Isaac Meir as a penalty for his peculiar movements in the course of praying.

337. J. L. Elzet, *Le-Korot ha-Ḥasidut,* "Rabbi Mendel mi-Kock," in *Ha-Ivri,* tenth year, copy 19, 4 Sivan, 5680 (1920).

338. Cf. *Emet ve-Emumah* 624:142; Marcus, *Ha-Ḥasidut,* p. 183.

339. *Emet ve-Emunah,* no. 624, and also cf. ibid., no. 141.

340. *Emet ve-Emunah,* no. 141.

341. The saying is cited in the collection of M. Lipson, *Mi-Dor le-Dor* (Tel Aviv, 1929), no. 702.

342. A derisive epithet about the "white cloaks," applied by R. Mendel to zaddikim and the dangers of heresy preceding the advent of the Messiah.

343. *Emet ve-Emunah,* no. 495.

344. *Siaḥ Sarfei Kodesh* 2:63:26.

345. Ibid., 1:166:34.

346. Exod. 23:7.

347. *Shem mi-Shemuel, Parashat Ẓav,* p. 87.

348. *Siaḥ Sarfei Kodesh* 1:617:118.

349. *Shabbat* 55a.

350. *Emet ve-Emunah,* no. 481; cf. also *Siaḥ Sarfei Kodesh* 1:248, where the saying is ascribed to R. Simḥah Bunem.

351. *Siaḥ Sarfei Kodesh* 1:329:68.

352. Ibid., no. 333.

353. *Emet ve-Emunah,* no. 493.

354. R. Meir of Opatów, *Or la-Shamayim, Be-ḥukotai,* p. 40b.
355. Shmuel of Shinavi, *Ramatayim Ẓofim on Eliyahu Zuta,* p. 75.
356. *Vayikra Rabbah* 9; cf. *Seder Eliyahu Rabbah* 1, and elsewhere in the Midrash.
357. *Emet ve-Emunah,* no. 449.
358. *Siaḥ Sarfei Kodesh* 2:329:94; Yeḥiel Moshe of Jadimów, *Niflaot Ḥadashot, Mishpatim,* p. 39.
359. Ibid., 1:536:97.
360. Ibid., 620:119.
361. Yeḥiel Moshe of Jadimów, *Niflaot Ḥadashot,* p. 55.
362. *Emet ve-Emunah,* no. 492.
363. *Mei ha-Shiloaḥ,* pt. 1 (Vienna, 1860), *Parashat Koraḥ.*
364. Yeḥiel Moshe of Jadimów, *Niflaot Ḥadashot, Parashat Shelaḥ,* p. 55.
365. *Sotah* 34b.
366. M. Walden, *Ohel Yiẓḥak* 3:30.
367. *Siaḥ Sarfei Kodesh* 1:141:28.
368. Yeḥiel Moshe of Jadimów, *Niflaot Ḥadashot, Balak,* p. 58.
369. According to a tradition of the Hasidim of Kock, the rebbe even expressed his admiration of Pharaoh for his obstinacy in not submitting even after the plagues had beset him: "Pharaoh was a *człowiek*!", i.e., a real man; cf. Elzet, *Le-Korot ha-Ḥasidut,* p. 10.
370. Shmuel of Shinavi, *Ramatayim Ẓofim* on *Seder Eliyahu Zuta,* p. 42; cf. *Emet ve-Emunah,* no. 70. In saying "I ate and I will eat," *Adam Ha-rishon* implied that his character was not of one who says "I will sin and I will repent," for at the time of the sin, repentance never even entered his mind.
371. *Siaḥ Sarfei Kodesh* 1:619:119.
372. *Emet ve-Emunah,* no. 299.
373. *Mei ha-Shiloaḥ, Pinḥas*; cf. the view of his master, R. Mendel, regarding the slaying of Zimri, *Emet ve-Emunah,* no. 153; concerning Pinḥas, Yeḥiel Moshe of Jadimów, *Niflaot Ḥadashot,* p. 60.
374. Shmuel of Shinavi, *Ramatayim Ẓofim* on *Eliyahu Zuta,* p. 40.
375. Ibid., on *Tanna d'Bei Eliyahu Rabbah,* p. 51.
376. *Siaḥ Sarfei Kodesh,* no. 311, p. 66; see his expression "I set them straight," *Emet ve-Emunah*, no. 728.
377. *Emet ve-Emunah,* no. 901.
378. *Kol Simḥah, Toledot,* on the verse "And all the wells which they had dug . . . ," p. 14a.
379. *Emet ve-Emunah,* no. 31.
380. Ibid., no. 21.
381. Shmuel of Shinavi, *Ramatayim Ẓofim,* p. 96.
382. *Emet ve-Emunah,* no. 448.
383. Shmuel of Shinavi, *Ramatayim Ẓofim, Zuta,* p. 44; cf. *Shem mi-Shemuel, va-Yakhel,* p. 285.
384. Ibid., commentary on *Tanna d'Bei Eliyahu Rabbah,* p. 129.
385. Ibid.
386. *Emet ve-Emunah,* no. 629; R. Mendel bases this norm upon the statement in *Midrash Tanḥuma, Pinḥas,* no. 10: "Even as the physiognomies of human beings differ from each other, so are they not alike in their opinions."
387. *Siaḥ Sarfei Kodesh* 3:130:484.
388. Ibid., 2:284:85; the basis in the Bible verse is provided by his peculiar etymology of *ovot* (ghosts) as desired, from the verb *avoh*, namely, *to will* or *want*; in contrast, the derivation of *yidoni* from the root *yadoa* (to know) is certainly right.
389. Shmuel of Shinavi, *Ramatayim Ẓofim,* p. 39.

390. *Emet ve-Emunah,* no. 212; according to the *Midrash Bereshit Rabbah* 58: Even as they are whole (unblemished), so are they whole (unblemished) in years. In the Yiddish original the ingenious exegesis of R. Mendel is founded on the translation of *ba* as "went along": "*ba beyamim* he went along with the days, he never was retrogressive."

391. Yeḥiel Moshe of Jadimów, *Niflaot Ḥadashot,* p. 87.

392. *Emet ve-Emunah,* nos. 411, 623; See also no. 161.

393. *Siaḥ Sarfei Kodesh* 2:5:23.

394. Shmuel of Shinavi, *Ramatayim Ẓofim, Zuta,* p. 40.

395. According to Jer. 13:17: The deduction from the verse in the Song of Songs is based on the etymological interpretation of *bane 'alim* (in sandals) as "locked up."

396. *Siaḥ Sarfei Kodesh* 1:383:74.

397. Ibid., 326:68; the first principle is cited by R. Isaac of Warka in the name of R. David of Lelov; cf. M. Walden, *Ohel Yiẓḥak,* p. 120.

398. *Emet ve-Emunah,* no. 576, in a commentary on the expression of consolation in the Gemara (*Shabbat* 12b): "It is the Sabbath and one must not cry out."

399. *Siaḥ Sarfei Kodesh* 2:402:107.

400. *Emet ve-Emunah,* no. 898.

401. *Siaḥ Sarfei Kodesh* 1:255:54.

402. M. Walden, *Ohel Yiẓḥak* 258:106. R. Mendel formulated his words as a commentary constituting a play on the words of the Gemara (*Erubin* 21b): When Solomon ordained the laws of *Erubin* and the washing of hands a divine voice issued forth and proclaimed (Prov. 23:15): "My son, if thy heart be wise, My heart will be glad, even Mine."

403. Cf. p. 282.

404. *Emet ve-Emunah,* no. 613; there is an element of similarity in the saying of R. David of Lelov, "If the Jews would make one hand [i.e., unite]—it would reach up to heaven." Cf. Ḥanokh Ẓevi Ha-Kohen, *Ye-Khahen Pe'er,* pt. 2 (Warsaw, 1936), *Derushim*, p. 86.

405. *Emet ve-Emunah,* no. 812.

406. Isa. 55:6.

407. Judah Mamlak, *Abir ha-Ro'im* (Piotrków, 1935) 2:61.

408. *Siaḥ Sarfei Kodesh* 2:328:94.

409. Ibid., 3:218:71.

410. Ps. 115:16.

411. *Shem mi-Shemuel, Pekudei,* p. 328.

412. Ibid., *Yitro,* p. 245.

413. *Siaḥ Sarfei Kodesh* 4:168.

414. Ibid., 1:122:25.

415. Ibid., 2:345:97.

416. Ibid., 1:127:26.

417. Ibid., no. 134; according to other versions, the chosen (élite) Hasidim had to stand on the rooftops and cry out "the Lord, He is God," or "Hear, O Israel"; cf. also ibid., 3:15: "I thought I would have only four hundred men, and I would go with them into the woods, to give them *manna*, so that they would recognize the might of His kingdom."

418. Ibid., 3:27:27.

419. Ibid., 3:388:109.

420. *Pesaḥim* 68b.

421. *Siaḥ Sarfei Kodesh* 3:513:136.

422. *Emet ve-Emunah,* no. 664.

423. *Siaḥ Sarfei Kodesh* 1:257:55.

424. Cf. ibid., 229:49; the proof from the verse is based on the explanation of *ḥil* in the sense of *mora* (fear, reverence), i.e., *hasid* (pious) and *domem* (quiet) as a sobriquet for a wise person, for "silence is a fence around wisdom." This saying was transmitted in the name of R. Naphtali of Ropczyce, with variations: If one is only a Hasid, he is a fool; if one is merely wise, he is a thief.
425. Ibid., 4:89; Yeḥiel Moshe of Jadimów, *Niflaot Ḥadashot,* p. 88.
426. *Shem mi-Shemuel, Bereshit,* p. 37.
427. *Emet ve-Emunah,* no. 43.
428. *Shem mi-Shemuel, Vayikra,* no. 239.
429. *Emet ve-Emunah,* no. 577.
430. Ibid., no. 96.
431. *Mei ha-Shiloaḥ*, pt. 2 (Lublin, 1922); *Vayikra,* p. 44; cf. also *Kedoshim*, ibid., p. 50.
432. Ibid., *Vayeḥi,* p. 22.
433. *Mei ha-Shiloaḥ,* pt. 1 (Vienna, 1860); *Vayeshev,* p. 26.
434. Ibid., pt. 2, *Yehoshua,* p. 85; cf. also pt. 1, *Bereshit*, p. 4.
435. Ibid., pt. 2, *Ki Tisa,* p. 41; *Melakhim I,* p. 87.
436. Ibid., *Yitro,* p. 30.
437. Ibid., pt. 1, *Vayeẓe,* p. 27.
438. Ibid., *Bereshit,* p. 4.
439. Ibid., pt. 2, *Yeshayah,* p. 88.
440. Ibid., *Teẓave,* pp. 35–36; *Yitro,* p. 31; *va-Etḥanan,* p. 68.
441. Ibid., *Vayakhel,* p. 42.
442. Ibid., *Terumah,* p. 35.
443. Ibid., p. 35.
444. Ibid., *Ki Tisa,* p. 38.
445. Ibid., *Tehillim,* p. 94.
446. Ibid., *Mi-keẓ,* p. 19 (in a commentary on the verse "God hath found out the iniquity of thy servants").
447. Ibid., *Vayeḥi,* on the verse "Ben Porat Yosef," p. 18 (Joseph is a fruitful vine).
448. Ibid., pt. 2, *Yitro,* p. 32; *Beha'alotekha,* p. 56; ibid., pt. 1, *Vayeshev,* p. 26.
449. *Gittin* 60a, passim.
450. Cf. p. 276.
451. *Mei ha-Shiloaḥ,* pt. 2, *Mi-keẓ,* p. 19; cf. also *Vayeẓe,* p. 14; *Behar,* p. 141; *Lekh Lekha,* p. 10.
452. Ibid., *beḥukotai,* p. 54.
453. Ibid., *Vayikra, Miluim.*
454. Ibid., *Vayeḥi,* p. 22.
455. Ibid., *Be-Shalaḥ,* p. 27.
456. Ibid., *va-Etḥanan,* p. 68.
457. Ibid., *Ki Teẓe,* p. 75.
458. Ibid., *Vayeẓe,* p. 14.
459. Ibid., *Mi-Keẓ,* p. 20; pt. 1, *Vayeḥi,* p. 37.
460. Ibid., pt. 2, *Va-Etḥanan,* p. 68; *Masekhat Berakhot,* p. 109; *Shmuel* 1, p. 86; *Ḥukat,* p. 64; *Malachi,* p. 93; pt. 1, *Beha'alotekha,* p. 95; pt. 2, *Va-Etḥanan,* p. 69; pt. 1, *Ha'azinu,* p. 128; pt. 2, *Be-Har,* p. 53.
461. According to *Shabbat* 89b.
462. *Mei ha-Shiloaḥ,* pt. 2, *Yeshayah,* p. 89; cf. pp. 295–296 on his view in the matter of Zimri and Pinḥas in "their outer garb" and in their inner selves.
463. *Emet ve-Emunah,* no. 466.
464. Ibid., no. 752.
465. *Siaḥ Sarfei Kodesh* 3:94:45.

466. *Mei ha-Shiloaḥ,* pt. 1, *Likutei Shas,* p. 156.
467. Ibid., pt. 1, *Likutei Shas,* p. 151; *Likutei Tehillim,* p. 139; pt. 2, *Ki Tisa, Miluim,* p. 146; *Ve-zot Haberakha, Miluim,* p. 149.
468. Ibid., pt. 1, *Likutei Shas,* pp. 156, 169; pt. 2, *Yitro,* p. 31.
469. Ibid., pt. 2, *Vaera,* p. 25.
470. Ibid., pt. 2, *Yeshayah,* p. 37; pt. 1, *Vayigash,* p. 33; *Ḥukat,* p. 100.
471. Ibid., pt. 2, *Yeshayah,* p. 93; *Yoel,* p. 91; *Vayigash,* p. 21; *Tehillim,* p. 100; cf. also ibid., *Devarim,* p. 67: "Sanctity was never cut off from the holy place."
472. Ibid., pt. 1, *Kedoshim,* p. 23; *Toledot,* p. 20.
473. Ibid., pt. 2, *Shelaḥ,* p. 39; *Ki Tisa,* p. 40; *Koraḥ,* p. 62.
474. *Siaḥ Sarfei Kodesh* 3:309:93; *Meir Einei ha-Golah* 89:24.
475. Ibid., 403:112.
476. Cf. Cherniḥa, *Niflaot ha-Saba Kadisha,* p. 14: There is a tale about the son of *ha-Yehudi* of Przysucha, Reb Jeraḥme'el, who tarried in Tomaszów in the course of his journey; in the evening the Hasidim of Kock congregated around his inn, smashed the windows, flung stones through the broken windows "and cut off his beard."
477. Cf. Elzet, *Le-Korot ha-Ḥasidut*; H. Adelbaum, "R. Mendel of Kock," *Ha-Olam* (1927), p. 79; both of them fix 1839 as the year of crisis for R. Mendel, but according to an *aggadah* of Ger, the incident occurred "circa 1841"; cf. *Meir Einei ha-Golah* 1:360:113. According to the tradition of Izbica, their rebbe began to reveal his doctrine in 1840 (cf. introduction to *Mei ha-Shiloaḥ,* pt. 2, p. 5) in consonance with a prediction in the *Zohar* regarding the revelation of the wisdom in that year.
478. *Siaḥ Sarfei Kodesh* 3:378:15, 108; 4:29:69.
479. *Meir Einei ha-Golah,* 26; 483.
480. Ibid., no. 481.
481. Ibid., pp. 65–66; Shatzky, *Geshikhte fun Yidn in Varshe* (New York) 2:101–10.
482. J. Shatzky, *Yidn in Varshe* 2:81–97, 284–85 (the proclamation of the rabbinate for the year 1849 was copied from the periodical *Izraelita* no. 18 [1871]); *Meir Einei ha-Golah* 1:121–31; *Kwartalnik Żydów w Polsce* 1:21:131–36.
483. *Siaḥ Sarfei Kodesh* 1:18:11.
484. Ibid., 215:46.
485. Ibid., 366:72.
486. *Meir Einei ha-Golah*, p. 128; *Emet ve-Emunah,* nos. 140, 270: "He said to them: in the beginning the Jews wore Brandenburg-kaftan and fringes and they began to change [their mode of dress] but there is no need to let oneself be martyred over this."
487. *Meir Einei ha-Golah* 2:89.
488. *Siaḥ Sarfei Kodesh* 1:40.
489. *Abir ha-Ro'im* 1:118; cf. also 2:43.

Chapter 10

1. Cf. chap. 3.
2. Tugendhold expressed this view without any embellishments in his report to the authorities in St. Petersburg for the year 1852; see chap. 8.
3. Appendix: document 13a. The report of the police chief was returned by the Committee for Internal Affairs to the viceroy; the copy, which had been made by this committee for the Committee on Religions has not been preserved among the documents of the committee. A summary of the report was submitted on the

order of the Committee for Internal Affairs, dated February 24, 1824, to the *Województwo* Committee of Podlasie; see appendix: document 13e.

4. Cf. R. Mahler, "Statistik fun Yidn in der Lubliner Voyvodstve, 1764–1765," table 2, in *Yunger Historiker* 2 (1929).

5. B. Wasiutyński, *Ludność żydowska w Polsce w wiekach 19 i 20* (Warsaw, 1930), p. 34.

6. R. Nathan David of Parczew and his son Elimelekh: cf. A. Z. Ascoly, *Ha-Ḥasidut be-Polin, Bet Yisrael be-Polin* 2:104.

7. *Emet ve-Emunah, Divrei Torah Me-Reb Menaḥem Mendel mi-Kock,* 5708, no. 325.

8. Ibid., no. 431.

9. Cf. chap. 8.

10. Cf. chap. 8.

11. The following are the parallel texts in the original:
"WIADOMOŚĆ: . . . herszt ich udziela im do ugruntowania szkodliwych zabobonów dążące niedorzeczne wykłady pisma. . . ." (From Appendix, doc. 13c.)
"Doresh tov: . . . eleh morei sheker ham'avtim et kitvei ha-kadosh be-viurei tofel hem yosifu leheḥazik emunot havlei shav . . ." (From *Doresh Tov*, p. 37b.)

12. The letter of the Committee for Religions to the Synagogue Supervisory Board and its reply are cited by I. Schiper in his book *Żydzi Królestwa Polskiego w Dobie Powstania listopadowego* (Warsaw, 1932) pp. 24–25. The documents of the Archives of the Jewish community in Warsaw.

13. In the Ashkenazic-Polish pronunciation the *Kametz* is rendered as "u," and aside from this, they were not precise in the articulation of the *dalet* with a quiescent *sheva* at the end of the word, pronouncing it like a *tet*. In any case the sound of the word *Hasid* came out sounding like *Husyt*, and in line with this was pronounced *Husyci* in the plural.

14. In Kozienice, the seat of the zaddik was occupied at that time by R. Moshe, the son of the *maggid* R. Yisrael.

15. These repressive measures are contained in a report of the *Województwo* Committee of Płock for the year 1825 to the Old Testament Believers Committee about the reform of the Jews: see D. Kandel, "Komitet Starozakonnych," *Kwartalnik Żydów w Polsce* 1:2:94. Kandel does not give the exact date of these dispositions against the *minyanim* in the Płock region, but according to the documents published here there is no doubt that they occurred in the spring of 1824.

16. Stanislaw Staszyc, a priest, active as a statesman in the days of the Great *Sejm*, in the Duchy of Warsaw and the Kingdom of Poland, was the author of hostile writings against the Jews.

17. The writing here is not clear.

18. Józef Ksalanty Szaniawski, distinguished author who was the right-hand man of the Minister of Religions and Education in Congress Poland, Stanislaw Grabowski; director of the Department of Censorship and Schools in his ministry, and the pillar of clerical reaction after he became a "penitent."

19. Possibly identical with the author Józef Lipinski. Concerning him see A. Brückner, *Dzieje Kultury Polskiej* (Cracow, 1946) 4:313, 347, 356.

20. It is apparent that this is the statesman and renowned author, friend of the Jews, Wawrzyniec Surowiecki; for details see R. Mahler, *Divrei Yemei Yisrael be-Dorot ha-Aḥaronim* (Merḥaviah, 1954) 1:3:64.

21. D. Kandel ("Komitet Starozakonnych," p. 94) erroneously gives the date of that order of the Committee for Religions regarding the Hasidim as July 8, 1823, and I. Schiper copied the error from him, in his *Żydzi Królestwa Polskiego,* pp. 24–26.

22. Cf. appendix: document 17.

23. This memorandum is undated. It is true, the Committee for the Affairs of Old Testament Believers was only set up in 1825. However, in the collection of its sources on Hasidism, documents of the year 1824, such as transcripts of the orders of the viceroy and the Committee for Religions forbidding the *minyanim* of the Hasidim and their gatherings, were also included. This collection begins with documents from the year 1798. Cf. appendix: document 17.

24. In the original, *manow,* in accordance with the Latin term *manes*, which applies both to the spirits of the dead and to household idols.

25. This is the exact translation of the well-known talmudic saying "the Merciful One requires the heart" (*Sanhedrin* 106b).

26. As is known, it was the Maskil Jacques Calmansohn—in his essay on the Jews of Poland, which appeared in Warsaw in French in 1796 and in Polish translation in 1797—who told of common ownership of property among the Hasidim; however, he apparently had in mind those "residing" at the court of the zaddik and his distribution of charity, as evident from the sentence "Tous leurs biens sont en commun et presque toujours à la disposition de leurs chefs" (cf. Graetz, *Geschichte der Juden*, 3d ed. [Leipzig, 1870] 2:595: n. 2. The version in the Polish translation is: "U nich majątki wszystkie są wspólne i prawie zawsze rządzą niemi Starsi . . ." J.C., *Uwagi nad ninieyszym stanem Zydów w Polsce y ich wydoskonaleniem; z francuskiego* [Warsaw, 1797], pp. 18–19). It is possible that the author of the "Comments" received his information in this matter from Calmansohn, particularly if note is taken of the similar formulation: . . . *mieć wszystko wspólne z towarzyszami* . . . (cf. appendix: document 14c).

27. Cf. chap. 9. This characteristic similarity of opinion concerning the Kabbalah prompts the conjecture that perhaps R. Simḥah Bunem himself was among those who provided the author of the "Comments" with information about Hasidism.

28. Cf. appendix: document 17.

29. See appendix: 15a–g.

30. Cf. chap. 9.

31. See appendix: document 16.

32. In 1799 central Poland was partitioned between Prussia, which took its western part, and Austria, which ruled over its eastern part, naming it "Western Galicia." It may therefore be surmised that what is meant here is the order of Emperor Franz for the year 1799, which—according to the report of R. Israel Löbel—prohibited gatherings by the Hasidim (cf. chap. 3).

33. See appendix: document 18.

34. The members of the "Congregational Board" in Warsaw in 1834 were: Zalman Posner, industrialist and owner of land-estates, distinguished for his communal activity; Solomon Eger, the son of R. Akiba Eger, the renowned Rabbi of Posen; Samuel Herzfeld, Zalman Abramson, and Jacob Epstein, who had formerly served as an officer in the Polish army. Cf. Schiper, *Zydzi Królestwa Polskiego*, p. 29, n. 17.

35. This memorandum was published by I. Schiper (ibid., pp. 28–29) from the documents of the Warsaw Jewish Community Archives; in the copy, evidently only the year of the memorandum was indicated.

36. In the transcript of the replies that were received from the Archives (appendix: document 19), no date is specified, but in view of the request of the Committee for Internal Affairs and Religions that an answer be given "at the earliest possible time," it may be assumed that the reply was, at any rate, not sent later than the end of that year, 1834.

37. R. Yeraḥmiel, the son of R. Jacob Isaac *ha-Yehudi* of Przysucha, who succeeded to his father's seat.

38. "The Organic Statute" of 1832 established the basic laws of the Kingdom of Poland under the new regime after the suppression of the Polish insurrection; it included some limited rights for citizens.

Glossary of Hebrew and Yiddish Terms

(Plural in parentheses)

aggadah (*aggadot*) the nonlegal, illustrative material (such as parables, legends, proverbs, and fables) in the Talmud and rabbinic literature, as opposed to Halakha. Also: a tale or legend.

bet din (battei din) a rabbinic court.

bet ha-midrash (battei midrash) a house of study.

dayan (dayanim) a rabbi's assistant, charged with deciding questions of ritual cleanliness and settling minor disputes.

dybbuk (dybbuks) an evil spirit or soul of a dead person residing in the body of a living individual.

gematria (gematriot) one of the aggadic hermeneutical rules for interpreting the Torah, consisting of explaining a word or group of words according to the numerical values of the letters.

Halakha the Oral Law stemming from the Torah.

Haskalah the Jewish Enlightenment movement.

ḥeder (ḥadarim) the old-fashioned elementary school for the teaching of Judaism in eastern Europe.

kehillah (*kehillot*) the autonomous administration of the Jewish community.

kohen (kohanim) a priest, an Aaronide.

Maskil (Maskilim) an adherent of the Haskalah.

melamed (melamedim) a teacher in a *ḥeder*.

mikveh (mikvot) a ritual bath.

Mitnagged (Mitnaggedim) an opponent of Hasidism within Jewish Orthodoxy.

miẓvah (miẓvot) commandment.

mohel (mohalim) a circumciser.

moreh hora'ah (morei hora'ah) a rabbi, one who decides matters of rabbinic law.

Reb traditional Jewish title of address, prefixed to a man's first name.

rebbe (rebbes) a Hasidic rabbi, a zaddik.

sefirah (sefirot) a kabbalistic term denoting one of the ten stages of emanation that emerge from "The Infinite" and form the realm of God's manifestation in his various attributes.

sheḥitah ritual slaughter.

Shema the declaration of God's unity, the Jewish profession of faith.

Shemini Aẓeret the eighth day of Sukkot, treated as a separate festival.

shoḥet (shoḥatim) a ritual slaughterer.

yod he vav he the hebrew letters of the Tetragrammaton.

zaddik (zaddikim) a "Just Man," the Hasidic leader whose charismatic personality made him the paramount authority in the community of his adherents.

Ẓe'enah u-Re'enah a Yiddish exegetical translation of the Pentateuch, the *haftarot*, and the five Scrolls, composed at the end of the sixteenth century by Jacob b. Isaac Ashkenazi. It is traditionally read chiefly by women.

Index